MUSICAL BELONGINGS

One of the pioneers of popular music studies, Richard Middleton has made an important contribution not only to this particular field but also to the critical and cultural theory of music more generally. Sixteen of his essays, dating from the late 1970s to the present day, have been selected for this collection, most of them previously published but some of which are new. The musical topics vary widely, from Mozart and Gershwin to rock and rap, from music hall to blues and jazz, from Elvis Presley and John Lennon to Patti Smith and Mariah Carey. But throughout, the author is concerned to locate appropriate ways of understanding 'the popular', and suggests that this task is crucial to any critical musicology worth the name. In a substantial introduction, he places his own intellectual development in the context of the development of the discipline, offering his latest thoughts on the past, present and future of critical musicology and its place in the critique of modernity. The overall theme, 'musical belongings', is revealed as a key not only to the relationship between music and the politics of *possession*, but also, by extension, to the investments made by musicology, critical and other, in those politics.

ASHGATE CONTEMPORARY THINKERS ON CRITICAL MUSICOLOGY

The titles in this series bring together a selection of previously published and some unpublished essays by leading authorities in the field of critical musicology. The essays are chosen from a wide range of publications and so make key works available in a more accessible form. The authors have all made a selection of their own work in one volume with an introduction which discusses the essays chosen and puts them into context. A full bibliography points the reader to other publications which might not be included in the volume for reasons of space. The previously published essays are published using the facsimile method of reproduction to retain their original pagination, so that students and scholars can easily reference the essays in their original form.

Titles published in the series

Critical Musicology and the Responsibility of Response
Lawrence Kramer

Music and Historical Critique
Gary Tomlinson

Taking Popular Music Seriously
Simon Frith

Music, Performance, Meaning
Nicholas Cook

Reading Music
Susan McClary

Sound Judgment
Richard Leppert

Music, Structure, Thought
James Hepokoski

Musical Belongings

Selected Essays

RICHARD MIDDLETON
Newcastle University, UK

ASHGATE CONTEMPORARY THINKERS ON
CRITICAL MUSICOLOGY SERIES

ASHGATE

Published by
Ashgate Publishing Limited
Wey Court East
Union Road
Farnham
Surrey GU9 7PT
England

Ashgate Publishing Company
Suite 420
101 Cherry Street
Burlington, VT 05401-4405
USA

Ashgate website: http://www.ashgate.com

ISBN 978-0-7546-2841-5

British Library Cataloguing in Publication Data
Middleton, Richard.
    Musical belongings : selected essays. – (Ashgate
    contemporary thinkers on critical musicology.
    1. Popular music–1991-2000–History and criticism.
    2. Popular music–2001-2010–History and criticism.
    3. Music–Social aspects.
    I. Title II. Series
    781.6'4'09-dc22

Library of Congress Control Number: 2009928373

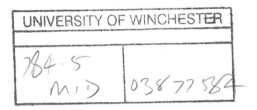

Mixed Sources
Product group from well-managed
forests and other controlled sources
www.fsc.org Cert no. SGS-COC-2482
© 1996 Forest Stewardship Council
FSC

Printed and bound in Great Britain by
TJ International Ltd, Padstow, Cornwall

Contents

Acknowledgements

The author and publisher wish to thank the following for permission to use copyrighted material:

Ashgate Publishing Ltd for 'Afterword' [re-titled here as 'Global, National, Local: Or, a Hysteric's Account of Negative Dialectics'], in Popular Music and National Identity, ed. Ian Biddle and Vanessa Knights, 2007, pp. 191–203.

Cambridge University Press for 'Articulating Musical Meaning/Reconstructing Musical History/Locating the Popular', Popular Music, 5, 1985, pp. 5–43; 'O Brother, Let's Go Down Home: Loss, Nostalgia and the Blues', Popular Music, 26 (1), 2007, pp. 47–64; 'Can We Get Rid of the "Popular" in Popular Music? A Virtual Symposium with Contributions from the International Advisory Editors of Popular Music' [extract], Popular Music, 24 (1), 2005, pp. 143–5.

Författarna for 'The Real Thing? The Spectre of Authenticity in Modern Musical Thought', in Frispel: Festskrift till Olle Edström, ed. Alf Bjönberg, Mona Hallin, Lars Lilliestam and Ola Stockfelt, Skrifter från Institutionen för musikvetenskap, Göteborgs universitet nr 80, 2005, pp. 476–87.

Liverpool University Press for 'Work-in(g)-Practice: Configurations of the Popular Music Intertext', in The Musical Work: Reality or Invention, ed. Michael Talbot, 2000, pp. 59–87.

Radical Musicology (http://www.radical-musicology.org.uk) for 'Last Night a DJ Saved My Life: Avians, Cyborgs and Gendered Bodies in the Era of Phonographic Technology', 1, 2006, 28 pars.

Taylor & Francis Group LLC for 'Locating the People: Music and the Popular', in The Cultural Study of Music: A Critical Introduction, ed. Martin Clayton, Trevor Herbert and Richard Middleton, 2003, pp. 251–62; 'Mum's the Word: Men's Singing and Maternal Law', in Oh Boy: Masculinities and Popular Music, ed. Freya Jarman-Ivens, 2007, pp. 103–24; 'Performing Culture, Appropriating the Phallus', in Voicing the Popular: On the Subjects of Popular Music, 2006, pp. 98–109.

Taylor & Francis (http://www.informaworld.com) for 'Authorship, Gender and the Construction of Meaning in the Eurythmics' Hit Recordings', Cultural Studies, 9 (3), 1995, pp. 465–85.

The Regents of the University of California, University of California Press for 'Musical Belongings: Western Music and Its Low-Other', in Western Music and Its Others: Difference, Representation, and Appropriation in Music, ed. Georgina Born and David Hesmondhalgh, 2000, pp. 59–85.

The University of Southern Mississippi for 'All Shook Up? Innovation and Contunuity in Elvis Presley's Vocal Style', The Southern Quarterly, 18 (1), Fall 1979, pp. 151–61.

Von Bockel Verlag for 'Were the Rockers Right? Revolution and Legitimation in British Pop Music of the 1960s', in Musik/Revolution, Vol. 3, ed. Hanns-Werner Heister, 1997, pp. 141–67.

Wiley-Blackwell for 'The "Problem" of Popular Music', in Music in Britain, Vol. 6, The Twentieth Century, ed. Stephen Banfield, 1995, pp. 27–38.

Introduction

Just remember darling, all the while, You belong to me.
This land is your land, this land is my land... This land belongs to you and me.
Going to Chicago, sorry but I can't take you.
Crying, Lord, will I ever get back home?[1]

Can a collection (even if a selection; especially a selection) count as 'critical'? Surely a critical impulse implies disassembly, incision, separation, subversion. What gives the essays brought together here the right to belong together? To whom or to what do they belong?

I can't deny the proprietorial relation; these things – as the bard had it – I must acknowledge mine, and there is a certain authorial responsibility that can't be forsworn. The sequence tells a story, if only a mundane story of chronology (the chapters are arranged chronologically, for reasons that I'll come to). Whether or not the authorial subject of the earlier works recognises the one of the latest (or vice versa), there is certainly a genealogy, marked by the proper name, by the properties of name and naming – extending not only to the modest rewards these children have earned for their progenitor but also to the desire, the longing, hidden within belonging itself.

We have, let's say, a *corpus*; linked in turn, in ways hard to fathom for certain, to another body: a body, for sure, with a biogrophemic status but one too that, at the times of writing, felt the sense of a real presence. This corpus has, here, its day in court; and as corpse (as dead letter), lines up its precession of spectres, the ghostly animations that, for authors, help to keep death at arms length. As usual, these spectres tell more than the author expects; and it turns out that all along the object – the desire, the longing – that drove the process of authorial exploration (which of course should always be seen as an act of territorialisation) was nothing but itself the subject of *belonging*, of *musical belongings*; or so (in what is no doubt an act of retroactive self-construction) it now seems. These animations, then, each neatly embalmed within its own chapter, would be the *voices* belonging to this corpus: voices that (seem to) cohere around a topic (a *subject*), but can never be reduced to this – at least not so long as they contain a spark of life.

Self-love, Freud suggested, is the primal mode of desire, from which all others take their cue. Writing always bears the marks of narcissism since its product cannot avoid reflecting back its author's motives. Critical musicology, which has sometimes wanted to represent

---

1   I'm tempted to suggest that this introduction has already been written (perhaps better) in the lyrics of popular songs. These extracts come from (in order): 'You Belong to Me' (Pee Wee King, Redd Stewart and Chilton Price, 1952); 'This Land is Your Land' (Woody Guthrie, 1940); 'When the Levee Breaks' (Kansas Joe McCoy and Memphis Minnie, 1929); 'Cool Water Blues' (Tommy Johnson, 1928).

itself as in the business of exposing the self-interest allegedly implicated in many previous scholarly engagements with music, is actually, one might say, itself doubly culpable, for on top of its unavoidable involvement in that first level from which no author can escape, its eager profession of a superior *self-awareness* – we *know* we're self-interested and are proud to advertise the fact – might be thought simply to massage the ego twice over. And, of course, playing with this point in the paragraphs so far (prettily, predictably, tiresomely, according to taste), I have fallen into this trap (but *knowingly*, needless to say). But if the 'hermeneutics of suspicion' can always re-double itself, biting the hand that feeds it, this doesn't mean that no crime has been committed, rather, that 'crime', in this sense, is without origin and without end. And, you know, this isn't so bad once you get used to the idea.[2]

It's on this basis that I feel reasonably relaxed about putting some elements (well, let's say – remembering to press the self-awareness button – a specific, thematically motivated selection of some elements) of my intellectual autobiography on display. That, and the point that the 'illness' I have just described is, I think it's clear, an endemic disease of contemporary culture in general. After the 'death of God', the 'end of politics', the 'deconstruction of the subject', the 'implosion of the canon', the 'un-disciplining of musicology', we can't believe *anything* without question (indeed, we can't easily identify a 'we' to do the disbelieving). In this sense, the trajectory followed by anyone closely involved in the activities associated with critical musicology over the last thirty years or so might be expected, regardless of its own intentions as it were, to speak to and about the wider course of development.

But this development is itself hard to separate from the wider conditions within which it took place. Its peak – in terms of both controversy aroused and influence exerted – is to be located, I think it will be agreed, in the period from the late 1980s to the late 1990s. If this is its moment, if critical musicology *belongs* to this moment, we should ask why this is so and what it means. A purely internalist explanation – perhaps identifying Joseph Kerman's 1985 book, *Musicology*, as firing a starting gun – would run counter to some of the core tendencies of critical musicology itself. In the 'external' world, it's hard to miss the fact that the Berlin Wall came down in 1989, the Cold War ended (apparently), and a unipolar world of neo-liberal hegemony was proclaimed under US leadership. A 'new musicology' – as Americans named it, at least temporarily – for a 'new world order'? Was this conjunction just happenstance? If it was more than that, was the relation one of reflection or even causation? Or was it, by contrast, one of violent *dis*junction, subversion, negation? Or do we need to think in a different way altogether, one that refuses that sort of binaristic approach; one where, maybe, such a refusal is actually the point, even if its effects take different forms in different spheres? I write as one who was involved in, and would want to defend much of, the critical musicology project, and I would certainly want to refute any attempt to reduce its politics to an epiphenomenal mechanics. Yet the conjunction is uncomfortable; and it's difficult to avoid noticing that 'new musicology' was first named as such in the American academy and has its home overwhelmingly in the Anglophone territories, precisely the locus from where finance-led turbo-capitalism has led the attempt – with limited success it now appears – to remake the

---

2   On the (ambivalent) pleasures of musicological discipline, see Ian Biddle, 'Fifth Column: On the Radical in Musicology', *Radical Musicology*, 1 (2006), http://www.radical-musicology.org.uk (4 March 2009), 14 pars.

political economy of the entire world. Perhaps, to put it no higher, it would be worth searching here for the source of the political difficulties into which critical musicology has sometimes fallen (and to which I'll return). There's certainly nothing particularly new in attempting to think intellectual and political trajectories together in this way. Fredric Jameson's exploration of the complex relations between so-called postmodernism and the formations of the new phase of capitalism identifiable in late-twentieth century modernity provides an inspiring example – and in addition, to the extent that the new musicology itself identified with currents in postmodernism, is specifically relevant to analysis of the 1990 moment.[3] The interplay between '1968' and its after-effects on the one hand and contemporaneous and subsequent developments in 'French theory' on the other is, similarly, a commonplace of intellectual history; and, again, is directly relevant to the case here, given the debts musicology came to owe to certain currents in this theory.

As this begins to suggest, we're unlikely to understand the historical significance of critical musicology if we confine our focus to the 1990s rather than following up earlier roots and lineages. The influence of structuralism and semiology was already being felt within musicology in the 1970s, as was that of music sociology, along with responses to a wave of English translations of T.W. Adorno, foremost representative in the musical sphere of Frankfurt School critical theory. These can all be seen, in a variety of ways, as reactions against the prevailing spirit of positivism, its dominance apparent on both analytical and historical sides of musicology (and its epistemological basis, arguably, a key component of the 'scientific' underpinnings of Western Cold War ideology). But this is even more striking in the emergence, at much the same time, of new, radical strands in ethnomusicology (John Blacking, Charles Keil) – radical both in subject-matter and in political argument – and of popular music studies (Simon Frith, Dave Laing, myself, Philip Tagg). In both these sub-disciplines, a prevailing culturalism of tone and method set itself against the hegemony of musical 'facts' as such, and indeed, in the case of popular music studies, was partly grounded in the broader development at the time of British cultural studies, with its background in older traditions of cultural critique (F.R. Leavis, Richard Hoggart, Raymond Williams, Stuart Hall) as well as, increasingly, the Frankfurt School and other currents in 'Western Marxism'. A significant initiative here, at least in Britain, was the launch of the Open University undergraduate course, *Popular Culture* (in which I was a participant) in 1981; given the national (indeed international) reach of the OU, the widespread dissemination in the course materials of both the native cultural studies tradition and the ideas of a range of 'Continentals' (Gramsci, Althusser, Foucault, Barthes, Lacan) marked a highly significant moment. The same year saw the foundation of the International Association for the Study of Popular Music, and the first issue of what would become the leading scholarly journal in this field, *Popular Music*.

---

3   Fredric Jameson, 'Postmodernism: The Cultural Logic of Late Capitalism', *New Left Review*, 146 (1984), 53-92. Jameson is far from being the only commentator to note the congruence, which in some circumstances can appear more like an affiliation, between postmodernism's epistemological project – 'sliding' of the signifier, deconstruction of subjectivity, erasure of 'presence' – and contemporary consumer capitalism's prodigious appetite for the fluid circulation of meaning-light multiplicitous commodity under a regime of 'flexible accumulation'.

Following genealogies in this way, we're pushed inexorably further and further back. (After all, the most significant 'critical musicologist' of the twentieth century was undoubtedly Adorno, who died in 1969 and who was publishing ground-breaking work by the late 1920s.) Indeed, if we pursue the lineages of critique retrospectively through the nineteenth century, we will find ourselves eventually – and predictably enough – in the Enlightenment, in territory where the basic problematics were set out that would in due course provide the very issues with which late-twentieth century critical thought, including critical musicology, would struggle, not to mention many assumptions that postmodernism would reject. We find ourselves, then, with Kant, in a sense the inventor of critique as a distinct mode of thought, whose 'Copernican revolution' placed the epistemological status of the reasoning, acting, judging subject centrally at issue; with Hegel, and his dialectic of self and other, subject and object, influentially applied to the psycho-history of the relationship of 'masters' and 'slaves' (a discourse of particular significance to both ethnomusicology and popular music studies); with Marx, who of course turned the dialectic on its head, giving it a materialist basis, and whose account of alienation, which he linked to the effects of commodity-fetishism, would have long-lasting influence on critical thought within all the human sciences; and with Nietzsche and Freud, with both of whom, albeit in differing ways, the human subject splinters further, and whose accounts of *will* (Nietzsche) and of *desire* (Freud) would prove fertile for interpretations of musical processes. Again, we should place this lineage, as Marx certainly would have done, in relation to the wider history, marked by the consolidation of class society, slavery (industrial and colonial), scientific racism and the growth of 'administered society' but also by movements of democratisation, socialism and nationalism, and distinct stirrings of cultural (including gender and race) politics. In the light of this last point, it's not surprising to find that the birth of critique as a mode of thought was accompanied by the birth, too, of the idea of 'culture', in the modern sense (notably in the work of Herder); and that this idea could in fact then function, in a variety of ways, as a force within the very operations of critique. Perhaps this helps explain why, for some, 'cultural musicology' is a more helpful descriptor than 'critical musicology'.[4]

The case of Nietzsche is particularly difficult for popular music scholars, since he espoused an 'aristocratic' aesthetics and scorned the 'resentful' slave mentality of the 'herd'. Indeed, for Nietzsche, *Kultur* as such was a synonym for 'illness', albeit one that was necessary for human progress and the possibility of higher forms of beauty. I would want to assert the potential for creativity and beauty to emerge from out of the seething life of the masses, the mob, the multitude; to proclaim (though it requires an effort of will that Nietzsche himself might appreciate, for there is much evidence presently to set against this): the People *contra* Nietzsche! How – briefly – might one do this? I'd like to return to the Herderian moment – a moment that enabled Herder to pre-empt what would shortly be codified as Kantian universalism, and also cut across what Hegel would, a little later again, posit as the dialectic of master and slave, on which Nietzsche would then draw; but I want to do this in a way that

---

4   I have discussed the parallel and intertwined histories of 'critique' and 'culture' in my 'Introduction: Music Studies and the Idea of Culture', in *The Cultural Study of Music: A Critical Introduction*, ed. Martin Clayton, Trevor Herbert and Richard Middleton (New York: Routledge, 2003), 1–15.

links up to a grasp of where the democratisation process, and with it the People-idea, has got to nowadays.

Herder posits a distinction *within* the category of 'slaves': '*Volk heisst nicht der Pöbel auf den Gassen, der singt und dichtet niemals, sondern schreit und verstümmelt.*' ('The people are not the mob of the streets, who never sing or compose, but shriek and mutilate.');[5] a distinction between urban *mob* (*Pöbel*, or for the Greeks, *ochlos*) and *people* (but people of a particular type – the *Volk*, or *ethnos*: the [predominantly rural] race-nation); and a distinction that would subsequently, of course, drive the different focuses of popular music studies and ethnomusicology, at least for some time. What object motivates Herder's distinction? I would say, *commodity* – the object that lies between, that drives apart, the images of folk music and commercial song. But of course the role of commodity has become more complex and more pervasive than in Herder's world. The *Volk/Pöbel* as a whole buy and sell their own songs, chase their own tail, prostitute their own tale, cannibalise themselves. This has long since become so taken for granted as to be invisible; commodity has the status of what, in the Hegelian language given renewed currency by Jameson and Žižek, we can call a 'vanishing mediator'. To the extent that this regime has been spread worldwide, what started as specific to late-eighteenth century Europe has become, at least as tendency, universal. And to the extent that musicology, particularly ethnomusicology and popular music studies, are complicit in this process – scholarly reification the flip side of commodity fetishism – it has been a colonising force in a far deeper sense even than postcolonial critique has realised.

And, why is Herder's language so fierce, so brutal? It stands in a lengthy tradition of 'educated' discourse about the culture of the mob which fixates on images of violence: the singers 'distort', 'mutilate', 'torture' tunes, words, voices. Why does this discourse point towards beastliness – for us, unavoidably, towards the sounds of the torture-chamber, concentration camp, farm factory, slaughter-house: industrialised meat? The tradition is still active in the twentieth century (and probably continues today), for example in Adorno's discussions of jazz, in which he ascribes sado-masochistic qualities to performers' 'mutilations' and 'distortions' of given material, and to listeners' pleasure in them. Writing of the jitterbugs, he observes that 'To become transformed into an insect, man needs that energy which might possibly achieve his transformation into a man.'[6] By this point, clearly, a new level of social self-consciousness has been reached, as pointedly revealed when Adorno, eliding animal and machine as the Other of the human, links the traits he identifies explicitly with the psychology of fascism. But this movement of thought needs another push. A further turn in the dialectical circle – the dialectic of enlightenment which Adorno and Horkheimer themselves have taught us 'is totalitarian' from the start[7] – reveals Adorno's own entrapment within its relentless machinery. From a later standpoint (one with a Deleuzian colouring,

5   G.W. Herder, *Sämtliche Werke*, vol. 25, ed. Bernhard Suphan (Hildesheim, 1967), 323.

6   T.W. Adorno, 'On Popular Music' [1941], in *Essays on Music*, ed. Richard Leppert (Berkeley CA: University of California Press, 2002), 437–69 (468). Adorno's theory of sado-masochism in jazz appears in several publications (see *Essays on Music*, Part 3), but is perhaps most clearly outlined in his review of Wilder Hobson's *American Jazz Music* and Winthrop Sargeant's *Jazz Hot and Hybrid*, *Studies in Philosophy and Social Science*, 9 (1941), 167–78.

7   T.W. Adorno and Max Horkheimer, *Dialectic of Enlightenment*, tr. John Cumming (London: Verso, 1997 [1944]), 6.

perhaps attending too to current ecological concerns), the possibility of an empathetic 'becoming-insect' (becoming-bird, animal, plant, soil...) might be precisely what stands between competing potentials for human transformation or extinction. How so?

The question returns us to enlightenment's culturalist, specifically its anthropological, project as such, within which Herder may be positioned. The quest of what has been called the 'anthropological machine'[8] is for the true nature of man – his species-essence, as the young Marx would call it. John Blacking's *How Musical Is Man?* is the classic ethnomusicological gesture in this tradition. But what if man qua species has no monopoly of music? What if the Neanderthals also sang, as Stephen Mithen argues?[9] Not to mention the other hominids. What about the great apes, whales, frogs, birds – and insects (ants, for example, communicate through 'songs' produced by rubbing body parts together; and the caterpillar of one species of butterfly turns this to its advantage: having facilitated its own capture, it sings for its supper – the ants' own grubs – fooling the ants by mimicking their song)? Or again, what about the mixed creatures of mythology – sirens, mermaids, angels – or those of modernity: vocoders, sampling devices and other cyborgian mut(il)ants? Species boundaries blur before our gaze. The search for a true voice – for the sound of the authentically human, whether originary (Herder) or promissory (Adorno) – is always as much a search for the self as for the missing object which is its ostensible preoccupation. The anthropological machine always ends up dissecting not so much this Other, its exotic historical and cultural object, as its subject – modern man. The Lacanian 'object voice' – voice as such; at the limit, the shriek stuck in the throat, language mutilated beyond meaning – registers the impossible-real knowledge of the internal fractures that form this creature.

In a moment that, to many, feels post-historical, it's not difficult to identify (even, for many, to celebrate) the death of the Folk, of the People, of Man himself. But the fractures cleaving the human animal animate also the social formation of the human (and meta-human) family – the hierarchies of race, gender, class and sexuality (and species); in a society structured in dominance 'nature' is always an ambivalent value, and so long as the nature of the Low, nature as low, the low as apparently natural, continue to shape these hierarchies, so long will the vernacular – the Roman *verna*, enslaved but also native born – insist that there is history, still, to be lived, struggle to be waged. 'Perhaps the body of the anthropophorous animal (the body of the slave) is the unresolved remnant that idealism leaves as an inheritance to thought'[10] – a disjunction put at issue more than ever by the machinery of today's technological mediations; can this now-increasingly-cyborgian remnant speak, sing, think? Yes: the shriek I hear is one of protest at its own mutilation – which at the same time references a self-mutilation by the Low's oppressive Other, masked by the projection of bestiality always inherent in the Herderian discourse as a whole.

In this light, it becomes possible to recognise something of the history-to-come nestling within Herder's gambit; a history crossed, perhaps, by what Agamben calls 'zones of indeterminacy', where category-making decisions are to be made; a history calling up the

---

8   See Gorgio Agamben, *The Open: Man and Animal*, tr. Kevin Attell (Stanford CA: Stanford University Press, 2004).

9   Stephen Mithen, *The Singing Neanderthals: The Origins of Music, Language, Mind and Body* (London: Phoenix, 2005).

10 Agamben, *The Open*, 12.

suggestion that 'Democracy' – democratisation being the name of the genealogy signalled here (and by the way I'm not confining this to what currently passes for democracy in the neo-liberal capitalist states) –

> Democracy exists in a society to the degree that the *demos* exists as the power to divide the *ochlos*. This power of division [... ,] whereby any multitude affirms and manifests itself as such, [...] is the path followed by a *One* which is no longer that of collective incorporation but rather that of the equality of any One to any other One.

A One, then, whose vehicle of articulation would raise the question, what would be 'the "voice" of a "people," insofar as a people would not be *a subject*, and as its voice would pass through a place, a mouth, apart – and separated from itself'?[11] This surely begins to adumbrate the shape of a political problematic where we find raised precisely the issues, distinctions, questions and possibilities that have occupied so much of the work of critical musicologists, which has focused to an enormous extent on thematics of *difference*. Even so, I'm forced to wonder whether, taking this body of work as a whole, it has yet assimilated the full measure of the challenge posed by ethnomusicology on the one hand, popular music studies on the other; if the power of the *demos* to forever divide itself, multiply, re-assemble, create new alliances – to continually form new *belongings*, we might say – were fully recognised as determinant of the musical field, could musicology, as a practice that primarily reflects interpretatively upon the contingencies of text and context, survive at all?

Following Jean-Luc Nancy's lead, just cited, we might pursue such questions by addressing more explicitly the question of *voice* (by which I mean not just musical voices but any enunciation that is taken to originate in a subject, individual or collective: 'the people', for example; even if this subject, as we've just heard, is not One). This is a topic that has been increasingly explored by musicologists in recent years, and is central to the concerns of critical musicology, both for its role in ideology critique (can voices be believed? Do they mean what they think or say they do?) and for its role in identity (whose voice is this? What mode of subjectivity does it produce?). It's clear that relations created or construed, both in historically located material and in contemporary practice, between enunciation and reception, address and addressee, speaking and hearing – between, that is, composers, performers and listeners or their putative personae, not to mention the larger social constituencies they're taken to speak for – are crucial to any understanding of how music is implicated in the processes and formations of identity-construction. This throws us back, headlong, into the problematic of belonging, or, as I'd like to refer to it now, of *possession*.

Stephen Connor has pointed to an important historical shift in the mechanics of ventriloquism, whereby possession *by* (e.g. a spirit) is supplemented or supplanted by possession *of* (another subject; the ventriloquist's dummy).[12] I think an analogous (and related) dialectic of possession is deeply implicated in the dynamics of music under the regimes

---

11 Agamben, *The Open*, 38; Jacques Rancière, *On the Shores of Politics*, tr. Liz Heron (London: Verso, 2007 [1995], 32; Jean-Luc Nancy, *The Birth to Presence*, tr. Brian Holmes et al (Stanford CA; Stanford University Press, 1993), 142. I discuss these ideas in more detail in Chapter 16 below.

12 Stephen Connor, *Dumbstruck: A Cultural History of Ventriloquism* (Oxford: Oxford University Press, 2000), 191–225, 249–89.

of modernity. This clearly applies to the structure of vocality: subjects possess voices, are possessed by them, mark their belongings – of social position, political authority, cultural competence, territorial location – by means of identifications at specific points within the vectors of enunciation; and what's more, such identifications can hide as much as they reveal, since music is the practice *par excellence* that can render voice with the qualities of the Freudian uncanny (*das Unheimliche*, to use the more resonant German term). More broadly considered, music not only possesses *properties*, what is *proper* to itself, as music, and to its specific genres, locations and moments; these properties are in turn inscribed within a deeper framework of *dialogue* (of which the structure of vocality is an important part), which is cultural and, ultimately, political: subjects (individual and collective) address each other here, in ways that are inseparable from the social and economic structures of possession (of which the relationship of masters and slaves is an important part). I have elsewhere referred to this framework, following Lacan, as the dialectic of *having and being*. For Lacan, this refers to a gendered difference: men 'have' the phallus; women's role is to 'be' the phallus (for men). But the logic applies more widely and is taken from Marx as well as Freud; it's a logic of law, property and desire (a logic of masters and slaves in fact), within which both commodities (for Marx) and subjects (for psychoanalysis), divided by class in the one case, by gender (and other social differentiations) in the other, are seen to be produced by analogous mechanisms of fetishism and reification. The result is that, under modernity,

> this structure of property and being – production/reproduction, penetration/penetrated, active/ passive, capital/labour, master/slave, or at bottom of course, culture/nature – dramatised by the representational work of the exchange economies, can be seen to traverse the whole range of social registers: not only gender but also race and, needless to say, class.[13]

'Music' – to whom the poets, knowing more than many musicologists, have often given a proper name – names a key site, a body politic if you will, where such exchanges take place.

The dialogues are, at one level, subject-to-subject. This is the stuff of 'identity'. But at another level they also involve objects, including subjects *as* objects: music is implicated not only in circuits of encounter but also possessive relations with objects – commodities, technologies, fetishes, objects of desire, reified sediments of ideology within ourselves. So, not only Bakhtin, Barthes and Levinas but also Lacan, Althusser, Baudrillard and Žižek. If critical musicology has tended to cultivate the first level at the expense of the second, this

---

13 Richard Middleton, *Voicing the Popular: On the Subjects of Popular Music* (New York: Routledge, 2006), 29–30. The role of gender difference in this structure is far from metaphorical and is not easily written out by anti-Lacanian critics. Women – as objects of possession, conflict and exchange – were arguably the first proto-commodities. The point has been made by historical anthropologists, but is clearly signalled in myth, as Adorno and Horkheimer have explained (*Dialectic*, 72–5). It may be as well to stress, however, that the logic of the structure is nevertheless indeed dialectical, and hence historically variable. As Adorno and Horkheimer point out, not without comedy (ibid., 203), the dynamics of the Freudian psychic economy map uncannily to those of 'corner-shop', 'small business' capitalist enterprise. Writing at a moment when capitalism was changing profoundly, Freud was in a sense dealing with aftershocks. When exploring the having-and-being economies of the twentieth and twenty-first centuries, it's important to take seriously the methodological caution this implies.

may explain why I sometimes find its political positions too fuzzy, too pliable. We should, though, be concerned not just with epistemology and ontology but with ethics too; not just having (knowledge, law, mastery) and being (a subject, an object, a property) but also *acting*. Here, perhaps, Nietzsche (proponent of the performative) comes after all to join Marx and Freud as mentors: the unholy trinity at the head of the critique of modernity outside of which critical musicology can't be understood; and it's telling then to register the resurgent influence of Nietzsche in much recent thought, an influence not without effect in the final essays in this book.

It would be far-fetched to claim that the discussion here can *explain* the trajectory demonstrated by the essays that follow, which I guess runs broadly from a Gramscian variant of culturalism, through an assimilation of semiotics and other hermeneutic theories, then of discourse theory, deconstruction and psychoanalysis, to end up in an approach that draws on recent 'post-Marxist' and 'post-Lacanian' philosophies of politics, voice and body.[14] At most it functions as a post facto meditation, which, I hope, places the evolution into a context. Looking back, I find it easy to see the lacuna in Marxism where a worked-out theory of the subject needs to be and to acknowledge the contributions that poststructuralism, deconstruction and psychoanalysis can make to filling it. It's equally clear to me that the attenuation in much post-Derridean, post-Lacanian work of any political project, of any even tactical foundational commitment, is debilitating. The trajectory mapped in this book thus follows many of the contours evident in the broader intellectual history of critical thought in this period, but to some extent refracts them through a personal lens. The end-point is no grand synthesis. Indeed, there are many loose ends. The project is incomplete – a condition that I would in fact want to claim as a necessary property of the theory.

◊ ◊ ◊

Needless to say, readers aren't compelled to follow this trajectory; you may prefer to read selectively, perhaps thematically. (Some of the themes outlined below can be followed further in other publications, to which I give a few pointers.)

The most straightforward way in which this book is about musical belongings is in relation to the various social categories of identity:

Class (chapters 2 and 5);

Race (chapters 6, 12, 15 – and, less explicitly, 1 and 5; see also *Pop Music and the Blues*, although the subject is discussed there more in terms of ethnicity than race, and chapter 2 of *Voicing the Popular*);

---

14 I'm intrigued to recall, having outlined this trajectory, that my earliest journal articles (not included here) were essays in psychoanalytically inflected interpretation. Apparently, systematising theory, whether Marxist or semiotic, couldn't prevent this temporarily marginalised investment from returning!

Gender and Sexuality (chapters 3, 9, 11, 13 – and, less explicitly, 1; see also chapter 3 of *Voicing the Popular*).

These categories come into a more specific focus in relation to discussions of:

The People/the Popular (chapters 2, 4, 8, 16 – and, implicitly, 6 and 7; see also the first chapters of both *Studying Popular Music* and *Voicing the Popular*).

But the popular exists too within larger political frameworks, for instance, that of:

The Nation (chapter 14);

which in turn is to be related to frameworks operating at lower and higher levels of organisation, that is, to what have come to be known as processes of:

Globalisation (chapters 14, 15, 16 – and, less explicitly, 6).

For a cultural practice such as music, belonging demands to be thought not only in terms of the social categories that it constructs or represents but also in relation to processes of production – to the sense that music is 'owned' by those who make it; so this introduces consideration of:

Authorship (chapters 3 and 7),

which in turn raises questions of:

Authenticity (chapter 10, a substantially expanded version of which appears as chapter 5 of *Voicing the Popular*); and:

Creativity (chapters 7 and 16).

As already suggested, a key role in processes of authorship – not least when issues of authenticity and creativity are in question – is occupied by:

Voice, a theme that runs right through the book (chapters 1, 3, 9, 11, 13 and 16), and becomes central in *Voicing the Popular*; but this is always – and increasingly, since the opening of the phonographic era – mediated by apparatuses and deployments of:

Technology (chapters 7, 11 and 16).

One of my central arguments in this book, however, is that the identities, selves or subjects that are at issue in all these constructions of belonging owe their specificity to – and are therefore to be understood in terms of – their relationships with what lies beyond or outside them; that is, to the structures of:

Otherness, or **Alterity**: this is the principal theme of chapter 6, but is also implicit in chapters 12 and 15 – and of course, to the extent that the subject of 'the People/the Popular' only exists within the terms of these structures, it's a constant background to the book as a whole (it's a constant background too in the sense that the musicological embrace of the popular itself functions in these terms).

As to method:

Analysis, I would want to claim, figures throughout, though quite rarely in forms familiar in most musicology, traditional or critical; I have done my time in the systematics workshop (see e.g. chapter 6 of *Studying Popular Music*), but actually I wonder why (it sometimes feels as if it was more like Kafka's penal colony). I'm comfortable now with an acceptance of methodological contingency, which I would describe as *conjunctural analysis*: chapter 1 is a clear example of what I mean by this, and in this sense, chapters 2, 3, 5, 6, 7, 9, 11, 13 and 15 (at least) follow a similar course, in at least some of their elements. I see this method as derived from Gramscian and cultural-studies sources, but as drawing also on Walter Benjamin's notion of 'constellation'; indeed, I might adapt Benjamin at this point: To articulate music analytically does not mean to recognise it 'the way it really is'. It means to seize hold of a cathectic attachment as it flashes up at a moment of danger.[15]

In music, a particularly important role in articulating conjunctures – in articulating them as sites of belonging – is taken by techniques of:

Repetition: I have written extensively on this topic; these writings are already readily accessible and therefore aren't included here (see Selected Bibliography, including chapter 7 of *Studying Popular Music* and chapter 4 of *Voicing the Popular*), but aspects of my understanding of this theme appear in chapters 7 and 11.

Moments of danger, seized analytically, offer a means whereby the assertions of belonging this involves can in turn be submitted to a larger rhythm of awareness – larger in terms both of movements of time and of social theatre; that is, can begin to write, to be written by, history. A late-twentieth/early twenty-first century vantage-point occupies a moment when, at various levels, 'history' seems to have run out of road; and it's this, it would seem, that has produced a particular, and particularly common, memory-flash (to salute Benjamin again), whose organising perspective might be summed up in the question, How does it stand, now, with enlightenment? (This is why, no doubt, Adorno and Horkheimer's great book, *Dialectic of Enlightenment*, came to seem a natural companion while I was writing this Introduction.) Or, to put this in a different way, what does it mean to say we're in a crisis of:

---

15 The adaptation is of Benjamin's critique of positivist historiography: 'Theses on the Philosophy of History' [written, 1940], VI, in *Illuminations*, ed. Hannah Arendt, tr. Harry Zohn (London: Fontana, 1973), 255–66 (257).

Modernity? The 'history' at issue in this book concerns this crisis, and also, therefore, the concept and course of development of modernity that it implies. And my argument would be that we will not understand the concept and the development, nor be able, therefore, to even broach an explanation for the crisis, without the awareness that modernity – by which I mean here what flows from the eighteenth-century Enlightenment and the political and economic revolutions that accompanied it – is always already structured by its engagement of the politics of the popular, which is to say, the politics of its struggles with the Low-Other, and the impress this leaves behind: a drama of what has been called 'love and theft'.[16] While the whole book is relevant to this theme, chapters 2, 6, 7, 12, 14, 15 and 16 are especially pertinent.

In this understanding of history, the moment of crisis explodes out of a constellation in which memory, revolution and the popular intersect; for, returning to Benjamin,

> History is the subject of a structure whose site is not empty, homogeneous time, but time filled by the presence of the now [*Jetztzeit*] [...] The French Revolution viewed itself as Rome incarnate. It evoked ancient Rome the way fashion evokes costumes of the past. Fashion [like popular music] has a flair for the topical, no matter where it stirs in the thickets of long ago; it is a tiger's leap into the past. This jump, however, takes place in an arena where the ruling class gives the commands. The same leap in the open air of history is the dialectical one, which is how Marx understood the revolution.[17]

◊◊◊

I'm convinced now that the schema of 'situational moments' that I put forward as a framework for grasping the historical development of popular music in modernity (see chapter 2) gets the twentieth century rather skewed. The 'moment of pop culture' around rock 'n' roll didn't, I now think, mark situational change; it was conjunctural. Instead, situational upheaval comes at the turn of the twentieth and twenty-first centuries, with digitisation, post-punk pluralism, a step-change in the operations of global capitalism and the widespread collapse of faith in values, systems and narratives built on a sense of a priori foundations and totalities. This moment – this 'suspension', as Jean-Luc Nancy calls it – is 'our time'; it spaces time, suspends it, puts it in place by spacing it, re-making history as a sense that precisely 'history', as pre-given narrative, is impossible. This, for Nancy, is 'finite history' – a spacing that offers 'the possibility of saying "we" and "our" [...] the possibility of being *in common*'. 'History', he argues, 'is community, that is, the happening of a certain space of time – as a certain spacing of time, which is the spacing of a "we."'[18] We're used to the idea that music says 'we'. Popular music, of course, searches for and addresses a specific 'we' (albeit one that isn't stable or uncontested). Popular music studies tries to identify the location of that 'we' and, within the rubric of critique, to put it in question. But, within the spacing of 'our time',

---

16 Eric Lott, *Love and Theft: Blackface Minstrelsy and the American Working Class* (New York: Oxford University Press, 1993).

17 Benjamin, 'Theses', XIV, 263.

18 Nancy, *Birth to Presence*, 151. Nancy's neo-Benjaminian theory seems to posit this 'suspension' as a novelty. But, as often happens, it may mark a historically contingent revelation that unwittingly opens to view a universal potential. This would be the sense of Benjamin's 'tiger's leap into the past'.

how might we go about defining the makeup of the 'we' of popular music studies? Or that of any musicological 'we' *tout court*? For Nancy, this 'we' is performative: '"History" […] has to be taken as an offer and to be decided […] We have to decide to enunciate our "we", our community, in order to enter history.'[19] But if this 'we' is declarative, how would we prevent its (self-) possessiveness, its 'our'-ness, re-entering the drear cycles of having and being?

Critical musicology was a declaration against the illusion of disinterestedness, revealing it as up to its neck in a certain structure of *ownership*. But critique exerts its own claims to possession, as we have seen. Strangely (or perhaps not), this tortuous movement (which is also often painful – torturous) seems to run parallel with an analogous tightening convolution in the instrumentalised use and control of music itself. This process reaches an extreme in the deployment of music *as torture*, a phenomenon incisively explored in recent writings by Suzanne Cusick.

In a moving meditation on this phenomenon, and its implications for her own work as a musicologist and for musicology in general, Cusick points out how the inter-connected sets of practices we thought we could identify as 'music' and as 'musicology' (whether old or new) are both brought up short, made foreign to themselves, rendered dumb or, precisely, *voice-less*, when confronted with details of the use of music or sound more generally as an instrument of torture.[20] What we thought was *ours* becomes *theirs* – a trauma all the more painful for scholars, and fans, of popular music, since this is the weapon of choice. We rejoin here the discursive trajectory identified earlier in Herder, as it reaches a moment of unsurpassed sado-masochistic (one might say, Adornian) perversity. In the blackest of ironies, music of the people, itself 'mutilated' to death, is deployed against the people: government of the people, by the people, for the people – a true dialectic of enlightenment!

Searching to understand why musicology falls silent at this point – or almost so – Cusick identifies, in effect, a sort of equivalence between the scholarly and military practices: both are ruled by quests for knowledge and assertions of power which are destructively negative (for, to put it in my own terms, critique tortures its object too, and hence ends up eating itself). Drawing on Eve Kosofsky Sedgwick's distinction between 'paranoid' and 'reparative' modes of reading (itself grounded in Kleinian psychoanalysis), Cusick pinpoints the 'hermeneutics of suspicion' as 'paranoid': the part-objects carved out of the world are sources of anxiety, disbelief, aggression, the search is for knowledge, and the dominant affect is hate. By contrast, reparative reading looks to re-assemble the part-objects into a whole with which the self can identify, the search is for pleasure, and the dominant affect is love.

Yes, but… But, what if there never was, and never could be, any whole for objects to belong to? (This would be the gist of a Lacanian response to the Kleinian position, but I intend a broader philosophical point.) Admittedly, Cusick, again following Sedgwick, emphasises that this would be 'not necessarily like any preexisting whole'.[21] But what if the very idea of a whole, if treated as any more than a (perhaps fruitful) fantasmatic 'as if', is politically

---

19 Ibid. 166.

20 Suzanne G. Cusick, 'Fifth Column: Musicology, Torture, Repair', *Radical Musicology*, 3 (2008), http://www.radical-musicology.org.uk (7 March 2009), 24 pars.

21 Eve Kosofsky Sedgwick, 'Paranoid Reading and Reparative Reading, or, You're So Paranoid You Probably Think This Essay is About You', in *Touching Feeling: Affect, Pedagogy, Performativity* (Durham & London: Duke University Press, 2003), 123–51 (128).

fraught, and love is, precisely, a recognition of this? Perhaps, rather than seeking integration, we should follow a different maxim: *let the other be; leave the objects where they are*. This isn't to deny that, in the inevitable processes of dialogical exchange or dialectical movement, objects, even the objects of human production and self-production, shift their significance for consciousness, that is, in a certain sense, they mutate. It is, though, to recognise a limit; indeed, at each successive moment of encounter, the strength of this limit beyond which consciousness cannot go increases. Love *means* the recognition of this noumenal core, beyond boundary, beyond name. This 'beyond' used to possess a name – namely, 'God' – until we found that we made this too. Once we accept this space – this grave beneath and enveloping the corpse (and corpus) – new shoots can begin to grow. This, in relation to music as much as anything else, would be love without theft.

The specifics of Cusick's material, which are drawn from the global US 'dark prison' network, are absolutely irreducible. Yet they belong to a genealogy. This instance repeats structurally a baleful pattern, in which music has often been implicated with violence, albeit in varied ways, most obviously in the 'culture' of the Nazi camps. Culture and barbarism have perhaps always been bedfellows – this is a key strand of the dialectic of enlightenment – and every document of culture is also a document of barbarism, as Benjamin observed. The broader instrumentalisation of culture is autonomous art's other side – feeding on its status as a legitimating exclusion – which helps to explain why musicology, traditionally autonomous music's ideological handmaiden, has struggled to deal with it. I wonder, then, if at bottom (the phrase launches me on a 'paranoid' reading, for which I hope I will be forgiven), the source of Sedgwick's distress, and Cusick's, isn't so much the paranoid quality of the hermeneutics of culture – for as both point out, suspicion is still often a justified tactic – but more the impotence of culture itself. Over the period when critical thought has infected the academy, to the point where a spiralling feedback crisis in its (auto-) immune system has brought it close to death, official politics in its triumphalist neoliberal mode has shrunk its sphere of operation almost entirely to the territory of culture: the mundane biopolitics of life-style choice (of which the war on those whose choices are other is a deadly mirror). Politics has appropriated culture as style. The torture industry carries to the limit the extreme instrumentalisation of cultural policy in general. Perhaps the appropriate reaction to this is that culture should *become* political (again) – and this should certainly include the cultivation of love (which, as paranoid theory has never tired of telling us, is always already political).

Modernity repeats, as all its most insightful critics, from Baudelaire through Nietzsche and Benjamin to Lacan, Derrida and Deleuze, have noticed. The culture/barbarism relation is one of modernity's repeating antinomies. Untying Ulysses from his mast and drowning – whether in love or song – is no more feasible than when Adorno and Horkheimer made the Sirens story the central myth of enlightenment. A musicology that is not just reparative but also declarative demands an act of faith – faith that the *economy* of possession might one day give way to an *ecology*; law of the household, where masters and slaves still torture each other, to a spreading enunciative discourse of filiation.[22] Family romance, the territory where popular song typically makes its home, and the originary site of at least two (un) holy trinities

---

22   Economy: *oikos* (= household) + *nomos* (= law). Ecology: *oikos* + *logos* (= discourse); here a *logos* that is always also an *energeia*.

(faith, hope, love; liberty, equality, fraternity), demands to be re-worked as *kinship*, conceived in its fullest possible intra- and inter-species extent, as that which joins and separates *at the same time*, which joins *through* separation. This is my hope for song, for music – and for the people. And what – at a moment when, as I write, the nature of the deepening world crisis demands that economic and ecological understandings of *oikos*, the common home, be grasped together, and invites a stand in favour of those who will undoubtedly be the principal victims of this crisis, the people, the lowest of the people, indeed the low in all its species dimensions – what would be the proper hope for musicology? That it *make a stand*; that, as it follows and engages with the routes of a rhyzomatically spreading musical practice (again both joining and separating), critique is able to metamorphose into something that, yes, puts down roots once more, but roots that sustain rather than drain; that fight towards the light (for the day of enlightenment entices still), while still planting themselves deliberately in the strata where the low make their homes; that neither appropriate nor expropriate but procreate, with legacy not genetically or generically selective but diasporically promiscuous, wild in disseminating and invaginating dispersal; metamorphose, then, into a truly *radical* musicology.[23]

---

23 Act as if you already believe; hence the journal which I have already cited, and is here cited again: *Radical Musicology*, http://www.radical-musicology.org.uk, cited both for its overall political strategy and for the specific discussion of 'radicality' in Biddle, 'Fifth Column', pars. 8–14.

Selected Bibliography

Books

Voicing the Popular: On the Subjects of Popular Music (New York: Routledge, 2006).
Studying Popular Music (Milton Keynes: Open University Press, 1990).
Pop Music and the Blues: A Study of the Relationship and Its Significance (London: Gollancz, 1972).

Edited Volumes

The Cultural Study of Music: A Critical Introduction, with Martin Clayton and Trevor Herbert (New York: Routledge, 2003), with a contribution (Chapter 8 of the present work) and an introduction (listed below).
Reading Pop: Approaches to Textual Analysis in Popular Music (Oxford: Oxford University Press, 2000), with an introduction and contribution (listed below).
Popular Music, Vol. 5: Continuity and Change, with David Horn (Cambridge: Cambridge University Press, 1985), with a contribution (Chapter 2 of the present work) and an introduction.
Popular Music, Vol. 4: Performers and Audiences, with David Horn (Cambridge: Cambridge University Press, 1984), with an introduction.
Popular Music, Vol. 3: Producers and Markets, with David Horn (Cambridge: Cambridge University Press, 1983), with an introduction and a contribution (listed below).
Popular Music, Vol. 2: Theory and Method, with David Horn (Cambridge: Cambridge University Press, 1982), with an introduction.
Popular Music, Vol. 1: *Folk or Popular? Distinctions, Influences, Continuities*, with David Horn (Cambridge: Cambridge University Press, 1981), with an introduction.

Essays not Included in this Volume

'Towards a New World? The Vicissitudes of American Popular Music', in *The Cambridge History of World Music*, ed. Philip V. Bohlman (Cambridge: Cambridge University Press, forthcoming, 2009).
'In Search of the Popular Music Text', *Bulgarian Musicology*, 31: 1 (2007), 3–19.
'Du concept de *people* dans la musique populaire', *Rue Descartes*, 60 (2008), 8–19.
'Introduction: Music, Modernisation and Popular Identity', in *Popular Music in France from Chanson to Techno*, ed. Hugh Dauncey and Steve Cannon (Aldershot: Ashgate, 2003), 1–6.

'Introduction: Music Studies and the Idea of Culture', in *The Cultural Study of Music: A Critical Introduction*, ed. Martin Clayton, Trevor Herbert and Richard Middleton (New York: Routledge, 2003), 1–15.

'Pop, Rock, and Interpretation', in *The Cambridge Companion to Pop and Rock*, ed. Simon Frith, Will Straw and John Street (Cambridge: Cambridge University Press, 2002), 213–225.

'Musikalische Dimensionen. Genres, Stile, Aufführungspraktiken', in *Rock- und Popmusik, Handbuch der Musikwissenschaft des 20. Jahrhundert*, Vol. 6, ed. Peter Wicke (Laaber: Laaber Verlag, 2001), 61–106.

'Introduction: Locating the Popular Music Text', in *Reading Pop: Approaches to Textual Analysis in Popular Music*, ed. Richard Middleton (Oxford: Oxford University Press, 2000), 1–19.

'Form', in *Key Terms in Popular Music and Culture*, ed. Thomas Swiss and Bruce Horner (Oxford: Blackwell, 2000), 141–55.

'Rock Singing', in *The Cambridge Companion to Singing*, ed. John Potter (Cambridge: Cambridge University Press, 2000), 28–41.

'"Over and Over": Notes towards a Politics of Repetition – Surveying the Ground, Charting Some Routes', http://www2.rz.hu-berlin.de/fpm/texte/middle.htm (1996). In Italian as '"Over and Over": Appunti verso una politica della ripetizione', *Musica/Realtà*, 55 (1998), 135–50, 56 (1998), 169–80.

'Who May Speak? From a Politics of Popular Music to a Popular Politics of Music', in *Popular Music Studies in Seven Acts*, ed. Tarja Hautamäki and Tarja Rautiainen (University of Tampere: Department of Folk Tradition, 1996), 8-22; reprinted in *Repercussions*, 7–8 (1999–2000), 77–103.

'The Rock Revolution', in *Music in Britain, Vol. 6, The Twentieth Century*, ed. Stephen Banfield (Oxford: Blackwell, 1995), 79–106.

'Popular Music Analysis and Musicology: Bridging the Gap', *Popular Music*, 12:2 (1993), 177–90; reprinted in *Reading Pop: Approaches to Textual Analysis in Popular Music*, ed. Richard Middleton (Oxford: Oxford University Press, 2000), 104–121.

'The Politics of Cultural Expression: African Musics and the World Market', in *Poverty and Development in the 1990s*, ed. Tim Allen and Alan Thomas (Oxford: Oxford University Press, 1992), 362–78.

'Sulla ripetizione', in *Il senso in musica: Antologia di Semiotica musicale*, ed. Luca Marconi and Gino Stefani (Bologna: Cooperativa Libraria Universitaria Editrice Bologna, 1987), 287–98.

'Popular Music, Class Conflict and the Music-Historical Field', in *Popular Music Perspectives, Vol.2*, ed. David Horn (Göteborg, Exeter, Ottawa and Reggio Emilia: International Association for the Study of Popular Music, 1985), 24–46.

'In the Groove or Blowing your Mind? The Pleasures of Musical Repetition', in *Popular Culture and Social Relations*, ed. Tony Bennett, Janet Woollacott and Colin Mercer (Milton Keynes: Open University Press, 1985), 159–76. Partly reprinted in *The Popular Music Studies Reader*, ed. Andy Bennett, Barry Shank and Jason Toynbee (New York: Routledge, 2006), 15–20.

'Articolare il significato musicale. Ricostruire una storia della musica. Collocare il popolare', *Musica/Realtà*, 15 (1984), 63-85, 16 (1985), 97–118. Reprinted in *Musiche/Realtà*, ed. Franco Fabbri (Milan: Unicopli, 1989), 69–112.

'Play it again Sam: Some Notes on the Productivity of Repetition in Popular Music', *Popular Music*, 3 (1983), 235–70. Reprinted in *Popular Music: Critical Concepts in Media and Cultural Studies*, ed. Simon Frith, vol. 3 (London: Routledge, 2003), 136–69.

'Popular Music of the Lower Classes', in *Music in Britain, Vol. 5, The Romantic Age, 1800–1914*, ed. Nicholas Temperley (London: Athlone Press, 1982), 63–91.

'After Wagner: The Place of Myth in Twentieth-Century Music', *Music Review*, 34:3/4 (1973), 307–27.

'Stravinsky's Development: A Jungian Approach', *Music and Letters*, 54:3 (1973), 289–301.

'Cage and the Meta-Freudians', *British Journal of Aesthetics,* 12:3 (1972), 228–43.

Review Essays and Shorter Articles

'"Popular Music" Does Not Exist', *Il saggiatore musicale*, 11:2 (2004), 395–8.

'Between Mediation and Articulation in Music-Historical Method', in *Musikwissenschaftlicher Paradigmenwechsel? Zum Stellenwert Marxistischer Ansätze in der Musikforschung*, ed. Wolfgang Martin Stroh and Günter Mayer (University of Oldenburg, 2000), 131–6.

'Pop Goes Old Theory' [Review Essay of Allan Forte, *The American Popular Ballad of the Golden Era 1924-1950*], *Journal of the Royal Musical Association*, 122:2 (1997), 303–20.

'Repeat Performance', in *Music on Show: Issues of Performance*, ed. Helmi Järviluoma, Tarja Hautamaki and Simon Frith (University of Tampere: Department of Folk Tradition, 1997), 209–13.

'Interpreting the Popular Music Text: Towards an Agenda', *Working Papers of the Institute of Popular Music*, 5 (University of Liverpool, 1994).

'Towards a Theory of Gesture in Popular Song Analysis', in *Studi e Testi 1: Secondo Convegno Europeo di Analisi Musicale,* ed. Rossana Dalmonte and Mario Baroni (University of Trento, 1993), 345–50.

'Two British Responses to Black American Musical Styles: the Beatles and the Rolling Stones', in *Report of the Twelfth Congress of the International Musicological Society*, ed. Daniel Heartz and Bonnie Wade (Kassel: Bärenreiter, 1981), 572–4.

Substantial Articles in Reference Works

'Ballad (North America)', in *Continuum Encyclopedia of Popular Music of the World, Vol. O: Genres*, ed. John Shepherd, David Horn, Dave Laing, Paul Oliver and Peter Wicke (London: Continuum, forthcoming, 2009).

'John Lennon', in *Oxford Dictionary of National Biography*, vol. 33, ed. H.G.C. Matthew and Brian Harrison (Oxford: Oxford University Press, 2004), 349–56.

'Semiology/Semiotics' and 'Class', in *Continuum Encyclopedia of Popular Music of the World, Vol. 1: Media, Industry and Society*, ed. John Shepherd, David Horn, Dave Laing, Paul Oliver and Peter Wicke (London: Continuum, 2003), 122–6, 176–8.

'Singing', 'Songwriter', 'Voice (as Instrument)', 'Form', 'Solo' and 'Song', in *Continuum Encyclopedia of Popular Music of the World, Vol. 2: Performance and Production*, ed. John Shepherd, David Horn, Dave Laing, Paul Oliver and Peter Wicke (London: Continuum, 2003), 164–68, 202–6, 455–7, 503–20, 638–42, 642–44.

'Lo studio della popular music', in *Enciclopedia della Musica*, Vol. II, ed. Jean-Jacques Nattiez (Turin: Casa Editrice Einaudi, 2002), 718–37.

'Pop' (part), 'Popular Music' (part) and 'Rock, in *The New Grove Dictionary of Music and Musicians*, rev. edn, ed. Stanley Sadie (London: Macmillan, 2001), vol. 20, 101–102, 111–16, 128–53; vol. 21, 485–6.

'The Beatles', in *Die Musik in Geschichte und Gegenwart*, rev. edn, ed. Ludwig Finscher (Kassel: Bärenreiter Verlag, 2000), *Personenteil Band 2*, 567–74.

CHAPTER 1

All Shook Up?
Innovation and Continuity
in Elvis Presley's Vocal Style

One way of looking at Elvis Presley is as a great American success story. From a life of anonymity and poor-white Southern poverty to enormous wealth and the kind of fame so pervasive that "all one has to do is appear";[1] undisputed king of popular music from 1956 to the advent of the Beatles, with world record sales estimated in 1971 as about 155 million singles and 25 million albums; top of the American popular record charts for 55 out of 104 weeks in the period from 1956 to 1958; and so on, and so on. Yet paradoxically this triumphant progress can also be read as a kind of failure. Certainly most rock critics take this line, seeing Elvis's career as a progressive sell-out to the music industry, a transition from "folk" authenticity (the Sun singles of 1954–55) to a sophisticated professionalism (epitomized by the ballads and movies of the 1960s) in which the dollars multiplied but musical values went by the board. Greil Marcus is the only writer on Elvis I have come across who tries to resist this Faustian scenario—which in essence is just as romantic as the great American success legend, its apparent obverse—but even he, when he comes to make his crucial distinction, places it between the Sun Golden Age, "a space of freedom," and a subsequent decline into a "riskless aesthetic of smooth-it-away" which "gives an all-encompassing Yes to his audience."[2]

There are big theoretical difficulties with such an analysis. Cultural fields, particularly in modern mass societies, do not work in this simple way. Of course there *are* different markets and different kinds

[1]Greil Marcus, *Mystery Train* (Omnibus Press, 1977), p. 139.
[2]Ibid., pp. 141, 166, 199.

152   *All Shook Up?*

of music but the processes of creation, production and consumption are too dynamic and interactive to permit rigid historical, typological or evaluative dividing lines. It is probably safe to say that in post-war America a pure "folk" role, untouched by commercial influences, had become impossible. The dissemination of music by radio and gramophone record permeated the whole country and every social stratum. The performers whom the young Elvis heard, and presumably learned from—gospel music singers, bluesmen like Arthur Crudup, Bill Broonzy, Junior Parker and Howlin' Wolf, country-and-western stars such as Bob Wills, Hank Williams and Roy Acuff—were *commercial* artists; they, like Elvis himself, did not separate themselves off from the whole wash of music that was available. When Sam Phillips, founder of Sun Records and "creator" of Elvis Presley, said "If I could find a white man who had the Negro sound and the Negro feel, I could make a billion dollars,"[3] the twin motivations, artistic and commercial, were not separated or separable.

If we look at the music Elvis produced through his career, we find equally strong *empirical* objections to the "decline-and-fall" view. All too often commentators stress a change in "sound" (for example, the "primitive"—hence "authentic"—acoustic of the Sun records giving way to the "sophisticated"—hence "manipulative"—methods of RCA, with their more elaborate use of amplification, vocal backing groups, strings) at the expense of other characteristics of the musical style, which may show continuity. I want to argue for the existence of important continuities.

Compared to his two great rock and roll contemporaries, Chuck Berry and Little Richard, the *scope* of Elvis's significance is limited. Unlike them, he was not a songwriter; unlike Chuck Berry, he was not an important instrumental stylist. Musically his contribution lies almost wholly in his singing, and it is this I want to discuss. His productivity was enormous, covering singles, albums and movies, but the center of his work was the single, and because of this, and to limit the boundaries of the discussion, I shall confine my examples to his

---

[3]Quoted in Jerry Hopkins, *Elvis: A Biography* (New York: Simon & Schuster, 1971), p. 66.

most successful singles, as compiled on RCA's "Golden Records" series, together with the earlier singles made at Sun.[4]

Elvis's two most notable contributions to the language of rock and roll singing are firstly, the assimilation of "romantic lyricism" and secondly, what I shall call boogification. Both techniques can be found in classic form in his first national hit, "Heartbreak Hotel" (1956). This was by origin a country song but its vocal has the shape of a typical blues shout. Nevertheless the rough tone, spontaneous, irregular rhythms, and "dirty" intonation that most blues singers would have used are for the most part conspicuously absent from Elvis's performance; his tone is full, rich and well produced, his intonation is precise, stable and "correct," the notes are sustained and held right through, and the phrasing is legato. All this is particularly clear on the words "broken hearted lovers," "been so long on lonely street" and "take a walk down lonely street," but the lyrical spirit is important throughout. At the same time this lyrical continuity is subverted by boogification. As in boogie-woogie, the basic vocal rhythms are triplets (♩♩♩ , ♩♪) and , again as in boogie-woogie, the *off*-beat quaver is often given an unexpected accent (e.g. ♩♪), producing syncopation and cross-rhythm. The effect is physical, demanding movement, jerking the body into activity. Elvis, however, extends the technique. He adds extra off-beat notes not demanded by words or vocal line, often splitting up syllables or even consonants, slurring words together, disguising the verbal sense. So we have

Occasionally, when it would not really be possible actually to notate subdivisions of the beat, there is on a "sustained" note something like a rhythm vibrato (in triplet rhythm): listen for instance to "Although" at the start of the second and last choruses, "Now" at the start of the third, and "Well" at the start of the fourth. Boogification is often

[4]*The Elvis Presley Sun Collection* (RCA HY1001, English), *Elvis' Golden Records*, vols. 1, 2, 3 and 4 (RCA 1707, 2075, 2765, 3921).

154   *All Shook Up?*

accompanied by characteristic "vocal orchestration": usually this involves deep, resonant chest-tone, designed to sound erotic, but Elvis also uses simulation of physical effort and distress, by means of spitting out words and gasping for breath. The overall effect of the boogification technique is of course sexy but it is also a bit jittery and absurd. The sensuality seems almost out of control, perhaps one of the earliest examples in rock of irrational "living for kicks," and indeed it may be that Elvis's development of the technique stems from his own erotic movements as a performer, which it is clear were, originally at least, spontaneous and involuntary.[5] The combination of boogification with romantic lyricism in "Heartbreak Hotel"—the two elements are perfectly integrated, or rather held in tension—produces a style already, at this early stage in Elvis's career, teetering on the edge of that melodrama into which he was so often to fall.

In fact, the same fusion of techniques can be found even earlier, while Elvis was still recording for Sun. "Milkcow Blues Boogie" (1955) is perhaps the best example since, again, the techniques are so well integrated, though Elvis's treatment of the song is at such a quick tempo that the operation of the techniques themselves is less clear than in "Heartbreak Hotel." The lyrical approach—the rich tone, the singing *through* the note, the sustained legato, the controlled phrase-endings—is most apparent for the last line of each chorus. Boogification pervades the entire vocal, though the quick tempo means there is less scope for *accenting* off-beat notes, and often the effect is so fast as to be a rhythm vibrato. The tempo also makes accurate notation harder. However, at the beginning we hear something like this:

(here the quavers are very short: almost an aspect of the articulation—slurring the words together—rather than of the rhythm).

[5]See Henry Pleasants, *The Great American Popular Singers* (London: Gollancz, 1974), pp. 271–2.

And again:

Well-ll   ah   tried ev' ry   thi - ing   to   git   a- long with-a - you - ou —

Again boogification is accompanied by vocal orchestration, this time including sudden falsettos.

A third important vocal technique appears in "Milkcow Blues Boogie"—though in terms of Elvis's overall development it is less important than the two already mentioned: this is the influence of gospel music. Obviously this derives from his upbringing (attending services and revival meetings at the Pentecostal church his parents belonged to in Tupelo—though in any case the music, white and black, was all around in the culture in which Elvis grew up), and it shows up in vocal tone (ecstatic—listen especially to the introductory "Well" at the start of the first chorus and again at Elvis's re-entry after the guitar solo) and in the use of elaborate melismata, a typical gospel technique. In "Milkcow" these occur most prominently in the last line of each chorus, on one particular word (italicized here): ". . . since that *cow* been gone," ". . . treating *me* this way," ". . . when your *baby's* not around." In a way "gospelization" is an equivalent in the area of pitch to what boogification does in the area of rhythm. In both cases the squareness and regularity of the lyrical traditions of white popular song are broken up, on the one hand through off-beat accents and rhythmic complexity, on the other, through "off-*tune*" melodic patterns. In both cases rational control is heard as being threatened by hints of ecstasy, physical or spiritual, and therefore by a touch of the irrational. The relationship is particularly clear when, as is often the case, the two techniques are combined in the same song. "Trying to Get to You" (1956, though recorded in 1955) is a good example, its rocking medium-tempo boogie rhythm perfectly matching the gospel-ish phrasing and tone of the vocal.

Gospelization was not just a "folk" technique which Elvis sub-sequently forgot. As with boogification and romantic lyricism, he continued to use it in his early Victor recordings—and indeed throughout his career. "Anyway You Want Me" (1956) is in a direct line from "Trying to Get to You" (the only important change being the

156   *All Shook Up?*

addition of a backing vocal group), and later songs like "One Night" (1958) and "Fame and Fortune" (1960) carry on the tradition.

What we do see in that tradition, however, is an example of a kind of stylistic specialization. This is also true of the other vocal techniques I have mentioned. While all of them continue to appear throughout Elvis's career, songs which *integrate* them, like "Milkcow Blues Boogie" (or "Mystery Train") in the Sun period or "Heartbreak Hotel" in the early Victor period, become less common. In particular the two main techniques, lyricism and boogification, tend to diverge, the former channelled into ballads, the latter into a particular kind of rock and roll song which I shall call mannerist. Elvis's huge ballad repertoire needs little commentary here, save to point out that it derived from both country and Tin Pan Alley sources—"I'll Never Let You Go" *and* "Blue Moon" (both 1956, though recorded in 1955 and 1954 respectively)—and that it began not with the move to RCA but at Sun, "Love Me Tender" (1956) and "That's When Your Heartaches Begin" (1957) being preceded by equally sentimental ballads cut for Sam Phillips; indeed, it began earlier: when as a boy Elvis was entered for a talent contest at the Mississippi-Alabama Fair, it was "Old Shep" that he sang. Mannerist rock is more interesting. It is associated most clearly with a series of songs, many written for Elvis by Otis Blackwell, starting with "Don't Be Cruel" (1956) and "All Shook Up" (1957) and stretching down to "Please Don't Drag that String Around" (1963). The techniques of boogification are exaggerated, over-played, even parodied. Placed in a context where they are not tempered by rock and roll shout, gospel ecstasy or lyrical passion—in short, by anything *serious*—and where instead they are associated with (deliberately introduced, tongue-in-cheek?) musical clichés, they move from the area of sexual excitement towards that of laughter. By pushing the techniques of "living for kicks" into mannerism, Elvis distances himself from their demands, physical and psychological. In "All Shook Up," for example, the old techniques are there:

a-well-a-bless-a-my soul-a-what's-a-wrong with me

but the triviality of the lyrics (from the powerful blues sex-imagery of "Milkcow" to a portrayal of love as no more than "itching like a man in a fuzzy tree" is the size of the transformation) and Elvis's light, amused vocal tone (no "vocal orchestration" here) tell us that this is not serious, it is a performance.

Mannerism is usually seen as an RCA development; Charlie Gillett, for instance, describes it in terms of the decline-and-fall myth.[6] But once again we find that it was already developing during the Sun period, notably in "Baby Lets Play House" (1955). The boogification here is very fast and complex, and, coupled with sudden falsettos, it produces a hiccoughing effect which is almost absurd. Certainly it is deliberately exaggerated so that it now expresses not instinctive enjoyment but self-aware technique: Elvis's confidence in his own powers is so unquestioned as to reach the level of ironic self-presentation. Stylistically each chorus divides into two. The first half is rock and roll shout, and contains threats to his girl ("You may go to college . . . but . . .," "I'd rather see you dead little girl Than to be with another man," etc.); the second half is mannerist and expresses Elvis's refusal to take himself seriously, the easy self-confidence of parody. To use a vogue concept, the myth to which the song speaks is "deconstructed" and the deconstruction takes place *in the song itself*.

Just as there are no easy distinctions to be made between Sun and Victor recordings, so commonly made categorizations based on "black" and "white" material are hard to maintain too. Both at Sun and at RCA the two principal techniques, romantic lyricism and boogification, were used indiscriminately in songs derived from or in either the rhythm and blues tradition or the country and western tradition. Elvis's first commercial release (1954) couples a rhythm and blues number, Arthur Crudup's "That's All Right," and Bill Monroe's country song, "Blue Moon of Kentucky." He sings the blues with all the lyrical control at his command, his tone rich and sustained, his phrasing rather square and precise, his intonation for the most part legitimate, the phrase-endings beautifully finished off. Blues lament is turned into confident self-presentation. Conversely "Blue Moon of Kentucky" is speeded up and the vocal boogified (though the lyrical style is retained for the "bridge")." Again the final effect of Elvis's version is of a celebration of his own charisma and power. Much the

[6]Charlie Gillett, *The Sound of the City* (Souvenir Press, 1971), pp. 66–7.

158   *All Shook Up?*

same still happens in some RCA recordings. Elvis's version of Chuck
Willis's "I Feel So Bad" (1961) is a lyricized blues to compare with
"That's All Right," while even a ballad as sentimental as "Good Luck
Charm" (1962) has a vocal carrying traces of boogification. The usual
interpretation of such songs—Elvis was crossing cultures and singing
the blues on a country song, creating "hillbilly blues" or rocking up
ballads—is far too simple, as Marcus has pointed out.[7] Elvis was
transforming all of these into something new, something unique,
something of himself—or as Sam Phillips put it in the recording studio
while Elvis was working out his "Blue Moon of Kentucky," "Fine,
fine, man, hell, that's different! That's a *pop song* now, little guy! That's
good!"[8]

Elvis's originality, then, lay not so much in the cultural mix which he
helped to bring into being—that was in the air and would have
happened anyway—as in what he did with it. He himself, when asked
by Sam Phillips' assistant who he sang like, quite justifiably replied,
"I don't sound like nobody."[9] And this was not the result of an unself-
conscious "folk" process (which subsequently gave way to a more
"professional" production-line approach at RCA): even at Sun the
evidence is that he was a self-aware artist who worked hard at building
up a style, rehearsing a recording and creating a performance technique.[10] From the start his music had an "authentic multiplicity"[11] of
styles. When he first turned up at the Sun studio and was asked what
kind of song he did, his answer was "I sing all kinds."[12] He was always
a performer. As Marcus says, "It may be that he never took *any* of it
seriously, just did his job and did it well, trying to enjoy himself and
stay sane—save," he adds, "for those first Tennessee records"[13]—
though I would argue that the seeds of "performance" are already
present in those Sun days, in "Baby Lets Play House" for example.
The ballad style for which he has been so criticized by rock writers
was not a fall from grace; it was always inherent in his singing, as

[7]See Marcus, pp. 191–3.
[8]Quoted Ibid., p. 192.
[9]Quoted in Hopkins, p. 64.
[10]See Marcus, pp. 172–3; Hopkins, pp. 70–1, 85–6, 149–52.
[11]Marcus, p. 185.
[12]Quoted in Hopkins, p. 64.
[13]Marcus, p. 143.

"That's All Right" shows. Even at that early stage, "Elvis was . . .
hellbent on the mainstream. . . . With Southern power in his music,
Elvis had mainstream savvy in his soul."[14]

The only workable categorization of Elvis's output is not historical
but by song-types. These run continuously throughout his career.
Admittedly different types do correspond to some extent to different
vocal techniques—though, as we have seen, this is not the whole story
since any one technique can be used in several song-types; moreover,
the best songs are beyond category, integrating the different techniques. What *does* happen historically is that integrated songs become
gradually less common through the course of Elvis's career. The
song-types tend to diverge, as the relatively small, well defined audience of the Sun days gives way to a large, heterogeneous market
demanding different types for different sub-sections. Elvis is all
things to all men *throughout* his career, but the nature of the audience
changes. At least the following song-types can be identified:

(1) Blues (from "That's All Right" [1954] to "I Feel So Bad" [1961])
(2) Fast rock and roll (from "Good Rocking Tonight" [1954] through
    "Hound Dog" [1956] to "A Big Hunk o' Love" [1959])
(3) Mannerist rock and roll (from "Baby Lets Play House" [1955]
    through "All Shook Up" [1957] to "Please Don't Drag that String
    Around" [1963])
(4) Slow ballad, out of country music or Tin Pan Alley (from "I Love
    You Because" or "Blue Moon" [1956] to "Are You Lonesome
    Tonight" [1960], "It's Now or Never" [1960] and a multitude of
    other examples)
(5) Up-tempo ballad (from "Blue Moon of Kentucky" [1954] through
    "A Fool Such as I" [1959] to "His Latest Flame" [1961])
(6) Gospelized ballad (from "Trying to Get to You" [1956] through
    "Anyway You Want Me" [1956] to "It Hurts Me" [1963])

The unifying factor is Elvis himself—or more precisely, Elvis constructed as a particular category: "Elvis as romantic hero." He turns all
his songs into celebrations of his own power, exercises in self-
presentation. Even the blues are transformed from a lament in the face

---

[14]Ibid., pp. 182, 198.

160 *All Shook Up?*

of evil reality into a charismatic transcending of reality: "Elvis's blues were a set of musical adventures, and as a blues-singing swashbuckler, his style owed as much to Errol Flynn as it did to Arthur Crudup. It made sense to make movies out of it."[15] He always knew he would be somebody (his mother told him). The hints of narcissism about his character and his music gain currency from the evidence of his parents' attitude to him (he was heavily spoiled as a child), from the outrageously flashy clothes he wore even as an unknown adolescent, and from the fondness he showed for his long, continually groomed hair (he went to a beautician, not a barber).[16] Indeed, if one is looking for psychoanalytic evidence within childhood, the combination of apparent ordinariness (Elvis seems to have been shy, unnoticed, *average*) and parental pampering might go far to explain the intensity of his search for self-fulfillment.

Elvis managed to combine in his singing and his image both the principal strands in what can perhaps be called "commercial romanticism": first, the desire for peace, escape, a dream-world where everything is safe and lovely, and secondly, the fascination, half obsessive, half afraid, with "the dark side," the irrational world of wild revolt and self-gratification. Needless to say, these are associated in the music with the techniques of romantic lyricism and boogification respectively, and the fact that they are not opposed but complementary—both can be seen as "escapes" from mundane everyday existence, the one into fantasy and self-transcending tears, the other into the self-abnegating madness of "Saturday night rebellion"—explains the fact that both musical techniques can be used, often together, in *different* song-types, and also the seemingly strange mixture in Elvis's character and "image" of rebelliousness and conservatism. To locate these elements a little more precisely, one can find them in that familiar fusion of "good old Southern conservatism" on the one hand and "good old Southern (especially poor-white) stubborn, sometimes sullen revolt" on the other. Like any other Southern poor-white boy, he had to kick over the traces, and his culture made him enough of an outsider vis-à-vis the American mainstream to enable him to do it; at the same time, he felt himself intensely as part of a community, with its

[15]Ibid., p. 182.
[16]See Hopkins, pp. 22–24, 37–40, 61–62, 273–74.

own myths and values, its own ways of dealing with and escaping the hardship of everyday reality. In a South which since pre-bellum days had represented "a cosmic conspiracy against reality in favour of romance" (W.J. Cash), a conspiracy intensified by defeat, isolation and neglect, Elvis's singing can be seen as the re-articulation of an old cultural dynamic, worked out, however, in a form that, because of changing social circumstances and economic structures within America and indeed the Western world as a whole, could appeal to a national and international audience equally hungry for rebellion and a fantasy of freedom.

CHAPTER 2

Articulating musical meaning/re-constructing musical history/locating the 'popular'*

In thinking about how to locate popular music within music history, I start from two propositions. Firstly, that attempts to isolate and define musical types, functions and effects by purely empirical means are likely to be unhelpful. Understanding 'popular music' – for example – in terms of a quantitively measured 'popularity' (sales figures) is not only methodologically difficult to do coherently but, more important, it hypostatises what is in reality a result of living, historically changing relationships. Secondly: if, then, musical categories should be grasped as part of social processes, it does not however follow that in this relationship (between musical type, concept or practice on the one hand, social group, factor or formation on the other) the relata are in a one-to-one correspondence. Thus – quoting again examples from commonly assumed positions – the idea that 'popular music' is 'really' confined to authentic proletarian self-expression is no less misleading than the Adornian notion that it is part of an undifferentiated blanket of leisure-goods imposed on the unresisting masses by a monopoly-capitalist 'culture industry'.

In contrast, it is better to locate musical categories *topographically* (even if, as Franco Fabbri argues, the topography is multi-dimensional: see Fabbri 1982). To quote Stuart Hall, 'popular culture is neither, in a "pure" sense, the popular traditions of resistance . . . nor is it the forms which are superimposed on and over them. It is the ground on which the transformations are worked.' (Hall 1981, p. 228). The key terms are 'process', 'relationship', 'transformation', and 'contradiction'. What the term 'popular music' tries to do is put a finger on that space, that terrain, of contradiction – between 'imposed' and 'authentic', 'élite' and 'common', predominant and subordinate, then and now, theirs and ours, etc., – and to organise it in particular ways. The relationships crossing this terrain take specific forms in specific societies, and must be analysed in that context. And, since they are

* An Italian version of this article first appeared in *Musica/Realtà*, 15 and 16. I am grateful to the editors for permission to publish an English version here. Parts of the article also appear in Middleton 1979, Middleton 1982 and Middleton forthcoming. The last gives a longer account of the basic theoretical framework.

6   *Richard Middleton*

also active, the field never quiescent, the possible meanings of
'popular music' must be historically located too.

Another way of approaching this area is in terms of the *relative
autonomy* of cultural practices, and it is helpful to introduce Gramsci's
insight that the relationship between actual culture, consciousness,
ideas, experience, on the one hand, and economically determined
factors such as class position, on the other, is always problematical,
incomplete and the object of ideological work and struggle. This is
linked to Gramsci's general conception of the relationship between
economic forces and superstructural elements. While retaining the
primary determinative role of the former, he insists on the relative
autonomy of the latter: these have their own modes of existence, their
own inertia, their own time-scales, such that we have to speak of a
'necessary reciprocity' between economic/social and cultural/ideologi-
cal levels. Cultural relationships and cultural change are thus not
predetermined; rather, they are the product of negotiation, imposition, resistance, transformation, etc. In class societies this process will
obviously be mediated primarily – though not exclusively – through
class relationships and class conflict. Thus particular cultural forms
and practices cannot be attached mechanically or even paradigmati-
cally to particular classes; nor, even, can particular interpretations,
valuations and uses of a single form or practice. In Stuart Hall's words,
'there are no wholly separate "cultures" . . . [no 'bourgeois' hit-song,
no 'proletarian' industrial folk song, no 'petit bourgeois' musical
comedy, or 'working-class' rock and roll] . . . attached, in a relation of
historical fixity, to specific 'whole' classes – although there are clearly
distinct and variable class-cultural formations' (Hall 1981, p. 238). 'The
domain of the "cultural" . . . is not the homogeneous expression of a
class-belonging but is composed of distinct and specific practices in a
process of *formation* and *negotiation*.' (Mercer 1978, p. 27). The best
approach is one that 'treats the domain of cultural forms and activities
as a constantly changing field . . . looks at the relations which constantly structure this field into dominant and subordinate formations
. . . [and] at the *process* by which these relations of dominance and
subordination are articulated' (Hall 1981, p. 235)

If musical elements, forms, types, are not owned by particular
classes, if their existence is not explained by a single expressive need
but is the product of multiple determinations, how are they appropriated for use by particular classes or groups of classes? Hall used the
word 'articulate', and Chantal Mouffe (1979) and others, drawing on
Gramsci, have talked of a 'principle of articulation'. The argument is
that while elements of culture are not directly, eternally or exclusively
tied to specific economically determined factors such as class position,

Re-constructing musical history   7

they *are* determined in the final instance by such factors, through the operation of articulating principles (sets of values) which *are* tied to these factors. These principles operate by combining existing elements into new patterns or by attaching new connotations to them. The result – or rather the *desired* result, for the articulative process is always open to contestation – is a particular construction of what Gramsci calls the 'national-popular': the repertoire of cultural/ideological elements which are available to, and at stake in, attempts to build or subvert hegemony.

The theory of articulation recognises the complexity of cultural fields. It preserves a relative autonomy for superstructural elements (musical structures, for example) but also insists that those combinatory patterns actually constructed do mediate deep, objective patterns in the socio-economic formation, and that the mediation takes place *in struggle*: the classes fight to articulate together constituents of the cultural repertoire in particular ways so that they are organised in terms of principles or sets of values determined by the position and interests of the class in the prevailing mode of production. This theory seems to me the most sophisticated method available of conceiving the relationship between musical forms and practices, and class interests and social structure. More sophisticated, say, than theories of homology put forward by, for example, some ethnomusicologists and by British subcultural theory, which suggest the existence of structural 'resonances', or homologies, beween the different elements making up the culture, consciousness and social position of a particular social group (see Chambers 1982, pp. 31–2; Willis 1978, pp. 189–203; Hebdige 1979, pp. 133ff.) However, I would like to hang on to the notion of homology in a qualified sense. For it seems likely that some signifying structures are more *easily* articulated to the interests of one group than are some others; similarly, that they are more easily articulated to the interests of one group than to those of another. This is because, owing to the existence of what Willis calls the 'objective possibilities' (and limitations) of material and ideological structures, it is easier to find links and analogies between them in some cases than in others. Consider, for example, János Maróthy's distinction between what he calls 'collective-variative' methods, which he connects primarily to proletarian musical practice, and the symmetrical solo song forms typical of bourgeois music culture, from the Middle Ages on (see Maróthy 1974). It would be a mistake to regard these two categories as simple products of class needs. But it is clear that, for objective structural reasons, it was, during a certain long historical period, *easier* for the bourgeoisie to make meaningful use of the second, the working classes the first, than *vice versa*. Similarly, working-class musical

8   *Richard Middleton*

practice found it hard to deal with the elements of bourgeois solo song
except by acquiescing in the norms of the dominant musical culture, or
by treating them parodistically or through other methods of distortion.

Moreover, however *arbitrary* musical meanings and conventions are
– rather than being 'natural', or determined by some human essence or
by the needs of class expression – once particular musical elements are
put together in particular ways, and acquire particular connotations,
these can be hard to shift. It would be difficult, for instance, to move
the 'Marseillaise' out of the set of meanings sedimented around it –
hence around other tunes of the same type too – which derive from the
history of the revolutionary French bourgeoisie. Similarly, it is not easy
to disturb the connotations of those types of 'folk song' constituted by
bourgeois romanticism as signifying (sentimentalised) 'community',
an organic social harmony. The romantic-lyrical ballad style of twentieth-century Tin Pan Alley clings stubbornly to its role in the representation of gender relations within the norms set by the stereotype of the
bourgeois nuclear couple, despite attempts made from time to time to
move it into new patterns with new meanings. Thus a theory of
articulation does not mean that the musical field is a pluralistic free-
for-all. It is not *un*determined, but *over*-determined, and the ruling
interests in the social formation take the lead in setting the *pre-
dispositions* which are always trying to constitute a *received* shape. As
Gramsci points out, 'the bourgeois class poses itself as an organism in
continuous movement, capable of absorbing the whole society, assimilating it to its own cultural and economic level' (Gramsci 1971, p. 260),
and this would-be universalising push provides one of the most
important elements in music history of the last two hundred years.
Thus underlying the other side of Gramsci's picture – the continuous
construction of class alliances, with its articulative dimension in the
cultural domain – there is a basic dichotomy, organised around the
relationship of 'hegemonic' and 'subordinate' blocs (the content of
each term and the terrain controlled by each subject being precisely the
object of cultural as well as economic struggle).

It should be added that each of these subjects is defined not only by
class position – central though that is – but also by other social factors,
notably age, gender, ethnicity and nationality. Each of these can
mediate any or all of the others. Indeed, as the underlying dichotomy
in the social formation has, during the development towards and
through monopoly capitalism, become ever starker, space for the
construction of local, often short-lived 'constellations' ('subcultures'),
formed at intersections of the various factors, has grown. Thus, it can
be argued that the impact of the young Elvis Presley was due to the
way in which, taking a range of pre-existing musical, lyric and per-

formance elements, he re-articulated them into a new pattern set by the intersection and inter-mediation of certain images of class (proletarian), ethnicity (black/poor white), age ('youth'), gender (male) and nationality (American South). The articulating principle governing the social meaning of this music for its audience must be defined in terms of a conjunction of new representations of leisure, the body, gender relations and capitalist consumption, tied in turn to the objectively new social-economic position of this audience in post-war capitalist society. This is how the romantic-lyric elements in Elvis's style, for example, could take on new meanings, mediated as they were by country and western's and black music's previous appropriations of them, by the 'underview' of the Southern working class on the American Dream, and by an awareness of a new freedom in adolescent leisure behaviour.

Of course, the effects of such a 'constellation' is nuanced by the social situation of *listeners*. The 'nationality' factor in early Elvis signified rather differently for English adolescents in the mid-1950s; it was mediated through the image presented by the 'American South' within their national tradition, and, more widely, through the rather different gender, generational and class structures obtaining in that tradition. (This is no more than to say that within the operation of articulation processes production and consumption are inextricably tied together – a consideration of immense importance which deserves far more discussion than can be given here.) Similarly, the effects of early Elvis (and of early rock 'n' roll in general) change over time, as the articulating factors change. Sometimes this affects the production of the music; in any case, it always affects the ways in which it is received. Thus the class orientation of early Elvis was shifted as his music was articulated to the interests of the dominant elements in the music business; at the same time, his generational sharpness was muffled. Subsequently, revivals re-invest in meanings closer to the originals but inevitably transformed by the effects of the intervening struggles over the ownership of rock 'n' roll and of its meanings. Elvis – that particular musical agglomeration – never *belonged* to anyone in particular, then; he – it – was there to be fought for.

This is an example of the way synchronic and diachronic axes delineating the musical field interweave in analysis. Locating important conjunctures – by slicing through the relationships obtaining at any one time in the social/cultural formation – and recognising their dynamic structuring, which gives rise to a variety of transmutations, continuities and ruptures, is equally important. In Gramsci's discussion of this, there is a distinction between two types or levels of structure: the 'situation' and the 'conjuncture'. 'Situation' refers to the

10   *Richard Middleton*

deepest, the organic structures of a social formation; movement there
is fundamental and relatively permanent, the result of crisis. 'Conjuncture' refers to more immediate, ephemeral characteristics, linked to the
organic structures, but changing at once more rapidly and less significantly, as the forces in conflict within a situation struggle to work out
their contradictions. For Gramsci, these two levels are dialectically
interlinked. But at the same time it is clear that some periods display
radical situational change, while others, in between these, are periods
of relative situational stability, when day-to-day conjunctural movement assumes a more prominent position in the historical picture. (See
Gramsci 1971, pp. 175–85.) In this way of analysis, the importance of
changes in the 'base' is retained – it is at the level of the situation that
homologies, in the sense defined earlier, may be thought to operate –
while greater relative autonomy for superstructural elements is
secured at the conjunctural level, for these elements may change at
differing speeds, in differing ways.

In sketching out a music history for the last two hundred years, one
can identify, I believe, three 'moments' of radical situational change.
These seem to be found in all the developed Western societies, though
the dating differs. It is on these moments that, at the present stage of
knowledge, research could perhaps most profitably be concentrated,
since they reveal most clearly the processes of formation of musical-
ideological fields.

First is the moment of the 'bourgeois revolution', marked by complex and overt class struggle within cultural fields, by the permeation
of the market system through almost all musical activities, and by the
development and eventual predominance of new musical types associated with the new ruling class (a development pursuing – to speak very
generally – a trajectory from heroic, progressive thrust towards a
stifling, oppressive conservatism). Conventional music history's
delineation of the period through rigid classical/romantic periodisa-
tions or 'great man' physiognomies hides a complex web of interactions – involving concert music, middle-class domestic genres, theatre
music, dance, the mass choral movement, political and protest songs,
and working-class broadside and street-song – which were the object
of active struggle, as old and new elements were articulated into a
variety of patterns and meanings. In Britain, this moment has several
phases during a long and turbulant period from the late-eighteenth
century to the 1840s. In most other West European countries it would
appear to begin rather later but to give way to a more stable period
around the same time, after the 1848 revolutions.

The second moment, I would suggest, is that of 'mass culture',
running from the late nineteenth century to around 1930. It is characterised by the development of monopoly-capitalist relations, by the

Re-constructing musical history   11

modes of what has been called social imperialism, and by a simplifica-
tion of class struggle into forms which, however various on the
ground, can be subsumed under Stuart Hall's overall 'power bloc
versus popular classes' dichotomy (Hall 1981, pp. 238–9). National
lineages remain important, but as one pole of a tension counter-
balanced by a growing internationalisation of culture, associated particularly with an emerging American hegemony. This shows itself both
in musical content – the impact of ragtime, jazz, Tin Pan Alley songs,
new dance forms and so on – and in new methods of mass production,
distribution, publicity: in short, a drive towards 'one-way communication' in homogeneous markets. Nevertheless, this should not lead to
an underestimate of the conflicts involved in establishing the new
system, now admittedly sited almost entirely at the point of consumption (since the productive apparatus was increasingly in the hands of
the large industrial concerns). As has often been pointed out, from
Walter Benjamin onwards (see Wicke 1982, for example), the
emergence of 'the mass' itself as a qualitatively new factor in the
musical process raises the possibility of new political dimensions to
musical meaning; moreover, many of the novel musical elements
incorporated at this time from black American sources carry the
potential for subverting ruling musical norms and entering into new
articulatory alliances – with the 'collective variative' techniques of
many older workers' traditions, for instance. Still, by the late 1920s or
early 1930s the relative settlement of the social crisis, in the establishment of fascism or, elsewhere, more liberal-reactionary regimes, is
paralleled by the widespread assimilation of Afro-Americanisms into a
synthesis ruled by older bourgeois musical traditions and the articulation of their meanings to an ideology of consumerist escapism (the
crooners, large dance-bands, etc.). (A parallel dialectic can be observed
within élite concert music during the 1890–1930 period, though here
this is more clearly at work in the sphere of compositional technique,
which, as Adorno points out, tended to veer in the direction either of
Schoenbergian 'critical isolation' or of Stravinskyan mechanism and
'social celebration'. This struggle, too, subsided into the conservative
neo-classical hegemony typical of the 1930s and 1940s. As with the
popular genres, no single element of musical technique in isolation –
total chromaticism, additive rhythms, ostinato patterns, etc. – possessed fixed meaning or can be assigned to particular social tendencies.
Rather they were articulated into different arrangements according to
principles assimilable to different social interests. Weill and Eisler, and
Bartók and Janáček, show that many of the same techniques could be
articulated to other interests – broadly, socialist and liberal-progres-
sive, respectively.)

The third moment begins sometime after the Second World War –

12   *Richard Middleton*

most strikingly with the advent of rock 'n' roll – and can perhaps be termed the moment of 'pop culture'. In this period the dichotomous model which is, to a considerable extent, applicable to the situation of 'mass culture' is, while not destroyed, noticeably *fissured*, through the development of an assortment of quickly changing, often would-be subversive styles and subcultures. At the same time, changes in technology (*electronic* systems take over from the *electro-mechanical* mode typical of 'mass culture', just as that had taken over from the purely *mechanical* production and distribution methods of the earlier bourgeois period, epitomised by music printing) create the potential for new production methods – magnetic tape replaces music scores, the 'three-chord' electric guitar puts in question the existing professionalised instrumental skills; and there are accompanying changes in relations of production, most importantly, the first significant encroachment on music production resources by young, especially working-class young amateurs, together with the opening up of a new market, that of 'youth', which is structurally less tied to established class roles than older generations. This group, with its 'margin for rebellion', looks to new musical sources, notably in black American rhythm and blues, many aspects of which are predisposed to connotations clustered around feelings of 'oppression' on the one hand, relatively non-alienated use of the body (potentially subversive of capitalist work disciplines) on the other. (Note that parallel upheavals occur at roughly the same time in élite music fields: jazz, where modern and *avant-garde* styles, and, in a different way, the revivalist movement, challenge the swing/commercial dance-band/crooner mainstream; and concert music, where the Adornian antinomy is transformed into one between total serialist and other forms of 'systemic integralism' on the one hand, and the 'critical disengagement' typified by indeterminacy, on the other. Since the late 1960s, an increasing number of crossovers between these areas, and the popular genres too, demonstrates in concrete terms the indisputable fact from a social-ideological, if not always a musical-technical, point of view of the unity of the musical field.)

Admittedly, the efflorescence of rock 'n' roll, and of the 1960s rock movements, took place against the background of a new social-historical phase, that of 'welfare capitalism' and an expansive ideology of liberal tolerance. Such official permissiveness was seen to be justified as at both moments, 'rebellion' was largely incorporated into the hegemonic system, articulated to predominantly safer musical patterns with less subversive meanings (mostly having to do with leisure consumerism, adolescent safety-valves, pin-up fantasy-romance, etc.). The real test for this conflict would come with a more critical

Re-constructing musical history   13

socio-economic climate – which is the measure of punk's assault, both on established musical conventions and meanings, and on the established mode of production. We are still living through the post-punk struggle – a point to which I shall return later.

For all three of these moments the delineation here is no more than a sketch, hence schematic rather than descriptive. One implication, however, is that research into these periods, instead of taking the conventional routes of studying genres or individuals or historical traditions, should concentrate on musical categories or elements which, within the articulative process, migrate from genre to genre, tradition to tradition, assuming new positions in different patterns, taking on varied meanings. For the moment of bourgeois revolution, for example, attention might focus on three categories (the stock bourgeois types?): the four-four march; symmetrical solo lyric melody (itself breaking into sub-types: *bel canto*, domestic, *volkstümlich*); dance (waltz, galop, etc.). Equivalents for the mass culture moment might be pentatonically-shaped melody; ragtime-based syncopated rhythmic structures; late romantic/impressionist ballad melody/harmony. And for pop culture, perhaps, boogie-style (eight-to-the-bar) rhythms; riff structures; antiphonal forms. Others can no doubt be identified.

If, in complex, differentiated societies, it is dangerous to ascribe a false harmony to the structure and meanings of musical styles, genres, types, or an 'essential' quality to the relationship between them and their users, it is clear from what has been said above that the principle most likely to govern these phenomena has to do with *internal contradiction*. By this is not meant that styles, genres and types do not often achieve an apparent coherence, which may be long-lasting, or that contradiction is always at work in the same way or to the same extent: this depends on social variables, not to mention the nature and richness of the available musical resources. What I am suggesting is that coherence is 'unnatural' – the product of cultural work; that musical units are assemblages of elements from a variety of sources, each with a variety of histories and connotation-clusters, and these assemblages can, in appropriate circumstances, be prised open, the elements re-articulated in different contexts. Sometimes internal contradictions are obvious, as when parody (in the widest sense of the term) is used. (This is a favourite technique for musicians of subordinate groups.) At other times they are relatively hidden, smoothed over by extensive cultivation, familiarity and the techniques of what Bourdieu calls 'legitimation', only to be revealed when constituent elements are wrenched away and placed in a new setting. This happens, for instance, when the *volkstümlich* tunes so popular in early nineteenth-century bourgeois domestic song (where they signify

14   *Richard Middleton*

according to romantic conceptions of nation and community) are used by working class singers for disaster ballads; when sentimental Tin Pan Alley ballad melody is 'gospelised' by Ray Charles or Otis Redding; or when the rhythm of the four-four heavy march is appropriated by the early punk bands, as a mode of critique (see Laing 1985, pp. 61–3). The strength with which particular potentially contradictory relationships are held together depends on the strength of the articulating principle involved, which is in turn connected with objective social factors. John Lennon's 'Imagine', so powerful when one is listening to it, quite easily afterwards deconstructs into its mutually contradictory elements: radical text, ballad melody and orchestration, singer-songwriter ('confessional') piano, soul/gospel-tinged singing. What is tying these together is an ideal, or to put it more concretely, a certain position associated with alienated intellectuals in late capitalist society. This hard-fought-for (and affecting) 'coherence' lacks sufficient material support (in terms of defined social interests) and ideological legitimacy (or threat) to sustain itself as more than a personal, transitory (i.e. 'bohemian', thus assimilable) re-orientation of the musical traditions concerned. When the tune appears as backing to a TV commercial – as happened in Britain – one is not taken aback.

It is instructive to apply this perspective to early rock 'n' roll – to Elvis Presley, let us say; for the conventional readings of this music fall into the essentialist trap warned of above. At first rock 'n' roll was generally seen in terms of *rebellion*: this was viewed positively, by fans and fellow-travellers, or negatively, by outraged defenders of established cultural interests; in any case, it was a *new music*, set against existing popular types. Subsequently a more sophisticated interpretation historicised this account, describing what happened to popular music in the late 1950s and early 1960s in terms of the *incorporation* or *co-option* of rock 'n' roll into the repertoire of the hegemonic bloc. Still, though, the vital point is missing – that rock 'n' roll was internally contradictory from the start: not just boogie rhythms, rough sound, blues shouts and physical involvement but also sentimental ballad melodies and forms, 'angelic' backing vocal effects and 'novelty' gimmicks.

In the case of Elvis, this problem is particularly striking because within the rock discourse he has been widely seen as both the music's first hero and its most prominent backslider. Most rock critics take this line, seeing Elvis's career as a progressive sell-out to the music industry, a transition from 'folk' authenticity (the Sun singles of 1954–5) to a sophisticated professionalism (epitomised by the ballads and movies of the 1960s) in which the dollars multiplied but musical values went by the board. Greil Marcus is the only writer on Elvis I have come across who tries to resist this Faustian scenario, but even he, when he comes to make his crucial distinction, places it between the Sun Golden Age, 'a space of freedom', and a subsequent decline into a 'riskless aesthetic of smooth-it-away' which 'gives an all-encompassing Yes to his audience' (Marcus 1977, pp. 141, 166, 199). But in post-war America a pure 'folk' role, untouched by commercial influences, had become impossible. The dissemination of music by radio and gramophone record permeated the whole country and every social stratum. The performers whom the young Elvis heard and learned from – gospel singers, bluesmen like Arthur Crudup, Bill Broonzy, Junior Parker and Howlin' Wolf, country and western stars such as Bob Wills, Hank Williams and Roy Acuff – were *commercial* artists; they, like Elvis himself, did not separate themselves from the whole wash of music that was available. When Sam Phillips, founder of Sun Records and 'creator' of Elvis Presley, said 'If I could find a white man who had the Negro sound and the Negro feel, I could make a billion dollars' (quoted, Hopkins 1971, p. 66), the twin motivations, artistic and commercial, were not separated or separable. If we look at the music Elvis produced throughout his career, we also find strong objections to the 'decline-and-fall' view. Commentators often stress a change in 'sound' (for example, the 'primitive' – hence 'authentic' – acoustic of the Sun records giving way to the 'sophisticated' – hence 'manipulative' – methods of RCA, with their more elaborate use of amplification, vocal backing groups, strings, etc.) at the expense of other characteristics of the musical style which may show continuity.

Elvis's two most notable contributions to the language of rock 'n' roll are firstly, the assimilation of 'romantic lyricism' and secondly, what I call 'boogification'. Both techniques can be found in classic form in his first national hit, 'Heartbreak Hotel' (1956). This was by origin a country and western song but its vocal has the shape of a typical blues shout. Nevertheless the rough tone, irregular rhythms and 'dirty' intonation that most blues singers would have used are for the most part conspicuously absent in Elvis's performance; his tone is full, rich and well produced, his intonation is precise, stable and 'correct', the notes are sustained and held right through, and the phrasing is legato. At the same time this lyrical continuity is subverted by 'boogification'. As in boogie-woogie, the basic vocal rhythms are triplets (♪♪♪, ♩♪) and, again as in boogie-woogie, the *off*-beat quaver is often given an unexpected accent (e.g. ♩♪), producing syncopation and cross-rhythm. The effect is physical, demanding movement, jerking the body into activity. Elvis, however, extends the technique. He adds

16   *Richard Middleton*

extra off-beat notes not demanded by words or vocal line, often splitting up syllables or even consonants, slurring words together, disguising the verbal sense. So we have ♩♩♪ ♩♩♪ and

lo - one - ly   Stree - ee - eet

♩♩♪ ♩♩♪ ♩♩♪ , ♪♩ ♪♩♩♪ ♩♩♪ and

be - e   so   lo - one - ly   ba - a - by   heart-break   ho - tel - l - l   I'll - ll   be

♪ | ♩♩♪ ♩♩♪ ♩♩♪ ♩♩♪ | Occasionally, there is

they'll   ne' - er'   ey   'e - 'er   look   ba - ack   'll   make   you   so

on a 'sustained' note something like a rhythm vibrato (in triplet rhythm): listen for instance to 'Although' at the start of the second and last choruses, 'Now' at the start of the third, and 'Well' at the start of the fourth. The overall effect of the boogification technique is of course sexy but it is also a bit jittery and absurd; the sensuality seems almost out of control. The combination of boogification with romantic lyricism in 'Heartbreak Hotel' – one element deriving from established Tin Pan Alley lyrical technique, the other from the black American subculture, the two together perfectly integrated, or rather held in tension – produces a style already, at this early stage in Elvis's career, teetering on the edge of that melodrama into which he was so often to fall. The articulation of the two together, in terms and in a context set by the values of the new youth culture, epitomises the overall problematic proposed by this music-historical moment; broadly speaking, we can think of romantic fantasy 'made young', 'given flesh', made to 'move' physically, while conversely an increased corporal freedom is presented, in line with the experience of adolescent sexuality in protestant bourgeois society, in a guarded, personalised, even ironic manner.

The same fusion of techniques can be found even earlier, while Elvis was still recording for Sun. 'Milkcow Blues Boogie' (1955) is perhaps the best example since, again, the techniques are so well integrated, though Elvis's treatment of the song is at such a quick tempo that the operation of the techniques themselves is less clear than in 'Heartbeak Hotel'. The lyrical approach – the rich tone, the singing *through* the note, the sustained legato, the controlled phrase-endings – is most apparent for the last line of each chorus. Boogification pervades the entire vocal, though the quick tempo means there is less scope for accenting off-beat notes, and often the effect is so fast as to be a rhythm vibrato. The tempo also makes accurate notation harder. However, at

the beginning we hear something like this: ♩ ♩ ♪ ♪ | ♩ ♪ ♩♩

Well ____ ah   wo - oke up ____

♪♩ ♪ | ♩ ♩ ♩ ♪♩ ♪♩ | ♪♩ ♪♩ ♩ ♪|♩

this __ a - morn-ing a - and ah - ah loo-ooked ou-ou-out the door __ .

Later:

you're gonn- a   nee - eed your - a - lo - o - vin' - a -   da - a - ddy here__ some   day .

Well - ll __   ah   tried   ev' - ry   thi - ing __   to   git a - long with- a   you - ou __ .

Both romantic lyricism and boogification not only date back to the
beginnings of Elvis's career but also continue to be used throughout its
development. There is no watershed, or 'fall from grace'. What we do
see, however, is a kind of stylistic specialisation. Songs which *integrate*
the techniques like 'Milkcow Blues Boogie' (or 'Mystery Train') in the
Sun period or 'Heartbeak Hotel' in the early Victor period, become less
common. The techniques tend to diverge, romantic lyricism being
channelled into ballads, boogification into a particular kind of rock 'n'
roll song which I shall call 'mannerist'. Elvis's huge ballad repertoire
needs little commentary here, save to stress again that it began not
with the move to RCA but at Sun, 'Love Me Tender' (1956) and 'That's
When Your Heartaches Begin' (1957) being preceded by equally sentimental ballads cut for Sam Phillips; indeed, it began earlier: when as a
boy Elvis was entered for a talent contest at the Mississippi–Alabama
Fair, it was 'Old Shep' that he sang. 'Mannerist rock' is more interesting. It is associated most clearly with a series of songs, many written for
Elvis by Otis Blackwell, starting with 'Don't Be Cruel' (1956) and 'All
Shook Up' (1957) and stretching down to 'Please Don't Drag that String
Around' (1963). The techniques of boogification are exaggerated, over-
played, even parodied. By pushing them into mannerism, Elvis dis-
tances himself from their demands, physical and psychological. In 'All
Shook Up', for example, the old techniques are there:

a – well - a - bless - a - my soul - a -what's-a- wrong with me __

but the triviality of the lyrics and Elvis's light, amused vocal tone tell us
that this is not serious. Mannerism is usually seen as an RCA development; but once again we find that it was already developing during the
Sun period, notably in 'Baby Lets Play House' (1955). Clearly, it is the
certain amount of 'slack' within the articulative relationships, the fact
that the combination of techniques does not fix any constituent one
hundred per cent to the others, that explains the possibility of differential development of elements in the mixture – rather than 'changes in
style'.

Elvis's importance, then, lies not so much in the as-it-were abstract
mix of elements (blues/country/Tin Pan Alley) which he helped to
bring into being in rock 'n' roll, but in what he did with it. He

18   *Richard Middleton*

transformed them – articulated them – into particular patterns. The only workable categorisation of Elvis's music, as we have seen, is not by historical period but by song-type – or more precisely, by apparently self-contradictory assemblages of musical elements as they are mediated by the differential demands of varied songs at various moments. What *does* happen historically is that integrated songs become gradually less common through the course of Elvis's career, while the song-types tend to diverge, as the relatively small, well-defined audience of the Sun days gives way to a large, heterogeneous market demanding different types for different sub-sections. Elvis is all things to his audience *throughout* his career, but the nature of the audience changes, and with it the nature and range of the articulations of the musical materials. The unifying factor is Elvis himself – or rather, Elvis constructed in particular categories, acting as embodiments of particular articulating principles, tied to particular sets of social needs and interests. These sets – the most striking, delineated earlier, is that associated with the moment of early rock 'n' roll – are associated with particular social contexts. Given the imperatives of mass musical reproduction, that moment, that set of social interests, needed Elvis, needed a *star*, to focus its challenge to the cultural hegemony; but equally this star was the product of those objective social interests – and was available for re-articulation, his image and thence his performances re-worked or re-interpreted, for different audiences.

Without this kind of analytical framework, respecting the complex levels of mediation involved and their relative autonomy, Elvis becomes simply the plaything of naked political forces (rebellious/ manipulative); and the fact that, for example, the young rock 'n' roller sang ballads from the start, that the older Hollywood star could still sing rock 'n' roll songs and was still respected by rock 'n' roll fans, that his 'blues' were 'romantic' (a kind of fantasy), his ballads often 'realistic' (given flesh), or that he could make boogification ironic: all this is inexplicable.

The complexity and energy of the early rock 'n' roll moment is probably symptomatic of its role as a manifestation of quite deep situational change. There is a richness of musical resources – many previously unavailable to a mass audience – and an excitement about new technological possibilities, new social relations and new kinds of musical behaviour which accounts for the fact that cultural struggle could take place here within musical production itself. It is instructive to turn, by contrast, to a period which is more settled, less varied in available musical resources, and characterised, apparently, by heavily

Re-constructing musical history 19

weighted relations between the class-cultural formations. The second half of the nineteenth century in Britain seems to be such a period.

Ned Corvan was a song-writer, fiddler and performer in the working-class concert halls and pubs of Tyneside in north-east England during the 1850s and early 1860s; in his final years he also worked in the first of the new kind of music halls, owned by commercially ambitious entrepreneurs and orientated more towards a nationally organised market and production system. Corvan's career was sufficiently close to the industrial struggles and Chartist agitation of the turbulent 1840s to draw inspiration from them; but British working-class musical culture in general, in this period, seems to have been settling into relative quiescence, characterised by consumption of music hall song (produced increasingly by large commercial organisations), the replacement of old tune-types by newer types originating in bourgeois theatre and drawing-room, and a transition from protest, street music and spontaneous sing-song to formalised performance in choirs and brass bands. In the second half of the century the outlines of a qualitatively distinct workers' music culture become ever mistier.

Despite strong regional cultural traditions, Tyneside was affected by these developments. But Ned Corvan, it seems, continued to work for a solidly working-class audience and address working-class concerns. How did he do it? He had relatively restricted resources: tunes drawn from rural and urban proletarian traditions and from new bourgeois sources; text-methods, turns-of-phrase and verse forms derived from drawing-room, popular theatre, broadside and working-class entertainment. Many of the originally proletarian elements had been appropriated and re-orientated by petit-bourgeois writers and publishers during the previous half-century. To re-articulate them back to working-class interests required considerable ideological *work*. Yet Corvan 'established himself as spokesman-in-song for his own class'; his first published song collection was dedicated to his

'Friends and Patrons', the 'Skippers, Colliers and Working Men in general, of Tyneside and Neighbourhood'. Instead of his songs being *about* workers, for the delectation of a petit-bourgeois readership, Corvan's 'Collection of local Songs and Ballads, Illustrative of the Habits and Character of the "Sons of Coaly Tyne"' was written *for, on behalf of* – and, in effect, *from within* – that network of communities, by a fellow-worker whose only difference was that the division and specialisation of labour now made economically (and culturally) possible the role of full-time professional working-class artist.

(Harker 1981, pp. 48–9)

The first important point to the argument here concerns Corvan's choice of tunes. There are no newly invented tunes; like almost all proletarian performers at this time, rural and urban, he draws on existing melodies. But at a time when tunes from bourgeois sources were increasingly popular and when traditional, so-called 'folk' tunes were in decline, certainly in the music hall, Corvan used comparatively few of the former and actively retained many of the latter. In a study of his four published *Song Books*, I found that of the forty-two tunes I could identify (four I could not), some sixty per cent are 'traditional', mostly of rural origin (the bulk Scots), while only about twelve per cent come from comic music hall songs and about twenty-five per cent from bourgeois sources (parlour ballad, light opera). Furthermore, three of the parlour ballad tunes and one of the comic song tunes contain pseudo-'folk' elements; and two of the 'bourgeois' tunes derive from American minstrelsy and have a melodic style similar to that of some Anglo-American 'folk' traditions.

It may be argued, of course, that in themselves these facts demonstrate comparatively little. 'Folk' tunes, especially of Scots origin, had long had a strong presence in the North-East regional culture; and, as in other areas of the country, they had also been taken up by middle-class circles. But the weight of received connotations is important here. Given a continuity of working-class usage of such tunes, a substratum of associations in the culture facilitated their articulation towards working-class needs. Their long-lived presence made it possible for them to act as a kind of semi-permanent critique of newer cultural trends. Whether that process *would* take place clearly depended very much on the texts to which the tunes were put, and the way the songs were performed. Contemporary reports suggest strongly that Corvan's performance style was dramatic, quasi-spontaneous, intimate and highly dependent on audience rapport – as against the more fixed, formalised renderings of the tunes which would be typical of performances in bourgeois drawing room or ballad concert.

As far as texts are concerned, consider Musical Ex. 1.*

For this attack on speculative urban development, which has resulted in the disappearance of the open spaces where working-class children used to play, Corvan obviously draws on the 'traditional' associations – the feelings of continuity – clustered around the old Scots tune to support his nostalgically cast complaint. Similarly, for a song about the plight of the suffering pitmen, which led many to resort to emigration (often to Australia: 'Astrilly'), Corvan makes use of the traditional tune, 'All Around My Hat', with its history of texts to do

---

* All the Corvan songs referred to here except 'The Sunday Morning Fuddle' are reproduced in full, together with many others, in Gregson 1983. I am grateful to Keith Gregson for permission to reproduce these extracts.

Re-constructing musical history   21

Example 1.   Tune: No Good Luck About the House

1. Noo, O dear me, what mun aw dee, aw've nee pleyce noo ti play,___ Wor

can - ny Forth an' Spit- al te, eh man, they've tune a - way,___ Nee

pleyce ti bool wor peyste eggs noo, to lowp the frog and run, ___ They're

ai - ways beel din sum-muck new they'll spoil New- cas - sel seune ___

2 The toon improvement's made greet noise, but aw heard my feyther say,
Thor was summick mair then little boys kept wor wise heeds at the play;
Thor is bonny wark amang thorsels, but aw mun haud my jaw;
But still thors folks 'boot here that smells the cash buik wiv its flaws.
Chorus: Oh dear me

3 Bedstocks that canny gam's noo dune, an' three hole teaser tee,
They've tune away wor best o' fun, so, lads, what mun aw dee
Aw'll bubble tiv aw dee, begox, or teyke some arsynack;
Then corporation men may funk when aw is laid on maw back.
Chorus: Oh dear me

4 Noo a' ye canny folk that's here, just think on what aw say
An recollect yor youthful days, when ye were fond o' play
Ye say yor schule days was the best, so help me in maw cause,
An cheer poor Bobby Snivvelnose by gean him yor applause.
Chorus: For Oh dear me

with farewell and absence, here transposed from the sphere of love to
that of work (see Musical Ex. 2).

Example 2.

1. Noo, mar-rows, aw's gawn ti leave ye, an' sair, sair, 'twill grieve ___ me Ti

leave wor can _ ny Tyne side shores where aw've had ma - ny a spree Tho it's

22   *Richard Middleton*

Example 2 – *cont.*

sair a-gainst maw li - kin tiv A - stril - ly aw'il gan hy - kin For

mai - sters keeps us strik - in', so what mun a pit man de?___

A similar theme in 'The Sword-dancers' Lament' is given the traditional tune of the pitmen's sword-dance (Musical Ex. 3).

Example 3.

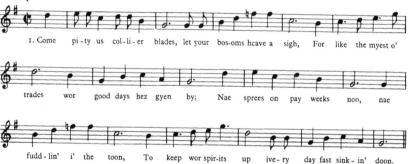

1. Come pi -ty us col -li- er blades, let your bos-oms heave a sigh, For like the myest o'

trades wor good days hez gyen by; Nae sprees on pay weeks noo, nae

fudd - lin' i' the toon, To keep wor spir-its up ive- ry day fast sink - in' doon.

While the deeply serious 'The Queen Has Sent a Letter, or The Hartley Calamity', written after a tragic pit disaster, gets an arching Irish-style tune, joining a long tradition of laments and plaints to this kind of tune (Musical Ex. 4).

Example 4.

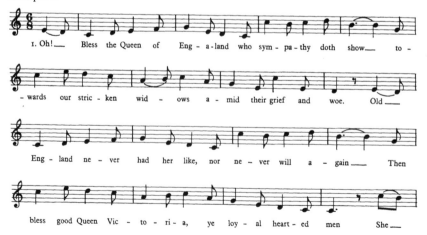

1. Oh!___ Bless the Queen of Eng - a-land who sym - pa-thy doth show___ to -

- wards our stric - ken wid - ows a - mid their grief and woe. Old ___

Eng - land ne - ver had her like, nor ne - ver will a - gain___ Then

bless good Queen Vic - to - ri - a, ye loy - al heart - ed men She___

Re-constructing musical history   23

sent   a   let – ter   stat – ing   I___   share   your   sor – row   here   to

sooth   the   ach – ing   hearts   of   all   and   dry   the   wid – ow's   tear.

2 Above two hundred miners are numbered with the dead
    Whose wives and children ne'er should want their bit of daily bread
    And while death's shadow overhangs the miner's cot with gloom,
    Let us calm the widow's heaving breast for those laid in the tomb;
    And ye that round your glowing fires, life's comforts daily share,
    Think of the helpless orphans and widows in despair.

4 The collier's welfare, as he toils, more interest might command
    Among the wealthy owners and rulers of the land.
    Are they like beasts of burthen, as Roebuck once did rave,
    Will government in future strive the collier's life to save?
    Why should the worn-out collier amid his object gloom
    Eke out the life his maker spared to share the pauper's doom?

Corvan also uses 'traditional' tunes to articulate celebrations of working-class life and characters: again cultural *continuity* within social
change is affirmed, and constructed; and other claims on these tunes,
other re-workings of these traditions, are resisted. The virtues of the
'Lads o' Tyneside' are described to the modal Scots tune, 'Lawd o'
Cockpen' (working-class 'lairds', these!) (see Musical Ex. 5).

Example 5.

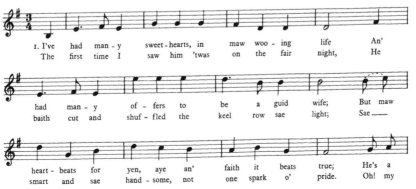

1. I've   had   man – y   sweet – hearts, in   maw   woo – ing   life   An'
The   first   time   I   saw   him   'twas   on   the   fair   night,   He

had   man – y   of – fers   to   be   a   guid   wife;   But maw
baith   cut   and   shuf – fled   the   keel   row   sae   light;   Sae___

heart – beats   for   yen,   aye   an'   faith   it   beats   true;   He's   a
smart   and   sae   hand – some,   not   one   spark   o'   pride.   Oh!   my

24   *Richard Middleton*

Example 5 – *cont.*

And 'The Factory Lass' gets a similar tune, 'Sunny Banks of Scotland' (Musical Ex. 6).

Example 6.

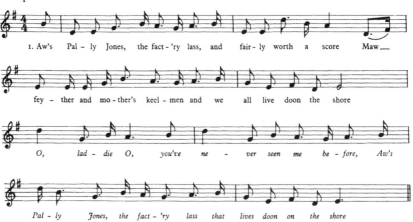

2 Oh! maw mother's sic a canny body her mouth hads three pennorth o'rum
  An' feyther likes his whisky toddy, but aw like beer begum
  Chorus: O, laddie ho! ye've niver saw me before.
          But aw's Pally Jones the factory lass,
          That leeves doon the shore.

3 An' Bobby Nun, that's deed an' gyen, used ti fiddle doon the shore,
  Often said, he niver saw yen could touch me on the floor,
  Chorus: O, laddie ho!

Re-constructing musical history   25

4 New sixes, casts offs, sylphs an' reels, aw could de them a like fun;
  Folks said aw was sae polkerfied, awd sic a bonny run.
  Chorus: O, laddie ho!

5 Aw've set the men folks ravin' mad, thor's twe wants me to wed,
  But aw've a canny blacksmith lad, folks call him bonny Ned.
  Chorus: O, laddie ho!

A famous fairground entertainer, Jimmy McKenny, is celebrated to the
Scots fiddle tune, 'The Tinker's Wedding' (Musical Ex. 7).

Example 7.

And the English tune, 'Derry Down', is used for one of Corvan's
humorous narratives, describing a practical joke, 'The Pitman and the
Kippered Herring' (Musical Ex. 8).

Example 8.

26   *Richard Middleton*

Example 8 – *cont.*

fun - ny queer spokes; But when we get a drop be - er we're a full o' glee, we make

mon - y a blun-der when we gan on a spree *Sing - ing* *fal* *dal,* *lal the dal le*

All the tunes I have mentioned so far are, as it were, rescued from the hands of the collectors and anthologisers of traditional 'folk' song, and those of 'refined' performers, with piano accompaniments, in bourgeois parlours; Corvan's texts articulate them to the needs of *his* class, at a particular moment in its history. But he also makes use of tunes from bourgeois sources – and transforms their meanings in the process. The tune 'Bow, Wow, Wow' originated in the London ballad opera/pleasure garden/harmonic society repertory of the late eighteenth century. In 'Jimmy Munro's Troubles' (Ex. 9) Corvan uses the banality of its phrasing, repetitions, sequences and harmonic structure to help construct a mock-simpleton persona, which enables him to cloak the bite of his social criticism in humour; he plays at 'acting the fool', in tortuous verbal constructions and juxtapositions of the serious and the trivial – just as the 'Bow, Wow, Wow' song originally did – but the real problems of railway accidents, rent and ragged clothes turn the joke around (Musical Ex. 9):

Example 9.

1. Ex - cuse me friends if trou - ble-some, may aw trou - ble ye a - while,— Sirs for

troub - lin' you, for troub - lin' me, to trou - ble you to smile,— sirs, Ye'll

ma - bies say its dou - ble trou - ble 'void it nae man can,— Sirs We've been

born in trou - ble, bred in trou - ble since the world be - gan— Sirs

Bow *wow* *wow* *The* *trou - bles* *of* *the* *times* *are* *ver - y* *bad* *just* *now.*

2 Nae, Cursmis time comes once a year, wi' roast beef lots to feed at,
    An' Cursmis bills they trouble then, but some folks niver heed that;
    The landlords trouble you for rent, and smile so when one pays it,
    Other poor souls sigh and say they're toubled hoo to raise it.
    Chorus.

3 Some married folks that hez nae bairns seem troubled hoo to get them;
    Others in the street to cadge noo varry often set them;
    Railway accidents trouble us, directors say they cannot mend them,
    So they varry often trouble us, an' sometimes wor troubles end then.
    Chorus.

4 Some cheps are troubled noo-a-days hoo to get a wife, Sirs,
    Others get them withoot any, then troubles start for life, Sirs,
    For scoldin' troubles then set in, an' iv chance yor wife ye mill, Sirs,
    They'll pop ye intiv gaol six months, to live in trouble still, Sirs.
    Chorus.

5 Aw've maw troubles like the rest o' folks, as on through life aw jog, Sirs;
    To tell the truth, aw's troubled sair hoo to reinsuit my togs, Sirs.
    Tailors' bills don't trouble me, but the bobbys they take note, Sirs,
    An' take me on suspicion 'cause there's nae change in my coat, Sirs.
    Chorus.

6 Napoleon hez been troubled since he tuik his cityashun,
    Infernal *bums* hez troubled him to cause assassinashun;
    Eugenia, tee, she's troubled sair, wiv her husband's life at stake, Sirs—
    Wor Bobby swears they'll pop him off if he isn't wide awake, Sirs.
    Chorus.

7 But in spite ov a' the troubles that trouble us poor devils,
    Wor Princess gat wed the tother day, an' noo in wedlock revels;
    In Prussia wiv her canny man, for life they've settled doon, Sirs;
    My eyes! what royal sport they'd hev beneath the honey moon, Sirs.
    Chorus.

8 Noo, friends, excuse the troublous rhymes aw've chanc'd to hev a voice in,
    Here's may yor troubles ellways end in merry hearts rejoicing,
    And as we toddle on through life banish care with all its buddies
    And shout success to coaly Tyne, wiv an end tiv all wor troubles.
    Chorus.

Similarly, Corvan takes the tune of 'The Mistletoe Bough', originally a mock-'gothic' ballad mixing melodrama and sentimentality, and typical of the early nineteenth-century bourgeois romanticism which created it, and puts it to words describing a situation of *real* emotion for working people: a rise in the price of household coal during the coldest weather of the winter (see Musical Ex. 10).

28   *Richard Middleton*

Example 10.

1. The snaw fell doon fast, an' poor folks seem'd shy, Clos'd up i' thor hyems as the
storm pel-ted by; An they wished roond their nooks such times soon wad pass, For pro-
-vis-ions had ris-en an' they'd saved lit-tle brass, And as mon-ey an' fir-in' was
melt-in' a-way Thor seemed nowt but caud dops for us poor sons of clay, The
wo-men folks flew ti' fill thor coal holes, To the de-poe but hang them they've
raised wor small coals. *O what a price for sma' coals (Hinny) how they've raised wor sma' coals_*

2 Gosh cap, what caud weather, wor Dickey did shoot,
   Mother fetch some coals in, wor fire's gannin' oot,
   Some coals, lad, thou's fond an' she geyped all amazed,
   Thou maun eat less an' drink less, the sma' coals are raised.
   But, hinnies, that's nowt, aw's still sore beset,
   Coals is thruppence a betement all meyn for to get,
   The only bit comfort maw body consoles,
   They've teyn off at last when they raised wor sma' coals.
   Chorus: O What a &c.

3 Aw went to the depoe, aw think that's the nyem,
   Aw stood tiv aw shivered, aw really thowt sheym:
   Amang sec a gang had ye seen me that day,
   Thou'd mebbis come seuner than aw did away;
   They fowt like fair deevils aw's sure an' far warse,
   For they kenn'd what it was for to hev a caud a–e;
   But if poor folk had sense they'd fill a' ther holes,
   Wi' cindes ti spite them for raisin' sma' coals.
   Chorus: O What a &c.

4 Yen jaws aboot seats but aw geyped wi' surprise,
   Ti see sic a squad wi maw pair o' eyes;

Thor was scrushin' an' pushin' sec a mixture o' folks,
Wiv sweels, pillow slips, cuddy cairts, an' long pokes;
But the aud wives bang'd a' for screaming they sings,
Canny man gis a pennorth ti warm wor aud skins,
Au've tatties ti boil, says another aw've stew,
Canny man, put your shuil in an gis a wee few.
Chorus: O What a &c.

5 Some keelmen 'bove the bridge, aw heard a wife say,
Had been frozzen up an' could scairsh get away;
They thowt aw thor fuddlin' days dune at last,
So they doon on thor knees ti meyke up for the past;
How, marrows, cries a bully, aw've an idea some price,
We'll find Sir John Franklin if we howk through the ice,
First let's find the north powl it's someway aboot
Then get on the top on't an' give him a shoot.
Chorus: Aw'll tell him they've raised &c.

6 They ken hoo ti swindle poor folks wi' thor loads,
Pretendin' thor raised, and that snaw stopped the roads,
But a pitman tell'd me ti stop up sic jaw,
For it niver rained hailstones nor snawed doon belaw.
An' he says if thou'll teeyke advice fra a feul,
When thors a greet vast o' weather, get thaw holes a chock full
An while thou's warmin' thaw shins by the fire, as the snaw
Drops doon through the loom, think o' the pitmen belaw.
Chorus: For they toil hard and sair for sma' coals, hinny, how they toil for sma' coals.

And the 'hymnic' parlour ballad tune 'Jeannette and Jeannotte' is used for the exhortatory words of 'Work for 1000 Men' (Musical Ex. 11), its 'dignity' and 'solemnity' re-articulated to the expressive needs of an appeal to end the evil of unemployment.

Example 11.

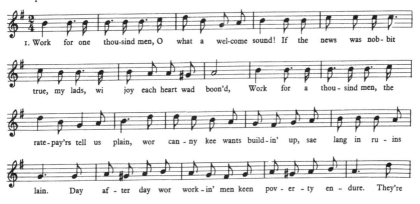

1. Work for one thou-sind men, O what a wel-come sound! If the news was nob- bit
true, my lads, wi joy each heart wad boon'd, Work for a thou- sind men, the
rate-pay'rs tell us plain, wor can - ny kee wants build-in' up, sae lang in ru - ins
lain. Day af - ter day wor work - in' men keen pov - er - ty en - dure. They're

30   *Richard Middleton*

Example 11 – *cont.*

oft com-pell'd to call up-on the Guard-ians of the Poor. But when

pov-er-ty be sets us em-ploy us ye who can, for

want should nev-er be the lot of an hon-est work-ing man.

2 Work for one thoosand men, aw wish the time was nigh,
   We're tired iv stannin' in the streets star'd at by passers by,
   Work for one thousand men, ye wealthy men be quick,
   Let Waiters hae the sites, in spite of Corporation clique.
   Put doon faction in wor Coonsil, obstructions then mon flee,
   An' honest hands earn honest bread, noo plung'd in poverty.
   Chorus: But when

3 Work for one thousand men! We need it ye'll believe
   When ye see us stannin' in the streets half starv'd frae morn to eve;
   Wor wives an' families te support, wor case is sad indeed;
   Its hard for working men to hear their bairns cry oot for bread.
   Think of strong men oot of work, wives destitute and pale,
   An' cry shyem upon the busy few that such miseries entail.
   Chorus: But when

4 Work for one thousand men! Improvements will be made;
   Wi' reet men in reet places we'll hae nae stop to trade.
   Work for one thousand men! Twad banish care and grief,
   For we subsist but varry poor upon the poor out-door relief.
   Then strain a nerve to help us, ye men that hez the reins,
   Think more of poor humanity and less of petty gains.
   Chorus: But when

5 Work for one thousand men! Oh would that we could prize
   What we stand so much in need of, then happy days would rise.
   Work for one thousand men makes work for thousands more,
   Who hand in hand with poverty keep moving to the door.
   Then let us pray for better times, wi' labour full in store
   With a fair day's wage for a fair day's work, we'll ask for nothing more.
   Chorus: But when

As an alternative to such subtle re-articulations, Corvan can provide straightforward parody. The insufferably sentimental parlour ballad 'Before the Bells Did Ring' is given new words which turn it into a comic epic about Sunday morning boozing, in which the hero ends up so 'fuddled' he is arrested (see Musical Ex. 12).

Example 12.

Original text
'Twas on a Sun - day morn - ing be - fore the bells did peal ____ A

Corvan's text In

note came thro' my win - dow with Cup - id on its seal ____ And
tiv a pub - lic hoose sae sly bin the back door aw did steal ____ Suen a

soon I heard a whis - per as soft as se - raphs sing ____ 'Twas
gill or two aw guz-zled up then doon my brass _ did fling ____ It was

on a Sun - day morn - ing be - fore __ the bells did ring.

Corvan's achievement, then – with a narrow stock of materials and against a background of retrenchment, in which the bourgeoisie's musical values, like its money, were increasingly setting the framework of socio-musical relationships – was to articulate those materials to the needs of his own particular audience. In a clearly stratified society, the interests of this audience were predominantly defined by class. Horizons were inevitably limited, the weight of various traditions heavy. The variety of articulated patterns was necessarily restricted, the invention of new techniques and modes of expression negligible. Corvan's basic method was that of parody: transforming the meaning of a tune through new words (and by performance methods). Even this kind of intervention in the productive process could not long survive him: the means of musical production were taken more and more into the hands of large commercial interests, while parody as a method retreated into informal niches in the fabric of working-class life.

The case of Corvan, and to a lesser extent that of early Elvis, are relatively straightforward, as far as analysis of their social meaning is concerned. In the first case, the shape into which the social formation is predisposed to settle, though contested, is obvious and is a powerful influence on the culture; the second – despite an underlying complexity in the musico-cultural relationships – possesses brilliant if temporary clarity arising from its historical position at the beginning of a period of great situational adjustment. How, though, would the method used here perform if applied to a subject right in the middle of complex situational change, where the social formation and the musical culture are characterised precisely by heterogeneity and seemingly transient affiliations? My final example – an approach to the so-called progressive rock of the mid- and late 1960s – may clarify this question.

Within the rock discourse of the time, progressive rock was widely regarded as associated with, indeed as the music of, the 'counterculture'. How, theoretically, this connection could be said to work was rarely explained (for an attempt, using a theory of homology, see Willis 1978); and, indeed, its existence and nature are problematical. There is an argument that the major determinant of the development from mid-1950s rock 'n' roll to late-1960s rock is 'professional': that is, it arises from an interest in exploring the technological and musical possibilities of the new conditions and conventions of production set up in the rock 'n' roll moment. How, in that case, could late-1960s progressive rock be specific to the counterculture? And how would such an affixation cope with the evident fact that the techniques, modes of expression and performers claimed by the counterculture as their own were apparently so easily appropriated by the established music industry interests, and the music spread into every social corner and function? Another problem is the sheer eclecticism of progressive rock, both in terms of the variety of sources on which it drew and the range of styles contained within the genre. By the mid-1960s the rock code as a whole was hardly a monolithic one; but progressive rock was a particularly heterogeneous genre (compared to, say, rock 'n' roll, which is fairly tightly defined). This may be a result, partly, of a move away from a determining social function (dance) towards a stress on the *listening* context and, concomitantly, an interest in non-popular musics, such as modern jazz, folk-protest and *avant-garde* music, which *are* musics for listening. Is progressive rock, then, a single phenomenon at all? If so, what makes it such? Is the variety itself signifying something? Is it connected with the variety of radical movements actually making up the counterculture? And how can the use made of elements and attitudes characteristic of 'legitimate' or relatively legitimate musics be squared with the counterculture's 'oppositionalism'? A brief 'reading' of four diverse but typical recordings will reveal examples of these characteristics – eclecticism, 'art' influences, 'professionalism' – together, also, with clear countercultural references, and thus will make the inner contradiction more concrete.

A comparison of the Beatles' 1967 single 'Strawberry Fields' with rock 'n' roll, or early Beatles for that matter, immediately reveals a much greater variety of instruments – 'orchestral' instruments (woodwind, brass and strings) and electric keyboard are added to drums and guitars – and they have obviously been 'scored' for: written arrangements creating varied textures have replaced a simple, consistent rock band texture, produced largely 'by ear', 'in performance'. Much of the sound has been produced through electronic 'treatment'. These two changes – instrumentation and electronic treatment – suggest two points immediately: that this is music created in a recording studio using quite complex equipment and recording techniques (the Beatles had in fact just given up live performance); and that it is music for listening rather than dancing. This is suggested too by the coda, which transforms the structure of the song and makes use of collage. The structure is also disrupted by the way the regular phrase-lengths and pulse usual in popular songs are subverted. In the first phrase, for example, the normal eight bars are stretched to nine. Throughout the song the rhythm of the vocal follows not the regular periods of dance music but the irregular accents of the words. The harmonic language has become more complex, less predictable, too.

What does the song 'mean'? The electronic treatment suggests 'abnormal experience' (presumably – so the lyrics suggest – psychedelic or hallucinogenic): this is achieved through reference to (dialectical articulation with) *normal* timbres previously used in pop songs, which are about 'real life' (love, dancing, etc.). However, this kind of sound was so widely copied in the progressive rock of the period – and more generally – that it quickly became a norm itself, a conventionalised sign, and soon permeated everyday musical practice and interpretation. The use of collage may signify 'in the unconscious' (which often manifests itself in a-logical jumbles of material). But this reading probably only suggests itself because a general signification related to 'random juxtaposition' (as in much *avant-garde* art) is narrowed down through articulation with the conjunction of electronically manipulated timbres, irregular rhythms, the lurching harmonies and the implications of the lyrics. Finally, the heterogeneous texture, the ever-changing relationships of instruments, may on one level simply suggest 'influence of art music'. On another, the varied perspectives and changing landmarks may signify 'a complex landscape' (which, given the other signifiers mentioned, is mental not physical). Pursuing Philip Tagg's argument (see Tagg 1979, pp. 99– 147) that conventional melody/accompaniment relationships signify the relationship of individuals (foreground) to their environment (background), it may be suggested that the shifting perspectives, as instruments zoom into the foreground, then out again, together with the relative lack of foregrounding of the voice, signify the *dislocation* of the individual's dominant position and of the single point of view. The (mental) environment displaces the ego from centre-stage – an important countercultural theme, of course (though once again articulated using *inter alia* musical techniques familiar in the *official* culture).

If 'Strawberry Fields' represents one important trend in the pro-

34   *Richard Middleton*

gressive rock style of 1966–68 – increasingly complex treatment of harmony, structure and recording techniques – a different trend, in some ways opposite to this, was also important. This used a restricted range of basic harmonic and melodic materials, favoured improvisation as a means of building structures, and achieved its most characteristic results in live performance. Usually it drew heavily on blues traditions. Cream's 'Spoonful', which appeared on their first LP and is a version of a song written by the Chicago blues bassist and composer, Willie Dixon, for one of the most celebrated Chicago blues singers, Howlin' Wolf, is a good example. Like many Chicago blues of the 1940s and 1950s, it draws heavily on the traditions of rural Mississippi blues – evident for instance, in the vocal (basic falling shapes, largely pentatonic, lots of repetition of phrases and short motifs, not much 'tune' – instead close to speech, shouted as much as sung) and secondly, the use, throughout, of only one chord – a kind of drone. After each verse there is a refrain, which is heavily dependent on repetition. (This repetition means that the refrain is easily extended, creating choruses of irregular length, and that is what Cream do, notably in the final chorus.) Other features most noticeably derived from blues are the use of a riff (the two-note idea which starts the song off and forms the basis of the refrain), the use of call-and-response (between vocal and guitar), and the instrumental styles, especially that of the guitar.

The simple harmonic structure has the effect of *freeing* melody and form; melodic lines are not constrained by having to fit changing chords and the form is not constrained by a particular harmonic sequence. This encourages improvisation, and enables the improviser to play at length and elaborately, as in the guitar solo by Eric Clapton. The building of extended forms over drones or very simple harmonic progressions (often two alternating chords) or riffs was of course to become a staple of hard rock and 'heavy metal' music, and encouraged the development of virtuosic soloists, especially guitarists. Thus while most of the blues-derived techniques I have mentioned appear to set the music in opposition to the dominant musical language (including that of many contemporary pop songs), this usage is developed in such a way as to lay stress on individualistic virtuosity and personal expression, achieved through 'professional' mastery of instrumental technique; and this could be seen as at least *compatible* with the traditions of bourgeois art.

Of course, blues-derived rock was not specific to the counterculture. It is interesting to compare the style of a recording like Cream's 'Spoonful' with that of earlier British rhythm and blues (the Rolling Stones or the Who, for example), which also makes use of basic blues materials; for this may throw light on differences between (apparently equally oppositional) subcultures. The musical difference seems to have to do with the *exploitation* and *refinement* of basic resources which are made by Cream, and these are the products of *improvisation*. Earlier rhythm and blues ('My Generation', or 'Satisfaction' for instance) *states a position*: its meanings are collective; Cream extract from this musical language the possibility of individual statements and relationships. Does the appeal of Cream to the counterculture reside here, in the possibility of spontaneity, personal expression and the hippie cult of freedom? It can be argued that techniques of drone and repetition (especially repetition of short units – what I call musematic repetition: see Middleton 1983) are particularly sympathetic to connotations having to do with 'collectivism': they play down 'difference', privilege the 'typical'. (Compare Maróthy's description of the collective-variative methods common in pre-bourgeois popular, and proletarian, traditions.) By superimposing on these techniques an ideology and a practice of personal self-expression, Cream's music seems to establish a dialectical relationship between the two, articulating each via the other into a new position.

A rather different trend in progressive rock was represented by the work of Pink Floyd, known for *avant-garde* experiments, often making use of collage, electronics and 'free-form' techniques. In a recording like 'Astronomy Dominé', a relatively compact example, there are no obvious divisions into the conventional chorus structure of popular song; instead the impression is of a piece *composed* as a whole. There is no really memorable melody, and the complex structure and varied rhythms and harmonies suggest this is music 'for the mind' rather than a simple pop song or dance music. However, there *is* a basic four-chord harmonic sequence, used as a structural underpinning for much of the piece; in a conventional rock song this might well have been deployed as a riff or worked into predictable phrase-structure patterns. But here it is 'covered over' with collages made up of vocal, instrumental and electronic materials, ranging from pre-recorded effects to improvised solo lines. What happens is that a short chord progression, which in Cream or the Rolling Stones might have been foregrounded, is pushed into the background, the joins between its statements disguised, links, an introduction and a coda added, so that the music seems to flow on continuously. The effect is that the structural level on which our attention fixes is the whole piece; and, to use the terms of Andrew Chester (1970), we listen *extensionally* as much as *intensionally*: that is, a complete work is built up by putting small fragments together into a freely structured whole rather than a given unit (for example, a chorus) being explored 'inwards' in ever-varied details (as in 'Spoonful').

36   *Richard Middleton*

Similarly, elements of rhythm and blues *phraseology* remain (drum techniques, guitar phrases and techniques) but they are subsumed within a heterogeneous mixture of styles.

In the terms of subcultural theory, this heterogeneity could be described as a kind of *bricolage* (see Hebdige 1979, pp. 102–6). But here the elements barely seem to hang together; or rather, radical disjunctions are part of the effect. Pink Floyd were influenced from outside rock; similar experiments (free form, electronics, wild improvisation, collage) were taking place among the jazz and 'classical' *avant-gardes* during the same period. And if the diverse references of the materials used in 'Astronomy Dominé' and similar pieces do have a coherence, it mainly rests on a kind of formalist and/or surrealist playing with sound-combinations and their mental associations and images, characteristic – in its implied position of social isolation – of almost all *avant-garde* music in the twentieth century. This certainly makes it more difficult than with Cream or the Beatles to appropriate this music to the needs of the hegemonic interests. At the same time, the references, especially rhythmic, to the rock tradition, are really all that serve to affix the music to the position of the pop culture audience.

If Pink Floyd's music displays the influence of, or at least a congruence with, *avant-garde* developments from outside rock, then Procul Harum's 'A Whiter Shade of Pale' (a big hit in the summer of 1967) can stand as an example of a complementary trend: the influence of 'classical' art music sources. The basic materials derive from a harmonic sequence (with melodic elaboration) taken from a cantata by J. S. Bach. On the one hand, this illustrates a tendency which sets something of a pattern in progressive rock: various rock/'classical' fusions were attempted, by Yes, Emerson Lake and Palmer, Mike Oldfield and others. On the other hand, it asks questions about the *rock* roots of the music: how can such a fusion take place? What happens to rock techniques? What does the fusion mean?

The influence is of a particular kind, from a particular source. Late Baroque music tends to be relatively formulaic and intensional in structure. Typically, it uses conventionalised harmonic progressions, melodic patterns and structural frameworks, and operates through imaginative combinations, elaborations and variations of these, rather than developing extended, through-composed forms. It also tends to have a regular, strongly marked beat; indeed, its *continuo* section could be regarded as analogous to the rhythm section of jazz and rock. The harmonic sequence I mentioned is used as a riff. It appears as the instrumental introduction (and two instrumental interludes), it comes four times in each of the two choruses, and it is still going when the song fades out. In all, there are eleven complete statements (plus the fade). Structurally, *there is nothing else.* The phrase itself is, by rock standards, quite complex harmonically (though to Baroque musicians it was something of a cliché). The use of a repeated harmonic progression is typical of rock. However, it also occurs quite often in Baroque music. There is no conflict here. The walking bass which underpins it is less characteristic of rock – the way the bass, which is semi-foregrounded, creates a two-voice counterpoint with the melody (organ or vocal) is a feature of Baroque music, and of a good deal of jazz, but not usually of rock, where bass parts generally have a harmonic function (they play riffs) but less often a melodic function. I suspect that the 'classical' source Procul Harum chose, and the use they made of it, account for the song's success. We can say that between the two codes involved – Baroque and rock – there are differences but also a relatively high syntactic correlation; surface details differ but deep structures are similar. Many other examples of rock/'classical' fusions fall apart because this element is lacking. This tells us something about the limits to fusion as an articulative method (as against other methods: parody, deliberate disjunction, acculturative adaptation, re-semanticisation) and about the limits to the expropriation of meaning: some syntactic structures are simply incompatible. It tells us something also about the *weight* with which received connotations attach to long-established traditions: it was probably the pre-modern (or at least pre-industrial), and at the same time the quasi-ritualistic motoric-gestural associations clinging strongly to the high Baroque style which attracted the rock group, and their counter-cultural followers.

Nevertheless, these associations *are* articulated into a new pattern, and it is the vocal which plays an essential part in that process, in making the song a *rock* song. Procul Harum superimpose on the Bach harmonies a vocal derived directly from rhythm and blues roots. In fact, the most obvious specific source here is soul music. This influence manifests itself in melodic shapes (largely pentatonic falling patterns, but, unlike, say, Chicago blues, also lyrical, sustained, long-breathed), vocal timbre (rich, open-throated, sensuous) and the use of melisma. To carry the argument further, it might be suggested that 'A Whiter Shade of Pale' adapts the genre of 'soul ballad', created by Sam Cooke, Ray Charles, Otis Redding and others; typically, such ballads also stretch vocals of the same type as this over complex chains of slow moving chords (which, as here, often involve repetition and riffs). Once again there is a congruence of codes – from classical music and from rhythm and blues – but once again, also, the non-congruent elements in each source act to re-orient the effects of the other. 'A Whiter Shade of Pale', we might speculate, marks a trend within the

38   *Richard Middleton*

counterculture which sees itself as, so to speak, 'sensuously spiritual' (Bach mediated by soul singing) and is 'immanently oppositional' *vis-à-vis* bourgeois culture (rock made baroque).

These discussions of a mere four songs establish the outlines of a problem which homology or reflectionist or immanent theories of musical meaning are equally incapable of solving. There are many – though not always contiguous – links between the music and elements of countercultural ideology; at the same time there are many references to facets of hegemonic cultural traditions. There *are* unifying factors – an ethos of 'personal' expression, for example – but equally there is a radical eclecticism of style and method; indeed, it is no easier to determine the limits defining the musical genre than the exact social composition and boundaries of the counterculture. The subcultural specificity of the songs is hard to establish; all contain techniques which continually threaten to widen the field of cultural reference. Subcultural ownership of music is very hard to protect. Within the counterculture, moreover, the response to each of the songs would have been different among different subgroups.

The main analytical requisite is, once again, an awareness of the internal contradictions running through the music and the culture; and the concomitant, a recognition that these must not be considered in isolation but within the larger musico-cultural field, to which the lines of contradiction relate. Undialectical methods lead to circular arguments. Thus, psychedelic elements in the musical style – blurred or tinkly timbres, for instance – are typically interpreted as such by reference to a subculture of drug-usage; in other words they are defined in this way primarily because hippies said they should be. A whole group of connotations, arising from our knowledge of the drug culture, then settles on the music. But this culture has already been defined in this way partially because of the existence in it of this particular kind of music. The meaning of drug usage is affected by the meaning of the associated music. And so we go on. The theory is perfectly structured internally (Willis calls the relationships reciprocal) but has no necessary connection to anything outside itself; there is no analytical *purchase* on it from without. In contrast, blurred or tinkly timbres should be understood in the context of general timbre-codes in popular music (and, more generally, in Western music as a whole). These considerations set limits to meaning – what Willis, aware of the difficulty, calls 'objective possibilities' – while at the same time they leave open a space within which the actions of other elements in the music, its context and reception, can pull them into a more specific place in the network of social meaning, in line with the work of the articulating principles involved. This explains, for instance, how elements of bourgeois 'art' music can, without losing their relatively

Re-constructing musical history 39

autonomously fixed limits of meaning, be re-articulated through the operation of different organising principles, so that their meaning is re-orientated.

Clarke *et al.* (1976) have described the individualism and diversity of the counterculture in terms of their roots in the ideology of the dominant (parent) middle-class culture, particularly in the context of that culture's enforced adaptation to new, more consumption-orientated forms of capitalism arising in the post-war period of affluence.

. . . some of these [countercultural] groups aimed for a systematic inversion, a symbolic upturning, of the whole bourgeois ethic. By pushing contradictory tendencies in the culture to extremes, they sought to subvert them, but from the inside . . . [their parents] mis-recognised the crisis *within* the dominant culture as a conspiracy *against* the dominant culture. They failed (as many members of the countercultures also failed) to see the cultural 'break' as, in its own traumatic and disturbing way, *profoundly adaptive* to the system's productive base . . . the new individualism of 'Do your own thing', when taken to its logical extremes, seemed like nothing so much as a looney caricature of petit-bourgeois individualism . . . (*ibid.* pp. 62, 65, 67).

The fact that the principles articulating the counterculture's position were partly oppositional, partly mediatory of dominant cultural interests, explains the mode of organisation of the progressive rock genre and its associated structure of meanings. To use terms derived from Clarke *et al.*, if typical working-class subcultures (teddy boy; rocker; mod; skinhead) have been governed by principles which can be generalised as 'collectivist', if the dominant bourgeois culture can by analogy be characterised in terms of 'possessive individualism', then the principle underlying the counterculture's *bricolages* is a kind of 'fraternal individualism' – or perhaps 'fraternal individualist bohemianism' (sometimes aestheticist, sometimes mystical, sometimes hedonist). The disparate sources on which the music draws are not arbitrarily assembled, their meaning simply expropriated; they are selected, in the light of the articulating principle. They do not lose the overall parameters of meaning which they bring with them, but the precise meanings these take on in practice are orientated through the effect of the new context in which they find themselves. Thus, in 'Spoonful' the meanings of the corporeal rhythms of rock 'n' roll are, without being destroyed, *shifted* somewhat (by the complex rhythmic overlays, the instrumental technique, lyrics and so on), so that they mean something slightly different. In 'Strawberry Fields' and 'Astronomy Dominé', the principle of extended forms is re-worked, still having an implication of 'thinking', but now thinking of a different kind from that suggested by, say, Beethoven.

This approach also explains why the music of the counterculture could be so easily co-opted and its radical implications defused. For, as Clarke *et al.* make clear, the articulating principle of hippie ideology is, in the final analysis, and despite its potential for opposition, embedded within the ideology of the dominant culture itself. Bourgeois individualism has a long history of subversive bohemian variants; and the struggle for control of the elements of countercultural musical style was a struggle between different aspects of the same principle. 'Fraternal individualism', for instance, is easily metamorphosed into 'élitist exhibitionism' (musically, this is the development from Cream to what has often been described as the 'empty virtuosity' of many late 1960s 'guitar heroes'); similarly, the 'thinking' of unpredictable extended forms, given the predictable lulling rhythms and bland timbres of Mike Oldfield is turned into LP-length 'easy listening'; the 'psychedelic sound' becomes exactly that: a fetishised label, isolated from the radical harmonic/rhythmic context it has in, say, 'Strawberry Fields', and pinned on to simple Top Ten dance tunes, as a tribute to the middle-class ideology of riskless hedonism.

It is not surprising, then, that in the early 1970s, having fulfilled its adaptive function for the bourgeoisie, and under pressure, externally from a reactionary backlash in society, and internally from growing 'professionalism', countercultural rock should for the most part subside into various forms of titillating superficiality. Only to be awakened by punk. Punk itself is dead, but the struggle initiated by the punk assault is still in progress. In one way, this assault can be regarded as a renewal of rock 'n' roll's struggle for some control of the productive apparatus. But at the same time punk, seeing the contradictions in the rock tradition's relations with the ruling culture, positioned itself in opposition not only to the ruling culture but also to the rock tradition, including its supposed oppositional aspects. Punk questioned the meaningfulness *of it all,* either nihilistically or from a positive political viewpoint. The way punk was able to re-work elements of rock 'n' roll on the one hand, *avant-garde* rock techniques on the other, and articulate them into forms of internally, as well as externally, directed critique, provides further material for the study of articulative processes; but it also suggests a need to stress another aspect, namely the relative *open-ness* of musical codes, compared to other signifying practices. This is the final point to be made here. By openness is meant both that specific musical elements are usually less firmly embedded in particular syntactic and semantic structures than are, for example, words, and that those conventions of meaning and syntax which do exist are more general, less precise, leaving greater freedom to make specific orientations in specific contexts. This is not to contradict the earlier argument that these general frameworks – the limits, or objec-

Re-constructing musical history   41

tive possibilities, mentioned previously as operating at the 'homologi-
cal' level – enclose syntactic and semantic spaces which, however
'free', are *in practice* over-determined, in line with a structure produced
by musical traditions and social pressures. Moreover, control of these
spaces and control of productive musical resources tend to go together
(this is, in the specifically musical sphere, the implication of Marx's
dictum, 'The ideas of the ruling class are, in every age, the ruling ideas:
i.e. the class which is the dominant *material* force in society is at the
same time its dominant intellectual force.'); though, as we have seen,
the relationship is complex, mediated and contested.

There are many ways of trying to close off the relative openness of
musical codes, of *fixing* meaning; a few are discussed above. It is worth
noting that one of the most common methods, for both subordinate
and hegemonic groups is to conjoin with a musical message the
relatively more precise significations of words or visual images. Some
examples have already occurred. For example, Ned Corvan, with
limited musical resources and restricted access to musical productive
skills and knowledge, relied mainly on his texts to 'fix' the meaning of
the tunes in the niche he wanted. Greater access to musical production, as with early rock 'n' roll, reduces the importance of words;
indeed for the rock 'n' roll culture it can be argued that the tendency to
treat lyrics as aspects of the musical texture rather than precise
denotative systems was advantageous, in that it resulted in a relative
openness which enabled fans to 'override' the music's internal contradictions and articulate it to their own needs. Whenever early rock 'n'
roll songs have lyrics of significance – almost inevitably at this time Tin
Pan Alley-style lyrics – their radical force is reduced. In fact, the
addition of more precise lyrics, of professionally constructed types, in
the late 1950s and early 1960s was one way in which rock 'n' roll, its
meaning thereby articulated to the needs of 'teenage consumer' or
'highschool' culture, was incorporated by the ruling interests. In
addition, TV and film were used to 'fix' rock 'n' roll meaning, through
the power of visual conventions. Elvis (from the waist up, or placed in
familiar Hollywood contexts) was defined in terms of romantic movie
or show-biz images, and the music correspondingly re-channelled. A
parallel process can be observed in the 1930s, when Hollywood played
an important part in settling the syncopated music of the 1920s into
functions of romantic escapism.

Punk's assault not only on musical content but also on the apparatus
and mode of production is now being answered in the same way. The
video 'boom' is being used to try to 'fix' musical meanings, close off
listeners' interpretative autonomy, and at the same time focus attention on a new technology under the control of the music and leisure

42   *Richard Middleton*

industries, and the advertisers. Not surprisingly, familiar images of escapism, 'star' poses, romantic glitter and bizarre jokes are reappearing alongside new types of visual gimmick. The music finds it hard to resist, and the partial articulative freedom achieved, for musicians and listeners, in the punk and post-punk musical culture of the late 1970s is in danger. A new phase in the articulation of musical meaning has begun, a new attempt to construct musical history into 'acceptable' channels; the popular response will be crucial.

References

Books and articles

Chambers, I. 1982. 'Some critical tracks', *Popular Music*, 2, pp. 19–36
Chester, A. 1970. 'Second thoughts on a rock aesthetic: The Band', *New Left Review*, 62, pp. 75–82
Clarke, J., Hall, S., Jefferson, T., and Roberts, B. 1976. 'Sub-cultures, cultures and class', in *Resistance through Rituals: Youth Subcultures in Post-War Britain*, ed. S. Hall and T. Jefferson (London), pp. 9–69.
Fabbri, F. 1982. 'Musical genres and their metalanguages', paper delivered to the ISME conference, *Pop and Folk Music: Stocktaking of New Trends*, Trento 1982
Gramsci, A. 1971. *Selections from the Prison Notebooks*, ed. Q. Hoare and G. Nowell-Smith (London)
Gregson, K. 1983. *Corvan. A Victorian Entertainer and His songs* (Banbury, Oxfordshire)
Hall, S. 1981. 'Notes on deconstructing "the popular"', in *People's History and Socialist Theory*, ed. R. Samuel (London), pp. 227–40
Harker, D. 1981. 'The making of the Tyneside concert hall', *Popular Music*, 1, pp. 27–56
Hebdige, D. 1979. *Subculture: the Meaning of Style* (London)
Hopkins, J. 1971. *Elvis: A Biography* (New York)
Laing, D. 1985. *One Chord Wonders: Power and Meaning in Punk Rock* (Milton Keynes)
Marcus, G. 1977. 'Elvis: Presliad, in *Mystery Train* (London)
Maróthy, J. 1974. *Music and the Bourgeois, Music and the Proletarian* (Budapest)
Mercer, C. 1978. 'Culture and ideology in Gramsci', *Red Letters*, 8, pp. 19–40
Middleton, R. 1979. 'All shook up: continuity and change in Elvis Presley's vocal style', in *Elvis: Images and Fancies*, ed. J. L. Tharpe (Jackson, Miss.), pp. 151–61; reprinted London, 1983
   1982 (with John Muncie). *Pop Culture, Pop Music and Post-War Youth: Counter-cultures*, Open University course U203, *Popular Culture*, Unit 20 (Milton Keynes)
   1983. ' "Play it again, Sam": some notes on the productivity of repetition in popular music', *Popular Music*, 3, pp. 235–70
   Forthcoming. 'Popular music, class conflict and the music-historical field',

paper delivered at the Second International Conference of IASPM, Reggio Emilia, 1983

Mouffe, C. 1979. 'Hegemony and ideology in Gramsci', in *Gramsci and Marxist Theory* (London), chapter 5

Tagg, P. 1979. *Kojak – 50 seconds of Television Music* (Gothenburg)

Wicke, P. 1982. 'Rock music: a musical-aesthetic study', *Popular Music*, 2, pp. 219–43

Willis, P. 1978. *Profane Culture* (London)

Records

Beatles. 1967. 'Strawberry Fields', Parlophone R 5570

Cream. 1966. 'Spoonful', on *Fresh Cream*, Polydor CP 594–001

Pink Floyd. 1967. 'Astronomy Dominé', on *The Piper at the Gates of Dawn*, Columbia SX 6157

Presley, Elvis. 1954–67. *The Elvis Presley Sun Collection*, RCA HY 1001; *Elvis' Golden Records*, vols. 1, 2, 3, 4, RCA 1707, 2075, 2765, 3921. These LPs contain all the recordings mentioned, and many more.

Procul Harum. 1967. 'A Whiter Shade of Pale', Deram DM 126

CHAPTER 3

AUTHORSHIP, GENDER AND THE CONSTRUCTION OF MEANING IN THE EURYTHMICS' HIT RECORDINGS[1]

Abstract

Pop songs are often interpreted, by fans, critics and even academic analysts, in relation to traditional notions of 'authorship'. But in recent pop, such as the Eurythmics' hits, these notions are at the very least in tension with a more fragmented construction of subjectivity. This article seeks to develop a method for analysing such constructions, both generally and in specific Eurythmics songs.

The method draws on Mikhail Bakhtin's *dialogic* theory of subjectivity and meaning, presenting the various parts of songs (i.e., both textural lines and structural sections) as interactive 'voices', each with its characteristic style-features. Such features are always culturally marked, through their multiple associations and their different positionings within various discursive domains. It is possible, therefore, to locate the styles, their features and their interrelations on a range of discursive axes (gender, ethnicity, etc.), making up a 'map' of the musico-discursive terrain, then to place the 'dialogue' constructed in a specific song in relation to these axes, this map.

For the Eurythmics, the *gender* axis is the most (though not the only) important one. It functions through the differential positioning of constituent styles (pop, blues, soul, disco, ballad, etc.) on this axis; in relation to other axes of meaning; through articulation in the specific socio-historical context of 1980s British pop; and via interaction with visual images (e.g., on accompanying videos).

After an analysis of eight songs, the article concludes with some implications of the method for the interpretation of gender – and more generally of the construction of subjectivity – in music.

Keywords
popular song; Eurythmics; gender; dialogics

Authorship or agency?

It may seem perverse, in a 'postmodern' world, to approach musical meaning from the perspective of 'authorship'. But if cultural studies no longer takes this romantic myth at face value, it is by no means clear that the popular music culture itself has followed suit. Journalistic criticism no less than fan discourse still very often speaks the language of 'originality', 'self-expression' and 'authenticity';[2] and, as Frith (1992), Cohen (1991) and Finnegan (1989) all make clear, this ideology remains at the heart of rock production. Even in the supposedly postmodern sphere of sampling technology, romantic claims of authorship survive (Goodwin, 1990). There are good reasons, then, to interrogate these claims.

In the tradition of Western art music, the individual composer so to speak 'signs' the work as his (or hers), and this 'sign' points to a unique creative source. The work joins others in a repertory, marked by genre, medium, style and function, so that, certainly up to the twentieth century, a fairly clear image of audience location is usually available as well. Of course, things are not quite so simple as this. Sometimes celebrated performers have a role in a work's genesis. Sometimes arrangers, orchestrators or editors muddy the waters. Sometimes composers imitate other composers, pastiche existing styles or borrow material. Increasingly works migrate between audiences and the boundaries of repertories crumble. Nevertheless, I think I describe accurately enough the paradigm case in this tradition. Of course, it is a tradition rooted in a much wider cultural history (see Stallybrass, 1992), and, in music as in other signifying practices, this relationship between 'authorship' and 'individuality' has strong implications for interpretation of style and meaning: it suggests who is speaking and in what context.

This is much less clear in the case of folk music and many other orally and electronically transmitted musics – even though bourgeois folk revivalists have tended to inaugurate a new definition of 'creative authenticity', attaching it to the 'unique identity' felt to be reflected in genuine 'folk' performance. In many non-Western traditions, the originators of pieces are unknown or mythical. Pre-revival 'folk' musicians generally worked with collectively owned material, and have rarely claimed much individual creative status. In twentieth-century popular music, increasing division of labour has turned production into a collective job, shared between performers, producer, sound engineer, and star singer (maybe) as well as writers. For the listener, the 'composition' is most likely to be the recording, and the ontological disjunction between this moment and any previous 'compositional' work merely dramatizes what is a general characteristic of electronically mediated dissemination: pieces refuse to sit still, generically, stylistically, socially; they are always sliding off the edge of one cultural site into another.

However, in the sixties, in rock, *auteur* theory reappeared. In part it drew on the folk revival ideology of 'authenticity', founded on 'truth to experience'; in part it tapped into the ideology of bourgeois art, especially as mediated by various kinds of bohemianism. Many rock performers composed their own songs. Often they got involved in production too. Stylistic originality and self-expression became the guidelines. There was an attempt to mark off a repertory – described as 'genuine' rock – and the rock audience thought of itself as quite tightly defined (even though this had little sociological solidity).

The Eurythmics had nineteen Top Forty hits in Britain between 1983 and 1990, about half of them reaching the Top Ten. While all of them appeared also on albums, their presentation and success as singles gives them the appearance of a coherent repertory, which could be defined by genre (chart pop), medium (amplified rock instruments, synthesised sound, multi-track recording studio), audience and function. At first glance, there seems to be a good case for describing their production in terms of 'authorship' and organizing our interpretation of them around this. The music and lyrics of all the songs were written by Dave Stewart and Annie Lennox, who together made up the Eurythmics. Other performers were brought in as necessary to do specific tasks on specific records. Both participated fully in the recording, mixing and production processes, and Stewart became a highly regarded producer. They deliberately organized their career so as to maximize their own control, forming their own publishing and management company, and insisting, as far as possible, on setting their own artistic agenda (see O'Brien, 1991: 88, 91; Waller and Rapport, 1985: 68, 73–4). Stewart's career began in folk clubs and a folk-rock band; Lennox was a student at the Royal College of Music in London when they met. Both backgrounds could have contributed elements of an ideology of authorship and authenticity. Female song-writers are unusual in popular music – except in the 'singer-songwriter' category, exemplified by Joni Mitchell – and Lennox's status as composer may have brought with it the connotations of 'confession' and autobiography which accompany that genre. She claimed to have been influenced by Mitchell. In the early years of her association with Stewart, their relationship was personal as well as musical. Given that virtually all the songs are about sexual relationships, it is hard not to read autobiographical elements into them.

This is certainly the line taken in many contemporary record reviews and in other journalistic comment (e.g. Sutcliffe, 1988; McNeill, 1983; Fitzgerald, 1983; Waller and Rapport, 1985: 84–5; O'Brien, 1991: 67, 75, 130–2; for instance: 'Annie's strength lies in her ability to channel this pain [arising from the break-up of her personal relationship with Stewart] into her song-writing': O'Brien, 1991: 75). Even a 'knowing' critic like Dave Hill links the self-managed, self-directed quality of the Lennox–Stewart career and the ups-and-downs of their relationship with the emotions and images portrayed in the music, and connects both to a wider 'rise and rise of the cult of the individual' (Hill, 1986: 35). Similarly, at the academic end of the spectrum of response, Wilfrid Mellers relates the songs to 'personal experience . . . a process of discovery' (Mellers, 1986: 226, 227). Lennox herself, in many interviews, goes along with this. 'A lot of the writing is introspective. It expresses how I feel myself' (Waller and Rapport, 1985: 98). 'I don't have much of an objectifying capacity as a composer' (O'Brien, 1991: 130); rather, she writes songs 'just to articulate how I feel' (Du Noyer, 1984: 7), and when she performs, she says, 'I'm showing myself through them' (Jackson, 1987: 26). 'If you have some degree of integrity', she insists, 'it's unbearable to live with an identity that's just slapped on you by someone else and isn't really representative of you' (Jackson, 1987: 26).

In a revealing joint interview, both Lennox and Stewart react violently to a New York dance re-mix of tracks from their *Touch* album: 'It was nothing to do with us', says Stewart; 'I can't stand the principle of it. It's songs that I've already recorded and mixed to the best of my ability' (Du Noyer, 1984: 6). The songs, it seems, are personal possessions.

Despite all this, to link the music's meaning to authorial experience and intention in any direct way is misguided. Just as the lyrics tell many different stories from many different points of view, so the music draws on a far greater variety of styles than could easily be taken to represent any unified perspective. Some might want to play down the significance of this. When musicians acquire a succession of styles, this is often treated as reflecting increasing technical mastery or artistic maturity. But more, always, is involved than this, for styles carry their own discursive baggage with them. A style offers a voice or voices, it makes available perspectives on the world, positions for listening subjects; it locates them socially. However, in the Eurythmics' case, there is a historically specific aspect to this as well. The stylistic allusions display a persistent sense of irony, and sometimes this reaches the level of pastiche. The visual image of the band was presented in a similarly shifting and ironic way, as we shall see later. The styles used summon up images of their own stereotypic audiences, and it seems likely that the market for the records was a very composite one. With so many differing allusions and markers, the music was from the start always seeping outside the boundaries of the chart pop repertory.

A moment's historical contextualization helps us to understand this. In the 1970s, as Frith (1989) explains, David Bowie, by literally and self-consciously 'inventing' himself through the construction of a succession of dramatic personae, had cracked open the rock myth of expressive honesty and subjective integrity. The 'new pop' of the early eighties was founded on the idea of the 'pose': ironic play with both musical and visual style. The new pop criticism which grew out of this moment celebrated 'postmodern' irony as an antidote to rock subjectivity. The rise of 'indie' music in the mid-eighties, as Reynolds (1989) makes clear, further complicated the situation, standing against both rock's straightforward commitment and the equally simple address to adolescent pleasures of typical chart pop. By this time, both critics and musicians were, consciously or unconsciously, often drawing on the language of poststructuralism to explain their strategies. To some extent, the Eurythmics' multifaceted style can be regarded as a microcosm of wider developments.

That this was a deliberate strategy is clear from statements by Annie Lennox herself. Confusingly mixed with claims to expressive authenticity are descriptions of how she played with 'artificial identities' (Du Noyer, 1984: 51); in particular, 'I played with my sexuality' (through manipulating androgynous and contradictory visual images and gestures). This sort of manipulation is related to a certain ambivalence about the self: 'sometimes I'm not too sure just how much is me and how much is someone else's story' (Jackson, 1987: 26); 'There's fifteen thousand different Annies. Within the one person there are a million types of . . . personas according to the environment you're in' (O'Brien, 1991: 100). But this is subsumed back into autobiography, as Lennox describes her inventions of, and identifications with, a multiplicity of roles virtually as a response to adolescent alienation: 'I didn't belong. I didn't know what role to take on. I didn't know who I was' (Irwin, 1986: 24). The 'unitary subject' is cracking – but reluctantly.

This subject had been exposed as a fiction some time before the poststructuralist assault. But what the poststructuralist critique has done is to make clearer some of the ways in which subjectivity, far from being an a priori experiential ground, is constructed in discourse – particularly language, but also other cultural practices (such as musical styles). One way of putting this, which I want to pursue, is that associated with Mikhail Bakhtin.

For Bakhtin, 'there is no experience outside its embodiment in signs' (quoted in Todorov, 1984: 43). Since signs are social products – that is, discourse is always 'inter-textual', always and unavoidably referring to previous discourse – subjectivity is created in dialogue with other subjects, other discourses. Thus 'the self . . . is not a presence wherein is lodged the ultimate privilege of the real, the source of sovereign intention and guarantor of unified meaning' (Clark and Holquist, 1984: 65); 'the self must be thought of as a project' (72), and 'the reason for the invisibility of the author is the same as that for the invisibility of the self: the author is not a single, fixed entity so much as a capacity, an energy' (88). We can say that 'the self is an act of grace, a gift of the other' (68); hence, while 'the author is profoundly active . . . his activity is of a . . . dialogical nature' (Bakhtin quoted in Clark and Holquist, 1984: 244).

This approach to creativity enables us to retain a concept of agency, in a particular, closely qualified sense, while refusing the mystifications of traditional notions of authorship. This is important, because the active contribution of Annie Lennox to the production process of Eurythmics songs itself creates meaning, especially for feminists. As Susan McClary writes in relation to Madonna, for a woman to insist on taking her representation into her own hands already constitutes a powerful act of meaning production (McClary, 1991: 149–50).

Style, voice and polyphony

The Bakhtinian concept of the 'dialogic subject' seems tailor-made for the Eurythmics' multi-styled repertory. They draw on styles from (at least) rock, chart pop, disco, the synthesizer or 'techno-pop' of the early 1980s, blues, soul, and ballad – and possibly 'classical' and 'folk' as well. And these are not just stocked up, one after the other, as if to demonstrate expertise, but are interplayed, interworked, in ways that relate to lyric themes. In the light of this, we can go further than just picturing the Eurythmics as a microcosm of the stylistic diversity of popular music in the 1980s. On the level of style-ideologies, the image of 'authorship' which they themselves present is not monolithic, but seems to vary in accordance with the associations attached to the different styles. Thus the irony of 'new pop' bounces off the unitary certainties of rock expression, or the antiphonal collective subject of soul ideology; synthesizer pop tends to write the subject out in favour of the machine; ballads allude to a tradition in which singers often transform already existing songs, obliterating the 'author', against a lavishly 'produced' and knowingly 'artificial' instrumental background. In a sense, then, the Eurythmics are playing with the conventions of various styles as these touch on ideologies of authorship. From the very start, we are confronted with the question, 'Who is this?'; 'Who is speaking here?'

Mainstream music semiology might classify the various style-features as 'topics' (see e.g., Agawu, 1991). But this somehow fails to catch the way that, in popular music anyway, styles are intersected by multiple discourses, so that they stand at the conjunction of a variety of axes of social meaning. Nor does it deal adequately with the fact that, often, in actual textures, manifestations of the styles overlap and coincide, so that they have the character of interacting 'points of view'. Given that these songs, judging by their lyrics, are little narratives or at least 'discursive tableaux', it is important to mark the styles as players in a social drama, and I would rather think, following Bakhtin, in terms of dialogic 'voices'.[3]

If theoretical justification is required for this, we can note that Bakhtin himself often described discourse, especially literature, and most especially the novel, as 'polyphonic', a quality achieved through 'orchestration' of the 'voices', counterpointing their varied social 'overtones'. For him, even a monologic utterance is structured in dialogue (between author and addressee), while the range of literary genres vary in the extent to which dialogue and linguistic diversity – 'heterology' – is explicitly built into the form. A similar range seems to exist in music, with a repertory like the Eurythmics' being analogous, in its way, to the 'polyphonic' novel. As Adorno reminds us (1973: 18), 'polyphonic music' – always, just because it is polyphonic – 'says "we"'. Even mono-stylistic pieces can be regarded as the interactions of different 'voices'. Barbara Bradby (1990; 1992; also Bradby and Torode 1984) has done excellent work on Buddy Holly, Madonna and the sixties girl-group repertory, showing how the vocal textures and narratives – interactions of lead and backing singers, for example – can be read in terms of social dialogues, touching particularly on constructions of gender and sexuality. This perspective has not been much applied outside popular music, although there are exceptions; nor has it been much applied to instrumental voices.[4]

Of course, while instrumental parts may carry gender markings, sung voices can hardly avoid doing so. John Shepherd (1991, chapter 8) has sketched something of the range of vocal styles deployed across the bifurcated territory of 'hard' and 'soft' rock – or as I am calling them 'rock' and 'pop'.[5] The typical male voice of hard – or as it is sometimes called, 'cock' – rock is hard and raspy, produced in the throat; this is the voice of aggressive, macho sexual demand. With great effort, it can be appropriated by women singers – Janis Joplin, for example – when it seems to suggest attempts to take over characteristically masculine constructions of possessive sexual desire. The classic male pop voice is thin and light, often a head voice; the image is of the vulnerable male adolescent, the 'feminized' male, craving (maternal) protection. The possibility of women appropriating this voice may turn on the availability of an appeal to the pre-gendered 'mirror phase' of Lacanian psychoanalysis. Kaplan (1987: 58–60, 93–101), in her discussion of pop video categories, describes this strategy, which would presumably rest on constructions of singer and imagined listener as androgynously, narcissistically reflecting each other's gaze. More often, however, women pop singers, in Shepherd's schema, use either a warm chest voice (woman as nurturer, sexual provider mediated by Ideal Mother), or a development of this which is given a greater edge, a head-tone sheen; here the singer's offer, a more calculated one, is of herself as willing sexual object.

As Shepherd notes, singers can move between categories within a song. Moreover, the gender positions which the categories construct are not fixed for all time; they can be renegotiated, in changing social and musical circumstances. There are, too, more categories than these available, especially if we widen the stylistic range. For instance, there is a particular female ballad voice – husky, 'lived-in' – which, especially if there is influence from the European cabaret or jazz night-club traditions, seems to position the singer as a 'woman of experience'. Annie Lennox uses this sometimes, as she does also a pure-toned 'virginal' timbre suggesting, perhaps, chastity, innocence, or, alternatively, a kind of rationalized or spiritualized control, a refusal to play sexual games. The precise meanings here may depend on where the voice is heard as coming from: from 'classical' singing, perhaps, or from 'folk-pop' (Joan Baez, Judy Collins, Mary Hopkin, the Carpenters); very rarely does Lennox's use of this voice seem to relate to any construction of a 'Lolita' persona, as Madonna's does (albeit teasingly, ironically). Which raises a particularly important point: that vocal styles do not work autonomously but are mediated by wider considerations of style. Both the dirty, raspy tones of 'cock rock' and the warm timbres of 'earthy' female pop singers take on different meanings when they appear in soul music; the head tones and falsettos of funk and disco-pop (James Brown, Michael Jackson) carry different implications from similar sounds in soft rock. Modes of singing help to delineate styles but they also move across them, responding to them, perhaps changing meanings as they go.

The Eurythmics' first hit, 'Sweet Dreams', is a good example of their use of stylistic multiplicity and of the way the styles can interact. The basic dialogue is between verse on the one hand, chorus and bridge on the other (see Figure 1). The verse suggests pop-ballad, with a low-pitched, narrativistic, worldly-wise vocal backed by synthesized string figures (strings being a traditional ballad accompaniment). But the vocal pitch contour is bluesy, and increasing pitch and rhythm inflections intensify this influence as the song goes on. The 'mechanical' synthesizer figures suggest 'techno-pop', while the straight-four-bass drum thud derives from disco. Against this constellation of style-influences, the chorus, which also appears as an introduction and an instrumental interlude, poses a soaring, wordless, melismatic vocal with sung backing, and the bridge is built from responsorial cries ('hold your head up') over a held, hymn-like I-IV (tonic-subdominant) chord sequence; both of these stem stylistically from soul music. In the chorus, too, the rhythm acquires a strong backbeat accent, a technique most associated with rock or rhythm 'n' blues. The dialogue between these two multi-voiced perspectives (verse on the one hand; chorus/bridge on the other) seems to affect the course of the song. After the first bridge, the succeeding interlude keeps the chorus's backbeat and also picks up a new, bluesy string phrase. The backbeat continues through the next verse; and then in the playout on the final verse, not only backbeat and bluesy string phrase are superimposed on the original verse music but also the melismatic soul-style vocal from the chorus. The interplay of styles seems, then, to create some sort of musical narrative as well as a dialogue. But what does it mean? To tackle this question, we need an interpretative framework.

Constructing meaning, constructing gender

For Bakhtin, not only is heterology – the dialogic interplay of discourses – a structural condition of subjectivity; it is also the source of meaning.

> Every word [or musical effect] gives off the scent of a profession, a genre, a current, a party, a particular work, a particular man, a generation, an era, a day, and an hour. Every word smells of the context and contexts in which it has lived its intense social life ... In the word ... contextual harmonies are unavoidable.
>
> (Bakhtin quoted in Todorov, 1984: 56–7)

As voiced utterance, music constructs identities, offering subjective positions associated with particular social locations. These positions are contextualized, and when the contextualization is especially consistent, we can speak, with Bakhtin, of 'chronotopes' – 'spatial and temporal indicators ... fused into one carefully thought-out, concrete whole' (Bakhtin, 1981: 84). Musical styles often place us in specific historical and geographical moments, and offer specific ways of experiencing imagined place and felt time.

But these experiences are always mediated by discourse. And one way, analytically, into this might be to envisage styles as speaking and interacting with each other on a variety of discursive planes: 'class', 'gender', 'ethnicity', and so on. If discourse is dialogic, styles will signify in relation to each other, in a field of meaning, which is 'structured in difference'; thus we can picture them as being positioned, for any given discursive plane, along axes of meaning: 'individual'–'collective', 'spiritual'–'sensual', 'black'–'white', for example. By drawing out these axes on the various planes, we can put together a series of discursive maps of the style-terrain.

For the Eurythmics, the gender map is particularly important. The multiple discursive constructions of gender and sexuality, together with their inevitable internal contradictions, make this a rich field for articulation

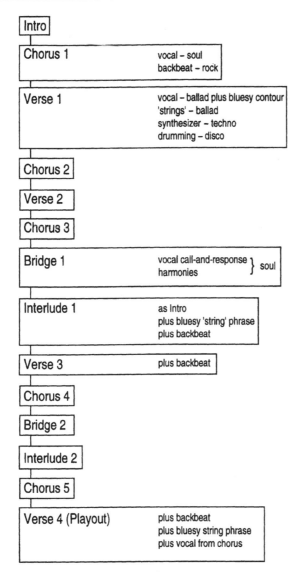

Figure 1. Sequence of verse, chorus and bridge in 'Sweet Dreams'.

by musical styles. As Birch has pointed out (1992: 50–5), the conflict within Western culture between the notion that art, and especially music, are somehow 'feminine' and the simultaneous tendency to exploit art's location in the (Lacanian) symbolic order so as to align it with structures of patriarchal authority, leads to a gendered distribution of styles and genres, some being regarded as more 'masculine', others as more 'feminine' (see

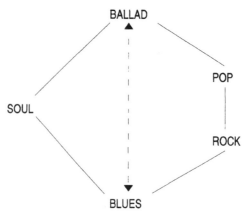

Figure 2.   The gender map.

Figure 2). The ballad, drawing on the code of 'romance', is clearly located (stereotypically) in the 'feminine' sphere and can be placed at one pole of the axis. Just as in the literary romance the heroine, while acceding to the conventional passivity of her role, ensnares her man by 'feminizing' him (Radway, 1987), so female ballad singers, while offering themselves for consumption, insist on the primacy of 'emotion' over 'sex'; and male singers have to be 'feminized'. At the opposite pole stands the clearly 'masculine' sphere of blues, a music that (again stereotypically) celebrates 'sex' rather than 'romance', and usually in the form of aggressive male desire. Here, female singers (Bessie Smith, for example) have to be 'masculinized'.

In practice, styles usually interact – hardly surprising, given that 'gender' is unstable. Indeed, the basic polarity is mediated by the positioning of other styles. One line of mediation seems to run through pop and rock. In line with the established contrast between 'cock rock' and 'teenybopper pop' (Frith and McRobbie, 1978),[6] rock is positioned closer to blues, pop closer to ballad – although clearly each style has its own specific associations (relating, for instance, to aspects of adolescence, male narcissism, etc.). The other main line of mediation runs through soul music, widely perceived as representing some sort of 'spiritualized eroticism'. Drawing on gospel music as well as blues and ballad, soul has offered new positions to both male and female singers, sometimes an androgynous blurring of roles, sometimes a proto-feminist egalitarianism, almost always a politics of solidarity. Disco (and to some extent subsequent styles of 'black pop' – funk, house) extends androgyny (there are links with gay culture), relating both to soul eroticism and pop-mediated romance (see Dyer, 1990).

Exploration of new gender positions in recent popular song has often been associated with the influence of soul and post-soul styles. But, given the (chauvinistic) messages of many lyrics (from soul down to rap), and soul music's historical links with black nationalism (not always renowned for progressive perspectives on gender), there is a need for care. Nevertheless, the link is not a false one. Just as male soul singers are often constructed as either relatively weak and needy or relatively trustworthy and responsible, so the music's rhythmic style is usually less aggressive, less thrusting, than that of blues and rock. The figure of the mature, matriarchal woman which features strongly in black American music traditions can be called up; and – a more specific chronotopic connection – the gospel lineage makes available images and associations of the leadership role of women in the black church, epitomized in the music by Rosetta Tharpe and Mahalia Jackson. Finally the general aura of *power* and *solidarity* attaching to soul through its link with black consciousness ideologies (James Brown being the best examplar) can fairly easily be rearticulated from an ethnic to a gender politics; a key chronotopic moment here is the cover of Otis Redding's celebration of black pride, 'Respect' (1965), by Aretha Franklin in 1967.

Although gender is the subject of a particularly important discursive map, certainly for the Eurythmics, it is not the only such topic. Moreover, maps interact. For example, we can envisage a 'nature'–'technology' axis, structured round a polarity of soul (where instruments are always 'vocalized', recording techniques 'humanized') and 'techno-pop', whose point is precisely to 'technologize' all sound sources. This could be seen as mediated by, for instance, disco in one way ('mechanized eroticism'), ballad in another ('glossy' orchestrations, 'mechanized' quality of old-fashioned show-biz), rock in a third (the expressive use of electric instruments signifying the masculine control of technology). There is interplay between this map and that of gender. Women, featured almost always as singers, not instrumentalists, are stereotypically associated with the body, via the 'natural' qualities of the voice; male instrumentalists, producers and sound engineers, by contrast, exemplify patriarchal mastery of the rationalized realm of technology (see Bradby, 1993; King, 1992). On the face of it, the Eurythmics seem to fit into this pattern: Lennox, the voice; Stewart, the instrumentalist/ producer. Just as the division of production was not so straightforward, however (Lennox played instruments and participated in arranging and production), so Lennox's voice is sometimes used as an instrument, or is even 'technologized', while synthesized imitations of 'natural' instruments, as well as fiercely 'vocalized' electrically produced tones, also query the conventional equation.[7]

A third important discursive map is organized around a 'sacred'–'secular' axis, with soul at one pole (spiritualizing the secular), opposing the relentlessly secularizing quality of vernacular pop, especially the more 'techno' variants. Principal mediations here are provided by ballad on the one hand, blues on the other. Blues, traditionally known as 'devil's music', is religiously charged (unlike pop) but relates by negation to the gospel–soul lineage; this is a style which, via interplay with the gender plane, often constructs women, and 'sex' itself, as evil, and men's powers and follies as demonically ordered. Ballad intersects sacred and secular orbits in a different way. Its idealization of the sexual relationship resonates with old-established confusions of carnal and spiritual love, addresses to the ethereal feminine ('my angel') summoning up images of the Virgin, which, in the context of interplay with the gender plane, stand in dialogue with complementary images (in blues and rock) of the Whore. There is plentiful historical sediment to call on, from Victorian 'sacred ballads' through protestant hymns (their passionate personalized address and typical harmonic progressions both influential on ballads), and mystical poetry, back to the confusions of sacred and secular, Madonna and Heloise figures, in mediaeval song and lyric.[8] A more speculative interplay of discourses would be to see the quasi-maternal positions available to women singers in soul as relating to matriarchal ('earth-mother') religion.

In the case of the Eurythmics, style-dialogue, and the resulting constructions of gender, were located in a very specific historical context, marked on the one hand by rising feminist consciousness and new definitions of sexuality and gender, and on the other by Thatcherite political reaction, attempting to hold back such change. Of course, the wave of 'gender-bending' in popular culture had its historical antecedents. Not only did it build on a tradition in pop music going back through Jagger and Bowie to Little Richard and Elvis, but this tradition too can be connected to earlier examples in twentieth-century entertainment (Liberace, Valentino, Josephine Baker); and to some extent the whole lineage connects to still older patterns of excess and license characteristic of theatrical performance (opera *castrati*, music hall drag artists, pantomime dames, boy actors, etc.). Nevertheless, as Garber (1992) points out, such subversive behaviour took on a new profile and new social resonances in the early 1980s. By the middle of the decade, 'cross-dressing', particularly 'male' styles for girls, was ubiquitous fashion. Ironically, Thatcherite individualism facilitated both the economics of 'second-hand dressing' and its narcissistic body politics (see McRobbie, 1989). But in a context marked by the rising influence of gay culture, changes in the structure of the family and the employment market, and post-punk experiment in pop music, 'gender-bending' possessed greater cultural power than this might suggest.

Moreover, the wave of cross-dressers which swept into pop (from Michael Jackson to Madonna, Boy George to the Pet Shop Boys) contained, for the first time, a strong representation of women performers, building on the examples of Millie Jackson, Grace Jones, Patti Smith and an array of punks. When Annie Lennox describes her 'I Need a Man' video as 'like a woman dressed as a man dressed as a woman . . . so there's a lot of sexual ambiguity in the whole thing. It's almost a homosexual statement as well' (O'Brien, 1991: 97), she acknowledges in retrospect what her notorious drag impersonation of Elvis at the 1984 Grammy Awards ceremony signalled at the time: her entry into what had become a 'continuum of strong women and feminised men who have, intentionally or not, used pop to trash gender boundaries' (Jon Savage, actually describing the 1990s band, Suede: *Guardian*, 14 July 1993).

The Eurythmics' very deliberate play with a range of visual images for Annie Lennox acquires its full meaning in this context, and these images in turn reflect back on the dialogue of musical voices. The initial, shocking androgynous persona (1983) had Annie in a man's suit, with cropped hair, dyed orange; and several other looks played on the theme of appropriating male power. Lennox and Stewart were often photographed to look like androgynous twins. But increasingly Annie also played ironically with traditional images of femininity (flouncy dresses, lace, soft-focus blond curls, etc.), and with markers of an equally stereotypic raunchy sexuality (black leather, low-cut bra and so forth). Outfits overflowing with show-biz glitter, such as her 'Liberace' suit with keyboard-effect lapels, put the whole game in quotation marks.

Equally carefully constructed were the visual images – and indeed the visual scenes and narratives – contained in the videos accompanying the Eurythmics' records. And while it is possible to exaggerate the interpretative importance of pop videos – after all, most listening takes place without them – they do in this case often confirm or amplify the musical meanings. Besides, visual images popularized in videos tend to seep into a more general consciousness, influencing subsequent listening even in the video's absence. This was perhaps especially true in the early 1980s, when the video form was an exciting novelty. And its effects may have been particularly felt on gender readings of Eurythmics songs, given that relatively few videos featured female stars (Kaplan, 1987). I shall not be going into any great visual-analytic detail in the interpretations that follow, nor drawing with any thoroughness on film theory – though it is clear that long traditions of stereotyped images, poses and gestures lie intertextually behind pop video technique, and that Annie Lennox feeds richly on these. Nevertheless, it would be misleading to discuss her positionality solely or even mainly in terms of, say, the scopophilic male 'gaze'; and even her visual negotiations and critiques of this (for it is rare in Eurythmics videos, except for purposes of irony, for the camera to position her for the classic male 'look') form only part of the dialogic texture, alongside the interactions of vocal timbres, of polyphonic voices and of musical styles.

Video theorists who neglect the music risk missing a good deal of this textural richness – which amongst other things precludes univocal con-structions of listener/viewer response. Garber (1992) argues that cross-dressing always acts as an index of 'category crisis', gender markings map-ping on to other axes of difference (ethnicity, class, cultural value, etc.), so that to upset established meanings in one sphere often puts others in jeop-ardy too.[9] Elvis, for example, conflating gender, ethnic and class subver-sions, was a 'living category crisis' (Garber, 1992: 367). Here musical ethnicity – a discursive plane not discussed in the topography sketched above – becomes vital.[10] Just as for black performers ethnic tension has often been displaced on to gender subversion (for instance, 'selling out' to white audiences being portrayed as 'emasculation'), so in the Eurythmics' music black/white and gender confusions are intermingled. The Eurythmics could 'pass for black' on US radio, just as Annie Lennox the woman could pass for . . . [what?], and when she sings 'white soul', one can think of this as a kind of 'aural cross-dressing'.

Given such rich discursive chains within the texts, it would be difficult to argue for anything but multiple listener positions. The dialogic interplay of 'voices' offers a range of possible points of identification: not just this style but also that, not just lead vocal (itself often split in gender implications through stylistic diversity) but also other voices in the texture. Polyphonic music provides the means to subvert any monologic 'gaze' at the same time as the classic pop texture (lead vocal dominant) strives to maintain it. Moreover, listeners themselves bring to the music a range of pre-existing investments in gender and other representations, which affect the direction of their 'look'. As Frith (1992) has pointed out, the pop audience is in any case gendered in complex and, to some extent, socially unconventional ways; and in the gender-bending context of the early eighties, this may well have led to that radically heterogeneous audience response theorized, in music and more widely, by many feminist critics (see Kaplan, 1987; McClary, 1991; Gamman and Marshment, 1988; Bonner *et al.*, 1992). But if we are imagining a 'more complicated scenario, one which allows fluid relations of activity and passivity across multiple identifications ... [involving] a whole variety of looks and glances – an interplay of possibilities' (Moore, 1988: 55, 59), this means that the interpretations that follow, while built (I hope) on evidence both in the texts and in the music-historical context, can only aspire to persuasiveness through inter-subjective scrutiny.

Some interpretations

Re-reading 'Sweet Dreams' in the light of the previous section, a quasi-narrative schema emerges, structured round the sequence of verse – the bleak, abusive setting of modern alienated society – chorus – a cry of feeling – and bridge – a soul-derived collective self-assertion ('hold your head up'). The voice moves from anonymous 'voice of experience' through the more 'expressive' pain and passion of the soul-influenced chorus, to the call-and-response of the bridge, which could be interpreted in terms of a general politics of solidarity or conceivably as the voice of a feminist sisterhood. As we saw earlier, characteristics of the chorus/bridge sections 'leak' into the verse sections, as the song is progressively 'humanized', through the 'vocalization' of the strings, the 'sexualization' of the drumming through the backbeat, and the increased role of sung voices in the texture. Parallel to this, visual images of 'nature' increasingly invade, or take over from, the representations of technology/business settings which we see at the start. Thus, the strings come to represent 'the human as natural', as we see Lennox and Stewart playing cellos in a field and in a boat. Similarly, Lennox's voice is increasingly pictured as 'natural' through 'tactile' close-ups of her face and mouth, imagery at odds with the portrayal which is dominant earlier, in which a masculinized appearance accompanies 'inhuman' gestures of mastery and domination. Surreal shots superimposing computers and cows ('nature'? or 'nature abused'?) emphasize the part played by the technology–nature axis in constructing gender in this song.

However, the implications for gender position are ambiguous. In the verse music, the ballad/disco mix suggests 'romance gone wrong', and the pop element defines this romance as of a post-1960s (hedonistic?) type; the suggestions of 'techno' define *how* it has gone wrong: through mechaniz-ation ('some of them want to use/abuse you; some of them want to be used by you/to be abused'). But the gender roles are unclear: the hints of torch song in Lennox's vocal seem to represent the protagonist as 'the woman as victim'; but the visual images of Lennox, in conjunction with the relentlessly 'techno' backing, could be taken to be presenting *her* as the abuser. Similarly, the use of soul style-features in chorus and bridge makes available both 'strong woman' and 'responsive man' positions; and sure enough, in the later parts of the video, Dave Stewart's appearance and movements are as 'feminine' as Lennox's are 'masculine'. So both stages in the dialogic process are androgynously peopled, and this facilitates a search towards a recovery of human dignity and solidarity *without* necessarily mapping this on to a stereotyped transition from 'male' ('technics') to 'female' ('nature') – or on to an equally stereotyped progression from 'woman as victim' to the Janis Joplinesque 'woman with phallus' (a progression which a purer ballad-rock sequence might have produced). That our picture here of what 'sweet dreams' are seems less ironic at the end of the song than it did at the beginning may be tied up with a redefining of sexual desire in relation to the map of gender roles.

Many songs, especially from the earlier stages of the Eurythmics' career, offer variants of the kind of style-dialogue we find in 'Sweet Dreams'. For example, 'Love is a Stranger' plays off a disco-techno-ballad mix in the verse against a chorus and bridge which introduce more urgent, higher-pitched singing in sensuous parallel thirds, a style suggesting soul, or even nineteenth-century opera. The dialogue is between third-person description ('Love is a stranger . . .') and first-person cry ('I want you . . .'); between love as threat (its victims presented as addicts of a ubiquitous commodity) and an attempt to assert desire as control. In this song, however, the style-elements interpenetrate the various sections to a considerable extent. Thus, the 'mechanical' drum/synthesizer backing runs continuously – imprisoning the desire embodied in the chorus vocal; at the same time, the IV-I harmonic sequence (the 'Amen' gesture beloved of soul music) which is most prominent in the chorus also underlies (in reverse: I-IV) the structure of the verse, so that its 'reassuring' quality[11] 'softens' the harsh environment pictured there. The result overall is a rather inconclusive feel. In the video, Lennox appears in three radically different guises: in long, peroxide-blond curls and fur coat; in her man's suit and cropped hair look; and in punky leather, with sadistic overtones. This reinforces the inconclusiveness, but at the same time helps prevent any possibility of an orthodox positioning of the victim–desire dialectic in relation to the gender axis: Annie insists that, if this is how 'love' is in the modern world, she will be jailer as well as prisoner.

In 'Who's That Girl?' the 'story' is clearer (in the music if not in the lyrics). The verse's ballad format has Lennox singing in low-pitched, throaty, torch-song style of unrequited love, backed by synthesized strings and sustained ('cello') bass-line. This gives way in the chorus to pop-disco:

regular-beat drumming with backbeat, repeating chord-sequence, synthesizer riff; the 'timeless' setting of ballad anguish is given chronotopic specificity. And in *this* (1980s) context, the protagonist is clearly not going to submit to the passivity of private melancholy: her insistent question, 'Who's that girl?', is delivered in assertive soul style, with extravagant melismatic backing phrases and (unison) vocal group support on the repeated 'Tell me'. This chorus puts the video Dave Stewart, showing off his various new women, in his place – a move confirmed visually when Lennox switches from her 'feminine' to her 'masculine' persona, then is shown (in both simultaneously) kissing 'herself'. What happens to the listener's positioning here? A musical equivalent of the visual hermaphroditism would be if (s)he, moving through identification with Lennox's vocal, incorporated the sharp-edged instrumental riff, or the backbeat drumming, into its (her?) perspective, pulling them into its orbit (rather than adopting their ('masculine') positions as alternatives).

Sometimes the style-mix is even more clear-cut. 'Would I Lie to You' combines rock and soul. In a more explicit assertion of independence, Annie is showing the door to a lover who is no longer welcome. The verse's aggressive rock groove, use of guitar distortion, and hard-edged vocal tone suggest a female appropriation of the cock-rocker's sneer. In the chorus, the riff (over a IV-V chord-alternation), the use made of brass and vocal group, the melismatic vocal overdubs, all come from soul, providing the emotional and social foundations for her self-confidence. In the video, Lennox arrives by motorbike, clad in black leather, then performs in 'sexy' black dress, with an extravagant take-over of the male rock singer's strut. But the camera does not fetishize her body (she often turns her back, disappears from centre stage, and is shot at an angle), and her freedom of movement, together with the unfeminine hair, suggest a 'new woman' redefining male freedom in terms of her rights to her own body.

In 'I Need a Man', which is blues-rock rather than soul-rock, adoption of a 'reverse-macho' stance is pushed over an extreme into parody. The harsh, raspy timbre and exaggerated arrogance of the vocal are matched by the heavy bass riff and Keith Richard-style guitar, and by Lennox's outrageous flaunting of herself and the phallic suggestiveness of her mike-handling. This is one-way sexual demand, a reverse image of Mick Jagger – except that for a woman to assume such a position, she has to start from the basis of her received role as object rather than actor: hence the peroxide curls, heavy make-up, low-cut dress. But the performance is, musically and visually, so over the top that, as Lennox herself was aware (see above), this parody of a man-eating vamp can hardly conceal other, deeper layers of interpretation. Behind it lies the suggestion that this performer is a male, in drag; and, further back again, we know (or do we?) that this male is only being played by a woman. The complexity is in the performance here, and this twisting of the received connotations of the blues and rock traditions (a clear case of Bakhtin's 'double-voiced utterance') is why the style-mixture of the song can be so relatively simple. This sort of ambivalence is absent in the stylistically similar 'Missionary Man' (the Eurythmics' 'Jumpin' Jack Flash'); but here the articulation of predatory sexuality with the sacred–secular axis (devil's music *versus* missionary man) results in musical modifications: the missionary man's message, in the bridge, is accompanied by a build-up of held, organ-like chords; and throughout (but especially in the play-out), occasional interjections of ecstatic, melismatic soul-style vocal fills attempt to recall a less conflictual relationship of sensuous and spiritual.

'There Must Be an Angel' treats the relationship of sexuality and religion very differently. The lyrics and the accompaniment, with its swooping strings and heavenly choir, signify 'ballad', but a ballad pushed by the vocal shapes with their literally fantastic melismata towards soul, and with a virginal purity of vocal tone which is indebted to 'sexless' ideals of classical singing. The playing off of erotic ecstasy, romantic longing and unearthly purity is focused by the video setting: Annie Lennox in virginal white gown; asexual angels flitting about; a neo-classical 'sensuality without sex'. The transmutation of ballad cliché ('there must be an angel playing with my heart') into a more socially generalized bliss ('an orchestra of angels') is readily explained once we interpret the song as appealing on the level of the pre-gendered mirror phase of Lacanian psychoanalysis.[12] The theatrical setting of the video performance, in front of androgynously clad king and courtiers at the Versailles court, provides a historical framing effect to facilitate listeners' regression to this phase.

The intersection of the gender and sacred–secular discursive axes in this song is made clear in the bridge, when heavenly chorus turns into black gospel choir, their characteristic and erotic syncopated rhythm backing a Lennox solo far more clearly derived from soul and with much richer, dirtier timbre. (Note, however, that the syncopated rhythm runs through the bass in the verse as well, tying 'heaven' and 'earth' together.) The ballad/soul mix produces an articulation of carnal and spiritual ecstasy which is somehow more 'radiant' than the pop disco/ballad fusions characteristic of Madonna's excursions in this area.

The soul connection, and its feminist potential, are explicit in 'Sisters Are Doing It for Themselves', in which Annie Lennox duets with soul singer Aretha Franklin, in a song which is virtually mono-stylistic. The political power of the style is deliberately drawn on to put a feminist message. And just as the musical texture builds up a composite female subject through call and response between the soloists and between them and the backing singers, so the video constructs a montage of historical women, intercutting this with shots of the (female) audience, and of the two stars: the one presented as androgynous 'new woman', the other as black matriarch;[13] far from being monolithic, the position offered here for women consciously embraces a range of possibilities (and apparently Aretha was not too thrilled by Annie's sexual politics: see O'Brien, 1991: 83–4), though it is noticeable that all the vocal relationships (unison doubling, echoes, decorative descants) are supportive rather than describing structural contrasts.

The music is erotic, but, through the use of long shots, angled shots and quick intercutting, the camera never fetishizes either Annie or Aretha. Similarly, the supposedly phallic power of the rock backbeat, appropriated for soul, is captured for a less oppressive eroticism. Interestingly, the guitar solo by Stewart, in a wah-wah style derived from heavy rock, is 'framed', not only musically – coming between sections with women singing – but also visually: it is intercut with shots of the two women soloists, and in the succeeding verse he is framed literally on a giant video screen behind them. In a neat reversal of the norm, *they* control *him*. Coming immediately after a bridge asserting that, whatever some may think, 'sisters' have no wish to rule out heterosexual love, this treatment of the guitar solo – which in rock conventionally signifies sexual desire from the male point of view – suggests how such desire can be redefined in a new context.

Some implications for method

Arguably, even songs that are close to being mono-stylistic, like 'Sisters', are heard dialogically, not only in the limited sense that they offer a range of polyphonic voices for us to identify with, but also because the style's 'others' are present *in absentia*, within the surrounding musical field. The style makes sense only in the context of what it is not. 'Sisters' and 'I Need a Man' could be seen as feminist attempts to take over and redefine a traditionally male strategy of suppressing heterology *within the text* by means of an imposed monological purity – an authoritative voice. McClary (1991) has suggested that as a rule it is *refusal* of closure and a single-point-of-view that is the mark of the feminist voice in music. This would imply that the stylistic multiplicity which is characteristic of most Eurythmics songs can be placed within a longer history; but, as well as denying to feminists the possibility of tactical appropriations of monological authorship, it would also tend to cut across interpretations tying the Eurythmics' multiplicity to the specifics of its 1980s (postmodern) moment, a moment when style-pluralism was by no means confined to explicitly feminist projects. It seems better if we steer clear of a dangerous essentialism, and emphasize the need to assess strategies in relation to specific historical conditions.

In a broader methodological perspective, the implications are that the interpretative approach put forward here need be confined neither to overtly heterological pieces nor to gender analyses. It appears to offer promise in the wider task of understanding musical textures as a location for the composition of human subjectivity.

Notes

1 An earlier version of this article was presented to the annual conference of the Royal Musical Association at Southampton University, March 1993.
2 For a recent demonstration of this, see Toynbee (1993).
3 This is not meant to deny the importance of other levels of interpretation – for example, that more 'introversive' level treated by Agawu (1991) in terms of quasi-rhetorical structure – and discussed elsewhere by myself in terms of 'gestural' structure (Middleton, 1993). Nor is it to deny the importance of interplay between levels. In fact, although I leave such other levels to one side in this article, it is interesting to wonder whether – in, for example, the sphere of

'sexuality and gender', to be treated shortly – (gendered) perspectives outlined on the level of 'dialogic semiotics' may 'feed back' on the performance of gestures, gendering them; and, vice versa, whether the gesturology of a piece (gendered? pre-gendered? cross-gendered?) might affect the precise shape taken by the social dialogue.

4 McClary (1991) pays considerable attention to gender coding of vocal styles and textures, across a range of genres; see, e.g., pp. 36–7, where she discusses seventeenth-century opera. Abbate (1991) sets up a theory of multiple 'voices' in the textures of nineteenth-century opera, and these may clearly be 'unsung' (they are just defined as 'localised in . . . invisible bodies': Abbate, 1991: 13); but disappointingly, in an otherwise brilliant work, she more or less confines her analysis to the singing characters. Kramer (1990), in another highly suggestive work, does broach the possibility of textural voices in nineteenth-century instrumental music, in his final chapter ('As if a voice were in them').

5 Behind this lies a more general discursive topography related to gender codings of vocal qualities and behaviour in our culture, covering aspects of pitch, register and timbre; for example, 'feminine' voices are expected to be high pitched but not shrill. See Henley (1977: 75–6).

6 Widely criticized by theorists, but still catching assumptions commonly held by listeners and in the music industry.

7 Such voice/instrument 'crossovers' are common in African-American musics – another reason why they contain so much potential for subversion of gender images. See Middleton (1990: 264).

8 Interestingly, it is precisely by drawing on ballad on the one hand, blues (via rock) on the other, and building her disco-ized pop that way, that Madonna is able to construct her Virgin-Whore persona, one of her big themes. McClary (1991: 163–5) and Bradby (1992) have analysed the roots and mechanisms of her 'sexualised virgin-Mary persona'.

9 This seems the best route towards solving what is otherwise a problem in McClary's analyses (1991). Reading such techniques as cadential closure in terms of patriarchal authority (and hence refusal of cadential closure as a feminist move), while persuasive in many contexts, misses out the point that such techniques appear to signify also in important other ways, on other discursive planes. Thus cadential closure, and the typical tonal narratives in which it operates in European music, have been read by Shepherd (1991, chapters 6 and 7) in terms of *class* oppression. Garber's (1992) approach enables us to think of how these different discursive spheres are connected, in producing 'category crises' (or alternately, of course, in operating 'category stability').

10 Despite the difficulties in ascribing ethnicity to musical styles ('black music' being the most familiar case: see Tagg, 1989), the importance of this practice to the way people locate them within the discursive topography cannot be denied.

11 On the effect of the IV-I gesture, see Middleton (1993). The harmonic 'reversal' means that the 'open' I-IV structure of the verse is in effect answered and completed by the IV-I closure of the chorus, pointing up the 'danger' portrayed in the former and strengthening the possibility of fulfilment for the desire expressed in the latter.

12 See p. 471. Kaplan (1987) has one of her categories of pop video (her 'romantic' type) working on this level – though she does not address any musical corollaries.

13 Some of the video analysis here is indebted to Kaplan 1987.

References

Adorno, Theodor Wiesengrund (1973) *Philosophy of Modern Music*, translated by Anne G. Mitchell and Wesley V. Bloomster, London: Sheed & Ward.

Abbate, Carolyn (1991) *Unsung Voices: Opera and Musical Narrative in the Nineteenth Century*, Princeton: Princeton University Press.

Agawu, Kofi (1991) *Playing with Signs*, Princeton: Princeton University Press.

Bakhtin, Mikhail (1981) *The Dialogic Imagination*, translated by Caryl Emerson and Michael Holquist, Austin: University of Texas Press.

Birch, Dinah (1992) 'Gender and genre', in Bonner *et al.* (1992): 43–55.

Bonner, Frances, Goodman, Lizbeth, Allen, Richard, Janes, Linda and King, Catherine (1992) editors, *Imagining Women: Cultural Representations and Gender*, Cambridge: Polity Press.

Bradby, Barbara (1990) 'Do-talk and don't-talk: the division of the subject in girl-group music', in Frith and Goodwin (eds) (1990): 341–68.

—— (1992) 'Like a virgin-mother?: materialism and maternalism in the songs of Madonna', *Cultural Studies* 6: 1: 73–96.

—— (1993) 'Sampling sexuality: gender, technology and the body in dance music', *Popular Music* 12: 2: 155–76.

Bradby, Barbara and Torode, Brian (1984) 'Pity Peggy Sue', *Popular Music* 4: 183–205.

Clark, Katerina and Holquist, Michael (1984) *Mikhail Bakhtin*, Cambridge, Mass: Harvard University Press.

Cohen, Sara (1991) *Rock Culture in Liverpool: Popular Music in the Making*, Oxford: Oxford University Press.

Du Noyer, Paul (1984) 'Well suited', *New Musical Express*, 10 November: 6–7, 51.

Dyer, Richard (1990) 'In defence of disco', in Frith and Goodwin (1990): 410–18.

Finnegan, Ruth (1989) *The Hidden Musicians: Music-Making in an English Town*, Cambridge: Cambridge University Press.

Fitzgerald, Helen (1983) 'Lovers and strangers', *Melody Maker*, 9 July: 20–1, 30.

Frith, Simon (1989) 'Only dancing: David Bowie flirts with the issues', in Angela McRobbie (ed.) *Zoot Suits and Second-hand Dresses*, London: Macmillan, 132–40.

—— (1992) 'The cultural study of popular music', in Grossberg, Nelson and Treichler (eds) (1992): 174–82.

Frith, Simon and Goodwin, Andrew (1990) editors, *On Record: Rock, Pop and the Written Word*, New York: Pantheon.

Frith, Simon and McRobbie, Angela (1978) 'Rock and sexuality', *Screen Education* 29: 3–19.

Gamman, Lorraine and Marshment, Margaret (1988) (eds) *The Female Gaze: Women as Viewers of Popular Culture*, London: The Women's Press.

Garber, Marjorie (1992) *Vested Interests: Cross-Dressing and Cultural Anxiety*, London: Routledge.

Goodwin, Andrew (1990) 'Sample and hold: pop music in the digital age of reproduction', in Frith and Goodwin (1990): 258–73.

Grossberg, Lawrence, Nelson, Cary and Treichler, Paula (1992) editors, *Cultural Studies*, New York: Routledge.

Henley, Nancy (1977) *Body Politics: Power, Sex and Non-Verbal Communication*, Englewood Cliffs: Prentice-Hall.

Hill, Dave (1986) *Designer Boys and Material Girls: Manufacturing the '80s Pop Dream*, Poole: Blandford Press.

Irwin, Colin (1986) 'Thorn of crowns', *Melody Maker* 22 November: 24–5.

Jackson, Alan (1987) 'Out of her box', *New Musical Express* 7 November: 26–7.

Kaplan, E. Ann (1987) *Rocking Around the Clock: Music Television, Postmodernism and Consumer Culture*, London: Methuen.

King, Catherine (1992) 'The politics of representation: a democracy of the gaze', in Frances Bonner *et al.* (1992): 131–9.

Kramer, Lawrence (1990) *Music as Cultural Practice, 1800–1900*, Berkeley, Los Angeles and Oxford: University of California Press.

McClary, Susan (1991) *Feminine Endings: Music, Gender and Sexuality*, Minneapolis: University of Minnesota Press.

McNeill, Kirsty (1983) 'Second bite is the sweetest', *New Musical Express* 19 March: 22.

McRobbie, Angela (1989) 'Second-hand dresses and the role of the ragmarket', in McRobbie (ed.) (1989) *Zoot Suits and Second-Hand Dresses*, London: Macmillan, 23–49.

Mellers, Wilfrid (1986) *Angels of the Night: Popular Female Singers of Our Time*, Oxford: Blackwell.

Middleton, Richard (1990) *Studying Popular Music*, Buckingham: Open University Press.

—— (1993) 'Popular music analysis and musicology: bridging the gap', *Popular Music* 12: 2: 177–90.

Moore, Suzanne (1988) 'Here's looking at you, kid!', in Gamman and Marshment (1988): 44–59.

O'Brien, Lucy (1991) *Annie Lennox*, London: Sidgwick & Jackson.

Radway, Janice (1987) *Reading the Romance: Women, Patriarchy and Popular Literature*, London: Verso.

Reynolds, Simon (1989) 'Against health and efficiency: independent music in the 1980s', in McRobbie (1989): 245–55.

Shepherd, John (1991) *Music as Social Text*, Cambridge: Polity Press.

Stallybrass, Peter (1992) 'Shakespeare, the individual and the text', in Grossberg, Nelson and Treichler (1992): 593–610.

Sutcliffe, Phil (1988) 'Just think . . . ', *Q* 2(5): 44–8.

Tagg, Philip (1989) 'Open letter: black music, Afro-American music and European music', *Popular Music* 8(3): 285–98.

Todorov, Tzvetan (1984) *Mikhail Bakhtin: The Dialogical Principle*, Manchester: Manchester University Press.

Toynbee, Jason (1993) 'Policing Bohemia, pinning up the grunge: the music press and generic change in British pop and rock', *Popular Music* 12(3): 289–300.

Waller, Johnny and Rapport, Steve (1985) *Sweet Dreams: The Definitive Biography of the Eurythmics*, London: Virgin.

DISCOGRAPHY AND VIDEOGRAPHY

All records discussed are available on Eurythmics (1991) *Greatest Hits*, BMG PD 74856. The videos are compiled on Eurythmics (1991) *Greatest Hits*, BMG Video 791 012.

CHAPTER 4

THE 'PROBLEM' OF
POPULAR MUSIC

'All the mass-based entertainment in the world cannot add up to a half-pennyworth of great art.'

(Michael Tippett)

I: Categories of Music

Most societies, certainly all class societies, recognize different categories of music, some 'higher', some 'lower'. Usually, however, distinctions are related to differences of social function or social group, and are not regarded as problematic; only in the twentieth century has popular music, in its modern guise – what Tippett calls 'mass-based entertainment' – become a 'problem'. It is precisely the historical developments characteristic of this period, notably the mass democratization of society and the commodification of culture, that explain why this is so; and any effort to understand it must be historically specific.

Defining popular music is notoriously difficult (see Middleton 1990: 3ff). The proliferation of crossovers today – Brian Eno, Steve Martland, Mike Westbrook, Michael Nyman and many others – makes this especially clear.

But this is a phenomenon that can be traced back, through Richard Rodney Bennett, Carl Davis, Malcolm Arnold, John Dankworth, to the beginnings of our period (Eric Coates, Cyril Scott, Billy Mayerl . . .), and to Elgar and before. Locating 'light music' and theatre music often creates confusions (what is Richard Addinsell's *Warsaw Concerto* or Andrew Lloyd Webber's *Phantom of the Opera?*), as does the substantial, if ever mutating, 'national residual' category: music that

MUSIC IN CONTEXT

everybody knows, from 'Land of hope and glory' to 'We shall
overcome', from 'You'll never walk alone' to the '*William Tell* theme'.

Commercialism cannot be the crucial factor. Again this is crystal-
clear today, as mass marketing of 'classical' music explodes.
Commercial sponsorship is widely accepted; the Arts Council (1985)
speaks the language of 'investment' and 'productivity'; Nigel
Kennedy and others are sold with production and image-making
techniques derived from the pop industry; opera draws rock-
stadium audiences. But again there is a history: for example, the
marketing of David Munrow or, earlier, of Britten', 'promoted . . . as
single-mindedly as Unilever would promote a new washing powder'
(Cole 1978: 56).

'Nymphs and shepherds', Ernest Lough's 'Hear my prayer',
Caruso and Fritz Kreisler were huge sellers in the early years of
the record industry, and from the beginning of the century, 'art'
musicians had no hesitation in accepting subsidy from the more
profitable 'popular' side of the business (Peacock and Weir 1975: 43).
In truth, from well before this date, the whole musical field existed
within the principles of the market – even if some sectors were
unhappy, even rebellious, about this.

If we try different distinctions, we find they are no less elusive.
The 'incompetence' attributed to some popular musicians, fuelled
by a venerable tradition of artists who cannot play or sing, who fake
performances, whose harmonies, orchestrations or records are
really created by anonymous professionals, is a product of a lack of
understanding of changes wrought by new technologies and production methods; how the music comes into existence is actually of
no significance. Besides, in many cases – singers as varied as Annie
Lennox, Van Morrison, Cleo Laine and Anne Briggs, for example –
consummate artistry is readily apparent if only appropriate criteria
are applied. Turning, then, to value distinctions, we find that these
are seldom rigorously argued (is all 'art' music automatically good?).
Even style differences are less conclusive than might be supposed,
and often work as codes for cruder explanatory grids, discredited by
ethnomusicologists, which operate with distinctions between simple
and complex, banal and original, or primitive and civilized (see
Blacking 1976, 1987).

In fact, the musical categories are *discursively* constructed, products
of *ideology*. The seemingly opposed concepts of art-music canon on
the one hand, commercialized, corrupted popular music on the
other, developed symbiotically, but slowly, during the nineteenth

THE 'PROBLEM' OF POPULAR MUSIC

century, as responses to industrialization. Macdonnell (1860) still had to explain to an educated readership how 'classical' music differed from opera and ballads (it was intellectually more demanding). Concert programmes continued mixed right up to the end of the century. The social accommodation between the aristocracy and new bourgeoisie, coupled with the prevailing idea of music as a social grace, tended to drain all categories of the bite of difference (Banfield 1981a: 14–18). Even 'vulgar' genres, it was often thought, had their appropriate social place, and in any case the hierarchy was readily traversed through the ladder of 'self-improvement'. Only tremendous turn-of-the-century changes in political, social and economic life turned Matthew Arnold's earlier warnings into common currency. The beginnings of mass democracy, socialism, the modern leisure apparatus, the mass media: all signalled that the age of the common man had arrived. Against an intellectual context of Nietzschian anxiety about the threat of the totalitarian crowd, 'mass culture' and, in élitist self-defence, 'art for art's sake' emerged together, bred by 'competitive commerce' from the 'fatal division of men into the cultivated and degraded classes' (W. Morris 1962: 139). 'Highbrow' and 'lowbrow' were born, and by the 1920s the new structure mapped by these new terms was firmly in place.

The role of the mass media was crucial. All types of music were dragged from previously separate locations and assembled in the same social space, where they both defined and were forced to respond to each other. The BBC, for example, 'undertook the standardization, classification and placing in rank order of the *whole field of music*' (Scannell 1981: 259). While Constant Lambert regretted that 'classical music is vulgarized and diffused through every highway and byway, and both highbrow and lowbrow are the losers' (1934: 235), the greater hardships were suffered by the popular side. The debate between high and low 'was in truth a disguised dialogue on the state of society' (Bigsby 1975: 20), arising out of the threat of general access to leisured culture. 'Discourses of art . . . depend on the "commercialization" of "mass" culture to set up, by contrast, their own superiority. If "mass" culture did not exist, high culture would have invented it (arguably it *has* invented it)' (Sinfield 1989: 176). The category of popular music, then, is the scapegoat required by the attempt to defend an élite tradition of artistic integrity against the pressures of modern society.

MUSIC IN CONTEXT

II: Attacking Popular Music

General attacks, drawing usually on a confused compendium of ideas about cultural provenance, moral effect and aesthetic value, have been common. The 'cesspool of popular music' (Rosselson 1979: 42), this 'disease' with its 'unworthy rubbish' and 'disgusting sounds' (Dwyer 1967: 115), 'primitive and uncouth' (Tippett 1974: 154), is aimed at listeners of 'bottomless vacuity', their 'open, sagging mouths and glazed eyes, [their] . . . hands mindlessly drumming in time to the music' revealing a 'generation enslaved by a commercial machine' (P. Johnson 1964: 17). Earlier (in 1942) Bliss wanted the BBC to segregate these 'Calibans' on a 'dirt tract', a 'continual stream of noise and nonsense put on by untouchables' (Scannell 1981: 258). By comparison, Macpherson's language in 1910 ('shallow', 'ephemeral', 'obvious') was restrained (1940: 11–12), linking him to late Victorian critiques (see Middleton 1981: 63).

Most commonly, however, condemnation has been directed against specific styles. Between the wars the 'barbaric rhythms' and 'foul noises' of jazz, as Sir Hugh Allen called them (quoted in 'Feste' 1921: 98), were a constant subject of critical discourse. Jazz was 'noisy and incredibly stupid' (Sir Hamilton Harty, in LeMahieu 1988: 116), 'propaganda for vulgarity' and 'deliberately evil' (J. W. N. Sullivan, quoted in 'Feste' 1932: 410). 'A subject for the pathologist', jazz put itself 'outside the pale of music' (Sir Arthur Bliss, W. H. Hadow, in Cole 1978: 146), especially when indulging the 'whinings and sobbings of the so-called "crooners"' ('Feste' 1932: 410). In the fifties, rock 'n' roll received similar treatment. Wain described fans 'screaming aimlessly, like animals' at 'this big phony slob . . . gyrating up and down' (Sinfield 1989: 168). Elsewhere we learn that 'our teddy-boys and girls are essentially primitives, untouched by the Western European culture of which they ought to be the heirs instead of merely the waste by-products', and rock 'n' roll is compared to 'certain forms of music [which] induce mass-hysteria in certain primitive peoples' (anon 1956: 203). As this suggests, racism is rarely far away from this discourse – though its language has seldom been so blatant in recent decades as it was in the 1920s, when African-American musicians were routinely described as 'savages' and 'Sambos' (see, for example, 'Feste' 1924: 797), their music as having a 'debasing effect' on 'the prestige of the white races' (Henry Coward, quoted in anon 1926: 78). For Clive Bell, 'niggers' could be 'admired artists without any gift more singular

THE 'PROBLEM' OF POPULAR MUSIC

than high spirits'; 'so why drag in the intellect?' he asked (LeMahieu 1988: 116–17).

It is characteristic that new styles have been attacked because they seem to threaten an established style – and the structure of the musical field associated with this – even if, at a previous stage, this too had been subject to quite similar attack. Steve Race found 'rock-and-roll technique . . . the antithesis of all that jazz has been striving for over the years – . . . good taste and musical integrity' (1956a). Between the wars, when jazz was the enemy, it was often compared adversely to music hall, which had by then come to be seen as possessing 'honest sentiment' and 'sound tunes'; it was indigenous and traditional, coming from the grass roots, unlike imported dance music (Scholes 1938: 601; see also Bonavia 1928). But earlier, for Parry and Sharp, it was music hall that was the enemy, and its prey was folksong, while for Robert Blatchford, in 1894, the 'real music' against which music-hall 'howling' was counterposed lay even further back, in a culture when glee and madrigal singing was commonplace (see Frith 1983: 40). At each stage, a seemingly settled musical field, having assimilated a previous incursion and put it – socially and culturally – in its place, is threatened by further upheaval, forcing historical relocation of the mythical Golden Age (whose ideological potency, however, remains undiminished). But in this historical schema jazz and rock are special, and hence attract special vehemence. Unlike music hall, the 'well-made' inter-war popular song and the mainstream post-war ballad, they have threatened not only the stability of the existing relationships between musical categories but also the very definition of what music, in the European tradition, is and how it is made.

III: A Changing Culture

In the aftermath of the First World War, antipathy to popular music was grounded in fears about materialism, egalitarianism, social and cultural homogeneity and Americanization – all of which seemed aspects of each other.

Elitists such as T. S. Eliot and F. R. Leavis, whatever their differences of motive and policy, were agreed that culture should be a hierarchy and that high culture must be reserved for a minority, who understood its carefully cultivated standards. The rest, 'docile, smiling and obedient . . . [were] capable only of mass indignation, herd pleasures

MUSIC IN CONTEXT

and community singing' (Lambert 1934: 181); their lot was the 'uninterrupted bawling' of the loudspeaker (Leavis and Thompson 1937: 108). The great spectre was 'levelling down': 'in our headlong rush to educate everybody, we are lowering our standards' (Eliot 1962: 108). Even on the left many agreed, pitching an idealized vision of working-class life against the threat of the passive consumerism of Americanized mass culture (Waters 1989–90).

Such a response to the crisis could lead to missionary work among the lower orders, as with the attempt, drawing on the considerable influence of Cecil Sharp, to propagate 'traditional' music and dance in schools and elsewhere (see Harker 1985). Similarly, for the paternalistic BBC of John Reith's dreams, 'few [listeners] knew what they wanted, fewer what they needed' and radio's job was 'giving people what one believes they should like and will come to like . . . the supply of good things will create the demand for more . . . the amenities of culture are available without discrimination' (quoted in Minihan 1977: 207; LeMahieu 1988: 146–7). Reith despised entertainment, including popular music, and the BBC treated it critically (cleaning it up, trying to suit it to the respectable middle-class hearth) and, at the same time, as the first rung on a ladder of cultural improvement.

As a BBC official put it, 'Every man wants in his heart to be a highbrow' (LeMahieu 1988: 147). This belief controlled the programming and presentation policies for 'classical' music, with their educational aims, and led to the highly popular 'music appreciation' talks broadcast by Percy Scholes and Walford Davies.

The BBC's 'democratization of music' strategy was part of a broader project, its ideological roots traceable to Victorian ideas of 'improvement'. The wider 'music appreciation' movement; the development of Associated Board exams, rural music schools, new school music teaching methods, childrens' concerts; the competitive festival movement; the importance of concert programme notes, such as those of Tovey; the educational programmes run by the big record companies: together these can be seen as a general attempt, at this time, to broaden the social base for 'good' music while counteracting the attractions of 'cheap' entertainment. At the BBC this led to continual conflict between programme planners and the Music Department, which was increasingly concerned to improve performance standards and widen the repertoire, in short, to appeal to connoisseurs, rather than educate Bliss's 'Calibans'. By the late 1930s, the cutting edge of their campaign was provided, firstly, by

THE 'PROBLEM' OF POPULAR MUSIC

chamber music and, secondly, by unfamiliar modern works – for their derision was directed at the hackneyed orchestral repertoire with popular (*sic*) appeal as much as light and dance music.

What the Music Department was fighting, we can now see, was the outline of a new common culture, a 'middlebrow' culture, part of which was an 'attempt of the BBC to make classical music popular (and popular music classical by vetoing the more dubious material)' (Pearsall 1976: 14). The *Radio Times* wanted listeners who 'were not only tolerant but eclectic in their taste . . . who can . . . enjoy either Bach or Henry Hall' (quoted in Scannell and Cardiff 1991: 206), an attitude embodied in the first disc jockey, Christopher Stone, whose anti-élitist catholicity of taste was designed not to provoke; it was 'the equivalent of a bath and a change for the tired man's and the tired woman's mind' (Stone 1933: 88). The BBC's 'idealized version of a fragile, never fully realized, middle-class cultural tradition which it then proclaimed to be the natural and authentic culture of the nation' (LeMahieu 1988: 182) lay close to J. B. Priestley's 'broadbrow' strategy, rooted as that was in a rosy Edwardian Golden Age. And, in a wider perspective (the taming and 'civilizing' of jazz; the formalizing and domesticating of the new 'barbaric' dances of the 1920s; the blurring of the light/classical boundary), it can be seen as part of an attempt to 'settle' the new, disruptive popular musics within a re-mapped hierarchy, drawing the crude high/popular bifurcation into a more subtle, manageable field structured by older ideas of cultural unity and value. The watershed was probably the late 1920s, when enthusiasm for 'symphonic jazz', cultivation of 'syncopation' by Lambert and others, and the serious jazz criticism of Spike Hughes seem to be symptoms of a historical node, whose crossovers (as we would now call them) then quickly lost any radical potential and slid into comfortable consensus. By the mid-1930s, the BBC was codifying 'popular music' itself, distinguishing between 'music for connoisseurs' (jazz, swing), 'music for entertainment' and 'music for dancing' (Scannell and Cardiff 1991: 191–3).

This settlement was transitional and could not survive the upsurge of populism released by the war (and prefigured in changes to the BBC's programming policy in the late 1930s), the renewed pressures of 'Americanization' that followed, and the growing importance of working-class people in the cultural market. Resistance took on extra vehemence as the cultural economy's adjustment of social focus made it clear that mass culture would increasingly be organized around the 'lowest' values. Waugh's novels document the new

MUSIC IN CONTEXT

terrain, 'flat as a map' (quoted in Hebdige 1981: 41), and the laments ring out: 'we shall have to . . . live a Woolworth life hereafter' (Harold Nicolson, quoted in Sinfield 1989: 45). 'It was the simultaneous articulation of *accessibility* and *reproducibility* (a million streamlined Chevrolets, a million streamlined radios) which finally proved disturbing to so many cultural critics' (Hebdige 1981: 54), for it led to 'barbarism with electric light . . . a cockney tellytopia, a low-grade nirvana' (C. Curran, quoted in Chambers 1985: 4). The influence of Leavisism expanded (see D. Thompson 1964, R/1973), its posing of 'critical discrimination' against the 'false needs' aroused by advertising and the 'standardized pulp' sold to satisfy them becoming something of a middle-class orthodoxy. On the left, Orwell saw the 'comeliness' of traditional working-class life threatened by the 'cheap palliatives' of Americanized mass culture (Orwell 1937, R/1962), while Hoggart, similarly, contrasted the 'shiny barbarism', 'candyfloss world' and 'spiritual dry-rot' of rock 'n' roll and the 'juke-box boys' with the 'warm and shared humanity', the folk-like 'archetypal quality', of the 'big-dipper' vocal style found in the working men's clubs of his youth (Hoggart 1957).

Such poorly focused anxiety and nostalgia offered little more than a variant on what was now a fully fledged analytic paradigm, developed from romantic–modernist ideology: on the one hand, intransigent, 'authentic' art; on the other, everything else. (Such a position was never as rigorously argued in Britain as it was, elsewhere, by T. W. Adorno, but its assumptions permeated the culture of the 1940s and 1950s: see, for instance, Tippett 1974.) William Glock's single-minded campaign at the BBC to make Radio 3 the voice of the modernist élite built on the logic of the three-channel hierarchy established in 1946 (and no doubt the tiny audience – less than 1 per cent – confirmed the implied social analysis). Assaults on this system often served, ironically, to shore it up – at least at first. For a long time, folk music had been presented as an 'authentic' alternative to the commercial song system, and hence could serve as a 'popular art'. In the 1930s, a minority adopted jazz – 'real' jazz, black American jazz, as distinct from what seemed to them the vapid imitations peddled by British dance bands – as an alternative art, at once uncommercial and expressively honest, and culturally rebellious. This enthusiasm was associated particularly with a new intelligentsia, grammar-school educated, lower middle class, excluded by or uninterested in traditional high culture. Philip Larkin was one of them. 'This was something we had found for ourselves, that wasn't taught

THE 'PROBLEM' OF POPULAR MUSIC

at school . . . and having found it, we made it bear all the enthusiasm usually directed at more established arts' (Larkin 1970: 3). By the 1950s, jazz – thoroughly mixed up with the Art Schools, Beat poetry and leftist politics – was the basic sound of middle-class bohemia (as in *Look Back in Anger*). Rock music, born partly in the same ambience, took from the examples of folk and jazz the ideas of authenticity and of bohemia. Its artists claimed the legacy of romantic critique. Amid the social upheavals and 'cultural revolution' (Marwick 1991) of the 1960s, its legitimation proceeded fast. By 1963, William Mann was reviewing the Beatles in *The Times* (27 December), and Richard Buckle in *The Sunday Times* (29 December) proclaimed them 'the greatest composers since Beethoven'. The BBC, after earlier reluctance, capitulated. Serious critical writing became common. Academic studies, journals and societies followed, and some university departments introduced popular music as well as jazz to their syllabuses. The Beatles' *Sgt. Pepper* album (1967) was widely admired and the jazz-rock band Soft Machine appeared at the 1970 Promenade Concerts. But this time the question whether upheaval would settle back into renewed consensual hierarchy was to be much less easily decided.

Could the conceptual distinction between 'high' and 'low' survive such constant revisions of boundaries? For a 1964 Government White Paper it was 'a question of bridging the gap between what have come to be called the "higher" forms of entertainment and the . . . brass band . . . the music hall and pop group – and to challenge the fact that a gap exists'. But Raymond Williams still insisted that, while 'jazz is a real musical form . . . the latest Tin-Pan drool . . .[is] not exactly in the same world' (Williams 1965: 364); and Donald Hughes (1964, R/1973: 153) went back to re-drawing hierarchies, distinguishing between 'folk' ('genuine, spontaneous'), 'Radio One pop' ('stereotyped . . . assembly-line product') and 'progressive pop' ('pop as a culture, in which a developing growth may take place'). At the same time, the possibility that both the laws of commodity production and of the romantic ideology of self-expression were now universalized throughout the musical culture might suggest that 'the interplay of artifice and authenticity is central to everyone's lives . . . In looking at the shifting ways in which the love–hate relationship of the artist and society has been worked out in pop, we simply find the dialectic in graphic outline' (Frith and Horne 1987: 180).

MUSIC IN CONTEXT

IV: After Hierarchy?

In a sense, the Cold War struggle – the need to validate 'democracy' –
meant that cultural equality *had* to be conceded. And if the choice
was between 'Bolshevism' and 'Americanization', it was obvious
which direction British society would follow. Cultural libertarianism
and economic affluence were two sides of this coin. According to
pop art theorist Lawrence Alloway, in 1959, 'the aesthetics of plenty
oppose a very strong tradition which dramatizes the arts as the
possession of an élite' and propose instead a 'long front of culture',
'the exercise of multiple choices across a wide spectrum' (quoted in
Hewison 1986: 46). It became difficult to maintain grounds for
value distinctions.

Under what some call a postmodern system, authority has
collapsed no less in culture than in society and politics. Universal
access to the ceaseless flow of images and reproductions destroys
uniqueness and even the sense that a given piece of music (say) has
any connection with 'reality'. The triumph of commodity form
means that all sense of aesthetic difference is mocked by the homo-
genizing effects of exchange values. The growing visibility of Asian
and African-Caribbean musics, added to the existing proliferation
of available styles, historical and subcultural, increases the sense
of an unavoidable relativism. The triumphs of 'sociologism' and
'ideological critique' (see, for instance, Shepherd et al. 1977), and
the influence of ethnomusicology, in higher education and to some
extent on school teachers, provide intellectual underpinnings for
this perspective. Protests became plaintive rather than self-con-
fident, Lord Goodman in 1966 lamenting that 'the pop groups are
winning the battle' against 'the worthwhile things in life' (quoted in
Sinfield 1989: 283) and his successor as Arts Council Chairman, Roy
Shaw, attacking the idea that 'anything goes' as a threat to 'all
objective standards of taste' (Shaw 1978: 6); or else they turned
eccentric (R. C. Taylor (1978) regrets the acceptance of jazz because
this removes its capacity to mock the pretensions of high art).

Nowhere is the trend clearer than in schools. Attempts to introduce popular music to CSE syllabuses, followed by the introduction
of the GCSE, which made stylistic and cultural pluralism one of its
fundamental principles (see Green 1988), led to the 1991 proposals
for National Curriculum music, based, with impressive impartiality,
on 'a wide variety of past and present musical cultures, styles, idioms
and traditions' (anon 1991a: 10). These proposals, together with the

THE 'PROBLEM' OF POPULAR MUSIC

controversy they aroused, reveal much about both underlying tendencies and resistance to them. The Minister's request that more attention should be paid to the 'repertoire, history and traditions of music' was a thinly veiled demand for more 'great art'; in the *Guardian* musicologist Geoffrey Chew attacked the elevation of Chuck Berry at the expense of Beethoven (5 March 1991), and critic Michael Kennedy pilloried the capitulation to the 'commercial pop industry' and to 'free-for-all mediocrity' (*Daily Telegraph*, 14 February 1991); while right-wing philosophers Roger Scruton and Anthony O'Hear formed a Music Curriculum Association to demand courses 'concentrating on our [sic] proper musical heritage from Palestrina onwards' (*The Times Educational Supplement*, 22 February 1991). Many 'classical' composers and performers – including Tippett, Boulez and Birtwistle, Simon Rattle, Charles Groves and Colin Davis – were supportive, however, and 83 per cent of public responses to the proposals were too. Nevertheless, the government's National Curriculum Council watered them down and insisted on a predominant profile for the 'Western heritage'. The Minister's final proposals represented something of a compromise – though he did not bow on the principle that 'the dominant examples for study . . . [should come from our] own cultural tradition'.

The theoretical tools to explain such developments are to hand – though they have not been applied rigorously and in detail to music. Ever since Benjamin's pioneering analysis (1970), it has been clear that mass reproduction and dissemination of art-objects destroys their 'aura' of uniqueness and autonomy, locating them instead in mundane everyday life alongside other kinds of commodity, and replacing aesthetic hierarchies with quasi-political struggle. 'We moderns have no safe principle of selection, so we collect . . . The cathedral of culture . . . [is] now a supermarket' (Eisenberg 1987, 18, 24). As Mannheim (1956) explains, this development is part of a more extensive destruction of 'distance' resulting from the comprehensive democratization of experience and social relationships; mystery is unmasked, and everybody and everything are, in principle, subjected to an egalitarian coexistence. At the same time, social power continues to be unequally held, and possession of the bourgeois 'aesthetic disposition', reproduced and transmitted through class-privileged modes of socialization and education, continues in its role of building 'cultural capital', marking social distinction and excluding those with unapproved tastes (Bourdieu 1980). As the collapse of cultural divisions accelerates, therefore,

MUSIC IN CONTEXT

legitimation procedures become ever more frantic, the 'most arbitrary distinctions . . . [being] drawn up into fiercely patrolled aesthetic boundaries' (Chambers 1985: 21).

A hesitant mix of old and new criteria abounds. Probably few 'serious' musicians are now antagonistic to popular music as such; but many perhaps share Robert Saxton's insistence, while rejecting 'hairshirt' modernism, that 'artistic integrity' demands the rejection of 'light listening': to give people 'only what they want', to 'go along at one . . . level', leads to 'a pretty awful cul-de-sac' (Saxton 1991). Responses to Pavarotti's giant Hyde Park concert in July 1991 revealed that many critics, unable either to escape or to cope with the implications of a culture marked by radical democratization of styles and at the same time by continuing disparities of status, fell back on old dogmas, mouthed mechanically, no longer linked to the social realities which gave them birth, but hurled desperately into the aesthetic void. Reactions varied from snook-cocking populism ('He delighted us with a rousing rendition of O Sole Mio, which even I had heard of because it was made famous by the Cornetto advert on TV', *Sun*), to élitist sneer ('With the popular songs, the banal is close at hand – in Mama he is almost the ice-cream tenor', *Financial Times*), to petit-bourgeois self-congratulation ('Mick Jagger's appeal is limited to the basics because he is a slob. Pavarotti, if at all, is a slob only in girth. Hyde Park 1991 is youth's revenge on Woodstock 1969', *Daily Telegraph*; all 1 August 1991).

Given this level of confusion, prognosis and prescription are equally difficult. Pluralism, however desirable, leaves a strange feeling of emptiness. '"No more walls" is a fine slogan, but not if you want to build a home' (Eisenberg 1987: 87). If comparative evaluation is to be rehabilitated, on new grounds, it may be necessary to find ways of reclaiming those parts of the modernist project that are still of use – notably a belief in the capacity of the human species for self-directed progress – while accepting the postmodern insight that culture is a game everyone is entitled to play.

References

Anon. 1926. Untitled article, *Musical Mirror*, vi (April), 78.
Anon. 1956. 'Notes of the Day', *Monthly Musical Record*, lxxxvi, 201-3.
Anon. 1991a. *Interim Report* (National Curriculum Music Working Group).
Arts Council. 1985. *A Great British Success Story*.
Banfield, S. 1981a. 'The Artist and Society', in *Music in Britain*, vol. 5, *The Romantic Age 1800-1914*, ed. N. Temperley (London), 11-28.
Benjamin, W. 1970 [1936]. 'The Work of Art in the Age of Mechanical Reproduction', in *Illuminations*, ed. H. Arendt, tr. H. Zohn (London), 219-53.
Bigsby, C.W.E. 1975. *Superculture: American Popular Culture and Europe* (London).
Blacking, J. 1976. *How Musical Is Man?* (London).
Bonavia, F. 1928. 'The Music of the Halls', *Musical Times*, lxix, 118-19.
Bourdieu, P. 1980. 'The Aristocracy of Culture', *Media, Culture and Society*, ii/3, 225-54.
Chambers, I. 1985. *Urban Rhythms: Pop Music and Popular Culture* (London).
Cole, H. 1978. *The Changing Face of Music* (London).
Dwyer, T. 1967. *Teaching Musical Appreciation* (London).
Eisenberg, E. 1987. *The Recording Angel: Music, Records and Culture from Aristotle to Zappa* (New York).
Eliot, T. S. 1962 [1948]. *Notes towards the Definition of Culture* (London).
'Feste' [Grace, H.]. 1921. 'Ad Libitum', *Musical Times*, lxii, 98-101.
'Feste' [Grace, H.]. 1924. 'Ad Libitum', *Musical Times*, lxv, 797-801.
'Feste' [Grace, H.]. 1932. 'Ad Libitum', *Musical Times*, lxxiii, 407-11.
Frith, S. and Horne, H. 1987. *Art into Pop* (London).
Frith, S. 1983. *Sound Effects: Youth, Leisure and the Politics of Rock 'n' Roll* (London).
Green, L. 1988. *Music on Deaf Ears: Musical Meaning, Ideology, Education* (Manchester).
Harker, D. 1985. *Fakesong: The Manufacture of British 'Folksong, 1700 to the Present Day'* (Milton Keynes).
Hebdige, D. 1981. 'Towards a Cartography of Taste 1935-1962', *Block*, iv, 39-56.
Hewison, R. 1986. *Too Much: Art and Society in the Sixties 1960-1975* (London).
Hoggart, R. 1957. *The Uses of Literacy* (London).
Hughes, D. 1973 [1964]. 'Pop Music', in *Discrimination and Popular Culture*, ed. D. Thompson (Harmondsworth), 133-55.
Johnson, P. 1964. 'The Menace of Beatleism', *New Stateman*, 28 February, 17.
Lambert, C. 1966 [1934]. *Music Ho! A Study of Music in Decline* (London).
Larkin, P. 1970. *All What Jazz: A Record Diary 1961-68* (London).
Leavis, F.R. and Thompson, D. 1933. *Culture and Environment: The Training of Critical Awareness* (London).
Lemahieu, D.A. 1988. *A Culture for Democracy: Mass Communication and the Cultivated Mind in Britain between the Wars* (Oxford).
Macdonell, J. B. 1860. 'Classical Music and British Musical Taste', *Macmillan's Magazine*, i, 383-9.

Macpherson, S. 1910 [1940]. *Music and Its Appreciation: or The Foundation of True Listening* (London).

Mannheim, K. 1956. 'The Democratisation of Culture', in *Essays on the Sociology of Culture* (London), 171-246.

Marwick, A. 1991. *Culture in Britain since 1945* (Oxford).

Middleton, R. 1981. 'Popular Music of the Lower Classes', in *Music in Britain*, vol. 5, *The Romantic Age 1800-1914*, ed. N. Temperley (London), 63-91.

Middleton, R. 1990. *Studying Popular Music* (Milton Keynes).

Minihan, R. 1977. *The Nationalisation of Culture: The Development of State Subsidies to the Arts in Britain* (London).

Morris, W. 1962. *Selected Writings and Designs*, ed. A. Briggs (Harmondsworth).

Orwell, G. 1962 [1937]. *The Road to Wigan Pier* (London).

Peacock, A. and Weir, R. 1975. *The Composer in the Market Place* (London).

Pearsall, R. 1976. *Popular Music of the 1920s* (Newton Abbot).

Race, S. 1956a. Untitled article, *Melody Maker*, 5 May, 5.

Rosselson, L. 1979. 'Pop Music: Mobiliser or Opiate?', in *Media, Politics and Culture*, ed. C Gardner (London), 40-50.

Saxton, R. 1991. Interview, BBC Radio 3, 11 July.

Scannell, P. 1981. 'Music for the Multitude? The Dilemmas of the BBC's Music Policy 1923-1946', *Media, Culture and Society*, iii, 243-60.

Scannell, P. and Cardiff, D. 1991. *A Social History of British Broadcasting, vol. I 1922-1939: Serving the Nation* (Oxford).

Scholes, P.1938. *The Oxford Companion to Music* (London).

Shaw, R. 1978. *Elitism versus Populism in the Arts* (Eastbourne).

Shepherd, J., Virden, P., Vulliamy, G. and Wishart, T. 1977. *Whose Music? A Sociology of Musical Languages* (London).

Sinfield, A. 1989. *Literature, Politics and Culture in Postwar Britain* (Oxford).

Stone, C. 1933. *Christopher Stone Speaking* (London).

Taylor, R.C. 1978. *Art, an Enemy of the People* (Hassocks).

Thompson, D. (ed.) 1973 [1964]. *Discrimination and Popular Culture* (Harmondsworth).

Tippett, M. 1974. *Moving into Aquarius* (London).

Waters, C. 1989-90. 'The Americanisation of the Masses: Cultural Criticism, the National Heritage and Working Class Culture in the 1930s', *Social History Curators Group Journal*, 22-6.

Williams, R. 1965. *The Long Revolution* (London).

38b

CHAPTER 5

Were the Rockers Right? Revolution and Legitimation in British Pop Music of the 1960s[1]

Music can on occasion have a role in political revolutions. It can also go through revolutions of its own, when styles change radically. Neither of these scenarios is irrelevant to the story of pop music in the 1960s; but what interests me more here - and what is ultimately more important, I think - is a third perspective, to do with the music's part in the Gramscian 'war of position' continually waged over the cultural terrain of late capitalism.[2] At issue is the contribution changing musical values made to the re-negotiation of political and social hegemony. My argument will be that the potential apparent in early rock 'n' roll for a decisive shift in conceptions of musical practice was largely dissipated in the 1960s, as evolving pop/rock was assimilated into, recuperated to, existing bourgeois aesthetic values, and legitimised. Of course, this interpretation is hardly new. It is a commonplace of rock history to see the 'simplicity' of rock 'n' roll giving way to growing stylistic variety, seriousness and artistic ambition, and at the same time the initial 'threat' giving way to social acceptance. What remains to be explained, however, is exactly **how** this happened - what social forces were involved? - and **why**. There is also a further issue. If, as Simon Frith has persuasively argued[3], much of the appeal of rock to bourgeois youth lay in a romanticism of the street, a liminal fantasy of unrespectable pleasures, how is this to be squared with the motif of legitimation, which pictures the history as an ascent to higher aesthetic ground?

Early rock 'n' roll, skiffle and then early Merseyside Beat seemed to offer possibilities for new social practices of music production[4]. At the same time, there is a sense in the music of a desire to re-conceptualise relationships between

1   An earlier version of this paper was given to a seminar of the Sixties Research Group in the Faculty of Arts at the Open University, Great Britain. Thanks to participants for their comments.
2   For my version of Gramscian cultural theory, as applied to music history, see Chapter 1 of Richard Middleton, *Studying Popular Music*, Buckingham 1990.
3   Simon Frith, *The Cultural Study of Popular Music*, in: *Cultural Studies*, edited by Lawrence Grossberg, Cary Nelson and Paula Treichler, London 1992, pp. 174-86
4   Peter Wicke, *Rock Music: A Musical-Aesthetic Study*, in: *Popular Music* 2 (1982), pp. 219-43; Peter Wicke, *Rock Music: Culture, Aesthetics and Sociology*, Cambridge 1990.

'music' and 'everyday life' by challenging music's confinement to categories of 'art' or 'leisure'. This entails both an anti-art ideology of 'trash' and the influence of African-American music's 'vernacular aesthetic'. The inversionary logic of 'trash' makes it easily susceptible to a re-aestheticising move - and this duly appeared, in punk. But black vernacularism remained accessible - at least in principle. Quite early, however - in a record like Elvis Presley's *All Shook Up*[5], for example - any 'threat' seems to be assimilated into an ironic, even mannerist presentation of self, 'liberation' to be shifted from the social sphere to a narcissistic indulgence close to familiar modes of bourgeois hedonism. The speed with which the cultural and political establishment accepted the Beatles in 1963-4 points towards the accuracy of the title that George Melly gave his late-sixties account of the period: 'revolt into style'[6], and the process ends up in the rock-classical fusions of bands like Genesis and Deep Purple. A useful marker is the appearance of progressive rock band Soft Machine at the Henry Wood Promenade Concerts in London (20/8/70). "At last Soft Machine have the recognition they deserve", wrote one fan, while *Melody Maker*'s reviewer thought that "it was an absorbing example of how rock is expanding its frontiers in every direction"[7]. Band member Robert Wyatt was quoted as saying: "It was a very nice evening, socially speaking, and it was good that the audience seemed to enjoy the Terry Riley and Tim Souster pieces just as much as our stuff...[however] we've done a lot of gigs and the Proms doesn't stand out as one of the important ones. But I can also see that it seems to have been important in terms of public relations...for a start, the little old ladies round our way used to think that we were a load of nasty, dirty hairies, but now they all say 'Good morning, Robert' very nicely'."[8]

Not everyone, still, welcomed rock. Probably most musicologists (though not all) agreed with Oxford Professor of Music, Sir Jack Westrup, that "the world of pop is largely a featureless desert"[9], and there were right-wing commentators who followed Paul Johnson's line ("a bottomless chasm of vacuity")[10]. By and large, though, the picture is one of a music seeking, and achieving, a status of some

---

5   Elvis Presley, *All Shook Up*, HMV POP 359, 1957.
6   George Melly, *Revolt into Style: The Pop Arts in Britain*, Harmondsworth 1970.
7   *Melody Maker, 22.8.70, pp. 30, 22.*, Melody Maker (henceforth *MM*) was the leading British pop music paper at the time.
8   *MM*, 5.9.70, p. 15.
9   Jack Westrup, *Editorial*, in: *Music and Letters* XLIX/1 (1968), p. 1.
10   *New Statesman*, 28.2.64, p. 17.

legitimacy. John Lennon, in 1972, thought he understood what had happened: "The people who are in control and in power and the class system and the whole bullshit bourgeois scene is exactly the same except that there is a lot of middle-class kids with long hair walking around London in trendy clothes. But...the same bastards are in control, the same people are running everything, it's exactly the same. They hyped the kids and the generation...we are a bit freer and all that, but it's the same game, nothing's really changed."[11] Society **had** changed, however - changed just enough to accommodate the 'cultural revolution' and turn it to advantage. Régis Debray's remarks ten years after 1968 are relevant: "May 68 was the cradle of a new bourgeois society. It may not yet realise this, but it is time someone told it so... The sincerity of the actors of May was accompanied, and overtaken, by a cunning of which they knew nothing...they accomplished the opposite of what they intended...Capital's development strategy required the cultural revolution of May."[12] It required too the cultural revolution of rock.

Not all pop fans welcomed the music's legitimacy. Melly[13] spotted working-class skinheads and rockers aggressively expressing their disaffection at progressive rock concerts. And Paul Willis's ethnographic study of hippies on the one hand, rockers on the other[14], documents the rockers' opinion of countercultural rock's pretensions: it was 'stupid', 'daft' and 'dreary'. The rockers preferred the everyday simplicities which they found in early rock 'n' roll. So, **were the rockers right**?

Routes of reception

Liberal-minded classical musicians were quick to claim approved aspects of pop for familiar critical narratives. William Mann's notorious article in the London *Times*[15], in which he analyses the Beatles' harmony for its modal progressions and 'pandiatonic clusters', is less important for its misunderstandings - which have often been pointed out - than for what it is trying to turn the music into. Deryck Cooke[16] takes Mann to task for using inappropriate criteria but does something

11   Quoted in Jan Wenner, *Lennon Remembers: The Rolling Stone Interviews*, Harmondsworth 1972, pp. 11-12.
12   Regis Debray, *A Modest Contribution to the Rites and Ceremonies of the Tenth Anniversary*, in: *New Left Review* 115 (1978), pp. 46, 48, 49.
13   Melly, p. 122.
14   Paul Willis, *Profane Culture*, London 1978.
15   William Mann, *What Songs the Beatles Sang...*, in: *The Times*, 27.12.63.
16   Deryck Cooke, *The Lennon-McCartney Songs*, in: *The Listener*, 1.2.68, pp. 157-8.

similar himself. For Cooke, the Beatles are impressive because they combine 'appealing tunes' with 'rhythmic or harmonic originality', and his analysis of 'Strawberry Fields' and 'Yesterday' focuses on how the irregular phrase structures connect to unexpected chord choices. But he misses *everything else* in the music and the result is to tie the Beatles to a familiar sort of perspective, commonly applied to a composer like Mozart: harmonic-rhythmic norms transfigured by genius. Meirion Bowen[17] offers a more sensitive survey of developments carrying rock towards 'art', but this is an art linked to a broader avant-garde: "a more *inclusive* conception of music - one in which European, oriental and Afro-American elements subsist side by side; one which draws in avant-garde electronics; one that links up with the other arts and other media"; still, however, it is a case of pop moving towards art: "Both jazz and popular music in this century have tried to heal the rift between themselves and so-called serious music. They have tried to expand their own content and range, especially by linking up with other sorts of music and media"[18]. Wilfrid Mellers, in writings from the early sixties onwards, saw pop developments in terms of a move from a kind of 'folk' to a sort of 'art', but again art with links to a broader avant-garde marked by a widespread neo-primitivism: "the finest music of Dylan and the Beatles can take its place alongside the best of modern jazz and some of the near best concert music; is this deeply significant, or does it merely mean that they've ceased to be pop and that, their youth ending, they'll cease to be myth heroes and will become intermittent and occasional 'artists'?"[19] By the time of his book on the Beatles[20], Mellers has a fully worked out theory of folk, pop and art as stages in an implicitly evolutionary socio-aesthetic narrative.

The general critical perspective within which Mellers was working was that of Leavisism, a dominant paradigm for liberal intellectuals in Britain at the time, spreading into educational institutions and 'quality' journalism alike (pop criticism featured in the *Sunday Times, Observer, Guardian, New Statesman* and *New Society* from the early sixties; only slightly later, 'serious' TV and radio programmes, such as John Peel's, were competing with chart-based shows on a liberalising broadcasting apparatus). F.R. Leavis's key critical method -

---

17   Meirion Bowen, *Musical Development in Pop*, in *Anatomy of Pop*, edited by Tony Cash, London 1970, pp. 32-57.
18   Bowen, pp. 38, 39.
19   Wilfrid Mellers, *Sixties*, in: *New Statesman*, 24.2.67.
20   Wilfrid Mellers, *Twilight of the Gods: The Beatles in Retrospect*, London 1973.

'discrimination', based on the criterion of 'emotional authenticity' - had already been extended to folk and jazz, where the grounding of such authenticity in Leavis's notion of 'organic community' could plausibly be demonstrated. It was now applied to pop, where it constituted a liberal amendment to older reactionary critiques of mass culture. As literary critic Michael Woods put it[21], "Intellectuals are always looking for alibis for their seriousness. But when writers on pop start to flash their credentials - how we waited in the rain to hear Chuck Berry when we were 14 - they are offering more than an alibi. They are hinting at a canon, a history...The new public is made up mainly of defectors from jazz and folk, plus a few classical fellow-travellers...it's surprising how little the ideology changes in the transfer."

An early stage in this development is illustrated in Hall and Whannel's 1964 book *The Popular Arts*[22]. Careful distinctions are made between 'folk art', 'popular art' and 'high art', and these are then set off from 'mass art', which is 'stereotyped', 'manipulative' and 'slack'. 'Popular art' is "essentially a conventional art which restates, in an intense form, values and attitudes already known; which reassures and reaffirms, but brings to this something of the surprise of art as well as the shock of recognition"[23]. The best that pop music can hope for is to be 'popular art', and , within mass-mediated music culture, the benchmarks for this category are set by blues and jazz. Throughout the book, there is a wavering between, on the one hand, an intuitive attraction to pop's 'vitality', and an appreciation of its folk-like roots, and, on the other hand, the application of Leavisite standards, which reveals a stratum of 'authentic expression' overwhelmed by commercial exploitation, and hence only a little potential for 'inner growth'. Similarly, Donald Hughes, writing in another 1964 book, *Discrimination and Popular Culture*, edited by the Leavis disciple Denys Thompson, sets his standards by folk and blues as well as classical music, and against this horizon his view of pop is bleak: "Just as the words take a basic, universal theme, denude it of any real individuality of utterance, and serve it up for mass commercial consumption, so the music is standardised to a pattern"; at most, it is a "form of release", and the author's advice is to "look beyond the pops back to their origins"[24]. Significantly,

---

21   Michael Woods, *The One Language that Remains*, in: *New Society*, 2.1.69, p.23.
22   Stuart Hall and Paddy Whannel, *The Popular Arts*, London 1964.
23   Hall and Whannel, p. 66.
24   Donald Hughes, *Pop Music*, in: *Discrimination and Popular Culture*, edited by Denys Thompson, Harmondsworth 1964, pp. 167, 163, 171.

however, by the time of the revised 1973 edition, Hughes's views have moved on. He now recognises skiffle and early Beatles as 'folk', enthuses over Dylan and 'folk protest', and describes progressive rock as "a culture in which a developing growth may take place". The new rock musicians "aim to express themselves with some seriousness of purpose"[25], and further development of this tendency is linked to the need for a deepening of democracy, in what amounts to a definite left-liberal educational project.

Interestingly, thinking within the marxist New Left followed a similar trajectory. An editorial in the first issue of *New Left Review* describes "the task of socialism today..[as being] to meet people where they *are*", and "teen-age culture ...[as] directly relevant to the imaginative resistances of the people who have to live within capitalism"[26]. Yet the issue also contains an article attacking the attention increasingly being paid to rock 'n' roll and applying Leavisite categories of discrimination to the field: "Rock 'n' roll is a splendid *outlet*; it should not be something to 'believe in'."[27] This is followed by an approving piece on the politicised 'folk songs' of Ewan McColl. For the next few years, almost all the writing on music in *NLR* was devoted to modern jazz and country blues; but in 1966, in a distinctly new step, Alan Beckett (issue 39) discussed the aesthetics of 'underground' pop, and in 1968 Michael Parsons (issue 49) introduced to the journal's pop coverage a new stress on the **internal** structures of the music, the Rolling Stones' musical forms being compared favourably to the 'standardised' patterns of most pop. In 1969 (issue 54) Beckett presented and discussed a 'map' of current pop/rock styles and placed them in evaluative categories. Then, in 1970 (issues 59 and 62) Andrew Chester offered a methodology for immanent analysis of the music, based on a distinction between 'intensional' and 'extensional' musical types[28]. This was to be highly influential within cultural and popular music studies, largely on the basis that allocating pop more to the intensional category said to be characteristic of African-American (and indeed most non-Western)

---

25   Hughes (second edition, 1973), pp. 153, 144.
26   *New Left Review* 1 (1960), p. 1.
27   Brian Groombridge and Paddy Whannel, *Something Rotten in Denmark St*, in: *New Left Review* 1 (1960), p. 54.
28   Andrew Chester, *Second Thoughts on a Rock Aesthetic*, in: *New Left Review* 62 (1970), pp. 75-82. By 'intensional' Chester meant variation through pitch and rhythm inflections of a given structural framework - a *rag*, say, or a chord-sequence; by 'extensional' he meant one-off, large-scale developmental forms generated from the manipulation of small thematic motifs.

music rather than to the extensional techniques of European classical music seemed to offer, at last, an appropriate way of analysing the music. But what was at least equally significant was the implicit aim to validate pop **as music**: by providing a method of assessing pop in terms of the complexity of its structures and the autonomous development of its techniques, Chester in effect located pop **alongside** classical music, different but equally legitimate.

Melly's book, previously mentioned, comes as near as most critical works of the period to escaping the Leavisite legacy. Melly saw rock 'n' roll as instinctive "screw and smash music" and described subsequent developments as "teetering on the edge of becoming art"[29]; but he is ambivalent about this: acute accounts of art-school elements in progressive rock[30], of the use of rock by suburban middle-class youth as a means of 'symbolic revolt', and of the Beatles 'classics', especially *Sergeant Pepper*, cannot disguise an element of nostalgia for pop innocence. Melly's interests in dada and surrealism, and in working-class jazz, predispose him to an anti-art platform and a cult of the vernacular: he **wants** rock 'n' roll to have been instinctive. The construction (often by intellectuals) of simplicity as an Other to intellectualism comprises a second important (though subordinate) discursive trajectory in the 1960s. It has its dangers of course (dangers which, it may be as well to acknowledge, cannot be completely shrugged off by the present writer, either).

Similar debates, during the same period, were also taking place **within** the pop music culture (which increasingly can be seen to have been generating its own intellectuals). From the middle sixties, struggles between the values of commercial pop and those of the emerging underground, between single and album, between radio chart shows and countercultural programmes like John Peel's on the BBC's pop channel, Radio 1 (started, 1967), become ever clearer. The debate can be followed in the pages of the weekly paper *Melody Maker*, which eventually came down as solidly progressive in its position (previously it had served the jazz audience, so there may have been an ideological link), but whose features, reviews and letter columns resounded for a time to the sounds of

---

29   Melly, pp. 36, 121.
30   On the importance of the art schools as sites of bohemian intellectualism where an aesthetic theory of pop was developed, see Simon Frith and Howard Horne, *Art into Pop*, London 1987.

battle, especially around 1967, when 'rock' can be seen gradually separating itself out from the sphere of 'pop'.[31]

As critic Chris Welch puts it, "A schism is hitting pop...The schism is the division between the hippy and the common (or garden) pop fan. Pop music is now reaching the stage where a small coterie of rather self-conscious young men are permanently devoted to lifting the realms of pop out of the banal into the creative and valid."[32] Fellow critic Karl Dallas[33] contrasts the "pre-packed, homogenised, supermarket muzak" of "today's plastic-dominated charts" with the "real sounds...real lyrics...real music" of the underground groups. Many musicians agreed: "singles are horribly out of date" - they require "working to a formula"; "people are brainwashed into thinking that the number one record represents the best music available"[34]. By contrast, a fan wrote in (unconsciously echoing many listener responses to other movements of 'advanced art' earlier in the century, as well as representing the views of many *MM* letter-writers): "Having just seen the Pink Floyd, I am absolutely bewildered. Can someone please explain what this psychedelic crap is all about? Their performance bore no connection with music and after three monotonous, ear-blasting numbers I walked out in disgust."[35] Pink Floyd's management responded to such attacks in the authentic tones of the avant-garde: " Now the Pink Floyd are accused of 'killing pop music'...so yes, the Pink Floyd are killing pop music because there are a large number of people whose minds are too closed to accept what the Pink Floyd do as anything other than a threat to most people's ideas as to what pop music is. To them all, the boring, repetitive, false glitter, the leers, the swinging clothes and rave gear, in other words the expensive packaging is music...The Pink Floyd is not packaged, they just are. Eighty per cent of Pink Floyd music is improvised...So the Pink Floyd are largely unpredictable both to the audience and to themselves. They can be sublime. They can be awful. So can audiences and generally the audiences get what they deserve and what they feel. The Pink Floyd is you. If you feel they are

---

31   Of course, a magazine like *Melody Maker* cannot be regarded as providing a transparent window on to 'reality' (anymore than the literature surveyed above can). But it was an influential site where discursive struggle took place and where discursive norms were established.

32   *MM*, 26.8.67, p. 5.

33   *MM*, 30.12.67, p. 11.

34   Eric Clapton, *MM*, 18.11.67, p. 18.

35   *MM*, 5.8.67, p. 16.

killing something for you, then you are their accomplice."[36] Or as a letter-writer put the argument: "What's wrong with the avant garde anyway? Without musicians like the Cream, music would never have advanced further than a hairy ape man drumming on a tree trunk."[37]

Some foresaw problems. Pete Townshend of the Who lamented that "All Radio1 has done is slash pop into two scenes - one basic and one art, and we fall into the middle...Enjoyment is the basic ingredient of pop, and I don't care if people understand it or not."[38] And the reviewer of the Rolling Stones album *Their Satanic Majesties Request* advised readers to "forget the Stones of rocking guitars and Mick shouting up-front days. This is heavily instrumental, experimental and demanding. It is also self-indulgent...This could be art for art's sake...No great melodies emerge. Nothing is particularly exciting. But music need not be melodic and exciting. It can be cacophonic and anarchistic, as lovers of 'serious' music and jazz would agree. But...pop groups enter the big league of music at their peril."[39]

By and large, however, *Melody Maker* staff writers were happy with progressive developments, and this reached a climax with *Sergeant Pepper*: "'The Beatles revive hopes of progress in pop music'; proclaimed a recent headline in the *Times*. And, as if it wasn't enough that Top People were reading serious matter about Pop People, William Mann - the Times Music Critic and author of that article - was later involved in a TV discussion with Paul Jones and George Martin in which the question was asked: 'Is pop music art?' No-one seemed inclined to give a definite answer to the question, but the mere fact that it could be seriously discussed proves that a proportion, at least, of today's pop music can no longer be dismissed as music for errand boys to whistle or as fit only for adolescent consumption...A high percentage of all pop music will always be rubbish - its existence, after all, depends on its appeal to the musically naive. But the fact that there are musicians, singers, producers, composers, arrangers and record companies who are now willing to produce music for its own sake - and not

---

36   *MM*, 30.12.67, p. 30.
37   *MM*, 5.8.67, p. 16.
38   *MM*, 30.12.67, p. 5.
39   *MM*, 2.12.67, p. 21.

purely with an eye to the largest possible sales - makes this one of the most
exciting prospects in the whole history of popular music."[40]

By 1970, the discourse of 'art', 'serious listening' and (by contrast) 'selling out' was
pervasive in *Melody Maker*. "Without going into whether or not Rock is art",
writes Pete Townshend, its 'revolution' (he uses the word a lot) happens on a
spiritual and emotional plane, facilitating self-knowledge[41]. When Jonathon King
complains that "the progressive scene is an old scene...with very old
attitudes...[and] rock has been a ghastly music form ever since it started"[42],
sheaves of letters descend defending 'good music'. Elitism was inevitable: "If you
look at Top of the Pops, and I rarely do that, all you see are 15-year-olds and
knickers. I don't see how they fit in with rock music. For that matter I don't see
how Top of the Pops fits in with today's rock music."[43] Critic Michael Watts, in
somewhat more sardonic vein[44], maps the rock/pop musical division on to a
distinction between the discursive spheres of 'groups' (associated with the
'bubblegum and teenybopper' categories; 'basically trivial', 'polished', 'well-
groomed'; often fronts for session musicians) and 'bands' (associated with the
'underground', 'which means that it might be very meaningful, often hotly political,
and frequently pretentious'; 'uncouth' in appearance; technically and often
technologically expert). Jimi Hendrix, interviewed just before his death, makes it
clear which side he is on: he plans to "gather everything we've learned musically
in the last 30 years, and ... to blend all the ideas that worked into a new form of
classical music"[45].

Social forces

The sociological evidence[46] supports what the drift of the contemporary literature
(selectively surveyed above) overwhelmingly implies: namely that an emergent
discursive formation, centred on the pop/rock division and marked by debates
over the relationships between art and commerce, authenticity and exploitation,
simplicity and complexity, aesthetic value, leisure and social behaviour, connects

---

40   Bob Dawbarn, *MM*, 10.6.67, p. 8.
41   *MM*, 22.8.70, p. 7.
42   *MM*, 11.7.70, p. 21.
43   Ritchie Blackmore of art-rock band Deep Purple, *MM*, 15.8.70, p. 15.
44   *MM*, 22.8.70, p. 19.
45   *MM*, 5.9.70, p. 7.
46   e.g. Simon Frith, *The Sociology of Rock*, London 1978.

with changing modalities in the structure of social class relations. Cultural and discursive struggles for ownership of the music, its definitions and its meanings, while not expressions of class conflict in any crude sense, can nevertheless be seen as mediating changes in the balance of social forces. The social compromise represented by post-war social democratic/welfare capitalist consensus; compulsory secondary education (from 1944) and expansion in the higher education sector; growing technocratically-oriented economic activity, resulting in a sizeable upwardly-mobile working-class fraction; a large increase in white-collar middle-class jobs; the emergence of a new intelligentsia, self-made, ambitious but often culturally unassimilated: the intersections of these developments created highly-charged frictions around cultural boundaries, and placed a premium on the establishment of cultural legitimacy. Moreover, the legitimising project which manifested itself in the development of rock (and elsewhere in popular culture) had an economic as well as a cultural trajectory. It is well known that most sixties 'revolutionaries' ended up with good jobs in media businesses, public relations, education, other consumer goods industries, and so on; and we know, too, how quickly underground rock was taken over by the large record companies. According to Frith[47], "when an increasingly fraught tension between creative and sales processes began to be experienced within record companies' pop divisions...towards the end of the 1960s, it was a sign that art discourses were beginning to be applied to 'commercial' sounds". But 'commerce' has rarely experienced difficulty in selling 'art'. Indeed, the relationship is arguably a symbiotic one, the ideology of 'art' distracting attention from the grubby pursuit of exchange value going on 'underneath', while commercial vulgarity sets in relief art's lofty 'otherness'[48].

Bourdieu[49] argues that a correspondence between social location and cultural taste lies at the core of the organisation of capitalism. To put this in his own terms, "class habitus" - the matrix of practices characteristic of the group - maps on to "cultural disposition" - the characteristic mode and values of cultural activity. "Taste classifies, and it classifies the classifier. Social subjects, classified

---

47   Simon Frith, *Performing Rites: On the Value of Popular Music*, Oxford 1996.
48   See Jon Stratton, *Capitalism and Romantic Ideology in the Record Business*, in *Popular Music* 3 (1983), pp. 143-56.
49   Pierre Bourdieu, *Distinction: A Social Critique of the Judgement of Taste*, London 1984.

by their classifications, distinguish themselves by the distinctions they make."[50]. Since the classes are ranked hierarchically, so too are their tastes: "To the socially organised hierarchy of the arts, and within each of them, of genres, schools or periods, corresponds a social hierarchy of the consumers. This predisposes tastes to function as markers of 'class'."[51] At stake here is the ability of a class to maintain the legitimacy of its taste, and hence to reproduce its social and economic power. Cultural "competence", passed on through family and school, generates "cultural capital" - which subsequently is transferrable into economic capital (the right taste 'buys' a good job, social advance, the best contacts).

More particularly, Bourdieu is concerned to distinguish what he calls "aesthetic" and "popular" dispositions, and, via a critique of Kant, to replace the supposed universality of the former with an explanation of its class specificity. De-mystifying Kant's opposition of higher and lower pleasures (pure contemplation on the one hand, sensual gratification on the other), Bourdieu attributes the "pure gaze", demanding cultivated, disinterested apprehension, and grounded in the theory of autonomous artistic production, to the bourgeois attempt to locate his own taste above the vulgarities of ordinary life. By contrast, the "popular disposition", for Bourdieu, refuses the gap between art and life, treats artistic representations as real, and appropriates cultural forms directly and sensually. But such a practice is inevitably subaltern: "The pure disposition is so universally recognised as legitimate that no voice is heard pointing out that the definition of art, and through it the art of living, is an object of struggle among the classes."[52] It is tempting to align the rockers' tastes - perhaps also some early rock 'n' roll reception, and the taste of sixties mods and skinhead subcultures for black dance music - with Bourdieu's "popular disposition". Equally, the positioning of progressive rock within the values of the "aesthetic disposition" seems clear. Moreover, those who were doing the positioning, from liberal intellectuals through young professionals and media workers to grammar school and university students, and middle-class drop-outs, were situated, or striving to situate themselves, within the broad ranks of the upper social strata, while flashier, more

---

50   Bourdieu, p. 6.
51   Bourdieu, pp. 1-2.
52   Bourdieu, p. 48.

visceral, more functional pop styles seem to have been largely the preserve of working-class youth.[53]

Even so, rock could not be legitimised without a struggle. But the aesthetic disposition is "transposable". Competence, once possessed, can extend its classifying power into 'foreign' domains, aided "by the whole corporation of critics mandated by the group to produce legitimate classifications and the discourse necessarily accompanying any artistic enjoyment worthy of the name"[54]. Through processes of "recuperation", rock was partially appropriated for aesthetic discourse. This led to conflict **within** the dominant class itself, "site par excellence of symbolic struggles"[55]. Aestheticising rock gave the 'new bourgeoisie' entry to a site of cultural authority, set off at one and the same time from the reactionary tastes of established ruling-class interests and from the 'popular disposition' below. But "the conflicts between artists and intellectuals over the definition of culture are only one aspect of the interminable struggles among the different functions of the dominant class to impose the definition of the legitimate stakes and weapons of social struggles"[56]. Whether pop should be classified in terms of cultural or economic capital was precisely one of the stakes of struggle. Far from the legitimation of rock being a simple story of one class expropriating another, then, the focus should fasten more on its role in the reconstruction of the bourgeoisie, as socially rising fractions, newly enriched with educational capital but relatively poor in economic wealth, attempted to usurp established interests. What was **not** at risk was the rules of the game itself. As Bourdieu argues, countercultures "merely contest one culture in the name of another, counterposing a culture dominated within the relatively autonomous field of cultural production and distribution (which does not make it the culture of the dominated) to a dominant culture; in so doing they fulfil the traditional role of a cultural avant-garde which, by its very existence, helps to keep the cultural game functioning"[57]. Perhaps this is what really lay at the root of John Lennon's frustrations.

---

53 Needless to say, there is some exaggeration in this observation. Particularly important is that class was articulated with gender: for example, middle-class girls often liked *pop* styles (but pop styles with older romantic elements going back to pre-rock 'n' roll popular traditions).
54 Bourdieu, p. 28.
55 Bourdieu, p. 254.
56 Bourdieu, p. 254.
57 Bourdieu, p. 251.

Fruitful though application of Bourdieu's model is, its usefulness is qualified by a certain element of essentialism - does working-class popular culture always fit the rules of his "popular disposition", or is it not sometimes, say, experimental rather than realist, or liminal rather than down-to-earth? - and a certain tendency towards an a-historical functionalism: certainly he has little to say about the specificities of distinct historical moments, and in particular he arguably over-estimates the 'fit' of class to cultural formation under the conditions of late capitalism. Why was there a social and cultural crisis in the 1960s, and what was its particular nature? Were the two great classes of marxist tradition actually still walking around the stage, distinctively costumed, their tastes so completely set apart?

A Gramscian turn - emphasising the constant **negotiation** of cultural and ideological elements required in the continually mutating, never closed process whereby hegemony is secured, challenged, re-made - would help mitigate these problems. A not dissimilar approach, applied to the specific period under discussion here, can be found in Habermas's book *Legitimation Crisis*[58]. For Habermas, the various 'systems' making up the social formation (economic, political, cultural, etc), rather than intermeshing via an over-determining class articulation, as in Bourdieu, interconnect according to principles related to the mode of organisation of the particular formation at a particular historical stage. 'Legitimacy' obtains where the connections are felt as normative; crisis in one system, resulting in incredulity towards dominant representations of what is 'natural' and 'right', leads to **legitimation crisis**. In advanced capitalist society, existing modes of organisation are modified by an increasing need for state intervention, public planning and class compromise. The expansion of the public sphere at once intensifies the role of culture as a site for the securing of legitimacy, and at the same time points up contradictions between the social and political inclusiveness apparently promised by this expansion and the official ideology of privatism (which includes the private mode of aesthetic consumption, as applied to 'autonomous' art). "The class compromise that has become part of the structure of advanced capitalism makes (almost) everyone at the same time both a participant and a victim."[59] As lower-class groups are drawn into the mainstream (as consumers, as citizens, as self-motivated skilled workers

---

58   Jürgen Habermas, *Legitimation Crisis*, London 1976.
59   Habermas, p. 39.

154

necessary for economic expansion), ideological fractures show up, class mobility increases, and at the same time a variety of alternative moral, social and cultural models appears. "Advanced capitalism creates 'new' needs it cannot satisfy"[60] - cannot, because to extend the 'superiority' of bourgeois life-style and culture to all in whom the desire for them has been awakened would destroy the exclusivity on which their authority rests. There is not enough 'cultural capital' to go round. This disjunction results in "socio-cultural crisis", which occurs "when the normative structures change, according to their inherent logic, in such a way that the complementarity between the requirements of the state apparatus and the occupational system, on the one hand, and the interpreted needs and legitimate expectations of members of society, on the other, is disturbed".[61]

For Habermas, the growth of the leisure sphere, the lengthening of adolescence and of the 'educational interlude', and a relaxation in family structure and sexual behaviour together go to construct the site of a youth culture which, drawing on the capacity for critique which modern art extracts from the traditions of bourgeois art, amounts to a definite **counter-culture**. He thinks that this counter-culture - "arising from the centre of bourgeois society itself"[62], as he significantly puts it - inherits modernism's "post-auratic" re-writing of the aesthetic function, in which the 'escape' from social reality offered by previous bourgeois art is transformed into critique. But, as Bürger[63] and others have pointed out, modernist art by and large never lost aesthetic aura, and its shocks have been successfully recuperated to the interests (and profit) of the social and cultural establishment. Similarly, the critical power of pre-modernist art was severely limited, especially after the early nineteenth century, as the society grew expert in managing art's 'dissonances' for its own purposes (i.e. of recreation and spiritual self-validation). The aesthetic disposition is functional to the society, as Bourdieu makes clear.

Habermas acknowledges that dissent can be managed through 'repressive tolerance', just as "social conflicts can be shifted to the level of psychic problems"[64]. He accepts that new cultural values can be "monetised" - that is,

---

60   Habermas, p. 49.
61   Habermas, p. 48.
62   Habermas, p. 85.
63   Peter Bürger, *Theory of the Avant Garde*, Manchester 1984.
64   Habermas, p. 129.

commodified and turned into sources of economic capital - and a rising demand for legitimate cultural meanings bought off by "rewards conforming to the system"[65]. Yet he seriously under-estimates the functionality to the system of the counterculture itself, for, as Bourdieu explains, by accepting the rules of the aesthetic game, it confirms their social power. Arguably, Habermas also under-plays the deeper economic ramifications of the new social developments which he identifies. Growth in cultural industry production; the commodification of leisure; modernisation and pluralisation of cultural tastes; expansion of the cultural-educational professions, and acknowledgement of their interests: these were precisely what was required to power capital's demand for increased consumption and an increased supply of brain-workers. 'High quality' cultural goods, such as progressive rock, were at the centre of the product repertory, with an important ideological as well as economic role. This, presumably, is exactly what Debray (writing only shortly after Habermas) had in mind (see p. 143 above).

What we see in the 1960s, then, is a substantial re-configuration of the field of legitimate musical taste - that is, of the aesthetic sphere - but one which, while brought on by system crisis, was ultimately compatible both with older cultural values and with the demands of a changing socio-economic formation. Bürger[66] describes the 'avant garde', by contrast with mainstream modernism, as being defined by the aim of smashing the institution of 'art' itself - of destroying Bourdieu's aesthetic game. On the level of vernacular practice, early rock 'n' roll perhaps hinted at a not dissimilar strategy. By 1970, however, this strategy had been left stranded in half-hidden corners of the "popular disposition". Small wonder that the rockers were disenchanted!

Interpreting the music

The legitimation of pop did not depend solely or even primarily on re-evaluation of the early styles. As we have seen, during the sixties the styles changed, and so it should be possible to follow the processes through which legitimation was produced not only through analysis of changing discourses but also through interpretation of developments in the musical practice. In a sense, what has been described so far as a struggle over popular musical values can be construed as a conflict concerning divergent representations of 'the people', modulated by

---

65   Habermas, p. 73.
66   Bürger, *Theory*.

changes in the class formation. All musical practice can be seen in terms of attempts to represent the cultural identities and values of its participants. In class societies it will be unavoidably **hybrid**, bringing together features, techniques and effects from a range of sources and trying to fix the combination as 'natural'; and in popular musics the different components, which we can regard as **actants** in a style-drama, each bringing associations from previous lives and contexts, are all aiming to construct particular figurings of 'the people'. This is a **dialogic** theory of musical meaning[67]. The production of meaning originates in 'dialogues' between a given style-element and its fellows in a piece, style or repertory, and between them and other elements in the wider musical field, present and historical; for all musical utterance comes clothed with the effects of having been 'always already' heard. Nothing in this approach authorises definitive interpretation: discursive struggle to include or exclude particular associations, to fix particular histories and dialogic connections rather than others, is endemic. The readings that follow (inevitably a highly selective sample) attempt to re-construct interpretative traverses which seem likely to have been active within the reception culture of the time (whether or not they were articulated or consciously held) and which arguably, we can now recognise, were going into the building of incipiently dominant positions within the processes of hegemonic negotiation.

A brief discussion of Elvis Presley's *All Shook Up*, described earlier as exemplifying a narcissistic domestification of rock 'n' roll, will illustrate the interpretive method (see Example 1)[68]. The vocal here stems from blues - thus locating the white adolescent in relation to a whole complex of meanings attaching to the position of African-American vernacularism within the broader patterns of the "black Atlantic"[69]. But the pitch smears and off-beat accents are pushed to such a mannerist extreme as to suggest Elvis, so to speak, **watching** himself perform. The bass patterns relate to boogie woogie - but the rhythmic plainness of the broken chords also connects to vamps in white Country music and entertainment styles, which in turn might be traced back to Classical 'Alberti'

---

67   Derived from the work of Mikhail Bakhtin; for a more detailed account, see Richard
      Middleton, *Authorship, Gender and the Construction of Meaning in the Eurythmics'*
      Hit Recordings, in: *Cultural Studies* 9/3 (1995), pp. 465-85.
68   All music examples are (selective) transcriptions from the recordings. They are at best
      partial representations of the sounds and there is no substitute for listening to the
      records.
69   Paul Gilroy, *The Black Atlantic: Modernity and Double Consciousness*, London 1983.

figures: we are reminded of Mozart portraying Papageno as a simpleton through a sort of clockwork rationality. Similarly, the corny guitar vamp helps to re-locate the poly-corporeal gestures of the rock 'n' roll sources within show-biz lineages of self-presentation. Already, then, pop is starting to accede to older, top-down representations of 'the people'.

NB 1: *All Shook up* - Verse 1 [∕and∖ denote glissandi]

Still, however, *All Shook Up* retains much of the relatively direct energies of early pop. By 1967, much has changed. In the Beatles' *Strawberry Fields Forever*[70] we are initially located by the mixed-modality vocal, sung with typical Lennon 'grain', in Mersey-pop territory (English provincial youth constructing itself into a partially mid-atlantic borderland) (see Example 2A). But the strikingly rich and varied textures, with predominantly low pitch focus, lead us back - via film score romanticism (note the colouristic orientalisms) - towards nineteenth-century art music (Wagner?), and also (such is the oddity of many of the contrasts) towards surrealism. At the same time, the square, scalic and broken-chord, 'classical' cello figures insist that this flux is **controlled** (see Example 2B). The outcome, perhaps, models the processes of formation of a popular-bohemian social fraction, pulled between 'thought' and 'feeling', cosmopolitan 'art' and provincial roots: a model stereotypically matched to the self-image of the art school-educated 'new intelligentsia'.

NB 2: *Strawberry fields* - A: opening of vocal.

B: Typical cello bass line

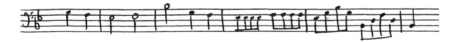

---

70   The Beatles, *Strawberry Fields Forever*, Parlophone R 5570, 1967.

NB 3: *A whiter Shade of Pale* - basic chord sequence.

In the contemporaneous *A Whiter Shade of Pale* by Procul Harum[71] the bass-line and chord-sequence, adopted from J.S. Bach[72], immediately make the claim for legitimate aesthetic status (see Example 3). But the link is specifically to an **early** point in the art music tradition (referencing the early music movement of the sixties?), suggesting an appeal both to a Leavisite sense of 'organic' community and to pre-modern religious traditions; the 'popular' here implicitly blurs class boundaries and harks back to a less fractious social formation. The organ style oscillates between ersatz Bachian twiddles, meandering improvisation of a style common to Anglican church organists (thus locating the piece within a distinctly 'English' strand of bourgeois culture), and jazzy glissandi. The latter connect up with a vocal timbre and phrasing derived from Soul music, and we are left overall with an image of a sort of decorous 'white(r shade of) negro' constructed through aesthetically sophisticated allusions to a pre-modern Other: an alliance of the exotic and archaic.

Pink Floyd were presented explicitly as an avant garde band (see descriptions earlier), and their *Astronomy Domine*[73] pursues a dialogics which is as much extra- as intra-generic: the music works in terms of what it is **not** (i.e., not what one expects in rock), at the same time as it implies links with various modernist strands. The collage-like electronics, for example, align the listener's ideological point of view with 'experiment' and 'technical progress' , as well as summoning up

71   Procul Harum, *A Whiter Shade of Pale*, Deram DM 126, 1967.
72   Specifically from an aria in the cantata *Vergnügte Ruh, beliebte Seelenlust* (BWV 170 Nr 1).
73   Pink Floyd, *Astronomy Domine*, on: *The Piper at the Gates of Dawn*, Columbia SCX 6157, 1967.

160

the 'gothic' combination of science and the irrational that is typical of popular science fiction (similar effects are found in sci-fi film soundtracks). The vocals sound vaguely 'modern' (for instance, the use of parallel triads) but also 'childlike' (similar to nursery rhymes): a sort of Debussy-ish exoticism, which heightens the image of a 'modernising popular' constructed with high-tech innocence (see Example 4).

NB 4: *Astronomy Domine* - sketch of vocal verse (rhythms simplified).

Slightly later, Soft Machine's *Slightly All the Time*[74], recorded about the same time as their Prom appearance, illustrates a somewhat different route to aesthetic legitimacy. The absence of vocals (commonly a point of engagement for a mass audience), the occasionally unusual chord choices, the 'shapeless' instrumental melodic lines, played with jazz phrasing, the loose form and foregrounding of improvisational technique: all play into an image of hip intellectualism, by this time the received aura surrounding modern jazz. The result is a perfect embodiment of Chester's 'intensional' process, conceived as high-status aesthetic domain.

Needless to say, these examples - by the Beatles, Procul Harum, Pink Floyd and Soft Machine - all come from the progressive, experimental, even avant garde side of the emergent rock formation (though it is worth noting that the first two were big hits as singles, the album containing Pink Floyd's piece also was a big

---

74   Soft Machine, *Slightly All the Time*, on: *Third*, CBS 66246, 1970.

seller, and even Soft Machine's recording spent six weeks in the album chart).
What could be said, in relation to the argument here, about the 'harder', more
'basic' styles of late-sixties rock?

NB 5: *Foxy Lady* - Verse 1 [♩ = spoken ✗ = Falsetto]

The style of Jimi Hendrix's *Foxy Lady*[75] derives most obviously from 'hard' blues
(Chicago styles, for instance); the vocal intonations and timbre, the guitar's
phraseology and use of 'vocalised tone' - these are unmistakeable pointers, and
the signals are to macho sexuality and 'real' emotion (see Example 5). If in a sense
the lineage runs parallel to rock 'n' roll's, by this time 'blues', processed through
'folk revival', had been appropriated into rock's ideology of 'community'; on this
level, then, the claim to legitimacy is less through the aesthetic sphere than

---

75   Jimi Hendrix, *Foxy Lady*, on: *Are You Experienced?*, Track 612 001, 1967.

through an almost Leavisite construction of folk-like 'authenticity of feeling'. At the same time, this style-tradition is laced with a hip intellectualism: note the jazzy virtuosity and the calculated use of noise through electronic feedback (Pete Townshend and others were consciously working out an aesthetic theory of rock noise at this time). It is passed, also, through the filter of the big riffs of West Coast acid rock - an emergent lineage re-working jazz/blues structure through a 'mind-blowing' aesthetic with older associations in European Romanticism. Bohemia beckons. Perhaps the connections go still wider. The programmatic use of repetitive noise goes back, through Stravinsky, to Beethoven - and Burke's concept of the awful Sublime. Here, perhaps, we have the Black-Other, asserting freedom from stereotype, and at large in the territory of Western modernism.

NB 6: *Jumpin' Jack Flash* - Verse 1

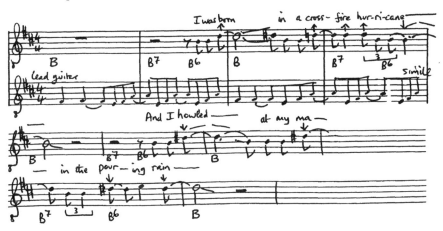

By contrast, in the Rolling Stones' *Jumpin' Jack Flash*[76], a white equivalent - equally blues-referenced, equally macho - we may hear the Black-Other **captured**, after a fashion which has roots deep in the history of bourgeois culture. Characteristically, the strategy veers between the exaggerations of stereotype and

---

76   Rolling Stones, *Jumpin' Jack Flash*, Decca F 12782.

the reduction of black difference in line with mainstream norms. On the one hand, the vocal mannerisms of pitch and accent distortion - surely more than is required - show Mick Jagger striving desperately for authenticity; on the other, the rather crude half-beat syncopations of the almost march-like guitar riff hark back to ragtime's assimilation to white rhythmic frameworks (just as Jagger's self-presentation as stud-hustler may be related to typical coon song images), and the equally over-regular ♫| ♩ upbeat figure from the introduction may even summon memories of the *William Tell* Overture (see Example 6). 'Square' and 'hip' are uneasily yoked together!

Aestheticising the style-elements of 'basic' rock became a definite strand in the progressive strategy. The signs of the vernacular are placed in quotation marks, passed through the distancing lens of an aesthetic-cultural programme. The legacy of this can easily be heard in heavy metal, whose roots in countercultural rock, otherwise hard to explain, have often been noted. The conjunction of the self-consciously 'artistic' and the equally self-consciously 'primitive' is already present in proto-heavy band Led Zeppelin, and the effects can be traced in subsequent heavy metal tendencies to parodic self-presentation, ostentatiously stripped-to-the-basics power-blues, and Classics-influenced instrumental virtuosity[77].

Searching for an everyday music

Bearing in mind both the discursive and musical analyses, what we find coming into view is a range of related trajectories with a tendency towards fixing the 'popular' within outlooks consonant with, or even originating in, long-lived, familiar bourgeois traditions. At the same time, we should remember that these trajectories provoked, in a dialectically linked development, the emergence of a 'teenybop' pop which at times comes as close as popular music ever has to justifying the Adornian anathema. In combination, the two provoke something of a sense of powerful forces trying to focus the culture around top-down figurings of 'the people' - in the one case, through processes of aesthetic elevation, in the other, through maximum compression of the musical energies into alienated moments of exchange-value. Writing in 1970, Richard Mabey captures the essentials of the moment exactly: "Can pop re-establish its links with everyday life, or will it continue to remain part high art, part trivial backcloth? Is there a

---

77   See Robert Walser, *Running with the Devil: Power, Gender and Madness in Heavy Metal Music*, Hanover NH 1993.

place for music-based ceremonial in our lives, or are we already too sophisticated to stomach such posturing? Is pop music necessarily the prerogative of the young and of the 'counter-culture', or could it form a means for invigorating the larger culture in which we all, willy-nilly, live (as it seemed it might during the first year or two of the Beatles)?"[78]

It is no easier now than it would have been for Mabey then to answer his final question with an unequivocal yes. The sixties, generally pictured as a historical fulcrum in the narrative of the **liberation** of pop music (in which it supposedly stood in for wider cultural forces) was, to a much greater extent, a fulcrum for a different reason: as a phase in a sequence of recuperation-negotiations in which long traditions of bourgeois culture attempt periodically to rejuvenate themselves with energies from below in order to preserve their authority.

In his recent book on the Beatles[79], Ian McDonald's rehabilitation of the sixties reveals the continuing power of the older story. He accepts the counterculture myth, opposing it to bourgeois norms - **but** at the same time describing underground rock in the quintessential terms of bourgeois aesthetics: "imaginative freedom", "living expression", etc. As a result, he misses the music's complicity with social developments: it becomes merely a "revolution in the head"; but this is precisely what most music within bourgeois culture was limited to, ever since the counter-revolutions of the early nineteenth century (and those nineteenth-century revolutions in the head had their social function anyway). McDonald praises sixties pop at the expense of the "Frankenstein's monster" of recent "mechanised, standardised" dance music and rap; it builds on a melodic/harmonic idea rather than being layered over a foundational rhythm track (so it does - to a large extent anyhow: just like bourgeois art music!). So, as progressive rock fades, "something in the soul of Western culture began to die during the late Sixties"[80].

A different perspective on this history would be to point out that the styles of recent dance music - house, rave, techno, etc - can be traced back to what were perhaps the **truly** radical tendencies of the 1960s. Growing out of many of the

---

78   Richard Mabey, *Who Called the English Teacher Daddy-O? Pop Music and Everyday Life*, in: *Anatomy of Pop*, edited by Tony Cash, London 1970, pp. 77-92.
79   Ian McDonald, *Revolution in the Head: The Beatles' Records and the Sixties*, London 1994.
80   McDonald, p. 299.

same post-war vernacular black musics as rock 'n' roll, and relatively unnoticed, dismissed or patronised by white critical discourse, the lineage of black dance-pop was largely confined to the mod, skinhead and 'Northern Soul' subcultural 'ghettos' in sixties Britain - only to re-emerge in disco, and, more forcefully, in late-eighties rave culture. The most influential figure in this lineage was soul/funk star James Brown, whose 1970 record *Superbad*[81] has been used by David Brackett[82] as the centrepiece of his exposition of black music's "Signifyin(g)" black difference: Brackett's basic point, drawing on African-American literary theory, is to show how a kind of 'vertical' process of constant variation - a "changing same" - is rooted in the vernacular schemas and rhythms of black culture (conversation, historical memory, ethics, religious belief, etc).[83] In this context, the belittling and ghetto-ising of such musical difference, within the broader popular music culture, can be seen as an attempt to **discipline** the Black-Other - just as the Jumping Jack Flash figure can be regarded as a **projection** of difference on to a stereotype, the two strategies making up bourgeois culture's traditional twin-track approach to managing its forbidden fears and desires.[84]

One might then see present-day dance music as an attempt (in a context that is in many ways quite changed, of course) to **re-run** the sixties, taking analogous starting-points off in a different direction, building on James Brown rather than the Beatles. What might that mean for the legitimation crisis so painfully resolved in the 1960s, and the reconstructed bourgeois hegemony put together then? But that is another story.

This should not be taken to imply a picture of dance music as a single track development (rather, it is multi-valent, its politics contradictory, its culture far from utopian). Nor is there any intention to deny the capacity of the music industry to coopt it - or even aestheticise it. It is to suggest, however, that intellectuals should transfer their energies from searches for pop's aesthetic potential (no less than from quests for its revolutionary correctness) into the

---

81   James Brown, *Superbad*, King 45-6329, 1970.
82   David Brackett, *Interpreting Popular Music*, Cambridge 1995.
83   The typography of "Signifyin(g)" (paradigmatic variation) signifies the difference from conventional 'signifying' (syntagmatic chains of meaning): so, not **representation** (the drawing of 'life' into 'art') but **practice**.
84   These strategies are explored in more detail in Richard Middleton, *Western Music and Its Low-Other*, in: *Western Music and Its Others*, edited by Georgina Born and Dave Hesmondhalgh, Berkeley CA forthcoming.

possibilities of 'thinking the vernacular' - with the implications for their own social positioning which that implies.[85] Again, it would be stupid to argue that in any conceivable organisation of society music will not have a variety of functions, some more singular and self-focused, others more ubiquitous and behaviourally embedded. But in the society we have, the category 'art' can **only** mystify (which is not to say that existing art music cannot be discursively re-positioned,[86] nor that new art music cannot through critique deconstruct its own status); 'everyday life' , though hopefully it may not be forever all that capital leaves available for self-legitimating practice, is for the moment the site where fruitful change, if not 'revolution', is most likely to arise.

85   I explore the implications for intellectuals of 'thinking the vernacular' in Richard
       Middleton, *Who May Speak? From a Politics of Popular Music to a Popular Politics
       of Music*, in: *Bordercrossings*, edited by John Shepherd et al, New York forthcoming.
86   Probably this has always happened; for two perspectives on strategies of 'popular
       listening', see Nicholas Cook, *Music, Imagination and Culture*, Oxford 1990,and Gino
       Stefani, *Melody: A Popular Perspective*, in: *Popular Music* 6/1 (1987), pp. 21-35.

CHAPTER 6

Musical Belongings:
Western Music and Its Low-Other

Music can never "belong" (to me).[1] It is always already "other," always located elsewhere (than here), in the matrix of dialogically constructed codes and historical debris responsible for its specific forms. Its interiority—in one sense real enough, because it is grounded in a sense of the bodily processes of sound production—has been turned into a myth of origination and possession. This is a hard argument for cultural property-owners to accept, but taking that step is—paradoxically—a precondition for any possibility of superseding musical alienation, of losing ourselves in the music, as the phrase goes. The price of any reconciliation between subjectivity and (musical) nature is an acknowledgment of the irreducible mediated sociality of both; for to belong to music (to a music)—as distinct from treating it as a belonging—must mean not some pseudoatavistic regression but a reflexive acceptance of the self's dependencies.

The sense of music's "autonomy" intensified in the late eighteenth century, setting off a development in Western music which resulted in the growth of that monstrous superstructure of meaning surrounding musical processes today. An increasingly powerful awareness of music's specificity, set within wider tendencies of rationalization in post-Enlightenment culture, had the effect of reformulating music's position in the cultural field as, first and foremost, a vehicle of expression and representation, and an object of interpretation and discursive elaboration. The nineteenth-century history is well known.[2] But at the same time, this fullness produced a lack. In a complementary movement, there is located "below" the sphere of meaning and reflexivity an image, or a kind of memory, of musical immediacy—of prediscursive musical practices, or musics of nature, often identified with a range of others (archaic, folk, popular, foreign, exotic), whose musics are taken to really, authentically, belong to them. Ironically, it is the development of elaborate alienating meaning systems in the Western musical culture that makes possible the depiction and annexation of these others: only when a sophisticated method of manipulating (mediating) semiotic difference is in place can immediacy be portrayed. At the same time, the fact that in the deconstructive late twentieth century the peculiarities of this apparatus are increasingly visible suggests the start of a new historical phase in which it is becoming clear that only when others are freed to pursue their own trajectories can Western music properly acknowledge the multiplicity of differences lying beneath its authoritarian binaries and become productively other to itself.

This new phase, if such it is, cannot be fully understood outside of a knowledge of the previous history. That in turn demands that we grasp the continuous interplay between the ways in which Western music has treated its others and the broader issue of how difference is articulated in all music. Music as such, it can be said, works by manipulating difference, both structurally—in terms of degrees of repetition, variation, and change—and semiotically, in terms of the dialogues coded into the polyphonies of both musical practice and repertory. In the music-historical field under consideration here, however, these processes are articulated to the network of interests active within social and ideological formations which are structured in dominance. Exploring this interplay between difference-in-general and difference-in-particular, we need to consider how it works within, and connects to, the whole sweep of Western musical developments taking place under the sign of the post-Enlightenment "modernity project." Of special interest are the configurations of what Paul Gilroy has called the "Black Atlantic"—the black other conceived as an active constituent in modernity itself;[3] though I want to think more broadly of a "Low Atlantic," which poses popular against elite, and of how, within that, "low" and black relate to each other.

Nineteenth-century discourses around the philosophy of music continually display the effects of the basic contradiction outlined above: between awareness of music's expanding meaningfulness, on the one hand, and, on the other, a quest for its essential immediacy (sometimes manifesting itself in an unwillingness to shift music as such out of a sphere of pure spontaneity). This tension tracks a parallel one in the contemporary musical practice: an exponential growth in talk about music—from criticism to compositional programs—proceeding alongside the romantic intuition that the "real" meaning of music lies *beyond* words (an intuition formalized by Schopenhauer in his doctrine that music directly embodies the primordial, inarticulate movements of Will, free from any attachments to external objects or rational thought). Nietzsche pointed out that the very idea of the prereflective in music (the naïve, to use Schiller's formulation) is the product precisely of an advanced stage of intellectual reflection. Nevertheless, he himself constructs a history in which music is progressively enveloped by symbolisms and

systems of interpretation of various kinds, and he seems to see a level (a "primitive stage of music") that is prior to this history—a level where music operates directly, "of and in itself," "before" the imposition of meaning.[4] This historical model harks back to Rousseau, for whom the origins of both music
and language lay in a kind of primitive speech-song which, without recourse
to any semiotic convention or conscious manipulation, directly expressed
the movements of "spontaneous desire." This "voice of nature," Rousseau
argued, was gradually overwhelmed by the growth of harmony, counterpoint
and the other "civilized" complexities of compositional technique.[5]

Rousseau's theory, the subject of postmodern critiques by Derrida and
De Man,[6] is the most important source for the romantic myth of musical authenticity. It can be felt, for example, behind Kant's more measured tones.
Kant places music relatively low in his typology of the arts precisely because
it "speaks . . . without concepts," leaving no "food for reflection"; it is thus
"more . . . enjoyment than . . . culture."[7] Kant is concerned to distinguish
beauty from mere enjoyment, and to some extent he can rescue classical music by means of an appeal to the beauties of its formal coherence—though
at the expense of a fastidious demotion of sensuous pleasures, such that, as
Lawrence Kramer suggests, he seems to be responding "less to an absence
of thought than to the presence of danger";[8] but the attraction as well as the
threat of this sensuous underside is palpable. Hegel reformulates and his-
toricizes the Kantian critique, seeing the triumph of "independent" (i.e., instrumental) music as directing music's content increasingly into areas of abstract, "sterile" technique. Paradoxically, by describing music in terms of
"sounding inwardness," representing subjectivity directly to itself,[9] Hegel can
account for music's centrality in nineteenth-century culture—it is the cutting edge of Spirit—but only in such a way that the resulting sterility inevitably
leads to the "end of art," as its function within his historical schema is taken
over by philosophical reflection. The prereflective, as summoned up by
reflexivity, can only function either as myth (as in Rousseau) or by trans-
muting into reflexivity (as in Hegel) and self-destructing. Small wonder that
Hegel saw the "unreflective" culture of Africa as lying quite outside history,
entirely fitted to be "slave" to the Western "master."[10]

It is this sterility, in a culture which he saw as ruled by "criticism," "his-
toricism," and "academicism," that is the starting motivation behind Nietzsche's search for the roots of the "Dionysian spirit," in which "nature itself . . . rises again to celebrate the reconciliation with her prodigal son,
man."[11] Richard Wagner, Nietzsche's favored vessel (at least at first) for the
longed-for rebirth of a Hellenic fusion of Dionysian and Apollonian tendencies, found the sources of his primitive other in Nordic myths. Ironically, however, he could only clothe it in the most up-to-date compositional
and orchestral technique. In an immense, egotistic assimilative move (which
is repeated elsewhere, as we shall see), one version of the drama of moder-

nity and its others is played out within the self-contained Wagnerian music-world.

This is one strategy. Its complement is that of projection, where the other, far from being assimilated, is externalized in a sphere of apparent social difference. It is this strategy which explains the attractions of the many thousands of "peasant dances," "Volkslieder," "bohemian rhapsodies," "Scottish" or "Slavic" character pieces, "plantation melodies," and so forth which throng the nineteenth-century repertory. A parallel development is the emergence of musical folklore and anthropology—with their typical romanticizing and exoticizing tendencies—from Herder, the Grimms, Ossian and Scott through to Vaughan Williams and Bartók. Sometimes the two strategies intersect, as at the 1932 Congress of Arab Music in Cairo,[12] where Europeans, including Bartók (who drew on "exotic" folk musics in his own compositions), begged the Arab musicians not to "modernize"; or in the involvement of English Musical Renaissance composers—Vaughan Williams among others—in folk song collection;[13] or in the influence of the early German folk song collectors, such as Herder, on Schubert. In all three of these cases (and many others) it is interesting that the approved other is defined as a defense against a threatening usurper: for Bartók this was city music; for the English composers and collectors, music hall; and for Herder, "the mob of the streets, who never sing or compose but shriek and mutilate."[14] We see that the differentiated sphere can be coded either positive or negative, and many tactical moves, on the part of composers or theorists, concern the interplay that can result.

However divergent their tactics, the aim of both assimilation and projection strategies is to manage the threat posed by potentially infinite difference to the authority of the bourgeois self, by reducing such difference to a stable hierarchy. This may be configured either through binary distinctions, dividing center from periphery, or through co-option of the peripheries into the center's sphere of influence. But the cast of others contains a range of characters and is rarely entirely passive; hierarchic closure is difficult to maintain. I shall be concentrating here on the relationship between Western music and what has been called its "low-other";[15] but, as we shall see, the various types have been to some extent interchangeable, and from the first, the whole range (peasants, primitives, exotics, women, bohemians, lumpen) are liable to be slipped into, connected to, conflated with each other. Yet this in turn only increases the chance that something will not fit—that control will break down.

SHACKLING PAPAGENO

What is at issue here is what Stallybrass and White have called "the formation of the cultural Imaginary [the forbidden zones, denied but desired] of the middle class in post-Renaissance Europe," a process involving "an internal distancing from the popular which was complex and often contradictory in its effects."[16] As mid-eighteenth-century musical style developed a range of internally more differentiated forms, together with the ability to portray a range of social types, behavioral characters and emotional gestures, so the twin strategies of assimilation and projection emerged. Comic low figures, differentiated musically, were a feature of opera from the beginning of the eighteenth century; and "exotics" also appeared, clothed for example in "Turkish" music, or in the pseudobarbaric strains given to the Scythians in Gluck's *Iphigénie en Tauride* (1779). In the famous ballroom scene in *Don Giovanni*, Mozart has three orchestras play simultaneously three dances: a minuet for the aristocracy, a *contre-danse* (urbanized "country dance") for the bourgeoisie, a waltz for the peasants. In instrumental music, such differentiated realms could be assimilated into the composer's controlling vision, as with the popular tunes used by Haydn, or—above all perhaps—through the refining treatment of dance rhythms. The concert use of minuet, then waltz, is especially interesting, enabling the rational bourgeois to deal with the disturbing fascination of the degenerate aristocracy on the one hand, the earthy peasantry on the other.[17]

The new structural principle of sonata was particularly conducive to the depiction of "other" spheres, either through differentiation of themes (for instance, the second theme of a sonata-principle movement was routinely described as "feminine," by contrast with the "masculine" first theme), or differentiation of keys. In 1755 Joseph Riepel published a treatise on key structure,[18] in which the interrelationships of the keys to which a piece was most likely to modulate were portrayed in terms of the social structure of the (high) bourgeois household. The tonic was the "master" key, while dominant, subdominant, and their relative minors represented various grades of servant; thus distant parts of the social sphere could be visited, but in the end they owed their meaning, and must give way to, the hegemony of the paterfamilias. (It is interesting that the relationships of masters and servants is a pervasive theme in Mozart's operas. The figure of the servant [especially female: nurses, maids], both as a marker of social distinction and as a route to forbidden, low-cultural zones, remains a common one into and throughout the nineteenth century.[19]) Fascinatingly, the tonic minor, a much more distant key, and one always suggesting something disturbing, foreign, an outburst of irrationality, is personified by Riepel as *Die schwarze Gredel* ("Black Maggie," Queen Margaret of Sweden, who was notorious for her swarthy complexion). While it seems unlikely that Riepel had heard any black music, it is significant that systemic disturbance to the established musical language is already associated with "blackness." Much later, the minor-ish tendencies of African American "blue notes," and the minor-pentatonic tonality of many blues, would give this association more substance.

Eighteenth- and nineteenth-century techniques of structurally differen-

64   RICHARD MIDDLETON

tiating areas of otherness, through thematic, tonal, or expressive means, have
been discussed by several musicologists, notably Susan McClary and Lawrence
Kramer.[20] For the romantics such moments are often marked by qualities of
lyrical "inwardness" and "immediacy"; they offer a glimpse of something constructed as beyond the grip of bourgeois rationality. While they may be projected on to social others, especially in opera and program music, in absolute
music, as Kramer points out, they are usually integrated within the orbit of
the monologic gaze of the controlling authorial intent. Where this control
is weakened—in some works by Tchaikovsky and Mahler, for example—the
form may threaten to fall apart. But this carries our story into the moment
of the modernist crisis; for illustration of the more balanced approach to
the low-other characteristic of the high-bourgeois phase of European music, we need to move back historically, and no better example can be found
than Mozart's opera *The Magic Flute* (1791).

It is a commonplace that this work, a *Singspiel* with Enlightenment and
Masonic themes, effects a marvelous interplay and fusion of high and popular elements. What is less often remarked is the *range* of others deployed
(women; blacks, in the persons of the "moorish" Monostatos and the slaves;
and plebeians, in the form of the comic birdcatcher, Papageno). Of special
interest is Mozart's handling of Papageno. This Enlightenment Caliban is,
as he tells us himself, a "child of nature," a happy simpleton, whose long-
ings reach no further than food, drink, a good woman, and floods of children. And his music, drawing on the popular ballad style of the *Singspiel* tradition, certainly sets him apart from the high characters. At the same time,
however, his simplicity sounds mechanical (see example 1.1): the tick-tock
rhythms, the elementary tonic-dominant progressions, the predictable
melodic sequences, the banal phrase-structure, produce an effect less like
folk song than like rational classicism reduced to its nuts and bolts; or rather,
like an image of "folk song" from above. This is a vision of what folk song
ought to be (i.e., simple) and at the same time what it has become (i.e., rationalized, enchained—just as Papageno's birdcatcher's panpipes rational-
ize the vagaries of birdsong into the first five notes of the major scale).
Conflating the "people" with a Newtonian clockwork nature, this presents
the Enlightenment's idea of the low: *under control,* at once a caricature of
the other and a mirror-image of the rational self.

When Papageno and Monostatos come face to face, they terrify each other
equally ("that is surely the Devil!"); and they are equated musically, singing
their halting, frightened phrases in parallel. Later, in the finale of act 1, when
the princely hero Tamino charms (Orfeo-like) the birds and beasts with his
magic flute, his tune is in a refined *Singspiel* ballad style; and then, when he
hears Papageno's pipes, he imitates their scalic figure: thus culture draws on
nature, high on low. Immediately, in an echoing invocation of music's magical possessive power, Papageno, with an almost parodically simple tune on

Example 1.1 Mozart, "Der Vogelfänger bin ich ja," from *The Magic Flute*

his magic bells, enchants Monostatos and his slaves, so that they leave off their pursuit and withdraw. A hierarchy of projections is set up, with Papageno as its mediating focus: as the low is to Tamino (i.e., "natural"), so blacks are to Papageno. (Monostatos's later aria, "Alles fühlt der Liebe Freuden," is about as "Turkish" as Papageno's songs are "folky": in both cases, then, the other is heavily mediated by High-Western refinement.)

A parallel structure of relationships links Papageno and Woman.[21] Papageno is woefully lacking in courage ("Be a man!" Tamino says to the terrified birdcatcher; "I wish I were a girl," he replies). He is a "chatterer." The first of the Masonic initiation tests for him and Tamino is that they stay silent, resisting the blandishments of the Three Ladies; "a man thinks before he speaks," he "seeks proof," whereas women are associated with bewitchment, treachery, gossip, and falsehood. But Papageno cannot hold his tongue, and he survives only with Tamino's help (the high solicitously lifting up the low). Early in the opera, Papageno lies to Tamino, and his punishment is to have his mouth padlocked (a scold's bridle?!). The link between his femininity and his "natural" qualities appears musically in the clockwork style of his songs, for, as Huyssen has suggested, the eighteenth century's love of automata quickly developed in such a way that the threat of the robotic machine was conflated with the threat of Woman: the automaton, seen in terms of a clockwork theory of Nature, became coded as feminine (since Woman represented Nature).[22] Mozart himself composed pieces for mechanical mu-

66   RICHARD MIDDLETON

sical toys, and the music he wrote for Papageno's magic bells (especially in his act 2 aria and the subsequent Finale) reminds us of this, as it fuses together the magical and the mechanical: the childlike Papageno (unreflective, easily amused) plays at rationality.

So simple is this child of nature that, in the act 2 Finale, united at last with his Papagena, the two of them can only stutter ("Pa—pa—pa"), as if relearning the power of speech.[23] But Papageno can be *taught*. In act 1, as he struggles to speak through his padlocked lips, his musically basic lines to "hm" are echoed and filled out by the tutelary Tamino. In the ensemble that follows (padlock removed), his line becomes somewhat more complex, for musically he is now captured and under guidance. Similarly, in his duet with the heroine Pamina ("Bei Männern, welche Liebe fühlen"), he copies her first phrase; it is simple, but rather too hymnlike, too elevated, for his normal style. Her second phrase gets too difficult for him, and he just adds to it a straightforward bass. By the time the final stages of the opera are reached, this tutoring process enables Papageno, in despair at apparently losing his Papagena, to move from his usual simplicity (tonic-dominant movement, scalic pipe interpolations) into music which is emotionally and harmonically more complex. This final assimilative gesture, its "humanizing" warmth limited by the underlying comedy (of course Papageno lacks the courage to hang himself), marks the boundary beyond which the Enlightenment's anthropology could not push, at the same time as the subtlety and complexity of Mozart's work represent one of that anthropology's high points.

CRIPPLING PORGY

After *The Magic Flute*, it is often argued,[24] the balance of high and popular elements achieved there was unrepeatable; they tended to split apart. What is more interesting to consider is the myriad strategies that evolved for dealing with this situation. Projective exoticism and assimilative self-assertion (for example, in theories of popular music as nothing more than *gesunkenes Kulturgut*—"cultured" musical materials that have descended, diluted, to be taken up by the uncreative masses) chased each other around the nineteenth-century musical field. And these tendencies continued to energize twentieth-century developments, taking ever new forms. With the spread of African American styles, notably jazz, conflations of black and low took on a greater intensity, resulting in complex, two-way negotiations within white popular music.[25] Indeed, it is increasingly in white responses (musical and verbal) to "black" styles that the clearest musical and discursive representations of bourgeois feelings about subterranean cultural experience are to be found. Depictions of early jazz as "primitive"—both positively and negatively charged—have been well researched;[26] just as characteristic were *denials* of the music's particularity, assuming their most sophisticated form in Adorno's reduction of jazz to "diluted romanticism," its internal differences to "pseudo-individualization."[27] It is clear too in Adorno's discussions how the historical context—the emergence of monopoly capitalism, the rise of mass culture, artistic modernism—gave these impulses a new sharpness. In the shadow both of World War I and of emerging Depression and totalitarianism, the bourgeoisie and intelligentsia of the 1920s and early 1930s readily located a challenge to "civilization," welcome or not, in the threat posed by the new popular musics.

In the U.S., the period was highly racially charged as well; and George Gershwin's opera *Porgy and Bess,* with its all-black cast and its use of "black" musical idioms, excited controversy from its very first performance in 1935. It is a kind of *Carmen* set in a folk South, in which the heroic but naive Porgy is physically crippled: he is never going to succeed in the "real world." The relationship in the opera between the "folk" world of Catfish Row—innocent and arcadian—and the values of a modernizing America—grown-up, sophisticated, corrupt—which are forever intruding can be linked to the central debates which have surrounded the work, focusing as they do either on the question of exploitation (does Gershwin steal from black music? does he patronize his characters?) or on that of aesthetic status (does the piece succeed in the grown-up world of opera?).[28] *Porgy and Bess* also reminds us of *The Magic Flute.* We feel Gershwin striving after a Mozartian encompassing balance of styles and social layers. At the same time, compared with the earlier work, his opera does move its center of gravity significantly toward the low: virtually all the characters are black and poor, and their important moments of musical otherness are painted in stand-out colors. Against this, telling the story not in speech but in florid recitative (as neither Mozart nor Bizet in *Carmen* does) yanks the aesthetic fulcrum back toward high art convention.

David Horn, in an attractive argument,[29] has suggested that we relax the critical pressure on Gershwin and allow the characters to speak in their varied specificity. Yet for all the musical eclecticism of *Porgy and Bess* and the tensions that result, one feels that the authorial Gershwin is always pulling at the strings. The characters are allowed a range of idioms, which, in the context of the overall stylistic location of the work, are not difficult to interpret; they range from Sportin' Life's slithery sensual chromatics to Porgy's folky-cum-heroic lyricism, from the "ecstasy" of the religious pieces to the neoprimitive abandon of the picnic scene. Yet in the end this differentiation of the other is circumscribed by the framework of genre: the black idioms are encased, put in their place, by the style, orchestration, and structural conventions of late-romantic opera. By choosing to write in this genre, Gershwin is unavoidably constrained by received power-relationships between high and low; his attempt to unify the work through use of the Wagnerian leitmotif technique is symptomatic of his hope that "the element within him that was Porgy might one day come to terms with the element that was Sportin' Life."[30] Thus the Gershwin psyche is the chief character. Against the pull, perhaps, of his own marginal status (his Jewishness, his Tin Pan Alley background, both of which must have motivated his identification with his low-others), he has situated himself where he is inevitably heir to the nineteenth-century strategy of imposing monologic authorial control on disparate materials, and where the only method available to him of representing "low-life" is through the code of the picturesque.

Like Neil Leonard's description of Gershwin's *Rhapsody in Blue* as "Liszt in blackface," Rudi Blesh's criticism of *Porgy and Bess* is cruel but revealing: "It is Negroesque. . . . [Like] the earlier travesty of minstrelsy . . . the Negro . . . is set forth as an entertainer singing a music that the white public finds to be just like *its own*."[31] This catches the work's dilution of "authenticity" in the picturesque, and at the same time the tension set up between appropriation and assimilation, difference and control. Gershwin himself insisted that he had composed "folk music"; but he also explained that he "decided against the use of traditional folk materials because I wanted the music to be all of one piece. Therefore I wrote my own spirituals and folk songs." His 1927 comment relating to *Rhapsody in Blue* is in similar vein: "Certain types of it [jazz] are in bad taste, but I do think it has certain elements which can be developed. I do not know whether it will be jazz when it is finished."[32]

The clearest examples of otherness, projected on to black characters, are the folky set-pieces: the children's song (act 3, scene 3); the prayers and shouts of the religious Serena; the chorus "I Ain't Got No Shame" (act 2, scene 2—the picnic scene), with its frenzied pseudoprimitive drumming; the fishermen's spiritual/work song (act 2, scene 1); the street-sellers' cries ("Here come the honeyman," for example). Even here, however, the authentic is *presented* to us; we see through Gershwin's eyes. Thus the honeyman's haunting pentatonic cry is surrounded by a harmonic "haze" created by drones and ostinatos, which has the effect of magically placing the scene in a distant landscape within the composer's mind—a place of trance and lost innocence. Porgy's minstrelized "I Got Plenty o' Nuttin'" draws on a different stereotype. But the musical differences between its simple scalic tune, with rag-style syncopations and banjo-strum accompaniment, and the pentatonics and blue notes of the other pieces mentioned does not disguise the ideological link, which lies in the picturing of simplicity.

"I Got Plenty" is an equivalent to the Enlightened folk songs that Mozart wrote for Papageno: civilization's parody of the precultured. And this assimilative impulse comprises the other pole in Gershwin's aesthetic strategy. At the beginning of the opera, the orchestral Introduction, with its repetitive pentatonic figurations over static harmonies and ostinati, is meant to transport us to an imagined Eden, as Mellers writes;[33] but it is a New Yorker's

Example 1.2 Gershwin, Porgy's theme, from *Porgy and Bess*

Eden, mediated through glittery symphonic sound—a canvas of exotic colors and showy rhythmic oomph. Jazzbo Brown's "lowdown blues," which follows, encases its bluesy phrases in fashionable (at the time) Tin Pan Alley piano chromatics (the style of Gershwin the nightclub pianist, in fact). "Roll Dem Bones," the chorus which then introduces the crap game, is an imitation spiritual—but the orchestration (string tremolandos and high-register violins doubled at the octave) turn this into melodrama. Similarly, when Porgy enters, he is announced by his orchestral leitmotif, a blues cliché (example 1.2). But this is delivered in Puccinian violin octaves, accompanied by "modernistic" parallel-sliding triads: the folk-hero is romanticized (in more than one sense—he is both folklorized and elevated).

As in *The Magic Flute*, assimilation slips into paternalism. The marvelous love songs for Porgy and Bess work by extending their bluesy modal starting ideas into long-breathed, upward-straining Puccinian lyricism, complete with lump-in-the-throat chromatic modulations. Porgy and Bess have to learn that, while "black" idioms are fine for Eden, grown-up emotions like personal love require the manner of European late romanticism. Bess's "divorce" from Crown turns her "from woman to lady" (act 2, scene 1), and Porgy, who buys her release, turns from innocent beggar to patriarchal provider. As they imagine leaving the folk, their music crosses the class-cultural barrier.

Like *The Magic Flute*, Gershwin's opera both exposes and exploits to the utmost the limits imposed on its project by genre convention and cultural situation. In large part its terrific power arises from the resulting tension, in particular the tension associated with the effort to bring musical (and social) multiplicity into line with the simpler structure of a high/low binary. Working on the composition, Gershwin made a research trip to South Carolina. It represented less an "exploration," wrote Dubose Heyward (author of the original novel and part librettist of the opera) than a "homecoming." One day, Gershwin heard a prayer-meeting of "shouting Negroes." He joined in—but he outshouted them: he "stole the show."[34] He loved what he heard,

70   RICHARD MIDDLETON

as what perhaps seemed to him to encapsulate an important part of himself; but—and here is the strategy of *Porgy and Bess* in a nutshell—difference was effaced, as projection and assimilation merged in the assertion of authority: he had to be master.

PAPAGENO/PORGY ANSWERS BACK

The composer Virgil Thomson commented acutely on the strategy of Porgy and Bess: "Folklore subjects recounted by an outsider are only valid as long as the folk in question is unable to speak for itself, which is certainly not true of the American Negro in 1935."[35] How, then, did this other speak? Can the low answer back?

Much of George Gershwin's education in low-life and black music took place in the nightclubs of Harlem, increasingly at that time a playground for affluent white slummers.[36] This white invasion was connected to a broader crisis in, and restructuring of, white bourgeois values evident since the turn of the century, but in the context of the jazz age, it took on a new intensity and meaning, focusing its exploration of low culture on "the Negro"—who at the same time could be kept conveniently at arm's length in the ghetto.[37] For Nathan Huggins, "Harlem seemed a cultural enclave that had magically survived the psychic fetters of Puritanism." "White folks," wrote Claude McKay, "discovered black magic there." James Weldon Johnson observed the visitors "seeking to recapture a state of primitive joy in life and living; trying to work their way back into that jungle which was the original Garden of Eden; in a word, doing their best to pass for colored." Rudolph Fisher remarked that "Now Negroes go to their own cabarets to see how white people act. And what do we see? Why, we see them actually playing Negro games . . . and they do them all better than I!"[38] Nowhere was this ersatz exoticism more in evidence than at Harlem's Cotton Club, where black dancers and musicians performed for all-white audiences, against a "jungle" decor, putting on shows with "a primitive naked quality that was supposed to make a civilized audience lose its inhibitions."[39] A typical program from 1929 advertised a "Congo Jamboree . . . an exhibition of unrestrained Nubian abandon."[40] Here Duke Ellington's "Jungle Band," in residence from 1927 to 1932, was responsible for the pseudoprimitive musical ambience (which was relayed across the U.S. on network radio).

Ellington was to criticize the "lamp-black Negroisms" of *Porgy and Bess*.[41] Criticisms of a similar sort, applied more widely to the whole phenomenon of black popular music's new-found appeal, came from many Harlem Renaissance intellectuals, who saw the songs, dances and shows as a new minstrelsy, simply updating stereotypes.[42] Ellington, master of the "pure put-on,"[43] seems to have played his role at the Cotton Club with equanimity; yet he was intensely serious about his music, rejecting the "jazz" label and claiming that African American musical forms "are as much an art medium as are the most profound works of the famous classical composers."[44] Ellington the man was equally as complex as the situation in which he and other black musicians found themselves, and there are no simple ways to resolve this apparent contradiction. We can start to understand its dynamics, though, by looking first at his upbringing in black middle-class Washington, D.C., and second at his working methods.

The Washington black bourgeoisie was proper and ambitious, its ideology of betterment centered on a sense of racial aspiration. Ellington never lost the combination of courtesy (which could include an ironic use of the minstrel's mask) and drive, nor the ambition of writing (and extending) the story of "his people." At the same time, he mixed easily with other classes, and his musical training mostly came, informally, from low-class musicians. Yet many of these—Will Marion Cook, for instance—were working for a serious popular music, insisting on the need for respectability in order to counter destructive stereotyping.[45] Working within this mix of social and ideological forces enabled Ellington to play off the different strategies against one another. Of course, this does not rule out the possibility of simply assimilating to white bourgeois norms; and arguably this sometimes happens—in some of the later large-scale concert works, for example.[46] More commonly, I would say, the cultural context that nurtured Ellington, marked by awareness of multiple black histories, could make available a "jungle to Harlem" narrative capable of *relocating* the jungle into a modern here and now—a narrative, then, which, rather than assimilating completely to Darwinian models of social and racial progress, worked to inscribe them in a project organized around the laying out of a quite "new territory."[47] Central to this strategy was an acceptance of difference within black music. Just as Duke mixed easily in different class spheres, so he both brought together disparate ideas and idioms and treated his band as a source of *collective* composition, encouraging and learning from his players' contributions.[48] It is possible to exaggerate Ellington's easy-going tolerance of diversity; yet even in pieces that demonstrate the imprint of his structural planning, the content rarely succumbs to a Gershwinian single-mindedness. This is not to say that the authorial Ellington just relinquishes control. Given the legacy of "double consciousness" deeply imprinted within African American culture, the constellations of self/other relations must in fact take on peculiarly complex forms here—a point with important implications for interpretation of the music, as we shall see.

Jazz historians have generally neglected Ellington's Cotton Club period, treating it at best as formative for later, more important developments.[49] This is rather unfair to some excellent music and, more important here, ignores the light it can cast on ways in which subaltern others can "answer back." Inheriting the nineteenth-century disposition to musical pictorialism,[50] Ellington was easily capable of meeting the demand for fashionable Orientalism (e.g., in "Japanese Dream" and "Arabian Lover," both 1929—replete with gongs, tinkly piano, woodblocks, etc.); and of transferring this exoticizing aesthetic to the strand in his own music that was becoming known as his "jungle style." In "Diga-Diga-Doo" (1928), the clichéd phrases over tonic drone chord come over now as comically simplified, the cymbal crashes as extravagant, the heavily strummed beat as "primitive" and the growled trumpet solo as melodramatically "barbaric"; is this Papageno/Porgy, tongue firmly in cheek, performing for his betters?[51] But the jungle style was an autonomous development, emerging some years before the Cotton Club residency,[52] and for other reasons. It was in large part the creation of trumpeter Bubber Miley and trombonist Joe Nanton, whose "talking" plunger-mute techniques derived from New Orleans sources; and when Ellington heard Miley's "gutbucket" stuff, he said (with slight exaggeration), he forgot all about "sweet music": "As a student of Negro history I had, in any case, a natural inclination in this direction."[53] In the 1927 "Black and Tan Fantasy" (credited to Miley and Ellington),[54] all the ingredients of the style—"growling" brass, heavy stomping four-beat rhythm, minor key with blues inflections—are used to intensely serious effect; but the "jungle" sections are cobbled together with an alto sax solo of nightclub sensuality and a piano bridge in cabaret style— with no attempt to finesse the differences into a single perspective.

Definitive interpretation of Ellington's "jungle" music is impossible, however. No doubt contemporary response varied, in part along lines driven by racial and class divisions and by differing cultural-political sympathies. One might nevertheless hear in Ellington's output from this period something of a passage between (to use the words of a contemporary critic) "stunts" on the one hand, and, on the other, "'effects' that are effects" (that is, which effect something "original and striking").[55] Even so, it is still possible to hear many recordings in more than one way, as they resist ideological closure. "Jungle Blues" (1930), for example, frames its growled solos with an introduction and coda which superimpose dissonant horn chords ("modernistic"?—or "comically braying"?) over a drone-like open fifth ("powerful"?—or "pointedly crude"?) in the rhythm section. "Jungle Nights in Harlem" (1930) collects together the usual growled trumpet solo, with stuttering ("pre-linguistic"?) repeated notes, extravagant screeches and swoops from Johnny Hodges's alto, and scale figurations from Barny Bigard's clarinet which might sound almost manic; background unison sax riffs outline the atmosphere, popular in jazz at the time, of melodramatic, minor-key foreboding, while Sonny Greer's continuous whiplash rim-shots could easily suggest barbaric ritual. The result, arguably, is an almost garish jungle evocation, delivered however with a gloss which distances the musicians from the message: "Man, look how terribly primitive we are!" they seem to say.[56]

There are other pieces, however, where, leaving the mask where it is, their gaze seems to swivel round, now pointing inward, into the new territory that the style makes available. "Echoes of the Jungle" (1931; credited to trumpeter Cootie Williams) draws on the same mixture of (basically simple) elements, but welds them into a richly elaborate variety of textures which capture the listener, pulling us into a quite new sound-world, functioning on its own terms. "Old Man Blues" (1930) pursues the same line of development, at faster tempo: pounding open fifths and talking muted-trumpet chords leave behind any purely "stunt"-like quality they might once have had, and now strike one as marks of cultural self-confidence.[57] This is a line that in one direction decisively colored Ellington's particular variant of 1930s big-band swing, and in another was to lead to his large-scale concert work of 1943, *Black, Brown and Beige,* "A Tone Parallel to the History of the Negro in America."[58] Nineteen years earlier, Paul Whiteman's famous Aeolian Hall concert, at which Gershwin's *Rhapsody in Blue* was premiered, had highlighted the assimilation of a tamed jazz to a middle-class white agenda (or, to put it in Whiteman's words, had signalled "that it was a great deal more than savage rhythm from the jungle"[59]). Ellington's badly received Carnegie Hall performance, criticized ever since for pretentiousness and formal incoherence, may on the contrary be taken to mark not any "jungle to concert hall" (minstrelsy to assimilationism) career move but an experiment whose indulgence of pluralism envisions a new world: a world conceived not as "populated by endangered authenticities—pure products always going crazy. Rather it makes space for specific [and diverse] paths through modernity."[60]

From 1926 to 1939 Ellington was managed by Irving Mills—a man who made his initial reputation in the music business, typically for of the 1920s, by buying "blues," *any* blues, from their composers, for flat $20 fees, and whose efforts as promoter, publisher, and agent certainly played a large part in Ellington's commercial success, particularly with white audiences, at the Cotton Club and more widely. Mills's other star performer was singer, bandleader, and showman extraordinaire Cab Calloway (who followed Ellington into the Cotton Club). Calloway's mixture of "scat" singing, "jive" lingo and "freak" instrumental effects, set in the context of pieces that conjured up a hepster's Harlem (complete with arcane references to weird characters and drug-filled lifestyles), might offer a clue to interpretation of Ellington's jungle style, on which Calloway drew. Both coupled an exotic appeal to captivated whites (probably engineered to a considerable extent by Mills) with a new and quite specific "path through modernity"—an urban-jungle subculturalism, rooted in black popular tastes but routed toward the hip, hybrid modernistic art of bebop.[61]

STRATEGIES OF SIGNIFYING

Henry Louis Gates identifies "Signifyin(g)"—continual reworking of a "changing same"—as the master-trope of black cultural practice.[62] Drawing on a distinction (and on terms) introduced by Houston Baker in his discussion of African American modernism and the Harlem Renaissance, we can identify two different yet overlapping strategies of Signifyin(g). On the one hand, *mastery of form* denotes the minstrelesque "liberating manipulation of masks," while on the other, *deformation of mastery*, by counterposing to the norms a knowingly alien discourse, performs an act of territorialization, an assertion of self which is "never simply a coming into being, but always, also, a release from a BEING POSSESSED."[63] As we have seen, both strategies would seem to be exemplified in Duke Ellington's music. Baker stresses that they are not mutually exclusive alternatives but continuously interacting possibilities, sliding between each other; and we can actually observe such a slide in one critic's response to Ellington's "Black and Tan Fantasy." Writing in 1932, R. D. Darrell recounts that "I laughed like everyone else over its instrumental wa-waing and garbling and gobbling. . . . But as I continued to play the record . . . I laughed less heartily and with less zest. In my ears the whinnies and wa-was began to resolve into new tone colors, distorted and tortured, but agonizingly expressive. The piece took on a surprising individuality . . . a twisted beauty that grew on me more and more and could not be shaken off."[64] As the music is heard as freeing itself from the demands of the mask, so Darrell, freed in turn from the burden of his controlling gaze, is able to accede to the *music's* demands, to *belong* to it.

Twentieth-century popular music has continued to be strung between the various discursive and ideological forces sketched in the previous two sections—drawn in particular between the pull of authenticity on the one hand and of legitimation on the other—while on occasion essaying momentary "deformations of mastery." Of course, white popular styles are (as was Gershwin) in a peculiarly complex position. Not only do they stand as other to the "high" cultural levels in our society, but they often act at the same time as the hegemonic self in relation to the other of black music.[65] African American culture has remained at the point of maximum sensitivity—"He who would enter the twenty-first century, must come by way of me," said James Baldwin[66]—but in recent decades, as the global economy and postcolonial politics have expanded the cast of characters available to the Western cultural drama, the category of "world music" has entered the field of debate as well. Nowhere have the effects been more dramatic than in South Africa.

Fueled by racial oppression and latterly by the structures of apartheid, minstrelsy has been a constant presence.[67] The very terms of discourse (civilization on the one hand, roots on the other) were set by the master-culture, and many of the available models came from European and U.S. (especially African American) sources. "Tribal" musics were easily linked with the "homeland" ideology. Apparently simple "township jazz" styles—jive, *kwela*—

could offer an image of colorful, dancing, happy-go-lucky blacks, show-cased also in musical shows like *Ipi Tombi* (1974). Working against this historical background, neotraditional musicians of the 1980s—*mbaqanga* star Mahlathini, *mbube* vocal group Ladysmith Black Mambazo, for example—inevitably faced the criticism that they were acceding to the projections constructed in white myths of black music (and the "ethnic" stations of the South African Broadcasting Corporation certainly had no difficulty in aligning them with their own "separate development" ideology). In both cases, however, there is also the possibility that Signifyin(g) on received elements was taking place. Ladysmith Black Mambazo, for instance, cooled the extravagant "bombing" style of *mbube* which they inherited (as if to say, look, we blacks may be reassuringly primitive but we can sing these ethnic riffs sweetly, and in tune!),[68] while Mahlathini set the call-and-response and growled vocals of rural Zulu tradition in an aggressive (electrified) township context (the jungle urbanized). Behind the mask, then, moves of "liberating manipulation" could perhaps be found.[69]

Assimilationism has an equally long history, in the hands both of whites and middle-class blacks (for example, the hymns and refined "ragtime" of Reuben Caluza[70]—or indeed, the anthem of the African National Congress, and now of the new South African state as well, "Nkosi Sikele iAfrica"). A revealing moment is represented by Paul Simon's 1986 album *Graceland*, which uses compositions, performers, and recordings with a variety of origins (American and South African—including Ladysmith Black Mambazo), mixing them together in New York. Many songs fuse aspects of different genres and styles. Yet, like Gershwin in *Porgy and Bess*, Simon clearly dominates, both musically and commercially (he takes the lion's share of royalties), cleaning up and interpreting his ethnic sources so that they support the visions of a white, middle-class American singer-songwriter. "The Boy in the Bubble" is representative, overdubbing an existing record by Tao Ea Matsekha in the driving, accordion-dominated *sheshwe* style with Simon's vocals and new guitar and synthesizer parts. The South African sound becomes a support for Simon's elliptical lyrics, and by the end it is swamped by the predominantly synthesized texture. Andrew Tracey complains that "Africa provides the rhythm section, the body of the pop music world, while Europe provides the melody, the head. . . . It is the Black man's job to help the White man do his thing. . . . Is African music only good for backings, not frontings?"[71] The fit Simon effects is powerful and imaginative, and certainly is a technological "miracle and wonder," as the lyrics have it; but, again as in *Porgy*, the limitations imposed by genre and by context (here economic as well as ideological) seem to me decisive, for, while "these are [indeed] the days of lasers in the jungle," the end result here is that the jungle is beamed back home, domesticated, to our New York loft.[72]

Example 1.3 John Knox Bokwe, "Ulo thix'o mkhulu" (The Great Hymn). Transcribed by Veit Erlmann from a recording by the Zwelitsha Choral Society of Kingwilliamstown, Cape Province, directed by S. T. Bokwe (the soloist), recorded by Hugh Tracey (International Library of African Music AMA TR-26, 1957).

The South African history, however, displays patterns of far more complex negotiation than the simple schema sketched above indicates.[73] Thus, for instance, John Knox Bokwe's "Great Hymn" (c. 1880), a cornerstone of early middle-class black nationalist culture, is already couching its Europeanized triads and simple triple meter in overlapping call-and-response textures and an alternating two-chord structure derived from Xhosa sources (example 1.3).[74] And a later variant, "Ilezwe Ngelethu," sung by trade union choirs in the 1980s, gives it a political rather than religious text and a vigorous, syncopated rhythm, carrying it clearly into "new territory."[75]

Such "deformations of mastery" have become more common in recent years: they can often be found, for example, in the work of pianist-composer Abdullah Ibrahim. In his *Soweto Is Where It's At*,[76] the basic material—a four-chord sequence repeated virtually unbroken for the whole twenty-minute

Example 1.4   Theme from Abdullah Ibrahim, *Soweto Is Where It's At* (*Tintinyana,*
Kaz LP 103, 1988 [track recorded 1975]). Transcription by author.

performance—could easily have become stereotypically other: the sequence, and its structural use in this way, derive from earlier black urban
styles (*marabi, kwela, mbube*) and before that from the use of pitch cycles in
rural South African musics; and "endless repetition" is endemic throughout the region. But the variety of textures used, the mixture of improvising
styles in the superimposed solos, and the jazz phrasings in the horn theme
and backings rule out any single, "authentic" cultural location. However,
the chord sequence (example 1.4) actually points, culturally, both ways:
while the I-IV-I$^6_4$-V^7 progression is a classic of South African popular styles,
it is also a classical music cliché—typically Mozartian (or, even more, Rossin-
ian). In that European context it functions as a cadence figure—a way of
signaling closure, exerting control. Indeed, Rossini uses it, as part of the
notorious "Rossini crescendo," to build a final climax, inciting his audience
to tumultuous applause. What happens in Ibrahim's piece, then, is that closure is rewritten as process, cadence as endless chain—an open-endedness
energized by rhythmic drive and constant rhythmic, melodic, and textural
shifts. The monologic gaze is rejected, perspective opened out. The people,
pictured by Rossini (according to some critics) as puppets, mindlessly clap-
ping at what they have been given, are refigured as a participating body—
a body politic.

The "double consciousness" implicit in Ibrahim's piece has been associated with the African American experience ever since W. E. B. Dubois wrote
about its quality of "second sight . . . this sense of always looking at oneself
through the eyes of others"; and Dubois already extended the idea to postcolonial peoples in general: it figures, for example, in Aimé Césaire's conception of *négritude*.[77] It may be characteristic of *all* others who become conscious of their position, and are enabled to open up the internal dialogics
inherent in their cultural miscegeny.[78] And such consciousness may be a
precondition of productive strategies of Signifyin(g) (or "answering back");
as Baker puts it, today "any conceivable global modernism . . . must be ar-

ticulated through Caliban's [Papageno's, Porgy's] expressive traditions—traditions that sing a joyful song on the far side of an acknowledgment of the fictional character of 'self' and 'other.' "[79]

In such strategies, the demands of meaning are inescapable. No retreat is available from the increasingly intense play of representations so characteristic of the cultural sphere under the conditions of modernity. Thus struggles over music's meaning—for particular discursive translations of musical signifiers—cannot but be fought. Yet there have been arguments that much of music's power stems from a capacity to slip the leash of these discursive mechanisms, engaging us on a less reflective level—a level that, elsewhere, I have conceptualized as one of "gesture."[80] It is possible that it is in this arena where the most radical attempts at "deformation of mastery" take place: where, for example, Abdullah Ibrahim's treatment of his four-chord sequence does not so much contest its meaning as redesign its implications for our sense of the body's location in time and space. The result is to produce a sense of a particular "gestural habitus"—a place where, as an embodied organism rather than a reflecting consciousness, one can *feel at home.*[81]

There is a danger here of reinstating romantic myths of immediacy. Yet such myths misrecognize a truth. If we conceive the gestural sphere not as that of some kind of mystical unmediated "presence" but as simply that of practical, as opposed to discursive, consciousness, we see that what the romantic theories get wrong is the structure of possession. While music can never belong to us (as myths of authenticity would wish), belonging *to* a music (making ourselves at home within its territory) is distinctly possible.[82] As we have seen, however, for low-others this sort of possession normally functions as a kind of tenancy, for they themselves are possessed—their home belongs to the master. Deformation makes possible strategies which, because they break down binaries, freeing the other to express his or her internal differences, also free the master-discourse to accept its own differences to itself (rather than projecting them outwards or assimilating them into false identity). Needless to say, this can never guarantee the new position against a further move of projection or assimilation. Short of utopia—or at least an end to gross social hierarchies—a permanent condition of negotiation represents the limit of the musical politics available to the low-other.

NOTES

1. Whatever faults might remain, this chapter owes a good deal to helpful comments made not only by the editors but also by Dave Laing and David Horn.

2. The usual historical image of the eighteenth century, which sees the rise of Viennese Classicism as signalling a move *away* from explicit meaningfulness into "pure form," is misleading. As Agawu has shown (*Playing with Signs* [Princeton: Princeton

University Press, 1991]), this music is ruled by an elaborate semiotics of musical "topics." Neither can nineteenth-century formalism be offered as a counterargument. Whether Kantian or Hanslichian, such formalism does not deny meaning, but is concerned just to distinguish external associations from what is taken to be the untranslatable significance of "the music itself."

3. See Paul Gilroy, *The Black Atlantic: Modernity and Double Consciousness* (London: Verso, 1993).

4. Friedrich Nietzsche, *Human, All Too Human*, trans. R. J. Hollindale (Cambridge: Cambridge University Press, 1986), 99.

5. Jean-Jacques Rousseau, "On the Origin of Language" (extracts), in *Music and Aesthetics in the Eighteenth and Early-Nineteenth Centuries*, ed. Peter Le Huray and James Day (Cambridge: Cambridge University Press, 1981), 92, 105.

6. Summarized in the contributions by Alastair Williams and Christopher Norris to *Music and the Politics of Culture*, ed. Christopher Norris (London: Lawrence and Wishart, 1989).

7. Immanuel Kant, *The Critique of Judgement*, trans. James Creed Meredith (Oxford: Oxford University Press, 1952), 193, 194.

8. Lawrence Kramer, *Music as Cultural Practice 1800–1900* (Berkeley: University of California Press, 1991), 4.

9. There is an incisive critique of Hegel's theory of musical immediacy in Lucy Green, *Music on Deaf Ears* (Manchester: Manchester University Press, 1988), 12–16.

10. G. W. F. Hegel, *Lectures on the Philosophy of World History*, trans. H. B. Nisbet (Cambridge: Cambridge University Press, 1975), 173–90.

11. Friedrich Nietzsche, *The Birth of Tragedy*, trans. Francis Golffing (New York: Doubleday, 1956), 23.

12. See Ali Jihad Racy, "Historical Worldviews of Early Ethnomusicologists: An East-West Encounter in Cairo, 1932," in *Ethnomusicology and Modern Music History*, ed. Stephen Blum, Philip V. Bohlman, and Daniel M. Neuman (Urbana: University of Illinois Press, 1991), 68–91.

13. Vic Gammon has dissected the ideology behind this moment; see his "Folk Song Collecting in Sussex and Surrey, 1843–1914," *History Workshop Journal* 10 (1980): 61–89.

14. Herder quoted in Peter Burke, *Popular Culture in Early Modern Europe* (London: Temple Smith, 1978), 22.

15. Peter Stallybrass and Allon White, *The Politics and Poetics of Transgression* (London: Methuen, 1986).

16. Ibid., 193.

17. On the parallels constructed in the eighteenth-century bourgeois mind between these higher and lower groups, see ibid., chapter 2.

18. *Grundregeln zur Tonordnung insgemein* (1755).

19. For example, in Victorian Britain, Arthur Munby secretly married his servant Hannah Cullwick. She had to abase herself for his voyeuristic pleasure, black up and dress as a slave, but also take him on her knee like a child. See Stallybrass and White, *Politics and Poetics*, 151, 154–56. Only a few years after Mozart's operas were written, Hegel, in his celebrated and influential discourse on "masters and slaves," was laying out the terms with which the relationship between the self/other dialectic and the structure of bourgeois consciousness could be discussed; see *The Phenomenology*

80   RICHARD MIDDLETON

of Mind, trans. J. B. Baillie (New York: Harper and Row, 1967; first published 1807), chapter 4.

20. Kramer, *Music as Cultural Practice,* especially chapter 6; Susan McClary, "Pitches, Expression, Ideology: A Exercise in Mediation," *Enclitic* 7 (1983): 76–86, and "A Musical Dialectic from the Enlightenment: Mozart's *Piano Concerto in G Major, K.453,* Movement 2," *Cultural Critique* 4 (1986): 129–69.

21. For a feminist reading of *The Magic Flute,* see Catherine Clement, *Opera, or the Undoing of Women,* trans. Betsy Wing (Minneapolis: University of Minnesota Press, 1988), 70–76. Clement also remarks on the importance of class relationships in the opera but does not pursue the musical implications of this point.

22. Andreas Huyssen, "The Vamp and the Machine: Fritz Lang's *Metropolis,*" in *After the Great Divide* (Bloomington: University of Indiana Press, 1986), 65–81. Popular culture also became coded as feminine (passive, irrational, garrulous, repetitive, etc.) in the nineteenth century, creating a threefold system of equations: Machine–Woman–People. See Huyssen, "Mass Culture as Woman: Modernism's Other," in ibid., 44–62; Tania Modleski, "Femininity as Mas(s)querade: A Feminist Approach to Mass Culture," in *High Theory, Low Culture: Analysing Popular Television and Film,* ed. Colin McCabe (Manchester: Manchester University Press, 1986), 37–52.

23. Would it be far-fetched to think of this reinitiation into the symbolic order of language as invoking the Lacanian Law of the Father ("pa-pa")?

24. For example, in Theodor W. Adorno, *Introduction to the Sociology of Music,* trans. E. B. Ashton (New York: Seabury Press, 1976), 22.

25. On the black-low relationship, see e.g. Gilroy, *The Black Atlantic.*

26. E.g., in Neil Leonard, *Jazz and the White Americans: The Acceptance of a New Art Form* (Chicago: University of Chicago Press, 1962).

27. This view can be found in any of Adorno's writings on jazz; for a survey, see J. Bradford Robinson, "The Jazz Essays of Theodor Adorno: Some Thoughts on Jazz Reception in Weimar Germany," *Popular Music* 13 (1994): 1–25.

28. On the debates surrounding *Porgy and Bess,* see Richard Crawford, "It Ain't Necessarily Soul: Gershwin's 'Porgy and Bess' as a Symbol," *Yearbook of Inter-American Musical Research* (1972): 17–38; David Horn, "Who Loves You Porgy?" in *The American Musical in Context,* ed. Robert Lawson-Peebles (Exeter: University of Exeter Press, 1994), 109–26; David Horn, "From Catfish Row to Granby Street: Contesting Meaning in *Porgy and Bess,*" *Popular Music* 13 (1994): 165–74.

29. Horn, "Who Loves You Porgy?"

30. Wilfrid Mellers, *Music in a New Found Land: Themes and Developments in the History of American Music* (London: Barrie and Rockcliff, 1964), 412. On leitmotif technique in *Porgy,* see Lawrence Starr, "Toward a Re-evaluation of Gershwin's 'Porgy and Bess,'" *American Music* 2, no. 2 (1984): 25–37.

31. Leonard, *Jazz,* 84; Blesh, quoted in Crawford, "It Ain't Necessarily Soul," 33. Emphasis in original.

32. Gershwin, quoted in Crawford, "It Ain't Necessarily Soul," 26; in Hollis Alpert, *The Life and Times of Porgy and Bess: The Story of an American Classic* (London: Nick Hern Books, 1990), 81; and in Leonard, *Jazz,* 84. Amusingly, just as Gershwin arguably condescends to his musical sources, so some of the critics condescended to him. A series of displacements is set up as Virgil Thomson describes *Porgy's* "freshness . . .

the hall-mark of *les grandes natures*. . . . I like its lack of respectability, the way it can be popular and vulgar. . . . He didn't know much . . . but his musical heart was really pure." (Quoted in Crawford, "It Ain't Necessarily Soul," 25–26.)

33. Mellers, *Music in a New Found Land,* 393.

34. Quoted in Edward Jablonski, *Gershwin* (Garden City: Doubleday, 1987), 273. For an account of Gershwin's trip to South Carolina, see Alpert, *Life and Times,* 88–90.

35. Virgil Thomson, quoted in Crawford, "It Ain't Necessarily Soul," 30.

36. Ed Kirkeby documents this aspect of Gershwin's life; see the quotation from him in Samuel A. Floyd Jr., "Music in the Harlem Renaissance: An Overview," in *Black Music in the Harlem Renaissance: A Collection of Essays,* ed. Samuel A. Floyd Jr. (Westport, Conn.: Greenwood Press, 1990), 22. (Floyd also argues that "Summertime," from *Porgy and Bess,* is derived from the spiritual "Sometimes I Feel Like a Motherless Child"; see Floyd, "Troping the Blues: From Spirituals to Concert Hall," *Black Music Research Journal* 13, no. 1 [1993]: 31–51.) Gershwin was also apparently present at the notorious party given by white author, socialite, and black culture propagandist Carl Van Vechten at which blues singer Bessie Smith performed: see Chris Albertson, *Bessie* (London: Barrie and Jenkins, 1972), 139–45; Nat Shapiro and Nat Hentoff, *Hear Me Talkin' to Ya* (Harmondsworth: Penguin, 1962), 241–42.

37. Lewis A. Erenberg, *Steppin' Out: New York Nightlife and the Transformation of American Culture 1890–1930* (Westport, Conn.: Greenwood Press, 1981) explores the broader context admirably. On white slumming in Harlem, see also Leonard, *Jazz;* Nathan I. Huggins, *Harlem Renaissance* (New York: Oxford University Press, 1971); Gilbert Osofsky, *Harlem: The Making of a Ghetto* (New York: Harper and Row, 1968).

38. Huggins, *Harlem Renaissance,* 89; McKay quoted in Osofsky, *Harlem,* 184; James Weldon Johnson, *Along This Way* (New York: Viking Press, 1968), 328; Rudolph Fisher, "The Caucasian Storms Harlem," *American Mercury* 11 (1927): 398.

39. Lena Horne, quoted in Jim Haskins, *The Cotton Club* (New York: Random House, 1977), 132. Haskins's book has a good feel for the Cotton Club primitivism, as well as giving details of the musical policy and repertory.

40. Quoted in Mark Tucker, "The Genesis of *Black, Brown and Beige,"* *Black Music Research Journal* 13, no. 2 (1993): 71. A much-quoted description of a typical Cotton Club "jungle sketch" can be found in Marshall Stearns, *The Story of Jazz,* rev. ed. (New York: Oxford University Press, 1970), 183–84.

41. A phrase used in a 1935 interview with Ellington, carried in *New Theatre* magazine; see Mark Tucker, *The Duke Ellington Reader* (New York: Oxford University Press, 1993), 114–17. There is some question about the credibility of this interview; Ellington certainly objected to the appearance of some of the phrases attributed to him. However, there seems no doubt that he did criticize *Porgy and Bess,* nor that his grounds were that it exploited and stereotyped rather than genuinely represented "Negro music."

42. See Floyd, "Music in the Harlem Renaissance"; Haskins, *The Cotton Club,* 21. The Harlem Renaissance was a movement of African American artists and intellectuals in the 1920s.

43. Mark Tucker, *Ellington: The Early Years* (Urbana: University of Illinois Press, 1991), 3.

44. Quoted in Mark Tucker, "The Renaissance Education of Duke Ellington," in *Black Music in the Harlem Renaissance*, ed. Samuel A. Floyd Jr. (Westport, Conn.: Greenwood Press, 1990), 122.

45. On Ellington's upbringing and its cultural context, see Tucker, "The Renaissance Education," and Tucker, *Ellington: The Early Years*.

46. Similarly, many Renaissance intellectuals saw black folk music as raw material for the production of high art. See Floyd, "Music in the Harlem Renaissance," 1–9.

47. The phrase comes from Houston Baker Jr., *Modernism and the Harlem Renaissance* (Chicago: University of Chicago Press, 1987). Interestingly, black history was a central object of study in the Washington schools of Ellington's boyhood. Also shows (theatrical and musical) with a "jungle to Harlem" theme were common in the 1920s; several were staged at the Cotton Club. See Tucker, *Ellington: The Early Years*, 69–72. Of course, *Porgy and Bess* has a kind of "jungle to New York" story too—though here New York represents not a relocated jungle but *escape*. The contrast is instructive.

48. Almost any book by or about Ellington casts light on his working methods, but Shapiro and Hentoff, *Hear Me*, 222, and Tucker, *The Duke Ellington Reader*, 96–102, are especially revealing.

49. The best discussion is Gunther Schuller's in *Early Jazz* (New York: Oxford University Press, 1968), 318–57, esp. 339ff. But even he stresses most of all the Cotton Club's role in Ellington's career: "The need for new background music for constantly changing acts . . . *required* Ellington to investigate composition (rather than arranging) as a medium of expression" (340). Schuller, a "schooled" composer himself, is wanting to push Ellington toward an ideology of compositional integration.

50. "Painting a picture, or having a story to go with what you were going to play, was of vital importance": Duke Ellington, *Music Is My Mistress* (London: Quartet Books, 1973), 47. On his pictorialism, see also Tucker, *Ellington: The Early Years*, 231–37.

51. Duke Ellington, "Japanese Dream" and "Arabian Lover," *The Works of Duke*, vol. 3 (RCA 741 029); "Diga-Diga-Doo," *The Works of Duke*, vol. 2 (RCA 741 028).

52. As early as 1924 ("Choo Choo"). Duke's use of the minstrelsy mask also predates the Cotton Club: see Tucker's discussion (*Duke Ellington: The Early Years*, 122–23) of his 1925 song "Jim Dandy (A Strut Dance)."

53. Ellington, quoted in Shapiro and Hentoff, *Hear Me*, 228; and in Haskins, *The Cotton Club*, 53. Interviews with the young Ellington and reviews of his work, reprinted in Tucker, *The Duke Ellington Reader*, confirm the impression of a man who identified his ambition of developing a serious black music with the cultivation of black historical difference; he "believe[s] that in the heart of the Africa a man can travel into today there lies a great secret of music" (1930; quoted in ibid., 43).

54. Duke Ellington, "Black and Tan Fantasy," *The Works of Duke*, vol. 1 (RCA 731 043).

55. The critic was R. G. Darrell, reprinted in Tucker, *The Duke Ellington Reader*, 34.

56. Duke Ellington, "Jungle Blues," *The Complete Duke Ellington*, vol. 3 (CBS 88000); "Jungle Nights in Harlem," *The Works of Duke*, vol. 4 (RCA 741 039).

57. Duke Ellington, "Echoes of the Jungle," *The Works of Duke*, vol. 6 (RCA 741 068); "Old Man Blues," *The Works of Duke*, vol. 5 (RCA 741 048).

58. Duke Ellington, *Black, Brown and Beige* (live recording of first performance, Prestige P-34004).

59. Whiteman speaking about *Rhapsody in Blue*, quoted in Leonard, *Jazz*, 80. Leonard is good on the significance of the concert, and so is Crawford ("It Ain't Necessarily Soul," 19).

60. James Clifford, *The Predicament of Culture: Twentieth-Century Ethnography, Literature, and Art* (Cambridge, Mass.: Harvard University Press, 1988), 5. For the reception of *Black, Brown and Beige*, see Tucker, *The Duke Ellington Reader*, 153–204; *Black Music Research Journal* 13, no. 2 (1993).

61. On Calloway's "popular modernism," see Gunther Schuller, *The Swing Era* (New York: Oxford University Press, 1989), 326–50. From 1939 to 1941 the young bebop pioneer-to-be, Dizzy Gillespie, played with (and wrote for) the Calloway Band. At the core of bebop, of Ellington's "jungle" style, and of a great deal of hot Harlem jazz of the 1930s, including Calloway's, was blues; and it is worth noting Ellington's 1930 declaration on the subject: "The Negro is the blues. Blues is the rage in popular music. And popular music is the good music of tomorrow." (Quoted in Tucker, *The Duke Ellington Reader*, 45.)

62. Henry Louis Gates, *The Signifying Monkey: A Theory of African-American Literary Criticism* (New York: Oxford University Press, 1988). "The absent *g* is a figure for the Signifyin(g) black difference" (46).

63. Baker, *Modernism*, 25, 56, and passim.

64. In *disques*, June 1932, reprinted in Tucker, *The Duke Ellington Reader*, 58. We can follow the evolution of Darrell's Ellington criticism between 1927 and 1931, in extracts included in ibid. 33–40 (from which I quoted earlier).

65. Usually these complexities are implicit and have to be teased out, but occasionally they are more obvious—as in the case of the British house/hip-hop offshoot called "jungle"; practiced and enjoyed by both blacks and whites, this style displays allusions to itself as a primitive other in lyrics and in discourse about the music, and it has become an object of debate in questions of racial musical politics.

66. In a Sunday afternoon church performance! Quoted in Baker, *Modernism*, 61. There is further complexity here, however. Baldwin's blasphemous aphorism certainly catches the centrality of the African American experience for postcolonial modernity; but on another level it perhaps also points towards the way in which African American music has been assimilated into the hegemonic global designs of the U.S. music industry. "Double consciousness" indeed!

67. American minstrel troupes visited South Africa as early as the 1850s. See Veit Erlmann, *African Stars: Studies in Black South African Performance* (Chicago: University of Chicago Press, 1991), 21–53. African American influences remained crucial.

68. See Veit Erlmann, "Conversation with Joseph Shabalala of Ladysmith Black Mambazo," *World of Music* 31, no. 1 (1989): 31–58.

69. For one earlier example of creative manipulation of the mask, see Erlmann's discussion of the development of the Zulu *ingoma* dance: Veit Erlmann, "'Horses in the Race Course': The Domestication of Ingoma Dancing in South Africa 1929–39," *Popular Music* 8 (1989): 259–73. Rich documentation of complex responses to received models, stereotypes, and pressures can be found in Christopher Ballantine,

84   RICHARD MIDDLETON

"Concert and Dance: The Foundations of Black Jazz in South Africa Between the Twenties and the Early Forties," *Popular Music* 10 (1991): 121–45.

70. See Erlmann, *African Stars,* 112–55.

71. Andrew Tracey, "A Word from the Editor," *African Music* 6, no. 4 (1987): 3.

72. Louise Meintjes argues persuasively ("Paul Simon's *Graceland,* South Africa, and the Mediation of Musical Meaning," *Ethnomusicology* 34, no. 1 [1990]: 37–74) that *Graceland* is open to a variety of readings, relating to a variety of political positions. No doubt *Porgy and Bess* and *The Magic Flute* are open to varied readings too, and we saw how difficult it is to provide definitive interpretations of the politics of Duke Ellington's music. Here, though, the question of *dominant* readings becomes inescapable, assuming that the dimension of power is to be taken at all seriously.

73. In addition to the works cited in notes 67 and 69, see David Coplan, *In Township Tonight! South Africa's Black City Music and Theatre* (Johannesburg: Ravan Press, 1985); Richard Middleton, "The Politics of Cultural Expression: African Musics and the World Market," in *Poverty and Development in the 1990s,* ed. Tim Allen and Alan Thomas (Oxford: Oxford University Press, 1992), 362–78.

74. The "Great Hymn" had been derived from an earlier, probably very *un*-European piece by the early Christian Xhosa convert Nkitsana Gaba. See Veit Erlmann, "Black Political Song in South Africa—Some Research Perspectives," in *Popular Music Perspectives 2,* ed. David Horn (Gothenburg, Sweden: IASPM, 1985), 187–209. Richard Middleton and the editors would like to thank Veit Erlmann for permission to reproduce this transcription from his "Black Political Song in South Africa—Some Research Perspectives," in *Popular Music Perspectives 2,* ed. David Horn (Gothenberg: International Association for the Study of Popular Music, 1985), 203.

75. Braitex Workers, "Ilezwe Ngelethu," *South African Trade Union Worker Choirs* (Rounder 5020, 1986).

76. Abdullah Ibrahim, *Soweto Is Where It's At,* on *Tintinyana* (Kaz LP 103, 1988).

77. W. E. B. Dubois, *The Souls of Black Folk* (Chicago: McClurg, 1903), 3. On Césaire's *négritude,* see Clifford, *The Predicament of Culture,* 6. On "double consciousness," see also Gilroy, *The Black Atlantic.*

78. The implications of this for white Western popular music history have hardly been investigated, let alone theorized. It is worth noting that Baker, in principle, does not limit Signifyin(g) to African and Afro-diasporic cultures.

79. Baker, *Modernism,* 61. For a similar view, see Huggins, *Harlem Renaissance,* 244–45.

80. Some arguments of this kind are summarized in Richard Middleton, *Studying Popular Music* (Buckingham: Open University Press, 1990), 239–44, 261–67. For "gesture" see Richard Middleton, "Popular Music Analysis and Musicology: Bridging the Gap," *Popular Music* 12 (1993): 175–90.

81. The concept of "habitus" and the idea of a practice-based "disposition" come from Pierre Bourdieu, *Outline of a Theory of Practice* (Cambridge: Cambridge University Press, 1977).

82. In the sleeve notes to *Buena Vista Social Club,* an album of Cuban music he produced (World Circuit WCD050, 1997), Ry Cooder puts this beautifully; this music, he writes, "takes care of you and rebuilds you from the inside out." Cooder's

participation in the performances, captivated yet modest and supportive, may be fruitfully compared with Paul Simon's role in *Graceland:* the intricately variegated styles of this Caribbean/Spanish/African/American hybrid music culture survive intact, both "very refined and deeply funky" (as Cooder says), "different" yet also "modern."

CHAPTER 7

Work-in(g)-Practice: Configurations of the Popular Music Intertext

There is scope for debate over the exact historical period when the concept of the musical work was established, still more over the moment when musicians started to produce works, but we shall surely agree on the central defining characteristics of this category: a work, as Lydia Goehr puts it, is 'a complex structure of sounds related in some important way to a composer, a score, and a given class of performances'.[1] There is a suspicion that this type of musical production is peculiar, at least in its origins, to that system, with all its associated social, aesthetic and discursive apparatuses, which Leo Treitler has termed the WECT: the West European Classical Tradition.[2] (Acronyms can serve the reificatory function, useful on occasions, of displaying the object for the fascinated scrutiny characteristic of the museum visitor.) As the authority of this system apparently implodes in the late twentieth century – at the same time, ironically, as it completes its dissemination to the last corner of the globe – it seems natural to question the sustainability of the work-concept. The contemporaneous rise in prominence of pop music provides a particular and pressing context for this question, since popular music, as Goehr points out, seems generally to be uncomfortable with 'work' thinking. It is not surprising, then, that a key theme in popular music studies since its beginnings some thirty years ago has been a concern to place a politics of pop **practice** in opposition to the apparently quasi-religious inventory of iconic classical **objects**.

The pop critique, explicit in much of the scholarship, implicit

---

1. Lydia Goehr, *The Imaginary Museum of Musical Works: An Essay in the Philosophy of Music*, Oxford, Clarendon Press, 1992, p. 20.
2. Leo Treitler, 'Towards a Desegregated Music Historiography', *Black Music Research Journal*, V.l. 16 (1996), pp. 3–10.

(arguably) in the music, is three-pronged. Popular music pieces can only rarely and in heavily qualified ways be attributed to a single author: a composer. More commonly, their production is a collaborative process, which may involve lyricists, songwriters, singers, instrumentalists, arrangers, orchestrators, producers, engineers, set designers, video directors and more. Transmission of these pieces between musicians is as much – and often more – through aural and oral channels as it is through scores; notation is rare today, and even when used is, and has been, generally no more than a sketch, an outline, a starting-point, or else an attempt to approximate what has already been achieved, in performance or recording studio, through non-literate methods. There is little sense, finally, that performances going under the same title make up a distinct class of events related in a consistent way to a pre-existing ideal form; rather, they comprise a potentially infinite series of events, related through family resemblances, which may move variable distances from siblings and from any notated 'parent'. Moreover, the extensive use in popular music of **borrowing** – the importance of 'tune families', the reliance on common-stock models, formulae, grooves and riffs, the privileging of variation over originality – compound this effect, which amounts to a thorough blurring (or non-recognition) of the boundary between 'performance' and 'composition'. Even when, in the nineteenth century, an older focus on public domain material began to give way to the publication of newly produced sheet music, identified and protected in due course by copyright legislation, songs were identified as often as not with their most celebrated performers rather than with their composers; if *Champagne Charlie* 'belonged' to anyone, it was to singer George Leybourne, not its writer, Alfred Lee. With the coming of records, this order of priorities could assume more luxuriant expression, the resulting proliferation of song versions acquiring the term 'covers'. In the second half of the twentieth century, the centrality to song dissemination and identity of the 'star quality' of performers *qua* performers renders ever more porous the boundaries around the singular work. At the same time, the radical changes to a song that can result from performance in different contexts – concert, club, disco, drive-time radio with talkover DJ, supermarket muzak – point in a similar direction.

From a historical point of view, the fact that this difference between vernacular music and the WECT could emerge so strongly is not too surprising. Just at the time, around 1800, when 'popular music' as we understand it was emerging as a distinct category so, too, were developing all the ideological and institutional accoutrements of the work-concept: the autonomy aesthetic, the 'serious' listener, the canon, music academies, 'great man' music history, and so on. Popular music, defined with a new intensity as 'different' – in fact, as 'low' and 'trivial' – could to a large extent continue to operate differently precisely because of this placing in the hierarchy. Pop was saved from complete assimilation to work-thinking by its vulgarity.[3]

The best umbrella term for the popular music practices I have been describing is probably **intertextuality**. A key feature of intertextuality (a rather modish term since the heyday of post-structuralists such as Julia Kristeva) – the idea that all texts make sense only through their relationships, explicit or implicit, with other texts – can be found earlier in the century, in theories as diverse as Peirce's 'infinite semiosis' and Bakhtin's 'dialogics' (to which I shall return). Indeed, this notion can no doubt be traced back still further (all theories of borrowing, parody, quotation, allusion, glossing, punning, etc. are germane), just as intertextual types of practice are rampant even in pre-1800 European art music (as Goehr points out). 'Intertextuality' is a good term for our purposes because it can cover such a range of techniques, requiring only that a text refer to other texts; but in exactly this respect, of course, it pushes against the tendential self-sufficiency of 'works'.

The popularity of post-structuralist perspectives, including the much-trumpeted 'death of the author', fed a loudly celebratory strand in cultural theorising, keen to trample on the élitist claims of art-objects in the interests of a supposedly postmodern politics of difference. And this theoretical move coincided with what appeared to be a significant shift in the practice. The dethroning of modernism, the rise of 'pop culture', and a quantum leap in the mass reproduction of the classics all pulled at the terms of the debate. The end of 'aura', foreseen by Walter Benjamin, was welcomed in the name of Baudrillard's 'simulacra' – copies without an original. Right across the culture, but particularly clearly in the sphere of music, there was a distinct technological factor to this shift. Digital technology – easily controlled sound-synthesis and signal processing, samplers and computer-controlled mixing equipment – offered a radically new

---

3. For the *vulgus*, it might be said, is 'common' (in more than one sense) rather than individualistic.

compositional setting, one that seemed to signal that works were now always works-in-progress, and that music was just material for reuse. Particularly in the sphere of electro-dance music, the ubiquity of sampling and multiple mixes appeared to some to go so far as to threaten the legal status of musical works and the identifiability of their producers – a development which, for many activists and left-leaning theorists, was entirely to be celebrated.[4]

Into the Mix

Remix culture, then, is seen by some iconoclasts as the final nail in the coffin of work-thinking. As critic Richard Williams puts it:

> One thing that seems to have disappeared from popular music in the last few years is the idea of a unanimously approved masterpiece, the single fully achieved and inviolable piece of work which achieves the status of a classic text. Re-mix culture more or less did away with it, with some help from new playback formats and the availability of such a vast quantity of music that the notion of consensus began to seem futile. In exchange we get the new idea of music as a continuing process, permanently open to radical revision. In the future, perhaps, all music will be effectively 'unfinished'; and the idea of authorial attribution may become as obsolete as the 32-bar Broadway ballad.[5]

Williams is discussing two CDs by the American bass-guitarist and producer, Bill Laswell, the first a 'reconstruction and mix translation' of pieces by jazz trumpeter Miles Davis, the second a set of 'ambient translations' of songs by reggae singer Bob Marley.[6] In both cases, Laswell (quoted by Williams as believing that 'tape memory has replaced composition')[7] got hold of the original master tapes and used them to produce new music which, in the range of its reconstructive

---

4. The best exploration of the implications of digital technology for musical practice and thought is Paul Théberge, *Any Sound You Can Imagine: Making Music/Consuming Technology*, Hanover, Wesleyan University Press, 1997.
5. Richard Williams, 'Fixing It in the Mix', *The Guardian*, 23 January 1998, G2 section, pp. 16–17, at p. 16. (In the year that saw Tony Bennett headlining at the Glastonbury Festival, the idea that the Broadway ballad is obsolete might be thought somewhat tendentious!)
6. Bill Laswell, 'Panthalassa: The Music of Miles Davis 1969–1974', Columbia CK 67909 (1998); Bill Laswell, 'Bob Marley Dreams of Freedom', Island 524 419-2 (1997).
7. Williams (1998), p. 16.

practices, casts fascinating light on the status of the work-concept at the end of the twentieth century.

There is a poignancy in choosing Davis for a remix project, for, having previously created instantly sanctified masterpieces for the emergent jazz canon, the great trumpet soloist found his late sixties and early seventies recordings (the ones that Laswell uses) attacked by jazz aestheticists for withdrawing from the challenges of authorial responsibility and retreating behind the open-ended anonymous vulgarities of funk-rock groove. Apparently, Davis showed little interest in what appeared on the albums. The dominant rôle in the mixing, choice of takes and formatting of the LPs was that of producer Ted Macero, and large quantities of material were left unused. Davis, despite his notorious prickliness over his own creative status, was already challenging the masterpiece aesthetic.

His 'In a Silent Way' LP tailors its form to the album format.[8] The first side is devoted to a single piece, *Shhh/Peaceful*, although at the end its hypnotic tonic-chord groove simply fades out: the performance could evidently have been prolonged indefinitely. Side 2, by contrast, encases a lengthy funk-styled improvisation, with solos for guitar, trumpet and tenor sax (*It's About that Time*), between two statements of *In a Silent Way*, a much slower, lyrical theme in unmeasured rhythm: a conventional ABA structure, then, though apparently rather arbitrary in its conjunctions of material. Two compositional modes are evident, both of which avoid the jazz conventions of periodic structure: the first consists of simple, 'out of time' thematic statement (*In a Silent Way*), the second of open-ended modal improvising over drones and riffs (*Shhh/Peaceful* and *It's About that Time*).

Initially, the most striking features of Laswell's reworking lie in the sphere of sound. Digital technology enables him to separate out the various instrumental parts with marvellous clarity, bringing many of them further up in the mix, but without cluttering the texture. Overall, the sound becomes much 'fuller', with much greater 'depth' (soloists right in the listener's face, for example). Sound quality is altered, too. In line with changing aesthetic norms, drums and (especially) bass become more prominent, altering the focus of the texture and, through the use of prolonged sustain on the bass, increasing the force of the drones. The guitar becomes more plangent, often with

8. CD reissue: Miles Davis, 'In a Silent Way', CBS 450982 2 (originally issued in 1969).

heavy reverb. Electric piano and organ sounds are filtered and 'eq-ed' to alter their timbres (and may also be sampled and modified to produce 'new' sounds). A good example of how such processes can change the whole effect can be found in the initial trumpet statement of the *In a Silent Way* theme. Davis's trumpet (with added digital delay) becomes much 'larger', more 'outdoors', its original halting breathiness expunged in favour of something more 'panoramic'. Similarly, the delicate filigree accompaniment is boosted into more enveloping washes of sound, while the continuous deep bass drone resonates around the listener's body. Here, and throughout, Laswell's soundscapes could not have been imagined before the experience of ambient music, electro-funk and dub.

At least as interesting, though, is what Laswell does to the form (see Tables 2 and 3). He makes one coherently organised piece, tightly cut from 38 to just over 15 minutes, out of what had been two (or possibly three). The sections are reordered, so that *In a Silent Way* (B) opens and closes the piece, and Laswell drastically shortens both *Shhh/Peaceful* (A) and *It's About that Time* (C) – by contrast, B acquires a new introduction and a new codetta – so that the balance of material is altered. By drawing on the pauses in Davis's A, extending them and adding to them from elsewhere, he creates links between sections that help to produce an effect of seamless flow. Naturally, Davis's sequence of tonal centres gets changed as well, from D-E-F-E (with modal implications) to E-D-E-F-E (still modal, but now beginning and ending on the same tonic, and, because of the adjustment of section lengths, laying much more stress on E). Moreover, Laswell uses the 'modulations' in subtle ways, shifting from E to F and then back from F to E through passages of bitonality; there is a particularly beautiful effect in the course of the latter when a trumpet A flat in F-oriented material from Section C (over a bass drone E) is then treated as a G sharp in the *In a Silent Way* tune (over the same bass drone).

Overall, Laswell exposes the family resemblances between the various materials and makes them live together; at the same time, he makes the performer Davis much more dominant (most of the guitar and sax solos are cut), and it is a particular Davis: the elegiac, lyrical soloist (he is excised from the funky Section C, which in any case is drastically shortened; note also that the first bass riff in this section, which in the original gives it much of its funk character, is mixed so low as to be almost inaudible). But in showcasing Davis, making him

Table 2: Miles Davis *In a Silent Way*

Section	Time	Tonal Centre	Description
A	0.00	D	organ chords, el. pno tinkles, gtr noodles, A–D bass riff, hi-hat groove, all over D tonality
	1.30		pause
	1.35		resume + tpt solo (1.45)
	5.20		tpt out – 'background' groove only
	6.00		gtr solo
	9.15		tenor sax solo
	10.45		sax out – 'background' groove only
	11.55		pause
	12.00		resume – 'background' groove only
	13.25		pause
	13.30		resume + tpt solo
	17.15		tpt out – 'background' groove continues, to fade
B	0.00	E	bowed bass drone (E), gtr tune (x2), el. pno tinkles – unmeasured
	2.12		tpt repeats tune (x2), with similar backing
C	4.15	F	quicker, funk texture, snare drum 4 (or 8) to bar, bass riff I (♫ ♪), + tpt solo
	5.00		bass/drums continue, el. pno interlude with important chordal motif
	5.45		gtr solo over similar backing
	8.25		gtr out – bass riff II (jazz-rock style)
	9.15		bass riff I, tenor sax solo
	10.35		tenor solo continues, with bass riff II
	11.40		tpt solo, with bass riff I
	12.45		tpt solo continues, with bass riff II
	13.15		continuation, but with bigger drum part
	13.55		continues, but with bass riff I
	14.45		continues, but with bass riff II
	15.20		tpt out
	15.40		riff out
B	15.45	E	recap of B tune, on gtr (x2)
	17.50		tpt repeats tune (x2)
	20.00		end

Table 3: Miles Davis: *In a Silent Way/Shhh/Peaceful/It's About that Time*
(realised by Bill Laswell)

Section	Time	Tonal Centre	Description
B	0.00 1.15 3.20	E	bowed bass drone (E), with 'electronic' sounds gtr tune (x2) over bass drone, el. pno, 'sounds' tpt tune (x2) over similar backing (but plus guitar)
Link	5.20	E	new gtr solo, over bowed bass drone, followed by tpt solo over 'ambient' sounds
A	6.45	D	tpt solo, over A–D bass riff, organ chords, el. pno figures, hi-hat groove (7.00)
Link	10.05 10.20 10.40 10.55	?	pause on organ chords (+ el. pno tinkles) continues – but held bass E enters chordal el. pno motif from Section C enters, in F (still over bass E) bass E out
C	11.15 12.10	F	tenor sax solo, over snare 8-to-the-bar plus el. pno chords (plus bass riff I – but this almost inaudible) tenor solo continues, over bass riff II
Link	13.20 13.35	?	bass riff out, sax out – chordal el. pno motif (in F) tpt solo (from Section C), in F but over held bass E
B	14.15 15.20	E	tune on tpt (x1) end

if anything more of an *auteur* than he originally was, Laswell also thrusts himself forward. When an individual takes so much trouble to produce both a particular emotional effect and a coherent formal shape, we are surely tempted to think of him not only as a remixer but also as a **composer**. (At the same time, we are reminded of dance-club DJs, with their love of seamless segues and control of mood-flow.)

When Laswell turns to Bob Marley, his approach is in one sense the exact opposite, for one of his first decisions was to remove completely Marley's singing voice from the music. While Marley stamped the personality of a global superstar on what had previously been largely a collectively produced style (and Laswell's refusal to tamper with his voice might be read as a mark of untouchability), this move would seem to open the way to radical possibilities of restructuring. Moreover, reggae itself had always been a remix-sympathetic music, especially since the rise and influence of its 'dub' variant from the 1970s onwards; from this point of view, reggae was an obvious choice for a 'translation' project.[9] Yet Laswell prepared by immersing himself in Marley's biography and background, and, according to Williams, 'we are invited to use our imaginations, and to feel his spirit suffusing these carefully textured reconstructions'; if, then, the result is that Laswell 'makes the music sound more like itself', the question is raised again, as it is in the case of the Davis remixes, of exactly how this musical 'self' is being conceived and where it is located.[10]

Marley's original version of the soul-ballad *One Love (People Get Ready)* is dominated by his vocal.[11] The straightforward verse–chorus form, built on conventional triadic chord-sequences and a simple reggae groove from the rhythm section, would be nothing – it would seem – without it, even though there is an important rôle, too, for backing vocal harmonies, especially in the choruses. What Laswell does with this material is extraordinary. The instrumental timbres are comprehensively remodelled and the textures clarified, as we expect by now (for instance, the foregrounded piano of the original disappears); more striking, though, is the addition of great washes of electronic sound, including many wind, water and birdsong-like noises. In effect, Laswell has invented a new genre – 'ambient-gospel' – since

9. Dub, beginning in the late 1960s with the work of such artists as King Tubby and Lee 'Scratch' Perry, is a form of reggae in which vocal (and often other) solos are excised, leaving just the rhythm tracks. The dub version, often issued on the 'B' side of a record and usually subjected to remixing and electronic sound-processing, can be used just as dance music or as backing for MC 'talkover' and 'toasting' (improvisatory rapping).
10. Williams (1998), p. 17.
11. Both Marley tracks discussed here can be found on 'Exodus', Tuff Gong TGLCD 6 (originally issued in 1977).

the other side of his reconstruction is the spotlight that removing the lead vocal throws on the backing singers, whose gospel-styled harmonies are mixed right up and forward, and given structural centrality. The piece starts with ambient sounds, and the basic reggae groove gradually emerges from within this; at this point the texture is so thematically empty that we are expected, it would seem, to be referring to the original recording, to hear Marley's singing in our inner ears. As the 'backing' singers emerge and come to the front acoustically, their harmonies become the focus; and then their backing (the rhythm section) fades out, and we are left with an a cappella gospel hymn (this is what the backing harmonies were, latently, all along), surrounded by electronic ambient sounds, which fade out to conclude the piece.

By turning the texture inside out, Laswell has in one sense certainly discovered elements that were embryonically present and put them in the centre; and in doing that, he has reconnected the material to an older musical and religious tradition which had been important in its formation but which had been 'modernised', as gospel song was secularised into soul music. At the same time, this process shifts the original recording from its specific cultural setting, an African-American axis weighted towards black Jamaica, into a more 'global' one, with the ambient soundscapes in particular appearing to place this cultural tradition within 'modernity', and to connect the song's spiritual message (the 'one love' suffusing righteous human nature) with the image of a mediatised universal Nature.

Marley's *Exodus* is a longer and more loosely structured piece than his *One Love*. Quasi-improvised verses, of variable length, alternate with chanted choral refrains and with extended instrumental passages, telling the story of the long journey of the 'Jah people' (God's chosen people in the Rastafarian religion). But the music possesses a striking density. This applies both to texture (a clattering network of highly active voices – bass, drums, guitar, keyboard and horns – all positioned in a low-to-middle register) and to structure: once the groove is established, around a virtually unchanging A minor drone harmony, most change is small-scale, and there is a good deal of quasi-improvisatory riffing around a variety of similar figures, drawing on minor-pentatonic G-A-C-D-E scale-material). The style is very funky, an effect created especially by Marley's singing, wah-wah from guitar and keyboard, and driving, percussive horn parts similar to those employed by James Brown.

Losing Marley's vocal has a less dramatic impact than in the case of

One Love: so much more is going on, and in any case, it does not
carry much of a tune. But, as with *One Love*, Laswell seizes upon the
new prominence of the vocal group, extends the structural weight of
their refrains, and blows them up enormously in the texture. Their
voicing is widened, through octave doubling and mixing up the parallel harmonies (see Ex. 1), and they are given massive reverb and
echo. At the same time, the range of instrumental sounds is expanded
(for example, acoustic piano takes on an important role), the bass,
drums, guitar and keyboard lines are clarified (often with altered timbres), the entire middle of the texture is opened out, and the overall
range is extended upwards (through extra harmonics and the addition
of often high-register electronic sounds, not to mention the added
higher vocal parts). Laswell does not recompose the form in the obvious way seen in his work on Davis, but he does organise the essentially open-ended process through different means: Marley's
principle is largely thematic (via the verse/chorus alternation), but,
deprived of this possibility, Laswell relies more on changes in dynamic
level and in texture (for instance, several times the bass drops out and
then returns).

As with *One Love*, Laswell's *Exodus* seems to be removed, at least
in part, from its previous specific cultural space. It is noticeable that
the funky horns do not feature until near the end, and the blown-up
vocal chants leave behind the personal inflections typical of soul
singing to become the voice of a choral collective. The dramatic,
'wide-screen' textures suggest, once again, a more global vision, and
the ambient sounds are those of electronic modernity. Guitar lines

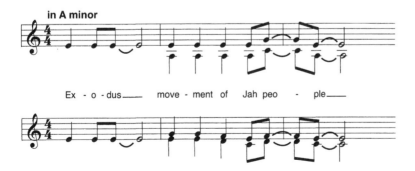

Example 1   For each continuation, the upper part gives Marley's lead voice, while
the lower part shows some of the harmonies made more prominent in Laswell's
version.

often have the larger-than-life 'twanginess' found in the soundtracks of Hollywood Westerns, and a particular keyboard phrase (Ex. 2) half-buried in Marley's recording but foregrounded in piano octaves by Laswell suggests the same provenance; we realise at this point that the minor-pentatonic melodic material of the piece is congruent with this particular movie sound-world, and cannot help wondering if, perhaps, Laswell has a Hollywood 'Exodus' in his mind.

Example 2

    The shift from cultural specificity to a more panoramic vision can, once again, be justified in terms of pointers in Marley's own music (emphasising groove and chant might be seen as a neo-Africanist move with which he would probably have sympathised, and the potential is readily available in his own *Exodus*); and there is, perhaps, a strange logic (albeit containing an ethnic inversion) to a link between reggae Rastafarianism and the black-and-white morality of the American Western. At the same time, Laswell's route to this achievement is surely stamped through-and-through with the mark of a quite personal perspective, an imagined world that is equally specific both to him and to a late-twentieth-century, globally-construed moment. Whose is the music, then?

    Laswell has (according to Williams) deliberately chosen music to work on from 'the beginning of the era that came after' the age of masterworks, 'the beginning of the language that we're speaking now'. For Williams, he has 'helped us towards an understanding of that new language's grammar and syntax'.[12] Yet categorising these recordings by Laswell does not seem to be quite this easy, as we have seen. How might they be classified? At times, when the relationship to the original is close, they feel quite like covers – or remixes. At other times, when the connection is less tight, the more flexible Jamaican music term 'version' seems more suitable. Sometimes, we are reminded more of categories familiar to us from Western art music history: the 'arrangement', the 'transcription', the 'parody'

12. Williams (1998), p. 17.

(which, in its fifteenth- and sixteenth-century version, seems technically not too far removed from Laswell's approach), or even the 'fantasia on a theme'. Are we in new times, or old? Is there an author in this work-house, and if so, who is it?

A fairly cursory survey suggests that record shops are filing Laswell's CDs not under his name but those of Davis and Marley; and, indeed, on the CD sleeves Laswell's name is presented in tastefully smaller type than theirs. On both recordings, however, he credits (as is common) a range of engineers and production assistants. To this he adds, on 'Dreams of Freedom', thanks to the Marley family, to The Wailers (Bob's original band), to other musicians who participated in the original recordings, and to three more who contributed new material for the remix (though not for the tracks discussed in this paper), not to mention Chris Blackwell (of Island Records) for 'creative direction and concept'; on 'Panthalassa', again, all the musicians from the original Davis recordings are listed. On both, also, the composers of the original pieces are credited – mostly Davis or Marley, but including, for example, keyboardist Joe Zawinul for *In a Silent Way*, and various others for some of the Marley tracks. Consulting CD reissues of the original albums, we find that producer Ted Macero's name features on 'In a Silent Way' as well; and production on 'Exodus' is credited to 'Bob Marley and the Wailers'. There is an extra intertextual interest concerning *One Love (People Get Ready)* in that composition is credited jointly to Bob Marley and African-American soul singer Curtis Mayfield, who, indeed, wrote a song called *People Get Ready*, which was a hit for his group, The Impressions, in 1965. It turns out that the verses of Marley's song function as a very loose cover of Mayfield's tune: Marley uses freely varied but recognisable versions of Mayfield's melody and its repeating three-chord harmonic progression, but with completely different lyrics (at the same time, there is certainly a thematic allusion to Mayfield's 'people get ready' sentiment).

Signs of Practice

It is too easy, then, to present the relationship between contemporary popular music and the work-concept in black and white, and over-radical, terms. My argument, in fact, is that (i) today's intertextual practices are to some extent the latest chapter in an old story, and are thoroughly embedded in long-lasting vernacular habits; and (ii) at the same time, their relationship with work thinking and its musical habitat is not one that can be defined in terms of a pure opposition: rather, the musical world we have to deal with here is singular, albeit one whose structure is warrened with ever-mutating networks of variants and divergences.

Some aspects of typical popular music compositional practices have already been described, but the ramifications of intertextuality can be pursued deeper into the textures and processes of vernacular forms. I have written elsewhere about the importance and nature of repetition in popular music.[13] Although repetition as such is plainly a privileged semiotic marker for music, as compared with other semiotic systems, it seems clear that iterative processes – repeating tunes, phrases, sections, rhythmic patterns, riffs, chord-sequences – are especially favoured in most sorts of popular music. Offering an element of the (so to speak) preformed, and standing over against the demands of painfully thought-through invention, such processes spurn the sort of uniqueness generally associated with 'works' (which is no doubt why, since Kant, music aestheticians have often been troubled by them). They generate the potential for infinitely extensible structures – a strophic song can have as many verses as can be made up, a West African 'timeline' or Cuban dance rhythm can be looped indefinitely, and a call-and-response dialogue can be repeated for as long as the musicians have stamina – and it is therefore no surprise to find recorded popular pieces often either ending at an arbitrary point or fading out, as if endless. Generative repetition can energise a repertory as well as an individual performance. If you can construct a song over a single riff, or a repeating 12-bar blues chord-sequence, then you can use the same riff or sequence to create a somewhat different song tomorrow; so can someone else. There is a seamless shift from this technique into the *maqam* principle on the one hand and the reproduction of standard generic formulae on the other. Within this whole range of contexts, repetition processes can be taken to signal the imprimatur of the collective, and point towards the anonymity not of 'the masses' (as élitist cultural critique would have it) but that

13. Richard Middleton, *Studying Popular Music*, Milton Keynes, Open University Press, 1990, Ch. 7; id., 'Repeat Performance', in *Music on Show: Issues of Performance*, ed. Tarja Hautamäki and Helmi Järviluoma, Tampere, University of Tampere Department of Folk Tradition, 1998, pp. 209–13; id., '"Over and Over": Appunti verso una politica della ripetizione', *Musica/Realtà*, Vol. 55 (1998), pp. 135–50.

which comes from standing in the interstices of social and generational exchange.

It is this understanding of repetition which has been theorised by African-American literary scholars as 'Signifyin(g)'. Signifyin(g), as found right across African and Afro-diasporic culture, is defined as the continual paradigmatic transformation, inter- or intra-textual, of given material, the repetition and varying of stock elements, the aesthetic of a 'changing same' (to use a phrase invented by Amiri Baraka). In its musical forms – constant variation of common-ownership material, intertextual reference, building performance on known frameworks, structural models and standard tunes – Signifyin(g) looks askance at the goal-directed drive for coherence typical of the mainstream WECT culture. It is worth noting, however, that Signifyin(g) is not only different, it also Signifies on the mainstream culture, for example, on the standard processes of signifying, with their syntagmatic chains always searching for closure: 'the absent *g* is a figure for the Signifyin(g) black difference'.[14] So there is not only otherness but also relation. And we notice the extraordinary coincidence whereby the gradual transformation of the popular musics of the Western world through African-American influence, beginning in the early nineteenth century with American minstrelsy and the spiritual songs of the 'Second Awakening', takes place over exactly the same period as the newly regulative work-concept makes its bid for hegemony – and does so not only elsewhere in the musical system, but also in relation to popular genres (the nineteenth century is, after all, when large-scale publishing of notated popular music pieces, with identified composers, begins). The two historical forces dance on together, like positive and negative electrodes defining the dynamics of the musico-magnetic field.

A common feature of the African-American tradition, though not confined to it, is the sense that there is more than one 'voice' in the texture (call-and-response, lead voice varying underlying framework, etc.). By contrast (at least in the paradigm case), the performers of a **work** must bend themselves to 'the composer's voice' (to quote the

---

14. Henry Louis Gates, Jr, *The Signifying Monkey: A Theory of Afro-American Literary Criticism*, New York, Oxford University Press, 1988, p. 46. Similarly, the optionally present *g* in the title of this paper, 'Work-in(g)-practice', is a figure for the Signifyin(g) pop difference, which also marks my debt to, and Signifyin(g) upon, Gates's theory.

title of Edward Cone's book).[15] Even if, in a certain sense, polyphonic music in itself says 'we', as Adorno suggests, in the WECT tradition the parts are felt to be subsumed into a single controlling authorial vision. And, anyway, as genuine polyphony declines in importance in WECT music over the nineteenth century, the effect of this mono-logic authority, suppressing all threat of the mess that dialogue might introduce, grows ever heavier.[16] Call-and-response, with its built-in ambivalence over both textural focus and start/end point, is a key technique in African-American music, directing us outside the con-fines of monologic closure. The 'vocalised tone' often applied to instruments, giving them a definite persona, and the personalisation of instruments (the guitar as lover, for example), tend in a similar direction. Right across the range of popular genres, the sense of a net-work of complementary voices – guitar comments, horn riffs, backing singers, active bass-lines, drum fills – playing off the vocal lead, which itself may well be 'conversing' with the voices of previous performers of the song, not to mention those of composer, songwriter, arranger and producer, is palpable. Who is speaking here, we are forever being driven to ask, and to whom?

Perhaps the most useful conceptualisation of intertextuality is the 'dialogical' theory of semiotics associated with Mikhail Bakhtin. For Bakhtin, the key moment in the communication process is not any of the pre-existing large categories (the language-system, the code, the message) but the **utterance** (the performance-event, we might say). And an utterance is always structured dialogically: an awareness of context, of addressees, of possible responses and of a whole history of previous usages of its terms, themes and intonations is built into its mode of operation. Thus

> Utterances are not indifferent to one another, and are not self-suffi-cient; they are aware of and mutually reflect one another ... The living utterance ... cannot fail to brush up against thousands of dialogic threads, woven by socio-ideological consciousness around the given

15. Edward T. Cone, *The Composer's Voice*, Berkeley, University of California Press, 1982.
16. Just as post-structuralist thought turned works into texts and announced the death of the author, so, too, it has sought to uncover the diversity of figures sup-pressed in this repertory by the composer's monologic voice: see Carolyn Abbate, *Unsung Voices: Opera and Musical Narrative in the Nineteenth Century*, Princeton, Princeton University Press, 1991.

object of an utterance, it cannot fail to become an active participant in social dialogue.[17]

There is in the utterance a 'double-voiced' quality – an allusion to other perspectives, subject-positions, moments, that is manifested also at higher levels as 'polyphony' (in texts) and 'heteroglossia' (in language) – which produces, and also originates in, the equally multi-faceted structure of subjectivity itself.

Bakhtin's argument is wide-ranging. But two aspects are of particular relevance here. Firstly, although the dialogic quality of human communication might be considered ubiquitous (and an unfettered 'polyphony', if not exactly the 'natural' condition of culture, at least an inspiring utopic trope), in practice its extent, forms and effects vary in line with both the conventions of genre and the impositions of social power. Class inequality means that dominant forces always try to reduce dialogue in favour of a centralised, monologic mode of discourse, and therefore cultivate genres which facilitate this; for Bakhtin, comparisons between, on the one hand, the closed single-point-of-view logic of legal, religious and academic (!) texts, the epic and the romance, and, on the other hand, the 'polyphonic' quality of the novel (especially as developed by Dostoevsky) and the 'carniva-lesque' excess and ambivalence of many 'low' vernacular genres furnish classic examples. This emphasis on the historical and social mediation of semiosis readily offers a persuasive explanatory framework for the emergent hegemony of the post-1800 WECT work-culture, and of its multifaceted relationship thereafter with popular (and especially African-American) genres.

At the same time, the alert reader will notice an apparent historical mismatch, since this rise to hegemony of the (monologic) musical work coincides with the golden age of the (supposedly 'polyphonic') novel. Novels vary in the extent of their 'polyphony', of course. Further (and paradoxically), the potential for critique opened by the very autonomy principle associated with the work-concept creates the possibility that the social turbulence of nineteenth-century bourgeois society could be represented in the forms and styles of musical works. Presumably, this would be why Abbate and others can uncover diversity beneath the apparent closures of this repertory. In fact, the most

---

17. Much of Bakhtin's work is now available in English; for a good, accessible selection, see *The Bakhtin Reader*, ed. Pam Morris, London, Edward Arnold, 1994. My quotations are taken from pp. 76 and 85 of this text.

unqualified manifestations of the spirit of monologic closure in this
period are probably to be found less in the output of a Schumann or
a Mahler and more in the broad 'middlebrow' repertory, with a bal-
ancing extreme at the other pole located in the multi-authored,
mixed-genre, performatively messy excesses of music hall and minstrelsy. To put this point in another way (and recall an earlier remark):
there is in this nineteenth-century music culture no rigid demarcation
between sites of work thinking on the one hand and practice thinking
on the other; rather, all the forces interact, in a variety of ways, across
the full topography.

The second point of particular interest lies in Bakhtin's concept of
creativity. Authorship for him is less a singular originary intention,
more a space in which the interrelationships of the dialogic voices, at
once characters in the text and fragments of subjectivity, are played
out; the construct of the unitary author (or composer), who speaks
through his characters, is regarded as an ideological imposition on
this space. Nevertheless, Bakhtin does not (with Foucault) see 'the
author' simply as a figure at large in certain forms of text and discourse, still less (with Barthes) as a fabrication to be destroyed in
favour of empowering the reader; rather, there is a definite relation
between the activity of authoring (and indeed the whole spectrum of
activities that we might describe as 'uttering') and real human beings,
living within real social relations. Even in the furthest flights of intertextual dialogue, the author (composer, performer, etc.) retains the
rights and responsibilities of **agency** – a key point for the politics of
popular music, and one to return to.

Still Work-ing ...

Bakhtin's sense of historical and cultural specificity can come to our
help when, swimming in the heady outpourings of the popular music
intertext (its repetitions, its Signifyin(g)s, its multiple voices), we are
suddenly brought up short by a thought in a different mood: surely
this intertext is the very same category whose individual products
have, especially in recent years, acquired such an insistent sense of
their individual identifiability and attributability as to require defence
through legal action when these are threatened. The several cases
hinging on unauthorised sampling stand in a longer tradition where
alleged plagiarism has been at issue. The circumscribing of popular
music as property, a process marked most clearly by the development

of music copyright law from the nineteenth century onwards, may have its peculiarities – the complexities and variabilities of contracts, of production systems and of dissemination modes mean that a host of parties, including composers, performers, publishers, record companies, managers and agents, may or may not get paid, in varying amounts, in different situations – yet it directs our attention to the fact that the absorption of the musical practice into commodity status has generated an administrative iron cage whose operation is absolutely predicated on the existence of a (financially rewarding) relationship between 'a composer, a score, and a given class of performances': not surprisingly, the usual definitional term in copyright law is 'the musical work'.[18]

In this situation, it is hard to ignore the significance of the composer's name on the record label or sheet music, or the extent to which the record form itself (by the 1950s taking over from printed music as the principal dissemination medium for popular music) has contributed to the 'fixing' of pieces in apparently definitive versions. When bands focus their live performances on accurate reproduction of their own recording, or when audiences complain that they have not succeeded, it seems as if we are watching an extension to the *Werktreue* ideal. Rock, blues and jazz critics assemble their 'classic' records into authoritative canons; CD reissues of 'complete works' (even of relatively minor performers), often including variant sources (alternate and unreleased takes) and extensive scholarly notes, match WECT collected editions for pedantic exactitude; discographers argue over the exact dates, personnel and outputs of recording sessions, like so many musicologists in search of the source history of even forgotten works. Obsessive listings ('The 100 Greatest Albums in the Universe' etc.) litter the specialist magazines, and late-twentieth-century 'trainspotters' mimic the reifying impulse of the eighteenth-century aristocrat or the nineteenth-century bourgeois, with their 'unique collections', at once fetishistic and marketable. In one sense, 'the shudder and ring of the [cash] register is the true music; later I will play the record, but that will be redundant. My money has already heard it.', but, although 'records make music cheap … the

---

18. 'A musical work … acquires copyright protection immediately it is committed to paper or fixed in some other material form, such as recording' (British Copyright Act, 1956, quoted in Simon Frith, 'Copyright and the Music Business', *Popular Music*, Vol. 7 (1988), p. 63).

disc too has its magic', and the collector's worship of the 'perfect' hi-fi sound is complemented by the way that records can turn performances into icons ('with records ... we experience the immortality of others'), recording into a search for the 'perfect' performance, and studio composition into the realisation of that ideal which score notations could previously only approximate.[19]

There is considerable ambivalence here, though. Assembling alternate takes on record not only documents a work's history but also lays before us a slice of that intertextual world of practice which gave it birth, enabling the listener to follow the Signifyin(g) dialogue between variants. Similarly, although recordings do in one sense freeze process into product, in another they do exactly what their name suggests – **record** a moment, a memory of a moment: and the aesthetic of the 'live recording' is only the extreme manifestation of a widespread approach that tries to give even the most laboriously and technologically constructed 'final mix' the effect of being a 'real performance' (this can extend to programming into the sequencing software signs of imperfection such as rhythmic unevenness). Recordings do take the emphasis on performed nuances so characteristic of the African-American tradition in particular and fix them for ever, as if in the glass-case of a museum, but at the same time, by capturing nuance which notation could only hint at,[20] they push the listener's attention squarely on to the focus favoured by that tradition; the endemic critical activity of comparing versions, the importance of covers, the enhanced status of performer-composers, all follow naturally from this, as (once the technology allows) does the practice of making multiple mixes aimed at different contexts (this appears to start with soul/funk star James Brown in the 1960s), and indeed the whole 'remix culture'. From here, it is a short step to using recordings as raw material; through sampling, scratching, talkover and live mixing techniques the record becomes an instrument of performance. While there is mileage still in Walter Benjamin's much-disputed argument that mechanical reproduction technologies such as records would dethrone the 'aura' of the traditional art-work, for they do democratise access and provide the ubiquitous furniture for a quite new

19. Evan Eisenberg, *The Recording Angel: Music, Records and Culture from Aristotle to Zappa*, London, Picador, 1987, pp. 20, 45, 46.
20. Or try to control, as WECT composers, from Rossini to Stravinsky and beyond, have notoriously attempted to make it do.

soundscape, located in some sense outside history, it is arguably his views on the potential of the new technologies to transform cultural **production** that are the more radical. 'Jungle' musician Goldie connects this potential explicitly to the possibilities of threatening the structures of cultural and social capital surrounding the old WECT system:

> The barbarians are breaking everything down. Conventional education has no status – that old passport isn't needed in the nineties, which are decaying through youth culture ever going forward, and the technology allowing us to shrink time. Youth culture has forced the hand of tradition, it's forced aristocracy to retreat. Aristocracy says, 'You can't do that with these machines,' but youth culture finds a loophole. There are no rules! The barbarians are taking over.[21]

Yet there is ambivalence here, too. Goldie has been described as a 'genius'; undoubtedly, he has 'aura' (and his private life is probed as much as Tchaikovsky's). Andrew Goodwin has suggested that the postmodern celebration of D-I-Y digital music technology tends to ignore the fact that in this culture, often, the producer (using the term broadly, to cover everything from studio composers through remixers to club DJs) picks up the charismatic mantle dropped by song-writers and singers.[22] The 'classic' 1981 collage by hip-hop pioneer Grandmaster Flash, *The Adventures of Grandmaster Flash on the Wheels of Steel*, draws virtuosically on material from six existing records: Chic's disco hit *Good Times* (1979), two numbers by pop/rock groups – Queen's *Another One Bites the Dust* (1980) and Blondie's *Rapture* (1981) – and three recent hip-hop records (Flash's own *Birthday Party*, *8th Wonder* by the Sugarhill Gang, and Spoonie Gee's *Monster Jam*).[23] The core of Flash's collage is the basic *Good Times* riff (a characteristic bass figure, together with a two-chord harmonic progression), and because both *Rapture* and *Another One Bites the Dust*

---

21. The *Guardian*, 23 January 1998, pp. 2–3.
22. Andrew Goodwin, 'Sample and Hold: Pop Music in the Digital Age of Reproduction', in *On Record: Rock, Pop, and the Written Word*, ed. Simon Frith and Andrew Goodwin, London, Routledge, 1990, pp. 258–73.
23. Grandmaster Flash, *The Adventures of Grandmaster Flash on the Wheels of Steel*, 'Jam! Jam! Jam! Sugarhill – the Legendary Label', Music Collections MUSCD 016; Chic, *Good Times*, Atlantic 3584; Queen, *Another One Bites the Dust*, EMI 5102; Blondie, *Rapture*, Chrysalis CHS 2485; Grandmaster Flash, *Birthday Party*, The Sugarhill Gang, *8th Wonder*, and Spoonie Gee and the Sequence, *Monster Jam*, all on 'Greatest Rap Hits, Vol. 2', Sugarhill SHLP 1002.

themselves make use of variations of this riff, while all the hip-hop numbers originate from the same Sugarhill stable that Flash himself belonged to, it is not difficult for him to find 'family resemblances' between his various materials.[24] The result is an entertaining intertextual exercise in which the Signifyin(g) relations traditionally connecting performances are transferred into the operations of 'tape memory'. Yet there is no doubt that the shape of *The Adventures* is unique and is the work of one man, Grandmaster Flash; and since he self-referentially cuts into his piece such rapped phrases (taken from his source records) as 'Flash is bad', 'Grandmaster cuts faster', and 'Say Flash, one time … two times … three times', he seems to accept in advance the adulation due to a composer. Bill Laswell's reputation, similarly, arises not so much from his bass-playing, which is unexceptional, but from his ability to bring together musicians from a variety of backgrounds (pop, avant-garde music, free jazz, African and Asian musics), work as a producer with them and create a characteristic sound-world. This is in a tradition going back at least as far as 1960s producer Phil Spector, whose grandiose studio arrangements for a range of pop singers and vocal groups were aimed, he said, at producing 'little symphonies for the kids'.

It is as if, with both vernacular traditions of musical practice and new technological potentials offering tools with which to undermine the foundations of WECT-style pantheons, new forms of aura rush in to fill the vacuum. The pop *auteur* has become a familiar figure since the rise of the singer-songwriter in the sixties. Bob Dylan, for example, despite his continued touring, despite the plethora of covers of his songs by other singers (and 'bootleg' recordings by himself), despite his frequent insistence that the essence of his work lies in performance, and despite the way he has drawn on pre-existing repertory and conventions in a range of genres, sits securely astride an *oeuvre* of classic recordings, obsessively linked by critics and fans to his own biography and to what they take to be the *Zeitgeist*. For all the obvious differences, comparison with a figure such as Handel seems as much in order as with, say, rural bluesmen.

Singers, too, have taken over aspects of the composer's auratic rôle,

24. Sugarhill Records (formed 1979): one of the first record companies specialising in hip-hop. The 'Good Times' riff was used in many other hip-hop and rap records around this time, functioning as one of many points of intertextual reference.

the star performers wrapping themselves in iconic allure and offering us at one and the same time privileged access to their innermost feelings (it would seem) and 'definitive' versions of the songs they perform. And this goes along with a history in which the appeal of dialogic textural voices, at some moments, in some contexts, has been matched by the attractions of lead and backing in others: a key pop texture, this, unmistakable when Celine Dion soars above the orchestra or Bruce Springsteen scythes through the electric guitars, and one that has been persuasively theorised by Philip Tagg in terms of the figure/ground (inner/outer, subject/object, individual/social) dichotomies so characteristic of a lengthy Western intellectual and cultural history. Soloism arguably takes on new meanings and a new intensity in modern society, in the context of a novel kind of mass individualism fed by market economics, the pursuit of individual pleasures fed by social mobility, consumerism and advertising, and a cult of the self fed by the collapse of religious belief and of social authority. These social processes mesh historically with the rise of the spectacular star performer since the nineteenth century. But there is ambivalence here, too, especially if we consider carefully what terms such as lead and solo have come to cover. What happens sociologically to a 'solo' guitar line, for example, when it is treated with heavy phasing and reverb effects, or when a vocal is double-tracked and 'chorused'? Who is it who speaks through the robotic-sounding vocoder-driven lead voice in Laurie Anderson's 1982 hit *O Superman*? Or the 'fattened' sound of the synth-bass's quasi-lead rôle in Berlin's *Take My Breath Away* (a big hit in 1986), played partly (though not quite completely) in octaves with the echoey lead vocal? To the extent that collaborative and technologised sound production processes (and even, in live performance, amplification and sound mixing) have 'socialised' voices, attenuating and even cutting the direct link between the 'persons' we see (or imagine) and those we hear, a space is opened up within which the question of who is speaking here becomes malleable. We realise that, traditionally in musical performance, a musical voice and a social voice are, so to speak, forced together. What happens now is that this monologic grip is at least potentially cracked open. The relationship between the social dynamics of the performance-event (real or virtual) and those of our broader experience which the former might be taken to represent (or at least to connect to) takes on a certain elasticity. At one extreme are 'works' heard as 'solos', even if performed by large polyphonic ensembles; they speak in the

composer's (or perhaps the conductor's) voice. At the other are solo
lines heard as speaking for a collectivity; Springsteen, for instance, as
a working-class Everyman. While we have certainly not witnessed the
death of the author, then, the electronic mask which this figure has
taken on has facilitated not only new routes of creativity but also a
new politics of listening.

Such masking or 'impersonation' is prefigured by the technique of
covering already recorded songs, for whom do we hear in this situation, the new performer or earlier ones, or both? The question can be
answered, yet again, only with an insistence on the variability of practice. The typology of covers is broad, from Natalie Imbruglia's 1997
hit *Torn* at one extreme (so close in every detail to an earlier version
by Norwegian singer Trine Rein as to occasion journalistic outrage),[25]
to at the other extreme The Verve's *Bittersweet Symphony* (also
1997), which, although closely based on an old instrumental version
of The Rolling Stones' song *The Last Time* as arranged by their man-
ager, Andrew Oldham, has changed and added enough to be legally a
new entity (albeit still the object of a court case for plagiarism). The
distance is that between something akin to a 'performance' in the
WECT sense and something actually on the boundary of a category
more like that of 'tune family'.

Frank Sinatra's celebrated *My Way* (1969), itself a cover of an earlier French song with new English words, has been imitated, adapted
and parodied many times. Sinatra, in his version, makes the most of
the emotionalism and the personal, even confessional, mode of
address, typical of the ballad genre. Digging into the verbal meanings,
his jazz-derived phrasing giving the singing the effect of authenticity,
he unquestionably ends up establishing the song in the popular mind
as **his** composition. Elvis Presley's 1977 cover follows the outlines of
Sinatra's version closely; it is inconceivable that he did not have this
version in his mind. However, the setting is stylistically shifted (from
large orchestra to rock band, from jazz-style rhythms to rock back-
beats, etc.). And Presley's singing, rhythmically less varied than Sinatra's, is much more dramatic in timbre and pitching: the echoey chest

---

25. It is interesting, of course, that what in a different musical sphere might have
been accepted as an adequate reproduction of an original is here denied credibility precisely because it is heard as adding nothing new. By contrast, 'copy
bands', whose sole *raison d'être* is to reproduce iconic performances with ritualistic exactitude, are regarded as perfectly acceptable.

voice and extravagant glissandi (for which he was well known) produce an effect that marks the 'way'of the song's title as emphatically
Elvis Presley's. The cover here, then, acts as a tribute, alluding to a
performance that we are assumed to know, but speaks from a different point in the music culture. Sid Vicious's 1979 version with the Sex
Pistols might also be described as a tribute, albeit a negative one. The
opening verse is turned into a parody of the tradition which Sinatra is
taken to represent (interestingly, Vicious's voice-production, diction
and 'sobbing' phrasing suggest that he associates this tradition with
classical music); the personal soul-baring is made to sound pretentious and self-indulgent. After this, a drastic punk restyling launches
itself violently at the conventions of 'classic' popular music, offering
the 'way' of punk with absolutely no apologies. Harmonies and
melody are stripped down to the basics, so that the focus is on the
aggressively speech-like vocalism (shout, sneer, snarl, with exaggerat-
edly demotic diction and deliberately bad intonation) and the ruth-
lessly regular rhythmic drive. The conjunction of disgust and
self-disgust is typical of punk. We might regard this recording as an
example of an ideologically motivated cover: there is a conscious
effort to make a statement which is in opposition to, and indeed
'mutilates', an existing aesthetic.[26]

Still, though, this could not work without a target. And, while we
can say that covers are located on a spectrum, moving from exact
copies at one end, through tributes, reinterpretations and distinct stylistic shifts, to ideological attacks at the other end, in all cases there is
a dependence on an **originating moment**: an existing version, a starting point or defining interpretation, against which the cover will be
measured, to which it will relate. This origin is not a 'first cause' but
more a transiently privileged moment of departure within networks
of family resemblances, bearing comparison with similar moments
within the networks of repetition, Signifyin(g) and remixing. It would
be misleading to view such moments as equivalent to 'works',
although we might, perhaps, consider them symptoms of 'work-ness'
(or the work-concept might be thought of as a historically specific
extrapolation from the more general system that I am describing in
terms of family resemblance networks). While the sheer variability of

26. Frank Sinatra, *My Way*, Reprise RS 20817; Elvis Presley, *My Way*, RCA PB1165;
The Sex Pistols, *My Way*, 'The Great Rock 'n' Roll Swindle', Virgin CDVD
2510.

process that has been sketched above renders any generalisation, still more any prophecy, dangerous, it may be that this sort of picture – networks of interconnected moments, coalescing into temporary hierarchies marked by the installation of 'root' points and specific input references – offers the best available model of a possible emergent politics of popular compositional practice.

Musical Works, Musical Labours

To pursue the progressive potential of this model very far would require much more than action on the level of compositional practices alone, for they are embedded in business structures that are completely predicated on the legally protected individuality of musical works, the financial hierarchies benefiting from this arrangement, and the quasi-romantic auras painted around these works and their 'creators' that are used to help sell them. It can hardly be accidental that the rise of the 'work' parallels and intermeshes with that of the 'commodity', nor that the history of that sort of 'individuality' necessary to the former coincides with that of capitalism, whose success was powered, as the work of Weber and Tawney gives us good reason to believe, by exactly the same species of property-conscious individualism. Fetishism of the work is not too far away from that fetishism of the commodity to which Marx drew attention, both in its characteristic psychology and in its social basis in the effacement of collective labour. Goehr attributes the success of work thinking to 'conceptual imperialism',[27] but it becomes easier to understand the political power that concepts can undoubtedly possess if we grasp the material forces in which they are rooted and which they help to sustain. The fact that digital technology and the world success of African-American musical practices, with their potential to subvert work thinking, have arrived at the same moment that the market has tightened its grip on musical production through ruthless maximum exploitation of ownership rights is one of the great ironies of the late twentieth century, but is readily explicable once we situate the rôle of transnational capital correctly in the analytical picture; this force will turn any 'raw material' into grist to its mill.

One way to address critically the conceptual level of this imperialism is to crack open the terms of its discourse. Just as 'recording' can

27. Goehr (1992), p. 245.

refer to a process, a moment in a network, as well as an object, so, too, 'work' can have an active and processual, as well as a reifying, sense; a musical work can be a **labour**.[28] Turning to Raymond Williams's indispensable *Keywords*, we find etymological corroboration of the way that 'the basic sense of the word, to indicate activity and effort or achievement' was shifted in favour of 'a predominant specialisation to regular paid employment' as a result of the development of capitalist productive relations.[29] It is easy to see how this might connect with the idea of the product of such relations being a 'work' (and the place of manufacture, a 'works').[30] The *Oxford English Dictionary* confirms that the earlier usage can be traced back well into the first millennium AD; it often seems to be connected with a sense of passing time (as in 'the work of a moment') and to have an ethical dimension (as in 'good works'). Examples of the second usage – work as product – can also be found before the year 1000, but seem to become much more common from the fifteenth century (which is about the date when the specialised application to 'art-works' begins, too). Williams shows as well how, in one usage, 'working' became associated with a particular social class, and how this history was intertwined with the etymological history of 'labouring' and 'labour': scope there, one would think, for some discursive labour by radical musicians and musicologists. James Brown's many recordings may well constitute a body of works, but when he is described as 'the hardest working man in show business', the significance of this phrase for his African-American audience, one suspects, is not limited to an awareness that Brown has been an exemplary black capitalist.

28. Is it possible that the word 'opus' contains an analogous dialogics? From around the sixteenth century, of course, this term can denote a musical work, although what exactly Listenius's '*opus perfectum et absolutum*' (*c.* 1527) means may be disputable, as Goehr points out (ibid., p. 116); but *opus Dei* in the Benedictine usage referred to the *activity* of prayer.
29. Raymond Williams, *Keywords: A Vocabulary of Culture and Society*, rev. edn, London, Fontana, 1988, p. 335.
30. Think of the Manchester-based company Factory Records, not to mention the commonplace image of 'assembly-line' musical production, applied not only to the Tin Pan Alley, Motown and Brill Building 'song-factories' but also to Haydn's symphonies, nineteenth-century Italian operas and English oratorios. The custom-built masterpiece resists the extreme extensions of this image, but also partly accedes, through the institutionalisation of compositional pedagogy (massed ranks of composers' apprentices); here we are more likely to be asked to think in terms of a discourse of craftsmanship, the 'composer's workshop'.

There is a lineage for such discursive critique among radical ethno-musicologists, where the late John Blacking and Charles Keil among others have emphasised a distinction between 'music as process' and 'music as product', often with (perhaps somewhat rosy-spectacled) appeals to evidence of non-commodity music-making in precapitalist societies or among marginalised groups within capitalist society. Lydia Goehr ends her book by asking how far the work-concept may have constrained and disadvantaged musicians, and concludes, eloquently, that

> Music as an end could never, on aesthetic grounds alone, fully justify the social or political means involved in its composition, performance and reception. The question, therefore, still asks for a more satisfactory answer, one that will force us to think about music, less as excused and separated, and more as inextricably connected to the ordinary and impure condition of our human affairs.[31]

While truly radical change in this direction might depend, I have argued, on a broader re-evaluation of 'individualism' and 'ownership' than seems presently to be in view, this seems no reason to question the value of attempts at change within the purely musical sphere – attempts to 'un-work' the practice, so to speak.[32]

Among the many implications that such moves would have, two are of particular interest here. First, the effects might be felt not only in the vernacular sphere, as one would expect, but also on the classical canon (which in any case now resides there to a considerable extent). If, for example, Richard Williams is right to suggest that Bill Laswell's reconstructions, by rewriting Miles Davis and Bob Marley in the light of later musical developments, reveal what they were 'really' (that is, latently) about, we might say that this is what good performance (and good composing too) in the WECT tradition has always done also:

31. Goehr (1992), pp. 285–86.
32. This would be somewhat analogous to contemporary movements to defend remaining environmental 'commons' – including the ecological and cultural knowledge of 'tribal' peoples. The project would be politically fraught, no doubt. Keil has called for a campaign to abolish music copyright altogether. I would be with Keil in spirit, but, as Steve Feld has suggested in his dialogue with Keil on this issue, it is far from certain that penniless musicians, especially those in 'third world' countries, for whom copyright represents one of the few routes out of poverty, would agree. See Charles Keil and Steve Feld, *Music Grooves: Essays and Dialogues*, Chicago, University of Chicago Press, 1994, pp. 313–24.

they take what is given and create the past through the ear of the present; this is the historical projection of intertextuality. Just as today's popular music practice is, as we have seen, somewhat less different from practice in that WECT tradition than is sometimes excitedly claimed, so, too, Western art-music practice (as distinct from the associated theory) may have been less faithful to *Werktreue* principles than is often supposed. One task now, therefore, may be to rescue historical performing practice from the *Diktat* of the composers and their philosophical, musicological and pedagogical allies.

A second interesting point brings us back to the question of authoriality. The move from 'work' to '(inter)text' can result, ironically, in a deepening of that very aestheticist isolation which troubles Goehr about the work-concept. In some postmodernist versions of this move, as the 'author' disappears, textuality as such appears to take centre-stage, writing 'humanity' out of the script. Swimming, distinction-free, in a sea of intertextual relativism, we (whoever 'we' now are) may lose all basis for resistance to an anonymous 'view from everywhere'. But all moments are not commensurate, and the ethics of musical practice that we badly need requires an identifiable agency – the Bakhtinian author – where responsibility can be seen to reside. The misogynistic strand in 'gangsta' rap can be defended on the grounds that it belongs to a much older Signifyin(g) thematics within African-American culture; similarly, the solipsistic political quietism typical of much recent dance-club culture can be explained in terms of self-referencing circularities in the music. In both cases, a dense, internally spiralling intertextual practice makes such hand-washing easy. But the singular moment, each performance-event, is ethically unique. Responsibility cannot be ducked, any more than it can (for intertextual relationships of a rather different type) in any case where a late-twentieth-century performance of *The Magic Flute* does not raise the issue of sexism, or where a *Ring* does not somehow, explicitly or implicitly, build in an encounter with the fascistic potential of Wagner's original. To imagine that the defence of such singularity implies a return to a culture of 'works' would be unimaginative. Rather, these moments, of a huge variety of types, operating within intricate cultural networks of resemblance and difference, are what I would like to term unique **instances**; they are, in short, examples of what may be called (and what we can try to feel our way towards) 'work-in(g)-practice'.

CHAPTER 8

Locating the People
Music and the Popular

Who are "the people"? The Founding Fathers of the United States of America had no doubt about the answer to this question: "We the people ... ," they declared in the new Constitution (1787), with the confidence proper to a new epoch. A few years later, Thomas Paine, defending the French Revolution with equal assurance, insisted that "the Authority of the People [is] the only authority on which Government has a right to exist in any country" (Paine [1791–92] 1969, 131). Such confidence was inspiring but oversimple. The Revolutionary Terror set a horrifying precedent for a host of subsequent attempts to establish popular authority by violence. The founding "we" of the United States was not universal but limited to men of property, excluding not only less-affluent white males but also Native Americans, all women, and (naturally) all slaves. The political moment was in any case part of a broader shift, in which, as Raymond Williams (1983) has shown, the rise of commodity culture led to an emergent and soon predominant usage of the term *popular* to mean "well-liked by many people." By the time that Alexis de Tocqueville was dissecting American society—the 1830s, a period when "Jacksonian democracy" was refocusing U.S. politics on the interests of the "common man"—he was as amazed that "The people reign in the American political world as the Deity does in the universe; everything comes from them, and everything is absorbed in them" (Tocqueville [1835] 1956, 58) as he was depressed by the prospect of leveling down that he saw resulting from the "tyranny of the majority."

From an early-twenty-first-century vantage point, the tiredness of the people idea seems self-evident. The grotesqueness of the concept of the Nazi *Volk* (from which Jews, gypsies, and homosexuals were excluded: no *Volkswagen* for them) was matched, for cynicism, by that of the "People's Democracies" of the Soviet bloc; Brecht's ironic advice to his masters, on the occasion of the failed East Berlin uprising of 1953, that they should perhaps dissolve the people and elect another, was the definitive riposte to "totalitarian populism" (Esslin 1959, 165). Popular Fronts for the Liberation of X (and, usually, the oppression of Y) have lost their allure (as marked by the comic demolition job on the phenomenon in the Monty Python movie *The Life of Brian*). Those of us living in Blairite Britain, with the reality of the "people's lottery" and "the people's Millennium Dome," not to mention the memory of the "people's princess" and of Margaret Thatcher's invocation of "the people" in the service of a multitude of reactionary causes, inhabit that farcical stage that, in familiar historical style, follows tragedy. Everywhere, distinctions between "the popular" and its others struggle to survive, it would seem, amid the assumptions of a vulgar relativism.

But the complexities were endemic from the start. The German Romantic W. G. Herder (1968, 323) carefully distinguished the folk-singing people (*das Volk*) from the "shrieking mob" (*der Poebel*), a distinction maintained in Arendt's *Origins of Totalitarianism* (1966); the "mob" was a key character in eighteenth- and nineteenth-century political and cultural discourses, and maintained its hold in the twentieth: the idea, explored by such diverse writers as George Orwell and T. W. Adorno, that capitalism's best hope for defending class injustice would lie in a program of cultural debasement of the masses is worth taking seriously at the same time that we note the element of condescension implicit in a perspective that fed a history of "moral panics" over "mobs" of ragtimers, jazzers, rock 'n' rollers, punks, and hip-hoppers. The nineteenth century saw a host of new communities imagined into being (Anderson 1991), in Europe and elsewhere, almost always with an appeal to a "national soul" embodied in their folk culture heritage. Small wonder that such a company of Celts, Magyars, Poles, Bohemians, generic Slavs (etc.—not to mention, further toward the margins, gypsies, Jews, "niggers" and orientals) dances and sings its way through the popular musical repertories of the period. Yet it jostles for space both with political and revolutionary songs fixed to class projects (from "La Marseillaise" through songs of the British Chartists, for whom, to quote one of their banners from 1848, "The voice of the People is the voice of God," to socialist anthems like "The Red Flag" and the "Internationale"), and with a huge expansion in market-oriented production, which by 1900 demanded that, in the words of Tin Pan Alley's Charles Harris, "A new song must be sung, played, hummed and drummed into the ears of the public, not in one city alone, but in every city, town and village, before it ever becomes popular" (Hamm 1979, 288). The character of the "people," despite its radical origins and potential, journeys through a landscape which, to use Althusser's phrase, is "structured in dominance," both in general and in the specific forms generated by the historical unfolding of capitalism; and in the maintenance of these hierarchized formations, cultural distinctions play an important role, as Pierre Bourdieu (1984) has taught us. Today, the historical trajectories, in exhausted anticlimax, precipitate inversion, detritus, and perversion, as in (to choose examples almost at random) the "turbo-folk" used as an instrument of ethnic cleansing in the Yugoslav wars of the 1990s; in the "Red Flag" simulacra passing for performances at Labour Party Conferences; and in the frankly celebratory sadocynicism of *Popstar* and *Pop Idol* (British TV talent discovery shows broadcast in 2001).

The people/popular concept, then, is irrevocably "dirty," and in two ways at least. First, it covers a discursive space whose content is mutable and open to struggle; just as, according to Bourdieu (1993a), there is no such thing as an objective "public" but only a shifting social character defined by varying survey methodologies, so, in the words of Stuart Hall (1981, 239), "there is no fixed content to the category of 'popular culture' ... [and] there is no fixed subject to attach to it—'the people.'" Second (and connected), the politics of the concept are "always already" corrupted (always already, because they are produced in a discourse with no clear origin), and, today, their rescue for progressive uses would require considerable cultural work—not least by intellectuals, so often popular culture voyeurs, but also would-be fellow travelers and even guides, for whom Fanon's injunction (1967, 187) to "work and fight with the same rhythm as the people" represents both a necessity and an impossibility.

The discourse we are uncovering is one specific to modernity. "The people" names a character seen as inhabiting an imagined social space (which is not to say that there is not a real social space in a relation with this). The configuration of this space varies historically and in accordance with ideological assumptions, and hence the character of "the people" is variably delineated too—as a social body, a political actor, a cultural voice—with implications for interpretation of its musical manifestations.

(We might suppose that many of the disagreements over definition—for example, of "the popular" seen as social-commercial success, as political representation either of tradition or of struggle, or as transformative figuring of an Imaginary—arise through confusing these registers. At the same time, we might also suppose that politically there is a point to trying to bring these into alignment: this would happen optimally when a music finds a way to speak with a fully politicized consciousness to and for a social bloc.)

The stage on which "the people" moves is commonly structured in alteritous fashion, and a variety of psychic mechanisms comes into play: projection, overcompensation, objectification, abjection. In general, "the people" is figured as a subordinate other—a periphery validating by difference both a central elite and a centered self. (In a happy coincidence, elite music acquired its first histories, became conscious of itself, in works published by Charles Burney and Sir John Hawkins in 1776, the same year as the American Declaration of Independence gave dramatic voice to the idea of popular sovereignty.) This figure is both gendered (the people inhabits a "motherland," and mass culture is "effeminate": passive, intuitive, affective, hysterical [Modleski 1986, Huyssen 1986] and racialized [the popular is imagined as "barbaric" and/or "exotic"—mapped, most commonly, onto "black"]). But peripheral elements can be appropriated by "the center," as they have been, arguably, in much of today's hegemonic popular music culture in the advanced societies. Alternatively they can answer back, as spectacularly evidenced in the long-lived, intricate workings of the "Black Atlantic" (Gilroy 1993); when, for instance, according to Lhamon (1998), an early-nineteenth-century New York cross-racial working-class fraction used the blackface mask to construct a subversive alternative to elite culture—a "Plebeian Atlantic"—at the very moment when the Founding Fathers were construing "we the people" as men of property and education. The working out of these tensions takes hugely varied forms. In Britain, the early beginnings of the late-modern phase constituted an important bourgeois fraction in the eighteenth century as a "polite and commercial people," with "popularity" defined by consumption patterns, within a by-now well-legitimated state; consequently the folk-national trope took the form not so much of a politically potent radicalism as an archaizing nostalgia or an instrument of English imperialism (Scots and Irish songs sounded endearingly quaint in London). In the United States, the agenda was fundamentally twisted by race (of course) and by the demotic triumphalism associated with a "Fordist" political economy. It was also mediated by the trope of migrancy, so the pioneer/hobo/beat/ ethnic outsider became a core popular type (prefiguring the postmodern cult of the border-crossing nomad).

The subject/object people is, then, necessarily fragmented, variable, and unstable: in the language of Freud and Lacan, *split*. As such, its very appearance is dependent on an apparatus—the regime of *representation*— specific to post-Renaissance (Cartesian) modernity (Foucault 1970), and given a new twist by Hegel's dialectics of subject and object, self and other. Earlier, the commoners were simply what was left over, but with the Cartesian revolution they became bound into a system whereby the out-there is a constituent of the problematic of the self: the representation of "reality" reflects, refracts, distorts, and guarantees the subject's presence, and the dynamics of popular and nonpopular interaction become an aspect of the processes of subjectivity. (Gary Tomlinson [1999] has explored this problematic for the realm of opera—but strangely the "people," whose nameless, numinous, but gross materiality, felt "from the near side" of discourse, acts as a guarantee of transcendent signification, is absent from his exposition, along with—more predictably—any hint, from the "far side," of their *speech*.) For Enlightenment thinkers, the evident contradiction between alterity (the inescapability of difference) and a politics of inclusivity could in theory be squared through the principle of universalism: all of humankind could potentially perfect itself in Reason. Mozart's *The Magic Flute* (1791) represents a neo-Kantian essay along these lines: Reason triumphs, with the "lower" characters located, musically and socially, firmly in the place appropriate to their cultural stage of development, yet at the same time narratively shadowing the revelatory trajectory followed by their "betters." By 1824, Beethoven's cry in the 9th Symphony, "O ye millions, I embrace you," has moved on to a neo-Hegelian reach for the Absolute. The shift from Kant's programmatic universalism of taste to Bourdieu's critique of distinction and its socioeconomic basis exemplifies a later skepticism. It remains true, however, that it was only with the advent of "modern" thought that this type of discourse became available at all. In the early eighteenth century, Giambattista Vico offered the innovatory means to think of all of a society, and even all of humanity, together, through a world historical image of human development. Tracing the journey from the Enlightenment to twentieth-century modernism reveals metaphors of cultural ladders (progress; upward mobility) joined by, perhaps giving way to, more synchronically structured models (highbrow-middlebrow-lowbrow; the interrelations of modernism, mass, folk, and primitive). At this point the figure of the *cultural field* (variably mapped to "corresponding" social and politicoeconomic fields) achieved a dominance eventually theorized by Bourdieu (1993b) among others, and in such concepts of Gramsci (1971) as "historical bloc," "hegemony," and the "national-popular."

Although the European Union's adoption of Beethoven's 9th Symphony "freedom tune" as its anthem might suggest that the Enlightenment project is still under way, it also marks its trivialization. Living (arguably) *after* the heyday of the modernity system, we often, it seems, find it problematic, embarrassing, or even ludicrous merely to name "the people." This grand subject appears to have turned into a simulacrum of subjectivity constituted in the reification of desire in advertising—"one market under God," as Thomas Frank's ironic rewriting of an earlier national-democratic ambition puts it (2002). At best, the people are elsewhere—in unnoticed Third World catastrophes, asylum camps, sweatshops; at worst, the popular is figured in terms of the mystifying flatness of self-improvement (the Blairite "people's meritocracy," with its boy and girl bands reflecting the self's narcissistic self-sufficiency). Digging within the musical repertories of this moment, can we find ways of reading the people back in?

Without proposing priority for any of the "fields" mentioned above— social, politicoeconomic, cultural—we concentrate here on the *discursive* sphere (using the term in the broadest, translinguistic sense). Whatever determinations and mediations are in play, the popular in music comes to us through the effects of sounds, words, and words about sounds: in short, through the work of the *signifier*.

Think of John Lennon's "Working Class Hero" (*John Lennon/Plastic Ono Band,* Apple PCS 7124, 1970). This is, evidently, a song about the people conceived in terms of class—or more exactly, about the disjunction of this relationship, that is to say, the culture forced on working-class people as a result of their lack of political consciousness; implicitly, it is also a song about leadership, or perhaps its lack or failure: "a working-class hero is something to be," as Lennon bitterly if ambivalently puts it. The style is terse, stern, and didactic, with lyrics foregrounded, melody plain, and accompaniment limited to simple acoustic guitar, summoning up memories of the equally spartan approach of the early Bob Dylan, down to the relentless ("deathly") guitar riff keeping the singer right on the straight and narrow message, forbidding all semiotic play. But an element of doubt about the references of pronoun shifters ("I," "we," "you," "they") clouds the issue: the flow of identifications is disrupted. Similarly, behind the stern paternal voice we hear a shadow—a would-be lyrical, "feminine" reach beyond the meaningful surface, audible in occasional tremulous cracks in timbre, anxious stretching for high notes, and little inflections and melismas around the main melody notes; and perhaps also in the disruption of the otherwise insistent minor tonic chord, once toward the end of every verse, by a single appearance of the "yielding" major chord on the subdominant (conventionally coded "feminine" in the Western tonal system, in relation to the "masculine" dominant). Will Lennon *cry*, we ask?

Historically, the song is richly contextualized. On a biographical level, it comes between, on the one hand, the traumatic Beatles breakup and Lennon's primal scream therapy earlier in 1970 with Californian psychotherapist Arthur Janov, when he spent much of his time crying and screaming, and on the other hand, the "silence" of the period 1975–79, when Lennon gave up musical production to be a ("feminized") househusband. In terms of cultural history, it punctuates the transition from "John Beatle" to "John Lennon," taking this to stand for the shift from the fetishizing, macho heroics of the 1960s star system (false hero worship, in Lennon's eyes) to the more skeptical, ironic, often gender-bending discourses around star presence characteristic of the 1970s. On the level of political economy, it engages the contemporaneous restructuring of class associated with the move away from social democracy toward the Thatcherism to come. "Working Class Hero" is both suspiciously insistent and revealingly fractured, signaling what Lawrence Kramer (1990) calls a hermeneutic window organized around scream/cry on the one hand and silence/death on the other. Lennon's figure of the people here is inscribed in the complex relationships set up at the intersection of shifting meanings attached to the tropes of "star" and "class," as these generate a tantalizing image of the popular other, desired but errant, and always receding from grasp.

For my argument in this chapter, the manifest content of "Working Class Hero," although obviously relevant, is less important than the exemplary interpretive lessons we can derive from its latent dynamics. Its voice, doubled and fractured, points clearly to the conclusion that, if popular songs can be related to underlying social formations, such relationships take culturally specific forms that, moreover, are never stable, always multivalent.

The Spice Girls' "Wannabe" (*Spice*, Virgin CDV2812, 1996), noisily surrounded by proclamations of "girl power," focused on gender rather than class. The singers issue instructions, give us their demands, tell us "what they really really want"; and the verses, where they do this, are delivered in a sort of rap style, borrowing and inverting the machismo of male hip-hop. No female group, however, can avoid summoning references to sixties girl groups, especially those of Motown, with their approach oriented around more traditional themes of "romance"; and sure enough, the choruses turn to a poppier style, complete with vocal harmonies, a melodic hook, and a stress on togetherness. The bridging of individual empowerment (verses) and collective feeling (choruses) is meant to target and construct girl power's own community (eliding the issue of class, of course). But verse and chorus are also contrasted: rapped call-and-response backed by rock-style minor-pentatonic bass riff in the first, major-key vocal harmonies in the second; it is as if the inclusivity strategy couples popular music's two main ideological categories and their gender associations, "feminine" pop fantasy being grounded by "masculine" rock realism—and further, calls up historical memories of dance-couplets (pavane and galliard, minuet and trio, etc.) reaching right back to the European Renaissance. The claim of contrast is deceptive, however. Verse and chorus flow seamlessly into each other, the rhythm track is continuous, and bits of vocal style from the verse increasingly find their way into the choruses; moreover, the bass/harmonic patterns of the two sections perform closely related gestures. Similarly, the dialogues within the verses are superficial: calls and responses from the different girls are much the same, and come from much the same place on the stereo spectrum. The song is a closed binary—nothing is left over—and the hint of teleology (tonally, the relationship of the two bass patterns—minor pentatonic and major, respectively—recalls that between *passamezzo antico* and *passamezzo moderno* that marked the dawn of "modernity" in the sixteenth and seventeenth centuries) leads nowhere.

Just as girl power offered a fake individual and collective empowerment at the extreme end of Thatcherism (there is no such thing as society, she told us), so "Wannabe" rehearses a simulacrum of difference, a wannabe teleology, a fantasy in which nobody fails and nothing is left out: rock and pop, romance and raunch, black (rap) and white (singalong), past and future are seamlessly stitched together. But the stitching (the suturing, as Lacan would call it) is overdone: it could not last—as became evident, on the level of biography, with the Spice Girls' disintegration, and, on the level of society, with the passage from Thatcherite postfeminism to the pseudomeritocratic populism that followed, accompanied as this was by a wave of emollient girl and boy bands on the one hand, and an underground subchorus of unorthodox gender poses on the other.

White rappers became commonplace in the 1990s. Most notoriously, the success of working-class white trash Eminem demonstrated the continuing potency of the blackface stance, his records exploiting (by implication) the blackface mask to proclaim white disempowerment. Produced by black rapper Dr Dre but most conspicuously successful (as with most rap by this date) with a middle-class white market, Eminem's extravagantly brutal, misogynistic, and homophobic narratives work against the background of a cross-race, class-based economic split in the United States (bourgeois affluence booming, workers impoverished, neglected, or imprisoned), but also draw the traditional *frisson* from the image of violence long associated with black ghetto society: rap's "posses" and "gangstas" reinscribe the discourse of mob and moral panic. Eminem's "My Name Is" (*The Slim Shady LP*, Interscope 490 287-2, 1999) adds further dimensions to the masking operation. The insistent repetitions in the choruses of the statement "My name is ... " summon memories of the long African-American tradition of naming games and rituals (the street game, the dozens, for instance); they also echo boxer Muhammed Ali's equally insistent question, "What's my name?" to his opponent Sonny Liston, soon after the name change accompanying his conversion to Islam, and Black Muslim refusals of slavery surnames (by Malcolm X, for example). Small wonder that the persona Eminem adopts here, named for us, significantly, by a distant, other, and highly technologized voice, way back in the mix, is "Shady."

In a sense, the narrative of the song, telling of Shady/Eminem's brutal, oppressive early life and schooling, and bringing together issues of identity, charisma, and class, works similar territory to "Working Class Hero." But the fragmentation of voice is much more overt here. Shady's apparent identity and location shift constantly, and are embedded in complex dialogues with other voices. The play of name, identity, and voice is a work of what black theorists such as Gates (1988) have termed Signifyin(g), a key practice in African-American culture that operates through manipulation of a "changing same" by constant variation of given material, disrupting the signifying chain in the interests of semiotic play. Another element in this intra- and intertextual work is the instrumental backing, shaped— typically for rap—from a sample, here a four-chord riff taken from Labi

Siffre's "I Got The," which repeats in varied forms throughout. Again, technology (digital sampling in this case) mediates a shift in the parameters of the popular music community. The process of Signifyin(g) makes fun (play; play as fun; funny, incongruous, or uncanny connections) of sense, of the signification process itself, its orientation around doing rather than meaning pointing toward the sphere of the body. Although "My Name Is" adheres to the typical rap duality of "rhymes" and "beats" (word and act, logos and body), the lyrics are noticeably "musicalized" through the operations of the vocal polyphonies, and the underlying riff, reduced to the basic drum/bass groove, is what fades out the song, inviting but always retreating from bodily response.

These three songs are offered as symptomatic rather than representative examples. Their intricate maneuvers around the registers of race, gender, and class remind us of Hall's point that there is no *essence* of the popular—"the people" can only be defined dialogically. Their points of address from "below," no less (and no more) than their positionings in the power textures of capitalist society, confirm that the discourse of "the popular" is closely tied to the project of modernity. This, as we have seen, guaranteed the subjectivity of the emergent Western self through an apparatus of representations of his others, "masters" and "slaves" warring on, but also maintaining, each other (to draw on Hegel's celebrated dialectical image, produced [1807] in the same moment that the "people," conceived as potential subject, made such a dramatic historical step forward).

   This does not of course imply that hierarchies of musical categories do not exist elsewhere. Indeed, probably "elite" and other categories (however labeled) have been found in all stratified societies. But the historically specific figure of "the people" as an agent in such dramas has been widely exported from "the West," as part of the globalization of the modernity discourse, and this has tended to restructure old hierarchies. Indeed, this process, although speeding up enormously in recent years, arguably began with colonialism as part of the birth of the modern itself. This hint of a universalism is alluring but tricky; on the level of the world picture, "modernization" has been uneven, variegated, and hybrid, and many "non-Western" societies—such as Japan, Argentina, and South Africa—have pursued quite specific paths for lengthy periods of time. Nevertheless, we can legitimately think in terms of a *dispersal of the modernity dialectic*, with all that this implies, both "here" and "there," for conceptions of "the people." For "us" in "the West," the question arising then (a postcolonial question) is: who can, who *may*, speak from "over there"? Respect for cultural difference should not exclude the possibility that one might surprise "others" where they are with an excavation of what is hidden from their gaze. Similarly, the reverse movement might reveal apparently premodern residues "here," strengthened by the effects of that internal colony, the "black Atlantic," but in any case offered a sympathetic home in popular music's permanent longing for carnival, its invitation to the body, its invocation of an excess beyond the purview of the symbolic structures of Western Reason.

Lacanian psychoanalysis has theorized an "object voice"—an impossible, transfinite object of desire, linked to the initial infant cry before the flooding in of culture (interpretation, representation, identification) rendered this forever lost. By analogy, we might posit an equally impossible "object act," linked to a presignifying body, where the organs worked "for themselves," not as extensions of the subject, and where the body existed, with fullness of gesture, as a field rather than discursive property. Just as the silenced object voice can nevertheless be invoked (albeit partially, stutteringly) in the voices we actually hear, so the object act can be enacted (acted, acted out) through fractures and windows in the putative coherence of actual performances. This stakes out ground where the apparently conflicting interests of universalism (still alive in such disparate narratives as Marxism and psychoanalysis) and cultural–historical difference can meet; where "masters" and "slaves" can negotiate new phases in a dialectic that from its beginning marked "the people" as irrevocably split; and where, through a metaphorical unbinding of the "mob" (the *mobile vulgus*—the people on the move), we might pursue the tantalizing if impossible task of bringing culture and politics, discourse and practice, into alignment.

Further Reading

Adorno, Theodor W. 1991. *The culture industry*. London: Routledge.

Bennett, Tony. 1986. The politics of the "popular" and popular culture. Pp. 6–21 in *Popular culture and social relations*. Edited by Tony Bennett, Colin Mercer, and Janet Woollacott. Milton Keynes, U.K.: Open Univ. Press.

Born, Georgina, and David Hesmondhalgh, eds. 2000. *Western music and its others: Difference, representation and appropriation in music*. Berkeley: Univ. of California Press.

262   Richard Middleton

Bourdieu, Pierre. 1984. *Distinction: A social critique of the judgement of taste.* Translated by Richard Nice. London: Routledge.

Gilroy, Paul. 1993. *The black Atlantic: Modernity and double consciousness.* London: Verso.

Levine, Lawrence. 1988. *Highbrow/lowbrow: The emergence of cultural hierarchy in America.* New Haven, Conn.: Yale Univ. Press.

Middleton, Richard. 1995. The "problem" of popular music. Pp. 27–38 in *The twentieth century, The Blackwell history of music in Britain.* Vol. six. Edited by Stephen Banfield. Oxford: Blackwell.

————. 2001. Who may speak? From a politics of popular music to a popular politics of music. *Repercussions* 7(8): 77–103.

Stallybrass, Peter, and Allon White. 1986. *The politics and poetics of transgression.* London: Methuen.

Williams, Raymond. 1983. *Keywords: A vocabulary of culture and society.* Rev. ed. London: Fontana.

References

Anderson, Benedict. 1991. *Imagined Communities: Reflections on the Origins and Spread of Nationalism*, 2nd edn (New York: Verso).

Arendt, Hannah. 1966. *The Origins of Totalitarianism* (London: Allen and Unwin).

Bourdieu, Pierre. 1984. *Distinction: A Social Critique of the Judgement of Taste* (Cambridge MA: Harvard University Press).

Bourdieu, Pierre. 1993b. *The Field of Cultural Production: Essays on Art and Literature*, ed. R Johnson (Cambridge: Polity Press).

Esslin, Martin. 1959. *Brecht, a Choice of Evils: A Critical Study of the Man, His Work and His Opinions* (London: Heinemann).

Fanon, Franz. 1967. *The Wretched of the Earth*, tr. C Farrington (Harmondsworth: Penguin).

Foucault, Michel. 1970. *The Order of Things: An Archaeology of the Human Sciences* (London: Tavistock).

Frank, Thomas. 2002. *One Market under God: Extreme Capitalism, Market Populism and the End of Economic Democracy* (London: Vintage).

Gates, Henry Louis III. 1988. *The Signifying Monkey: A Theory of African-American Literary Criticism* (New York: Oxford University Press).

Gilroy, Paul. 1993. *The Black Atlantic: Modernity and Double Consciousness* (Cambridge MA: Harvard University Press).

Gramsci, Antonio. 1971. *Selections from the Prison Notebooks*, ed. and tr. Quintin Hoare and Geoffrey Nowell-Smith (London: Lawrence and Wishart).

Hall, Stuart. 1981. 'Notes on Deconstructing "the Popular"', in *People's History and Socialist Theory*, ed. Raphael Samuel (London: Routledge), 227-40.

Hamm, Charles. 1979. *Yesterdays: Popular Song in America* (New York: Norton).

Hegel, Georg Wilhelm Friedrich. 1910 [1807]. *The Phenomenology of Mind*, tr. J. B. Baillie (London: Allen and Unwin).

Herder, Johann Gottfried. 1968. *Sämtliche Werke*, vol. 25, ed. Berhard Suphan (Hildesheim: G. Olms).

Huyssen, Andreas. 1986. *After the Great Divide: Modernism, Mass Culture, Postmodernism* (Bloomington: Indiana University Press).

Kramer, Lawrence. 1990. *Music as Cultural Practice, 1800-1900* (Berkeley CA: University of California Press).

Lhamon, W.T. 1998. *Raising Cain: Blackface Performance from Jim Crow to Hip-Hop* (Cambridge MA: Harvard University Press).

Modleski, Tania. 1986. 'Femininity as Mas(s)querade: A Feminist Approach to Mass Culture', in *High Theory, Low Culture: Analysing Popular Television and Film*, ed. Colin McCabe (Manchester: Manchester University Press), 37-52.

Paine, Thomas. 1969 [1791-2]. *Rights of Man*, ed. Henry Collins (Harmondsworth: Penguin).

Tocqueville, Alexis de. 1956 [1835]. *Democracy in America*, ed. Richard D. Heffner (New York: Mentor Books).

Tomlinson, Gary. 1999. *Metaphysical Song: An Essay on Opera* (Princeton NJ: Princeton University Press).

Williams, Raymond. 1983. *Keywords: A Vocabulary of Culture and Society*, rev. edn. (London: Fontana).

CHAPTER 9

Performing Culture, Appropriating the Phallus[1]

It's easy to see how we can speak about *cultures of performance* in music: the range of approaches to performance, and the way they depend on specific bodies of knowledge, signal clearly that musical performance is always culturally embedded. I'll be talking about a particular performance – albeit one preserved on record – a performance from the repertory of rock music, to be understood therefore within the conventions of rock music culture. But we can also speak about the *performance of culture*: I mean the idea that 'culture' isn't simply given to us, nor is it generated freely by human subjects; rather, its modes of operation, the subject positions it makes available for occupation, are contingent, continually performed out, and only hang together because of the strength and regularity of this pattern of enactment. This perspective comes to us from a variety of sources: interactionist sociology; cultural constructionism; semiological pragmatics; speech-act theory, for example. At its most provocative, packing the strongest political punch, it's associated with some recent currents in gender theory, notably the theory of performativity put forward by Judith Butler.[2] Since musical performers are always gendered, there's a special interest in this connection – not least in the case of vocal music, emanating unmistakeably from the sexed and gendered body. The performance I'll be discussing is a song, a song moreover from a genre where the gender conventions of performance, for both men and women, are relatively firmly fixed. But however strong the fixings, performance can go wrong, so to speak; this possibility of mutation or subversion is important to Butler, as it will be to me.

Of course, music provides a specific site of performativity. But as well as respecting this specificity – which the disciplines of musical analysis invite us to do – we need also to situate it in relation to its broader cultural work, which in this case might well have to do with the role of vocal utterance, of voice itself, in the performing out – the reproduction, modification, subversion – of sexed and gendered subject-positions. Here, another site of analytical work offers itself for our attention, its consulting-room furnished with a couch rather than score and loudspeaker. These two sites – of musical and psycho-analysis respectively – can be regarded as dialectically linked. How so?

In a 1982 paper – never published as far as I know – the sociologists Barbara Bradby and Brian Torode introduced the concept of 'song-work'.[3] It's unfortunate that this has

---

1   This is the text of a keynote address given to the Nordic Musicology Conference, Helsinki, July 2004. Substantially the same paper was given, again as a keynote, to the annual conference of the Society for Music Analysis, Hull University, July 2003. I'm grateful to participants at both events for their comments. The text subsequently grew into part of Chapter 3 of my *Voicing the Popular: On the subjects of Popular Music* (New York: Routledge, 2006).

2   See Judith Butler, *Gender Trouble: Feminism and the Subversion of Identity* (London: Routledge, 1990); *Bodies that Matter: On the Discursive Limits of "Sex"* (London: Routledge, 1993).

3   Barbara Bradby and Brian Torode, 'Song-Work: The Musical Inclusion, Exclusion and Representation of Women', paper presented to a conference of the British Sociological Association,

been given so little attention subsequently. What they had in mind was Freud's theory of dreams, according to which the 'manifest' meanings of dreams stand for, but at the same time misrepresent the 'latent' meanings expressing unconscious desires and fantasies. The transformations produced are, in Freud's quasi-economic model, the result of 'dream-work', and it's the task of the psychoanalyst to undo this work, that is, to interpret the dream. By analogy, songs – according to Bradby and Torode – transform unconscious desires, fantasies and anxieties into vocalised patterns and effects. Although I don't intend to follow through this Freudian analogy in great detail, I do find the concept of song-work useful: vocal labour channels, represents, constructs the flows of psychic energy going to form, de-form, re-form the patterns of human subjectivity; and, as with dream-work, the transformations inevitably leave traces, slips, aporias behind for the analyst to work on.

Needless to say, in attempting to bring into relation two modes of analysis, two sites of performance, I am myself putting on a performance – on a circus highwire, some might think. But the transference mechanisms implicated in scholarly conferences, though fascinating, are a subject for another conference; and I must leave my own dream-work to your interpretation.

The subject of my analysis is a song from Patti Smith's 1975 album *Horses*, a cover of Van Morrison's 1965 garage-rock classic, 'Gloria'.[4] And the course of treatment proceeds through three sessions, each superintended by a different analyst – Sigmund Freud, Jacques Lacan, Slavoj Žižek.

The original, by the Belfast R&B band Them, with Van Morrison singing the leering vocal, is a classic of what has become known as the 'cock-rock' genre, in which a strutting male voice, dripping with demand, imposes his phallic authority on a female object of desire.[5] Patti Smith's cover, as Mike Daley has pointed out in an article in *Popular Music*,[6] comprehensively re-works the original. She encases it in new material – actually a version

---

Manchester, 1982.

4   Van Morrison, 'Gloria', *The Story of Them, Featuring Van Morrison* (Deram 844 813–2, 1997 [1965]); Patti Smith, 'Gloria in Excelsis Deo'/'Gloria', *Horses* (Arista 07822 18827 2, 1975).

5   The classic text is Simon Frith and Angela McRobbie, 'Rock and Sexuality', in *On Record: Rock, Pop, and the Written Word*, ed. Simon Frith and Andrew Goodwin (London: Routledge, 1990), 371–89. Certainly Van Morrison's vocal performance conforms closely to 'cock-rock' convention, as Frith and McRobbie describe it: 'explicit, crude...aggressive...loud, rhythmically insistent, built around techniques of arousal and climax...shouting and screaming...swagger untrammelled by responsibility...' (ibid. 374).

6   Mike Daley, 'Patti Smith's "Gloria": Intertextual Play in a Vocal Performance', *Popular Music* 16:3 (1997), 235–53.

Little more survives from the original than the chorus line (which spells out the name 'Gloria' and throws it antiphonally between lead vocal and group response) and the basic narrative shape: he (Van Morrison), expecting Gloria's arrival (as usual), describes with lip-smacking relish her approach, down the street, into the house, into his room... Patti Smith's lengthy prelude ('Oath') establishes her protagonist as a blaspheming, amoral free spirit. The central narrative is considerably extended, the lustful tension built up in more detail, and the (sexual) climax described more explicitly and repeated, the whole of this passage making important play with tempo changes. Quasi-religious imagery (a looming tower, chiming bells) lays the ground for a dramatic half-time coda, pregnant with the judgemental menace evoked by the memory of Jesus dying for somebody's sins (but not hers), which is followed by the final triumphant, full-speed chorus and fadeout.

Needless to say, the discussion that follows in the main text will make more sense if readers can supplement this summary by listening to the records.

of a poem she had written some years before called 'Oath' – which foregrounds the moral dangers of her lustful desires; and she pushes her appropriation of Morrison's vocal persona to an extreme. Daley rightly brings out the way that Smith's vocal extremes – the switching of registers, which confuses gender norms, the vast range of vocal effects, the barely coherent climaxes – seem both to parody the conventions of cock-rock and appropriate them for herself, thereby inverting the traditional structure of sexual positioning. A straightforwardly feminist critique of oedipal norms, then?

There's no lack of material to fuel a Freudian analysis. Brought up by a mother who was a religious fanatic and an atheistic, blaspheming father, whom she adored, Patti Smith rebelled as a teenager against her earlier religiosity, substituting the religions of art and of rock 'n' roll, particularly its sexual permissiveness. An unmarried mother at 21, she gave the baby up for adoption – refusing, one might say, the conventional cure for penis-envy. Adolescent hallucinations appear to have mingled religion and sex: 'I used to dream about getting fucked by the Holy Ghost', she later said.[7] Although as a child she fiercely resisted feminine type-casting, as she struggled to make it in bohemian New York in the years after 1967, she seems to have worked through relationships with a succession of father-figures, including artist and photographer Robert Mapplethorpe, Dylan's friend Bobby Neuwirth, playwright Sam Shepherd, musicians Allen Lanier and John Cale, who produced *Horses*, and, at least in fantasy, Jim Morrison and Jimi Hendrix. These men, she herself said, she looked to for 'discipline'. Her performance style became celebrated for performative excess and sexual frisson, and among her specialities was the appropriation of songs associated with dominant male singers, not just 'Gloria' but The Who's 'My Generation', the Stones' 'Paint It Black' and 'Hendrix's 'Hey Joe'. Mapplethorpe's iconic cover photo for the *Horses* album portrays her ambiguous in gender but undoubtedly masterful and in control. 'I write to seduce a chick', she said, 'I write to have somebody'.[8] Plenty of evidence here, then, Dr Freud might say, of unresolved oedipal business.

What Freud might have paid less attention to is the wider context. In the early seventies, a specific New York rock music was coalescing – a sort of avant-garde art-punk – built on foundations provided by the twisted street-realism of Velvet Underground, with John Cale and Lou Reed to the fore, and the tradition of mostly unknown garage bands of the 1960s, continued by MC5 and Iggy Pop and the Stooges. Backed by the new rock magazine, *Creem*, with writers like Lester Bangs, Dave Marsh and Lenny Kaye, who became Patti Smith's lead guitarist, Suicide, the New York Dolls, Wayne County, Television, Blondie and the Ramones put together a provocative anti-hippie aesthetic characterised by noise, shock, avant-garde excess and self-proclaimed trash. Important to them also were gender inversion and a playing with sexual marginalities – both Wayne County and the Dolls, for instance, cultivated transvestite imagery – and these were to feed through into later punk's gender-bending. Influential in the wider background were free jazz and the performance art of Fluxus, Lamonte Young and John Cage – and indeed the whole bohemian New York scene: William Burroughs; Mapplethorpe, celebrating in his photos the gay S&M subculture; Andy Warhol, whose Factory was a centre of a 'post-moral' philosophy of sexuality and of a brand of performativity – a sort of cool, indeed blank narcissism – clearly influential on Smith.

---

7   Victor Bockris, *Patti Smith* (London: Fourth Estate, 1998), 20.
8   Ibid. 7.

The attempted shooting of Warhol in 1968 by Valerie Solanas, founder of SCUM, the Society for Cutting Up Men, reminds us that this was also the moment of second-wave feminism. Betty Friedan's *Feminine Mystique* had come out in 1963, and, much more radical in tone, Mary Ellman's *Thinking about Women* in 1968, Evelyn Reed's *Problems of Women's Liberation: A Marxist Approach* in 1969, and both Germaine Greer's *The Female Eunuch* and Kate Millett's *Sexual Politics* in 1970. The women's movement, intricately related to New Left politics and the civil rights struggles, was in ferment, especially in the USA; and was also entwined with the gay rights movement: the Stonewall Riots had taken place as recently as 1969; in 1972 David Bowie 'came out' as a self-proclaimed bisexual, and by the mid-seventies an image of bisexuality was decidedly 'cool'.

Notoriously, of course, feminists had problems with Freud – especially with his alleged phallocentrism. From this perspective, one can readily interpret Smith's 'Gloria' as an attempt to re-write the Freudian story: that is, as an attempt to invert the traditional relations of sexual power, and to lay claim to an active, quasi-'masculine' pleasure, with (assuming her vocal persona is unproblematically female – which we should perhaps not assume) a possibly lesbian tonality. And listeners who know their Roland Barthes will then have no difficulty in associating the fracturing of linguistic coherence, the extravagant graininess of the vocality, as symptoms of *jouissance*.[9] This analysis would certainly go with the historical grain. The 1966 book, *Human Sexual Response*, by Masters and Johnson, setting out the results of their exhaustive research into sexual practice in the USA, seemed to establish 'the myth of the vaginal orgasm', a conclusion seized upon by feminists, including Anne Koedt in her book with that title published in 1970. But if the clitoris is now the thing, this upsets Freud's theory, according to which infantile genital activity common to little boys and girls must give way, in the female, to acceptance of lack and of a proper sexual passivity. In this theory, female adolescent fantasies of masochism or narcissism are assuaged only when vagina replaces clitoris as focus, and impregnation and motherhood come to provide a substitute fulfilment for the lost phallic object; continuing clitoral activity, by contrast, produces neurosis or perversion. Millett's critique of Freud argues for an 'equalling up' of sexual autonomy; Greer's proposes rather a 'softening' of penile aggression and a rehabilitation of vaginal authenticity – a sort of generalising of Eros, after the manner put forward in Herbert Marcuse's sociological revision of Freud, *Eros and Civilisation*, which, in its 1966 second edition, had become a core text for both feminists and the New Left in general.

Either way, on this reading, Patti Smith's 'Gloria' has Freud – at least the Freud of caricature – retreating in some confusion; although he is probably muttering as he goes something about hearing signs of anxiety as well as lust in her performance, and speculating about neurotic tendencies….

On this first level of analysis, the exchange taking place is simply of a body-part. But doesn't sex happen in the head? For Freud, sexuality is always psycho-sexuality, and the phallus functions on the symbolic as well as the biological level – an approach pushed much further in Jacques Lacan's re-reading of Freud. But while we wait for our next session, we might ponder whether the first analysis is adequate to the sense of religious angst in the song – or indeed, to the representation of sexuality: isn't there something deeper than we have grasped so far? Desire seems both *over*-coded here – almost hysterically insistent –

---

9   Roland Barthes, 'The Grain of the Voice', in *Image-Music-Text*, tr. Stephen Heath (London: Fontana, 1977), 179–89.

and *under*-coded – not quite there musically, as if, in line with the Warholian voyeuristic tendencies of the New York avant-garde as a whole, it's being 'looked at' rather than felt gesturally, 'acted out' rather than grooved out. These are terms that might point towards one of Lawrence Kramer's 'hermeneutic windows'.[10] With the help of Dr Lacan, let's see if we can push through it.

Lacan's concept of the phallus is complex and by no means stable. The key point, though, is that, although he does keep a place for the real phallus – the penis as it functions in the register of the Real – in his mature thought this is far less important than the phallus as *image* – in this Imaginary register, it mirrors or reflects back desire – and the phallus as *symbol* – in the register of the Symbolic, it comes to stand for the whole structure of Law, the Law of the Signifier. Simplifying, we may locate the phallic image in the sphere of Lacan's *objets petits a* – the famous Freudian part-objects, for Lacan, object-causes of desire; and the phallic symbol in the sphere of the Lacanian Big Other – that radical alterity, the locus of language, culture, law, which precedes all individual subjectivity. The importance of *castration* is as a marker of the paternal threat. This isn't necessarily associated with a real person but is a metaphorical function, which Lacan therefore calls the Name-of-the-Father. The threat – whose authority is essentially a sham, since there is no final signifier in the Big Other – institutes the superego and founds 'culture' itself; and is mapped, in an asymmetrical structure, on to the field of sexual division: the possession or lack of a real phallus is taken retroactively as a figure for the unequal positioning of men and women in the symbolic field. Sexual difference, on this account, is thus entirely contingent – it stands for an inscription of a differential schema of subjection to a phallogocentric law – but it is nonetheless almost unbelievably powerful.

Jouissance is Lacan's term for a quasi-orgasmic bliss, a transgressive ecstasy which it is the role of the normative pleasure-principle inscribed under the sign of castration to forbid, and which is therefore also associated with pain. For Lacan, as for Freud, *jouissance* is essentially phallic; perhaps we may think of this powerful image-fantasy as standing at the head of the whole family of part-objects – *objets petits a* – and in that sense the signs of *jouissance* we noticed earlier in Patti Smith's vocal mark the coursing of her desire around Gloria's 'bits'. Indeed, 'voice', along with 'gaze', is Lacan's addition to Freud's list of part-objects; and the 'object-voice' is defined precisely as that impossible (because inaudible) surplus left over when the symbolic stratum of the vocal stream has been accounted for – the excess, the 'indivisible remainder', which can be at best disturbed when the subject is temporarily not at home, the signifiers not in place. To the extent that Smith's vocal performance approaches objectivity in this sense, it's the terrifying *jouissance* associated with an invocation of the object-voice that is at issue.

Applications of the *jouissance* idea usually link it to subversion of patriarchal law – the law of the Symbolic; this is the drift of Barthes's theory of geno-song – and still more of Julia Kristeva's theory of a pre-symbolic level which she calls 'semiotic', associating it explicitly with a pre-phallic developmental phase centred on the mother. Such applications over-simplify their Lacanian source, even though in his later years Lacan himself came to speculate about the possibility of a specifically feminine *jouissance*, a rather mysterious bliss

10 Lawrence Kramer, 'Tropes and Windows: An Outline of Musical Hermeneutics', *Music as Cultural Practice 1800–1900* (Berkeley CA: University of California Press, 1990), 1–20; re-printed in Lawrence Kramer, *Critical Musicology and the Responsibility of Response: Selected Essays* (Aldershot: Ashgate, 2006), 1–20.

'beyond the phallus' which, apparently, women may experience but know nothing of; and that's the point, for this *jouissance* can appear only through breaks and slippages in the order of knowledge, only as a fantasy-projection. For Lacan, there is no pre-discursive reality, no pre-symbolic body; for him, *jouissance* (what escapes in sexuality) and *signifiance* (what shifts within language) are inseparable, and the excess is therefore radically undecideable in its orientation. It can subvert the Law but it can also stick to it, the terrifying, superhuman, disembodied voice of the patriarchal god acting precisely as what lends a spurious authority to the dicta of the superego: *le-père-jouissance*, as Lacan calls it – the obscene ecstasy of control as such. It seems there are two object voices, 'voice against voice', as Mladen Dolar puts it. Or rather – since we are here in the territory not of complement but of supplement – 'the secret is maybe that they are both the same; that there are not two voices, but only one object voice, which cleaves and bars the Other in an ineradicable "extimacy"' ('exstimacy' being Lacan's coinage for the 'outsideness' of the 'inside', in the final analysis, the lack in the big Other which voids its guarantee of self-sufficiency). And this means, Lacan speculates, that one might 'interpret one face of the Other, the God face, as supported by feminine *jouissance...*[and] while this may not make for two Gods, nor does it make for one alone'.[11]

This does not – quite! – clear up our understanding of the song 'Gloria'. We are left wondering whether the glimpses of object voice mark a *subversion* of the phallic order; or rather an attempted *theft* of the phallus, an *appropriation*; or again, an eruption – 'between the lines' – of feminine *jouissance*; or alternatively, a same-sex masquerade traversing the routes between all of these (on a banal level, the repeating-climax structure, which Smith herself compared to the rhythms of female orgasm, might be taken to back up the apparently lesbian narrative setting). What we do know better, however, is the landscape we are in. This is a song of desire, but also one of *blasphemy*: the Law-of-the-Father is rejected (or rather, co-opted, the phallus appropriated), but the looming tower, the tolling bells, the half-time day-of-judgement moment are marks of terror and guilt, and the initial declaration of moral autonomy is delivered in tones redolent of both trauma and of the cocky, more-than-human self-staging of the rock god (notice how, with the strange episode in the lyrics where 'twenty thousand girls call their name out to me' in 'Roosevelt Stadium', there is a conflation of modes of *jouissance* attaching to sex, religion and rock stardom). The defences against the void opening up beyond the Law itself are only just maintained. 'Exstimacy' is also ex-communication.

Lacan has been little better received by feminist critics than Freud. But psychoanalysis stands not for utopias but for understanding. It is this realism – its 'always already' is its reading of original sin – that prompts Lacan's notorious aphorism, 'Woman does not exist' – by which he means to point to the unavoidably subjected status of the discursive figure 'woman', qua phantasmatic Absolute, within the phallogocentric symbolic order.[12] This has the merit of enabling us to recognise the sheer weight of *risk* entailed in Patti Smith's performance: this is no simple claim for equality of sexual pleasure; to challenge the ordering of desire is to challenge also the authority of Law itself.

---

11 Mladen Dolar, 'The Object Voice', in *Gaze and Voice as Love Objects*, ed. Renata Salecl and Slavoj Žižek (Durham NC: Duke University Press, 1996), 7–31 (27); Lacan, quoted in ibid, 27–28.

12 See Slavoj Žižek, 'Otto Weininger, or "Woman Doesn't Exist"', in *The Žižek Reader*, ed. Elizabeth Wright and Edmond Wright (Oxford: Blackwell, 1999), 127–47.

Does this mean that biology is irrelevant? By no means. Lacan's point here is precisely that deadlock in the symbolic order – the assymetrical layout of 'masculine' and 'feminine' modalities – is 'grafted' in an entirely contingent way on to the facts of anatomy and reproduction. Sexual difference is a non-natural suture sited at this point of disjunction. At one and the same time, this widens the space available to cultural work, including interpretive and political critique, both for Smith and for the listener, and enables a proper respect for the ambition, the sheer *danger*, of the performance.

And what about the listener? So far, I could be accused of transforming Smith's 'Gloria' from performance into text – to use a linguistic terminology, focusing on the dimension of the *énoncé*. But performance here – the dimension of the *énonciation* – is vital, albeit, as a recording, this is a complex type, its 'staging' of a quasi-live performance at the same time objectified by a technology that mortifies as it disseminates. There is a literature about this deadening quality of the phonograph, notably Friedrich Kittler's book *Gramophone, Film, Typewriter*: the phonograph, this medium which brings up ghosts, voices of the living dead, disembodied traces of an uncertain humanity, an *énoncé* always carrying the label, 'anon'; and it surely can be no coincidence that this medium achieves a cultural centrality over the same period as Freud and Lacan develop the theory of the part-object, object-cause of desire, *objet petit a,* including most importantly here, the object-voice. But this mortifying effect is to be read always in its dialogue with the vivifying quality of the *énonciation*, the performance-act as such.

In this intricately structured listening experience, then, who speaks? And to whom? And also, who looks? In both Van Morrison's original and Patti Smith's cover, 'Gloria' has an intensely filmic quality; the story is told through the scopophilic gaze of the singer. We might recall that voyeurism was very much a theme of New York art-rock, probably derived in part from Warhol, whose description of visual images as 'shots' is a symptom of his general alienated and voyeuristic approach to both art and stardom. In this sense Valerie Solanas's shooting of him can be regarded as an attempted phallic reversal via an example of what Lacan calls a *passage a l'acte*; real gun replaces symbolic photo-images, just as, in the Lacanian *acte*, an impulsive, quasi-psychotic action carries the subject temporarily out of the Symbolic altogether into the dimension of the Real, reaching for the status of an object. 'Gloria' doesn't go that far – even if, according to one biographer, Smith welcomed the suggestion that she might become a 'sex-object'.[13] Lacan makes a distinction between 'act', where the subject qua subject goes missing, exits the theatrical set-up of reality, and 'acting out', which takes place within the scene; and Smith's track has very much the structure of *fantasy* as Freud and Lacan describe it: a quasi-theatrical staging of a 'scene' within which the subject's unconscious desire is obsessively acted out, and which functions as a defence against trauma – veiling the unavoidable insatiability of desire, ultimately the lack in the Other.

To explore this further, we can turn to our third shrink, Slavoj Žižek; but, since much of his writing focuses on analyses of film, he will probably take us for our consultation to the cinema (not inappropriately, given that in a way this darkened fantasy-space re-locates the individual psychoanalytic transference as a mass cultural practice). Critical theory has been here before, notably in Laura Mulvey's classic but much-criticised article, 'Visual

---

13 Bockris, *Patti Smith*, 160.

pleasure and narrative cinema'.[14] Here Mulvey draws on Lacan's account of the origins of the Imaginary order in the child's so-called 'mirror phase' to offer a gendered theory of the pleasures of the cinematic gaze in terms of relationships of identification and scopophilia. But Žižek, like Lacan, insists that fantasy, including film fantasy, inscribes images in structures of meaning as well as identification; and that this operation must be understood in terms of the interplay of *énoncé* and *énonciation*, and its role in the splitting of the subject: *énoncé* writes the subject into existence through the structures of the text, while *énonciation* points to the site from where the unconscious speaks – the place where the leftovers of the subject's encounters with his others puts him at risk.

In 'Gloria', the voices can, at one level, be thought of as helping to put in place the structure of the fantasy-scene, constructing that symbolic fiction which we know as 'reality', speaking for characters to imaginary listeners. But on another level, that of object-voice, they disrupt this fiction. With Lacan, Žižek argues that, as objects, both voice and gaze occupy a place from which the subject is always already excluded, simply by virtue of his partiality of positioning; from the 'thing that sees' and the 'thing that sounds', he becomes an 'I', a looking, vocalising subject. Žižek's advance is to suggest that these two partial objects can supplement each other, the one filling the hole left in the field of the other, acting as the other's *objet petit a*: 'we hear things', he says, 'because we cannot see everything', and vice versa.[15] And in film, he argues, this can happen when the structure of montage – the network of intersecting gazes – necessarily implies a missing space – what has been excluded – which may be filled by an uncanny, unexpected voice, a sound that does not belong, or even a voice we strive to hear but cannot. One example must suffice. It is easy enough to hear the interplay of Smith and the 'boys in the band' as they combine to name Gloria in terms of an exchange of voiced gazes – a phallic exchange, centred on their joint, almost pornographic objectification of 'Gloria'. But where is 'Gloria' herself? Is she the surplus left over from the montage process, her voice traceable only in the senseless scream stratum of Smith's vocal, or alternatively in the force of her own voice's almost palpable absence – as that silent scream which, for Žižek, represents object-voice in its purest form? Or, is she to be read, again within Smith's vocal itself, but simply as a symptom of narcissistic (perhaps homosexual) fantasy; and, by extension, as the sound of voiceless feminine *jouissance*? Or, given that the boys speak for her, name her, is she standing for the passages of subjectivity itself? Žižek, following Hegel, regards the naming power of language as the very mechanism whereby 'pure self' – the void that represents the 'night of the world' – moves into the symbolic order and assumes the trappings of subjectivity.[16] And behind this process, sanctioning it through the figure of castration, stands the Big N, the Name-of-the-Father, which Smith tries to, but cannot, speak, but which is written in the song-title: 'Gloria in excelsis deo'.

In a song called 'Ain't It Strange' from the 1976 album *Radio Ethiopia*, Smith challenges God: she sings, 'Turn around God, make a move!' In an interview she said of this, 'I wanna be God's daughter. No…I wanna be God's mistress…I wanna be fucked by God. Not just once, a thousand times.' On 26 January 1977, she was singing this song live when – 'its after a part where I spin like a dervish and I say "Hand of God I feel the finger, Hand of God I

---

14 Laura Mulvey, 'Visual Pleasure and Narrative Cinema', *Screen* 16:3 (1975), 8–18.

15 Slavoj Žižek, '"I Hear You with My Eyes"; or, The Invisible Master', in *Gaze and Voice as Love Objects*, ed. Renata Salecl and Slavoj Žižek (Durham NC: Duke University Press, 1996), 90–126 (93).

16 Žižek, 'Otto Weininger', 136.

start to whirl, Hand of God I don't get dizzy, Hand of God I do not fall now.'" – when she fell dangerously off the stage, seriously damaged her neck and was laid up for three months. 'I fell... I did feel the finger push me right over...'.[17] And her music started to become more subdued, less turbulent, more 'feminine'.

In 1979 Smith retired and married ex-MC5 guitarist Fred 'Sonic' Smith. She raised a family and lived quietly, in apparent domestic tranquillity, for some years – amid persistent rumours of how she was subservient to Fred, deferred to him in everything – and even whispers that she suffered domestic violence.

So, was she 'cured'?

And, what has our own course of treatment achieved? Analysis's promissory note was always more like an IOU than a prescription – and we can confidently expect that the big O in the middle of this formula, at once beyond and grounding the (YO)U and the I, will be continuing to speak, as the analyst and her subjects fall, exhausted but performing still, into a fondly imagined but impossible silence.

---

17 Bockris, *Patti Smith*, 125; Clinton Heylin, *From the Velvets to the Voidoids* (London: Penguin, 1993), 198.

CHAPTER 10

The Real Thing? The Spectre of Authenticity in Modern Musical Thought

Authenticity has been having a hard time.[1] According to Born & Hesmond-halgh (2000:30), it's a concept that "has been consigned to the intellectual dustheap", outmoded in a culture ruled by the simulacrum—copies without an original, in the words of Jean Baudrillard—at a moment marked, we're told, by the "end of history". The Czech "velvet revolution", focused on Václav Havel's attempt to bind together artistic and ethical truths, looked increasingly like a last gasp as, after 1989, in an Americanised world, the stakes were reduced to a crude antinomy of power—with or against?—in which the hegemonic authority scarcely felt the need to hide its instrumentalism, whether in political, economic or cultural arenas. Just at the moment when "speaking truth to power" could scarcely be more necessary, the intellectual tools to guide and justify this have gone missing.

I want to ask whether the idea of authenticity can be, if not rehabilitated, at least re-fitted in a way appropriate to a supposedly postmodern age, in which the apparatus of Western Reason is in disarray, and all notions of origin, foundation, absolute truth have seemingly been banished. But in doing this, I'll also want to ask where this concept came from—to sketch in a genealogy, in the sense made influential by Nietzsche and Foucault: that is, an excavation of the historically specific institutional and discursive passages whereby "authenticity" was moulded into an ethical and cultural, even disciplinary force. For Foucault, consideration of "ideology" doesn't belong here: knowledge is equated with power, and power is everywhere. But the truth-claims inherent in the concept of authenticity ask us to at least consider the relativity or arbitrariness or alternatively the normativity of values; and, although we could decide to just follow Foucault's lead and assign such issues to the machinery of an entirely contingent discursive regime, unless we also follow him in the illogicality of supposing that his figure of "so-called man" can simply choose to cancel himself, we shall need to take the historical Telos of the authenticity problematic—that is, its utopian ambition—seriously; and for this reason I'll be doubling back later to the question of ideology.

---

[1] The initial version of this paper was given as a keynote address to a conference of the British Forum for Ethnomusicology, Goldsmith's College London, in November 2002. An expanded version will appear as part of my forthcoming book, *Voicing the Popular: On the Subjects of Popular Music*, due from Routledge in 2005.

Strangely, although "authenticity" seems, at least in many circles, to be intel-lectually almost dead, its discussion within popular music studies and ethno-musicology is not particularly well developed. Ask a student of pop—let alone a pop fan—what "authenticity" is, and almost certainly the answer will instance musical types: it's rock (rather than commercial pop), blues (rather than disco), early (rather than late) Elvis, Badly Drawn Boy (rather than well groomed boy bands). Similarly, ethnomusicologists—though less so than used to be the case—might talk about rural rather than urbanised, traditional rather than commercial, local rather than international, indigenous rather than hybrid, and so on; or, at a more sophisticated level, the discourse might be about the effects on musical practice of cultural imperialism, the transnational music industry corporations, postcolonial subalternity, new border-crossing identities, etc. Generally, in any case, the focus is on music; it's *music* that's authentic (or not).

I want to widen this out. Allan Moore, in a recent article in *Popular Music* (Moore 2002), has started to do this. He argues that authenticity isn't inscribed in music but ascribed, by people; and that it's they who are authenti-cated (or not), not the music as such. Actually it's both. We talk about people being true or false to themselves, and we worry about whether our actions, feelings and views are really, authentically, our own; and we also wonder if music expresses or represents us, or other subjects, in an honest way. And the interplay is important. Authenticity is a quality of selves and of cultures; and they construct each other. The etymology is interesting: *autos* meant "self", *authentikos* "warranted"; subject and object, self and other: I want to hang on to both sides of this coin—which, in a first approach, we might characterise in terms of a search for "the real thing".

Within popular music, the discourse of authenticity, even if (as noted above) it is not particularly well developed, is familiar enough. Typically, it marks out the genuine from the counterfeit, the honest from the false, the original from the fake –oppositions which in turn often map on to further dis-tinctions: feeling as against pretence, acoustic as against electric, subculture as against mainstream, people as against industry, and so on. As Simon Frith has shown (Frith 1981, 1988), the roots of this discourse lie in the bourgeois appropriation of folk music, constructed as an other to commercial pop, and in debates over jazz and blues, where, in a similar fashion, "authentic" strands were promoted over ersatz derivatives. On the level of scholarship, within cul-tural studies, subcultural theory, ethnic—for example, black—studies, and so on, the music features in terms of distinctions and political positions clearly indebted to older discourses in folkloristics, anthropology and Romantic *Kulturkritik*. Throughout this history, both people and music were involved: authentic music came from (perhaps even generated) authentic communities; the bogus stuff was produced by cynics and aimed at (perhaps even created) consumers mired in false consciousness: dope for dupes.

Kantspel

Feedback of discourse on to music production is common; indeed, we might say, in Foucauldian fashion, that music industry institutions—distinctions between record labels, music genres, radio channels, sales charts, typical A & R and journalistic practices—make it almost impossible to think outside the terms of this problematic. We can see John Lennon as an exemplary figure. Almost as soon as the Beatles became successful, Lennon was beginning to formulate his creative ambitions along the lines of a search for the "real me"– "John Lennon" as opposed to "John Beatle", to use his own images, an authentic self as opposed to the commodified, fetishised icon that he came to loath. Musically, culturally, politically, this search was articulated through a set of oppositions in which a series of Others was lined up against the inauthentic. This started with rock 'n' roll: "rock 'n' roll was real, everything else was unreal (…) You recognise something in it which is true, like all true art…If it's real, it's simple usually, and if it's simple, it's true" (Wenner 1972:100–101); and subsequently it took in singer-songwriter honesty and psychedelic visions, avant-garde iconoclasm and conceptual art, transcendental meditation and primal scream therapy, political anthems and politicised happenings, hymns to feminism and to black pride. The search for the real Lennon, it would seem, could only proceed through the cultural peripheries—through the Other. And, in a familiar figuration, these Others were conceived as attractively unreflective—models of *action*, in the face of over-intellectualised sophistication: the blues, for example, "is better [than jazz] (…) Because it's real, it's not (…) thought about, it's not a concept, it is a chair, not a design for a chair" (*ibid.*:103).

Lennon's 1970 album with the Plastic Ono Band stands as a highpoint in the articulation of this dialogue between inside and outside. Consider the track *"God"*. This is actually, in a fairly direct way, *about* "authenticity": the lyric lists a collection of authorities and myths (from Jesus and the Buddha to Elvis and Dylan) in whom Lennon no longer "believes", whose god-claims are punctured—"the dream is over"; the list climaxes in "the Beatles". And what's left? "Me"—the self—or the loved self: "Yoko and me"; "and that's reality". And this inner reality is secured through a musical reference to a "real" music—a self-grounding through the Other, here a Black-Other speaking in the signifiers of Gospelised Soul, marked most obviously by Billy Preston's piano and Lennon's vocal melismas but going right down to the *"Stand by Me"* chord-sequence.[2]

The album, if read as an implied response to the Beatles phenomenon, and beyond that to the sixties more broadly, can also act as a pointer towards the historical force-field constituting this period, framed by the Cuban missile

---

[2] The main chord-sequence of Ben E. King's 1961 Soul hit, *"Stand By Me"*—I-VI-IV-V—was familiar enough from previous Soul and Doo-Wop tunes but became iconically associated with King's song (much as George Gershwin's *"I Got Rhythm"* sequence became "the rhythm changes"). Lennon would have a minor hit with *"Stand By Me"* in 1975.

crisis of 1962, when instrumentalised Reason came close to destroying the whole human species, and the "events" of 1968 and their aftermath, when reconfigurations of Western Reason—proposed, co-opted, neutralised, marginalized—ended up initiating the decisive turn towards the formations of narcissism and consumer capitalism—the self obsessively cultivated but also privatised - within which we still find ourselves. Within vernacular philosophy, forms of existentialism and of situationism were strong—representing moves of the self inward and outward, respectively—and both were influential on Lennon; but in the intellectual wings, currents of post-structuralist thought were poised, against a backdrop of despair over political failure, to carry Western thought towards the problematic of relativism so familiar today.

The earlier history is lengthy and takes us back most importantly to the eighteenth century. A key figure is Rousseau who perhaps first lays out the concept of an authentic self—an individual identity whose "inner voice", if only uncovered beneath the babble of social conditioning, is what we should be true to. And of course, this voice of nature is most clearly represented—projected, we might say—in the figure of the Noble Savage—humanity prior to the evils of civilisation. (We might note the counter-argument of Rousseau's contemporary, Diderot, whose insistence on the constant and confusing interaction within the self of reason, desire and fantasy "leaves us", in Richard Rorty's words, "with the need to construct a self to be true to, rather than, as Rousseau thought, the need to make an already existent self transparent to itself" (Rorty 2002:15). Following this archaeological trajectory can take us further back—to the Age of Humanism, when the figure of the "individual" in the characteristic modern sense first becomes central to thought, represented in literary production in the genre of autobiography (Montaigne's Essays, for example), not to mention scientised in the work of Descartes. This is a period which is also, of course, the Age of Discovery, when emergent figures of travel, of exotic others, of centre and periphery, empire and colony, dramatise through formations of difference the uniqueness of the equally emergent Western self.

Such "encounters", as Philip Bohlman calls them in his recent *World Music: A Very Short Introduction*, play a large part in forming the history within which, from the Age of Discovery down to the present, changing images of "world music" play out. Montaigne, for instance, also wrote "On Cannibals", drawing on the accounts of the missionary Jean de Lery—accounts including a description of what Bohlman sees as "the first encounter between the musics of old and new worlds" (Bohlman 2002:2). At each moment in this history, musical norms are challenged by encounters with difference, disrupting but also reshaping both cultural politics and musical subjectivity.

The authenticity trope is deeply embedded in this problematic. It's inseparable from, and an engine of, the drama of "modernity" itself. After Rousseau, Herder is a central figure. Folk music collector, ethnographer, historical and

Kantspel

philosophical anthropologist, early proponent of Romantic *Kulturkritik*:
Herder was first to speak of cultures in the plural—ways of life distinctive of
particular peoples, each valid, all incommensurate with the others—just as,
now looking inwards, he insisted that each individual person had his own way
of being human: "Each man has his own measure (*Mass*), likewise his own
tuning (*Stimmung*)" (quoted, Taylor 1991:127). Rousseau's claim in the *Social
Contract*: "Man is born free, and everywhere he is in chains. One man thinks
himself the master of others, but remains more of a slave than they are", was
worked up by Hegel into his celebrated discourse of Master and Slave, which
points both inward and outward, mapping together dialectics of history,
philosophy and psychology. The background here is the powerful nineteenth-
century discourses of imperialism, orientalism and raciology; and of class—
what I have elsewhere (Middleton 2000) called the problematic of the Low-
Other. From here, Marx and Kierkegaard take divergent routes, and
Nietzsche, cutting away the foundations, leaves the field clear for the naked
assertion of will, on the one side, the imposition of totalitarian or administrative cages, on the other. This initiates a crisis of the subject addressed in differing ways by critical theory (Adorno, Marcuse), structuralism/post-structur-
alism (Saussure, Lacan), phenomenology (Husserl, Heidegger) and existentialism (Jaspers, Sartre), a constellation significantly re-oriented by the beginnings
of post-colonialist critique (Fanon, in the 1950s). At this point, the good ship
"authenticity"—under threat not only from philosophical critiques but also
the baleful lessons of fascism and Stalinism—seemed definitely holed below the
water; and yet so pressing, still, appeared its demands, as God, Reason, Progress, lay dead or at least unconscious, that in another way it steamed ahead
even faster, into the turbulence of the sixties, folk revivals, rock purism, punk
nihilism and world beat just some of its musical manifestations. Fanon
(quoted, Caute 1970) himself still spoke its language: "Let us try to create the
whole man, whom Europe has been incapable of bringing to triumphant birth.'

This is the language of "culture" itself. But the idea of culture, in its distinctive modern sense, arises, yet again, with the Enlightenment project
itself—as the response of Herder and the German Romantics to the perceived
failures or banality of actual civilisation. Whether in its Arnoldian, aestheticist
or anthropological development, it is therefore *critical*; it answers to lack. From
this point of view, authenticity fills out the absence which culture anxiously
diagnoses. But culture is also a response to the secularising tendencies of the
society, to the disenchantment of the world. In this sense, it is normative: it
tells us what we *should* think or feel, what people *should* do, what culture
should be like, when divine revelation is unavailable and unreflexive tradition
seems insufficient. From this point of view, authenticity is precisely
uncritical—it offers itself as *natural* (which is, of course, one of the standard
definitions of ideology). Squeezed forth in this way, authenticity appears as, so
to speak, a by-product of secular culture's political ambition and the drama of

the modern subject's self-construction which accompanies this. Its materials can be both introjected (as superego commands and modes of signification assimilated from elsewhere) and projected (on to desirable others); but they co-exist or struggle there with their opposites, forever drawing the distinctions by which we live, by which cultural values—in music, for instance—have their effects. For the young Marx, "Man (...) practically and theoretically makes the species (...) History is the true natural history of man". (Marx 1975:327, 391)—that is, we become human when get to work on nature, enter history, and produce ourselves as the human species. But this historical movement (self-production, self-knowledge) comes with a cost—alienation. As Terry Eagleton puts it, culture in all its guises is a response to "the failure of culture as actual civilisation—as the grand narrative of human self-development (...) It [culture] is itself the illness to which it proposes a cure". (Eagleton 2000:23, 31) Authenticity, as a name for value-claims positioned within the alteritously structured social and psychological fields of action where the cultural body is formed, is a symptom of this disease.

The crisis of authenticity thus represents a cultural crisis and also a crisis of subjectivity. In both spheres, foundations seem to have been knocked away—foundations of, on the one hand, the subject's agency and schemas of representation (of both self and others), and, on the other hand, foundations of cultural legitimacy and power. I want to look briefly at two recent attempts to address these crises, first the crisis of ethnography as I shall call it—how we construe and write our relations with cultural others—and second the crisis of selfhood—how we locate ourselves as thinking and acting subjects in the world.

By "ethnography" I mean here not only ethnomusicologists" recordings of their encounters but also reports of analogous "expeditions", literal and metaphorical, by popular music scholars, and by historical anthropologists—Philip Bohlman and Gary Tomlinson, for example; and even by historical musicologists reconstructing past performance practices: all our attempts, in fact, to make sense of, to represent, to fashion a story—a *true* story—about what is foreign but must also become familiar—the music of others and our engagement with it. I'll focus on Michelle Kisliuk's classic exposition of a method appropriate to doing ethnography after the reflexive turn associated with the 1980s—"(Un)Doing Fieldwork: Sharing Songs, Sharing Lives" (Kisliuk 1997).

Kisliuk rejects any pseudo-objectivity, and knows well that her subject—music cultures of the BaAka in central Africa—is not just "there for her" (indeed, in her book-length study of the BaAka, *Seize the Dance*, she is very careful to distance herself from previous stereotypes of "pygmy" culture[3]). What's persuasive about her method is precisely her insistence to write herself in, to

---

[3] Given the profile of "pygmy pop" over recent decades, such caveats were certainly necessary; on the exploitation of BaAka and other central African "pygmy" music, by a range of musicians from jazz and rock through to avant-gardists such as Brian Eno and dance music mixes like *Deep Forest*, see Feld 2000.

Kantspel

present the encounter as shared, a "conversation", yet to acknowledge, even foreground, her own inescapable authoring role. In the impulse to share, she seems to put her identity at risk: "Self-Other boundaries are blurred (…) our very being merges with the 'field'" (*ibid.*:23); but this self-conscious constructionism has a purpose: ethnographers "create themselves" as, in fieldwork, "the process of identity-making surges to the forefront of awareness" (*ibid.*:24, 25); and in a sense her aim is to define herself as she wants the BaAka to see her— in particular, to differentiate herself from "tourists" and "missionaries". Here the intense difficulties in her project begin to emerge. She sides with the locals in their refusals to play along with stereotypes and in their essays in "modernisation"; but of course she cannot avoid having an agenda of her own: she too has a sense of what is "real" in BaAka culture, and ironically, to defend this, she has to risk her own "authenticity", to "perform" the role she wants to represent her in the encounter. Although she's aware of the history she brings with her, and of the history going to create BaAka culture as she finds it, the foregrounding of immediate "experience" ("I tried to keep an open mind" (*ibid.*:29), she writes), effectively brackets this out. She knows, and she knows that we know, that she is (unavoidably) selective; but her criterion for selection—we should "ask ourselves whether an experience changed us in a way that significantly affected how we viewed, reacted to, or interpreted the ethnographic material" (*ibid.*:39)—pushes ethnography in the direction of *Bildungsroman*; in the end, BaAka music becomes, against her will as it were, "for her". In the conjunction, "Kisliuk and the BaAka", each term is in danger of becoming the mere ground for the other; something has gone missing, and it's in this unacknowledged absence that the images of authenticity—of experience, of representation, of belonging—spring up.

It would risk distortion to describe the centrality of the authorial "I" in Kisliuk's article as "narcissistic". But this quality—such a familiar feature of life in our late-twentieth/early twenty-first century society—is a core theme for the philosopher Charles Taylor in his book, *The Ethics of Authenticity* (Taylor 1991). For Taylor, it describes one of the effects of the "soft relativism" into which the *topos* of the authentic self has now so often sunk, accompanied by privatisation of the subject and the shrinking of the bounds of agency in the face of systemic "iron-cage" instrumentalism. His answer is, like Kisliuk's, "conversation"—or to use his term, dialogics. He points out that outside of dialogue with significant others, no sense of a "real me" can have meaning; difference only registers against a horizon of existing values, and "authenticity" thus demands, as a condition of existence, reference to schemas located beyond the isolated self. Identity depends on recognition, and oppression can be defined as recognition denied. Taylor responds to the post-structuralist critique of authenticity by—paradoxically but plausibly enough—aligning the poetic, rhetorical qualities of the Nietzschean lineage with the same roots in Romantic aesthetics—the will to self-creation—as also generated the authenticity paradigm itself; but at the same time, by so to speak eliding Dionysus with Prometheus, he misses the *fictive* and *phantasmatic* quality of the post-structuralist self—the constant cancelling which renders the subject "as if"—forever lost, incomplete or elsewhere. Similarly, his heroic strategy to break the bars of the iron cage, through re-harnessing instrumental reason to moral choices open to (dialogically constructed) real agents in the service of concrete political projects, is on one level inspiring but falls short of the necessary acknowledgement of the possible effects of the prison state itself on the very structures of self-understanding and self-construction. Again, something important is missing: "self" and "other", "subject" and "society", are made to ground each other, and the movements of "authenticity" articulate that process; but the larger field of articulation is present only through its absence.

One term for the missing element might be "ideology". The indispensable name of the game, as it is for both Kisliuk and Taylor, is indeed "dialogics". Yet, even in the scriptural texts of dialogics—the writings of Bakhtin and his circle—the dialogic exchange, within the operation of signifying practices or of the structures of subjectivity, is commonly written in the language of ideological conflict. And "authenticity", born in the same Enlightenment moment as "ideology", lives within that world—the world of "truth" and "falsehood", "reality" and "illusion".

But if a dialogical stance is the starting-point for any attempt to re-figure authenticity for a world where foundational authority must be regarded as humanly constructed, then there are several versions available—including some which factor in a role for ideology. The best-known is Jürgen Habermas's model of "communicative reason": "action oriented to reaching understanding" in which "the unforced force of the better argument" is counted on to bring interlocutors into alignment, always subject to "third-party" judgement of validity-claims (that is, ideology critique in the interests of "undistorted communication') (Habermas 1990:296, 130). Habermas derives his model from what he identifies as a counter-discourse within Enlightenment reason itself—thus he distances himself from the exclusionary tactics he associates with Foucault and Derrida—and indeed he can be criticised for a neo-Kantian return of universalism: "intersubjective understanding" exerts a "binding force", setting up a "dialectic of betrayal and avenging force" (*ibid.*:324, 325) that is ultimately indebted to a religious motif of faith. At a distance from such universalism stands the unalloyed pragmatism of Richard Rorty (e.g. Rorty 1991), whose refusal to look beyond an interests-oriented account of truth, again pursued through intersubjective negotiation, links his politics with Taylor's liberalism. In both cases, however, one is struck by the sheer *reasonableness* of the approach—as if "authenticity" can just be neatly stitched back in to an unfortunately disrupted coffeehouse conversation. But if authenticity appears historically exactly in the moment when the modern dialogics of Self and Other emerge, then to identity dialogue as the mechanism *on its own* that can

Kantspel

save it is to take as input what was in the beginning an effect. Authenticity was born in shock. Its conjoining of ethical and aesthetic imperatives—law with pleasure, a "you should" with a "you want"—introjects a turbulence into the signifying dialogues forming the subject that goes along with the withdrawal of the Father (for God is dead). The resulting trauma is what requires to be brought to light.

We shall not get far without the concept of ideology. The difficulty here, though, is that this concept has long since been moved beyond its earlier character of tying values to specific interests—typically, those of social classes—so that, especially since the post-structuralist turn, it's most often now conceived as pervading discourse in general. According to Slavoj Žižek, "We are within ideological space proper the moment this [any] content—'true' or 'false' (if true, so much the better for the ideological effect)—is functional with regard to some relation of social domination ('power', 'exploitation') in an inherently non-transparent way" (Žižek 1999:61). But if "truth", as Lacan puts it, "has the structure of a fiction" (*ibid.*), what then marks out ideology as different? For Žižek, this is the wrong question. Indeed, the denial of a non-ideological reality is the ultimate ideological move, the too-easy "it's all ideology" acting as the verso of the vulgar-relativist "it's all true (from its own point of view)": "although ideology is already at work in everything we experience as 'reality', we must none the less maintain the tension that keeps the *critique* of ideology alive (...) ideology is not all; it is possible to assume a place that enables us to maintain a distance from it, *but this place from which we can denounce ideology must remain empty, it cannot be occupied by any positively determined reality*—the moment we yield to this temptation, we are back in ideology." (*ibid.*:70)

We *can* after all, then, ground ideology, and hence truth also—but only in an absence, an impossibility. And how is this place to be specified? Žižek takes a fix on it through the dualities of inside and outside, spirit and body, one ideology over against another, ideology as external force (institutionalised in the Ideological State Apparatuses of Althusserian theory, for example) and ideology as internal spontaneity. This dialogics introduces a "reflective distance": ideology is always "ideology of ideology" (*ibid.*:72), and we can think perhaps of chains of "authenticities" in this way. But this is no comfortable "conversation". Its issue is a ghostly presence, for which Žižek adopts Marx's term, "spectre": "an elusive pseudo-materiality that subverts the classic ontological opposition of reality and illusion" (*ibid.*:73). Spectre, indeed, *supplements* what can be represented, covering for what is missing from our symbolisations of "reality". It is, then, "the pre-ideological kernel, the formal matrix, on which are grafted various ideological formations" (*ibid.*:73)—and the spectre (of "authenticity" for example) stands for the return of just what cannot be represented. Lacanians will recognise here that Žižek is drawing on the master's concept of the Real—defined as what always escapes from, is foreclosed by, the orders of the Symbolic (ruled by the signifier) and the Imaginary (where the identities of Self and Other are played out), which brings them along with itself into being in the very act of foreclosure. For Žižek, then, spectre appears in the gap between "reality" and the Real; "the pre-ideological 'kernel' of ideology thus consists of the spectral apparition that fills up the hole of the Real." (*ibid.*:74)

What is the nature of this "hole'? It stems from the fact that the totality, the absolute, which, by definition, our socially constructed symbolisations can never encompass, is necessarily riven by social antagonisms—class struggle, for example—the representation of which is always already distorted, even as the protagonists concerned lay claim to the whole symbolic terrain—to the totality, as it were. "The 'repressed' real of antagonism" (*ibid.*:77), to use Žižek's phrase, can never emerge because it would mean the mutual cancelling of incompatible visions—one "authenticity" and another, "working-class" and "bourgeois", self and other—whose thoroughly ideological self-presentation as *polarities* inserts a third term, a neutral ground—"truth", "God", "social harmony"—to ground them. It is in the traumatic gap between these "realities" and the repressed Real that the apparitions of "authenticitity", "real music", "honest expression", "people's culture", "truthful performance", etc. emerge: spectral fetishes, fetishised spectres that are the subject of our worship and our haunting—not "true" but not "false" either. We can begin to glimpse what is missing from Kisliuk's and Taylor's accounts: just that antagonism—that "cut" between what is and what can be conceived—whose exclusion makes possible the appearance of an ordered symbolic whole, social reality as such, throwing up in the process the spectres associated with the authenticity trope: truth to self, representations of the other, a quasi-universalistic human sympathy, and so on.

In this perspective, critique remains possible—that is, without reverting to the epistemology of the "God trick". Returning to Lennon's *"God"*, we could seek to uncover the historically specific antagonisms on which his polarisation of "dream" and "reality", iconic myth and inner truth, is founded, and which it represses; and on which the authentication of "black music", in relation to an implied other, is set up. There's a further dimension. The song is embedded in a discourse of exchange (an inventory of the values of false gods), as against use—the "real" value of the material here-and-now ("Yoko and me"). Žižek derives his figure of the spectre from Marx's theory of the commodity-fetish, which of course also confounds the false (ghostly) abstractions of exchange with the nonetheless "real" presence of the consumer good. We can add another twist to the approach if we see this not just as an analytic model but also as an historically specific condition; for authenticity arose *on the back of* commodity-fetishism: the two figures are co-dependent, each the under- or over-side of the other. These spectres are *Doppelgänger*—and the authenticity claims of musical commodities, such as Lennon's album, gleam through a dense and ghostly mist.

485

Kantspel

Politics also remain possible, in particular through tactics of *appropriation*—re-articulating particular elements of ideology from one social position to another, re-mapping the location of an "authenticity" in relation to the social formation, freeing authenticities from, breaking their bonds with, their others and deconstructing their (false) positivities. We can hear Lennon doing this vis-à-vis the discourses of rock, particularly countercultural rock, and the prior rock appropriation of black music; but his own appropriation is of course no less ideological, and is open to re-articulation out of its apparent fixing to a familiar bourgeois domestic solipsism. And we could easily follow the re-commodification of the John-and-Yoko myth in subsequent years; the intertwining of authenticity and commodity fetishes operates here too, and appropriation always threatens to re-appear as a capitalisation of cultural property.

Crucial to the functions of both critique and politics is the unmasking of "authenticity"'s reification, whether in relation to self or cultural form—that is, its configuration, in a precise Marxian sense, as an *authenticity-fetish*; and along with this, its analysis as, conversely, a *moment* in the endless flow of sub-jectifications and objectifications taking place in the exchanges of inside and outside, self and other.

Which brings us to the final turn in Žižek's analysis. Figuring "spectrality as that which fills out the unrepresentable abyss [the trauma] of antagonism" "(*ibid.*:79), that is, as what covers up the very foreclosure which makes repre-sentation possible, brings him to the suggestion that spectrality as such responds to a fear—the fear of *freedom*, conceived as that moment when an act of transgression temporarily cancels both "reality"—the flow of symbolisa-tions—and the power of the spectre. Žižek warns against "ontologisation" of this moment; and we have seen enough examples of totalitarian closure, attaching themselves to pseudo-authenticities, to recognise the danger—the social essence of human life itself rules that historically developing reality is incomplete as such: it can never be grasped as totalised. Yet this doesn't exclude the possibility that from time to time the vicious circle of closure can be disrupted. What this means in concrete terms is less than clear; yet in thinking this through, we can hold on to the idea that, although "authenticity" may be spectral, its kernel can also stand for "a dream within the dream"(*ibid.*:82), and there remains the chance that "reality" can fracture, under the shock-effect of "the real thing".

Richard Middleton: The Real Thing?

References

Bohlman, Philip 2002. *World Music: A Very Short Introduction* (Oxford: Oxford University Press)

Born, Georgina & David Hesmondhalgh (eds.) 2000: *Western Music and Its Others: Difference, Representation, and Appropriation in Music* (Berkeley: University of California Press)

Caute, David 1970. *Fanon* (London: Fontana)

Eagleton, Terry 2000. *The Idea of Culture* (Oxford: Blackwell)

Frith, Simon 1981. "'The Magic that Can Set You Free': The Ideology of Folk and the Myth of the Rock Community", *Popular Music*, 1, pp.159–68

Feld, Steven 2000. "The Poetics and Politics of Pygmy Pop", Georgina Born & David Hesmondhalgh (eds.): *Western Music and Its Others: Difference, Representation, and Appropriation in Music* (Berkeley: University of California Press), pp.254–79

Frith, Simon 1988. "Playing with Real Feeling—Jazz and Suburbia", *Music for Pleasure: Essays in the Sociology of Pop* (Cambridge: Polity Press, 1988), pp.45–63

Habermas, Jürgen 1990. *The Philosophical Discourse of Modernity: Twelve Lectures*, trans. Frederick Lawrence (Cambridge: Polity Press)

Kisliuk, Michelle 1997. "(Un)Doing Fieldwork: Sharing Songs, Sharing Lives", Gregory F. Barz & Timothy J. Cooley (eds.): *Shadows in the Field : New Perspectives for Fieldwork in Ethnomusicology* (New York: Oxford University Press), pp.23–44

Marx, Karl 1975. *Early Writings*, trans. Rodney Livingstone & Gregor Benton (Harmondsworth: Penguin)

Middleton, Richard 2000. "Musical Belongings: Western Music and Its Low-Others", Georgina Born & David Hesmondhalgh (eds.): *Western Music and Its Others: Difference, Representation, and Appropriation in Music* (Berkeley: University of California Press), pp.59-85

Moore, Allan 2002. "Authenticity as Authentication", *Popular Music*, 21/2, pp. 209–23

Rorty, Richard 2002. "To the Sunlit Uplands" (review of Bernard Williams, *Truth and Truthfulness: An Essay in Genealogy*, Princeton: Princeton University Press, 2002), *London Review of Books*, 31/October, pp.13–15

Rorty, Richard 1991. Objectivity, Relativism and Truth, Philosophical Papers, 1 (Cambridge: Cambridge University Press)

Taylor, Charles. 1991. *The Ethics of Authenticity* (Cambridge MA: Harvard University Press)

Wenner, Jan 1972. *Lennon Remembers: The Rolling Stone Interviews* (Harmondsworth: Penguin)

Žižek, Slavoj 1999. "The Spectre of Ideology", Elizabeth Wright & Edmond Wright (eds.): *The Žižek Reader* (Oxford: Blackwell), pp.53–86

Discography

John Lennon/Plastic Ono Band 1970. Apple PCS 7124

CHAPTER 11

'Last Night a DJ Saved My Life': Avians, Cyborgs and Siren Bodies in the Era of Phonographic Technology

Saving life, fixing the mix

I'm listening to Mariah Carey's version of the classic dance-tune, 'Last Night a DJ Saved My Life' (which appeared on the soundtrack of her disastrous feature film, *Glitter*). But Carey – arguably *the* female pop voice of the 1990s – isn't heard for the first minute of the track.[1] Instead, the scene is set by the intersecting imperatives of three male rappers, Busta Rimes, Fabulous and DJ Clue, and their orders brook no argument: 'Pay attention! ... Give it to me! ... Shake it and bounce around!' Throughout the song, Carey's voice (capable as it is of multi-octave virtuosity) is restrained, generally low in register, positioned in the middle-ground of the mix, behind the men, behind the rhythm track. It comes across as the willing object of a complex manipulative production. What is going on? 1

In a time-worn move, the film's narrative tracks the audience's knowledge of Carey's own mythic life-story – from childhood struggle to stardom, via chance and romance (the very first sound-film, Al Jolson's *The Jazz Singer*, set the trend). Her curvaceous but strangely homogenised body, draped in alluring poses and glittering, plasticated sheen around the CD booklet just as it is across the movie screen, seals the deal – the sale which buys celebrity. How does the DJ's life-saving performance fit into this narrative? 2

On one level the story told in the song is conventional enough: **3**
forget your troubles, lose yourself in song, find solace in dance.
But this scenario is insistently gendered. The rappers' voices
make explicit what we could anyway assume – that the DJ will be
male, and that the object of his ministrations will be female, here
'embodied' vocally (as it were) in the little-girl-lost voice offered by
Carey. The DJ stands for authority, an authority with pedagogic
power: 'Hey listen up to your local DJ/You better hear what he's
got to say/There's not a problem that I can't fix/Cause I can do it
in the mix.' As the multiple rap voices shoot across the sonic
space from all directions, surrounding Carey's low-key, centrally
positioned vocal, it's tempting to adapt the distinction commonly
made in film theory between a stereotypic male position – mobile,
free to enter and leave the visual scene, crossing boundaries at
will – and the equally stereotypic female position – passive, fixed,
an element of the space itself. As Teresa de Lauretis puts it, 'The
woman, fixed in the position of icon, spectacle, or image to be
looked at, bears the mobile look of both the spectator and the
male character(s). It is the latter who commands at once the
action and the landscape...'[2] Yet the lyrics I just quoted come
(towards the end of the track) from Carey, sliding between
subject-positions. She has, on the one hand, learned the lesson
which her posse of prancing rappers have handed down, but on
the other hand, she appears to stand in their place: echo, mimic
or (in some strange way, as if the positions of ventriloquist and
dummy were reversed), precondition or even source?[3]

I'll return to the issue of embodiment (and also to that of **4**
ventriloquism). For now, I want just to note that, in spite of the way
the recording makes elaborate textural and vocal gestures
towards the reproduction of a live event, actually all the voices
here have, strictly speaking, left any body behind.[4] The record
form itself, generically, marks this erasure. But it's amplified by the
digital technology used to produce this particular recording: all the
voices recorded in different studios, Carey singing her own
backing vocals, the mix created with the help of Protools software.
The voices come to us from..... from where? We have no idea –
except that we know, if we stop to think about it, that they emerge
from some apparatus, from a machine. This is canned music, its
ontology most clearly centred in *things* – the CD, the audio
equipment, the surrounding visual images of Carey; as a
persistent strand of criticism throughout the twentieth century told

us ('Keep Music Live', said the Musicians Union), this music is *dead.* How can a DJ, whose professional activity lies in the spinning, the spinning out, of this simulacrum of performance, possibly 'save a life'?

As is well known, the connection of phonograph technology with tropes of death stems from its very beginnings.[5] Preservation of the voices of the dead, it was envisaged, would be one of its principal functions. The editors of the *Scientific American* in 1877 'pronounced Edison the only man alive capable of raising the voices of the dead'.[6] 'Upon replaying the old cylinder,' writes Friedrich Kittler, '...it is a corpse that speaks.'[7] – a sensation whose uncanniness we should make every effort to reconstitute, for as the fictitious composer who features in Maurice Renard's short story of 1907 – a story reproduced by Kittler – puts it: 'How terrible it is to hear this copper throat and its sounds from beyond the grave!'[8]

In his early writings on the new recording technologies, dating from 1928 and 1934,[9] Theodor Adorno laments the fading of this uncanny, disruptive power following the domestication of the apparatus into a piece of bourgeois furniture. The gramophone horn, once 'brass', becomes 'muffled', both in design and material, and its messages mutate from 'fanfares of the street' into 'shrouds of the emptiness that people usually prefer to enshroud within themselves'. Even though this process of 'stabilisation' is apparently not complete – for 'the downtrodden gramophone horns reassert themselves as proletarian loudspeakers' – Adorno fails to pursue his own hint about the role of social variability, and his funereal imagery – it points towards a sort of 'second death', actually – seems to mark the end of records' role as 'disturbers of the peace'.[10] Nevertheless, Adorno does suggest that in principle the needle's direct (that is, unmediated) inscription of its message still retains the potential to summon up memories of a pre-lapsarian *Ur*-language. This 'machine-writing', 'delicately scribbled, utterly illegible[,]...committed to the sound that inhabits this and no other acoustic groove', points towards a condition marked by a kind of pre-subjective subjectivity, a state before the babble (Babel) of divergent meanings, when things could speak for themselves and art might become 'an archaic text of knowledge to come'.[11] Much later, Kittler picks up this idea: 'Ever since the invention of the phonograph, there has been writing without a subject... Record grooves dig the grave of the

author.'[12] (I'll come back to the overlapping territories of groove
and grave.)

At first sight, Adorno's position might seem to manifest a dismaying   7
nostalgia – or at best to draw upon the messianic strand in the
thought of his friend Walter Benjamin without fully assimilating it to
his own rather different project. As cultural technology, records enter
a social field that is always already formed – is alive and lively, one
might say – and their voices are always already subjectivated. The
image of the tortured parrot in a box presented in music-hall singer
Gus Elen's 1896 song, 'The Finest Flow O' Langwidge Ever 'Eard',
and discussed recently by Elizabeth Leach, comes to mind.[13]
Elen's 'phonygraff', as depicted on the song-sheet, is nothing more
than a parrot hidden in a hat-box, into which four listeners are
plugged via 'hearing tubes' (as so often with such images, the inter-
connection of the listeners through a central machine has a
cyborgian look to us today, and indeed medical technologies such
as the stethoscope played an important role in the emergence of this
new imagination of the sounding body, as Sterne has pointed
out[14]). The parrot is forced into speech (by prodding it with a pin,
dropping burning tobacco on it, putting pepper in its seed), but its
'songs', in successive refrains, engage common music-hall
scenarios, inhabited by stock characters (an irate landlord, a bookie
taken to the cleaners, a 'lady' jostled in the street). The scene may
be surreal, even uncanny, then – nature and machine conflated –
but the musical result is both socially specific and culturally familiar.
Thus the parrot may certainly be read as 'foreign' – an exotic other –
but has been domesticated too (a pet in a cage), and, although it
impersonates both men and women, its babbling subservience
positions it discursively, I would suggest, as feminine, its flow of
mechanical mimicry a nicely suggestive complement to the
contemporaneous figure of (silent) masculine fidelity offered by the
celebrated HMV dog, Nipper.[15] It is also low-class, its 'finest flow o'
langwidge' clearly (and not surprisingly, given the torture that
provokes it) a stream of obscenities which produces mixed
reactions, of amusement or of outrage, from the respectable
bourgeois listeners depicted on the song-sheet. Gus Elen, himself
positioned as a cockney coster (a lovable, working-class exotic), has
the role of a kind of *deus ex machina* (or *deus machinae*?), whose
'negotiation' of/with this feminised, rough-trade avian other at one
and the same time falls into a familiar pattern of music-hall cultural
politics and looks forward to what would become (as we shall see) a
standard dynamic within the cultural economy of recorded song.

As Leach makes clear, what is crucially at stake in Elen's song is 8
the status of 'writing', as this has been and can be figured across
a range of practices – from vocal performance through textualities
of various sorts to mechanically and electronically mediated
reproduction – and across a *longue durée* with roots deep in the
Classical equation of language and reason, passed on through
the traditions of Christian Platonism. In the beginning was the
word, which was with God and which wrote nature into existence.
If the book of nature is there, for science, to be read, it is also
there as an ambivalent stage-setting for the voice of Man, at once
source and threat. Elen's parrot stands not for nature in any
primordial sense but for nature on the rack, subjected – as Adorno
might well have pointed out – to the ravages of instrumentalised
reason, forced to reflect back to us our most inane blather. Leach
also points out that the parrot is not the only bird species to
feature in this discursive tradition; just as it stands for irrational
imitation, so the nightingale stands quintessentially for a kind of
natural (as against human) reason, each in its divergent way
being deployed to set off the distinctiveness of music proper. Yet
singers too have over the same period often been compared to
both parrots (silly reproduction machines) and nightingales
(artless vehicles of nature). Were they 'phonygraffs', or even
musical cyborgs, *avant la lettre*?[16]

For the Romantics, the book of nature was a *secret* one, and 9
Adorno – following Benjamin – picked up the idea of a pre-
representational 'hieroglyphic' system which, he suggested, it was
music's utopian role, hinted at in the directly inscribed form of the
record, to encrypt and to reveal. The parrot's mechanical 'flow o'
langwidge' might also remind us, then, of another mysterious
force of nature – the hypnotic effects associated mythically with
the singing of the Sirens, who would become important to
Adorno's argument as, in collaboration with Max Horkheimer, he
subsequently developed it, in *Dialectic of Enlightenment*: the
Sirens who, as Barbara Engh points out, are described as half
woman, half bird.[17] Adorno sees Odysseus's encounter with
them as standing for that fateful moment which marks the way
(male) logos would learn to resist the blandishments of (female)
pathos – if only by stopping up the ears and immobilising the body
– but for Adorno, Engh insists, this points not only towards the
historical trajectory of gender difference but also to the still more
basic problematic within which the human differentiates itself from

beastly nature.[18] Engh is right; and yet, the distinction of levels is hard to maintain with any rigour:

While they [the Sirens] directly evoke the recent past, with the irresistible promise of pleasure as which their song is heard, they threaten the patriarchal order which renders to each man his life only in return for his full measure of time... Men had to do fearful things to themselves before the self, the identical, purposive, and virile nature of man was formed...[19]

The Adornian narrative – like this discursive tradition as a whole – has a distinctly theological cast: 'the idea of music is the form of the divine name', and music's task is to 'name the name itself' in a form of 'demythologised prayer'[20] – a phal-logocentrism whose hierarchic effect is hardly overturned by those inversions in certain feminist moves which locate a foundational stratum instead in some pre-linguistic bodily 'knowledge' to which women (like birds? like Sirens?) have privileged access.

Clearly, the implications of Adorno's argument are far more subtle 10 than my initial sketch may have suggested. His apocalyptics are grounded not just in 'nostalgia' but also in a historically located account of the human 'traffic with technology' which presents its potential outcome as having positively 'post-human' implications: 'phonograph records', he argues,

are not artworks but the black seals on the missives that are rushing towards us from all sides in the traffic with technology; missives whose formulations capture the sounds of creation, the first and last sounds, judgement upon life and message about that which may come thereafter.[21]

Yet, although developing (and exploitative) social relations have a vital role in his historiography, its quasi-theocratic underpinning – based, ultimately, on a scriptural metaphysics – limits the value of his interpretations of actual recorded content. He would no doubt agree with the suggestion that, as the needle circles towards the central 'black hole', the inescapably metaphorical status of this movement makes clear that the social dynamics within which records are emplaced are always specific (hence always gendered, raced, classed); indeed, his own imagery – he writes of 'the scriptal spiral that disappears in the center, in the opening of the middle, but in return survives in time' – might almost be taken to foreshadow the Lacanian discourse of 'organ holes' (such as the mouth) through which the culture can continue to be, in Derrida's term, 'invaginated', and to summon up the equally sexualised connotations of the 'horny' loudspeaker, re-phallicising (hence dis-seminating) what the work of the needle had begun.[22] Still, I believe that Adorno got the positions here somewhat awry. In his account, female voices don't record effectively because they need the physical presence of their originating bodies, whereas the male voice – quintessentially for him that of Caruso – works precisely because here voice is identical with self, with logos we might say. To pick up Engh's psychoanalytic extrapolation, the phonographic machine, in a sort of Lacanian mirror-phase procedure, acts as the ideal form of the male body – it is, in Adorno's words, 'the sounding image of his own person', records being 'sounding photographs of their owners'; and the male's disavowal of loss – of his 'castration' – is made bearable through his demand that the female performing body fill in for his lack.[23] But in the actual music history, things are surely not like this. In the field of popular song, we might speculate (however reductively), the privileged objects are the voices of women, and by extension of blacks and feminised men. Meanwhile, control of these voices is normatively in the hands of white males – either exercised through an authoritative lead vocal or, more typically, through a 'voice off' in the studio[24] – or in the spinning hands of the DJ: that DJ whose 'performances' animate the traces in the record grooves, in a process of Derridean 'arche-writing' which will place any quest for an *Ur*-language in question but which will persist in its belief that only in his hands can technics save life.

Why is this outline reductive? Because we can easily think, for 11 example, of macho male pop singers – Presley, Lennon, Jagger – not to mention 'masterful' women and black DJs and producers.[25] Nevertheless, the principle stands, pegged in place as a base-line from which deviations are experienced as such. Within this tradition, to *perform* at all – especially through such a bodily intimate mechanism as singing – is to put a body on display, to flaunt it, offer it up: a role which of course is typically associated with, expected of, women. Indeed, in this discursive formation, to *own* to a body already produces a place of subordination, creating the potential to suffer (as Mariah Carey does: the entire music culture within which this music works insists that we imagine her body, even if the inescapable visual images didn't all the time remind us); meanwhile, the owners of discourse (Carey's rapper friends, for instance) are all words, bodies effaced from view no less than those of the record producers.[26] But vocal machismo is often ambivalent, its pumped-up demand tinged with a homoerotic tease (Presley, Lennon, Jagger); similarly, 'strong' women (Joplin, Franklin, Simone, Madonna) nevertheless play to deeply entrenched male fantasies, just as black men, even when constructed into the stud persona of racist stereotype, also find themselves willy-nilly spending the legacy of an 'emasculation' rhetoric rooted in the socio-sexual economy of slavery. All this confirms what we know well enough, that the sexual dynamics of gender (and race), however over-determined in their normative expression, can speak with many tongues – a complexity only intensified by the fact that, if the apparatus of recording acts as a mirror (as it surely does), it is an *acoustic* mirror that is involved. 'Reflections' of the vocal body, traversing anamorphically the gap between mouth and ear, have a capacity to short-circuit the 'normal' distinctions between inside and outside, self and other – for 'the moment we enter the symbolic order, an unbridgeable gap separates forever a human body from "its" voice. The voice acquires a spectral autonomy, it never quite belongs to the body we see'[27] – as well as entering a permanent query about the mutual fit of the psychoanalytic mechanisms of 'voice' and 'gaze'. Of what order are the bodies we desire or identify with as we listen to 'Last Night a DJ Saved My Life' (or as Adorno listened to Caruso), and through what processes are they produced?

What is a woman, what a man (and what a Siren)?

Others have begun to explore the social dynamics involved in the   12
gendering of the recorded voice. Barbara Bradby, for example, has pointed to the key divergence in dance music between male rapping and female soul-singing, the one centred on language, the other on embodied feeling.[28] From a similar perspective, John Corbett has discussed the implications of the typical pop hierarchy of lead and backing vocals:[29] while for Corbett, recorded music as such is in a sense 'entirely voice-over',[30] within this overarching scenario a lead voice typically articulates the narrative while backing vocals offer an often linguistically

nonsensical 'sonorous envelope'. The latter, he argues, are positioned normatively as female – and by extension, as also black; and hence as *castrated* – which (continuing the metaphor across the sexuating divide) produces a permanent threat of *bleeding* from one category to another, for example from female – that 'black hole where meaning drains out of the system', in Kaja Silverman's words[31] – to male. Corbett's argument points, rightly, towards a more nuanced picture than the binary from which, necessarily, interpretation starts. If, at the level of the technology, 'it is lack of the visual, endemic to recorded sound, that initiates desire in relation to the popular music object',[32] then this lack cuts, potentially, in all directions. (Think early Elvis. Does that groove 're-embody' the lead voice (and what gender, exactly, are those hips)? And if it does, is it in turn disrupted by Elvis's characteristic 'hiccups', 'dis-membering' a body turned back towards a *corps re-morcelé*? Is this body *black* – as early radio listeners famously assumed?) Thus recording technology, by apparently evacuating bodies from the scene of subject-production, places previous systems of both gender and race relations into crisis, a crisis which reassertions of familiar binaries will try to nullify – as in 'Last Night a DJ Saved My Life' – but whose underlying mode – usually hidden, sometimes visible – is one of *hysteria*.

Hysteria is, stereotypically, a female complaint; according to Lacan, its identifying question is 'Who am I? a man or a woman?', or, more precisely, 'What is it to be a woman?'[33] The complement here, on the male side, is obsession (a neurotic 'dialect' of hysteria, according to Freud) – but obsession mediated by a distinct strand of *fetishism*, manifested in masculine fetishising of records, both as collectable commodities and as carriers of aural fidelity, but in any case following the pattern of a familiar economy of possession and disavowal.[34] (Racial hysteria and fetishism follow similar patterns – allowing for the different terms in the structure.) But in a moment of crisis, both conditions migrate. Within the vocal field, the hysterical question, for the female, as Engh points out, concerns the threat of disembodiment, while for the male, it centres on loss of control over memory: whence, one might say, the fetishistic desire for and identification with a maximally abstracted sound – a voice of knowledge.[35] In Renard's story, his composer listens obsessively to the sounds held within a 'double-horned' sea-shell, which he compares to a gramophone; 'women were singing... inhuman women whose hymn was wild and lustful like the scream

13

of a crazed goddess... and the same maddening scene was repeated, periodically, as if by phonograph, incessantly and never diminished.' Driven to distraction by his inability to notate the 'sexual screaming' he hears (that is, to abstract it, to tie it down for memory), the composer falls down dead; and 'what if', asks the narrator, 'he died *because he heard the sirens singing*?'[36] But what about the Sirens, what happens to them? Is their hysterical question, mediated by the encounter with another (the phonographic) 'reproductive body', a question that takes the form of a demand for the return to them of phallic motherhood – of woman not as the source of infantile babble but the territory of maternal law, and beyond that, of a 'writing before writing', a vocal productivity which goes all the way down into nature itself?[37]

I want to move shortly to consideration of a second recording, one 14 that might throw extra light on the questions raised so far. But before this, I need to situate the record economy, however briefly, in something of its pre-history: a genealogy articulated in the intersection of several long-lived tropes in the late-eighteenth and early nineteenth centuries. First, Hegel's master-slave dialectic – permeating both social registers (Woman, Black, Low, all widely imagined as natural slaves) and the march of reason itself, with its outcomes in such technologies as the phonographic 'invisible master' demanding fidelity from the voices he deploys; second, the mapping of this 'slavery' condition to the psycho-social dynamics of commodity-production and commodity-fetishism (notice how records even look a bit like coins, and are collected – hoarded – as if they were); and third, the way this drama of having and being (as Lacan would describe it) provokes that decisive shift in the structure of ventriloquism described by Steven Connor, from possession *by* (a supernatural force) to possession *of* (a dummy, genie, stooge) – a shift that is predictably gendered.[38] Small wonder that the voices of women, blacks and feminised men have been favoured by the phonographic ventriloquists, nor that it's pre-eminently their bodies which have been put in question. For this genealogy as a whole places the body in crisis – and once again, Adorno and Horkheimer offer a telling insight. They present the Sirens episode as a master-and-slave allegory.[39] Both master (Odysseus) and slaves (his men) are 'disabled', the first immobilised and alienated from practice, the second reduced to a function, their labour alienated from their senses. In the crisis of the encounter, both too are *silenced*: Odysseus has no listeners (his men cannot hear) while they are just mutely 'yoked in the same rhythm'.[40] The master-slave structure of ventriloquism breaks down – or rather, both parties become subjects of a higher (invisible) master, who, for Adorno and Horkheimer, will turn out to be: capital. At the same time, both are also 'disembodied': Odysseus is bound, his body straitjacketed, while the men's bodies are turned into a mere instrumentalised force of reproduction (like women's?).[41]

How, then, does the technology of recorded song speak to this **15** still-evolving crisis? Disco might mark a key moment: when 'slaves' in all the categories I have mentioned – Woman, Black, Low, the 'living dead' rising from the grave of history – were summoned to the dance floor and took it over. The key issue then might become, not only the surface politics of possession – who controls whom – but also the deeper question of the structure of possession as such, and its implications for subjectivity.[42]

Machining voices, organising bodies

Here now, nurtured in the same dance-music lineage as gave rise **16** to disco, comes the freaky figure of Dr Funkenstein, one of funk music pioneer George Clinton's several aliases, which go along with his many band names: Parliament, Funkadelic, and, with particular resonance here, The Brides of Funkenstein. He is singing – if that's the right word – his eponymous song;[43] but he's not alone. Clinton developed a celebrated live show, centred on space-travel imagery – he tended to emerge, in a clear birthing metaphor, out of 'The Mothership' – and John Corbett has argued persuasively[44] that Clinton's claims to 'alien' origins connect not only with themes of alienation, madness and liminal identity but also with the Afro-diasporic experience of displacement and slavery: to be positioned, however repressively, outside species normality (as 'non-human' – either beast or robot) creates a margin for subversion – maybe even a pointer towards the 'post-human'. It's not surprising, then, that, as Corbett points out, zombie-related discourse figures centrally in Clinton's rhetoric, and (as he doesn't[45]) that such discourse has deep roots in Afro-diasporic culture; nor, perhaps, that in 'Dr Funkenstein' our mad funk-scientist is accompanied by a whole posse of – of what? Clones, the album title tells us – but clones, perhaps, with a history as slaves and zombies; and a future also – as duppy conquerors?[46]

Over a slow funk groove, its tonic-chord drone (interrupted only by   17
occasional IV-V-I curtain-raisers) embroidered with a polyrhythmic
interplay of bass, guitar and keyboard riffs, our (invisible) master
of funk introduces himself in relaxed proto-rap style. The boasting
is standard ('kiss me on my ego'), and his verses alternate with a
relatively unchanging choral refrain pronounced in rhythmic
speech-song by what are undoubtedly his creatures ('We love you
Dr Funkenstein, your funk is the best... Hit me on the one again; if
you want, hit me again'), but also, it seems, his creation. The
Doctor, fresh from the Mothership, so he tells us, positions himself
in a lab ('micro-biologically speaking', begins one of his verses,
before plunging into a torrent of pseudo-scientific gobbledy-gook),
but his discourse is also embedded in history: his fascination with
bones takes the form of an elaborate allusion to the old African-
American spiritual 'Dry Bones', itself based on Ezekiel's biblical
vision of the valley of bones. Thus the act of creating new life is
referenced both to the moment of Romantic crisis when, as Mary
Shelley's tale implies, the book of nature might indeed be read but
with fateful results, and to an even longer, in-effect mythological
history in which the life-and-death struggles of slavery were linked
to the work of divine providence ('Son of Man, can these bones
live?'[47]). Indeed, the track as a whole positions itself within the
complex dialogical networks of African-American Signifyin(g) (not
least through the use of soul/funk formulae: 'well, all right', etc.); in
structure, it could be heard almost as a parody of James Brown's
'Say It Loud – I'm Black and I'm Proud', with its chanted children's
refrain.[48]

In the last couple of minutes of 'Dr Funkenstein', however,   18
Clinton's voice gradually retreats from the foreground, burying
itself behind the sounds of his 'creatures', not to mention a freaky,
free jazz-style trombone solo (even before this, its authority had
begun to be put at risk through gender-problematising shifts of
register); a 'parliament' of voices takes over. Is Clinton here
subverting the structure of the master-slave dialectic; or even,
perhaps, refusing its terms altogether? If so, part of this move
might be a refusal of funk cliché, positioning the genre in the lab
(rather than 'nature') and claiming the black body for modernity –
a refusal that, in turn, might be read as also an attempt to side-
step an oedipal competition with Brown (Soul Brother Number
One, self-proclaimed inventor of funk, and epitome of the
labouring, sweating, 'funky' black body).[49] This is probably too

simple, though. Clinton no less than Brown constantly claims in his lyrics funk supremacy.[50] Moreover, in 'Dr Funkenstein' he is clear that his skeletal connections find their ultimate point[51] in 'movement of the hips' – dance as simulacrum of sex – while, conversely, Brown presents himself, not just as a force of nature, but – in the title of one his songs – as a 'sex machine': a phrase conjuring up, needless to say, a whole history of cyborgian imagery centred on the robotic reproductive labour of the slave at the same time as it insists on black sexuality's relevance to contemporary industrialised culture. Dr Funkenstein's hips may clank and grind, or they may groove (but doesn't 'groove' summon up industrial as well as organic connotations anyway?) – but what exactly are their offspring? Are we talking reproduction – or (clone-like) replication?[52]

To address this question, perhaps we should attend to the voices **19** of these creatures. And strange creatures they are, indeed – not clearly either monsters or cyborgs. The choir is one thing – or rather, it isn't, its slightly raggy robotic rhythms sounding either drilled or drugged or perhaps both. But pervading the whole track is an array of individual voices (voice-unders?), filling the sonic space with life, many of them back-of-the-throat squawks and gurgles, others comically ululating melismas (part cartoon, part pseudo-operatic: sirens for the age of the pop diva?), all of them strangely positioned in frame of reference between the simian and the avian.[53] The scene, apparently, could be either jungle or studio-laboratory – or both. (Despite the importance of Clinton's live shows, it's clear that, in a reversal of the conventional assumption, the principles of his multi-polar, fragmentary aesthetic were worked out first in the studio, were made imaginable by studio technology.[54]) But while this collective vocality is more variable than Clinton's lead, it is so only in degree; in both fields, it splits apart. Moreover it is, as we have already seen, far from clear, far from settled, where the lead is located. Is this a case of the authority normally associated with 'space-off' being subverted? At any rate, reading the 'sociology' of the song is certainly complicated. What genders are represented? Hard to say – and, while the groove is undoubtedly 'black', aren't there also (in the freakish sounds) echoes of Frank Zappa and Captain Beefheart, tribute to Clinton's earlier funkadelic fusion of acid and dance? (To quote the words of a slightly later Funkadelic album, 'one nation under a groove'.) One might diagnose symptoms of both gender and racial hysteria if the groove were not so relaxed – but for Lacan, 'hysteria' describes a certain social-symbolic structure as much as a clinical extreme: a structure that we can see in terms of an imaginary social anatomy, fragmented by inexplicable vectors of identity confusion.

The mad scientist's funk is engraved in the groove, the bodies – 20 organs of this social body? – animated by system loops. (In the etymological history, 'groove' and 'grave' have linked origins, but there are sexual connotations as well – in American slang, the groove could be the vagina – as well as drug overtones – being possessed by grooviness – and of course the record groove, connecting to connotations of industrialised reproduction, spins us into the heart of the mechanical or cybernetic apparatus. In this discursive nexus, life and death, subject and object, body and machine, are tightly conjoined.[55]) We have become used to the idea of funky machines – the robotic Grace Jones or Michael Jackson, 'slaves to the rhythm'. In Barbara Engh's discussion of Adorno and the Sirens, she points to an earlier episode in the *Odyssey*, where the hero, anonymous for the moment, *does* hear the song; unwelcome memories flood in, dissolving self-control, as he imagines himself a woman, a slave – by implication, an animal, 'panting and dying'.[56] As the record-apparatus threads its way, via transistor radio, walkman, iPod, mobile phone and the rest, into every social space, public and private, as sampling and re-mixing constantly re-animate what Engh, after Adorno, calls the 'archive of subjectivity',[57] we are far from the domestication that Adorno lamented, and moving – perhaps – towards a new understanding of the otherness of nature, of the nature of objectness, in which memory no less than images of possible bodies may circulate in a 'book' of digitised data. If we were to interpret 'Dr Funkenstein' in the light of Donna Haraway's project to reinvent 'nature' – problematising right across the categories of 'simians, cyborgs and women' – we would have to ask if we find here what she calls 'significant prosthesis': a new kind of embodiment.[58]

But – was the body ever really *lost*? Or, to put it another way, 21 hasn't it always already been 'lost' – a figure that the subject can hold together only with difficulty, under and against the pressures of particular, changing historical contingencies? Jonathon Sterne argues that the sense of trauma accompanying the initial phonographic moment marks the 'loss' of a prior fullness which this moment itself had constructed; the idea of aural 'fidelity' (along with a whole raft of associated concepts, including 'authenticity', 'live' as distinct from 'canned music', and Benjaminian 'aura') arises at precisely the point when technological change puts it at risk, thereby bringing it into being: 'reproduction precedes originality'.[59] This is to say that the most important effect of changes in cultural technology may be to reveal – that is, to enable us to think – what in a sense was already there. Certainly, if the advent of phonographic voice-over was traumatic, listeners seem to have got used to it fairly quickly; but this may be because, on some level, they were well aware that the body, as cultural construct, has always taken multiple forms, including what has been termed the 'vocalic body': 'the idea... of a surrogate or secondary body, a projection of a new way of having or being a body, formed and sustained out of the autonomous operations of the voice', an idea that can be given a strong sense of the complex energy flows involved, into, through and out of the various organs of ingestion, excretion and ejaculation, by means of the ancillary term, 'vocalimentary canal'.[60]

We have long been accustomed to assigning such vocalic bodies 22 to a putative source – an invisible cuckoo, a nightingale in the darkness, a mist-enshrouded foghorn (or siren), the thunder of the gods... By contrast, what might be called the 'acousmatic fallacy' characteristic of some theories of electro-acoustic music wants us to conceive of synthesised sounds with no 'body' at all – sounds in themselves, so to speak; but listeners immediately invent an imagined source for them, drawing on the contours embedded in their experience of the operations of the vocalimentary canal: the phallus (male or female) writes, the voice translates, and the mapping of this process to the structures of anatomical and other visual and tactile knowledge describes exactly how the sensuous and the symbolic create each other, through the Derridean networks of 'dissemination' and 'invagination'. All sounds, then, 'have body', as Roland Barthes almost said in his famous article, 'The Grain of the Voice' (an article that may be most productively read as being about the ways in which bodies, especially vocal bodies, *write themselves*). The acousmatic, on the other hand, often appears against this background as a re-inscription of the phallogocentric 'view (or rather, voice) from nowhere' – the 'sounds in themselves' familiar in theories of 'absolute music', which are so only because the omniscient 'invisible master' (or rather, the unacknowledged inaudible master standing behind His Master's Voice) is pulling the strings.[61] Adorno's vision of a self-writing music morphs too readily into this voice, neglecting (as

Benjamin did not) the implications of the possibility that in the beginning wasn't word at all, wasn't language (however universal), but *name*, and that naming requires an *act* – a bodily energy.[62]

From this point of view, what is important about the phonographic 23 moment isn't so much the technological changes themselves as the way an older economy of loss, embodiment and subjectivity is reconfigured, in a moment of crisis for understandings of the body; the cyborgian figures of recorded voice – vocalic bodies incorporating microphones, amps and the rest, all the way down to computers – are the symptom of this shift, a shift in which 'the apparatus had its own grain; the supposedly mute machines had many voices of their own', but which also puts the very 'human' status of the sounding subject in question, for 'the cyborg appears in myth precisely where the boundary between human and animal is transgressed.'[63] There is a suggestion that the trajectory put in place could be post-patriarchal, even post-oedipal: 'A cyborg body is not innocent; it was not born in a garden; it does not seek unitary identity... Unlike the hopes of Frankenstein's monster, the cyborg does not expect its father to save it through a restoration of the garden.'[64] What might such creatures be like? One is tempted to think of Deleuze's 'bodies without organs' – de-territorialising assemblages, or 'machines', opposing all centralised conceptions of *organism* in the possession of a subject. Deleuze's neo-Spinozan vision dismantles 'the body' but not, he insists, as a process of fragmentation:

"A" stomach, "an" eye, "a" mouth [and, presumably, "a" voice]: the indefinite article does not lack anything; it is not indeterminate or undifferentiated, but expresses the pure determination of intensity, intensive difference. It is not at all a question of a fragmented, splintered body, of organs without the body (OwB). The BwO is exactly the opposite. There are not organs in the sense of fragments in relation to a lost unity, nor is there a return to the undifferentiated in relation to a differentiable totality. There is a distribution of intensive principles of organs, with their positive indefinite articles, within a collectivity or multiplicity, inside an assemblage, and according to machinic connections operating on a BwO.[65]

As a vector of perpetual becoming (becoming woman/child/animal/etc.), the BwO is connected in a privileged way by Deleuze with his idea of music;[66] and yet the process of *dispersal* identified here is, for Deleuze, in constant play with a re-territorialising movement named as *refrain*, for which birdsong provides the privileged exemplar, but which also underlies the principles of musical structure.[67] The record form as such, one might think, should stand for him as a manifestation of parroting refrain, in the interest of (capital) accumulation and (social) body formation.[68] But the paradoxes of repetition – certainly real enough, and epitomised in the chants of the creatures in 'Dr Funkenstein', which are both tedious and perpetually re-contextualised, looped and entertainingly loopy – atrophy politically outside the purview of a field of subjectivity. As a programme, Deleuze's irrationalist vitalism, predicated as it must be on a wilful (hence self-contradictory) de-subjectivisation, makes Adorno's 'nostalgia' seem positively rational.[69] Žižek's inversion of Deleuze's trope, picking critically at the latter's disavowal of 'loss', of 'castration', aligns the 'organ without a body' with the psychoanalytic concept of the part-object. Such an organ – here 'phallus', but equally 'voice' or 'gaze' – is one that 'I put on, which gets attached to my body, without ever becoming its "organic part," forever sticking out as its incoherent, excessive supplement' – it is, then, a 'mask that I put on'.[70] In Žižek's view (building on the later Lacan) this organ can certainly speak – indeed, the 'body' can under certain circumstances seem to collapse into just a multiplicity of such organs each giving voice – but not as an effect of the loss of subjectivity, rather of the emergence of the subject (the 'pure' subject, the subject as, so to speak, meaningless blob, the subject before the processes of subjectivisation formed it into a self) from out of the coherent mirror-like image of the 'person'. This subject is the subject of *drive*, and in its impossible desire for the part-object which alone sustains it, itself assumes the position of an object.[71]

The difference between these two positions is crucial: it's the difference between a refusal of, and an engagement in, the problematic of (self-)'possession' – or, to put it another way, it turns on the survival or not of the possibility of a supplementary 'and yet...' Still, it's important to maintain both, as points of tension within a cultural force-field dealing with the contemporary sense of a 'body in pieces' – a force-field that, as we have seen, bears insistently on the issue of the relations between man, animal and machine.[72] This is all the more important because the two positions align so neatly with the twin tendencies sketched earlier of *hysteria* on the one hand, *obsessional fetishism* on the other. The BwO seeks always to evacuate from any fixed position of enunciation that would render the body into a determinate (gendered, raced) form. For Deleuze, 'music is a deterritorialisation of the voice'. The process of 'machining the voice' describes a constant play between the need for 'the abolition of the overall dualism machine, in other words, the molar formation assigning voices to the "man or woman"' [for 'Being a man *or* a woman no longer exists in music'], and, on the other hand, 'the requirements of capitalism, which wants a man to be a man and a woman a woman, each with his or her own voice'.[73] The OwB, by contrast, precisely *fixates*, and the Žižekian move is always in danger of what he himself calls a 'fetishistic short circuit'. The question here is whether the 'ancephalous subject who assumes the position of the object – or, from another direction, the position of an object that starts to talk, that subjectivises itself' – doesn't carry us 'beyond morality'[74], that is, towards a point in the economics of the ventriloquial shift (from possession to possessive) where elements of the possessive are mapped back on to a state of (ecstatic) possession, the (pure) subject spoken (still) by commodity (a real abstraction, slave of a higher power[75]).

Perhaps what the creatures populating 'Dr Funkenstein' have to 25 tell us is: like it or not (as in the children's game, 'coming, ready or not'), *there will always be bodies*; but, at the same time there will also always be *organs*. And what the phonographic moment makes easier than ever before to grasp is the potentially fluid and always problematic nature of this relationship – including social migrations of its hysterical and fetishistic states, and constant intersections within the sensorium between 'voice' and 'gaze', sound and sight, acoustic and visual mirrors[76] – not to mention its strictly *fictional* quality. In Žižekian language, these creatures are *spectres* – neither wholly material nor wholly spirit – whose role is to cover over the gap in the body of the Real, that gap which could close only in the event of complete symbolic collapse (that is, only with death).[77] Clinton's zombies are bodies/organs reclaiming voices, previously muffled while they lay – among the wreckage of history – at Benjamin's Angel's feet (the Angel that, in this context, is writing the groove of the record of history).[78] And what these spectral phenomena have to say is: *these bodies are the only ones we have*; this is what the 'loss' of the body documented in the record form actually reveals – that these bodies, the ones we (collectively, socio-cyborgianally) make for ourselves, *are the only ones we ever had*. It is within this space of invention – a space not so much between two deaths as between two lives – that recorded voice, including even the work of the DJ, can contribute to saving life.

DJ as saviour? No doubt there are some practitioners of this art – 26 lords of a spinning creation, carefully composing a universe, naming their names (at once imposing and forbidding translation) – who would welcome this description. Mariah Carey is saved in the night – the sacred night (we can perhaps assume) of the dance club. George Clinton works his spell in the equally dark, mysterious space of the laboratory – the sound-lab. We're summoned to Walter Benjamin's 'night of nature': 'works of art', he wrote, 'may be defined as the models of a nature that awaits no day, and thus no Judgement Day; they are the models of a nature that is neither the theatre of history nor the dwelling-place of mankind. The saved night.' What manner of 'man' might, prospectively, inhabit such a place, and how would the redemption of nature bear upon his own salvation? Benjamin's answer is opaque – but in one passage seems to suggest that the crux would lie in the 'severing' (the recognition?) of the 'mystery' within his own makeup (the contradictions within his bodily force-field?), a possibility he finds offered in the moment of sexual fulfilment:

Sexual fulfilment delivers the man from his mystery, which does not consist in sexuality but which in its fulfilment, and perhaps in it alone, is severed – not solved. This mystery is comparable to the fetters that bind him to life. The woman cuts them, and the man is free to die because his life has lost its mystery. Thereby he is reborn, and as his beloved frees him from the mother's spell, the woman literally detaches him from Mother Earth – a midwife who cuts that umbilical cord which is woven of life's mystery.[79]

Art; sex: where, pre-eminently, identity is hazarded in engagement with the promise of the other; where objects – phallic, vocal, other – are made to speak, where bodies write themselves. Yet the paradox (the 'mystery?') remains, for 'art' (the spiritual) is apparently aligned with nature while 'sex' (the natural) unbinds the fetters that tie man to life. Is this paradox the key to the 'severed' state, the cut of recognition? Knowledge of a loss of what cannot be saved but which will in any case return?

The religious motif is notable in both Carey and Clinton – even if 27 in one case it revolves around blind faith (faith in the DJ and in 'a song' – in the sirenic seduction of art), in the other around scientific knowledge (which, however, is put to the procreative purposes of a sex machine). This religious tonality is not unusual for pop music.[80] In an unexpected twist to the 'dialectic of enlightenment', Derrida has suggested that, far from religion and science being opposed, 'technoscience' *supports* a discourse of 'salvation': the two forces (faith and knowledge, precisely) 'always have made common cause, bound to one another by the band of their opposition'. It is worth quoting him at length:

Of a discourse to come... No to-come without some sort of *iterability*, at least in the form of a covenant with oneself and confirmation of the originary *yes*. No to-come without some sort of messianic memory and promise, of a messianicity older than all religion, more originary than all messianism... This *yes* will have implied and will always imply the trustworthiness and fidelity of a faith. No faith, therefore, nor future without everything technical, automatic, machine-like supposed by iterability. In this sense, the technical is the possibility of faith, indeed its very chance... Instead of opposing them, as is almost always done, they ought to be thought together, as *one and the same possibility*: the machine-like and faith, and the same holds for the machinal and all the values entailed in the sacrosanct (*heilig*, holy, safe and sound, unscathed, intact, immune, free, vital, fecund, fertile, strong, and above all "swollen") – more precisely in the sacrosanctity of the **phallic** effect... [an effect] which is not necessarily the property of man... The phallic... once detached from the body... is this not where one grasps... the potency of a logic powerful enough to account for... everything that binds the tele-technoscientific machine... to faith in the most living as dead and automatically *sur-viving*...?... One could ... connect everything in the semantic genealogy of the unscathed... that speaks of force, **life**-force, fertility, growth, augmentation, and above all *swelling*, in the spontaneity of erection or of pregnancy.... [But also to] covenants or founding promises in an *ordeal of the unscathed* that is always a circumcision, be it "exterior or interior," literal or... "circumcision of the heart."[81]

We might want to stress rather more than Derrida does the trans-gendering routes this phallic effect (potentially) travels. But the main point here is broader. If the phallus writes (as I have suggested), the outcome is an *automatic* writing. In the nexus that Derrida describes, sex, writing (representation; art) and faith are conjoined, in a 'machine' that works as if automatically on the problematic of *creation* (the one thing language – signification – cannot account for: 'In the symbolic nothing explains creation.'[82]). If the hysteric's question revolves around the issue of *procreation* (what is a woman, am I a woman, can I procreate?), and the obsessive's around the issue of *de-creation*, hoarding up simulacra of 'life' in an attempt to cheat death, then recording technology, as it organises these positions, comes to look like a metaphor for – or rather, a way of re-playing – the act of creation itself (creation/procreation/reproduction/replication...): the search for *origin* on the one hand, for *difference* (sexual, grammatological) on the other, on both of which, of course, the book of *Genesis* is eloquent. It's not only a question of the DJ as god, therefore, but also of God as DJ, and His creation as always already phonographic. And the record mimes not only His creation but also the divine loss: just as God cuts adrift His universe, so the phonograph (god *in* the machine) forgets its offspring as it disseminates them. For the trace is also a cut, the ontological 'circumcision' reflected in the technological groove. The mystery, then – so Benjamin tells us, I think – is just that there *is* no mystery.

The record groove – or rather, phonography as such – offers, **28** above all, *fidelity* – a potentially infinite memory and promise, confirmation of an originary yes. In the 'abysmal' structure of recorded performance – sample inside mix, mix inside tune, tune inside disc, disc inside set – the salvatory possibility devolves upon the iteration of a loss – of a self-loss – which, however, will always deliver a return, a return with interest, life in its dance with death. Phonography – a 'machine for making gods'?[83] Or at least, unearthly bodies – stars certainly but also sirens and others. A machine, then, which, while placing the natural body (apparently) under erasure (returning it to 'saved night'?), sets free what in an older language would be called the *soul*, in all its bodily ambivalences and spectrality. An old (religious) lesson: to save life demands that first we lose it.

Bonus Track

I'm listening to Björk's extraordinary 2004 album, *Medúlla*. Virtually **29** the whole album, including the (electronically mediated) 'beats', is generated out of 'voices' (Björk's own, one or two other solo voices, choirs), although there is a bit of synth and piano as well.[84] While a host of collaborators are featured, most of the tracks are written and produced by Björk – in this sense, the album stands at the end of a lengthy trajectory in which she has steadily taken an increasing amount of control of both the productions and her collaborations – so that on the one hand the music always seems to be referring to her (it is, one might say, an exercise in self-possession), yet on the other hand she is constantly subsumed into a larger and immensely rich soundscape. It would be possible to read many of the songs as dramatisations of the Odysseus-and-the Sirens story: seductive vocal textures (the sound of techno-sirens) are combined with repeating beats and, often, accompanying riffs (suggesting the endless labour of the oarsmen); except that the two spheres frequently cross over – vocal sounds are 'rhythmicised', beats are 'vocalised', as the Adornian binary of artistic contemplation and social practice is put at issue. It would often be impossible to know from listening what sort of 'body' the voices originate in, where they 'belong': what sound like synthetic sounds or processed vocal samples or 'real' voices aren't always clearly distinguishable, mutate into each other; and similarly the constant dislocation of language (which perhaps finds a point of reference in Björk's own well-established 'mechanical' style of vocal articulation) tends to put received notions of the voice/instrument distinction at risk. And yet, often enough, Björk's familiar soaring solo voice will take wing from out of the more complex textures, calling our attention back to a visual image we know well (albeit it has been given many forms, often somewhat cyborgian, over the years). In the same sort of way, the more complex tracks are interspersed with simpler songs where this solo voice, almost alone, delivers folksong-like melodies which anchor her modernity in history (or, perhaps, in myth).[85] The album represents no utopian, nor even a 'post-historical' moment, then – rather, it's just one symptom of new potentials. Björk has long insisted that for her 'nature' and 'technology' are not distinct;[86] and, as Donna Haraway might have predicted, for a woman to pursue the implications of this belief can only cast the gendering of phonographic technology in a new light. Whatever the nature of the vocal body (bodies) we hear on *Medúlla*, then, we would surely be justified in naming it (them): *Cybjörk*.[87]

In 'One-Way Street', published in the same year as the first of 30 Adorno's essays on the phonograph, Walter Benjamin, musing on the meaning of technology, argues for a recognition that 'technology is the mastery of not nature but of the relation between nature and man'. Is this what Björk is about? Some have read Benjamin's suspension of the opposition of man and nature – a characteristic example of his 'dialectic at a standstill' – as pointing towards the 'post-historical'.[88] However, he goes on, immediately, to affirm that 'Men as a species completed their development thousands of years ago; but mankind as a species is just beginning his. In technology, a *physis* is being organised through which mankind's contact with the cosmos takes a new and different form from that which it had in nations and families.' Just as there was writing before writing, there is, apparently, a history after history – all the more so because, according to Benjamin, the technological rape of nature is to be laid at the door of capital ('the lust for profit of the ruling class'), while the 'power of the proletariat' is required 'to bring the new body [the body of mankind] under its control... Living substance conquers the frenzy of destruction only in the ecstasy of procreation.'[89]

But I'll give the final word to Evan Eisenberg's friend, Clarence, 31 who, trying to catch the erotics inherent in the process whereby records make objects speak, pointed us in the same direction as Benjamin and Björk. 'Records,' he said, 'are inanimate until you put the needle in the groove' – until the thing gives voice, we might say – 'and then they come to life.'[90]

---

[1] This article started life as a paper presented to a symposium organized by the Centre for the History and Analysis of Recorded Music at Royal Holloway, University of London, 14-16 April 2005. I am most grateful to participants for their comments and the discussion that ensued. My thanks too to *Radical Musicology*'s anonymous readers for their stimulating comments.

The Mariah Carey track, 'Last Night a DJ Saved My Life', is on *Glitter* (CD, Virgin 7243 8 10797 2 0, 2001), track 8; a DVD of the film is also available: *Glitter* (DVD, Columbia C8212269, 2001). There have been many versions of the song, and it's a favourite for re-mixing. Its title has attained emblematic status, being borrowed for at least one book (Bill Brewster and Frank Broughton, *Last Night a DJ Saved My Life: The History of the Disc Jockey* [London: Headline, 1999]) and encapsulating for many the almost messianic role of the DJ in contemporary dance club culture (see e.g. Kai Fikentscher, "'There's Not a Problem I Can't Fix, 'Cause I Can Do It in the Mix'", in Lysloff, René T. A. and Leslie C. Gay (eds.), *Music and Technoculture* (Middletown CN: Wesleyan University Press, 2003), 290-315; Fikentscher's title quotes from the lyrics of the song – a line which I explore myself shortly).

But still, why this song (rather than countless others)? Some styles of musicological writing attract accusations of selectivity – either arbitrary or cunning – in their choice of musical examples. The songs I discuss in this article, both here and later on, are not offered as exemplars – representing a class, crystallising a type – but as symptoms, pointing, like ideological symptoms, towards features of the social, cultural and discursive formations that underlie them.

[2] See Teresa de Lauretis, *Technologies of Gender: Essays on Theory, Film, and Fiction* (Bloomington IN: Indiana University Press, 1987), 43-4, 98-9: 44.

[3] On the original recording of the song, by disco group Indeep, there is no rapping until the playout. It is initiated by the female lead singer, with the first couplet of the lyrics just quoted, and she then gives way to a male voice (probably the song's composer Michael Cleveland) for the second couplet. Thus the switch of subject-position remains gendered, which makes Carey's subversion of this division all the more striking. The Indeep version is available on many reissues, for instance *Funk/Soul Classics: The Ultimate 80's Soul and Funk Revival* (CD, Ministry of Sound, MOSCD84, 2004).

[4] On the phonograph and disembodiment, see Barbara Engh, 'After "His Master's Voice"', *New Formations* Vol. 38 (1999), 54-63.

Of course, if we watch the film, the body returns. Or does it? We certainly see images; but these cover a gap as much as the voice does (if in a different way). It's not just that technology – visual and aural – renders the body of celebrity virtual (though it does), but that – as Lacan famously puts it – 'reality' (which 'is structured like a fiction') stands in for the Real.

For Lacan, an important aspect of this formulation is a distinction between voice as carrier of meaning, as vehicle of the Symbolic (for instance, in song lyrics), and 'object voice': that inaudible, indeed impossible voice which would remain if all meaning could be stripped away, and which points, therefore, towards the Real. While I certainly want to explore this territory – a territory traversed by intersecting figures of voice, body, nature and machine – I would hope to put at issue any too-easy pictures of simple binary distinctions.

For a clear introduction to the concept of object voice, see Mladen Dolar, 'The Object Voice', in Salecl, Renata and Slavoj Žižek (eds.), *Gaze and Voice as Love Objects* (Durham NC: Duke University Press, 1996), 7-31; and for a wider-ranging exploration of its intersections with other kinds of voice, see Mladen Dolar, *A Voice and Nothing More* (Cambridge MA: MIT Press, 2006).

[5] See for example Engh, 'His Master's Voice', 55-6, 59-60; Jonathon Sterne, *The Audible Past: Cultural Origins of Sound Reproduction* (Durham NC: Duke University Press, 2003), 287-92, 297-8, 303-7. Sterne points out the deep

embedding of phonographic memorialising in broader turn-of-the-century discourse around 'preservation', including spiritualism and 'canning' (e.g. of food).

[6] See Barbara Engh, 'Adorno and the Sirens: Tele-phono-graphic Bodies', in Dunn, Leslie C. and Nancy A. Jones (eds.), *Embodied Voices: Representing Female Vocality in Western Culture* (Cambridge: Cambridge University Press, 1994), 120-135: 124.

[7] Friedrich Kittler, *Gramophone, Film, Typewriter*, tr. Geoffrey Winthrop-Young and Michael Wutz (Stanford CA: Stanford University Press, 1999), 83.

[8] *Ibid.* 53.

[9] T. W. Adorno, 'The Curves of the Needle' [1928], tr. Thomas Y. Levin. *October* Vol. 55 (1990), 48-55; 'The Form of the Phonograph Record' [1934], tr. Thomas Y. Levin. *October* Vol. 55 (1990), 56-61. Both are re-published in T. W. Adorno, *Essays on Music*, ed. Richard Leppert (Berkeley CA: University of California Press, 2002), 272-282.

[10] Adorno, 'The Curves', 52. The phrase 'disturbers of the peace' is almost certainly meant to summon up Freud's concept of Eros, the 'life-drives' (described as 'breakers of the peace' in the standard English translation of his 'Beyond the Pleasure Principle' (1920); see Sigmund Freud, *On Metapsychology: The Theory of Psychoanalysis* [London: Penguin, 1991, 337]). For Freud, these drives were in a complex dualistic relationship with the drive towards stasis, quiescence, entropy characteristic of the 'death-instincts' (Thanatos). We know that Adorno was reading psychoanalytic work, including Freud, from the mid-1920s, and in the original German texts Adorno's phrase is the same as Freud's: 'die Störenfriede'.

The idea of a 'second death' comes from Slavoj Žižek (and, through him, from Lacan): see Žižek, 'You Only Die Twice', in *The Sublime Object of Ideology* (London: Verso, 1989), 131-49. Between 'real (biological) death' and 'symbolic death' (the disintegration of the subject's place in the symbolic system or even of this system as such) lies a space where the Real can erupt, where peace can be disturbed. Adorno seems to suggest that, with the return of bourgeois good sense, the possibility of symbolic death dies (but at the same time listeners are, for him, also already dead, 'enshrouded' in emptiness).

[11] Adorno, 'The Form', 56, 59, 60.

[12] Kittler, *Gramophone*, 44, 83.

[13] Elizabeth Eva Leach, 'Parrots, Phonographs, and Other Imitators', paper presented to a symposium organized by the Centre for the History and Analysis of Recorded Music at Royal Holloway, University of London (30 October 2004). I am grateful to Liz for making this available to me.

[14] Sterne, *Audible Past*, 154-67.

[15] Parrots of course identify themselves as 'pretty Polly' and cannot stop talking; Nipper, by contrast, whom many early viewers of the original image took to be sitting on his master's coffin (see Sterne, *Audible Past*, 301-3), is all ears.

[16] The status of 'writing': a topic so huge that its limit must, especially since the Derridean deconstruction, be deferred indefinitely. Though I cannot treat it adequately, however, it will surface continually in the course of my argument. In light of Carey's racial identity (and even more so, that of George Clinton, whom I will discuss presently), one reference worth making here is to an argument prominent recently which, denying the conventional account of the African-American/European musical relationship as falling into an oral/literate binary, wants to describe African-American music as 'phonographic': this music, it is argued, actually deconstructs this binary through its emphasis on the materiality of sound, which is inscribed on the (dancing, gesturing) body, most importantly on the reproductive mechanisms of bodily registered memory. (For a concise summary of this argument, with references to other relevant literature, see Katherine Biers, 'Syncope Fever: James Weldon Johnson and the Black Phonographic Voice', *Representations* Vol. 96 [2006], 99-125.)

But this argument applies to voice as such (hence to all musics centred on oral reproduction), which is always already split, always already embroiled in the spacings of trace; that is, reproduces on its own level the binary that it supposedly deconstructs. Biers's position recalls that of Deleuze and Guattari, whose speculative anthropology of 'savage' modes of representation positions systems of 'voice-audition' and 'hand-graphics' as both 'inscribed' on the body but as mutually autonomous, hence inter-connected (Gilles Deleuze and Félix Guattari, *Anti-Oedipus: Capitalism and Schizophrenia*, tr. Robert Hurley, Mark Seem and Helen R. Lane [London: Continuum, 2004], 202-17). Despite paying lip-service to Derrida's insistence on the irreducibility of 'writing in the broad sense' (*ibid.*, 221) – the trace as ' the arche-phenomenon of "memory," which must be thought before the opposition of nature and culture, animality and humanity, etc... this trace is the opening of the first exteriority in general, the enigmatic relationship of the living to its other and of an inside to an outside: spacing' (Jacques Derrida, *Of Grammatology*, tr. Gayatri Chakravorty Spivak [Baltimore: The Johns Hopkins University Press, 1976, 70) – in practice Deleuze and Guattari cannot bring themselves to abandon the myth of 'a graphism that leaves the voice dominant by being independent of the voice' (*Anti-Oedipus*, 221.) Against this, 'phonography' – as a Derridean understanding of historical anthropology no doubt facilitated by our recent experience of actual recording technology – must be understood as positing, always, a 'writing before writing'.

There is, nevertheless, a specificity to the African-American case, to which Biers draws attention, and which is to do with the aftershock of slavery and the way this coincided with, precisely, the advent of recording technology. This, as she points out, made it possible for African-American music to play a key role for whites, as a point of displacement for their anxieties over mechanical reproduction and its implications for both voice and writing: 'fugitive waves' duly 'captured', in Edison's no doubt inadvertently double-voiced phrase (quoted in Biers, 'Syncope Fever', 113). This dimension will be important for my argument when I come to discuss George Clinton – but it's also relevant to the racial voicing in Carey.

Despite this specificity, it is still worth pondering the possible parallels, as well as differences, between the music culture Biers is discussing – ragtime, coon song – and that represented by Gus Elen: both performative cultures, both captured (to some extent) in notation and in record grooves. An obvious place to start research would be the work of African-American blackface vaudeville star, Bert Williams, whose early recordings are contemporary with those of Elen.

[17] Theodor Adorno and Max Horkheimer, *Dialectic of Enlightenment*, tr. John Cumming (London: Verso, 1997 [1944]), 32-43, 58-60. According to Giorgio Agamben (*The Open: Man and Animal*, tr. Kevin Attell [Stanford CA: Stanford University Press, 2004], 24), as late as the eighteenth century, serious scientists (Linnaeus, for example) still classified sirens with man on the one hand, with animals of various types on the other.

[18] Engh, 'Adorno', 134. In the Homeric epic, Odysseus stops up his rowers' ears with wax so that they cannot hear the Sirens' alluring song, and has them tie him to the mast so that he cannot respond to it. In at least one early twentieth-century image, from the cover of the July 1913 issue of *Telephone Review*, the new sound-reproduction technologies take up the Siren function. In this picture, entitled 'Her Voice Alluring Draws Him On', three attractive young women in the foreground use the telephone to work their wiles, while the mythological Sirens look on from the background. See Sterne, *Audible Past*, 171. As Dolar points out (Voice, 207 n. 6), there's a lengthy, Christian history to this sort of adaptation of the myth.

[19] Adorno and Horkheimer, *Enlightenment*, 33. The right conclusion here, perhaps, is that both Engh's reading and the feminist account she is implicitly critiquing are 'true' (that is to say, both the sexual difference and the difference man/nature have originary status); but only as logical moments in a dialectical paradox the full tension of which must be preserved if it is to measure up to the mystery of the emergence of human subjectivity. Like the Adornian 'nostalgia' itself, this paradox, appearing post facto, registers a memory of 'what will have been'.

[20] Adorno (1953), quoted in Thomas Y. Levin, 'For the Record: Adorno on Music in the Age of Its Technological Reproducibility', *October* Vol. 55 (1990), 41. Before 1909, when the Gramophone Company adopted the picture of Nipper as its emblem, their trademark had centred on images of a 'Writing Angel' inscribing the grooves with a heavenly quill (see *ibid.* 40 for reproductions); the shift from supernatural inscription to domestic respectability mirrors the trajectory of Adorno's lament (and note that the 'coffin' in the original Nipper picture was subsequently cropped out: see Sterne, *Audible Past*, 302).

[21] Adorno, 'The Form', 61.

[22] Adorno, 'The Form', 60. The original German text – 'die Schriftspirale, die im Zentrum, der Öffnung der Mitte verschwindet, aber dafür dauert in der Zeit' –

is not without its ambiguity. Max Paddison has pointed out to me (private communication) that Adorno is clearly touching here on one of his key themes, the temporalisation of space and the spacialisation of time in the relationships of performance, score and recording; the word *dafür*, he argues, is therefore best translated as 'for that reason'. However, Thomas Levin's 'in return' is also very plausible – and contains its own ambiguity: the suggestion both of a reciprocity of going and coming, and of the homeostatic effect of the repetitions contained within mechanical reproduction, can hardly fail to remind us of the Freudian *Fort-Da*, the game in which Freud's grandson played out a simulacrum of presence and absence by repeated manipulation of a cotton reel. The two interpretations may not be too far apart if the *Fort-Da* is taken as a model of Derridean arche-writing, in which *différance* is defined in terms precisely of the imbrication of deferral in time and scriptal marking (grooving out) in space.

On the psychoanalytic concept of 'organ-holes' as objects of desire and sites of subjectivity, and their relationship to Derrida's concept of 'invagination' (in turn related in terms of gender rhetoric to his concept of 'dissemination'), see Kaja Silverman, *The Acoustic Mirror: The Female Voice in Psychoanalysis and Cinema* (Bloomington IN: University of Indiana Press, 1988), 66-71. The sexualisation of the voice that is implied in my description of grooves, holes and horns might remind us of the old idea of the genital voice; this played a significant part in the history of ventriloquism (see Steven Connor, *Dumbstruck: A Cultural History of Ventriloquism* [Oxford: Oxford University Press, 2000], 54-5, 70-72, 166-75, 182, 195-208), which in turn forms important background to the phenomenology of records, and will return later in my argument.

As an addendum, I should acknowledge that between the historical phase about which Adorno is writing – the phase of grooves, holes and horns – and the digitized apparatus within which Carey works lies a narrative of extensive technological change – too big a story to go into here (the place to start would be John Mowitt, 'The Sound of Music in the Era of Its Electronic Reproducibility', in Leppert, Richard and Susan McClary (eds.), *Music and Society: The Politics of Composition, Performance and Reception* [Cambridge: Cambridge University Press, 1987], 173-97). Nevertheless, 'disembodiment' is a constant. Moreover, I suspect that the spiral-hole figure (Adorno's play of time and space, disappearance and return) is buried quite deep in the phonographic imaginary as a whole: discs still get inserted into machines, to be 'read' (and 'written'), and we know that the trace they carry will fade but always return; with the iPod, the hole is, even more directly than before, the (eroticized?) organ of the ear. Why has vinyl refused to die – indeed, come back to life? Carey's life-saving DJ mixes discs; and the point of his mixing is just to delay, ideally to infinity, the organ-hole moment.

[23] Adorno, 'The Curves', 54. Adorno's argument here gets tangled. (Leppert [in Adorno: *Essays*, 233] suggests that the article has a 'vague, at times almost free-associational' quality related both to the author's youth and that of the technology, and resulting in 'theoretical uncertainty'. I think this uncertainty has definite roots.) First of all, he suggests that what records best is the singing voice, 'best' meaning what is 'most faithful to the natural ur-image'; presumably this is the singing voice as such, i.e. across gender. Then he moves on to distinguish the recordability of male and female voices, as we have seen. He follows this with an argument about abstraction, according to which

gramophone sound has become so abstract that it needs to be complemented by 'specific sensory qualities of the object it is reproducing' – its 'full concreteness' – if it is to be 'graspable'. Where the object's 'natural substance' is itself already 'mechanically fractured' (he seems to be thinking of instrumental sound, separated from the body as this is), or is 'permeated by intentionality', the record cannot grasp it (idem). 'Permeated by intentionality' sounds like a (stereotypical) definition of male voice to me – yet Adorno has already told us that it's the female voice which recordings cannot grasp; how is the male vocal subject made concrete, then?   And, by locating his gender distinction in 'natural substance', isn't Adorno himself – against the thrust of his own theory – embedding abstraction in ontology (i.e. outside history)? One might wonder if the species of concreteness Adorno seems to ascribe to the male voice is not an example of what has been called a 'real abstraction' – a form of social effectivity (as in commodity consumption) driven by an abstraction (exchange relations; or, similarly, universalizing male discourse?) whose value is misrecognised as 'real' (i.e. concrete, whole, meaningful – as in the mirroring self-presence of the male body sounding off?) (see Žižek, Sublime Object, 16-21). Adorno hints at a connection in the record-economy between abstraction and commodity form (see 'The Form', 57) but doesn't follow it up; I shall do so, later.

A different gloss on Adorno's 'famous "antifeminist" remark' is offered by Slavoj Žižek (On Belief [New York: Routledge, 2001, 44-5]). For Adorno, Žižek argues, Woman is situated in between bodily identification and disembodiment, a position enabling (e.g. in her resistance to recording fidelity) a hysterical protest against that reification which men can only tolerate. The trope of hysteria is intriguing – I will return to it myself, later – and, although there is little support for Žižek's reading in Adorno's own text, it is true that Adorno did write about 'the woman question' in these terms elsewhere, as Engh has pointed out ('Adorno', 131-2). But Žižek's account surely does little more than re-cast the patriarchal binary in which Adorno is implicated, rather than deconstructing it; the argument I want to make is that recording technology puts this binary precisely at issue.

It may be revealing that Adorno's vocal mirror-ideal is Caruso. On one level this is perfectly predictable: in terms of commercial and critical success, not to mention his trail-blazing legitimation of phonographic technology, Caruso was certainly the master voice of the early record industry. At the same time, his repertoire, his reception and descriptions of his voice and singing style yield readily to tropes of gender hysteria with which the history of twentieth-century mass entertainment, from Rudolf Valentino through Elvis Presley to Michael Jackson, have made us so familiar. (His repertoire covered not only opera but also the 'feminine' genres of Neapolitan song, light ballads and American popular songs; his audiences – his 'hysterical public', as Michael Scott describes it – were famous for 'explosions of passion... intoxicating storm[s]... delirium... an electric charge', 'shrieking' and 'tears'; his singing was 'vulgar... opulent...luscious', its 'angelic sweetness' and 'seductive grace', 'voiced in instinct with sensuous quality' and 'almost feminine delicacy', suggesting, especially in its celebrated quasi-falsetto upper register, an orientalism easily associated with the exotic image of the 'swarthy' Neapolitan: Scott, The Great Caruso [London: Hamish Hamilton, 1988], 43, 33, 47, 72, xvii, xviii, 6, 9, 128, 145.) Caruso's recordings are widely available on reissues. Personally, I find no difficulty in succumbing to the delirious ambivalence conjured up by his vocalic body. Caruso's death in 1921 provoked a perhaps not dissimilar response from the composers of Tin Pan Alley: 'They Needed a Song Bird in Heaven (So God Took Caruso Away)' – a siren voice indeed! We can imagine the posthumous Caruso – his angelic vocal body half bird, half... what? – scribing the grooves inhabited by his successors (cf. note 19 above). (Of course, for his phonographic fans, the living Caruso was already 'disembodied' – or rather, perhaps, bodily indeterminate, mutable, spectral.)

No doubt it would be simplistically psychologistic to reduce Adorno's problem with popular culture to a case of male hysteria. Even so... (Engh's discussion – 'Adorno', 132-3 – evokes a picture of him lashed to the phonographic apparatus, like Odysseus to the mast – terrified, presumably, that his body might betray him. For male hysteria and popular singing, see Richard Middleton, 'Mum's the Word: Maternal Law and Men's Singing', in Jarman-Ivens, Freya (ed.), *Oh Boy: Masculinities and Popular Music* [New York: Routledge, 2007], 103-124).

[24] Again there's an analogy to film theory, here to the concept of 'space-off' – that space not visible in, but inferable from, what is shown in the frame. Note Teresa de Lauretis's point, however, that to subvert this relationship, by making space-off visible (audible), would potentially deconstruct its gendered structure; see De Lauretis, *Technologies of Gender*, 26.

[25] It is somewhat reductive as well because it neglects the wider structure of commercial music production, in which a multiplicity of actors within multi-media transnational corporate systems all have their say; which of them, and in what inter-relationships, are speaking through any particular record? The 'body' of capital, as well as of labour in all its intersections, also tends to disappear, rendered invisible ('voices off') by the commodity-fetish (which, although here there is yet another large-scale topic which I lack the space to cover properly, will return).

[26] This idea that the discursive structure of body-possession is gendered, and that consequently so too is susceptibility to pain, owes much to Elaine Scarry's *The Body in Pain: The Making and Unmaking of the World* (New York: Oxford University Press, 1985). For Scarry, the reduction of the self to a body, at its most intense in a state of physical pain, destroys language, standing at an extreme from the disembodying extension of the self out into the external world through the authoritative deployment of voice; this structure, she further argues, is mapped on to asymmetries of power – of gender for example (see especially *ibid*. 207, including note 20), or class (261-77). Carey's emotional suffering is not the same as physical pain but, given the typical sense that such suffering is 'inexpressible' and has physical effects (the DJ saves Carey from a 'broken heart'), I suggest it occupies an adjacent position in this structure. Carey's enfeebled vocal, backgrounded by the repeated injunction to 'shake and bounce around' (she ends the record in almost inaudible vocalese), is an index of this position. There is one injunction that is an exception to the rappers' focus on her body: 'Talk to me'; but this is satisfied when she takes up, 'parrots back' to them, the DJ's position of power, a move that renders any subversive effect (see Note 3 above) ambivalent at best.

[27] Slavoj Žižek, '"I Hear You with My Eyes"; or, The Invisible Master', in Salecl, Renata and Slavoj Žižek (eds.), *Gaze and Voice as Love Objects* (Durham NC: Duke University Press, 1996), 90-126: 92.

[28] Barbara Bradby, 'Sampling Sexuality: Gender, Technology and the Body in Dance Music', *Popular Music* Vol. 12 No 2 (1993), 155-176.

[29] John Corbett, *Extended Play: Sounding Off from John Cage to Dr Funkenstein* (Durham NC: Duke University Press, 1994), 56-67.

[30] *Ibid.* 60; within film theory, voice-over – voice of authority, its body effaced – is seen as normatively coded male: see Silverman, *Acoustic Mirror*, 47-54.

[31] Silverman, *Acoustic Mirror*, 62.

[32] Corbett, *Extended Play*, 37.

[33] Jacques Lacan, *The Psychoses: The Seminar of Jacques Lacan, Book III 1955-1956*, ed. Jacques-Alain Miller, tr. Russell Grigg (London: Routledge, 1993), 171.

[34] On this, see Corbett, *Extended Play*, 40-44; Keir Keightley, "Turn It Down!" She Shrieked: Gender, Domestic Space, and High Fidelity, 1948-59', *Popular Music* Vol. 15 No 2 (1996), 149-177; and Evan Eisenberg, *The Recording Angel: Music, Records and Culture from Aristotle to Zappa* (London: Picador, 1988). The most memorable character featured in Eisenberg's engaging book is Clarence, who lives, cold, hungry and in squalor, but surrounded by his collection of three-quarters of a million records. The combination of arbitrariness, narcissism and disavowal typical of the fetishistic obsessive is nicely caught by the fact that one of the categories Clarence collects is 'anything with "Clarence" on it' (*ibid.* 6). What is disavowed is, of course, loss (i.e. 'castration') – ultimately, de-subjectivation (death: for Lacan, the obsessive's question is, 'why is he here?', and 'why is he going to disappear?' [Lacan, *The Psychoses*, 179]).

[35] Engh, 'Adorno', 121-3, 132-4

[36] Kittler, *Gramophone*, 54, 55. Leach points out ('Parrots') that Gus Elen's phonygraff scene is notated; but even here, as she implies, the assertion of the superiority of a performance culture centred on scores is troubled, for the parrot's words aren't reproduced, only reported in Elen's narrative: what is he afraid of – a parroted 'sexual screaming', offering the choice of catatonia or hysteria?

[37] The phrase 'reproductive body', used with this ambivalence of reference, is Barbara Engh's ('Adorno', 130). This interpretation of the Sirens' loss is already pre-figured by Adorno and Horkheimer, who speculate that with Odysseus's 'success', their mythic power disintegrates, and who link this process with the subsequent disablement of song (and by extrapolation, we might add, the

subjection of women) (*Enlightenment*, 59-60).

Both Engh ('His Master's Voice', 62-3) and Dolar (*Voice*, 170-73) point out that in Kafka's version of the story the Sirens are silent; even more than their singing, it is this silence that is truly irresistible (see Franz Kafka, 'The Silence of the Sirens', *Shorter Works*, vol. 1, tr. Malcolm Pasley [London: Secker & Warburg, 1973], 106-7). Is this aphonia a (typical) symptom of their hysteria? A manifestation of object voice (a Munch-like 'silent scream'; 'voice at its purest... the ultimate weapon of the law' [Dolar, *Voice*, 171]; the epitome of 'writing before writing')? Is it the silence of the (phonographic) grave, of the Freudian death-drive? For Kafka, the Sirens' defeat is nothing to them: for they are, as Dolar puts it, not just bird-women but also automata – cyborgs merely imitating humanity (*ibid.* 173); their silence, we might say, is that of the still-functioning phonographic machine after the record has stopped. But Kafka is still more complex than this. He obfuscates the causality of the silence. Do the Sirens produce it by merely pretending to sing – or does Odysseus produce it by obliterating the song from his consciousness? Is this an acousmatic silence – a silence without definite origin, a 'pure resonance', the silence of nature, the 'pure void of the Other' as such (*ibid.* 181)? Or is the whole paradox just (just?!) a game? Kafka's final coup is to speculate that perhaps Odysseus really did hear the silence, that his performance was just that; the Sirens 'were going through the motions of singing; he was going through the motions of not hearing their silence.' (*ibid.* 172) But hysteria is, precisely, a form of theatre; hysterics 'act out' their fantasy. Who, here, is the hysteric? Who, or what, possesses whom? Questions from which listeners to records cannot escape any more than can Kafka's characters.

[38] Connor, *Dumbstruck*, 191-225, 249-89. It was women, typically, who up to the eighteenth century were possessed by spirits; conversely, how many ventriloquists since then – usually performing ventriloquists operating on dummies – have not been men?

The slave is in many ways the ultimate commodity, and also, commonly, the object of fetishistic desire, anxiety and obsessive control. Capital is the ultimate ventriloquist – an invisible master. The dialectic of having and being which is acted out here is, for Lacan, crucially figured in the drama of the phallus (typically, men have it; women are it) – a drama that in my view is historically embedded in this political-economic structure (and vice versa). For a more detailed exploration of this problematic, see Chapter 1 of my book, *Voicing the Popular: On the Subjects of Popular Music* (New York: Routledge, 2006).

[39] Adorno and Horkheimer, *Enlightenment*, 34-8.

[40] *Ibid.* 36.

[41] If, as Kafka has it (cf. note 37 above), the Sirens are silent as well, the invisible master might seem to be all-conquering – an eerie parallel to the Adornian second death (cf. note 10 above). But, as suggested there, the space of second death offers creative as well as funereal potential; the body cannot forever be muted – such, at least, would be my contention – and silence qua voice-as-such, voice at its zero point (cf. note 37), is always also pregnant, a non-space which, precisely because it is empty, offers room for Eros, the life-drives.

[42] From its beginnings, disco offered privileged spaces to blacks, women and gays. The original version of 'Last Night a DJ Saved My Life', by disco group Indeep, dates from this period (1982 to be exact). Mariah Carey's biographical positioning is worth noting here. As a woman of mixed race (Irish-American mother, Venezuelan-African father), she is also often described as emerging out of an upbringing, after her parents' divorce, marked by poverty and conflict; and, like many divas, she has become a gay icon. Her career is often presented as a struggle for (self-) possession; but at the same time, of course, divas (like Sirens?) possess their listeners.

Disco and the dance-music lineage it initiated also gave a privileged role to turntable technology (hence the narrative of 'Last Night A DJ Saved My Life'). Against this background, the emergence of digital machines (CD and MP3 players) might seem to extend the Adornian story of domestication – to de-eroticise the apparatus. But these are still 'reproductive bodies'. No voice-machine can escape an (inevitably sexualised) role in issues of (dis-)embodiment. What metaphoric imagery might surround, for instance, the CD sliding into and out of its player, offering its mirror-like surface to the burning light of the laser?

[43] Parliament, 'Dr Funkenstein', *The Clones of Dr Funkenstein* (CD, Polydor 8426202, 2001 [LP, 1976]).

[44] Corbett, *Extended Play*, 7-24.

[45] But Marina Warner does: see her *Fantastic Metamorphoses, Other Worlds* (Oxford: Oxford University Press, 2002); for Corbett's discussion, see *Extended Play*, 19-21.

[46] In Jamaican patois, a 'dup' is a ghost (and may be linked etymologically to the musical genre of dub, with its startling sound trickery). 'Duppy Conqueror' is a 1969 Bob Marley track, probably written and certainly produced by dub pioneer Lee Perry. According to Perry, dub is 'the funny stuff, that's what's inside comin' out, so you put it down on a record. That's what it is, the ghost in me coming out.' (Quoted in Corbett, *Extended Play*, 129).

[47] Ezekiel 37:3; the spiritual tells how ankle, leg, thigh, hip bone (etc) are all connected – at least they are if we 'hear the word of the Lord'.

[48] On the African-American aesthetic of Signifyin(g) – 'repetition of a changing same' – see Henry Louis Gates, *The Signifying Monkey: A Theory of African-American Literary Criticism* (New York: Oxford University Press, 1988).

[49] This suggestion stems from an interpretation initially put to me by Philip Auslander.

[50] In the early stages of his career, Brown apparently carried his record masters (sic) around with him: 'when I wanted to release something', he writes, 'I pulled the master out of the bag, and gave it to the record company... I called all the releases.' (James Brown, with Bruce Tucker, *James Brown: The Godfather of Soul* [London: Sidgwick and Jackson, 1987], 160).

[51] One is tempted to say, after Lacan, their *point de capiton* – that is, the

point where the play of signifiers is (albeit temporarily) pinned (buttoned, quilted, anchored) into a specific knot of meaning.

[52] This interpretation of 'Sex Machine' is indebted to a brilliant essay on the subject by my postgraduate student, Jenny Tamplin.

[53] Given the name of the band, it would be wonderfully apposite if Clinton had read Geoffrey Chaucer's The *Parlement of Foules* (1374-81?)! Chaucer's poem is in the form of a dream-vision, based on Cicero's *Somnium Scipionis*. Chaucer's dreamer is led by Africanus (sic!) to a 'parliament' of birds, assembled to celebrate St Valentine's Day and choose their mates. It's comic, satirical (of social hierarchy) and, of course, allegorical.

Adorno and Horkheimer point out in their discussion of Odysseus's encounter with the temptress Circe that, as 'representative of nature', she (and following her, Woman) is surrounded by 'obedient animals as her escorts' (*Enlightenment*, 71). But if Clinton is presented as a Circe figure, his 'creatures', as they 'name the name itself' ('we love you Dr Funkenstein'), seem to imply that 'she' still wants to play God. On the discursive coupling animal/Woman, see Engh, 'His Master's Voice', 59-61 – and also note 54 below.

Agamben describes the slave-like animality that supports the human in man as 'anthropophorous'. 'Perhaps', he writes, 'the body of the anthropophorous animal (the body of the slave) is the unresolved remnant that idealism leaves as an inheritance to thought.' (*The Open*, 12) Are Clinton's anthropophorous creatures inside or outside?

[54] See Corbett, *Extended Play*, 144-54. Indeed, it might be argued that Clinton's 'freak' sound-world does no more than continue a lineage of 'novelty' sound-effects going back to the early days of recording technology. But, although this embeds funk experimentalism – once again – in history, it shouldn't be taken to negate either the symbolic specificity of this world or the deep significance of its 'animalistic' qualities. One strand in the history can be traced back through African-American comedy records of the 1920s, drawing on vaudeville traditions and, before that, on the masquerades of the nineteenth-century minstrel show. Animal imitations often figured in the minstrel show (as indeed did cross-dressing), and can no doubt be linked to the still broader, Afro-diasporic trope of the 'Signifying Monkey' explored by Henry Louis Gates. The discursive territory here is that in which, in a variety of ways and not just for the obvious racist reasons, blacks were wont to be positioned, and often to position themselves, in close proximity to animals. At the same time, there's a technologically specific factor. Barbara Engh has pointed out ('His Master's Voice', 59) that the ephemera characterising turn-of-the-century phonographic culture overflow with animal and bird imagery (Nipper is of course the emblem of this, just as Gus Elen's parrot is a symptom), embedding the sonic tradition to which Clinton's 'creatures' belong in a long-established discursive habit. And, once again, the register of gender division overlaps the broader man/nature distinction: Engh's discussion (*ibid.* 61-3) of the even longer tradition whereby Woman is positioned on the side of the animal culminates in a reference to Kafka's story of Josephine the Singer, who is a mouse – a figure which Ian Biddle has shown to be deeply inscribed in the performativity of gender in this very same early twentieth-century moment (Ian Biddle, 'Of Mice and Dogs:

Music, Gender, and Sexuality at the Long Fin de Siècle', in Clayton, Martin, Trevor Herbert and Richard Middleton (eds.), *The Cultural Study of Music: A Critical Introduction* [New York: Routledge, 2003], 215-26).

[55] I discuss the groove/grave nexus in more detail in *Voicing the Popular*, 145-7.

[56] Engh, 'Adorno', 133-5.

[57] *Ibid*. 125.

[58] 'Embodiment is significant prosthesis; objectivity cannot be about fixed vision when what counts as an object is precisely what world history turns out to be about.' (Donna Haraway, *Simians, Cyborgs, and Women: The Reinvention of Nature* (London: Free Association Books, 1991), 195.

[59] See Sterne, *The Audible Past*, 1-29, 213-21: 221.

[60] The term 'vocalic body' is Steven Connor's; see *Dumbstruck*, 35-43 (the quotation is from p. 35). I introduce the term 'vocalimentary canal', an organ which I see as traversing the territory from head, through lungs and stomach to genitalia, in *Voicing the Popular*, 93. A Trobriand Islander once told Malinowski, 'The throat is a long passage like the wila (cunnus) and the two attract each other.' (Quoted, Eisenberg, *Recording Angel*, 71).

The pre-history of the 'talking machine', going back at least to eighteenth-century experiments in 'mechanical voice', suggests that the body/voice suture has long been understood as in a sense artificial, as a device of embodiment, however disavowed this idea might often have been. As Dolar puts this, 'The voice appears as the link which ties the signifier to the body. It indicates that... the bodily emission must provide the material to embody the signifier, the disembodied signifying mechanics must be attached to bodily mechanics...' (Dolar, *Voice*, 59).

[61] Admittedly, there's an ambivalence in the practice of acousmatic music, in which, sometimes, sounds are made to approximate to 'real-life' sounds. This parallels an ambivalence in the etymology, where the Greek *acousma* means 'a thing heard', and yet a key reference is to the way that followers of Pythagoras had to listen to their master's voice while he was invisible, positioned behind a screen. Word was all; body was a distraction. See Michel Chion, *The Voice in Cinema*, tr. Claudia Gorbman (New York: Columbia University Press, 1999), 18-19.

Even the reading of Barthes's article presented here can't save it entirely. Barthes misses the point that the pinning together of sound and body, voice and gaze (real or imagined), is always incomplete and paradoxical; that 'de-acousmatisation' (as Chion calls it: *ibid*. 27-9) always fails in the end; that ventriloquism is irreducible (see Dolar, *Voice*, 197 note 10). The acousmatic voice is a voice in search of a body – even if the body it finds turns out to be 'wrong' in some way (see *ibid*. 60-61). Can we say that, attached (even phantasmatically) to things, sounds become voices, i.e. that things *veut dire* (to use a Derridean formulation; see *ibid*. 191 note 2)? In which case, my own formulation of 'translation' is misleading also. Voice doesn't so much translate bodily gesture as transect and at the same time produce its imagined movement, creating (a little bit of) embodiment; as in the game of charades, its effects 'look like', 'sound like', meaning (or, as Barthes might prefer, like 'grain').

[62] Cf. Freud (*Totem and Taboo: Some Points of Agreement between the Mental Lives of Savages and Neurotics*, tr. James Strachey [London: Routledge and Kegan Paul, 1950], 161): 'in the beginning was the Deed'; Freud's context is his theory of a 'primal crime' (murder of the father), out of which 'culture' itself , including morality, guilt and language, could be thought to emerge, and he is quoting Goethe's Faust (which shows the price of such knowledge): 'Im Anfang war die Tat'.

There is a Christian version of this myth. St Augustine describes John the Baptist as the Voice which must precede, and then give way to, the Word (Jesus Christ). Voice – voice as bodily emission, 'voice which merely resonates and offers no sense, this sound which comes from the mouth of someone screaming' – has to die if logos, theological truth, is to emerge. Still (as Dolar points out), Word must (then) become flesh, i.e. flesh transfigured, 'flesh of ideality itself' (Dolar, *Voice*, 15-16, 191 note 6). But further, flesh itself, including vocalizing flesh, was, as far back in the myth as we can go, always already shot through with ideality, act with inscription. Derrida points out that, in giving the name Babel to stand, as proper name (i.e as origin), for 'confusion' (a common noun, thenceforth applied with impunity to the babble of foreigners, racial inferiors, women, children, apes, birds, nature itself), God introduced precisely confusion into the very interior of the name, and into the act of naming. 'Babel', as name, purports untranslatability, yet, as act, it sets up an originary multiplicity; it 'at the same time imposes and forbids translation' (a process we can understand as occurring within an initial production – 'translation' as originary, as phonographic (cf. note 61) – as well as between productions, as translation in the normal sense). Thus in the primal act of naming – Adorno's 'naming the name itself' – there is already deferral, a 'writing before writing', and the Babel story stands for 'the myth of the origin of myth'; even God's name, which he gives to himself, pleads for translation: 'before language, languages', before the divine body, bodies, before the primal act, already acts. (Jacques Derrida, 'Des Tours de Babel', in *Acts of Religion*, ed. Gil Anidjar [New York: Routledge, 2002], 104-34: 108, 104, 118. Derrida refers to two key texts by Walter Benjamin: 'On Language as Such and on the Language of Man', tr. Edmund Jephcott, in *Selected Writings*, Vol. 1, ed. Michael Bullock and Michael W. Jennings [Cambridge MA: Harvard University Press, 1996], 62-74; and 'The Task of the Translator', tr. Harry Zohn, in *ibid.*, 253-63).

'In the beginning': I have throughout resisted the search for origin (except, of course, as retroactive myth); man is the creature who produces his own origin. Nevertheless, it is interesting that in palaeo-anthropologist, Steven Mithen's account of the proto-language developing among the hominid ancestors of man (he names it 'hmmmmm' because it was Holistic, Multi-Modal, Manipulative, Musical and Mimetic), discrete holistic expressions functioned like names rather than words, and were acted out as well as spoken/sung. Even so, the sources of this proto-language go back (to the primates and beyond) as far as one could go. There is no point zero in evolution. See Steven Mithen, *The*

Singing Neanderthals: The Origins of Music, Language, Mind and Body
(London: Phoenix, 2006).

[63] Sterne, *The Audible* Past, 274; Haraway, *Cyborgs*, 152.

[64] Haraway, *Cyborgs*, 180, 151.

[65] Gilles Deleuze and Félix Guattari, *A Thousand Plateaus: Capitalism and
Schizophrenia*, tr. Brian Massumi (London: Athlone Press, 1988), 164-5. On its
first appearance (in *Anti-Oedipus*, 9-17) the BwO is presented as dead, inert;
yet it comes alive, as subsequent elaboration shows: it provides a surface for,
appropriates as it rejects, the flows of the desiring-machines – the organs. It's
the device Deleuze uses to acknowledge a remnant – beyond the machines –
without having to think organism. Yet without something like a death-drive, a
concept he rejects, this device remains speculative – a residue, we might say
(strangely, for a supposedly materialist psychiatry), that idealism leaves to
practice. But what if the BwO is itself a machine – a symbolic-discursive
machine? In Deleuze's account, it records the flows; it is, then, a recording-
machine – a phonograph. Recording not only memorialises but also defers,
prolongs, sur-vives (to use a Derridean word-play); recording is, immediately,
production.

[66] See *Thousand Plateaus*, 232-309, especially (for the music connection)
272: 'music is traversed by a becoming-woman, becoming-child... by
becomings-animal, above all becomings-bird, but many others besides.'

[67] See *ibid.* 299-350.

[68] And indeed, the inert body of the BwO is presented as the social body,
including the body of capital, on which the productions of the organs are
registered, and this process is described as 'recording' (Deleuze and Guattari,
Anti-Oedipus, 9-17). See note 65.

[69] One might think that Deleuze's 'molecular' ontology speaks of its times,
congruent as it is with excitedly deterritorialising models of both the emergent
digital media and the genetic revolution in evolutionary theory. Today it seems
clearer that what both the 'bitscape' and the 'genescape' make available is
more passages, more levels, more 'homes' for subjectivity rather than its
demise.

[70] Slavoj Žižek, *Organs Without Bodies: On Deleuze and Consequences*
(New York: Routledge, 2004), 87.

[71] See *ibid.* 170-176.

[72] Is this force-field the same place as the one Agamben describes (in
different terms) as a 'zone of indifference' where, constantly, decisions as to
'the articulation between human and animal' – and, we may add, between
human and machine – are made? For Agamben, this 'zone of indeterminacy in
which the outside is nothing but the exclusion of an inside and the inside is in
turn only the inclusion of an outside' is empty – empty save for the ceaseless
activity of decision. But what if this activity is itself determinate, even

passionately so, and the zone therefore full? Isn't this the territory where desiring-machines function (or not) and are converted (or not) into drive – that irreducibly hybrid (bio-machinic-human) force where jouissance and castration support each other endlessly, in the process circulating the first writing – writing before writing? (Agamben, *The Open*, 37, 38)

[73] Deleuze and Guattari, *Thousand Plateaus*, 302, 303, 304, 307.

[74] Žižek, *Organs*, 176, 177.

[75] 'Real abstraction': see above, note 23. The effect of commodity fetishism as real abstraction is to deposit the master-slave relationship in the social unconscious as foundational.

[76] In a telling pre-echo of this problematic as it would work itself out in subsequent media development, Alexander Graham Bell claimed for his newly invented device, the photophone (which transmitted sound through light), that 'I have heard articulate speech produced by sunlight! I have heard a ray of the sun laugh and cough and sing!' (Quoted, Sterne, *Audible Past*, 181.)

[77] For this conception of spectre, see Slavoj Žižek, 'The Spectre of Ideology', in Wright, Elizabeth and Edmond Wright (eds.), *The Žižek Reader* (Oxford: Blackwell, 1999), 53-86.

[78] For Benjamin's vision of the Angel of History, see his 'Theses on the Philosophy of History', in *Illuminations*, ed. Hannah Arendt, tr. Harry Zohn (London: Fontana, 1973), 255-66.

[79] Benjamin, *Selected Writings*, 389, 482 (translation slightly modified). I owe my awareness of these texts to Agamben, who discusses them in *The Open*, 81-4. Benjamin's 'antifeminist remark' (cf. note 23), resonating with the elements of patriarchalism in both the Carey and Clinton tracks, is disturbing, if perhaps unsurprising. What, one wonder, would Björk (to whom I turn shortly) make of it?

[80] Pop music is, of course, overwhelmingly secular (except for the important exception of country music). However, to mention just ballad (love of God or of the Virgin transferred to the sphere of human romance); blues (devil's music); soul (gospel ecstasy transposed to the sexual relationship); singer-songwriters (closeted in the confessional); even heavy metal (homage to the Anti-Christ), should be enough to establish that this foundation is shaky. If Christianity invented secularism, secular pop maintains a home for the religiophorous. And if the anthropophorous is the remnant that idealism leaves to thought, then perhaps the religiophorous is the remnant that secularism leaves to spirit.

[81] Jacques Derrida, 'Faith and Knowledge: The Two Sources of "Religion" at the Limits of Reason Alone', in *Acts of Religion*, 42-101: 43, 83-5.

[82] Lacan, *Psychoses*, 179.

[83] The phrase is Henri Bergson's, quoted in Derrida, 'Faith', 77.

[84] Björk, *Medúlla* (CD, One Little Indian TPLP358CD, 2004). Björk uses a variety of singers, including a throat singer and several 'human beat-boxes'. On her approach, she says: 'I used different methods with each person, but I encouraged everyone to express themselves and imagine they were a human drum loop or bassline. I also got the Icelandic choir to pretend to be insects and birds and other ancient creature. The difficult job was sitting at the computer afterwards deciding what to edit. I had so much material I'd say 80% of the time spent on this album was pure editing. Sometimes I just needed to swap chunks around, other times I had to add vocals from one track to another or strip everything down to a couple of notes. As much as everyone delivered live performances, there was a lot of weaving and layering needed to bring the whole album together.' (http://www.bjork.com/facts/about/what/On Medúlla/ (29 July 2005).

[85] According to Björk, *Medúlla* is 'folk music, but without any folk attached' (*ibid.*).

[86] For example: 'For me, techno and nature is the same thing. It's just a question of the future and the past. You take a log cabin in the mountains. Ten thousand years ago, monkey-humans would have thought, That's fucking techno. Now in 1997 you see a log cabin and go, Oh, that's nature. There is fear of techno because it's the unknown. I think it is a very organic thing, like electricity. But then, my father is an electrician - and my grandfather as well.' (http://www.bjork.com/facts/about/what/'On nature and techno' [29 July 2005]). Or: 'Synthesizers are quite an organic, natural thing. But I think it's always with mankind that every time something new arrives, like say when they invented fire, they were terrified: "Oh this is going to kill us all! It's doomsday!"' (http://www.bjork.com/facts/about/what/'On technology' [29 July 2005]). See also Charity Marsh and Melissa West, 'The Nature/Technology Binary Opposition Dismantled in the Music of Madonna and Björk', in Lysloff, René T. A. and Leslie C. Gay (eds.), *Music and Technoculture* (Middletown CN: Wesleyan University Press, 2003), 182-203.

[87] Are they bodies or organs? 'Medúlla is primitive, like before civilisation. It's the soft squidgy thing in the centre. After Vespertine I was going to do an album with intuition only, no brain please. I was thinking more visceral, flesh and blood, pregnancy... death metal.' (http://www.bjork.com/facts/about/what/On Medúlla/ [29 July 2005]).

[88] Agamben is one who cites Benjamin's insight (*The Open*, 82-3) and places it in just such a 'post-historical' context.

[89] Walter Benjamin, 'One-Way Street', tr. Edmund Jephcott, in *Selected Writings*, 444-88: 487. Of course, 'development' (*Entwicklung*) is not 'history' – at least not in the sense assumed in the paradigm beginning with Herodotus and ending, maybe, with Nietzsche, which is centred on human projects, with teleological import, recorded in a would-be objective narrative. But isn't this paradigm itself an (imperialistic) construct of Western reason? 'If what is called history is a dynamic and open social reality, in a state of functional disequilibrium..., then primitive societies are fully inside history'. (Deleuze and Guattari, *Anti-Oedipus*, 165) And, even if capitalism marks the end of history in

a certain sense (*ibid.* 168), this says nothing about how long this end might last, nor the extent of the vicissitudes along the way.

[90] Quoted, Eisenberg, *Recording Angel*, 28.

Bibliography

Adorno, T. W., 'The Curves of the Needle' [1928], tr. Thomas Y. Levin., *October* Vol. 55 (1990), 48-55.

------, 'The Form of the Phonograph Record' [1934], tr. Thomas Y. Levin. *October* Vol. 55 (1990), 56-61.

------, *Essays on Music*, ed. Richard Leppert (Berkeley CA: University of California Press, 2002).

Adorno, T. W. and Max Horkheimer, *Dialectic of Enlightenment*, tr. John Cumming (London: Verso, 1997 [1944]).

Agamben, Giorgio, *The Open: Man and Animal*, tr. Kevin Attell (Stanford CA: Stanford University Press, 2004).

Benjamin, Walter, 'Theses on the Philosophy of History', in *Illuminations*, tr. Harry Zohn (London: Fontana, 1973), 255-266.

------, *Selected Writings*, Vol. 1, ed. Michael Bullock and Michael W. Jennings (Cambridge MA: Harvard University Press, 1996).

Biddle, Ian, 'Of Mice and Dogs: Music, Gender, and Sexuality at the Long Fin de Siècle', in Clayton, Martin, Trevor Herbert and Richard Middleton (eds.), *The Cultural Study of Music: A Critical Introduction*, (New York: Routledge, 2003), 215-226.

Biers, Katherine, 'Syncope Fever: James Weldon Johnson and the Black Phonographic Voice', *Representations* Vol. 96 (2006), 99-125.

Bradby, Barbara, 'Sampling Sexuality: Gender, Technology and the Body in Dance Music', *Popular Music* Vol. 12 No. 2 (1993), 155-76.

Brewster, Bill and Frank Broughton, *Last Night a DJ Saved My Life: The History of the Disc Jockey* (London: Headline, 1999).

Brown, James, with Bruce Tucker, *James Brown: The Godfather of Soul* (London: Sidgwick and Jackson, 1987).

Chion, Michel, *The Voice in Cinema*, tr. Claudia Gorbman (New York: Columbia University Press, 1999).

Connor, Stephen, *Dumbstruck: A Cultural History of Ventriloquism* (Oxford: Oxford University Press, 2000).

Corbett, John, *Extended Play: Sounding Of from John Cage to Dr. Funkenstein* (Durham NC: Duke University Press, 1994).

Deleuze, Gilles and Félix Guattari, *A Thousand Plateaus: Capitalism and Schizophrenia*, tr. Brian Massumi (London: Athlone Press, 1988).

------, *Anti-Oedipus: Capitalism and Schizophrenia*, tr. Robert Hurley, Mark Seem and Helen R. Lane (London: Continuum, 2004).

Derrida, Jacques, *Of Grammatology*, tr. Gayatri Chakravorty Spivak (Baltimore: The Johns Hopkins University Press, 1976).

------, *Acts of Religion*, ed. Gil Anidjar (New York: Routledge, 2002).

Dolar, Mladen, 'The Object Voice', in Salecl, Renata and Slavoj Žižek (eds.), *Gaze and Voice as Love Objects* (Durham NC: Duke University Press, 1996), 7-31.

------, *Voice and Nothing More* (Cambridge MA: MIT Press, 2006).

Eisenberg, Evan, *The Recording Angel: Music, Records and Culture from Aristotle to Zappa* (London: Picador, 1988).

Engh, Barbara, 'Adorno and the Sirens: Tele-phono-graphic Bodies', in Dunn, Leslie C. and Nancy A. Jones (eds.), *Embodied Voices: Representing Female Vocality in Western Culture* (Cambridge: Cambridge University Press, 1994), 120-135.

------, 'After "His Master's Voice" ', *New Formations* Vol. 38 (1999), 54-63.

Fikentscher, Kai, '"There's Not a Problem I Can't Fix, 'Cause I Can Do It in the Mix"', in René T. A. Lysloff, and Leslie C. Gay (eds.), *Music and Technoculture* (Middletown CN: Wesleyan University Press, 2003), 290-315.

Freud, Sigmund, *On Metapsychology: The Theory of Psychoanalysis* (London: Penguin, 1991).

------, *Totem and Taboo: Some Points of Agreement between the Mental Lives of Savages and Neurotics*, tr. James Strachey (London: Routledge and Kegan Paul, 1950).

Gates, Henry Louis, *The Signifying Monkey: A Theory of African-American Literary Criticism* (New York: Oxford University Press, 1988).

Haraway, Donna, *Simians, Cyborgs, and Women: The Reinvention of Nature* (London: Free Association Books, 1991).

Kafka, Franz, *Shorter Works*, Vol. 1, tr. Malcolm Pasley (London: Secker & Warburg, 1973).

Keightley, Keir, ' "Turn It Down!" She Shrieked: Gender, Domestic Space, and High Fidelity, 1948-59', *Popular Music* Vol. 15 No. 2 (1996), 149-177.

Kittler, Friedrich, *Gramophone, Film, Typewriter*, tr. Geoffrey Winthrop-Young and Michael Wutz (Stanford CA: Stanford University Press, 1999).

Lacan, Jacques, *The Psychoses: The Seminar of Jacques Lacan, Book III 1955-1956*, ed. Jacques-Alain Miller, tr. Russell Grigg (London: Routledge, 1993).

Lauretis, Teresa de, *Technologies of Gender: Essays on Theory, Film, and Fiction* (Bloomington IN: Indiana University Press, 1987).

Leach, Elizabeth Eva, 'Parrots, Phonographs, and Other Imitators', unpublished paper.

Levin, Thomas Y., 'For the Record: Adorno on Music in the Age of Its Technological Reproducibility', *October* Vol. 55 (1990), 23-47.

Middleton, Richard, *Voicing the Popular: On the Subjects of Popular Music* (New York: Routledge, 2006).

------, 'Mum's the Word: Maternal Law and Men's Singing', in Jarman-Ivens, Freya (ed.), *Oh Boy: Masculinities and Popular Music* (New York: Routledge, 2007).

Mithen, Steven, *The Singing Neanderthals: The Origins of Music, Language, Mind and Body* (London: Phoenix, 2006).

Mowitt, John, 'The Sound of Music in the Era of Its Electronic Reproducibility', in Richard Leppert and Susan McClary (eds.), *Music and Society: The Politics of Composition, Performance and Reception* (Cambridge: Cambridge University Press, 1987), 173-97.

Scarry, Elaine, *The Body in Pain* (New York: Oxford University Press, 1985).

Scott, Michael, *The Great Caruso* (London: Hamish Hamilton, 1988).

Silverman, Kaja, *The Acoustic Mirror: The Female Voice in Psychoanalysis and Cinema* (Bloomington IN: University of Indiana Press, 1988).

Sterne, Jonathon, *The Audible Past: Cultural Origins of Sound Reproduction* (Durham NC: Duke University Press, 2003).

Warner, Marina, *Fantastic Metamorphoses, Other Worlds* (Oxford: Oxford University Press, 2002).

Žižek, Slavoj, *The Sublime Object of Ideology* (London: Verso, 1989).

------, ' "I Hear You with My Eyes"; or, The Invisible Master', in Salecl, Renata and Slavoj Žiže (eds.), *Gaze and Voice as Love Objects* (Durham NC: Duke University Press, 1996), 90-126.

------, 'The Spectre of Ideology', in Wright, Elizabeth and Edmond Wright (eds.), *The Žižek Reader* (Oxford: Blackwell, 1999), 53-86.

------, *On Belief* (New York: Routledge, 2001).

------, *Organs Without Bodies: On Deleuze and Consequences* (New York: Routledge, 2004).

Discography

Björk, *Medúlla* (CD, One Little Indian TPLP358CD, 2004).

Brown, James, 'Say It Loud – I'm Black and I'm Proud', *Startime* (CD set, disc 2, Polydor, 849 110-2, 1991 [single, King, K6187, 1968]).

------, 'Get Up (I Feel Like Being a) Sex Machine', *Startime* (CD set, disc 3, Polydor, 849 111-2, 1991 [single, King, 6318, 1970]).

Carey, Mariah, 'Last Night a DJ Saved My Life', *Glitter* (CD, Virgin 7243 8 10797 2 0, 2001), Track 8.

Indeep, 'Last Night a DJ Saved My Life, *Funk/Soul Classics: The Ultimate 80's Soul and Funk Revival* (CD, Ministry of Sound MOSCD84, 2004 [12 inch single, Sound of New York Records, SNY 5102, 1982]).

Marley, Bob and the Wailers, 'Duppy Conqueror', *Complete Upsetter Collection* (CD set, Trojan, TBOXCD 013, 2000 [single, 1969]).

Parliament, 'Dr Funkenstein', *The Clones of Dr Funkenstein* (CD, Polydor 8426202, 2001 [Casablanca 8426202, 1976]).

Videography

Glitter, dir. Vondie Curtis-Hall, USA, 2001 (DVD, Columbia C8212269, 2001).

CHAPTER 12

O brother, let's go down home: loss, nostalgia and the blues

Abstract

The blues genre is commonly (and not incorrectly) regarded as a key marker of African-American identity and one with 'deep' (folk, or 'down home') roots. But this status is inadequately understood unless it is placed in a context of inter-racial exchange, in which 'roots' are a product of a complex transaction between 'modernity' and 'tradition'. This territory is explored in terms of a thematics of loss, nostalgia and trauma, evident both in blues content and in the historical structure of revival to which the genre has been continually subject. A useful background is the film O Brother, Where Art Thou?, *a nostalgic celebration of nostalgia with a blues/bluegrass inter-racial dimension, and a productive theoretical framework is provided by Lacan's approach to fantasy, loss and nostalgia.*

Introduction (Take 1)

Three events from the beginning of the new century:

First, the White Stripes, a guitar-based duo from Detroit, emerge as 'the most exciting rock band in the world' (*The Guardian*, 29 March 2003), on a platform of emotional truth, pared-down simplicity, recall to tradition. Their style is centred on musical influences and an aesthetic of authenticity drawn from blues; their first two albums are dedicated to Son House and Blind Willie McTell, respectively. The White Stripes are only the most prominent of a number of like-minded bands. We seem to have yet another blues revival on our hands.

Second, in 2002 Alan Lomax, arguably the first significant folklorist to look for blues in the field (as distinct from tripping over them among other types of song), dies, and his book, *The Land Where the Blues Began*, which recounts his fieldwork experiences in the 1940s, 1950s and 1960s, is re-published.

Third, the Coen Brothers' movie, *O Brother, Where Art Thou?*, set in the 1930s and organised around the nostalgic appeal (but also the political potency) of 'old timey' music, is an unexpectedly huge hit. Although the focus of the soundtrack is on early hillbilly music – and it triggers another revival, this time of bluegrass – a racial theme, with a blues strand, is crucial. Early in the film, the three white heroes, led by Everett Ulysses McGill, are joined on their travels (which are part escape from prison, part search for the 'treasure' Everett has buried) by an African-American singer-guitarist modelled on a real bluesman of the time (whose name he carries), Tommy Johnson. (Part of the fun is that the initial meeting takes place at a crossroads, where, paying due homage to legend, Tommy has just met the Devil – he was white and had a 'mean look' – and, presumably, traded his soul for musical prowess. Tommy is on his way to Tishomingo; the real Johnson would more likely have been on his way to Jackson: but close enough.[1]) Our four heroes miraculously form themselves into a band, and their version of 'Man of Constant Sorrow', featured on local radio, is a smash hit, subsequently securing their pardons after they perform it at a political campaign rally in support of Governor Pappy O' Daniel. This song is a 'white blues': the 'standard' I–IV–V chord-sequence is truncated into a ten bar verse, with a four-bar refrain after each two-verse segment; the vocal follows familiar melodic shapes and drips with blue notes; Tommy's bluesy, riff-heavy guitar anchors the song 'down home'. In another important episode in the film, Tommy is rescued from the clutches of the Ku Klux Klan; the KKK's Grand Wizard is revealed to be O'Daniel's racist political opponent, who – appalled – describes our boys as a 'miscegenatin' band'. (The point is confirmed when, in the performance at the rally, Tommy's guitar fits effortlessly into the marvellously intricate textures of a full bluegrass band sound.[2])

Many things are going on in these three developments, but they have at least three aspects in common. First, 'revival': the past is conjured up, brought into the present, re-configured. At the same time, this past is a 'folk' past: what is conjured up is 'tradition', a home that has been lost. And finally, these transactions are unavoidably racialised: white rock musicians, white scholars, white film-makers drawing on black roots – only to find (at least in the movie) a white investment already in place, right back down home.

Introduction (Take 2)

In *Music Grooves* (1994), Charles Keil makes the scandalous suggestion that, far from fitting the 'folk' paradigm, blues in its origins was urban and modern rather than rural and archaic, was circulated and developed on records as much as (perhaps more than) through live performance and oral dissemination, and was from the beginning an inter-racial phenomenon – that, in a sense, it was even a white invention, with which black musicians then had to come to terms, which they reconfigured. Writing at a time when the claims of African-American identity politics were being shouted from the rooftops, Keil would probably be less than surprised that his speculations have not been widely pursued.[3] Of course we know (from the work of Tony Russell, in Oliver *et al.* 2001, for example) that in the vernacular musical practice of the South there was a cross-racial 'common stock' of tunes, songs, and vocal and instrumental techniques going back at least to the nineteenth century and including features and songs that we would now associate with blues (hence, for instance, 'Man of Constant Sorrow'). But although this is important and relevant (it provides the broader historical backdrop to Keil's more specific point), it is not the same argument. We may quibble with the idea of 'origin' (where in the endless relays of cultural practice does anything begin, and how could such an *ex nihilo* claim justify its authority?), but nevertheless when a genre is *named* and a certain cultural place discursively established, then we identify a moment possessing a particular historical power.

There is no significant historical evidence for the existence of a blues genre before 1902–1903, the period when Gertrude 'Ma' Rainey, Jelly Roll Morton and W.C. Handy all claim to have heard (or in Morton's case, made up) blues songs for the first time; all, however, were speaking (and naming the genre) with the benefit of hindsight.[4] During the next few years, several folklorists included verses looking like blues in published collections,[5] but they did not identify them as such nor show any special interest in them. The big moment came in 1912 with the first publications of blues compositions, including Handy's 'Memphis Blues'. In fact, Handy (a trained, middle-class musician, far from 'the folk') had put together his tune in 1909, as 'Mr Crump' (as yet without words) for his band to play in a political contest (another!) in Memphis; but he was beaten to publication by the white band-leader, Hart Wand, with his instrumental, 'Dallas Blues' – just as he was closely followed in 1913 by Leroy 'Lasses' White's 'Nigger Blues' (White was, ironically but appropriately, white and a blackface minstrel), which in turn became, it appears, one of the first 'blues' to be recorded, in 1916.[6] A torrent of publications followed. From the start, the blues craze set off by these publications involved white bands as well as black, and (preponderantly) white singers – Gilda Gray, Blossom Seeley, Marion Harris – until Mamie Smith's 'Crazy Blues' of 1920 (which is musically as much a torch song as a blues, actually). The female black singers following in Mamie Smith's wake, singing 'vaudeville blues', were part of this rich inter-racial culture of commercial song, including but not limited to blues, and they also, arguably, played the single biggest role in establishing a black performing presence within it, touring the South and disseminating their records there as well as in the Northern cities. But in the 1920s blues were also a key part of the repertories for many white singers, dance bands, both black and white, and theatre and jazz musicians. The first significant blues recordings by a black male singer came out in 1924, from the banjo-playing, minstrel-show songster, 'Papa' Charlie Jackson. No 'folk blues' records appeared until Blind Lemon Jefferson's in 1926, and, although his success initiated a downhome blues recording boom during the late 1920s and early 1930s, the most commercially successful male blues singers at this time were the jazzy Lonnie Johnson, and Leroy Carr – sophisticated in a different way, based in Indianapolis, with a style locating itself far from the cotton fields and levees.

This story is familiar enough. But the inferences that Keil would draw are less so. What had happened, it would seem, is that whites (together with a good number of middle-class and ambitious blacks such as Handy and Perry Bradford, composer of 'Crazy Blues'), working in a context defined increasingly by a sequence of black-tinted music fads – coon song, ragtime, jazz – and by conventions of blackface performance, had crystallised a new commercial song genre out of their appropriations of a bundle of African-American vernacular practices. As part of this process, white singers, drawing on images of black style, had created models of blues vocality, which black performers could not evade. From this point of view, 'Nigger Blues', usually dismissed as a wooden travesty, becomes interesting. Recorded by an up-market white 'character' singer from Washington DC, George O'Connor, its meanings flow when placed where it belongs, in a metropolitan drawing-room.[7] Like many of Handy's, White's song sticks together an assortment of lyric clichés, familiar from many other songs, and puts them to a formulaic blues melody over the standard twelve-bar changes. It is O'Connor's delivery that speaks to the regulative norms of the culture within which 'blues' would now exist. Whose voice(s) do we hear? Two at least, I would suggest, or even three: the singer's, itself split between that of the white elite, to which he belongs and which he addresses, and that of an imaginary object which he strives to imitate; and secondly, that of the object itself – or rather, the object wanting to subjectivise itself, to make its own desire heard, conjured up in our imaginations now. Here is the 'plantation South' transplanted to the white drawing room (and thence to our ears); the exotic reified (in dialect, in rhythm, in melodic gestures): desire, and lack, coursing through the gaps between the voice we actually hear, the voice O'Connor wants us to imagine and the voice blotted out but which we know is there, somewhere, could we but find it.

In a way, the 'nigger' has been folklorised here, a blues revival set in train even before its source has been sufficiently established to copy. (Cecil Sharp, who would shortly make his fieldwork visit to the Appalachians, would certainly have recognised what was going on.) The full folklorisation process comes later, however, starting in the 1950s. Thus the historical schema which follows from pursuing Keil's proposal is striking. The blues Golden Age[8] – when black re-appropriation gives the music sufficient relative autonomy to produce its moment of condensed historical force – is very short, running from the 1920s to the 1950s. It is preceded by a period when blues as an emergent pop fad covers over, but at the same time provides a hazy refraction of, a no doubt rich, multivalent vernacular practice. It includes two even shorter peaks of down-home assertiveness (Mississippi, late-1920s/early 1930s; Chicago, late 1940s/ early 1950s), which would subsequently provide the core sources for the (mostly white) pattern of folklorisation and revival that constitutes one pole of the afterglow, the other comprising the marginalisation of blues for African-Americans. The Golden Age coincides with a period of enormous tension, marked by forces pushing the 'modernisation' of the South on the one hand, explosive racist reactions, centred on such organisations as the Ku Klux Klan, on the other. *O Brother* sits in the middle of this period, exploring the tensions with a comedy as black as it is hilarious. 'Real' blues, it confirms, is a construction always mediated by white desire – which thus also enfolds blacks within this structure. Despite the pressures of identity politics, this position does not 'rob' blacks of the blues: the music's political potential as a cultural resource remains, but inescapably embedded in a larger racial dialogue.[9]

Mass communicatin' culture 'n' heritage

In *O Brother*, Governor O'Daniel, rushing into the radio station to do a show immediately after our heroes have made their record there, declares excitedly for modernity: he is 'mass communicatin'', he boasts. Communicatin' what? Well, the past: 'culture 'n' heritage', to use a well-worn and rather suspect Southern phrase, also deployed by O'Daniel's KKK opponent, disgustedly describing the 'miscegenating band': 'this ain't *my* culture 'n' heritage', he asserts. Blues too points both forward and back; it is modern, as we have seen, but from the start also sounds old. As a genre, blues comes into being with sheet music and records, and registers the social effects of Reconstruction and its failure, followed by the profound economic shifts – industrialisation, urbanisation – of the late nineteenth and early twentieth centuries. It speaks of 'culture shock': mobility, deracination, alienation, freedom – both sexual and more general. Even in the core of down-home territory, the Mississippi Delta, the social and economic geography was the result of quite recent developments – large-scale migration from the surrounding hill-country, drainage projects through levee building, settlement of new land, the coming of the railways (see Lomax 1993, pp. 64–70; Evans 1987, pp. 169–74), producing 'the conditions of an urban ghetto spread out over a rural landscape' (David Evans, quoted in Davis 1995, p. 47). Yet from the beginning blues *sounds old* – 'back then' is built into its aesthetic ('Times ain't now nothing like they used to be . . . I done seen better days but I ain't putting up with these . . .': Rabbit Brown's 'James Alley Blues' [1927]); and 'going back' (to that 'same old used to be', etc.) is as common as 'going to' (Chicago, Kansas City . . .): as Tommy Johnson puts it, 'Crying, Lord, will I ever get back home' ('Cool Water Blues' [1928]), and 'Well, I'm going back home, gon' fall down on my knees' ('Lonesome Home Blues' [1930]). The motif was there in the earliest proto-blues lyrics collected ('Well, I started to leave an' I got 'way down the track; Got to thinkin' 'bout my woman, come a-runnin' back. Wish to God some ol' train would run; Carry me back where I come frum'[10]). It was still there – indeed, not surprisingly, intensified – when Muddy Waters recorded such songs as 'I Believe I'll Go Back Home' in Chicago in 1948. At the same time it cannot be entirely separated from a much older trope: the mythological 'dear old Southland' of the minstrel show plantation, still clearly present in many early commercial blues songs (for example, Spencer Williams's 'Tishomingo Blues' [1917] and 'Basin Street Blues' [1928] and Handy's 'Way Down South where the Blues Began' [1932]).

From this point of view, blues, as Houston Baker puts it, is the 'always already' of African-American music; 'the song is no stranger . . . I been here before', and blues offers an ancestral voice, 'an anonymous (nameless) voice issuing from the black (w)hole' (Baker 1984, pp. 4, 64, 65, 5). In Paul Oliver's words: 'Blues had come from way back, but no one knew then, or even knows now, quite where, when or how they sounded' (Oliver *et al.* 2001, p. 2). And blues is 'always already' revived, bringing back up something already lost. Race record marketing commonly appealed to an 'original' authenticity: for example, Paramount advertised Blind Lemon Jefferson's first release as 'a real old-fashioned blues by a real old-fashioned blues singer . . . old-time tunes . . . in real southern style' (quoted in Charters 1975, p. 63), while earlier, in 1924, they had announced the first issues by Ma Rainey in a style which reads like an ethnographer's celebration of finding a lost tribe: 'Discovered at Last – "Ma" Rainey, Mother of the Blues!' (Oliver *et al.* 2001, pp. 262–3). A 1923 advertisement in *The Metronome*, probably placed by the music publishers E.B. Marks, states that:

Mechanical companies are tumbling over each other in their eagerness to discover 'real blues'. There are bushels of inferior compositions on the market labelled 'blues', but the genuine article by born writers of 'blues' is as scarce as the proverbial 'hen's teeth'. A 'real blues' . . . sways the hearer almost with every note, and underneath it all there is the wail of the aborigine. (Quoted in Evans 1987, p. 63)

In W.C. Handy's 1926 blues anthology, white enthusiast Abbe Niles in his 'Introduction', while locating blues as a new genre, insists on its status as folk music and describes his task as digging out 'their folk source', hidden in a range of previous folk genres, from beneath their popular success (Handy 1926, pp. 12, 20). Handy himself, in his autobiography, consistently portrays these pre-blues folk materials as 'rough diamonds' which he, as a skilled composer, would refine into more rounded and varied pieces; blues, then, is part of his 'mother tongue' and writing blues songs 'cannot be delegated outside of the blood' (Handy 1961, p. 231; and see pp. 137–51). First-generation blues singers, when interviewed later in life, sometimes bring out the moment early in the century when they encountered the new genre; Tommy Johnson's brother, LeDell, recalls family music-making in the early years of the century as based on 'love songs' and 'jump ups', but 'when all these late blues come out, that's all I studied' (Evans 1971, pp. 18, 19); similarly, a blind Clarksdale songster tells Alan Lomax how his repertoire of the early 1900s, jump ups and reels, gave way to blues: 'we were entering the jazz age and the old world was being transformed' (Lomax 1993, p. 55). Just as often, however, they refer to 'deep', mysterious pre-twentieth century origins: thus, for Memphis Slim, also talking to Lomax, 'Blues started from slavery' (*ibid.* p. 460), while for John Lee Hooker, 'it's not only what happened to you – it's what happened to your foreparents and other people. And that's what makes the blues' (Oliver *et al.* 2001, p. 203). No sooner had blues exploded into popular consciousness, it seems, than it was mythologised as 'old time'. The interplay of 'modernity' and 'folkloric' deeply embedded in blues discourses maps this dialectic of old and new, to produce an economy in which 'survival' – of individuals, a music, a culture – would always resonate to the anxieties of real or imagined loss.

The folklorisation process assumed the force of a movement in the 1950s and 1960s, but this is pre-figured by the collecting and publishing work of John Lomax, and especially his son Alan, in the 1930s and 1940s, and to some extent, with a rather different sort of focus, by activities associated with the Harlem Renaissance of the later 1920s. There is a clear lineage, constructed through the wider 'folk revival', via the Lomaxes, the Seegers and their associates, leading to young revival singers of the 1960s such as Bob Dylan, along with the British 'blues boom' of the same period. The iconic figure of Leadbelly has an important transitional status. 'Discovered' in 1933 by the Lomaxes in Angola state prison, Louisiana, his songs published three years later (Lomax and Lomax 1936), promoted as a 'folk singer', Leadbelly (Huddie Ledbetter) became a key point of focus within the early white American folk revival. Leadbelly was a songster, but he sang blues and had worked with Blind Lemon Jefferson; more importantly perhaps, he seemed to carry a disappearing culture. (The Lomaxes' aim in 1933 was 'to find the Negro who had had the least contact with jazz, the radio, and with the white man'; Lomax and Lomax 1934, p. xxx.) Moreover, he had charisma, not least because of his fearsome reputation for violence, which had put him in jail several times for assault and murder. It is hard not to suspect that, for many middle-class whites, here was the body of a noble savage on to which forbidden desires and anxieties could be projected,[11] a suspicion intensified by many of Alan Lomax's later descriptions of similar experiences to those on the 1933 trip. His romantic account of a Son House performance at the moment of his 'discovery' in deepest Mississippi in 1941 (actually House had made commercial records some ten years earlier) can stand for many:

His voice, guttural and hoarse with passion, ripping apart the surface of the music like his tractor-driven deep plow ripped apart the wet black earth in the springtime, making the sap of the earth song run, while his powerful, work-hard hands snatched strange chords out of the steel strings the way they had snatched so many tons of cotton out of brown thorny cotton bolls in the fall . . . Son's whole body wept, as with eyes closed, the tendons in his powerful neck standing with the violence of his feeling and his brown face flushing, he sang in an awesome voice the *Death Letter Blues.* (Lomax 1993, p. 18)

Alan's father had described his response to the music at a Texas dance on their 1933 field trip: 'I felt carried across to Africa, and I left as if I were listening to the tom-toms of savage blacks' (quoted, Wolfe and Lornell 1993, p. 112). But Leadbelly was no 'savage', nor a rural simpleton. He actually discovered blues (as distinct from other song genres) in the early 1900s, working in the red-light district of Shreveport; and at the same time he was picking up contemporary vaudeville and Tin Pan Alley songs as well, a process that continued throughout his career: established as a 'folk' singer, he added pop, jazz and country songs to his repertoire, including covers of Jimmie Rodgers yodels. The Lomaxes tried to dissuade him, arguing that he should stick to 'older folk songs'. For John Lomax, 'his money value is to be natural and sincere'; unlike contemporary commercial African American singers, 'Leadbelly doesn't burlesque. He plays and sings with absolute sincerity. To me his music is real music'. On the occasion of Leadbelly's folkloric debut – at a Modern Languages Association conference in Philadelphia in 1934, at which he was scheduled along with a performance of 'Elizabethan Ayres to the virginals' – Lomax was complimented on his 'talented aborigine' who produced 'a treat of uncontaminated "original" music' (*ibid.*, pp. 145, 2, 130, 135).

A little later, Big Bill Broonzy – though a very different character from Leadbelly – underwent a not dissimilar transformation. Mississippi born, Broonzy moved to Chicago as early as 1920, and played a key part in the evolution there, in the 1930s, of a citified, commercially orientated band-based blues style. With his career in decline after the war, he was picked up by the revivalists, toured Europe, and was re-made as a 'folk' artist. In Lomax's account, based on interviews with Broonzy, his 1930s trajectory was a forced response to the demands of 'villainous' and 'vulgar' record company bosses demanding 'slavish and uncreative imitation', 'cheap "novelty" blues', 'drowning the poignant and often profound poesy of the earlier country blues in oceans of superficial swill' (*ibid.*, pp. 446, 447). Charles Edward Smith's picture in his 'Foreword' for the 1964 edition of Broonzy's memoir (Broonzy 1964, pp. 11–25) is similar, presenting the singer's later career as a *release* into renewal of an earlier rural identity which mentally he had never left. Yet, as Charters points out (Charters 1975, pp. 177–80), this renewal was *also* a response – a response to Broonzy's sense of a new market, and many of his new recordings were transformations of songs that had first been recorded in band formats, or even picked up from records by others or from songbooks. What is interesting here, though, is that in both his Lomax interview and his own memoir, Broonzy goes along with the revival narrative. He defends his 'old time blues', describing them as 'the real blues' (Broonzy 1964, p. 31), and traces many of his songs back to youthful experiences in the South; it is as if he himself is 'inventing' a musical past that would substantiate his folk persona.[12] There is, it appears, a 'double consciousness' at work here – a mask which can always turn but which, from both directions, casts a particular light on the more obvious screen constituted by the blackface cork.

Black involvement in the folklorisation process can be traced back to the early years of the century. As mentioned previously, white folklorists at that time paid little attention to blues, despite booming interest in African-American folk song. (White [1928, p. 16] estimates that fifty-nine books on the subject, many of them collections, were published between 1914 and 1926.) This is not surprising. Conceptions of 'folk culture' were conventional. Dorothy Scarborough's, though perhaps rather cruder than most, gives the drift: she writes of songs with a 'rough, primitive charm', which 'show us the lighter, happier side of slavery, and re-create for us the rustic merry-making of the slaves'; this results from the fact that the Negro 'is closer to nature' – but this will not last, and there is an urgent need to collect these songs 'before the material vanishes forever, killed by the Victrola, the radio, the lure of cheap printed music' (Scarborough 1963, pp. 128, 161, 281–2).[13] It was hard to fit blues, 'that peculiar, barbaric sort of melody . . . sung in vaudevilles everywhere' (*ibid.*, p. 264), into this paradigm. The usual line was that blues were a regrettable commercial product with buried folk origins (Krehbiel's description [1914, p. v] of 'ragtime tunes' as folk song's 'debased offspring' followed the same perspective), but this product could in turn be taken back and folklorised. As White puts it (White 1928, pp. 25, 389), blues, 'which were originally folk material but which come back to the Negro, through phonographs, sheet music, and cabaret singers, as a factory product whose dubious glory may be attributed to both white and Negro "authors" ', have now reached a stage where the 'folk blues and the factory product are . . . almost inextricably mixed'. With a rather less jaundiced tone, Odum and Johnson (1926) also argue for this interplay – in effect, assimilating current recordings into the category of folklore; however, they still work with a standard 'folk-to-commerce' historical model – 'the student of Negro song tomorrow will have to know what was on the phonograph records of today before he may dare to speak of origins' – which construes the trajectory as one from 'natural' to 'artificial' (*ibid.* pp. 33–4). White (1928, p. 5) also points out that African-Americans, as they emerged from the folk stage (that is, as an aspect of modernisation), were starting to appreciate their own folk heritage. Much of this took place at Fisk University, which saw the publication of folk song collections by John W. Work (1907, 1915) and Thomas W. Talley (1922) – collections, however, which include no blues. (Even as late as Work's 1940 collection, which includes his interview with Ma Rainey together with a short discussion of blues, acknowledging that recorded blues can be folklorised, he gives no examples.)

A shift in educated African-American attitudes only came with the artistic and intellectual movement of the 1920s known as the Harlem Renaissance.[14] By now, spirituals had been accepted as folk heritage and Paul Robeson and Roland Hayes were singing them, along with other black folk songs, on the concert stage. As we have seen, W.C. Handy, with Abbe Niles's support, was insisting on the folk sources of blues but also on the need for professionals to aestheticise these sources. Renaissance intellectuals such as Sterling Brown, Waring Cuney and Langston Hughes began to deploy phraseology, themes and diction drawn from blues in their poems. B.A. Botkin's *Folk-Say* (Botkin 1930) included several of these (among them Brown's memorable 'Ma Rainey'[15]), and also Brown's critical study, 'The Blues as Folk Poetry' (*ibid.*, pp. 324–39). Here, in what is perhaps the first scholarly attempt by an African-American to assimilate current recorded blues to the criteria of 'folk song', Brown describes the border between 'authentic' blues and 'urbanised fake folk things' as vague, the work of Rainey and Bessie Smith as 'of the folk', and current blues songs in general, 'at their most genuine', as 'accurate, imaginative transcripts of folk experience' (*ibid.*, pp. 324, 339). By the time of *The Negro Caravan* (Brown *et al.* 1941), a landmark collection of literature of all kinds, partly edited by Brown, we find not only spirituals, traditional ballads, work songs and two of Langston Hughes's blues poems, but a whole section devoted to blues which includes examples by Handy and Morton, songs drawn from the Lomaxes' Leadbelly collection, and also transcriptions from records by Ma Rainey, Bessie Smith, Bill Broonzy, Lonnie Johnson, Memphis Minnie and Ida Cox. In a move typical of a modernist outlook, blues has been situated as on the one hand, folk culture, on the other, a source for art. We find also an article by the artist E. Simms Campbell, reprinted from *Esquire* magazine, 'Early Jam' (*ibid.*, pp. 983–90), claiming racial ownership of blues (and ragtime, jazz and swing), exalting its specific capacity to tell a cultural truth. Recalling riverboat performances experienced during his St Louis boyhood (perhaps around 1920), Campbell notes that 'Many of the popular tunes of the day were written by whites as well as Negroes but there was this undercurrent of music – this music behind even the blues – this forbidden land as it were, that only a kid with all eyes and ears could catch' (*ibid.* p. 989). In this romanticised memory, we hear, I think, the true note of blues nostalgia.

It is hard, nonetheless, to separate this turn in African-American perspectives from contemporary contributions by white enthusiasts. Newman White argues that, in the upsurge of black appreciation, white encouragement was crucial. This help could be literal. Scarborough reports that the 'Charleston group' (presumably a branch of the American Folklore Society) was 'teaching the Negro children their racial songs'; the group go to the plantations to learn 'the authentic songs', then teach them to the children orally (Scarborough 1963, p. 282). It is interesting to compare this to George Gershwin's 'research trip' to South Carolina, the results of which he fed into his 'folk opera', *Porgy and Bess* (see Middleton 2000, pp. 67–70). Gershwin, in fact, was pursuing an aestheticisation policy which ran parallel to Handy's; Paul Whiteman's celebrated Aeolian Hall concert, which included the premiere of Gershwin's *Rhapsody in Blue*, took place in 1924, two years before Handy's anthology appeared. By contrast, Carl Van Vechten – white critic, writer, socialite, 'undisputed downtown authority on [black] uptown night life' (Huggins 1971, p. 100), tireless supporter of all forms of African-American culture and a crucial mediator in the Harlem Renaissance – pushed a different line. Although he admired Handy and wrote enthusiastic reviews of both his blues anthology and his autobiography, Van Vechten wanted to travel back along the evolutionary ladder of blues history rather than pursuing it into an aestheticised future. In articles published in 1925 and 1926, he demanded more research not only into the Southern sources of 'primitive' blues, in order to locate their 'wealth of eerie melody, borne along by a savage, recalcitrant rhythm', but also into the folkloristic status of current blues records (his argument here, contemporary with that in Odum and Johnson 1926, anticipating Sterling Brown's by several years). 'The Blues', he thought, 'are well-nigh unplayable save by instinctive Negro performers', and his models were the two Smiths, Bessie and Clara, whom he famously invited to social events at his house. His description of a Bessie Smith concert is a classic of a certain type, stressing her 'rich, ripe beauty of southern darkness':

Walking slowly to the footlights, to the accompaniment of the wailing, muted brasses, the monotonous African pounding of the drum, the dromedary glide of the pianist's fingers over the responsive keys, she began her strange, rhythmic rites in a voice full of shouting and moaning and praying and suffering, a wild, rough Ethiopian voice, harsh and volcanic, but seductive and sensuous too . . . And now, inspired by . . . the power and magnetic personality of this elemental conjure woman and her plangent African voice, quivering with pain and passion, which sounded as if it had been developed at the sources of the Nile, the crowd burst into hysterical shrieks of sorrow and lamentation. (Kellner 1979, pp. 48, 52, 162–3)

There is no doubting Van Vechten's sincerity nor the importance of his support for black culture, widely acknowledged by African-American artists and intellectuals in the 1920s; his articles and reviews in *Vanity Fair* in the mid-1920s, from one of which the above description comes, played a key role in bringing vernacular black musics to the attention of middle-class whites. The sources of his romanticisation lie not in personal motivation but in the psychic dynamics of cultural power and desire. His was a liberalism which meant that, 'try as he might to illustrate that Negroes were much like other people, Van Vechten's belief in their essential primitivism makes him prove something else' (Huggins 1971, p. 102).

White investment would continue to be crucial. About the same time that *The Negro Caravan* came out, white artist, bohemian and anthropologist Harry Smith was starting to assemble the inter-racial repertory for his celebrated *Anthology of American Folk Music* – a collection that would act as a basic archive for the 1950s/1960s folk revival, documenting that 'old weird America', as Greil Marcus (1997) has called it. In effect, Smith turned earlier entrepreneurs like Ralph Peer into folklorists, for, in an innovative and revealing move, he sourced his anthology from (by then almost forgotten) commercial records of the late 1920s and early 1930s. This (the late 1930s/ 1940s, roughly speaking) was a veritable moment of revival (downhome blues, in Chicago; 'traditional' jazz'; bluegrass, as well as folk-blues and other folk musics) – although in a sense the moment simply folds a further phase into an already established recessive pattern. This is also the moment in which *O Brother Where Art Thou?* is set, and, as far as the structure of revival is concerned, the film is exemplary, for the movie itself enacts a revival of a culture which is already, in the film narrative, reviving its own past. The story seems to be set around 1937 – but O'Daniel's campaign-song, 'You Are My Sunshine', written in 1940 by country musician Jimmie Davis, was actually used in Davis's campaign for the Louisiana state governorship in 1944.[16] By contrast, an unknown Tommy Johnson is most likely to have been encountered travelling to Tishomingo (Jackson) during his early period of recording, in the late 1920s or early 1930s. Like a dream, then, the film diagesis condenses several moments in a historical transition on to a mythical moment, which can then serve as a node within an even longer pattern. The lynchpin song, 'Man of Constant Sorrow', is 'traditional'. It had been first published around 1913, in a pocket songster by the blind (white) Kentucky singer, Richard Burnett, collected in the field in the Appalachians in 1918 by Cecil Sharp, who published it as 'In Old Virginny' (Sharp 1932, II, p. 233), and first recorded in 1928, by hillbilly singer Emry Arthur (who knew Burnett). It was revived by bluegrass group, the Stanley Brothers, and influentially recorded by them at the Newport Folk Festival in 1959, which led to a spate of 'revivalist' versions in the early 1960s, by Bob Dylan, Peter, Paul & Mary and others. In the wake of *O Brother*, it of course became a hit all over again, together with the elderly Ralph Stanley himself. In this structure, the object of revival forever recedes from view.

Ironically (it might seem) this 'lost object' is disseminated in the film by *modern* technology. However, records, far from destroying what we have lost, are better seen (like photographs) as producing this loss itself – or rather, as contributing to a momentous reconfiguration of the inter-relations of loss, memory and presence. Records circulate disembodied voices: spectral emanations which at one and the same time seem to come from *beyond* (beyond the grave?) and to be contained *within* an object, re-animating it in a novel form of mimesis. Friedrich Kittler (1999) among others has exhaustively explored the associations of the early phonograph and gramophone with figures of death, memorial and the supernatural – and the striking conjunction of the technological changes with the birth of Freudian psychoanalysis (in which the unconscious is taken to write itself, its losses, memories and desires, in an equally uncanny way). Ethnographers were quick to take up the new technology, and tales of their subjects' uneasy reactions to its supernatural power are legion (see Brady 1999). Both Erika Brady (pp. 30–2) and Michael Taussig (1993, pp. 208–11), though, note that urbanised Westerners were equally likely to fall into a 'magical' interpretation, suggesting a projective/introjective structure that reflects a strange reciprocity between primitivism and modernity. But if records refigured otherness – the rush to preserve creating the very gap it recorded, in a move that Lacan's neo-Freudian theory would shortly enable us to interpret in terms of the 'object voice', that voice situated uncannily outside any locus of subjectivity[17] – they built on old-established foundations. The link between disembodied voice (as in echo, for example) and supernatural power is an anthropological commonplace, as are totemic ritual masks designed to enable the actor to represent godlike authority not only visually but also vocally. 'Primitive' responses to the new technology from rural African-Americans actually seem to be rather rare: Alan Lomax (1993, p. 9) tells of an old farmer who, on hearing the recording of his friend that Lomax has just made, exclaims, 'That's a ghost . . . It purely a ghost'; but he is immediately slapped down by the musician as 'old-fashioned'. Was this acceptance because, even in remote areas of the South, blacks were actually *moderns* – Lomax's anecdote is set in 1942, but even in the late 1920s, when the first blues recordings were made in the South, people were familiar with 'technology' (railways, steamboats, cotton gins, radio – and phonographs)?[18] In Ma Rainey's stage act she used to emerge from a huge cardboard Victrola, reconnecting the voice to the body and marking this easy acceptance (see Davis 1995, pp. 72–3). Or was this acceptance a residue of neo-African 'superstition' – voodoo voices, hauntings and the familiarity of the doubling strategies offered by masking (not least in the secular parody laid out by blackface performance)? Or a combination of both, perhaps? On this account, Edison's 'fugitive sound waves' (Brady 1999, p. 1) – always receding from grasp – represent a reconfiguration of an old dynamic, whereby fetishes externalise human powers (at the same time as making non-human nature speak). When, in *O Brother*, as the moment for Tommy's lynching approaches, the Grand Wizard mimes Ralph Stanley's spine-chilling song, 'Oh Death', through the mask of his (oh-so-white) shroud, the layers of cultural meaning run very deep.

This structure – the lost object forever fleeing through the psycho-cultural strata – maps precisely to the structure of nostalgia. Densely layered, without clear origin, or else with an origin repressed from view, the nostalgic moment in its typical obsessive repetition may be identified, using Freudian-Lacanian terminology, as a species of *fantasy*, its object located within the 'acting out' of a *fantasy scene*. In this sense, nostalgia is actually emblematic of modernity, for it is the fracturing of tradition that brings forth this particular figuring of loss – even though, as we have seen, the effect when it emerges, as part of the psychoanalytic excavation of the modern subject, is to reveal what was always already there: a structure built around a lost object, which is in one form or another a human constant. (For psychoanalysis, the quintessential mark of this structure is of course the metaphor of 'castration' – which in turn stands as a model for a range of other separations [from the breast, the womb, etc.]: a point not without interest here given the importance in blues of the thematic interplay between phallic insistence and its defeats.) The novelty brought by recording tech-nology is that the object lost is now itself objectified, fetish fetishised, the commodity-totem supplementing an already existing phantasmatic cathexis. And this process happens – time is compressed – with such force that the investments are at once obscured and placed at exceptionally high risk.

What is interesting about nostalgia in the specific genre of blues, therefore, is, firstly, that the play of modernity and tradition is *built in* to its own history and subject-matter, producing a peculiar bitter-sweet nostalgia, its object feared as well as desired; secondly, that both the nostalgia constituted in revival (in the sequence of *énonciations*) and the nostalgia embedded in the blues form (in the texts – the *énoncés*) are at issue, and their interplay is constitutive; and thirdly, that the dialectic of modernity and tradition is time-compressed with such force here as to squeeze out the effects of an entrenched racialised encounter into intense psychodrama.

Men of constant sorrow

But what exactly is the object of nostalgia in blues? *Loss* is the genre's core topos, usually *a propos* of love or a lover. But this is widely understood as a metonym for a broader loss – a 'defiant discontent' (Abbe Niles, in Handy 1926, p. 40) or a 'state of being as well as a way of suffering' in the words of Alan Lomax, who acutely links this both to alienation and racial terror in the Deep South in the early twentieth century and, more broadly, to the rootlessness of modern life (Lomax 1993, pp. ix–x, 472). In this context, even the more celebratory aspects of blues – sexualised boogie-woogie rhythms, the ribald fun of 'hokum', the rock-solid grooves of later, urbanised musicians like B.B. King, even the good-humoured dance-rhythms of 'jump' bands such as Louis Jordan's – take on a quality of fragility: almost an out-of-time, out-of-place 'as-if', experienced against a background of historical flux and racio-sexual neurosis.[19] If the blues is 'devil music', the loss it figures has the familiarity of the everyday – it is accepted, even embraced – while at the same time inhabiting a marginal moment, forming an endless dialogue of disempowerment and self-assertion. For Tony Russell, blues offers – for whites as well as blacks – an invitation to enter a different space: 'to step out in the guise of the blues is to step out of line. Blues confers a licence to break rules and taboos, say the unsayable, create its own dark carnival' (Oliver *et al.* 2001, p. 233).

One way into this territory is via the classic 'bad man' ballad, 'Stagolee', based on real events taking place in St Louis in 1895, which, however, quickly formed themselves into a legend generating hundreds of song versions, associated with both blacks and whites, and a myth with a potency – especially for African-Americans – that has lasted right down to gangsta rap. Common to most versions is that Stagolee shoots his antagonist in cold blood over the theft of his hat, and that the bragging machismo of this anti-hero produces awe-struck respect. Cecil Brown (2003) stresses the racial dimension. The real murderer – Lee Shelton – was a black pimp working in a red light district of St Louis, a 'marginal' area where blacks and whites could mingle, and was also involved in political struggles around the issue of the black vote. Attempts by 'progressive' politicians to clean up such areas went side by side with exoticising descriptions by slumming white journalists, drawing on blackface discourse (for instance, the 'razor-toting coon'). It is easy to see why 'Stagolee' could be a hero to the growing black lumpen class; but many early versions were associated with whites (including the first recordings), even though Brown traces the main thematic elements back into stories about anti-slavery rebels, and points out that many black versions end with the hero's descent into hell, where usually he throws out the devil (variably figured as a white man or another 'bad nigger') and takes over. Shelton knew Tom Turpin, composer of the first published rags, and Brown speculates that Turpin may have created the first 'Stagolee', but it first surfaces as a holler from ex-slaves moving into Mississippi levee camps; although not formally a blues, it is often described as such in song titles, and its macho theme certainly fed into blues traditions.

It seems possible that the blues nexus emerged in the early years of the century precisely through a graft of such highly charged and often morally ambivalent themes on to the evolving pool of proto-blues vernacular and commercial musical developments: a 'dark carnival' indeed. Mississippi banjo player Lucius Smith, who started performing in 1902, played old-style (pre-blues) dance music with Sid Hemphill's string band and was interviewed by David Evans in 1971, had fascinating views on the advent of blues:

The blues done ruined the country . . . It just make 'em go off at random, I'd say, frolicking, random, you see. More folks have got killed since they start playing the blues than ever been. It's just a, you know, just a out of order piece . . . the 'Memphis Blues' and all that, it done brought about a whole lots of it, you know, I'd say, trouble . . . Makes a racket, you know, with young folks, you see . . . The blues ain't nothing but a racket. A whole lot of drunk folks, you know, don't care for nothing, and they just bring eternity, the blues do. Heaps of folk love to hear it, but it just brings eternity . . . (Evans 1987, pp. 47–8)

Intriguingly, this sort of historical shift is exactly what Newman White outlined in 1928: he saw Handy's mediating role as crucial, but 'folk blues', he speculated, originated in the 'Negro underworld' (White 1928, p. 389) of cities like Memphis and St Louis, from where it passed through the streets and levees to construction gangs and rural workers.[20] It is interesting, then, to compare 'Stagolee' to 'Joe Turner', a song which also entered into legend and probably originated about the same time, and which (White pointed out) has a tune that, according to Niles, became the basis of all blues melodies. Bill Broonzy (1964, pp. 53–9) describes his version, learned from his uncle, as telling the real story of a kindly white slave-owner who helped out his slaves with food and clothes in times of disaster – but anonymously, through his black overseer (also called 'Joe'). It is an intensely nostalgic song of racial harmony. In other versions, however, the song is about a *bad* white man – a 'long chain man' who by trickery and brutality takes blacks away to the chain gangs and penitentiaries. Thus the perspective is different from that in 'Stagolee', but 'Joe Turner' too serves as a slippery symptom of the racial stratum in blues thematics, just as its key lyric – 'Joe Turner been here and gone' – crystallises blues' ambivalent sense of loss, nostalgia and violence.

In these two songs, the fixing of this sense to the specific topos of sex is still loose. Joe Turner variably maintains or shatters the black family; Stagolee fights over a symbol of his manhood, his Stetson (see Brown 2003, pp. 98–105). In blues, this knot is tied, with a vengeance. Blues foregrounds a knowledge that human beings have always needed, tried, sometimes failed to learn, that the sexual relationship always falls short (in Lacan's more radical aphorism, 'There is no sexual relationship'[21]); quarrels, mistreatment, break-up, absence dramatise this essential core, which situates the sexual act as always a species of nostalgia, a reference to a fulfilment forever lost – and a reference, therefore, that can stand in for all other disappointments and deprivations. The obsession with sex in blues marks out a territory where a particular topology of desire and rupture (specified culturally and historically) overlays and stands for the founding deprivations of subjecthood itself – at the limit, the cry of the fallen creature as such. As in all manifestations of nostalgia, the true object of desire is veiled – an absence fantasised as a presence which, however, is never quite there. 'The blues' is often personified ('Mr blues, how do you do?', etc.), but comes upon the singer unawares, appears behind one's back, in dreams, a ghostly presence; it is a spectre – a *conjuration*. (Some singers, including Tommy Johnson, have described their music as 'air music', referring to its mysterious, apparently supernatural source: see Evans 1987, pp. 114–5.) In Lacanian terms, it is an *objet a* (*objet petit autre* or object-cause of desire), around which actual movements of desire can only circle, which will always be missed.

We should, as the saying goes, be careful what we wish for; does the blues drama truly represent a desire to confront the loss on which it is built? For Lacan, the fantasy-scene functions as a repetitive image, protecting the subject from trauma (ultimately, from the terror of castration). It is located in a framed, theatrical space (that is, within the sphere of the Symbolic), which, however, invokes an unknowable Real, a space lying beyond the frame; and it is 'acted out' (performed) in response to an alienation – the other's refusal to listen (that is, it stands for a blockage). What is the trauma that is silenced here? Surely the murderous scene 'down home'. For blacks, this is obviously rooted in the history of slavery and since, but for whites too there is an investment via mechanisms of guilt, projection and appropriation. But for both groups, might not these specific symptoms also be standing for something deeper? – a 'primal' structure, made raw by the effects of modernity which find their point of most intense focus in images of black bodies, commodified by capitalism in its crudest form (slavery) and now at one and the same time simulated, evacuated and fetishised all over again in the objects of mass reproduction technology. This scene is a family scene, and the structure is of course oedipal; but it is also fratricidal (Cain and Abel; black and white; Oh Brother!), rooted in a particular horror, fear and guilt engendered by a competitive resistance, but also a secretly complicit accommodation, to the primal castration threat: a sado-masochistic fratricidal embrace, for 'there is no *racial* relationship' either, and blues is 'devil's music' because, in its exemplary determination to stare secularity straight in the face, the 'Name-of-the-Father' is forever at issue, forever displaced.[22]

You will find a fortune

The figure of blues nostalgia, and the traumatic hinterland it covers, locates us in an historical structure of meaning, allied on the one hand to the layered pattern of 'revival', but condensed also on to a concrete sexualised metonym which in turn relates to a network of racialised projections, introjections and abjections. If, after the fashion of Lacanian algebra, we write nostalgia as N, this is to locate it as a specific aspect of O – the Big Other, the Symbolic system as such. But N is forever fractured by the impossible claims of O (since there can be no final signifier, justifying its authority), forever as a result splitting off symptoms of n (*object petit n*) in the incessant coursing of subjective desire – unassimilable, spectral, allied to the founding trauma located in the Real (that is, outside the grasp of O). Thus: $\emptyset/N \rightarrow n(\$)$ that is, N, 'divided into' the barred (incomplete) Big Other, splinters off infinite numbers of n, which in turn help structure the barred (split) subject: a formula that should be given the dynamics of a vortex in which intersecting tropes of modernity, tradition and subjectivity pull us giddily towards an uncertain future.

The 'moment of danger' is no less clear today than it was a hundred years ago. Indeed, in many ways it is not dissimilar: a new phase in the reach of global capital, driven in part by a leap in technology (now digitisation – which, among other things, enables Moby and Tangleeye to sample Alan Lomax's field recordings); labour divided by race, now on a global scale; the resulting fractures finding a metonymic focus in the sexual relationship (as in rap); in music a deluge of revivals, most notably in the new category of 'world music', into which blues and bluegrass are partly assimilated, and which, like early blues, constitutes itself as a revival without a source – or rather with a mythic source which 'world music' itself brings into being. Back to the future?

Early in *O Brother*, our heroes – drawn by the lure of Everett's promise of buried treasure – encounter a mysterious black blind prophet (Homer's Polyphemus[23]); he is nameless and works for no man – a utopian figure indeed, outside the patrilineal world of capitalism, and Everett, an enthusiast for modern commerce, duly dismisses his prophecy: 'You will find a fortune – though it would not be the fortune you seek'. This is accompanied by a guitar blues: apparently non-diagetic, though perhaps it is preparing us for Tommy Johnson's entrance which will take place shortly. On one reading, Everett's 'fortune' is conventional: reconciliation (after a fashion) with his long abandoned wife. But this sexual twist has an allegorical glint. At the film's climax, our heroes, white and black, are saved from summary execution at the hands of their pursuing prison guards by a fortuitous flood: symptom of modernity (it inaugurates a hydro-electric scheme: the South is changing), this both submerges the tarnished trinkets they sought and stands, of course, like all floods, for whatever rebirth one might wish to imagine.

The fortune sought through revival appears to be 'roots', but this will not be what is found. In her study of Abdullah Ibrahim, Christine Lucia wants to rewrite the nostalgia she finds in his music as 'a whole climate of memory'. His 1970s recordings in particular are 'not so much an embodiment of nostalgia as a journey towards nostalgia' – towards 'an ideal past that the listener is invited to share, and one that we *can* share because it is an imaginary, archetypal terrain, the lost domain of childhood'. Quoting Michel de Certeau on such domains – 'sites that have been lived in . . . filled with the presence of absences' – she evokes the sense of a 'home' which is not just 'an illusion, blotting out the pain, a necessary fiction to survive the present' but the ground of a 'utopian dream' with the power to be 'part of the future' (Lucia 2002, pp. 128, 136, 138). Blues nostalgia seems to speak not just of loss but also, famously, of *resilience* – a particular inscription of absence in a present that will, at all costs, be survived; but, as we have seen, this 'necessary fiction' screens off (though never with complete success) a psychic undergrowth of virulent trauma (as, surely, must also be the case in the South African context). For Lacan, such 'fictions' are the stuff from which fantasy (including nostalgia fantasies) organises our sense of 'reality' and guarantees the subject's consistency. The aim of the 'talking cure' (and, one might add, the 'singing cure') is to enable the subject to 'traverse' his fantasy – to work through its arbitrary structure, achieve distance from its pleasures, unlock the fastening whereby a purely imaginary formation is taken to signify (that is, is connected, as its energising motor, to the Symbolic). Such an act is capable of unfreezing the immobile fantasy-scene, and making history move; but at the cost of revealing that terrifying imaginative space lying outside 'domestication'.

The lost object of blues is certainly to be found down home. Truly to re-visit this place, however, is – for whites as well as blacks – to conjure up a family scene which is always already beyond reason. Brothers (and sisters), where art thou?

Endnotes

1. The Faustian bargain was a widespread blues trope. Tommy Johnson certainly made the claim: see Evans (1971, pp. 22–3); Davis (1995, pp. 105–6). For further details of Johnson's life and music, see Evans (1971, *passim*).

2. It is a nice – and, as we shall see, a meaningful – irony that in the late 1930s this sound did not yet exist (although most of its constituent features did) and the label 'bluegrass' had not been invented. Already 'tradition' is being read back into the past and presented as more traditional than the real thing – a technique characteristic of revivals.

3. An initial version of Keil's piece was first published in *Dialectical Anthropology*, 10 (1985), pp. 119–30. Davis (1995) follows a somewhat similar, though not quite so radical line; but he does not list Keil's text in his bibliography. Otherwise, to the best of my knowledge, Keil's argument has not really been followed up.

4. Rainey was speaking to John W. Work (1998 [1940], pp. 32–3); she remarks that when, shortly after, she began to sing such songs in her

act, they were not yet called 'blues'. Morton was speaking to Alan Lomax in his Library of Congress interviews of 1938 (Lomax 1973[1950], p. 62); Morton also mentions other pieces which he heard, or created, around the turn of the century and which he refers to as 'blues' – but the exact dating is unclear and in many cases the examples he gives suggest ragtime features as much as those of what would come to be understood as blues. Handy was writing in his autobiography (Handy 1991[1941]), telling the famous story of hearing a bottleneck guitarist at Tutwiler railway station (*ibid.*, p. 74); Handy, admittedly, does also refer to a one-line tune he heard in St Louis in 1892, of a type which, later, he says, he would draw on to create his own blues songs (*ibid.*, p. 142). Clearly, then, elements which would later congeal into typical blues features were in play before 1900 – but that is a different point.

For an overview of the few sources that describe 'blues-like' music in the 1890s, see Evans (1987, pp. 32–3), and for similar

62   *Richard Middleton*

references to the early twentieth century, *ibid.* pp. 33–40. Some of the locations are rural but many are urban (including racially fluid New Orleans).

Keil (1994) has a footnote referring to an unpublished MA dissertation including descriptions of sheet music, by white composers, containing blues-like features and dating from several decades before 1900. Of course Peter Van der Merwe (1989) traces some such features back to sixteenth-century Europe . . .

5. See Odum (1911); Perrow (1912, 1913, 1915). The songs had been collected some years before publication. Lomax (1917) does identify a blues (see Note 20 below) but treats it not as part of a genre but as just a song – one that lives in the larger category of secular songs ('reels').

6. The very first blues record, also by a white singer, appeared in 1915. I mention 'Nigger Blues' and discuss it below because it is available in a modern reissue (see Discography).

7. George O'Connor (1874–1946) was a highly successful lawyer and businessman, a familiar figure in upper-class Washington DC society, an intimate of many top politicians, and well-known too in these circles as a singer of light opera and contemporary popular songs. Among a large amount of sheet music, his papers contain sixty-three 'coon songs'. Columbia put out quite a number of records by O'Connor, usually backed by other popular singers of the time, including Al Jolson; 'Nigger Blues', for example, is backed by Jolson's 'I'm Saving Up the Means to Get to New Orleans'. See http://www.library-georgetown.edu/dept/speccoll/oconnor.htm

8. As it might seem to us. For some in this period, the Golden Age was already gone, destroyed by 'modernity' (sheet music, records, commerce). This pattern of infinite regression is part of the process of folklorisation itself – and also (as we shall see) of the structure of nostalgia.

9. It is both an advantage and a disadvantage of speculative historiography that proof is impossible. In this case, presumably, it would entail establishing that all black blues singers were situated at the end of chains of musical learning at an earlier stage of which – perhaps beyond various mediating links – one would find white models. Walter Benjamin's advice (1973, p. 257), which I find persuasive, that 'To articulate the past historically does not mean to recognise it "the way it really was" (Ranke). It means to seize hold of a memory as it flashes up at a moment of danger' does not license distortion of materials. We now have the sources to show the explosive development of a rich commercial music culture, involving blacks and whites, often in close proximity, during the period from the 1890s to the 1920s; the spread of the new media technologies, including into rural areas, and the importance in the South of travelling shows; the important mediating role of white entrepreneurs (Ralph Peer; H.C. Speir; Frank Walker) in marketing blues from the South; and

the inescapable presence across these developments and processes of blackface performance conventions. To assemble all the evidence would require a large book – but still would not prove the point. What is at issue is a cultural unconscious which can be invoked, led to the couch and encouraged to speak (through interpretations of its textual signifiers) but not reliably documented. I am not of course assuming that, for African-American actors within this unconscious, the signifiers unthinkingly replicate what has been heard, only that they are involved in a network of reference structured by differential power. I will come to the 'moment of danger' presently.

10. Quoted, Perrow (1915, p. 190).

11. The *New Yorker* (19 January 1935) published a 'ballad' by noted poet William Rose Benét to mark Leadbelly's arrival in New York with John Lomax. It includes the words: 'He was big and he was black/And wondrous were his wrongs/But he had a memory travelled back/Through at least five hundred songs./When his fingers gave those strings a twang/Like a very god in heaven he sang' (accompanying booklet, Leadbelly [n.d.]). See Wolfe and Lornell (1993, pp. 167–8), and for further evidence of the frisson accompanying Leadbelly's arrival in New York, *ibid.*, pp. 1–4, 136–42. On Leadbelly as primitive, see also Davis (1995, pp. 164–71).

12. John Lee Hooker, speaking in 1968, was more straight-forward: 'My type of music, I got a variety – for the young folks and the older folks, and the folksingers . . . I have created about three different fields; a folk field, a blues field, and a jump field for the kids' (quoted, Evans 1987, p. 84).

13. For similar perspectives, see Krehbiel (1914); Lomax (1917); Talley (1922); Odum and Johnson (1925); J. and A. Lomax (1934). The first scholarly publication to claim folkloric status for commercial blues records was Odum and Johnson (1926).

14. The broad programme of the Harlem Renaissance saw African-American advance as tied to cultural modernisation. But attitudes were far from homogeneous, not least in relation to music and to black folklore. See Anderson (2001).

15. 'I talked to a fellow, and de fellow say:
She jes catch hold of us, somekindaway;
She sang "Backwater Blues" one day . . .'
[Then, after quoting Rainey's lyric]
'Dere wasn't much more, de fellow say:
She just gits hold of us, dataway'

16. Intriguingly, Davis also recorded white blues, was considerably influenced by black music and even recorded with a black musician, Oscar Woods; see Tony Russell's account in Oliver *et al.* (2001, pp. 206–9).

17. On this see Salecl and Žižek (1996).

18. In John Lomax's account of his and Alan's 1933 recording trip (Lomax 1934), the convicts they record seem to demonstrate absolutely no suspicion of the 'singing machine'.

O brother, let's go down home 63

19. Davis (1995, pp. 136–8) argues that even though 'hokum blues' like Tampa Red's 'It's Tight Like That' were clearly novelties, they were also meant to sound old, even corny. Similarly, Louis Jordan's amiable dance-tunes are inconceivable without the historical background of earlier African-American vaudeville humour, which in turn points back towards coon song and minstrelsy (some titles: 'Saturday Night Fish Fry'; 'Beans and Corn Bread'; 'Ain't Nobody Here but Us Chickens'). A different article might nevertheless explore the possibility that in the movement from blues to Rhythm & Blues, then to Soul, an as-if takes on a steadily increasing social concreteness and political efficacy. It might also consider the role of rock 'n' roll, which brings together several of these more 'celebratory' blues references; rock 'n' roll as 'the future of nostalgia'? (see Boym 2002).

20. John Lomax (1917, p. 143) gives a blues which, he says, he has heard many times under many different names (usually referring to a particular place: e.g. 'The Dallas Blues'), but first of all in a levee camp in Texas that was using imported Mississippi labour. The lyric contains a huge number of familiar blues phrases, many of which can be found in published songs such as Handy's and in later recordings, and some of which appear in White's 'Nigger Blues'. According to David Evans (sleeve notes, *Let's Get Loose*), 'Nigger Blues' entered the southern white and black folk repertoires and was recorded under a number of titles; no doubt the traffic went both ways.

21. Meaning that sexual difference functions not in terms of complement but of supplement: the two partners do not add up to a whole; rather, each represents a different modality (which, in both cases, fails – that is, as one might say, contains a hole). Part of the failure is that the relationship will always be asymmetrical. Lacan's patriarchalism weights this asymmetry in a predictable direction, one which we do not need to accept and on which the fraught and distinctive history of African-American gender relations offers a sharp commentary. Evans (1996, pp. 181–2) gives a concise explanation of Lacan's thinking on this subject.

22. For Lacan, 'the true formula of atheism is not *God is dead* – even by basing the origins of the function of the father upon his murder, Freud protects the father – the true formula of atheism is *God is unconscious*' (Lacan 1979, p. 59) – a formula confirmed throughout the blues, where God is a very present absence. Lomax acutely points out that many singers of the most agonised blues were actual orphans, but that this also stands for a broader sense of orphanage from society (Lomax 1993, pp. 361–2). In this context, the racialised discourse of (black) 'boys' and (white patriarchal) 'bosses' of course takes on a particular meaning.

23. The Coen Brothers' story is loosely based on that of Homer's *Odyssey* – hence Everett's middle name of Ulysses. What are we to make of the fact that the folklorist Howard Odum published a trilogy of novels centred on the travels of a fictional bluesman (the first evocatively entitled *Rainbow Round My Shoulder: The Blue Trail of Black Ulysses* [1928] modelling his hero on a real blues-singing hobo-songster, John Wesley 'Left Wing' Gordon – he had lost his right arm – whom Odum saw as epitomising the blues 'wandering outcast' topos; see Odum and Johnson 1926, pp. 206–20)? Or of the fact that John Lomax described one of his 'discoveries', James 'Ironhead' Baker, as a 'black Homer' (Wolfe and Lornell 1993, p. 112)? Were Odum and Lomax romanticising a certain marginality? Were the Coen Brothers? Am I?

References

Anderson, P.A. 2001. *Deep River: Music and Memory in Harlem Renaissance Thought* (Durham, NC, Duke University Press)

Baker, H., Jr. 1984. *Blues, Ideology and Afro-American Literature: A Vernacular Theory* (Chicago, University of Chicago Press)

Benjamin, W. 1973. *Illuminations*, ed. H. Arendt, trans. H. Zohn (London, Fontana)

Botkin, B.A. (ed.) 1930. *Folk-Say: A Regional Miscellany* (Norman, University of Oklahoma Press)

Boym, S. 2002. *The Future of Nostalgia* (New York, Basic Books)

Brady, E. 1999. *A Spiral Way: How the Phonograph Changed Ethnography* (Jackson, University Press of Mississippi)

Broonzy, Bill (with Yannick Bruynoghe). 1964[1955]. *Big Bill Blues: Big Bill Broonzy's Story as Told to Yannick Bruynoghe* (New York, Oak Publications)

Brown, C. 2003. *Stagolee Shot Billy* (Cambridge, MA, Harvard University Press)

Brown, S.A., Davis, A.P., and Lee, U. (eds.) 1969[1941]. *The Negro Caravan* (New York, Arno Press)

Charters, S. 1975[1959]. *The Country Blues* (New York, Da Capo Press)

Davis, F. 1995. *The History of the Blues* (London, Secker & Warburg)

Du Bois, W.E.B. 1999[1903]. *The Souls of Black Folk*, ed. H.L. Gates, Jr. and T.H. Oliver (New York, Norton)

Evans, D. 1971. *Tommy Johnson* (London, Studio Vista)

——— 1987. *Big Road Blues: Tradition and Creativity in the Folk Blues* (New York, Da Capo Press)

Evans, Dylan. 1996. *An Introductory Dictionary of Lacanian Psychoanalysis* (London, Routledge)

Handy, W.C. 1990[1926]. *Blues: An Anthology* (New York, Da Capo Press)

64   *Richard Middleton*

1991[1941]. *Father of the Blues: An Autobiography* (New York, Da Capo Press)
Huggins, N. 1971. *Harlem Renaissance* (New York, Oxford University Press)
Keil, C., and Feld, S. 1994. *Music Grooves: Essays and Dialogues* (Chicago, University of Chicago Press)
Kellner, B. 1979. *Keep A-Inchin' Along: Selected Writings of Carl Van Vechten about Black Art and Letters* (Westport, CT, Greenwood Press)
Kittler, F.A. 1999. *Gramophone, Film, Typewriter*, trans. G. Winthrop-Young and M. Wutz (Palo Alto, CA, Stanford University Press)
Krehbiel, H.E. 1962[1914]. *Afro-American Folksongs: A Study in Racial and National Music* (New York, Ungar)
Lacan, J. 1979. *The Four Fundamental Concepts of Psycho-Analysis*, ed. J.-A. Miller, trans. A. Sheridan (Harmondsworth, Penguin Books)
Lomax, A. 1973[1950]. *Mister Jelly Roll: The Fortunes of Jelly Roll Morton, New Orleans Creole and 'Inventor of Jazz'* (Berkeley, University of California Press)
    1993. *The Land Where the Blues Began* (New York, Pantheon) (Reprinted, New York, New Press, 2003)
Lomax, J.A. 1917. 'Self-pity in Negro folk-songs', *The Nation*, 105, pp. 141–5
    1934. 'Sinful songs of the Southern Negro', *Musical Quarterly*, 21, pp. 177–87
Lomax, J., and Lomax, A. 1934. *American Ballads and Folk Songs* (New York, Macmillan)
    1936. *Negro Folk Songs as Sung by Leadbelly* (New York, Macmillan)
Lucia, C. 2002. 'Abdullah Ibrahim and the uses of memory', *British Journal of Ethnomusicology*, 11/2, pp. 125–43
Marcus, G. 1997. *Invisible Republic: Bob Dylan's Basement Tapes* (London, Picador)
Middleton, R. 2000. 'Musical belongings: Western music and its low-other', in *Western Music and Its Others: Difference, Representation, and Appropriation in Music*, ed. G. Born and D. Hesmondhalgh (Berkeley, University of California Press), pp. 59–85
Odum, H.W. 1911. 'Folk-song and folk-poetry as found in the secular songs of the Southern Negroes', *Journal of American Folklore*, 24, pp. 255–94, 351–96
Odum, H.W., and Johnson, G.B. 1925. *The Negro and His Songs* (Chapel Hill, University of North Carolina Press)
    1926. *Negro Workaday Songs* (Chapel Hill, University of North Carolina Press)
Oliver, P., Russell, T., Dixon, R.M.W., Godrich, J., and Rye, H. 2001. *Yonder Come the Blues: The Evolution of a Genre* (Cambridge, Cambridge University Press)
Perrow, E.C. 1912, 1913, 1915. 'Songs and rhymes from the South', *Journal of American Folklore*, 25, pp. 137–55; 26, pp. 122–73; 28, pp. 129–90
Salecl, R., and Žižek, S. (eds.) 1996. *Gaze and Voice as Love Objects* (Durham, NC, Duke University Press)
Scarborough, D. 1925. *On the Trail of Negro Folk-Songs* (Cambridge MA, Harvard University Press)
Sharp, C. (with Olive Dame Campbell) 1932. *English Folk-Songs from the Southern Appalachians*, 2 vols., ed. M. Karpeles (Oxford, Oxford University Press)
Talley, T.W. 1922. *Negro Folk Rhymes* (New York, Macmillan)
Taussig, M. 1993. *Mimesis and Alterity: A Particular History of the Senses* (New York, Routledge)
Van der Merwe, P. 1989. *Origins of the Popular Style: The Antecedents of Twentieth-Century Popular Music* (Oxford, Clarendon Press)
White, N.I. 1928. *American Negro Folk-Songs* (Cambridge, MA, Harvard University Press)
Wolfe, C., and Lornell, K. 1993. *The Life and Legend of Leadbelly* (London, Secker & Warburg)
Work, J.W. 1915. *Folk Songs of the American Negro* (Nashville, Fisk University Press)
    1998[1940]. *American Negro Songs and Spirituals: A Comprehensive Collection of 230 Folk Songs, Religious and Secular* (New York, Dover)
Work, J.W., and Work, F.J. 1907. *Folk Songs of the American Negro* (Nashville, Work Brothers)

Discography

Anthology of American Folk Music, comp. Harry Smith. Smithsonian Folkways FP 251, 252, 253 (1997 [1952])
Leadbelly, *The Library of Congress Recordings*, comp. Lawrence Cohn. Elektra EKL-301/2 (ND)
Let's Get Loose. New World Records NW290 (1978)

Videography

O Brother, Where Art Thou? Universal MPO14V (2000)

Note

Much of the material in this article also appears in a slightly different form, in Richard Middleton, *Voicing the Popular: On the Subjects of Popular Music* (New York, Routledge, 2006).

CHAPTER 13

Mum's the Word
Men's Singing and Maternal Law

"He's got such an extraordinary voice—it could be black, white, male or female."[1] This was Simon Frith's comment on singer Antony Hegarty, of the band Antony and the Johnsons, on the occasion of their success in the 2005 Mercury Music Prize. The biggest surprise is that this vocal ambivalence should be thought surprising: pop music has always offered privileged space for gender and race play, and since records removed the body from sight, radical imaginings of the vocal body have been free to run riot within listening practices. It is tempting to follow, analytically, the particularly transgressive route taken by an Antony; it would, no doubt about it, throw light on the vocal variables of masculinity. But in a sense this is too easy. I want instead to focus on examples of "gender trouble" arising within what seems to be the more mainstream lineage of male singing—the "dark center" without which Antony's provocative sounds, with their transgendering implications, would lose their power (but which is itself defined only in relation to its exclusions and disavowals). I will note in passing, however, the potential importance of the generic territory that Antony occupies: as some critics have remarked, his exquisitely melancholic, even masochistic explorations of loss, hopeless love and death carry his Mercury-winning album, *I Am a Bird Now*,[2] towards the thematics of torch song, in origin and by tradition a female genre. Although there are precedents for this appropriation, in the work of gay singers such as Marc Almond and Boy George, playing provocatively with vocal register and

104 • Richard Middleton

timbre in the context of this specific generic choice remains unusual, and
I will return to this point.

My strategy might seem to run counter to an argument persuasively
made within queer theory (and presented with clarity by Judith Halberstam,
among others[3]) that, because normative (male) masculinity can appear as
such only through its positioning within a broader, highly variable range
of masculinities (including female masculinity), it is best deconstructed by
attending to the latter. There is both a theoretical and a political strength
to this argument. However, it ignores the extent to which the specific conventions of vocal performance exist in cultural territory where masculine
norms are always already troubled, indeed sometimes self-deconstruct-
ing; for men even to perform music—especially to sing—is itself already
to query these norms, to "feminize" themselves, at least incipiently.[4] At the
same time, patriarchal authority is of course stereotypically asserted by
male voices of command—but the shaky foundations of this power make
its mechanisms all the more inviting to theory. For this reason, might we
even find—to carry the argument to even more provocative lengths—that,
if normative masculinity is only defined in a context created by alternative
forms, it will sometimes be female masculinities performed by *men* that
have especially strong effects?[5]

Singing (to) Mum

Notoriously, the psychoanalytic traditions on which I shall be drawing
tend to normalize, or even naturalize, the mapping of sexual difference
to the standard gender binary, and, moreover, to embed this map within
the hierarchical structure of discursive power. While rejecting this as an a
priori, on epistemological (as well as political) grounds, I *am* impressed by
the power of psychoanalytic realism; that is to say, if we fail to recognize
the historically constituted strength of phallogocentrism, as it has been
called, within the performative mechanisms of the Symbolic order, then
our grasp both of these mechanisms and of their shaky foundations will
fall short. In singing, possession of the symbolic phallus, through which
the Law-of-the-Father circulates, typically follows the contours of linguistic authority but also clings to the modes of expression of male desire: narrative and emotional command, and normative masculine imagery, are
married together. My interest here lies in those moments when the mask
of self-confidence slips and signifying structures threaten to rupture—
moments when, perhaps, Mum has the word (that is, one might say, when
what had been secret—"mum's the word!"—is brought into the light). For
in the delineations of what is clearly an Oedipal drama, the location of the
vocal phallus is key; and, if the purpose of this drama is to locate young
males and females in their "proper" places in the symbolic as well as sexual

order, then any "misfire" may well summon up the figure of the Oedipal or Phallic Mother, holder of the Law in that "other time" before paternal "castration" barred access to the pleasures and tensions of the "preoedipal triangle" (mother-child-imaginary phallus) in which the circulation of vocal energies by the acoustic mirror (babbling, cooing, demanding, crying) played a central role.[6]

It would hardly be possible to imagine a rock singer who, in most of his best known work at any rate, adhered more closely to macho conventions than John Lennon. And those vocal qualities—the driving, sneering, stage-centered cockiness—run parallel to similar traits in the behavioral persona he constructed for himself. (Not that I want to naively align life and music—but there is room to consider the scope of interpenetrating author-functions at work in a subject's diverse textual and quasi-textual projects.) At the same time, however, Lennon notoriously had a mother-problem. This was probably linked—so popular biography suggests—with his sense of early abandonment by his natural mother, Julia, and her cruelly early death; but it also, I suggest, had much deeper roots, roots that lay in the tangled web of sexual possibilities offered by rock 'n' roll, and indeed by twentieth-century popular music generally. The 1970 *Plastic Ono Band* album[7] can be regarded as a crucial "hinge" in this aspect of his psycho-creative biography (as in so many others): before it lay the fraternal dynamic of the Beatles period—a band of rebellious (but also frustrated) brothers; afterwards came the New York period of (sometimes fractious) domesticity with Yoko Ono, who quite clearly assumed a quasi-maternal role for Lennon, within which, however, she was capable of cracking a whip that could subdue the most wayward child. The album is popularly supposed to document the effects of the "primal scream" therapy that Lennon had just gone through with the California psychologist Arthur Janov, although this may have been symptom rather than cause. At any rate, among the treasures that primal digging uncovered were two mother-songs: "Mother" and "My Mummy's Dead."

"Mother" is introduced by the pealing of church bells. A funeral? Who has died?—mother, obviously, but perhaps also Lennon himself—the old Lennon.[8] This ushers us then into the world of ballad—a soul-tinged ballad, sung in his most gorgeously mellifluous tenor, pushing into an incredibly high register, and with even higher excursions into a head voice. (Is this voice male, female, white, black?) In three rigidly repeating verses, Lennon laments the loss of mother, father, childhood. So far, then, in terms both of musical structure and of family relations, we seem to be on an even keel. Yet even here, there are occasional strange "lurches" in the vocal, both rhythmic and in pitch inflection, as if he is discomfited by but at the same time struggling to stick with the insistent tread of the slow-paced, unrelenting metrical-harmonic framework. Increasingly, the

106 • Richard Middleton

underlying instrumental movement has the feel of a bodily machine, summoning images of childlike, quasi-autistic rocking—a figure that is intensified in the lengthy coda, where, over a rigid V-IV-I riff, hammered out by
Lennon's own piano chording, his vocal phrases—entreating mother and
father to "come home"—evolve into throat-tearing, discordant howls. As
the repetitions take root and the vocal cries—tears of rage as well as tears
in the fabric of meaning—dominate the sound-space, language retreats
from our attention. This is, one might say, a Freudian *fort-da* with a vengeance. And whose is this voice, so multitextured, so rich yet constantly
cut open with a rapacious edge (a phallus in the throat)?—Nina Simone's?
(Lennon's performance, vocally and, so to speak, theologically, reminds
me of nothing so much as Simone's recording of "Sinnerman.")But if this
phallus is an offering to mother, it is—like Simone's—double-edged.

The "autistic" motion in "Mother" takes on additional resonance later in
the album when we hear the fragment, "My Mummy's Dead." Lasting less
than a minute, with Lennon's vocal recorded relatively dead over clanging,
metallic guitar (almost like a folk banjo: from hillbilly via "Mr. Tambou-
rine Man," taking the children away?), this song has the feel of a nursery
rhyme, its opening phrase mimicking the shape of "Three Blind Mice." It
is a nursery rhyme recovered through a haze of memory, though: Lennon's
"lifeless" singing over (or rather, behind) the robotic guitar strum forced
to be its own mirror, the singer lulling himself.

These two songs have particular import for my purpose here because
of their explicit subject matter. But they do not stand alone musically, and
indeed take on wider significance in the context of Lennon's overall trajectory. The ripped voice can often be heard in recordings of this period—in
"Cold Turkey" and "Well, Well, Well," for example—but also can perhaps
be traced back, paradoxical though it may seem, to Lennon's earlier hard-
rock voice: as if the "cock-rock" extreme, mutating towards object status,
betrays its own authority, revealing the gender-transgressive potential of
the male singing-act itself. On the other side, as it were, lie Lennon's surre-
alistic songs—"I Am the Walrus," "Glass Onion," and again an earlier lineage including "Lucy in the Sky with Diamonds" and "Strawberry Fields
Forever"—where, in a parallel mechanism, language subverts itself, this
time in child-like word-play. At the same time, there is a sequence of ballads—from "If I Fell" and "In My Life" to "Because" and "Julia"—whose
"feminized" orientation comes to full fruition in the "girly" ballads he
addressed to Yoko in the 1970s. Overall, the question that comes through
is how gender comes to be, and how vocal articulation, which seems as a
rule to pin it in place, can also open it up to doubt.

My suspicion—though it would require detailed investigation to document this—is that Lennon's articulation of this question stands in a lengthy

twentieth-century tradition. Not that the subject matter would always be overtly "maternal." However, in the work of an equally celebrated early-century singer, Al Jolson, this aspect does loom large—indeed, even larger than in Lennon. The classic example, first recorded for the movie *The Jazz Singer* (dir. Crosland, 1927), where it closed out this, the first sound-film, assuming a key historical status, is Jolson's "My Mammy" (he had been performing it since 1918).[10] As with Lennon, there is an intriguing biographical link. The film story, in which the Jewish hero refuses the role of rabbi laid out for him in favor of a career in show business and cuts himself off from his father in the process, loosely parallels Jolson's own history. In the movie, however, there is a final reconciliation, in which the hero, Jack Robin, forced to choose between a longed-for Broadway opening and standing in for his ailing father to sing the traditional "Kol Nidre" at the Day of Atonement service, opts for the latter. (During his performance, his father—in proper Oedipal fashion—dies.) But, although this might seem to settle for family norms rather than "prostituting" his vocal talent in the theatre, Jack's showbiz career in fact resumes in due course, and the next (and final) scene—which follows so quickly as to make comparison of the two contexts and their music unavoidable—relocates the family romance on to a stage organized around his performance of, and to, "Mammy."

Jolson's rendition made world-famous the hyperemotional gestures he had been working up for years: down on one knee, his arms stretched pleadingly wide, he sobs his appeal in a keening high tenor full of "cantorial" rubatos, passages of heightened, chanted parlando, mordents, glides and other ornaments, and "counterrepresentational" diction (strangled vowels, exaggerated consonants, accents in the "wrong" place). The camera positions us alternately with him, addressing his mother in the front row of the stalls, and with her, lovingly listening, its dialogic gaze-structure supplementing the vocal flow, filling in for her missing voice (we see her lips move but cannot hear her) and completing the mirror-relay. Jolson, like Lennon, pushes the qualities of a "masculine" vocal style—here an emotion-wringing operatic-cantorial tenor—to such an extreme that in effect they undo themselves, resulting in singing that is at one and the same time "feminized" and (not untypically for female vocalities as they are often imagined) out of control: the voice seems to be, as it were, operating itself, and Jolson's body, jerking this way and that, follows. But if Lennon situates the Mother-relation in a context of *loss*, Jolson focuses it on a trajectory of *return*: "I'm coming," he repeatedly exclaims, hoping fervently that he won't be too late.

As I suggested, we cannot but compare this performance with that of the "Kol Nidre." Not only are the vocal qualities and bodily gestures similar, but in both cases Jolson's "queering" of normative masculine vocality

108 • Richard Middleton

is enabled by the device of a *mask,* on the one hand the accoutrements of "blackface" (Jolson's standard performing persona since 1905, but widely used, still, in the 1920s, by some blacks as well as by whites), on the other the vestments of priesthood. In the synagogue, we might say, he stands in for and at the same time supplants his father—but in the shape of an "orientalized" feminine, who stands to the patriarchal God as bride (and to Mammy, therefore, when he subsequently sings to her, as child-bride?). The religious motif implicit but atrophied in Lennon (his "Imagine" is the song of an atheism for which the authority of a murdered god has been reinscribed in the emotional injunctions of celebrity-humanism) is explicit here: it is the "Kol Nidre," sung, significantly, on the Day of Atonement, that makes Jolson's secular success with "Mammy" possible, that legitimates its "feminine" sentimentality; if God is not in his voice, his mother says, his father will know. (For Lennon, the relations are inverted: vocalizing the guilt adhering to his fractured maternal bond is what authorizes his attempted murder of the father in himself, most clearly enunciated in the song "God."[11])

"My Mammy" is only the best known in a rich corpus of "Mammy songs" for which Jolson had long been famous, including "Coal Black Mammy" (1921), "Give Me My Mammy" (1921), "Chloe" (1923) and "Mother of Mine, I Still Have You" (1927). In turn, these songs fit into a broader repertoire of "Southern Plantation" material, indebted to nineteenth-century minstrelsy and the turn-of-the-century coon song; "My Mammy," for example, was one of three Jolson interpolations in the 1918 show *Sinbad,* the others being "Rock-a-Bye Your Baby to a Dixie Melody" and George Gershwin's "Swanee." Within this tradition, the "Southern Mammy" stereotype was a key trope. For Lennon, the favored African-American influences were blues and soul rather than coon song and ragtime, and there were contemporaries of his—Elvis Presley, Mick Jagger, Jimi Hendrix—and later artists, too—Michael Jackson, Eminem—whose debt to the legacy of blackface performance conventions was far more obvious. Nevertheless, placed in this context, Lennon's singing can hardly help but remind us of the importance of this lineage in twentieth-century popular music as a whole, in terms both of musical features and of the psychoracial dynamic that has accompanied them. And we are reminded then that a key strand within this lineage is its matriarchal twist. The familiar stereotypes—the "strong black woman," the haven of the maternal arms, the voice as enveloping as the bosom, set against the complementary clichés of male emasculation— are of course ideologically distorted tools in that psychoracial conflict; yet they are grounded in lived-out black identities with, certainly on the female side, a power that cannot be denied. In a similar way, the misogynistic cast of many of the "Phallic Mother" myths should not be allowed to disqualify the psychoanalytic significance of the figure of maternal law, nor its possible potency as a cultural resource. From blues pioneer Gertrude "Ma" Rainey to Nina Simone, "high priestess of soul" with a voice of "warrior energy," and beyond, there is a tradition here that offers a powerful inverse trajectory to the equally familiar lineage of black male raunch (from the down-home bluesmen through Muddy Waters to Ice Cube and 50 Cent).[12] Add to this the parallel case of the Jewish "matriarchate"—where again a controlling maternal presence goes along with figures of male emasculation, this time the product of a feminizing orientalism[13]—and register in its full importance (as is not often done) the centrality of the intertwining traditions of African-American and Jewish-diasporic vocalities to the development of American popular music as a whole, and one cannot help wondering if Al Jolson's mediation of the two—like George Gershwin, he was a Jew clothing his marginality in blackface—is not a symptom of a cultural mechanism of historic significance, in which the patriarchal cast of Western traditions is given a decidedly matriarchal twist.

Although I want to suggest that this mechanism has a deeply embedded continuity and that careful analysis might unpick symptoms, albeit often less clear-cut ones, at many points along its path of development, it is clear that some particularly revealing nodes do stick out. An obvious case is Elvis Presley, an acknowledged model for the young John Lennon and, although less directly connected to Jolson, a performer who in his early work can in many respects be situated in the wake of Jolson's passage: his voice moves enigmatically through a wide range of registers, including into falsetto; it pops, hiccups, strangles words and plays rhythmically with their dismantled components (vowels, consonants) in a way that, as it were, reembodies itself in the image of a dancing machine;[14] he caresses lyrical phrases like a cooing mother stroking her baby's skin; above all, perhaps, he sings "as if" black (an effect that, as is well known, led to widespread racial misidentification when his records were first broadcast). The young Elvis's education in black music is well documented, and this must have included an assimilation, if only unwitting, of blackface performance codes: the success of Jolson's late movies, *The Jolson Story* (dir. Green, 1946) and *Jolson Sings Again* (dir. Levin, 1949), revived his faltering career, and this is the period, too, when African-American performers with a penchant for "clowning"—Louis Armstrong, Dizzy Gillespie, Louis Jordan—began to be criticized for what modernizing opinion saw increasingly as variants (albeit less old-fashioned variants) of these codes. In the rural and small-town hinterland of Memphis, the legacy of a minstrelized racial dynamic was all around. Robert Fink has described how Presley's version of "Hound Dog" started its life as blackface comedy—"a witty multiracial piece of signifyin' humor, troping off white overreactions to black sexual innuendo"[15]; if his recording ended up being sung, furiously, *at* the media establishment who criticized his indulgence in such innuendo—which is Fink's argument—it may not be too fanciful to think that it was also sung, in tribute and gratitude, *to* the song's first proponent, Willie Mae "Big Mama" Thornton.

The histrionic qualities of Presley's early style—the title of "All Shook Up" can stand as its key trope—was matched by the hysterical character of its reception, particularly in the context of live performance.[16] As with Jolson, who blazed a trail for Presley in this respect, the symptoms of this mass hysteria were largely associated with girls, and their frenzied adulation reached new levels: according to Hollywood director, Hal Kanter, who watched a 1956 show, "I'm a man who saw Al Jolson on the stage, and I never saw anything like the reception that Al Jolson got until Elvis Presley—and he made Al Jolson seem like a passing fancy."[17] Presley did not have a repertoire of Mammy songs, but the biographical Elvis was very much a mammy's boy[18] and it is not difficult to imagine that both the female lovers he would address in his songs and the young women he addressed in his hysterical audiences functioned as displacement objects of desire, mediating his mammy-love. In this feminized emotional economy, an intricate triangular trade of identity and desire seems to be set up, in which—we might think—Elvis assumes a position of "phallic mediator" between his female fans on the one hand, the mothers they have lost and those they believe they must become (as in imagination they mother him), on the other. The "shook up" quality of his singing—fracturing sense, jerking the body uncontrollably, cooing like a baby, emoting like a woman—marks out a troubled territory that all gestures of "manliness" (even GI service) could not completely settle.[19]

Arguably, the nearest Presley comes to a Mammy song is his early classic, "That's All Right Mama." But isn't this song addressed not to mother but to a lover? Yes and no (perhaps).[20] Barbara Bradby and Brian Torode, in their analysis of Buddy Holly's "Peggy Sue," argue that metaphorical "baby" discourse in rock 'n' roll should be taken seriously.[21] For them, Holly's vocal performance—with register shifts, hiccups, and linguistic fractures that bear comparison with the young Presley's—is about his growing from boy to man, a process he achieves through addressing "Peggy" as a baby (addressing her in babyish language) and eventually "disciplining" her wayward rhythms, bringing musical and verbal "sense" into line with his masculine authority. But this relationship works like that between mother and child: "the crying of a baby is silenced not by words, but by the union of the bodies of mother and baby in a rhythmic rocking motion. 'Rock 'n' roll' songs take this bodily relation between mother and baby as a metaphor for the sexual relation between man and woman, in which the man rocks his 'baby,' the woman . . . 'man' stands in for 'mother' and 'woman' for 'baby' in the 'rocking' relationship."[22] Because Holly finally reaches a position of control, of fatherhood to come indeed, Bradby and Torode conclude that the performance in the end confirms a conventional model of male socialization. But where has "mother" gone? Holly not only speaks to his "baby"; like Presley in "That's All Right Mama" (where again words are scrambled, producing almost a babbling effect, and ending with a whole chorus sung to meaningless, "infantile" vocables—"Dee dah dee dee"), Holly sings *like* a baby. The trade is triangular (actually it is a four-some: the absence of the real father, positioned surely just off-mike, looms over the whole scenario); and the shifting relations encapsulated in the vicissitudes of the whole baby/mama discourse (which is not specific to rock 'n' roll but goes back at least to early twentieth-century song) identi-fies popular music as a scene of unstable family romance with much to play for.

If, in the context of the lineage I am reconstructing, rock 'n' roll mediates between Jolsonian minstrelsy and Lennonesque rock, we would expect to find similar historical mechanisms subsequently. Perhaps in rap music—certainly a field of tension implicating both racially and gender-defined protagonists: but here violently transmuted, with a decidedly negative twist, so that mammy-and-baby is rewritten as bitch/whore and—*mother-fucker*. (Not that this term is exclusive to rap. Indeed, from its early-twenti-eth-century origins, as the most extreme insult, its meanings expanded so that by the 1950s it could have positive as well as negative connotations—a history similar to that of "bad" and "wicked." Nevertheless, it assumes an unprecedented centrality in rap discourse, and a background of Oedipal frisson surely remains.[23]) What is placed before us, at least at first hearing, is a family of *orphans,* but one where the presence of the missing mother is all the more palpable because the rappers' continuing entanglement with her—typically displaced on to their "bitches"—takes such a venge-ful form.[24] The maternal voice imagined here is not the comforting one of Julia Kristeva's "choric fantasy," which she associates with a develop-mental stage before the "castrating" force of paternal law arrives, but that of the phallic mother, source of law (and often terrifyingly so). It is from this relation that the "perversion" of sadism/masochism arises—for where might we locate the first signifiers of deprivation and punishment but in the mother's acts and words of admonishment?—and the often noticed sadomasochistic cast of rap lyrics reminds us that, for Lacan, this complex is associated with one of the "partial drives" in particular, the invocatory drive: the maternal sounds that at one and the same time convey discipline and, as object-voice, immediately cut off from its body of origin, offer the lure of a quite specific *jouissance*.[25]

112 • Richard Middleton

But surely, it might be objected, rap is the genre par excellence where, not maternal, but paternal law is asserted; where masculine authority is imposed through, precisely, words—mastery of rhymes, aggressively delivered. Yet once again (indeed in particularly spectacular fashion) the signifiers of masculine control—speed of verbal articulation, dexterity of rhyming, percussively injunctive diction—are, often, pushed to such excessive lengths that they undercut their own ostensible goal, hysterical gabble matching grotesque bodily gestures and turning language into, not so much a tool of meaning, as an object of play that at the same time acts, by its own force as it were, on the surface of the body itself. This tendency reaches a peak, and rap its crisis point, in the 1990s. To listen, for example, to the Wu-Tang Clan's trend-setting first album from 1993[26] is to hear a surreal mix of "meaningless" repetitions, arbitrary jump cuts, and bizarre overlays of voices, often with grotesque timbres, sometimes "inhuman," sometimes in sequences of "childlike" rhyming. The backgrounds combine abstract, near-atonal riffs and nostalgic, even "cheesy" samples. The range of rap styles deployed here perhaps finds its most telling voice in the weirdly shifting, half-bark, half-singsong persona offered by Ol' Dirty Bastard (a.k.a. Russell Jones: has his father gone missing, in a pathology dating back to slavery?). Even allowing for the effects of cultural distance, explicit verbal meaning seems to me way below the listening horizon. Although rapping is conventionally read as a transplantation of the soundscape of the ghetto street (sometimes seen as a metonym of the "cut-up" culture of a postmodern globalopolis), I hear this music just as much as referencing a phantasmatic aural interior; perhaps that originary "umbilical web" of which Michel Chion writes, a maternal vocalized web that for him marks, all at the same time, desire for an object (a c(h)ord) that is lost, the cut that severed it, and the tentacular grip that it nevertheless retains.[27] The same inside-outside tension, at a different level, animates the character-istic interplay in rap between its claim to authenticity—rap reflects real life—and its status as high spectacle, a knowing performativity reflected in the masquerade of stage-names and doubles.[28] Indeed, too often "real life" has *become* a performance, verbal bullets confused with real ones, both (phallic) object-types marking, machining and dismembering the body. This foot-stamping tantrum is most memorably encapsulated by the Clan: "Bring the motherfucking ruckus!"[29]

From minstrelsy to hip-hop: a history of the family that at the same time documents a continuing if mutating crisis of masculinity. Three over-arching points are worth emphasizing:

- Not surprisingly perhaps, the moments I have picked out with my examples map easily to points of masculine crisis in the social history, and each is accompanied by a "feminizing" partner: Jolson (first-wave feminism; the threat of emasculation heard in crooning); rock 'n' roll (Cold War domestification and its anxieties; the camp of such performers as Little Richard); Lennon (second-wave feminism; the feminization heard in progressive and glam rock); rap (late-century "post-feminism"; post-disco dance music, and its gay elements).

- The "involuntary voice" in play in all the examples—the voice seemingly writing itself, outside conscious control, and in the process both separating itself from the body and gesturing it into a particular shape—can be regarded as one aspect of the Lacanian "object-voice," that impossible voice, inaudible as such, which is left over when all signifying processes have been accounted for, the voice which, in one form or another, is ultimately the voice of the Other. Although this voice, typically, stands alteritously to logos—and therefore, in the conventional psychoanalytic scheme, marks the place of a "feminine" *jouissance*—for the later Lacan, it is also what "sticks" to logos, what makes logos work, gives it its god-like authority; in this latter guise, voice is that senseless cry which gives law its force, which therefore summons its own ecstasy—*le-père-la-jouissance*. "There are not two voices, but only one object voice, which cleaves and bars the Other in an ineradicable 'extimacy'"; and, as Lacan himself put it, "why not interpret one face of the Other, the God face, as *supported* by feminine *jouissance*. . . . And since it is there too that the function of the father is inscribed in so far as this is the function to which castration refers, one can see that while this may not make for two Gods, nor does it make for one alone."[30] But to limit this structure to "support" is too grudging: surely it opens the way for the possibility of a reconfiguration of "castration" itself, based on recognition of the role of the phallic mother in weaving the "web" of the symbolic—a possibility that Lacan does not pursue.

- The symptoms we might expect of such a radical, indeed dangerous move—loss of vocal control, automatism, dismemberment or imaginary reconstruction of the body, confusion of gender signifiers, defensive reinforcement of patriarchal markers accompanying their simultaneous fracturing—are all over the examples I have introduced. They bring inescapably to mind a condition that was at the core of the psychoanalytic project from its beginnings, but that Lacan subsequently broadened into one of the modes in his typology of discourse—*hysteria*.

114 • Richard Middleton

What Is it to Be a Man?

Psychoanalysis offers no bar to the traditional assumption that hysteria is, typically, a female condition. Lacan, extrapolating from Freud, describes hysteria as structured by a question: "Who am I? a man or a woman?" or rather "What is it to be a woman?"[31] And the dissymmetrical form this question is given applies to male as well as female hysterics, because the skewed shape attributed to sexual differentiation—Man is normative, Woman is his symptom—makes the "problem" of femininity the key issue for both genders. But if "castration" were to be reconfigured, the mobility of the phallus fully recognized, then the question for hysterical masculinity would shift: What is it to be a man?

Freud made clear that the root of hysteria lies in sexual fantasy[32]—but the fantasy stands for a situation in which something has "gone wrong," the "normal" course of desire has been blocked or refused. Bodily symptoms "convert" this structure of repressed trauma into an "imaginary anatomy"[33] within which disorders, often interlinked, of the genitalia, digestion, lungs, throat and voice have a prominence that is, for my purposes here, particularly striking. What is more, the intertwining economies of sexuality and of the alimentary and vocalimentary canals often throw up tropes of *procreation:* in Freud's classic case study of "Dora," for instance, a bundle of symptoms hinging on mysterious abdominal pain is interpreted as a fantasy of childbirth; and in Lacan's reading of this study he describes how a particular male hysteric suffers a fantasy of pregnancy.[34] The hysteric's question can thus also be written as, "Am I capable of procreating?"[35] But in the case of male singers, what imaginary anatomy is involved in this? Rather than disablement or movement of a womb (the classical understanding of the female complaint), perhaps we should think of the movement of an imaginary phallus, from its "normal" place up into the throat. Here, suggests Lacan, the hysteric probes at the heart of things, for "In the symbolic nothing explains creation" and in the failure of the signifiers, his voice, exposing the object at the core of the subject, opens on to the Real.[36]

Of course, the singer is "only performing." But so, too, is the hysteric. His attacks "are nothing else but phantasies translated into the motor sphere, projected on to motility and portrayed in pantomime"; for him, "the technical term 'acting out' takes on its literal meaning since he is acting outside himself."[37] Freud's interpretative technique here is similar to his approach to "dream-work" (indeed, dreams often figure in hysterical case histories), and in a similar way our singers might be thought to offer examples of "song-work."[38] In both cases, what is performed is conflictual—the staging of a lack, of ambivalence, of "multiple identifications"; paradoxically, it is a "desire for unsatisfaction" that is presented to our gaze, an insistence on failure through which "the subject 'gives body' to his deadlock."[39] Lacan's rereading of "Dora" clarifies the structure of identification and desire typically entailed in hysterical performances. Her ultimate object of desire, he argues, is not Herr K., as Freud initially suggests, but Frau K., her father's mistress; she situates her ego, in effect, with Herr K., identifies with him as her ego-ideal, and uses him to mediate her (illicit, same-sex) desire.[40] For the hysterical subject, Lacan explains, "his ego is in the third party by whose mediation the subject enjoys that object in which his question is embodied."[41] And, picking up what Freud had already spotted ("the entire structure of the hysteric, with his fundamental identification with the individual of the sex opposite to his own by which his own [hetero-]sex is questioned . . ."[42]), Lacan also exposes the homosexual element which typically arises. One can hardly help remarking that, like "Dora," all the singers I have discussed—Jolson, Presley, Lennon, stereotypical male rappers—have a "father-problem" (he is absent, dysfunctional or rejected); nor that there are grounds for identifying a homoerotic charge to their performances, complementing the "feminizing" musical trends that accompanied their work, identified earlier. But if these singers situate their ego with Mother, what is their object of desire? Although the homosexual implication is important, surely their loving but fraught negotiations with the vocal object point us toward the centrality of—the *phallus*: that ambivalent object, circulating narcissistically (do they want to have it or to be it?) between mother and pregendered infant.[43]

Needless to say, there is no reason to think that any of the singers I have discussed could be diagnosed as clinically hysterical. Yet, just as for Freud "normality" is always a bit neurotic, so the later Lacan, thinking through a general model of discourse, included in it an important role for the "discourse of the hysteric." In this discursive mode, represented thus:

$$\frac{\mathcal{S}}{a} \rightarrow \frac{S_1}{S_2}$$

the key part (the function of agency, top left) is played by the always-already split subject ($\mathcal{S}$), whose refusal of "normal" interpellations, and insistence on his transgressive desire, has as its consequence and condition whatever object (*objet petit a*) can function to cover over his self-constitutive lack. This structure, performed out symptomatically, is addressed to, is routed via an identification with, a Master-signifier (S_1), which in turn posits a new value-system (S_2). Mark Bracher's explication—"The hysterical structure is in force whenever a discourse is dominated by the speaker's symptom—that is his or her unique mode of experiencing *jouissance*"[44]—helpfully

116 • Richard Middleton

adds that the function of object *a* can be filled by a range of sexualized body-parts, by another subject (a baby for example) but also by gaze and voice (especially mother's). When mum's the word, we might add, it is the "vocal phallus" that is a key rhetorical figure—a specific case of a general condition whose ubiquity is well caught in Žižek's Hegelian gloss: "the 'figure of consciousness' stages ('figures') the concealed truth of a position [its unspoken surplus or object *a*]—in this sense, every 'figure of consciousness' implies a kind of hysterical theatre."[45] Without placing music in the consulting room, then; without blurring the differences between everyday gender performativity and that specific to musical representations, we can note the contiguities and overlaps of spheres; and if then the twentieth century as a whole starts to appear as hysterically overdetermined—psychoanalysis starts there in the 1890s, heterosexual norms slide and shift hysterically throughout the period, singing acts out symptoms of trauma, desire and impossibility, conditions of mass cultural consumption hystericize star/fan relations (a pattern followed in general politics, from fascism through "1968" (Che?) to Thatcher, Milosevich and Bin Laden)—perhaps this is pointing where our understanding of the history needs to go.

Flaming Desire

In the context of the trajectory I have been outlining, even genres associated with conventional gender politics may come to seem "suspect." In country music, for example, the apparently rigid heteronormative conventions are so strong as positively to invite camp parody (this is the "I'm a lumberjack" factor, to cite the Monty Python song), a pattern that lays the ground for k.d. lang's lesbian appropriation. But in lang's *Absolute Torch and Twang* album, her subject position is particularly complex: here is some form of female masculinity (lang was not yet publicly "out" but her sexuality was well known), applied to country (including covers of songs "belonging" to men), yet also performing torch songs (a genre traditionally associated with submissive, suffering femininity—including in the country lineage, in the work for instance of Patsy Cline, a strong influence on lang).[46] Her bluesy articulations come from torch song, but are smoothly integrated into a full range of country vocal conventions (growl, falsetto, catch in the throat) so that the overall impression, particularly in light of her powerful, gleaming timbres produced through a wide range of registers, is one of (phallic?) control; "torch" is mitigated by "twang" ("pullin' back the reins," she rides "tall in the saddle"). If the identification is with a maternal phallicism, what lost object does she cling to? Her lament is for childhood—"memories of children . . . buried . . . deep down inside" which, however, "won't be denied."[47] This position assumes a special force if we listen with a knowledge of traditions of hysterical male and submissive female singing. In that perspective, lang so to speak dehystericizes the schematic female (same sex) hysterical relation; in following the male hysteric's path, she *normalizes* it.

In which case, the transvestite, transgendering Antony—also covering a repertoire that can broadly be described as torch song, but from within performing traditions more obviously amenable to transgressive gesture (performance art, cabaret)—may be said to rehystericize it. Ranging through the registers from chesty countertenor to powerful falsetto, his fast rhythm vibrato sometimes tremulous (read: torch song), sometimes strong and edgy (read: soul; Nina Simone?), Antony's unpredictable surges of phrasing and dynamics, and often jerky, disjointed rhythms connect him back to Jolson, Presley and Lennon, but position him, too, in complex generic territory where torch and soul meet crooning (read: sensitive, even "effeminate" male). Many of the songs thematize childhood or sisterhood, and empathize with women. Striving, perhaps, for a phallic mother identification (most clearly in the soul-shout, "Fistful of Love"), this quest seems confused by body dysmorphia—a misfire between imagined body and its appearance (or "clothing"). Frequent references to birds and flight suggest a desire for the spirit to flee this body, to cast off its burden—the burden of the phallus perhaps (is he a *castrato*?[48]).

Compared to lang's twanging authority, Antony's melodies circle naggingly around themselves; his lyrics return obsessively to themes of hopelessness and death. Obsessional neurosis—the condition towards which classic torch song points—was considered by Freud to be a "dialect" of hysteria. The formative question flips: from sexual identity, hence procreation, to existence as such, hence death; "why is he here?," the subject asks, and "why is he going to disappear?," his rituals designed to ward off the threat of death. Indeed, the obsessive refuses the question of sexual difference: "The obsessional is precisely neither one [sex] nor the other—one may also say that he is both at once."[49] Yet, as the Freud of *Beyond the Pleasure Principle* insisted, life and death create each other. Perhaps it is to this "beyond" that torch song, at the end of the twentieth century and the beginning of the twenty-first, building on all the vocal transgressions of previous decades, has the power to point, offering possibilities of new economies of desire, fueled by multitudinous routes and identifications of love. Fire consumes, but also clears the ground and lights the way. A bonfire of vanities—those vanities that sustain patriarchal norms—may turn out, too, to be a bonfire of profanity: that obscene "Thou shalt not" which brought Law into existence in the first place. And if, then, the word returns to mum,[50] perhaps it will reveal its originary surplus, at the level of the drives, as that act of creation which men either stole or dared not face.

118 • Richard Middleton

Notes

Thanks to Freya Jarman-Ivens and Ian Biddle for comments on an earlier draft of this chapter.

1. Simon Frith, quoted, http://www.timesonline.co.uk/article/0,,2-1769107,00.html.
2. Antony and the Johnsons, *I Am a Bird Now* (Rough Trade RTRADCD223), 2005.
3. Judith Halberstam, *Female Masculinity* (Durham, NC: Duke University Press, 1998).
4. For an example from what might appear the very heart of musical patriarchalism, heavy metal, see Robert Walser, *Running with the Devil: Power, Gender, and Madness in Heavy Metal Music* (Hanover, NH: University Press of New England, 1993), Chapter 4. As Walser observes, "Spectacles are problematic in the context of a patriarchal order that is invested in the stability of signs and that seeks to maintain women in the position of objects of the male gaze" (108).

    Halberstam argues that normative masculinity presents itself as "nonperformative": it does not need performance, it tells us, because it is taken to be natural; thus in the very few places where such performance does reveal itself, the masquerade can turn out to be very fragile (*Female*, 234–235). She hardly mentions music, but in fact her discussion of female Elvis impersonators (257–259) supports my point since, as she explains, their technique—which is one of hyperbole—can only work by exposing through exaggeration the outrageously constructed nature of their source (e.g., the performativity of the "real" Elvis, seen as already an impersonation of itself).
5. This suggestion may seem outrageous; at the least, it risks dismissal as just another male appropriation. Yet any antiessentialist theory of gender must surely allow the possibility of such multiphase (de-)constructions. How far could they go? Could a woman reappropriate such a male appropriation? Of course (cf. my discussion of k. d. lang later).
6. For a clear summary of Lacan's rewriting of the Freudian Oedipus Complex, in which a "first time" (the "preoedipal triangle") is succeeded by second and third times marked by paternal "castration," first of the mother, then of the child, see Dylan Evans, *An Introductory Dictionary of Lacanian Psychoanalysis* (London and New York: Routledge, 1996), 127–130. The idea that the voice might have a privileged role in the phallic function of the first time is implicit in many neo-Lacanian feminist accounts, but the speculation that this role might have a symbolic (that is, law-making) as well as imaginary dimension is most incisively put forward in Kaja Silverman, *The Acoustic Mirror: The Female Voice in Psychoanalysis and Cinema* (Bloomington, IN: Indiana University Press, 1988), 72–100. In effect, the status of the maternal-infantile voice-nexus as part-object (*objet petit a*) arises at this time out of its "substitution" (as it might seem subsequently) for what has yet to rear its ugly head.
7. *John Lennon/Plastic Ono Band*, EMI 7243 5 28740 2 6 (2000 [1970]).

8. Lennon's own commentary suggests, intriguingly, that the bells are meant to convey "the death knell of the mother/father, Freudian trip"; this is, then, an anti-Oedipus. (Lennon, quoted in Anthony Elliott, *The Mourning of John Lennon* [Berkeley, Los Angeles and London: University of California Press, 1999], 49. Elliott's interpretation of the song [49–53] is powerful.)

9. I discuss Nina Simone, including "Sinnerman" specifically, in the context of a theory of "phallic motherhood," in my *Voicing the Popular: On the Subjects of Popular Music* (London and New York: Routledge, 2006), 121-123.

10. *The Jazz Singer* (Warner PES 99321), 1988 [1927]. Jolson's 1928 audio recording of "My Mammy" (reissued on *Al Jolson: Great Original Performances 1926-1932* [CDS RPCD 300], 1992) is vocally even more extravagant than his film performance. W. T. Lhamon is characteristically brilliant on Jolson's performance style in *Raising Cain: Blackface Performance from Jim Crow to Hip Hop* (Cambridge, MA: Harvard University Press, 1998), 102–115. Stephen Banfield is good on his vocal technique in "Stage and Screen Entertainers in the Twentieth Century," in *The Cambridge Companion to Singing*, ed. John Potter (Cambridge: Cambridge University Press, 2000), 63–82.

11. "God" was included on the same album as "Mother" and "My Mummy's Dead"; "Imagine" followed closely afterwards, on the album *Imagine* (Parlophone 7243 5 24858 2 6), 2000 [1971].

12. According to jazz musician Danny Barker, "When you said 'Ma,' that means mother. 'Ma,' that means the tops. That's the boss, the shack bully of the house, Ma Rainey. She'd take charge." Quoted in Angela Y. Davis, *Blues Legacies and Black Feminism* (New York: Pantheon, 1998), 121. The "warrior energy" reference comes from singer Bernice Johnson Reagon, quoted in Brian Ward, *Just My Soul Responding: Rhythm and Blues, Black Consciousness and Race Relations* (London: UCL Press, 1998), 302. The lineage of such female black singers has continued to be productive, as may be heard in the work of, for example, Queen Latifah and Mary J. Blige.

    It is important to view the distorting myths of the "black matriarchy" through the lens of revisionist African-American scholarship, which has rescued its progressive political potential; Angela Davis, bell hooks, and Hortense Spillers are the key authors. I discuss their work, in the context of the "phallic mother" argument, in *Voicing the Popular*, Chapter 3.

    See also Judith Halberstam's chapter in this collection, on "Big Mama" Thornton.

13. For the nineteenth- and early-twentieth-century gentile mind, this emasculation was marked by the "perversion" of circumcision, while maternal control was confirmed by the matrilineal descent of Jewish racial identity.

14. Elsewhere I call this "boogification," the voice acting rhythmically as if it were a boogie-woogie pianist's right hand; see Richard Middleton, "All Shook Up? Innovation and Continuity in Elvis Presley's Vocal Style," in *Elvis: Images and Fancies*, ed. Jac Tharpe (London: W. H. Allen, 1983), 155–166.

15. Robert Fink, "Elvis Everywhere: Musicology and Popular Music Studies at the Twilight of the Canon," *American Music,* 16 (1998), 135–179 (169). In a further interesting connection, "Hound Dog"—along with many other rock 'n' roll songs—was composed by two Jewish writers, Jerry Lieber and Mike Stoller. As far as the Tin Pan Alley period is concerned, the importance of the African-American/Jewish alliance has often been noted; even at the time, Isaac Goldberg, in his 1930 book on Tin Pan Alley, had suggested that both groups shared "the sad, the hysterical psychology of the oppressed race," a comment whose terms will become intensely relevant to my argument later. Michael Billig, who quotes this comment (*Rock 'n' Roll Jews* [Nottingham: Five Leaves Publications, 2000], 77–78), has documented the continuation of the alliance in rock 'n' roll and rock music, where it has attracted less attention. Billig argues that Jews mediated black culture to WASPs, but the story he tells—that in this role they gradually retreated from the stage (Jolson, Eddie Cantor, Irving Berlin, Sophie Tucker, Fanny Brice, et al.) into song-writing and record production and then, by the 1960s, more or less disappeared from view—locates them as what Slavoj Žižek has termed a "vanishing mediator": they do their work then vanish from sight (see Žižek, *For They Know Not What They Do: Enjoyment as a Political Factor,* 2nd ed. [London: Verso, 2002], 182–197). Still, it would be worth asking whether Jews, as Billig argues, not only played a key role in "feminizing" rock 'n' roll (*Rock 'n' Roll Jews,* 90) but also contributed to African-American and thence rock singing an emotive, even histrionic approach, especially in ballads, that could even now be restored to critical view.

    On the blackface Elvis, see also Greil Marcus, *Mystery Train: Images of America in Rock 'n' Roll Music,* 4th ed. (London: Penguin, 1991), 152: "At the start, Elvis sounded black to those who heard him; when they called him the Hillbilly Cat, they meant the White Negro. Or as Elvis put it, years later: ' . . . made a record and when the record came out a lot of people liked it and you could hear folks around town saying, "Is he, is he?" and I'm going, "Am I, am I?"'"

16. It seems a pity that there is no etymological connection between "histrionic" (from Latin *histrio,* a stage-player) and "hysterical" (from Greek *hystera,* the womb); although we might note that the conditions of "histrionic paralysis" and "histrionic spasm" (muscular paralysis, or spasm of the face, respectively) were first named at exactly the same time (the late nineteenth century) as hysteria was being first defined as a neurosis by psychiatrists, including the young Freud. Had the two semantic territories intersected each other, perhaps unwittingly (the discursive unconscious at work)?

17. Quoted in Peter Guralnick, *Last Train to Memphis: The Rise of Elvis Presley* (London: Abacus, 1995), 374.

18. See, for example, Elaine Dundy, *Elvis and Gladys* (London: Pimlico, 1995).

19. This view of the feminized Elvis is far from new. The literature starts with Sue Wise's "Sexing Elvis," in *On Record: Rock, Pop and the Written Word*, ed. Simon Frith and Andrew Goodwin (London and New York: Routledge, 1990 [1984]), 390–398, and is expertly drawn on by Freya Jarman-Ivens in "Breaking Voices: Voice, Subjectivity and Fragmentation in Popular Music" (Ph.D. thesis, University of Newcastle, 2006), 226–244. However, this picture of Presley has not, I think, been located in the historical perspective I am attempting here.

    It is ironic that joining the army, far from "making a man" of Presley, has been regarded by mainstream (i.e., masculinist) commentary as a key factor in his "emasculation"; afterwards, so it is argued, rebellious erotics gave way to middle-of-the-road crooning. So was Elvis at his "sexiest" when his "masculinity" was at its most ambiguous—when, one might even hazard, most incipiently *female?*

20. The original that Presley is covering was by Arthur "Big Boy" Crudup. The nomenclature of "big boys," while no doubt a response to the diminutive "boy" of white racist discourse, also may function as a challenge to that of "big mamas" (as well as being a variation on the "papas" who were not uncommon in earlier blues; Papa Charlie Jackson, for instance). The discourse of the family romance is perhaps at its most discursively complex in the field of African-American music.

21. Barbara Bradby and Brian Torode, "Pity Peggy Sue," *Popular Music*, 4 (1984): 183–205.

22. Ibid., 201, 202.

23. The "motherfucker" trope sits in a broader African-American tradition of ritual insult that has the opponent's mother as its central object and that finds its most typical form in the street game known as "The Dozens"; see William Labov, *Language in the Inner City: Studies in the Black English Vernacular* (Philadelphia: University of Pennsylvania Press, 1972), 306–353; Lawrence W. Levine, *Black Culture and Black Consciousness: Afro-American Folk Thought from Slavery to Freedom* (New York: Oxford University Press, 1977), 344–358. Levine doubts the force of Oedipal explanations, but I think he is reading too narrowly. Roger D. Abrahams is surely closer to the mark when, in situating the discourse of male, often apparently misogynist African-American ritual boasting in the context of historically contingent black family structure, he emphasizes the *ambivalence* inherent both in the motherfucker trope and in the typical relationship of young male to mother-figure (both actual and displaced) that the trope maps. (Roger D. Abrahams, *Deep Down in the Jungle: Negro Narrative Folklore from the Streets of Philadelphia*, 2nd ed. [Chicago: Aldine Publishing Company, 1970], 20–35.)

    In rap the violence implicit in the term is rarely aimed explicitly at the mother herself, but Eminem's obsession with the subject of his allegedly abusive mother represents a rare moment when it is. In his song "Kill You," he fantasizes raping her.

24. Rap's typical grouping into posses, crews, clans, mobs, and tribes immediately suggests the dynamics of dysfunctional family romance—or perhaps recalls Freud's mythic figure (for such it surely is) of the parricidal "primal horde"; but in this case our murderous band of brothers find the Father has already disappeared, victim of a higher authority (the Man; the System), and the Mother—desired but feared—turns out not to offer what might have been hoped. See Sigmund Freud, *Totem and Taboo: Some Points of Agreement between the Mental Lives of Savages and Neurotics,* trans. James Strachey (London: Routledge and Kegan Paul, 1950).

25. For a critique of Kristeva's mother/child theory along the lines outlined here, see Silverman, *Acoustic,* 101–126. On sadism/masochism and the invocatory drive (with voice as its *objet petit a*), see Jacques Lacan, *The Four Fundamental Concepts of Psychoanalysis,* trans. Alan Sheridan (Harmondsworth: Penguin, 1979), 183–186. On sadism/masochism in rap, see Jarman-Ivens, "Breaking," 157–166.

26. Wu-Tang Clan, *Enter the Wu-Tang Clan (36 Chambers)* (BMG 74321203672), 1993.

27. Michel Chion, *The Voice in Cinema,* trans. Claudia Gorbman (New York: Columbia University Press, 1999), 61–62. Kaja Silverman's critique of this passage (*Acoustic,* 72–79) takes Chion to task, rightly I feel, for situating the "web" entirely in a mythical, quasi-uterine, symbolically impotent stage and transferring the baby's discursive helplessness on to the mother. The image can be rescued, however, if this web is seen as, among other things, an early materialization of the symbolic network itself.

28. Again Eminem, with his multiple personae, offers the most clearly worked-out example.

    "Spectacle" is a key trope in Russell A. Potter's *Spectacular Vernaculars: Hip-Hop and the Politics of Postmodernism* (New York: State University of New York Press, 1995). For Potter, this relates primarily to rap's place within, and resistance to, the "society of the spectacle" described by Guy Debord—where mass media signs become the most potent vehicle of commodification. Although rap is undoubtedly, and importantly, located in this place, I see its spectacular performance gestures (both live and recorded) as resonating more broadly: with the specular mechanisms of identity performance theorized by Lacan and Althusser, and, especially, with the specific African-American variant of such mechanisms evident in the extreme theatre (the "hysterical theatre," as I shall shortly want to call it) of blackface.

29. "Bring Da Ruckus," *Enter the Wu-Tang Clan,* track 1.

30. Mladen Dolar, "The Object Voice," in *Gaze and Voice as Love Objects,* ed. Renata Salecl and Slavoj Žižek (Durham, NC: Duke University Press, 1996), 7–31 (27); Lacan, in *Feminine Sexuality: Jacques Lacan and the École freudienne,* ed. Juliet Mitchell and Jacqueline Rose (London: Macmillan, 1982), 147 (my emphasis).

31. Jacques Lacan, *The Psychoses: The Seminar of Jacques Lacan, Book III 1955–1956,* ed. Jacques-Alain Miller, trans. Russell Grigg (London and New York: Routledge, 1993), 171.

32. For example, "at least *one* of the meanings of a [hysterical] symptom is the representation of a sexual phantasy." (Sigmund Freud, "Fragment of an Analysis of a Case of Hysteria," in *The Standard Edition of the Complete Psychological Works of Sigmund Freud,* vol. VII [London: Hogarth Press, 1953 (1905)], 3–122 [47].)

33. See Jacques Lacan, *Écrits: A Selection,* trans. Alan Sheridan (London: Tavistock Publications, 1977), 4–5.

34. See Freud, "Fragment," 101–103; Lacan, *Psychoses,* 168–171, 178–179. "Dora"'s symptoms include nausea, coughing, catarrh, genital discharge and loss of voice, and Freud links them, via processes of displacement, to a fantasy of fellatio. "Vocalimentary canal" is my term for the imaginary anatomy along which vocal energies—of ingestion and ejaculation, dissemination and invagination (to use Derridean terms)—might be felt to flow; see Middleton, *Voicing,* 93.

35. Lacan, *Psychoses,* 171.

36. Ibid., 179. Lacan, as he points out, is here following Freud in moving "beyond the pleasure principle" (179–180).

37. Sigmund Freud, "Some General Remarks on Hysterical Attacks," *The Standard Edition of the Complete Psychological Works of Sigmund Freud,* vol. IX (London: Hogarth Press, 1959 [1909]), 228–234 (229); Lacan, *Écrits,* 90. Freud's "pantomime" reminds us that *silence* (the hysteric's aphonia or muteness) can be seen as the extreme manifestation of the vocal subversion of language—object voice in its purest form.

38. The concept of "song-work," and the analogy with "dream-work," come from Barbara Bradby and Brian Torode, "Song-work: The Musical Inclusion, Exclusion and Representation of Women," unpublished conference paper, British Sociological Association, Manchester, 1982.

39. Freud, "General," 230; Žižek, *For,* 144, 142.

40. Lacan, *Psychoses,* 174–175.

41. Lacan, *Écrits,* 89–90.

42. Lacan, *Psychoses,* 249; Freud had argued that hysterical desire might be split bisexually: "Hysterical symptoms are the expression on the one hand of a masculine unconscious and on the other hand of a feminine one." ("Hysterical Phantasies and their Relation to Bisexuality," *The Standard Edition of the Complete Psychological Works of Sigmund Freud,* vol. IX [London: Hogarth Press, 1959 (1908)], 157–166 (165); and cf. "Fragment," 59–63, where Freud applies this argument to the case of "Dora," adding by the way that in his experience it affects male hysterics more than females.)

43. Why this (rather speculative) structure? Because of the dissymmetry of the Oedipal process to which Lacan, following Freud, persistently drew attention. Where the hysterical female, failing to pursue the "normal" course towards a maternal identification, will get "stuck" on father, or a father-substitute, the male, if his paternal identification is blocked or refused, can readily fall back on an earlier relation with mother. Of course, this assumes—wrongly, I suggest—that the dissymmetry is fixed. If the Oedipal process can be reconfigured, the way would be open for the female hysteric to follow the male path (Silverman, in *Acoustic,* 120–125, argues something similar). Is this part of what is at stake for female masculinity?

124 • Richard Middleton

44. Mark Bracher, "On the Psychological and Social Functions of Language: Lacan's Theory of the Four Discourses," in *Lacanian Theory of Discourse: Subject, Structure, and Society,* ed. Mark Bracher, Marshall W. Alcorn Jr., Ronald J. Corthell, and François Massardier-Kenney (New York: New York University Press, 1994), 107–128 (122, 114). If hysteria qua clinical condition stands in a metonymical relationship to the "discourse of the hysteric," we might be prompted to widen the social net of hysterical desire beyond the gender question on its own; recalling Elvis Presley's pregnant "Am I, am I?," for instance (note 15 above), we might wonder about the possibility of racial hysteria. Here, however, if "the symbolic is not merely organised by 'phallic power' but by a 'phallicism' that is centrally sustained by racial anxiety" (Judith Butler, *Bodies that Matter: On the Discursive Limits of "Sex"* [London and New York: Routledge, 1993], 184), a specific structure of overdetermination is clearly in play, one that casts light retrospectively on the Jewish/blackface strand of my argument.
45. Žižek, *For,* 143.
46. k.d. lang, *Absolute Torch and Twang* (Sire 7599–25877–2), 1989.
47. These two quotations are from "Pullin' Back the Reins" and "Nowhere to Stand," respectively.
48. Compare his sound to that of Alessandro Moreschi, on *The Last Castrato* (Opal CD 9823), 1987; or that of Dana International, a real castrate (we assume) rather than a virtual one, whom I discuss in *Voicing the Popular,* 131-134.
49. Lacan, *Psychoses,* 179, 249.
50. I intend to leave the exact implications of such a return to "mum's (the) word" hanging somewhat. The etymology is tantalizing, however. "Mum" is baby-talk of course (as we would expect here); but its source ("mamma") not only stems (allegedly) from a baby's "natural" first word but also means, lip-smackingly, "breast" (from Latin, *mamma*). At the same time, "mum" means "silence" too (Hush! Mum's the word)—we recall that the "silent cry" has been considered the purest manifestation of object voice—and from here we find that to "mumm" (to act in a mummer's play or dumb-show) carries us into the territories both of *mime* (including the "pantomime" of hysterical behavior, as Freud described it) and of *masquerade* (including blackface performance). We cannot rule out the possibility that the association of mother and silence marks a patriarchal act of, precisely, silencing; yet perhaps this rich nexus of, equally precisely, word-play also reveals a site of theatre where Law is *in the making,* where word is (also, still) act, and where such malleability opens the social formation of the Symbolic itself to change. Maybe song—"mum" in its final sense (mmm . . . : "an inarticulate sound with closing of the lips" [*OED*])—is the practice in which all these meanings can be stitched together.

CHAPTER 14

Global, National, Local:
Or, a Hysteric's Account of Negative Dialectics*

Like the editors of this volume, I am writing from the vantage-point of a university that recently introduced a degree course in 'folk and traditional music'. The core focus of the course is on 'the traditions of these islands' (the title of one of the modules). But immediately questions arise. First of all, questions of political nomenclature. How should we describe 'these islands'? Do they include a 'United Kingdom' (it has been notably less united since Scotland and Wales were granted a certain level of autonomy), 'Britain' or 'Great Britain' (the latter suggesting an uncomfortable hangover of imperial pretension), or even the 'British Isles' (but why are they 'British?')? Where does this leave 'Ireland', and should we speak of 'Northern Ireland' or 'the North of Ireland'? A second group of questions has more to do with the actual music cultures. For such has been the degree of cross-influence, historically, between 'English', 'Scottish', 'Welsh' and 'Irish' traditional musics, so important have been the broader links, for example into Continental Europe or now involving the net of 'Celtic Connections' (including Brittany and Galicia) or the diasporas (the Irish in the USA, the Scots in Canada), and, more recently, so radical has been the impact of newer styles with less specific geographical identities (rock music, dance beats, jazz, and – broadest of all – 'world music'), that it proves all but impossible to distinguish and delimit separate traditions of these islands, and to tie them to national or quasi-national homes. Both sets of issues come together in the 'Northumbria question'. Since the course is located at Newcastle upon Tyne, it is natural that the strongest focus of all should be on the traditions of the north-east of England – an area still named in many contexts as 'Northumbria'. It is many centuries since Northumbria was a kingdom, stretching from the Humber to the Clyde, from the North Sea to the Irish Sea (its power was at its peak in the seventh century AD), yet this historical background suggests why its music is both specific and irreducibly hybrid. Recently, the British government offered the people of the north-east a regional assembly with a rather small amount of autonomy. The offer was decisively rejected – even though, on the cultural level, the rise of the 'Geordie Nation'[1] (accompanied now by the policy aim, familiar in declining industrial areas, of pursuing economic regeneration through cultural regionalism) has been inexorable.

Newcastle University is also the lead partner in a regional consortium whose music programmes have been awarded the status of Centre of Excellence in Teaching and Learning. The Centre's title (and its agenda) is 'Music and Inclusivity'. The concept of inclusivity points towards many of the buzzwords – pluralism, hybridity, multiculturalism – that are thematized in the discourse of globalization, together with its dialogical partner of localism. And on this level

*This essay first appeared as an *Afterword in Music, National Identity and the Politics of location: Between the Global and the Local*, edited by Ian Biddle and Vanessa Knights. This explains some references which might otherwise seem mysterious.

it would seem hard to take exception to it. Yet one wonders how far it is from the Blairite 'Big Tent', a favoured image offered by a cynical power strategy that can be all things to all men (and occasionally women) only because it is not very much to any of them. If everybody and everything are inside, what is left outside? Is there anything – any music, any musical politics – to which we would want to object? At a moment when the multiple articulations of political identity, mediated by a host of other factors (most obviously religion), have become particularly pressing, and in some contexts have taken on such murderous forms, it seems less than adequate to offer a simple hymn to the virtues either of the global or of the local.

I start with these two examples of local perspective not in order to advertise Newcastle to the world, but to make the point that the book itself emerges from particular locations, with all that implies. As an intervention, it is itself inscribed in the processes it documents. At the same time, those locations are also multiple and complex – as a glance at the contributors' biographies will confirm. It is the single most striking achievement of the book, I think, that it exposes so richly that complexity, as it affects the processes of musical production, dissemination and consumption. To retrieve the language of the editors' introduction, if 'nation' (and its cognates, substitutes and close relatives) had taken on the status of a 'vanishing mediator', how strongly it has re-emerged into view! And in what a multiplicity of forms! Since Freud, we know that the repressed will always return – and, often, in unforeseen or, perhaps, uncomfortable guises. Slavoj Žižek often points out that affiliations to identities such as 'nation' are rational only up to a point. What really makes them stick is something extra, a surplus in the subject – an obscene if often surreptitious enjoyment that comes with acceding to the call of a master (here, race, blood, language, leader; or even, could it be, just 'tradition'?). This is at its most obvious under totalitarian systems (the case of Serbia in the Yugoslav wars is a good example),[2] but is by no means confined to them. While it is certainly imperative that we work to make visible what seemed to vanish, it does not follow, then, that the outcome will always be politically welcome. Still, what is clear is that, whether we think synchronically (so that 'nation' features as the middle term between 'local' and 'global') or diachronically (in which case the nation-state marks the passage between the pre- and late-modern), no simple three-moment schema can measure up to the complexity of actually existing world society.

It is useful at this point to return to Žižek's discussion of the 'vanishing mediator' in *For They Know Not What They Do* (Žižek, 2002: 179–97). In dialectics, he suggests here (with support from Hegel), we need to count not to three – as is conventionally assumed – but to *four*! How so? The argument is that between the first moment (the first 'immediacy' or 'positivity') and the second (the 'absolute' or 'external' negation of the first) comes a prior moment of negation. This 'inner negation' of the first moment emerges when we think about its conditions of existence – the internal antagonisms or 'lack' that alone make it possible. Having emerged, and having provoked the mediation represented by the second (external) negation, this first negation then 'vanishes' – it is the 'vanishing mediator' – but in the process it has pushed the dialectical movement to a four-step shape. Another way of looking at this, Žižek suggests, is to grasp that the first negation emerges *retroactively*: the effect of the second negation is to change our understanding of the very first moment because the inner contradictions that enabled that moment have now come into view – thus, as 'national' appears, the meaning of the moment that precedes it shifts: it becomes, precisely, 'pre-national'. Perhaps we could push the argument even further. If the middle term in the conventional triad relates to the first by double negation, maybe a similar relation holds between the second and third; negation doubled then squared. (This would fit with Hegel's view of totality – at least in Žižek's reading (2002: 99) – as always 'squared totalization': a system actually built out of a series of *failed* totalizations, each one leading 'logically' – that is, through its failure, to the next.) What is more, if retroactivity – a concept that Žižek takes from psychoanalysis – were to be fully realized, the always reversible relationship between 'origin' and 'effect' (as in the relationship between 'fantasy' and 'reality') might provoke us to speculate on the possibility of dialectical movement in *both* directions. This is not to imagine that we can 'go back' historically (which would amount to a symptom of 'vulgar nostalgia'), but rather that looking back along the chain of 'failures' might make them available for reinscription in new mediations. This, as I see it, would be to pursue to its fullest extent Žižek's frequent injunction to 'tarry with the negative'.

The question now becomes: where is the point of leverage (in other terms, the location of *agency*)? In an alternative reading of the second of his four moments, Žižek argues that it can also function as the moment of *event*, of maximum 'openness' – hence, as a moment of heightened subjectivity, when contingent choices become (what would subsequently come to seem) necessary (and the subject vanishes again). The issue is whether negativity is to be regarded as merely intermediary, a movement between two 'normalities', or as radical refusal. It is noteworthy that Žižek also translates this system into the form of a 'Greimasian semiotic square' (see Greimas, 1987). The idea of such squares is to lay out synchronically a particular semantic field in such a way that the full range of modes of difference is represented. Thus in Figure 1 the S1/S2 relationship represents an opposition or contrary, but another level – -S1/-S2, the level of contradiction or negation – is always implied as well, even if it is less overt, lying 'below' the level of the first. In terms of Žižek's dialectic, then, the movement would be from S1 through its internal contradiction to its contrary or antithesis (S2) and finally to the 'negation of the negation' (-S2). Figure 2 shows one of Žižek's examples.

For Žižek, as already pointed out, the critical movement – the most 'open' moment – is the second (marked X for this reason; the moment of the 'vanishing mediator', representing – if we put it in Lacanian terms – the subject's encounter with the Real). In Fredric Jameson's adaptation of Greimas (1972: 162–8; 1987: xvi), however, the key position – the one that typically takes longest to fill out and is therefore the most open – is the fourth, the negation of the negation. This may be the difference between a pre- and a post-psychoanalytic teleology. Nevertheless, it is worth noting that elsewhere in Žižek's account (2002: 117–37), when he discusses Hegel's 'modes of judgement', it is the *fourth* mode that, in completing

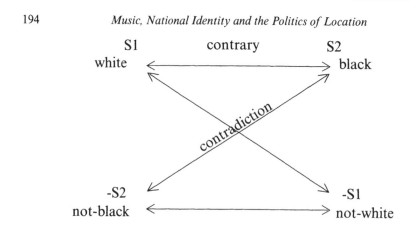

Figure 1   The Greimasian semiotic square

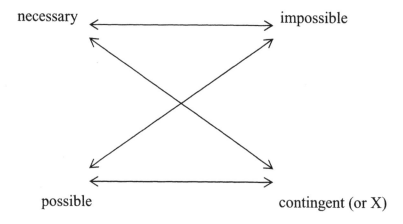

Figure 2   Žižek's Greimasian square

the dialectic, does so by positing contingency (retroactively) as necessity. This is the 'judgement of the Notion'– that is, how and under what circumstances an object measures up to its Notion – and it corresponds to the Hegelian proposition that the dialectic must take the form not only of Substance (necessity as self-movement) but also of Subject (contingency reformulated as necessity, the effect of particularizing subjectivity as it arises at the point of a gap in Substance, where Substance is inadequate to itself). Here is how Žižek puts it:

> 'Dialectics' is ultimately a teaching on how necessity arises out of contingency: on how a contingent *bricolage* produces a result which 'transcodes' its initial conditions into internal necessary moments of its self-reproduction. It is therefore Necessity itself which depends on contingency: the very gesture which changes necessity into contingency is radically contingent. (2002: 129)

The critical question now becomes which Subject will occupy this position. Far less significant is the arithmetical issue (second or fourth?); indeed, the confusion here might be taken as a symptom of the possibility already raised, that in principle *we can start at any point and move in any direction.* Is this how the famous 'negative dialectics' of Adorno can be sparked back into life?

Figures 3 and 4 – leaving all interpretation for readers to pursue – are two attempts to adapt the system to the subject matter of this book. (Here 'national' is a movable *actant* which might take different guises in different positions.)[3]

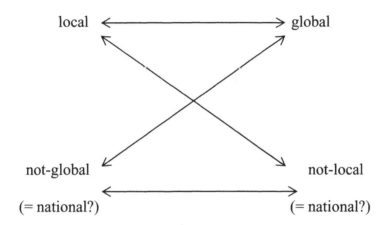

Figure 3   Local/global as a Greimasian square

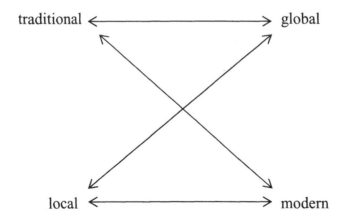

Figure 4   A second elaboration of the local/global as a Greimasian square

Although both Jameson and Žižek, in their different ways, translate the device of the 'semiotic square' into a form capable of representing dialectical movement

(into 'squared totalization' one might say), there remains, of course, a danger
with all such structuralist models that they pull thought towards synchronic
closure: there is no visible 'outside'. Strangely, much the same comment might
be made of this model's apparent intellectual opposite – what I will term, very
crudely, 'positivism', including such tendencies as the 'transcendental empiricism'
of Deleuze. Here too, albeit from a different direction, is an image of a One, an
absolute totality, populated by a multitude of laterally related forces, and again
there is no beyond. This is the world inhabited by two much discussed books
on the politics of globalization by Michael Hardt and Antonio Negri, *Empire*
(2000) and *Multitude* (2004). For Hardt and Negri, in the state of 'Empire' into
which the world is moving, the nation-state (even the USA) loses its leading role,
becoming at most a constituent in a multi-levelled network of powers, including
also transnational corporations and global institutions such as the World Bank
and International Monetary Fund, which together manage the global capitalist
system. Increasingly, the registers of the political, economic, social and cultural
coincide under the emergent hegemonic mode of 'immaterial' (that is, information-
and affect-related) production; the product, then, is social life itself, the authority
one of 'bio-power'. But resistance ('bio-political' resistance) also fills the social
space. No longer located purely in any single class, or any other social group, still
less in the 'people', this is identified with the 'multitude' – 'singularities that act
in common' (Hardt and Negri, 2004: 105),[4] whose home is indeed 'the common':
democracy moving beyond the structures of representation towards 'absolute
democracy', the rule of everybody by everybody.

In his review of *Multitude*, Tom Nairn (2005a) takes Hardt and Negri to task
– rightly, in my view – for their apocalyptic tone, in which careful political analysis
is subordinated to a quasi-religious, indeed millenarian rapture; the sense of a
utopian 'last time', grounded in a Spinozan absolutism, runs strangely parallel,
Nairn points out, to the fundamentalist fantasies of those they oppose – the 'end
of history' fanatics in Washington DC, both religious and secular.[5] Žižek's critique
of *Empire* (Žižek, 2004: 195–202) also focuses on this absolutism. Democracy
cannot be absolute, he argues, because any democratic articulation of a specific
position performs itself out in preference to those it excludes; by contrast, true
'absolute democracy' could actualize itself only through terror. Similarly, Žižek
goes on, 'multitude' can function only *as* resistance – that is, as countervailing
movements on a stage laid out by a contextualizing authority (here, global capital);
for the multitude to take power would inevitably produce the need for a substitute
Master-Signifier (most likely, a totalitarian leader). Although Hardt and Negri are
militantly anti-transcendentalist, their ontology of immanentist vitalism (which
has a philosophical lineage running from Spinoza to Deleuze, both of whom
they reference frequently) relies on an essence (what is common) that is treated as
logically preceding (rather than taking account of) any of the social antagonism
they describe. In Hegelian language, they are all Substance, and no Subject; and
yet, just as their text is actually full of subjects that do not declare themselves
('we can and must intervene': Hardt and Negri, 2004: 263), so their concept of a

multitudinous essence turns in effect into some kind of (surely transcendental) subject: 'the multitude is itself an active subject' and its task is nothing less than to bring into being 'a new race or, rather, a new humanity' (2004: 339, 356). Can we see here the 'millennial mysticism', identified in many 'world music' discourses by Martin Stokes (2003), pumped up to a particularly melodramatic point?

Despite the importance of these criticisms, however, we should credit Hardt and Negri not only with many telling arguments in both their books, but also with a thesis possessing an expansive and imaginative reach that, unlike many other globalization theories, at least attempts to measure up to the scale of the shift we are living through. Moreover, one of their key insights is pertinent to my own discussion here. This is the idea that, as the 'imperial' system approaches fulfilment – that is, as it fills the world – all sense of an *outside* – of an excluded Other – of the type which has sustained the identity of all previous social and political identities tends to be dismantled. We are not there yet. But we can see the moment rushing towards us when, on the one hand the world economy is, so to speak, *full* – that is, the supply of consumption capacity and of labour is insufficient to meet the demands of continuing expansion – and, on the other hand, the resources of natural capital (energy, water, minerals, soil productivity) come up to their limits against a backdrop of declining biodiversity and climatic efficacy. At that moment, sooner or later, 'there is no more outside' (Hardt and Negri, 2000: 186).[6] An awareness of this, usually unacknowledged or disavowed, is what now constitutes our political unconscious.[7] Characteristically, Hardt and Negri push their argument too far, suggesting that: 'In Empire, no subjectivity is outside, and all places have been subsumed in a general "non-place"' (2000: 353). On the contrary, the implications for subjectivity, and for the network of social, cultural and political affiliations on which it depends, are better understood in terms of a rebound mechanism: what used to be outside must be projected, in new ways or with new intensities, back inside. We can think of this as a new twist on the Lacanian deployment of the Möbius strip. Lacan uses this topological figure to point out the fuzziness of the boundary between 'inside' and 'outside': in traversing the strip (a rectangle twisted once, its ends joined up), we seem to cross from one face to the other but there is only one surface and only one edge – and we end up where we started. Lacan's concept of *extimité* marks the fact that the outside is always already inside the subject. While the psychoanalytic advance had thus already got to this idea – and indeed first enabled us to think it – Hardt and Negri give us a way to politicize it: by siting the idea itself directly on the social stage, they reveal its own *extimité*, for the outside was inside the body politic all the time. In a sense the Lacanian identity mechanism of the mirror phase is ratcheted up a gear, socialization doubled (as it were) producing the context for reflection squared: a sort of mirror dialectic, in which meaning can bounce, anamorphically, in many directions (and again one wonders if this is how the 'negative dialectic' might be forced back into movement).

It is in this context that the figure of the 'nation' must be rethought, not least for musical practice. It is important for the subject – musical or cultural no less than individual – that mechanisms of distinction and identification, including relationships with a Master-Signifier (a Big Other) continue to subsist; otherwise the result may be psychosis. But under hyper-*extimité*, identifications are 'scrambled'; as Others are internalized socially, borders are problematized. This, it seems to me, describes the situation that many if not all the 'world', 'national' and 'local' musics explored in this book inhabit. It is certainly the home for the many hybrid musics of the New Europeanness, as Philip Bohlman (2004: 276–331) calls it; since 1989, musical expressions of nationalism and other ethnic identities have undoubtedly been resurgent in Europe, but, as he points out, in new, mutable, multivalent and often inchoate forms. Consider the case of 'Irish music' as discussed by John O'Flynn (I mean the music labelled as such, not simply music produced in Ireland). At first positioned as subaltern – as the music of a self-consciously postcolonial state – this has moved to a hegemonic position within the symbolic economy of musical nationalism, functioning as the dominant fraction of the 'Celtic connection' and as a widely admired model for 'post-traditional' musical politics. This move clearly maps the shift of the Irish state itself from 'developing' status into a 'Celtic Tiger' incorporated within the core of the transnational economy (and, indeed, the music works as a brand within this economy as much as Guinness does). But at a deeper level what has happened here, surely, is that the music found that its previous Other had vanished, or at least had been transmuted into the shapeless flows of imperial capital; it was thus forced to fold back on itself (with a Möbius twist), assuming a position strangely *outside itself*. Or think of rap music. In the 1980s and early 1990s, this seemed clearly to be the voice of an internal colony in the USA, a 'hip-hop nation'; yet, since then American rap has become the dominant within a global rap coalition (willing or unwilling – the irony is, of course, particularly piquant in the case of France, as comes out in reading Brian George's chapter). Once again, an external limit has been reached and the music has folded back on itself, a slave becoming *at the same time* a master. Perhaps much the same applies to the case of Hispanic popular musics, both at the level of specific genres (for instance, the *flamencos jóvenes* discussed by the editors in their introduction, or the technobanda of the Los Angeles *barrios* discussed by Helena Simonett) and at the level of the musical 'latin' as a whole, as this has traversed the continents, internally and externally.

It is noticeable that all these music cultures are diasporic.[8] So, too, is Jewish music, unmentioned in this book but prominent in Bohlman's (2004) book, and another instructive example. Here is a culture that, of traumatic necessity, ended up filling the world, as it were, but then rebounding to a singular point – to Palestine/Israel, where a nationalist struggle, which is at once a symptom of a transglobal network of power, has conjured up a musical field riven by multiple ruptures (Euro/Yiddish/American/'Oriental') but at the same time with unmistakable global resonances: what had been expelled returns to the centre. Dana International's winning 1998 Eurovision Song Contest song, 'Diva', offers a striking focus. With an 'international' musical style out of Eurodisco, tricked out with orientalist gestures returning to haunt the metropolis that spawned them, the song's lyrics turn the singer's body inside out, into a body politic, 'larger than life', with 'senses nobody else has', on 'a stage which is all hers' – she is 'hysteria', 'an empire'. This is musical trash which indeed trashes borders, a point rammed home by the singer's transsexual identity.[9]

It is not surprising that diasporic musics feature prominently; their otherness has been forced to the edge of the world and has returned to the centre, on the rebound. That the two most striking cases – African-American and Jewish – became, ironically, indispensable components of the *mainstream* American popular song lineage of the twentieth century suggests that Jacques Attali (1985) was right all along – music may not exactly predict coming change in political economy but it certainly seems to have the power to encapsulate at an early stage what is coming to be – just as the fact that this extraordinary phenomenon goes largely unremarked is a sure sign that, as quasi-national mediators, they vanished. The 'double consciousness' model of subjectivity which W.E.B. Du Bois (1999 [1903]) theorized for African-American culture, but which (*mutatis mutandis*) may be generalized across to other diasporic cultures as well, should thus be rethought in the context of 'empire': with the end of outside, the self that is always already doubled with an other claimed as a self (and vice versa) is becoming normal. But to put identities in question in this way, to side-step interpellations, is inevitably to create instability, and the shaking voices (and often bodies too) of many African-American and Jewish singers point up the fact that at the root of these traditions lie founding traumas that may well mark this symptomology as a form of cultural hysteria.[10] To what extent might this also apply to other music cultures discussed in this book?

The mention of hysteria may rouse Lacanian minded readers (not to mention Žižekians) from their slumbers. And there is certainly grist that can be milled here. I am struck by the structural similarity between the 'dialectical squares' and Lacan's schema for the functions of discourse.[11] It would be nonsensical simply to conflate them; they come out of different intellectual contexts and are aimed at somewhat different problems. Still, in both cases we are dealing with formulae that understand the construction of meaning as bound up in *movement* – movement that implicates both subjects and social forces. It is telling too that, even though Lacan's schema takes the form not so much of a square linking dialectical moments as a formula linking discursive positions, here again there is a distinction between an upper level where overt factors are represented and a lower level where more implicit or repressed factors are located (Figure 5).

For Lacan there are four fundamental modes of discourse, which he associates with the Master, the University, the Hysteric and the Analyst, respectively. These are created by the variable positions in the formula taken up by four key factors: the Master-Signifier (S_1), the System of Knowledge (S_2), the (always already divided) Subject ($\$$) and lastly the issue of this division – the object of desire which covers the subject's lack and stands for excess, Plus-de-Jouir (a). The Discourse of the Master, for example, is shown in Figure 6.

200   *Music, National Identity and the Politics of Location*

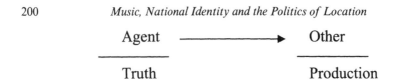

Figure 5   Lacan's schema for the functions of discourse

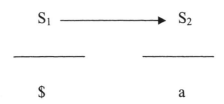

Figure 6   Lacan's Discourse of the Master

The position of agency is occupied by a Master-Signifier (in our context, it could be 'Nation' or it could be 'Capital'), which ties together for the subject – creates an identity from – the whole field of relevant knowledge (S_2). In the process, the entire system of the divided subject and his fantasies is suppressed – it is this that 'vanishes' – including even the divisions and supporting desires which structure those who take up the Master's position, who speak on his behalf. It is not difficult to see how this applies to the case of capitalist globalization, and how this Master learned his tricks from the pre-existing methods of nation-states (and Hegel – the Hegel of rational state theory – may be implicated in this).

How might we escape such totalizing structures? Unlike the Greimasian square, Lacan's schema includes the capacity for the four factors to move, clock-like, round the four positions in the formula.[12] The key lies in which factor occupies the position of Agent; thus to release what Masters make 'vanish' we need to supplant them in that position. Who is this 'we'? The Discourse of the Hysteric may point us in the direction of an answer. It should be pointed out that, although the clinical condition of hysterical neurosis has its specificity, nevertheless for Lacan (following Freud) there is also a sense in which, despite the fact that the hysterical subject is usually referred to in the feminine, all subjects are, to some extent, hysterics. Hysteria is normal. This Discourse places the divided Subject, in 'her' alienation, in all the negative conditions of her subjectivity (to recall Žižek's account of the dialectic), in the key position (Figure 7). The Hysteric, then, refuses official interpellations (master-signifiers), centring her desire (a) around a symptomatology which reveals her alienation as such. This subversion is addressed to an Other in the form of a demand for the provision of a new Master-Signifier (indeed, in the clinical condition, the desire is routed through an attempted identification with this Master), which in turn produces an alternative value-system (S_2). Thus, while the Hysteric's insistence that lack *is* Truth and that

Afterword   201

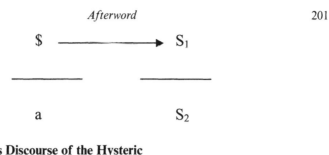

Figure 7   Lacan's Discourse of the Hysteric

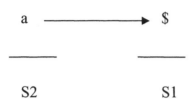

Figure 8   The Discourse of the Analyst

this situation is permanent marks her out as the only real realist, at the same time her discourse cannot move past the moment of contradiction: the negation of the negation, we might say, lies beyond her. What, then, would it mean, in the context of the struggle for musical identifications, if we were to set out to hystericize our politics?

For Lacan, the Discourse of the Hysteric is a step on the way to the Discourse of the Analyst, which is the only discourse where the possibility of *revolution* lies (Figure 8). Here the subject's fantasy (a) takes centre stage, coaxed into visibility; hence the subject, albeit never freed from networks of 'mastery', but reconciled to his own alienation, is enabled to construct new, more fluid, manifestly conflictual Master-Signifiers. Moreover, beyond the fantasy, once it has been 'traversed', lies the level of Drive – the pulsations of the fragmented body in its relation with the traumatic impossibility of the Real of *jouissance*. Žižek (2002: 272–3) has written of an *ethic of the drive*. If the imperative of a hysterical ethic is 'to keep the *desire* alive at any price' (2002: 271), the point of the analytic discourse, and of the level of drive it will tendentially reveal, is 'to mark repeatedly the trauma as such, in its very "impossibility", in its non-integrated horror ... This, then, is the point where the Left must not "give way": it must preserve the traces of all historical traumas, dreams and catastrophes which the ruling ideology of the "End of History" would prefer to obliterate – it must become itself their living monument' (2002: 273).

Some of those traumas are marked in the musics explored in this book; they are 'monuments', too, to dreams and catastrophes lying historically 'behind' the globalization ideology, 'before' but also possibly 'beyond' its moment. If, as seems likely, the self-introjection of the world-system calls up an increased demand for a psychoanalytic understanding of politics, a path that seeks the intertwining of hysterical and analytical discourses looks the right strategy. How exactly this will work is difficult to say. Perhaps we will not know until we try it.

Notes

1 For readers not from the UK, the term 'Geordie' may be unfamiliar: it is a term (somewhat contested) applied to those who were raised in Tyneside in the north-east of England and refers both to the identity and to the dialect which retains elements of Old English.

2 See Robert Hudson's chapter in this volume.

3 The term 'actant', taken from Greimas, refers to a set of semiotic elements within a narrative which together add up to some kind of uniform agency: it can work in ways similar to an 'actor' but need not be a single person.

4 This is really Deleuze's 'body without organs' (Deleuze and Guattari, 1988: 149–66) transposed to the level of the political body.

5 Some of Nairn's other criticisms (though not all) are less justified, I think.

6 I am aware that this perspective could look uncomfortably close to Hardt and Negri's absolutism and hence to the 'end of history' illusion. What distinguishes it (I believe) is the point that not only difference, but also antagonism, is likely to increase rather than disappear; if contradictions can no longer be 'resolved' by projecting difference outside, then we are going to have to get much more used to dealing, on social as well as on personal levels, with its introjection.

7 Interestingly, in writing about the 2005 Edinburgh G8 summit, Nairn comes close to the basic Hardt–Negri position. He points out that in all its previous stages capitalism had defined itself by contrasts and struggle with what it was against – but now it seems to itself to stand alone: 'capitalism needs symbiosis. Or to put it another way, it needs to breathe an air it can never itself manufacture or supply … Following the denouement of 1989, these historical assets had largely disappeared: what historical materialism had castigated as "bourgeois society" was not merely victorious but alone – condemned to the preposterous life-raft of neo-liberal orthodoxy.' However, 'there is no such thing as capitalism "as such" outside think-tanks … Its air has to come from somewhere else, and this cannot be pre-packaged, bought and sold' (Nairn 2005b: 20). I agree with Nairn that what will follow once the air begins once again to flow, once the process reaches a critical level, is less predictable than Hardt and Negri seem to allow; it is precisely what is at issue for political work.

8 As is the case of raï in Parvati Nair's chapter.

9 Bohlman (2004: 21–3) discusses the song in the context of the Eurovision Song Contest and I discuss the song and the performance in more detail in Middleton (2006).

10 My own favoured pair of exemplars, dating from a moment just before the mediatory role of these traditions 'vanished', would be Al Jolson and Cab Calloway; but readers may easily supply their own alternatives.

11 My presentation of this is simplified in the extreme. For a good summary and discussion, see Bracher (1994).

12 To be fair, Jameson, in his 'Foreword' to the English translation of Greimas's *On Meaning*, drew attention to the transformational and narratological dimensions of his semantic theory, and the potential for dialectical interpretation these produce. This,

he suggests, is most strikingly illustrated in 'the attempt, by rotating the square and generating its implicit positions, to find one's way out of the conceptual or ideological closure' (Jameson, 1987: xvi–xvii).

References

Attali, Jacques. 1985. *Noise: The Political Economy of Music*, tr. Brian Massumi (Manchester: Manchester University Press).

Bohlman, Philip V. 2004. *The Music of European Nationalism: Cultural Identity and Modern History* (Santa Barbara CA: ABC-Clio).

Bracher, Mark. 1994. 'On the Psychological and Social Functions of Language: Lacan's Theory of the Four Discourses', in *Lacanian Theory of Discourse: Subject, Structure, and Society*, ed. Mark Bracher, Marshall W. Alcorn Jr, Ronald J. Corthell and Françoise Massardier-Kenney (New York: New York University Press), 107-28.

Deleuze, Gilles and Guattari, Félix. 1988. *A Thousand Plateaus: Capitalism and Schizophrenia*, tr. Brian Massumi (London: Athlone Press).

Du Bois, W.E.B. 1999 [1903]. *The Souls of Black Folk*, ed. Henry Louis Gates Jr and Terri Hume Oliver (New York: Norton).

Greimas, Algirdas Julien. 1987. 'The Interaction of Semiotic Constraints', in *On Meaning: Selected Writings in Semiotic Theory*, tr. Paul J. Perron and Frank H. Collins (Minneapolis: University of Minnesota Press), 48-62.

Hardt, Michael and Negri, Antonio. 2000. *Empire* (Cambridge MA: Harvard University Press).

Hardt, Michael and Negri, Antonio. 2004. *Multitude* (London: Hamish Hamilton).

Jameson, Fredric. 1972. *The Prison-House of Language: A Critical Account of Structuralism* (Princeton NJ: Princeton University Press).

Jameson, Fredric. 1987. 'Foreword', in Greimas, Algirdas Julien *On Meaning: Selected Writings in Semiotic Theory*, tr. Paul J. Perron and Frank H. Collins (Minneapolis: University of Minnesota Press), vi-xxiii.

Middleton, Richard. 2006. *Voicing the Popular: On the Subjects of Popular Music* (New York: Routledge).

Nairn, Tom. 2005a. 'Make for the Boondocks', *London Review of Books*, 5 May, 11-14.

Nairn, Tom. 2005b. 'Democratic Warming', *London Review of Books*, 4 August, 19-20.

Stokes, Martin. 2003. 'Globalisation and the Politics of World Music' in *The Cultural Study of Music: A Critical Introduction* (New York: Routledge), 297-308.

Žižek, Slavoj. 2002. *For They Know Not What They Do: Enjoyment as a Political Factor*, 2nd edn (London: Verso).

Žižek, Slavoj. 2004. *Iraq: The Borrowed Kettle* (New York: Verso).

CHAPTER 15

Jazz: Music of the Multitude?[1]

Producing Jazz

In *The Producers*, Jewish-American writer and director Mel Brooks takes the measure of the Nazi dictatorship and its race crimes by means of ridicule.[2] His aim is the jackboot that stamps everything into sameness, his ammunition the materials of American pluralism, musical, cultural, sexual. His two Jewish protagonists, the producers Max Bialystock and Leo Bloom, plan a fraudulent and lucrative Broadway failure, *Springtime for Hitler*, which, however, turns into a shock success at the moment when the audience realises that its wildly over-the-top camp is a send-up. The alliance of Jew and African American that created the American musical produces (albeit unwittingly) a showbiz triumph that is used to mock Nazi visions of military hegemony. Fascism is turned into fantasy. There is irony of course in the fact that Hitler's victims – Jews, blacks, gays – get to win; but this is only by rendering him unnatural – emasculating him[3] – through their own exaggerated stereotype-hugging unnaturalness (the money-grubbing Jew; choreographic effects that reach back, through Busby Berkeley, to the routines of minstrelsy; etc.), and only at the price of 'failure' (the producers, having succeeded – against their intentions – end up in gaol).

The satire thus lies close to the bone. The aesthetic similarities revealed between showbiz extravaganza and the pantomime of fascist rallies point to a triumph of style over substance, a fetishism of surface, of *commodity*; the American Dream, manipulated by crooked producers, comes to reflect the resistible rise of the criminal dictator; the object of laughter, reflected in the mirror of entertainment, looks 'just like us'. The show is full of Oedipal (and Cain and Abel) references; this is *family* (in the gay as well as straight sense). But where is the *black* branch of the family? Visually, it's almost completely missing. But it's there in the music, and the music, as already implied, plays a central role in Brooks's strategy (he composed all the set numbers). Katherine Baber (2006) has argued that, just as Brooks in other films has

---

1   I'm grateful to participants in the Jazz Worlds/World Jazz conference held in Chicago in May 2006 for their comments on the original version of this paper. Particular thanks to Ron Radano for his subsequent detailed reading. This essay is due to appear also in a volume under the same title as the conference, edited by Philip V. Bohlman and Goffredo Plastino.

2   There are three versions of *The Producers*, the original 1968 film, a 2001 Broadway musical, and the 2005 film of the musical. I don't discuss the differences between these here, though they are revealing. The films are available on DVD: *The Producers*, Studio Canal 1002632 (1968); and *The Producers*, Sony CDT 40713 (2005).

3   This is particularly clear in the 2005 film. Roger de Bris, the gay choreographer, steps in at the last moment to play Hitler. As 'a silly, hysterical, screaming queen', this is his chance, so his equally gay assistant tells him, to give a performance 'passing for straight'. He fails (and so, in terms of the film narrative, he succeeds).

African-American 'sidekicks' assisting Jewish protagonists, so in *The Producers* music of African-American provenance plays the role of mediator. To be sure, there are significant 'Jewish' moments too – snatches of klezmer fiddle and *shtetl tanz* – but most of the key dramatic passages are marked by tributes to black music: ragtime, blues, scat, swing, cabaret jazz – not to mention tap dance. Admittedly, most of the score isn't like this. Rather, it resides squarely within the idiom of the mainstream American musical – which, however, is unimaginable without the appropriations of jazz materials and techniques that have marked its development from *Show Boat* and *The Jazz Singer* (both 1927) on. As Baber points out, *The Producers* therefore fits into a lengthy tradition in which Jews and African Americans have 'miscegenated' musically. This is a topic I'll return to. If the result is some sort of 'hybrid', what are the implications of its parentage? What is the meaning of the fact that, as a rule, the black side of the affair has been exploited, even excluded – that such marginalisation cannot help but position the result in the lineages of 'blackface'? What are the implications of this for our understanding of jazz?

Of course, the music of *The Producers*, for all its suggestive moments, isn't *really* jazz – is it? If we are to grasp jazz as a species of 'world music', we may need to relax the definitional corset. Brian Currid (2000) has suggested that the musicals *Singin' in the Rain* (1951) and *A Star Is Born* (1954) both play off an appropriation and at the same time a disavowal of blackface – that is, of a white imagination of black – in the construction of a National-Symbolic. In doing this, both reference *The Jazz Singer*, and specifically its blackface star, Al Jolson. Surely *The Producers* represents a further stage in this trajectory – a deconstruction of the myths on which these previous films, and Hollywood itself as a site of national identity-construction, rely; in this sense, it seems to posit 'America' itself, in all its ambivalent embroilment with political forces that explode the boundaries of the national, as a model which must give way to a subsequent phase, but which, in doing so, will not escape its past.[4] For Sampson Raphaelson, author of the story and play on which *The Jazz Singer* was based, 'Jazz is Irving Berlin, Al Jolson, George Gershwin, Sophie Tucker… Jews are determining the nature and scope of jazz more than any other race – more than the negroes, from whom they have stolen jazz and given it a new color and meaning.' (Quoted, Melnick 1999, 103) But, what did *he* know? Well, as Krin Gabbard reminds us (1995A, 1), in a certain sense, 'jazz was "invented" by whites' (just as, arguably, blues was too: see Middleton 2006A, 40–63); and, again in a certain sense, many black musicians have gone along with this, that is, have wanted to distance themselves from the term. Jazz, it's clear, is always produced (musically; discursively) under conditions that are indelibly marked by race. What, more precisely, then, is at stake when jazz is produced?

---

4   In the 2005 movie, as Bialystock languishes, abandoned, in jail, he dreams of his idyllic rural childhood; his Mammy calls to him (complete with Southern accent). Except that this isn't his mother, 'that's not my life'; he's remembering someone else's life – he's remembering, surely, Jolson's Southern Mammy-dreams. His accomplice, Bloom, meanwhile, whose dream at the beginning of the show of becoming a Broadway producer matches Jolson's *Jazz Singer* character, Jack Robin's longing to star on Broadway, is torn not between showbiz and synagogue (as is Robin) but between showbiz and the industrialised accountancy office in which he works (his unhappiness there represented by a 'Jewish' lament). For Brooks, 'Max and Leo are me, the ego and id of my personality': Baber 2006, 6.

Black Rhythm, Mask and Modernity

Black rhythm might be one answer to this question. As Ronald Radano (2000) has pointed out, the trope 'hot rhythm' attained a crucial prominence in discourse around African-American music in the first decades of the twentieth century. It was associated with excess, violence, intoxication, disease, physical display – and of course the body producing this 'syncopation gone mad' (474) was, provocatively, dangerously, enticingly, *black*. It's within this context that we must situate Cab Calloway's 1931 recording titled, precisely, "Black Rhythm".[5] This is a twelve-bar blues (with a bridge in the exotically moaning, minor-key style of Calloway's contemporary Minnie the Moocher numbers), and it starts unexceptionally enough with a bluesy trumpet solo. Once Calloway's vocal enters, however, the mood turns positively surreal, with a comic mélange of singing styles and accompaniment patterns. The result is clearly a satire on white myths of the black South and, in particular, myths of 'black rhythm'. Calloway's red-hot piano player 'down in Louisiana' plays, he tells us, what may sound like a wonderful 'symphony' but actually he is just improvising on a 'Southern mammy melody'; still, 'the blues that he'll compose will thrill you from your head to your toes', because he has 'hot rhythm in his hands' ('he can lay on the white ones [keys], can play on de black ones with ease'[6]). Calloway's vocal cuts between serious baritone and over-the-top high tenor bordering falsetto; and the arrangement 'cuts up' the piece with an assortment of sophisticated breaks, some in double-time, some with 'modernistic' harmonies or modulations (in the Whiteman style), others pointedly illustrative (stride piano, New Orleans clarinet, plunking banjo) – all of them caricatures in some sense of 'black rhythm'. But when all the winks have been winked, damn it, the piece *is* hot: the swing is infectious, the interlacing of materials and splicing of rhythms so precise, so *masterful,* that black rhythm, blues voice, come out on top of all stereotypes.[7] We can't understand a piece such as this except within a frame constructed out of the traditions and conventions of blackface performance, going right back to the nineteenth-century minstrel show; but still, it's as if blackface has been picked up, given a good shake, and then, still spinning, re-turned under new management.

It's an example, we might say, of *blackface negotiation.* Refusing object status, rejecting slavery, asserting mastery, deterritorialising itself, the music *answers back* to the instrumentalised role imposed by hegemonic power. How? Through what I call variously 'Harlem modernism' or 'cubist blues': Harlem modernism – a concatenation of dirty 'jungle' sounds, freaky vocal techniques and neo-primitivist rhythm; cubist blues – a blues that splinters formula, as much in Charley Patton as Charles Mingus, as much in Robert Johnson as Ornette Coleman, as much in Nina Simone as Cab Calloway.[8] This isn't to say, by the way,

---

5 On *Cab Calloway and His Orchestra 1930–1931*, Classics 516, 1990 [1931].

6 The contrast between 'white' and 'black' modes of pronunciation, as represented here, is clear in the performance. One wonders if Calloway had Irving Berlin in mind. Berlin, notoriously, could only play on the black keys (which he referred to as 'nigger keys') and was widely rumoured at this time to keep a 'little coloured boy' in his closet, who wrote all his songs. See Melnick 1999, 114–19.

7 I'm consciously writing in my own responses – yes, I'm susceptible to 'syncopation gone mad' too – an authorial move that is risky but, I believe, necessary.

8 On 'Harlem modernism' and 'cubist blues' see Middleton 2006A, 78–86. The idea that there is a distinctively African-American take on 'modernism' is far from new. Guthrie P. Ramsey (2003) refers to 'Afro-modernism'. But, although he acknowledges a 'pre-history', he places its epicentre, conventionally, in the 1940s, with bebop. I am more drawn to narratives (Baker 1987, Gilroy 1993,

that 'answering back' is all that jazz does – though I would argue that everything jazz does takes place in a context where the challenge posed by 'answering back' is unavoidable – nor that these are the only forms that 'answering back' can take: many other strategies can be found. Indeed, we should see these examples as components within a lengthy lineage, that which – to summon the terminology of Paul Gilroy (1993) – identifies black music as part of a specific *counterculture of modernity*.

This is to say that the music takes its place as a key actor within a long-running drama of alterity. The terms of this drama have become familiar in scholarship of recent decades, and I don't need to go into them in detail. In the 'pre-history', Hegel's dialectic – of subject and object, self and other, master and slave – marks an influential moment; but the basic orientation of this framework can be traced back at least as far as the Renaissance – which was also the Age of Discovery of course – and perhaps as far back as the Greeks. As the lessons of this way of thinking were absorbed, and critiqued, within subsequent critical philosophy, cultural theory and political thought, they eventually found points of particular prominence in two areas: politics on the one hand, in the shape of postcolonial theory; theory of the subject – phenomenology, post-structuralism, psychoanalysis – on the other. This fork, which never completely bifurcates, marks out an intertwining structure in which inside and outside produce each other. Slavoj Žižek puts it well:

> What characterises the European civilisation is…precisely its *ex-centered* character – the notion that the ultimate pillar of Wisdom, the secret *agalma*, the spiritual treasure, the lost object-cause of desire, which we in the West long ago betrayed, could be recuperated out there, in the forbidden exotic place. Colonization was never simply the imposition of Western values, the assimilation of the Oriental and other Others to the European sameness; it was always also the search for the lost spiritual innocence of OUR OWN civilization' (Žižek 2001, 67–8).

Although this analysis identifies a general condition, we can pick out key moments in the music history that achieve special symptomatic clarity – I would say that the moment around 1930, the moment of Cab Callaway among others, is one[9] – but jazz, and the lineages behind it, are always already constructed as an imaginary, hence a symptom *avant la lettre* of 'global culture' (as the white West has envisaged it). Speaking back (claiming autonomy) in this system means: I'm not speaking from where you think I am; not (for example) from the phantasmatic South but from *here*, from your own territory, where I, a subject of displacement – that process of displacement which had transformed the racial geography of the USA in this period – am now your neighbour (see Radano 2000, 470–75).

This is the territory of *encounter*, to use a term that has been given enormous resonance by Philip Bohlman among others (see e.g. Bohlman 2002). But the encounter is not only external but internal as well: internal to subjects, as I have already indicated, but also internal in a more obvious, political sense, internal to American society and its structures. Needless to say, on this level it's always asymmetrically structured too, structured around relationships of masters and slaves. Thus, as already indicated, race (or more broadly, formations of cultural, ethnic or national belonging) is integral to jazz – but it's not black or white, rather,

---

Radano 2000, 2003, and back to Jones 1963) that start earlier and that locate an enduring, racially configured structure of difference on which the contingencies of modernity then get to work.

9   Significantly, this was a moment when racial rhetorics in the USA display a distinct hardening and essentializing trend; see Radano forthcoming.

blackface. This is, then – for it follows – also the territory of what Robert Young (1995) has called 'colonial desire'. Again there's a lengthy back-story, tracing 'the emergence of [this particular form of] desire in history, its genealogy and its disavowal in the history of racialized thought,' and this story is intrinsic to 'culture', in the sense of this term that the West invented, as such (Young 1995, xi). But again, as Young points out (50–54), a specific shift at the moment of modernism is important: under pressure from forces of massification and egalitarianism, a hierarchical system previously applied to cultures (a model derived from Enlightenment thinking) was transposed 'inwards' on to a hierarchy linked to class; radical modernists distanced themselves from the 'popular' formations of their own societies, their elitism bolstered, ironically, by an appropriation of 'primitive' art from 'foreign' sources that had formerly often been dismissed. Jazz was a key player in this drama, a mediator of Low-Others, old and new.

In a sense, then, jazz can be seen as part of the broader modernist project, its resistance to cliché and stereotype, its persistent self-marginalisation, components of wider tendencies. I certainly want to argue that, from this point of view, jazz was modernist not from the moment of 'modern jazz' in the 1940s but from its very beginnings. At the same time, however, this role had a vital specificity. Jazz 'primitivism' was always already 'inside', just as its engagement with commercial material and with racist stereotype resulted in a hybridity that foreshadowed what would later come to be called (misleadingly) postmodern. If 'the whole program of modernism' was that 'there must be an object other than the fetish' (Dolar 2006, 69) – that is, aura must be destroyed, the authentic voice must be allowed to speak – then European modernism, unable to admit that the fetish-image was also a (racist) mask, was doomed to a failure which disruptive jazz was better placed to evade. Part of this advantage lay in black music's off-centre relation to 'technological modernism'. Always already 'phonographic' (Biers 2006) – its traces inscribed on bodily-mediated circuits of transmission – this music developed in symbiotic relation with the culture of recording, shining a particular light both on fetishism (recording *as* fetish) and on the modernist quest for *origin*, for authentic voice (which, as jazz both recognizes and contests, always fails). This locates jazz centrally within the 'discourse network' of 1900 (Kittler 1999); but at the same time, its historically embedded aesthetic of 'ragged time', deconstructing the 'archive' of established culture in ways unavailable to white élites, indicates that black modernism was thoroughly *prepared*, its 'telling inarticulacy ... a record of missed moments, a ragged voice' (Biers 2006, 118; see also Radano 2003, 230–77). It's in this light that the apparently problematic aspects of Zora Neale Hurston's celebrated delineation of the 'Characteristics of Negro Expression' (1998) begins to make perfect sense. The way that 'Hurston maps out a "vernacular" orthodoxy that builds rather obviously from modernist ... figures: asymmetry, angularity, pastiche, speed' (Radano 2003, 47) reveals itself as indebted not only to her personal style of 'ethnographic fiction' but also to the proto-modernism of the vernacular itself. And, as Nathaniel Mackey (1998) explains, the love of mimicry she emphasises, rooted in a culture where performativity is normal ('action came before speech': Hurston 1998, 298), is a *colonial* mimicry, where othering as creativity works as a counterbalance for people who are othered socially as subordinate. Fracturing the self ('New Black Music is this: Find the self, then kill it': Amiri Baraka, quoted, Mackey 1998, 522), the resulting ambivalence (Bhabha 1994) creates a space that is a blackface space – an apparatus for othering that deploys behind a mask, where marginality is a 'dislocating tilt' (Mackey 1998, 530) that contends with unequal social power.

In assessing black modernism, acknowledging this blackface stance is vital. Thus, while it's easy to talk about jazz traversing the globe, mediating and articulating cultural and political forces, and relations of power – and this is all true and necessary to say – more important is that jazz (at its most productive) always moves towards a border, an edge, a mirror, mask… If this, as it might appear, is to offer a poststructuralist reading of modernism itself – or at least to uncover points of ambivalence that it would require subsequent poststructuralist critiques to articulate – what is revealed is no soft celebration of difference for its own sake, but rather a hard-edged refusal to be pinned down to any centre of power. This is jazz's specific modernity: its negotiation with cultural power always tends towards an evacuation of the centre, to a move 'outside', refusing stasis. In this sense it was the first postcolonial music. Even when it has been ushered into the ante-rooms of legitimation (from the attempted assimilation of Armstrong and Ellington to more recent manifestations of canon-formation), alternative views from 'elsewhere' spring up, marking the structure as ex-static, eccentric, a critique of modernity from a position bridging its pre and its post. This is why definitions of jazz have been so difficult: it's not that jazz cannot be defined; it can always be defined (in particular; contingently), but it always eludes universalisation. The name works as a fetish covering a void around which multitudinous practices circulate.

The structure of *exception* has become a key topos in much recent critical thought. Giorgio Agamben, for instance, discussing the status of sovereignty (but also that of its symmetrical opposite, the outcast) focuses on that 'form of relation by which something is included solely through its exclusion': 'the rule applies to the exception in no longer applying, in withdrawing from it' (Agamben 1998, 18). Agemben compares this structure to that governing the sphere of language, which, in order to distinguish itself, needs to posit its own suspension, but can do so only in terms of its own presuppositions. As he explains, 'only the sovereign decision on the state of exception opens the space in which it is possible to trace borders between inside and outside and in which determinate rules can be assigned to determinate territories. In exactly the same way, only language as the pure potentiality to signify … divides the linguistic from the non-linguistic …' (Ibid. 21) And he has extended the comparison to Alain Badiou's deployment of set theory, in particular, the difference Badiou (2005) draws upon between *membership* and *inclusion*. In this theory, the exception falls between the categories, it's 'what cannot be included in the whole of which it is a member and cannot be a member of the whole in which it is always already included'; it corresponds, for Badiou, to his concept of *event* – 'an element of a situation such that its membership in the situation is undecidable from the perspective of the situation' (ibid. 25). What, though, might be the *appeal* of the exception, why should we be *interested* in the event? If jazz might be positioned within such frameworks, what are the dynamics that draw us towards it? Here theories drawing on psychoanalysis have more to offer. In the Lacanian re-reading of Freud, jazz might appear as an *objet a*, a bit of otherness splitting away from the subject yet always inextricably connected to it, an object-cause of desire, which can never be caught, and which Lacan also conceives as a surplus or remainder left over by the introduction of the Symbolic into the Real. Drawing on Hegel and Lacan, Žižek (1999B) has developed the idea of the 'non-all set' – an apparent totality which can only close itself by adding or subtracting a boundary-forming exception, a surplus that will not fit but that maintains the system by commanding desire. It's on the basis of this logic that Lacan declares, notoriously, 'Woman [the totality, the absolute, with capital W] does not exist' (see ibid. and also Žižek 2002, 42–6); and on this basis too that I have argued recently that 'Popular Music does not exist' (Middleton 2006A, 31–5). In this sense, 'Jazz' does not exist either.

Jazz and Empire

Paradoxically, it might seem, it's precisely the non-existence of jazz that explains why jazz was so quick, so ready, to become a world music. (The hegemony of American capital – another non-all set – has of course also been vital; indeed, the two formations are mutually imbricated, as we shall see.) The discourse of globalisation has become familiar in this context: 'Jazz – made in America, celebrated worldwide', as a well-known advertising slogan had it. As a rule, though, this discourse is couched in terms of traditional imperial power, albeit 'soft' power. As we have seen, jazz has always problematised such politics. Besides, the national/imperial model is inadequate to analysis of the current phase of capitalism, in which the global productivity of mobile speculative funds, the level of the Chinese currency and the exploitation of unregulated labour, wherever it's located, are more important to Wall Street than anything happening in the workplaces of Chicago or Detroit – or the talking-shops of Washington DC for that matter.

Chatter about 'globalisation' is everywhere, and is often facile and/or self-serving. Apocalyptics need to be qualified by history. In music, for example, the discovery and subsequent 'filling' of a world with musical (and racialized) difference has been a centuries-long process (Radano and Bohlman 2000, 16-18). Still, there is something potentially momentous about the present moment; and in trying to grasp an appropriate conjunction of historical awareness and political readiness, we can call upon a range of avenues of approach. Returning to Agemben (1998), for example, we find an argument that the relation between sovereignty, subjectivity and exclusion ('bare life'), as the very basis of politics, is both very old (it goes back to the Greeks) and progressively transformed as, from the seventeenth century, the rise and subsequent crisis of the nation-state generalises the state of exception across the population in the form of what, following Foucault, he calls 'biopolitics'. The margin moves inside – Foucault's 'great confinement' (Foucault 1991) is a response to this – as *homo sacer*, exception as bare life, 'gradually begins to coincide with the political realm, and exclusion and inclusion, outside and inside … enter into a zone of irreducible indistinction … in our age, the state of exception comes more and more to the foreground as the fundamental political structure and ultimately begins to become the rule' (9, 20). In a later book, *The Open* (2004), this political machine is supplemented by an 'anthropological machine' which, in a similar 'zone of indistinction', continually operates to decide on the question man/animal, humanity/nature – and by extension, one might add, also on the question (civilized/savage) of race – and again Agemben identifies recent political and technological forces that have the effect of cancelling the historically defined tasks allotted to nations and peoples in favour of generalised formations of management at the level of the species and its 'nature' as such.

In the background of Agamben's argument lie not only Foucault but also, in a less obvious way, Deleuze and Guattari's more economically oriented historical anthropology, in which, after a survey of the mechanisms of 'deterritorialization' and 'reterritorialization' operating in 'savage' and 'barbarian' societies, capitalism is identified as the limit case of all social development (Deleuze and Guattari 2004, 267–94). Here capital's need for constantly expanding production – constant 'decoding of flows' to use the authors' language – results in a 'field of immanence', where continual overflows of external limits are recuperated to relative limits installed within:

> The social axiomatic of modern societies is caught between two poles, and is constantly oscillating from one pole to the other. Born of decoding and deterritorialization, on the ruins of the despotic machine, these societies are caught between the Urstaat that they would like to resuscitate as an overcoding and reterritorializing unity, and the unfettered flows that carry them toward an absolute threshold. They recode with all their might, with world-wide dictatorship, local dictators, and an all-powerful police, while decoding – or allowing the decoding of – the fluent quantities of their capital and their populations. They are torn in two directions: archaism and futurism, neoarchaism and ex-futurism, paranoia and schizophrenia. (Ibid. 282)

What would happen when this movement comes up against the external limit set by the 'full body' of the earth (as Deleuze and Guattari call it)? The absolute limit of society as such is, they argue, schizophrenia. Is this – this particular, mutant form of 'hybridity' – the future?

The revisionist concept of 'Empire' put forward by Michael Hardt and Antonio Negri (2000, 2004) – on which the ideas of Deleuze and Guattari and of Foucault are strong influences – may offer some pointers.[10] Like Agemben, Hardt and Negri tell the story of 'sovereignty', but they are more interested in the geopolitical level. In the state of 'Empire' into which the world is moving, they argue, the nation-state (even the USA) loses its leading role, becoming at most a constituent in a multi-levelled network of powers, including also transnational corporations and global institutions such as the World Bank and International Monetary Fund, which together manage the global capitalist system. Increasingly the registers of the political, economic, social and cultural coincide, under the emergent hegemonic mode of 'immaterial' (that is, information- and affect-related) production; the product, then, is social life itself, the authority the Foucauldian instruments of 'bio-power'. But resistance ('bio-political' resistance) also fills the social space. No longer located purely in any single class, or any other social group, still less in the 'people', this is identified with the 'multitude' – 'singularities that act in common' (Hardt and Negri 2004, 105) – whose home is indeed 'the common': democracy moving beyond the structures of representation towards 'absolute democracy', the rule of everybody by everybody.

This millenarian absolutism is a problem, and has been the object of many criticisms, including my own (Middleton 2007, 196–7). Yet, we should credit Hardt and Negri, at least, with a thesis possessing an expansive and imaginative reach that, unlike many other globalisation theories, at least attempts to measure up to the scale of the shift we are living through. Moreover, one of their key insights is pertinent to my own discussion here. This is the idea that, as the 'imperial' system approaches fulfilment, that is, as it fills the world, all sense of an *outside* – of an excluded Other – of the type which has sustained the identity of all previous social and political identities in the West tends to be dismantled. We are not there yet. But we can see the moment rushing towards us when, on the one hand the world economy is, so to speak, *full* – that is, the supply of consumption capacity and of labour is insufficient to meet the demands of continuing expansion – and on the other hand the

---

10 The two books are actually rather different in focus and tone, *Empire* being more historically organised, *Multitude* more philosophically sweeping; moreover, the event of 9/11 came between them and clearly moved the second work in an even more apocalyptic direction than the first. I ignore these differences here, concentrating purely on the two organising concepts.

resources of natural capital (energy, water, minerals, soil productivity) come up to their limits, against a backdrop of declining biodiversity and climatic efficacy. At that moment, sooner or later, 'there is no more outside,' as Hardt and Negri put it (2000, 186). An awareness of this, usually unacknowledged or disavowed, is what now constitutes our political unconscious. Characteristically, Hardt and Negri push their argument too far, suggesting that 'In Empire, no subjectivity is outside, and all places have been subsumed in a general "non-place"' (ibid. 353). To the contrary, the implications for subjectivity, and for the network of social, cultural and political affiliations on which it depends, are better understood in terms of a rebound mechanism: what used to be outside must be projected, in new ways or with new intensities, back inside (only for new exclusions and projections to succeed them, in a continuing process in which both finitude and infinity are put in question).

Jazz, despite its insistent otherness, was always already 'inside' – born in the metropolis, in the belly of the capitalist beast, strangely familiar wherever it went, inside the citadels of power – at the same time as it was never completely assimilable. And, as inside and outside crash together, cancelling projections, forcing collisions, a hybridity (miscegenation, cross-breeding) that was always already at work is revealed as the secret of modern subjectivity itself. Jazz dirt displays what we always were, and what we need now to consciously become.

So, what of jazz and 'multitude'? Just as the concept of 'Empire' is flawed by its absolutism, so too is the 'absolute democracy' of 'multitude'; moreover, in the theory 'multitude' is fetishised and made to just *follow* the forces of Empire, that is, the equally fetishised form of global capital – it's (still) a *slave*. But 'commons' are inhabited irreducibly by antagonisms and fractures, peopled by always mutating, self-reflexive, self-cancelling protagonists. If jazz is taken to occupy this 'new place in the non-place' (a 'place defined by the productive activity that is autonomous from any external regime of measure': ibid. 357), this place is *noisy*. Moreover, while the Deleuzian rhetoric of (de/re) territorialization, on which Hardt and Negri rely, certainly catches something important about this 'new place', I would rather write it (and so would jazz, I suspect) in a more concrete language of power, as a drama of (dis/re) *possession*[11] – a drama that is thrown all the more into relief if we ask the question (the key question raised by 'world jazz'): what if the lesson of 'Empire' is to reveal that the very concept of 'totality' – that is, a way of thinking, in both ontology and in politics, founded on the concepts of 'set' and 'exception' – is specific to Western metaphysics and is reaching

---

11 Cf. my reference (Middleton 2006A, 78) to Houston Baker's take on 'Harlem modernism'. According to Baker, what is at work here is:

> a continuous interaction of two strategies: on the one hand, *mastery of form* – the 'liberating manipulation of masks' – and on the other, *deformation of mastery* – an act of deterritorialization, an assertion of selfhood that is 'never simply a coming into being, but always, also, a release from a BEING POSSESSED' – and a release into what Baker calls 'new territory' – a place that 'exists on no map'. (Quotations from Baker 1987, 15, 25, 56)

At the same time, as I also point out (Middleton 2006A, *passim*), the trope of possession (possession by, possession of) is of broader import, historically in the drama of masters and slaves, and politically, in the (ventriloquistic) dialectics of voice.

the end of its useful life?[12] If exception becomes the general rule, if multitude empowers difference everywhere, 'boundary' becomes, not irrelevant, but mundane – introjected and therefore ubiquitous – and the question of totality devolves to a more modest 'there is what there is (and might be)'. The new languages (jungle-speak; mumbo-jumbo) of Harlem modernism are far from abandoning the field of contestation (that is, of possession), but at the same time perhaps also anticipate a state-to-come where 'hybridity' would take on new kinds of significance. To grasp what this entails, we need to return to that earlier moment – to Cab Calloway, and also to Al Jolson.

Yiddish Blackface

Here I want to draw attention to Cab Calloway's pastiches of Al Jolson: Jolson, whose film, *The Jazz Singer*, smoothes over the sort of ruptures I have just been describing, offering the paradigm case of that ambivalent suture which allowed blackface mask to turn Jew – the paradigm outsider – into American, and at the same time, jazz into transnational commodity. Calloway opens the fractures up again. There are several ballads in which Calloway's references to Jolson are hard to doubt.[13] But they're even clearer in the vocal of his "St Louis Blues" (1930),[14] where his gabbling-on-a-note, declamatory register shifts and extravagant glissandi summon up images of Jolson's pseudo-cantorial style. This is a 'cubist blues', in which, as in "Black Rhythm", the vocal cuts abruptly between long held notes, quick-fire diction and scat, between high tenor and baritone registers, with imitations of freak instrumental techniques thrown in. In the latter part of the piece, the band – again as in "Black Rhythm" – 'cuts up' the flow, inserting staccato riffs and extravagant whinnying held chords in a way that intensifies the sense of dislocation encapsulated in Calloway's lyrics: 'I'm gonna leave this town, walking, talking to myself' – and he does, mumbling and shrieking. Actually, the Jolson connection is only part of quite an intricate intertextual web. Calloway's vocal starts with a stratospherically high note held for almost the whole of the first chorus before it drops an octave. The reference is almost certainly to Louis Armstrong's celebrated trumpet line in the final chorus of his "West End Blues". But Calloway's arrangement is also clearly modelled on that of Armstrong's own 1929 recording of "St Louis Blues" (the riffs in the out choruses, including the whinnying chords, are very similar, for instance). Calloway's tribute is thus not only to W.C. Handy's St Louis, not only to Al Jolson, but also to Armstrong

---

12 This isn't to gainsay the probability that the importance of boundaries is a human universal, organized around conceptions of the body ('The human body is always treated as an image of society … If there is no concern to preserve social boundaries, I would not expect to find concern with bodily boundaries': Mary Douglas [1970, 70]) or around the Derridean concept of the arche-writing (the trace as 'the arche-phenomenon of "memory," which must be thought before the opposition of nature and culture, animality and humanity, etc… this trace is the opening of the first exteriority in general, the enigmatic relationship of the living to its other and of an inside to an outside: spacing': Derrida 1976, 70) or around some other model. But the foundational status of absolute totality is a very specific case of this – one that always tends towards idealism. In this sense, Marx is an idealist as much as is Hegel or Plato, and dialectics *must* be re-thought (as I suggest later).

13 For example, "Yaller", "So Sweet", "Blues in My Heart".

14 On *Cab Calloway and His Orchestra 1930–1931*, Classics 516, 1990 [1930].

– to *Saint Louis*, who is placed before us, especially in Calloway's initial vocal chorus, as what? – a black Jew?

What opens before us here are the parallel tracks of marginality in American popular music: African-American/Jewish; and their intersection (from Berlin to Gershwin, Jolson to Eddie Cantor, Sophie Tucker to Fanny Brice, Mezz Mezzrow to Benny Goodman). This is a familiar story; the importance of Jewish involvement in music publishing, management, and song-writing, as well as performance, hardly requires establishing. But it does bear emphasis here. *The Jazz Singer* epitomises the genre of 'Yiddish Blackface'. In *The Singing Kid* (a movie from 1936) Jolson sings 'to Uncle Sammy and my mammy' on one New York rooftop while Calloway joins in on another. From the early twentieth century Jewish performers had become the main carriers of blackface: 'By the 1930s ... it had come to seem natural to many observers that Jews should have become the "best" – and best-rewarded – makers of "Black" art.' (Melnick 1999, 13) Tiptoeing carefully round the racist conflation of Jews, blacks and other 'inferior' races – the Nazis referred to 'degenerate Jewish-nigger music' but Henry Ford beat them to it with his description of 'moronic and sensuous Jewish jazz music' – we must recognise that the idea of jazz being born from a black/Jewish interaction was a commonplace: 'distorted, sick, unconscious of its destination', wrote Sampson Raphaelson, 'jazz linked polyglot, New World America to the ancient wandering Jew'; or, as Isaac Goldberg put it in 1927, 'It [jazz] reaches from the black South to the black North, but in between it has been touched by the commercial wand of the Jew.' Jazz in this period, moreover, was often housed discursively within the category of 'orientalism' (Goldberg wasn't alone in locating 'a common oriental ancestry in both Negro and Jew': quoted, Melnick 1999, 123) – which helps explain why the drug-fuelled location of Calloway's Minnie the Moocher often sounds like Chinatown. Behind the caricatures lies a genuine intersection and mutual dependency. This is Michael Rogin territory; indeed, most of the references just given come from his book *Blackface, White Noise* (1996).[15] Rogin writes brilliantly about a political alliance that assimilating Jews were able to deploy to both identify with, and distance themselves from, the black outcast: 'with no home to return to, this diaspora people creatively identified its fate with its new homeland'; the strategy of exchange, the masking strategy, was both economic and cultural: immigrant Jews, writes Rogin, were predominantly 'cultural and economic middlemen', disproportionately active in 'exchange' professions (business, media, entertainment), and their central sphere of activity was the construction of a 'melting-pot popular culture' as part of which a mainstreamed version of 'jazz' was turned into a music

---

15 References (apart from those to Melnick) from Rogin 1996, 5–6, 95–6, 98-9. This is also Jeffrey Melnick territory. Melnick (1999) documents the black-Jewish relationship in the musical sphere exhaustively, pointing out that the social dynamics of the process produced assumptions, among Jews, African Americans and others, about musical commonalities, both technical and emotional. Such assumptions are nicely encapsulated by Isaac Goldberg:

The Jew, racially, is also an Oriental and was originally much darker than he is today. He has the sad, the hysterical psychology of the oppressed race. From the cantor grandfather to the grandson who yearns "mammy" songs is no vaster a stride than from the Negro spiritual to the white "blues." The minor-major, what we might call amphibious, mode of the typical blues, with its blue notes, is by no means a stranger to the Jewish ear. The ecstatic notes of the Khassidim ... bear striking psychological analogies to the sacred and secular tunes of the Negro... The simple fact is that the Jew responds naturally to the deeper implications of jazz... (Goldberg 1930, 293–4)

for the all-American masses (ibid. 64–65). Just as the Hollywood moguls (almost all Jewish) 'Americanised themselves by interpreting gentile dreams' (ibid. 84), so too did the musicians and musical entrepreneurs; and the stuff of those dreams passed through the refracting lens of black culture. But Rogin is interested in the role of 'Jewish blackface' in the 'cultural production of America' (ibid. 11); I want to place it in a larger framework and timescale. Moreover, if I were to voice a criticism, it would be to ask whether Rogin, by reducing blackface to an instrumentally driven white expropriation, doesn't risk performing a similar exclusionary move, as far as African Americans are concerned, to the one he is criticising.

Taking the blackface mask seriously means acknowledging the full complexity of its doubling qualities – that 'double consciousness' extensively explored in black cultural theory on the basis of Du Bois's famous formulation but also the similar trope developing out of the Jewish Enlightenment: in Moses Mendelssohn's words, 'Be a Jew on the inside and a man on the outside.'[16] It also requires us, in this particular context, to grasp that the mask covers (as it reveals) a trauma: the doubleness is *damaged*; or (to turn to psychoanalytic language) is presented under the sign of *castration*. The historical-cum-mythic drama of the black phallus, and its encounters with fetishists and lynch-mobs, hardly needs comment here; its mirror image appears in the case of the circumcised Jewish penis, widely associated with castration, effeminacy and disease (see Gilman 1991). The effects are inscribed – so the myths suggest – all over the body (which is in the one case out of control, excessive, in the other distorted, pathological), and permeate the music too: the black trumpet-hero, for example, poised forever between figures of virility and threats of emasculation, at risk in the 'cutting contest' (Gabbard 1995B); the Jewish voice, thin, wavering, unnatural, uttering gibberish (Yiddish or the 'pidgin German' known as '*Mauscheln*': Gilman 1991, 10–37). Just as minstrel show jokes about huge black noses turn on genital references (see e.g. Lott 1993, 25–7, 162–3), so the Jewish nose was viewed as a displacement of the circumcised penis: the 'nose job' first became widely available around 1900 (Gilman 1991, 179–92). Isaac Goldberg, writing about the melancholy he hears in both black and Jewish singing, notes 'that *Weltschmerz* which the Jew seems to acquire with circumcision' (quoted, Melnick 1999, 183); as the body is cut, one might say, the *objet a* moves up into the throat. The relationship circled here reaches a point of particular intensity in the writing of Franz Fanon (sometime later, of course, after the holocaust had transformed the situation). As Gilman suggests (1991, 198–9), Fanon can identify (as black) with the Jew but only via a difference: under racism, the black is castrated but the Jew is killed or sterilised; this can only happen because of an implied contrast in Fanon's analysis – real body (black) as against abstract, that is racial body (Jewish); lynching/death camp; corporeal/symbolic – a contrast that rescues the black body from over-corporealization at the cost of reducing the Jewish (male) body to a racial symbol.[17]

16 Du Bois 1999, 10–11. Mendelssohn, quoted, Most 2004, 14. Most explicitly links African Americans and Jews around this 'doubling' model, and argues that all the major groups involved in development of the American musical (Irish and gays as well) used the genre, on this basis, as a form of 'self-fashioning'.

17 This could be put another way. If we follow Scarry (1985), to have a (real) body, i.e. one that can be damaged, is to be subaltern. The powerful, by contrast, have a voice (a voice of authority), which floats free of any specific corporeal positioning. On this account, blacks have bodies. Within the drama of possession, they can therefore be *dis*possessed. Jews share an abstract body, i.e. they mimic white gentile power. While this mimicry always falls short – so body returns, as a sort of spectre – it enables

These patterns might be thought in relation to the aetiology of *hysteria* – where a refusal of norms, and the blockage resulting from the impossibility of this refusal, are 'converted' into physical symptoms. Hysteria was commonly seen, in the early twentieth century, as a disease not only of women but also of (male) Jews; and indeed, several writers (Gilman 1991, Stratton 2000) have suggested that the elaboration of hysteria in early psychoanalysis is linked to its status as a 'Jewish science' (which then casts Fanon's remarks – the remarks of a black psychiatrist – in a quite specific light). Once started along this track, it becomes difficult not to place the contemporary reception of black music in the USA into a similar context. The fashionable late-nineteenth century complaint of 'neurasthenia' was seen as reflected in the fevered, out-of-control movements associated with coon song, ragtime and early jazz (Biers 2006); 'black rhythm', in all its contaminating heat and excess, mimicked and stimulated the gestures of hysterical bodies, subjects of its 'swoonings and ravings, nervous trembling beyond control', its 'ragged, hysterical effect', its 'syncope fever'.[18] The 'strain of hysteria' that Goldberg finds in jazz is, he argues, racial – 'the rising frenzy of the Negro's "ring shout" and the voluptuous ecstasies of the jazz ball are sisters under the skin' – and this encompasses also its Jewish participants, who share 'the hysterical psychology of the oppressed race' (Goldberg 1930, 292, 293), a psychology that, by the time he was writing, has made jazz, he says, into a symbol of 'world hysteria' (quoted, Melnick 1999, 24).

The condition of hysteria traverses the network of corporeal levels: physical symptoms register on the individual body the effects of pathological breakdown in the body politic and responses to its disciplinary insistences. Jazz, conceived as 'Yiddish blackface', presents a concrete materialisation of that 'biopolitics' which, following Foucault and Deleuze and Guattari, has come to pervade recent thought on globalised society – a society in which the principle encapsulated in the axiom *habeas corpus* takes on a new significance, and an intense urgency (Agamben 1998, 123–5). The range of available reference is dizzying. How is Foucault's 'political anatomy' (Foucault 1991) affected by the 'imaginary anatomy' which Lacan (1977, 4–5) ascribes to the hysteric? If jazz functions like blood circulating round (and 'infecting') the body politic, and its black protagonists like an organ all too often cut out from the American corpus, how might this structure relate to Marx's images of commodity circulation around the political-economic body (see Radano forthcoming)? Can the continual oscillation between 'body' and 'organs' figured in Deleuze and Guattari's celebrated image of the Body without Organs (2004, 8–17 and *passim*) – a metaphor that seems to underlie the mutual articulation of 'empire' and 'multitude' in Hardt and Negri's system – cast light on the body politics of jazz?

We certainly have to reckon with the fact that *that* body is 'beside itself' – that is, as a blackface body, is always positioned as an exception. If 'the Jew is the disease in the body politic' (Gilman 1991, 136), the black is 'the body of the anthropophorous animal (the body of the slave)' (Agamben 2004, 10), the beast that is forced to support his (white, gentile) betters. On the one side is a body that is damaged, one that would be normal but for what is missing,

---

them to stand for possession-as-threat (via myths of conspiracy and financial hegemony). These two trajectories circle round the 'hole' of capitalism, giving it 'body'. (The hole being the lack that gives rise to the commodity fetish, which acquires concrete manifestations in the forms of grotesque images of black and Jewish bodies.)

18 These are contemporary formulations, quoted in Radano 2003, 275, Biers 2006, 104, 105, respectively. Both works are good sources for the argument made here.

on the other a body that is excessive, instinctually overflowing, one that (as the caricatured imagery of minstrel show and coon song makes all too plain) is that of an animal. On the one side, loss; on the other, excess. Psychoanalytically, *excess* on the one hand, *loss* on the other (surplus as against disavowal and renunciation) have analogous structural functions; indeed, each *maintains* the other, via the topology of Law and Transgression, a topology mapped by the trope of *castration*, forever circling round the abyss of superego and *jouissance*: without fear – that is, acceptance of castration – no excess.

Jon Stratton has argued (2000, 52–83) that Freud's theory of the *uncanny* – the *unheimlich*, that which is at the same time strange and strangely familiar – is rooted in a particular (and particularly Jewish) sense of mimicry (that colonial mimicry which Bhabha describes as 'ambivalent' and which we may describe also as 'blackface'). The theory needs to be rewritten, therefore, as less a universal than a specific trope of modernity: what is displaced is an 'uncanny other' in the modern self, one that the Jewish 'threat' (and that of the black as well, we might add), being already inside the body politic, is pre-eminently called to represent. In the movements of this 'diasporic uncanny', may we see the African diaspora as the exception by *excess* (always another home, round the triangular trade route, always undermining Law), the Jewish diaspora as the exception by *excision* (circumcision: here there is no home; which is why it can represent the '*genus*' of belonging – belonging to Law, to culture – as such)? And then the collision of these two, so vital in the development of jazz: doesn't this present itself as a particularly powerful engine of musical response to 'Empire'? The discourses around 'travelling jazz' tend to remark on its strange *familiarity* – it seems at home everywhere, can always mix with native genes – but at the same time also home in on its *rootlessness* (the Nazi/Stalinist charge of 'cosmopolitanism' registers totalitarian alarm over this quality); multiple roots – no single origin – render jazz's multiple routes of travel a species of permanent evacuation.[19]

In their lengthy histories, these two diasporas have danced around each other. Rogin (1996, 20–21) points out that medieval theology often conflated these races as equally 'black' spiritually. More recently, in nineteenth-century racial 'science', Jews were standardly described as black, and this was commonly ascribed to inter-breeding with Africans during exile; even minute quantities of Jewish blood, it was assumed, would colour the offspring indelibly, just as the notorious 'one drop' rule in American states meant that 'passing' could

---

19 There is historical substance behind this mythology. As Stratton points out (2000, 84–136), the experience of the *ghetto* and the dialectic of *diaspora and return* are central to Jewish historical thought – just as they are too for African Americans. In both cases, maternal imagery – linked to Jewish and black mother figures – plays key roles in this formation, and we are reminded that for Freud the originary uncanny image is that of the mother's genitals, the place of one's birth. Home – *belonging* – is always gone but always at issue (another way of thinking the *possession* trope). Once again, though, there's also a contrast. According to Stratton, the specific quality of Jewish diaspora relates to a difficulty in representation – a *proscription* of representation, arising (in Freudian terms) from a refusal to murder the father; 'Jewish difference' stands for 'a blockage in the representational order of the modern, western state' (126–7), a blockage that manifests itself socially in 'incest' (marrying in). In the African-American case, however, the problem is surely one of *over*-representation – the father is always already dead, always already substituted by the Man – and the outcome is miscegenation. The stereotypical family structures – on the one side, tightly bound, set apart from the national 'family', on the other side, 'dysfunctional', broken by the intervention of the national 'family' – speak to this contrast.

only ever be skin deep (a mask).[20] By the early twentieth century, ideas of a shared racial heritage were circulating among both Jews and blacks in the USA (Gilman 1991, 99-103, 170-78; Melnick 1999, 95-102). The two diasporas come together, in the formation of modernity, as *shadows* – of each other, of the hegemonic centre – sacred and secular arms of a phantom body politic, the one standing typically for forbidden pleasures, the other for Law itself, in a bizarre configuration of Hegelian master-and-slave logic: both positioned as slaves yet at the same time both functioning, within the hegemonic imagination, as *fetishes* (of the body; of ritual law), which conjure up the shape of a new master, commodity.[21] Carried on the principle of universal exchange (money), the commercial establishment of African-American music, in which Jewish business (as well as performers and composers) played a key part, appears as a symptom pointing towards a central historical dialectic of modernity: this moves, tendentially, from the pagan body ('black rhythm'); through, second, Judaeo-Christian denial (the dirt of the body, symbolised by excrement, at once object of shame and gift to the other, generalised in the 'anal' form of money-exchange, the visual form of the blackface mask, the racial forms of pathology and exclusion);[22] thirdly, a secular sublation – jazz, from this perspective, is the first post-Christian music, for only 'slaves' (i.e. those on the receiving end of Christian guilt) were positioned where they could hope to carry this through.[23] And jazz's critical engagement with, indeed up-turning of, these two trajectories – its 'answering back' to stereotypes of primitivism on the one hand, and of masochistic discipline, law, commodity on the other (both stereotypes can be found in Adorno's view of jazz, for example[24]) – constitute a world-historical irony: jazz has universal currency, flows round the world like money (and indeed, to some extent on the back of money) but refuses to reduce itself to that fetishistic form.

There's an obvious objection to this analysis: although the Jewish Other indeed has a lengthy history in the West as a whole, it hardly has a significant presence in the USA, and certainly not in the operation of the popular music culture there, before the late nineteenth century, when Jews from Eastern Europe flooded across the Atlantic. Moreover, it fades

---

20 The 'science' was actually more convoluted than this account suggests. Jews were 'black' but at the same time, in order to contrast with the 'purity' of the white race, had to be 'mongrels', i.e. of mixed race as well; their blackness was thus often hidden (and all the more dangerous for that), whereas real blacks found 'passing' much more difficult. (See Gilman 1991, 101–3, 174–8.) Again, a difference within a similarity is revealed: blacks are, as it were, less than white while Jews are, in a way, more than (i.e. imitative of) white.

21 Given more space, this analysis should be gendered. One might start from Rogin:

If the patriarchal Jew of racist fantasy was the superego mirror of the hypermasculine, sexually rampaging black id, the hysterical or trickster Jewish man blended into the feminized blackface black. (Rogin 1996, 70)

22 There's a key moment in *The Jazz Singer* when Al Jolson sings "Dirty Hands, Dirty Face". 'Dirt' here can be read as referring not only to the blackface cork, not only to the 'dirt' of marginal cultures, especially that of black music, but also to the commercial success this performance heralds for Jolson's character, i.e. to dirty *money*. See Rogin 1996, 91–2; Lhamon 1998, 105–8.

23 I'm influenced here by the structure of historical ruptures put forward by Slavoj Žižek (2001, 106-51), though I don't follow it precisely.

24 See e.g. Adorno 1983, where, interestingly, the shackling of primitivism ('irrationality' and 'vitality' are his terms) by 'standardization' and 'commercialization' is interpreted in terms of a theory of castration symbolism. De-mystifying one myth, Adorno buys into another...

from view, in the music, after World War 2, limiting the real active force of this black-Jewish encounter to what we can term the 'long jazz age' (from ragtime, blues and coon song to swing).[25] The difficulty disappears if we identify the role of this phase as that of what has been called, by Jameson, Žižek and others, a 'vanishing mediator': a crucial mediating operator which carries out its historical work, exposing the contradictions within the previous situation and prompting the emergence of its successor, and then *vanishes* from sight, no longer required, indeed suppressed, by the new dispensation it has enabled (see Žižek 2002, 179–97). Note that for Žižek the moment of exposure (before the mediator then vanishes) is the dialectical moment of maximum contingency and openness. It's also, in a way, a moment of pure negation. It might be thought then to conjure up the 'void' or 'empty set' of Alain Badiou's ontological system (Badiou 2005, 52–69); in which case, the name of this void might well be: '*whiteness*' – the central yet disavowed organising trope of Western culture. In terms of dialectics, it's the first negation of two, thus making for a four-stage process overall. Thus it exposes the contradictions in the initial proposition, perhaps through parody or exaggeration: as here in the excessive Americanness of Hollywood fantasy, paralleled musically in, for example, Irving Berlin's show-biz jingoism, more 'American' than even 'natives' could match (from 'God Bless America' to 'There's No Business Like Show Business' encapsulates the range); a kind of screen, on which an alternative – the second stage of negation – can then be written. We can see the 'long jazz age' then as constructing such a screen for an African-American performance, but also, considered as a whole, as an indispensable prologue for what could only properly consolidate itself in more clearly postcolonial, globalised times – a time of 'Empire'. Could jazz have become quite so mobile, so readily translatable into multiple tongues, if it hadn't pioneered the encounter of diaspora and exchange – hadn't seen through the fetishes?

Go Forth and Multiply

The place coming into view here, a place that jazz has inhabited in exemplary fashion, might look uncommonly like the 'non-place' reserved for 'multitude'. Certainly, specifying the nature of this non-place – or rather (for political work is required), 'constructing, in the non-place, a new place' (Hardt and Negri 2000, 217) – is a key task for twenty-first century radicals. How is it best construed? Should we start from the impossible empty place that Žižek (1999A) reserves for ideological critique? From the (perhaps congruent) zones of indeterminacy where, for Agamben (1998, 2004), decisions of anthropological and political inclusion and exclusion must constantly be made? Or from Badiou's void (2005); or his 'evental site', a situation regarded as on the edge of the void, from where an 'event' might be precipitated? I have suggested elsewhere (Middleton 2006A, 233–8, Middleton 2006B, 23–

---

25 Between 1881 and 1930 some 2.5 million Jews, mainly from Russia and Eastern Europe, migrated to the USA. Over much the same period (actually 1882–1948) around 520,000, from much the same areas, moved to Palestine, a comparison that will become of interest shortly. (Figures from Stratton 2000, 164–92; Melnick 1999, 61.) Relative historical emptiness before this period is qualified by the importance of myth: biblical stories of slavery, exodus, Jordan and Promised Land were appropriated by African Americans to link them to the Jews, while Americans as such – subjects of myriad utopian quests, of multiple diasporas – had for many years often been seen as 'modernity's jews' (Stratton 2000, 179), a story that helped attract actual Jews to the USA.

25) that, at the level of subjectivity, such empty spaces are always also full – full of what Lacan calls *Sinthome*: not so much symptoms (of ideological interpellation) as a pre-ideological object at the heart of the subject, the object that founds desire – in other words, the formations of *drive*. What difference does this make to Badiou's notion of 'event', which seems to arise (or not) from an evental site quite outside any subjective mechanism; or to Agamben's bleak but logically impeccable presentation of the tendency to generalisation of the exception as reaching its paradigm case in the concentration camp, where, under conditions of a grotesque form of 'Empire', both nation and subject are reduced to anonymous bare life?[26]

If 'sinthomaticity' is, as I have argued (Middleton 2006A, 238–46), constituted historically, exclusion of filiation in this way is impossible. Under conditions of modernity (and increasingly so), such filiations will be hybrid. But, 'Is all hybridity the same?' (Radano and Bohlman 2000, 36) Is all hybridity desirable? Young, in considering this question (1995, 166–74), puts his trust in a Deleuzian concept of 'nomadism', conceived as a counter-practice at the level of the body (personal and social) to the forces of territorialization. But the Body without Organs – which, as formulated by Deleuze and Guattari, certainly frees up the desiring machinery of the multitudinous organs – needs the countervailing pressure of the Organs without a Body (i.e. organs subject to castration, as fraught *objets a*) if all agency of the subject isn't (once again) to be excised. Consideration of the historical oscillations of the body politic caught within the regime of such a force-field returns us to the Žižekian version of 'negative dialectics' introduced above. If, within the four-stage dialectic, the first negation only emerges as such from the standpoint of the second – that is, retroactively – which is what Žižek suggests, then the relationship is one of origin and effect, which, as psychoanalysis has taught us, is in principle reversible (indeed, was always already constructed 'in reverse' since 'originary' (rather than 'origin') appears only in the light of the supposed 'effects' that in fact produced it as such). This is not to imagine that we can 'go back' historically, but rather that looking back along the chain of 'failures' might make them available for re-inscription in new mediations. The hint here is of a kind of hybridity specific to 'Empire', where, in the incessant movements of the 'outside' back 'in' (Lacan calls this 'exstimacy,' Agamben 'estrarity'), the quest for totality will always fail but can never rely on mechanisms of exclusion to foreclose on further movement.[27]

---

26 See Agamben 1998, 119–88. 'The camp ... is the new biopolitical *nomos* of the planet.' (176) It would be fitting to add that the camp, as model of this condition, was preceded by the slave plantation. In both cases (without positing any facile historical equivalence), we see situations that in previous eras would typically have been located *outside* (i.e. outside politics as conceived within the system in question) shifted *inside*, blanks that nevertheless act as motors (economic and/or ideological) of the system itself. Yet in both cases, and contrary to what appears to be the drift of Agamben's account, residues of meaning, law, kinship survived. If the state of 'Empire' were to result not (or not only) in empowerment of multitude but in the generalisation of such enclaves or ghettos of the excluded, this survival is important. This residue of 'agency' will indeed be important to my argument shortly.

27 For 'exstimacy,' see Lacan 1992, 139. For 'estrarity,' see Agamben 1998, 110. I elaborate this version of the four-stage dialectic in more detail in Middleton 2007, 192–6 (reprinted, this volume, Chapter 14). I also explore there whether it could be brought into relation with Greimasian 'semiotic squares' and with Lacan's schema of modes of discourse (which again number four). In this schema, the 'discourse of the hysteric' is the mode of protest, of refusal. To move beyond this position – which, one might say, is the quintessential mode of twentieth-century modernist politics – requires a shift, Lacan suggests, to the 'discourse of the analyst', where the subject's fantasy (her *objet a*) takes centre stage,

In the early history of jazz, the vanishing mediator was black – 'Jazz is Irving Berlin, Al Jolson ...' – but later, under pressure from African-American identity-politics, it was Jewish. In *The Producers*, it's black again. But by this point there's a new context, in a way a context prepared by the earlier history – one we can summon up through the word 'klezmer'. While, needless to say, there are multitudes of hybridities going to form 'world jazz' at the end of the twentieth century, the case of klezmer, when placed in relation to the previous history, offers a point of maximum intensity. Radano and Bohlman (2000, 41–44) call attention to the prominence of klezmer in the 1990s, but point out that it not only looks forward (to 'millennial transit') but also back, and that within that retroactive look lies a difference: between Europe, which uses klezmer to recall the 1920s and 1930s when the black/Jewish alliance 'putatively resisted ... fascism' and therefore blurs the racial difference, and the USA, where klezmer functions as a site for the construction of Jewish modernity, a site, therefore, of revival, authenticity, survival. In both cases, we can say, though, klezmer references *belonging* – to New Europe, to old rituals. But this impulse is in latent contradiction with the diasporic force of (blackface) jazz. The contradiction emerges with full power when the problematic is shifted to Palestine – for instance, to the work of Israeli musician, Gilad Atzmon.

Atzmon doesn't play klezmer in any strict sense. But in his music – for example, in a piece such as "Al-Quds", featuring the Palestinian singer, Reem Kelani[28] – the hybrid mutations giving rise to klezmer at once intensify and shatter, revealing the ineradicable conflict between the forces of belonging (given paradigmatic focus in the politics of Zionism) and of perpetual diaspora; between, one might say, the models of old nationalism and new 'Empire'. Two diasporas (Jewish, Palestinian) are overlaid, on the same ground (musical, geographical), each splitting the other's home apart, both rendered moot by the testimony of a third, the hybrid lineage offered by jazz history. 'Al-Quds' is the Arab name for (the divided city of) Jerusalem (hence metonymically for the disputed territory of Israel/Palestine), and the piece is included, appropriately, on an album titled *Exile*. It's based on an Israeli tune associated with the 1967 war but with lyrics by Palestinian poet, Mahmoud Darwish, encapsulating love and loss of homeland beyond all racial or cultural particularity. Atzmon's reeds and Kelani's voice dialogue; the two musicians share compositional credits; Jewish tune, Arab melody and hectic post-bop improvising follow each other, as it were, seamlessly (they can do this largely because much of the piece is constructed over drones, allowing the highly inflected, highly ornamented melodic lines to flow), but stylistic differences, rather than being suppressed, seem to emerge naturally, even when abrupt. The fit is uncanny – that is, never quite at home.

Is this 'American music'? 'Jewish'? 'Middle-Eastern'? Is it 'world music'? Is it 'jazz'? Perhaps all of these, but also belonging to none alone. A hybridity, maybe, whose very concreteness locates it as near as we can imagine to a 'non-place'. If earlier encounters are seen in terms of vanishing mediators – hence perhaps as, in Badiou's terms, presenting but also covering over (retroactively) a *void* – could this irruption of concreteness be such as to qualify as belonging to an *event*, something unprecedented, unassimilable to the assumptions of the established situation? Out of the negative gesture magnificently thrown down by jazz

---

and the divided subject, reconciled to her constitutive trauma, embraces what Žižek (2002, 272–3) has called an *ethic of the drive*. To move beyond the 'hysteria' that has dominated resistant response to 'Empire', to truly empower 'multitude', perhaps demands just such a shift.

28 Gilad Atzmon and the Orient House Ensemble, "Al-Quds", *Exile*, Enja TIP-888 844 2, 2003.

universalism, which at its most imperialistically anodyne indeed offered a kind of blank space, emerges an insistent local, the very untranslatability of which, however, turns the tables on 'exile' and in effect universalises itself, standing for the genus of difference as such and bringing the outside back in. History and its rupture are both inscribed here, *simultaneously*; and multitude, in forgetting itself as totality, validates *singular event* – in Badiou's terms, a status of *belonging* which is however radically *unincluded* – as what produces the continuing political claims of jazz. Jazz 'noise' *raises Cain*, as the title of W.T. Lhamon's book on blackface performance reminds us. Jazz's shape-shifting travels conjure up for us the trope of Cain's mark, which, mythologically but also within the concrete histories of American blackface discourse, had prepared the ground for the encounter of Jewish and African exiles. Cain, a grower of grain, 'had been rooted. After he slew Abel, Cain was routed'; 'routed into cities', says Lhamon (1998, 124) – but I say, routed everywhere. The multitudes, all of us, under the sway of jazz carry his blackface mark.

Bibliography

Adorno, T.W. "Perennial Fashion – Jazz", in *Prisms*, trans. Samuel and Shierry Weber. Cambridge MA: The MIT Press, 1983.

Agamben, Giorgio. *Homo Sacer: Sovereign Power and Bare Life*, trans. Daniel Heller-Roazen. Stanford: Stanford University Press, 1998.

— *The Open: Man and Animal*, trans. Kevin Attell. Stanford: Stanford University Press, 2004.

Baber, Katherine. "'The Jew who Buried Hitler': Music and Identity in Mel Brooks's *The Producers*", *Institute for Studies in American Music Newsletter* XXXV:2 (Spring 2006): 6–7.

Badiou, Alain. *Being and Event*, trans. Oliver Feltham. London: Continuum, 2005.

Baker, Houston, Jr. *Modernism and the Harlem Renaissance*. Chicago: University of Chicago Press, 1987.

Biers, Katherine. "Syncope Fever: James Weldon Johnson and the Black Phonographic Voice", *Representations* 96 (Fall 2006): 99–125.

Bhabha, Homi. "Of Mimicry and Man: The Ambivalence of Colonial Discourse", in *The Location of Culture*. London: Routledge, 1994, 85–92.

Bohlman, Philip V. *World Music: A Very Short Introduction*. Oxford: Oxford University Press, 2002.

Currid, Brian. "'Ain't I People?': Voicing National Fantasy", in *Music and the Racial Imagination*, ed. Ronald Radano and Philip V. Bohlman. Chicago: University of Chicago Press, 2000, 113–44.

Deleuze, Gilles and Guattari, Félix. *Anti-Oedipus: Capitalism and Schizophrenia*, trans. Robert Hurley, Mark Seem and Helen R. Lane. London: Continuum, 2004 [1984].

Derrida, Jacques. *Of Grammatology*, trans. Gayatri Chakravorty Spivak. Baltimore: The Johns Hopkins University Press, 1976.

Dolar, Mladen. *A Voice and Nothing More*. Cambridge MA: The MIT Press, 2006.

Foucault, Michel. *Discipline and Punish: The Rise of the Prison*, trans. Alan Sheridan. London: Penguin, 1991.

Douglas, Mary. *Natural Symbols*. New York: Pantheon Books, 1970.

Du Bois, W.E.B. *The Souls of Black Folk* (Centenary Edition), ed. Henry Louis Gates Jr and Terri Hume Oliver. New York: Norton, 1999 [1903].

Gabbard, Krin. "Introduction: Writing the Other History", in *Representing Jazz*, ed. Krin Gabbard. Durham NC: Duke University Press, 1995A, 1–8.

— "Signifyin(g) the Phallus: *Mo' Better Blues* and Representations of the Jazz Trumpet", in *Representing Jazz*, ed. Krin Gabbard. Durham NC: Duke University Press, 1995B, 104–30.

Gilman, Sander. *The Jew's Body*. New York: Routledge, 1991.

Gilroy, Paul. *The Black Atlantic: Modernity and Double Consciousness*. London: Verso, 1993.

Goldberg, Isaac. *Tin Pan Alley: A Chronicle of the American Popular Music Racket*. New York: The John Day Company, 1930.

Hardt, Michael and Negri, Antonio. *Empire*. Cambridge MA: Harvard University Press, 2000.

— *Multitude: War and Democracy in the Age of Empire*. London: Hamish Hamilton, 2004.

Hurston, Zora Neale. "Characteristics of Negro Expression" [1934], in *The Jazz Cadence of American Culture*, ed. Robert G. O'Meally. New York: Columbia University Press, 1998, 298–310.

Kittler, Friedrich A. *Gramophone, Film, Typewriter*, trans. Geoffrey Winthrop-Young and Michael Wutz. Stanford: Stanford University Press, 1999.

Lacan, Jacques. *Écrits: A Selection*, trans. Alan Sheridan. London: Tavistock Publications, 1977.

— *The Seminar. Book VII. The Ethics of Psychoanalysis, 1959-60*, trans. Dennis Porter. London: Routledge, 1992.

Lhamon, W.T. Jr. *Raising Cain: Blackface Performance from Jim Crow to Hip Hop*. Cambridge MA: Harvard University Press, 1998.

Lott, Eric. *Love and Theft: Blackface Minstrelsy and the American Working Class*. New York: Oxford University Press, 1993.

Mackey, Nathaniel. "Other: From Noun to Verb", in *The Jazz Cadence of American Culture*, ed. Robert G. O'Meally. New York: Columbia University Press, 1998, 513–32.

Melnick, Jeffrey. *A Right to Sing the Blues: African Americans, Jews, and American Popular Song*. Cambridge MA: Harvard University Press, 1999.

Middleton, Richard. *Voicing the Popular: On the Subjects of Popular Music*. New York: Routledge, 2006A.

— "'Last Night a DJ Saved My Life': Avians, Cyborgs and Siren Bodies in the Era of Phonographic Technology", *Radical Musicology* 1 (2006B), 31 pars.

— "Afterword", in *Music, National Identity and the Politics of Location: Between the Local and the Global*, ed. Ian Biddle and Vanessa Knights. Ashgate, 2007, 191–203.

Most, Andrea. *Making Americans: Jews and the Broadway Musical*. Cambridge MA: Harvard University Press, 2004.

Radano, Ronald. "Hot Fantasies: American Modernism and the Idea of Black Rhythm", in *Music and the Racial Imagination*, ed. Ronald Radano and Philip V. Bohlman. Chicago: University of Chicago Press, 2000, 459–80.

— *Lying Up a Nation: Race and Black Music.* Chicago: University of Chicago Press, 2003.

— "Black Music's Body Politics", in *Jazz Worlds/World Jazz*, ed. Philip V. Bohlman and Goffredo Plastino, forthcoming.

Radano, Ronald and Bohlman, Philip V. "Introduction: Music and Race, Their Past, Their Present", in *Music and the Racial Imagination*, ed. Ronald Radano and Philip V. Bohlman. Chicago: University of Chicago Press, 2000, 1–53.

Rogin, Michael. *Blackface, White Noise: Jewish Immigrants in the Hollywood Melting Pot.* Berkeley: University of California Press, 1996.

Scarry, Elaine. *The Body in Pain: The Making and Unmaking of the World.* New York: Oxford University Press, 1985.

Stratton, Jon. *Coming Out Jewish: Constructing Ambivalent Identities.* London: Routledge, 2000.

Young, Robert J.C. *Colonial Desire: Hybridity in Theory, Culture and Race.* London: Routledge, 1995.

Žižek, Slavoj. "The Spectre of Ideology", in *The Žižek Reader*, ed. Elizabeth Wright and Edmond Wright. Oxford: Blackwell, 1999A, 53–86.

— "Otto Weininger, or 'Woman Doesn't Exist'", in *The Žižek Reader*, ed. Elizabeth Wright and Edmond Wright. Oxford: Blackwell, 1999B, 127–47.

— *On Belief.* Abingdon: Routledge, 2001.

— *For They Know Not What They Do: Enjoyment as a Political Factor*, 2nd edn. London: Verso, 2002.

CHAPTER 16

Vox Populi, Vox Dei.
Or, Imagine, I'm Losing My Religion (Hallelujah!):
Musical Politics after God[1]

In recent years, the ranks of popular music professors, distracted by the demands of empirical research agendas, have tended to allow their attention to withdraw from a question once central to their discipline: 'What is popular music?' An online debate on this question, published in 2005 in the journal *Popular Music* – sophisticated, well-informed and stimulating though it was – revealed a preponderantly pragmatic stance that posed little challenge to the prevailing millennial political stupor.[2] But, as the capitalist crisis now unfolding reminds us, 'the popular' was always political, and the discursive territory of 'the people', from its Greek beginnings in the contested intersections of *demos*, *ethnos* and *ochlos* (mob), guardians, masters, plebeians and slaves, always projected controversy, conflict, scandal. On one account, politics indeed begins here, for as Jacques Rancière recalls, politics

> is the apparatus whereby the people are kept within the visible sphere that the people's name rules over: as the subject that occupies the gap between the fiction of community on the one hand and the surfeit of reality of the populace on the other, the people serve both to link and to separate the two, themselves alternately taking on and losing definition as the features of the two intermingle.[3]

Here, any simple descriptivism struggles.

Readers of my book *Studying Popular Music* may recall that, for me, the point was not to *describe* 'popular music' but to position the name of 'the people' within the discursive matrix formed by the ever-changing interplay of forces to which Rancière refers.[4] But the key question for any neo-Gramscian approach, such as I attempted there, was always: how exactly does the 'articulation' of ideological elements get to work – or, more precisely, from where? Laclau and Mouffe's devastating critique of the economic essentialism surviving in Gramsci, and subsequently in Althusser (the myth of the economic 'final instance'), re-wrote 'class' as a subject whose discursive constitution can never be just 'superstructural', and opened the way to a 'post-marxist' politics of articulation.[5] But the price was a post-structuralist conception of the subject (perpetual sliding of the signifier and all that) which

---

1   This essay had its beginnings in papers given at Newcastle University in 2005 and 2008, and the University of Chicago in 2006. I'd like to thank participants for their comments.

2   'Can We Get Rid of the "Popular" in Popular Music? A Virtual Symposium with Contributions from the International Advisory Editors of *Popular Music*', *Popular Music*, 24:1 (2005), 133–45. The opening section of the current essay is adapted from my own contribution to this symposium.

3   Jacques Rancière, *On the Shores of Politics*, tr. Liz Heron (London: Verso, 2007 [1995]), 93.

4   See Richard Middleton, *Studying Popular Music* (Milton Keynes: Open University Press, 1990), Ch. 1.

5   Ernesto Laclau and Chantal Mouffe, *Hegemony and Socialist Strategy: Towards a Radical Democratic Politics* (London: Verso, 1985).

comes uncomfortably close to the crudest forms of identity politics. However 'popular music' is articulated, whatever we try to make it mean, 'the people' as subject is embedded somewhere within it, and with an emotional charge that will apparently just not go away. We need to account for that investment as well as the (necessary) mutability of content.

Following Slavoj Žižek's deployment of Lacan's rather notorious aphorism, '(The) Woman does not exist', we might say that '(The) Popular music does not exist'.[6] This doesn't mean that individual beings/objects/practices ('women'; 'songs'; 'the popular') located under the relevant concept don't have empirical existence, but that the category as such stands for an abstract ideal which at one and the same time covers over an internal blockage (it can never fully be what it wants to be, as it were), projects its lack on to its (equally lacking) antagonistic Other, and is hence in some sense always spoken from the position of that Other, from elsewhere. (My parenthesis round the definite article – in Lacan/ Žižek it's a bar through the word – marks this structure of lack.) This is why, just as (even more notoriously) 'Woman is the symptom of man', so 'popular music' is the symptom of its Other. On one level, there's a symmetry and you can try inverting the relationship (thus feminists can say, 'Man is the symptom of woman'), but such inversions don't destroy the binary structure, which is in any case at bottom asymmetrical: one side (the Master) is constructed as *universal*, the other (the Slave) as that particularity which makes the Master possible. You can read this position either as tough-minded realism (which would help explain, for example, why feminism hasn't yet triumphed and why most university music departments and degree courses are still given the universalistic title 'music' while 'popular music' courses have to be given their own marker) or as a problematic foreclosure of politics. Interestingly, Žižek's position, it seems to me, is congruent with Adorno's celebrated aphorism, to the effect that 'popular' and 'serious' are 'torn halves of an integral freedom, to which however they do not add up':[7] not as in a simplistic reading (the two sides have split apart and for historical reasons can't be stuck together again) but in the sense that they represent mutually contradictory conceptualisations *of the same field*. So is Žižek simply re-inscribing the dead end we find in negative dialectics? He says not: for him, the 'negation of the negation' doesn't freeze the dialectic but reveals negation as a sort of positivity referring back to the constitutive contradiction in the object itself.[8] Anyway, one way or another, I suspect the answer lies, somehow, in the status of that void – Adorno's 'do not add up', that is, what 'falls out', what cannot be symbolised, when the constitutive antagonism forms – which is presented as a condition of subjectivity itself.

Žižek's position is grounded, more broadly, in an anti-descriptivist theory of naming. Names ('the people', 'music', 'popular music'), he argues, don't acquire meaning through reference to given properties but through a 'primal baptism' followed up in a 'chain of tradition'. (You can test this: are there any properties whatsoever that would necessarily rule out a given musical experience from the category 'popular music'? I think the answer is, no.) Thus, 'popular music' is just: *that*. (This is also the moment of Jean-Luc Nancy's 'ecceity': a gesture, outside all specific qualities, all *telos*, all agency; an opening of the eyes

---

6   For Žižek's argument, see Slavoj Žižek, 'Otto Weininger, or "Woman Doesn't Exist"', in *The Žižek Reader*, ed. Elizabeth Wright and Edmond Wright (Oxford: Blackwell, 1999), 127–47.

7   Letter to Walter Benjamin, in Ernst Bloch, Gyorgy Lukács, Bertold Brecht, Walter Benjamin and T.W. Adorno, *Aesthetics and Politics* (London: Verso, 1977), 123.

8   See Slavoj Žižek, *The Sublime Object of Ideology* (London: Verso, 1989), 173–8.

[or ears] – 'behold!'[9]) But the moment of the baptism is mythical: it appears with the act of naming itself, an 'always already' implied retroactively by its effects once we're in the Symbolic. The name, qua master-signifier (the Lacanian *point de capiton*, or quilting-point), is *empty*; yet it does have a sort of objective correlative, namely, the famous Lacanian *objet a* – Žižek's 'sublime object', a little bit of the Real, what is in the object more than itself, what the symbolic process must exclude if it is to function at all, the object-cause of desire. This object corresponds, on the side of the subject, with the 'belief before belief' which makes subjectivation (the articulatory play of contesting subject-positions) possible. 'Popular music' interpellates its listeners (at least it does if they turn round when it says 'Hey!'); but why should we *want* to turn – or, more precisely, *what* is it that turns? Žižek's answer is: that meaningless piece of stuff, that object in the subject, which alone ensures its consistency; it's the Real which answers.

What, for us, is this object-cause of desire but 'the people' – or rather, that meaningless and impossible site of *jouissance* underlying and supporting all social fantasies of 'the popular'? Where else would we find the source of that siren call, the people's voice?

If, in the enfeebled state of political thought today, this suggestion elicits incomprehension or cynicism, such responses are nothing new. The nineteenth-century's celebrated encapsulation, 'Vox Populi, Vox Dei', was familiar (and also, perhaps, threatening) enough to attract mockery from Flaubert, Nietzsche and no doubt many others.[10] Yet its echoes persist, even now, long after the death of God was announced; after, too, so many betrayals of and by the People.

***

'Vox Populi, Vox Dei'; the voice of the people is the voice of God: a slogan which, while immensely popular in the nineteenth century, had a history going back long before this, at least to the Middle Ages, perhaps as far as biblical times. This is where my book, *Voicing the Popular*, starts – with the people speaking for God/God for the people; at any rate, with the people assuming sovereign powers.[11] I focus there on the people side of this equation: the implications for understandings of popular culture and music; but it will be impossible to grasp those implications fully without thinking about the God side: about the *authority*,

---

9 Jean-Luc Nancy, *The Birth to Presence*, tr. Brian Holmes et al (Stanford CA: Stanford University Press, 1993), 46–7. 'Ecceity' is what Giorgio Agamben (*Homo Sacer: Sovereign Power and Bare Life*, tr. Daniel Heller-Roazen, Stanford: Stanford University Press, 1998) might, by analogy with his concept of 'bare life', call 'bare presence'; it's the 'presence' of a being that is abandoned, under ban, that is, excluded – excluded from all systems of Law, all concepts, language (ultimately, from God). Later in his book, Nancy will stress that 'at the heart of thing-words, as at the heart of all things, there is no language', and that at this level, anterior to names, there is only a *voici*, a pronominal 'there is this', a 'some thing', the 'some' of which is a 'whatever' – an endless multiplicity. See *Birth to Presence*, 167–88 (168, 185). I will have occasion to return to many of the points signalled here.

10 Gustave Flaubert, *Le dictionnaire des idées reçues*, ed. E.-L. Ferrèrre (Paris: Louis Conard, 1913 [published posthumously from notes made in the 1870s]), 43; Friedrich Nietzsche, *Human, All Too Human: A Book for Free Spirits*, tr. R.J Hollindale (Cambridge: Cambridge University Press, 1996 [1878]), 255–6.

11 Richard Middleton, *Voicing the Popular: On the Subjects of Popular Music* (New York: Routledge, 2006), 1–6.

the *originary power*, exerted by His voice – ceded, it would appear, to a newer god. I'll return later on to the other term in this phrase – voice – and indeed this will function as a subterranean thread running throughout. But, to start with God. What happens, musically, to His authority when God dies? Two popular songs can help get the discussion under way.

John Lennon's 'Imagine'[12] sketches a post-religious socialist-humanist utopia ('imagine there's no heaven/no possessions', etc). But its would-be democratic vision – 'imagine all the people' – is undercut, even vitiated, by several features of the record. First, by the record's commodity status – it *is* a possession. This is, secondly, connected to the author-singer's celebrity status – Lennon possesses The Truth. Which in turn, thirdly, is *centred*, given a centre, musically; centred on two levels: on the one hand, in form – think of the sense of tonal closure, the manipulation of open and closed phrases, the associations of the ballad genre (Dave Laing traces the lineage of ballad romance to the discourse of 'courtly love', a secularisation of mediaeval Mariolatry, which in turn was an eroticisation of the Christian master-and-slave relationship[13]); and centred, on the other hand, in intense vocal presence: this adopts ballad's private, 'shrivelled' focus and, addressing *us* as unworthy disciples, acolytes, lovers, attempts to transmute it 'upwards' into a world-political claim – a would-be *cult*. Lennon is the God his song forswears.

Think now about the REM song, 'Losing My Religion'.[14] Here, by contrast, the centre refuses to appear: modal harmony obscures tonal centre; the vocal circles obsessively round the same few notes; Michael Stipe's vocal tone is flat, unchanging, refusing 'personality'; meaning is obscure – but seems to be designed to project an image, to project our gaze, elsewhere ('that's me in the corner/in the spotlight/I thought I saw/heard'), a place from which the singer has withdrawn.

The vocabulary of the lyrics positively compels a psychoanalytic reading: there's religion; confession; dream; tears; excess, loss and falling short ('I've said too much, I haven't said enough'); spotlight and corner; unidentified voices, heard or not, uncanny, spectral... The relentless groove and the instrumental fills produce a repeating architecture from which there seems no exit; perhaps this is a *screen*, beyond which lie unexplained mysteries, on which is projected a *dream*. If 'Imagine' offers a fantasy of a straightforward, programmatic type, 'Losing My Religion' seems to script a more uncanny, quasi-theatrical *fantasy-scene*. Somehow one is reminded of the Freudian dream, in which a father, with the body of his dead son lying in the next room, dreams that the son wakes him, crying 'Father, can't you see I'm burning?' Only to find, on waking, that a candle has fallen on the body, which really is burning. 'Father, can't you see I'm burning?' – such a resonant question, which Slavoj Žižek has described as the psychoanalytic version of the essential Christian moment: 'Father, why have you forsaken me?' What's the motivation of this dream? It is, says Lacan, the desire to relive, prolong, encounter again, what has always already been missed, been failed; 'what is he burning with if not...the weight of the sins of the father...?'[15]

---

12 John Lennon, 'Imagine', *Imagine* (Apple PAS 10004, 1971).

13 Dave Laing, *The Sound of Our Time* (London: Sheed and Ward, 1969), 57–60.

14 REM, 'Losing My Religion', *Out of Time* (Warner Bros 7599-26496-2, 1991).

15 Sigmund Freud, *The Interpretation of Dreams*, tr. Joyce Crick (Oxford: Oxford University Press, 1999 [1899]), 330–31; Slavoj Žižek, *On Belief* (London and New York: Routledge, 2001), 145; Jacques Lacan, *The Four Fundamental Concepts of Psycho-Analysis*, tr. Alan Sheridan (Harmondsworth: Penguin, 1979), 34.

I read the song as circling round such an encounter; as articulating a sense of a missing centre, a desire actually to miss what is at the same time desired and in any case cannot be evaded – but which can never appear and has irrevocably failed. This lost centre can go, I will suggest, under the name 'God'.

Or, in psychoanalytic metaphor (drawing on this discipline's Judaeo-Christian roots), Name-of-the-Father. Even with the so-called 'death of God' – even with the Foucauldian 'death of man' (which, arguably, is what stymies Lennon's project) – this figure survives; and must survive, in some form, if the symbolic system we call 'reality', and with it culture and politics, isn't to crumble completely. Without it – more precisely, without the Big Other of the symbolic order on the one hand, the nameless Thing, excluded, at which we can only tremble, on the other, guardians respectively of the interlinked forces of 'truth' and '*jouissance*' – without this structure, psychosis follows. As Lacan puts it, 'The father, the Name-of-the-Father, sustains the structure of desire with the structure of the law.' For Lacan, 'the true formula of atheism is not *God is dead* – even by basing the origins of the function of the father upon his murder, Freud protects the father – the true formula of atheism is *God is unconscious.*'[16] God has fallen asleep – but is still there, unconscious; or, from a different angle, He is *in* the (our) unconscious, murdered but as a result all the more powerful. Either way, God is split, barred, extimate, ex-static (at once inside and outside), and the two angles are correlative: as Žižek puts it, the 'impenetrability of God to Himself, discernible in Christ's "Father, why did you forsake me?,"… this total abandonment by God is the point at which Christ becomes FULLY human, the point at which the *radical gap that separates God from man is transposed into God Himself.*'[17]

The bereaved know that the loved one is never more present, more alive, than when dead. Although I am following here a psychoanalaytic path, the conclusion isn't dependent on such a route. Nancy's take on this creative de-production finds a particularly effective image in the paralysis suffered by the declining Nietzsche. In the madness of his fragmentary utterances, Nietzsche presents a sort of 'caricature' of the God whom he has himself killed off: 'God outliving himself, but paralyzed'; 'God presents himself dead…he is the incarnation of the dead…the absence of God caused anxiety, but the presence of God dead, and of his voice, paralyzes'. Nietzsche's 'I am God' is in a sense no more than the over-mighty subject's *ego sum*, and on both levels is strictly speaking mad, 'the statement of a subject who affirms himself to be anterior to his own production', to be identical to the 'null moment' (death) when no 'itself' was yet available. Thus '"I am God" means "I am dead".' This is what God is – 'the absolute and void self-knowledge of the complete night in which the subject produces itself, that is to say, paralyzes itself'.[18]

What does this problematic mean for secular belief – for a 'critical atheism' (to name my own position)? Žižek again: his theory of ideology posits, against both post-ideology and total-ideology models, the notion of an *empty space*, from where – if we can imagine the impossible task of occupying it – ideology critique is still possible; possible *provided* it remains empty of positive content.[19] Similarly, occupying the 'God-space' enables agency

---

16 Lacan, *Fundamental Concepts*, 34, 59.

17 Žižek, *Belief*, 145–6.

18 Nancy, *Birth to Presence*, 48–57; quotations from pp. 48, 50, 54 and 56.

19 See Slavoj Žižek, 'The Spectre of Ideology', in *The Žižek Reader*, ed. Elizabeth Wright and Edmond Wright (Oxford: Blackwell, 1999), 53–86.

– commitment, authority, action, creativity – provided it continually evacuates specific justifications, displaces content: that is (putting it another way), operates on *faith*, not *belief*. Or (another approach) this space must be occupied only by a proto-god who knows he does not know himself – whose bungling of creation, whose impotence, fully reflects our own.

The plausibility of my reading of 'Losing My Religion' matters less than the overall argument: that assessing music, certainly any popular music, from something like the perspective I have just outlined is the condition of musical politics today. Without it, musical politics is either written off (equivalent to the idea that we are 'beyond ideology') or reduced to New Age market choice (equivalent to the idea that ideology is inescapable, and any choice as good as another).

Excursus 1. This argument clearly has its starting-point in the experience of secular society – and its insistence should, one might think, be qualified by the fact that on a world scale the process of secularisation is very uneven. Moreover, in recent decades secularisation has called forth a dramatic and, for many, quite unexpected religious riposte, including instances of an intense, violent and fundamentalist nature – a move provoking, in turn, an equally fundamentalist response from representatives of simplistic atheism; if God is dead, he will apparently not fade away (and nor will His deniers). But if He is in the unconscious, or if he is paralysed, this isn't so surprising (and the whole dance of believers and unbelievers actually re-cycles an earlier phase, when, at the turn of the nineteenth and twentieth centuries, 'fundamentalism', both Christian and other, was invented, against the background of an anxious perception of 'modernist' threat: Darwin, Nietzsche and secular politics). Charles Taylor characterises the bottom line underpinning the whole shift in a way that is quietly devastating: 'Naïveté is now unavailable to anyone, believer or unbeliever alike.'[20] I would be prepared to be more provocative, for the crux may lie in that phrase 'called forth' which I used a moment ago: globalisation means that theocratic resurgence, much of which has a distinctly hysterical tinge, only registers against a horizon which is normatively, even where emergently, secular, while even in those developed societies where religious practice survives strongly, mainstream popular culture tells the truth about its changed conditions, acknowledging God as at most a haunting absence. Thus, even if any true secularism will have a religious colouring – or to put it in terms indebted to the philosopher Ernst Bloch, if all religion as practiced is a kind of pre-illumination of a utopian secular grace – I stick to my view that, precisely in the interest of pursuing the implications of such a trajectory, God will have to be killed over again, as often as it takes. Christianity always implied as much.[21] Feminists saw this early: why is God – why is, still, the Name-of-the-Father – *male*, and how, then, might women best stage His death (questions broached in some progressive branches of theology)? John Lennon, for all his late feminism and the influence of Yoko Ono, evades such questions in 'Imagine'; perhaps the blankly unerotic voice of the sexually ambiguous Michael Stipe, retreating in 'Losing My Religion' from any patriarchal centrality, raises them implicitly?

The most intriguing case of the mutual imbrication of secularity and religion is provided by the USA, home (actually or spiritually) of just such recordings as these. The 'secularisation of providence', in Rancière's apt phrase,[22] roots the Constitution in a rigorous separation of state and religion; and

---

20 Charles Taylor, *A Secular Age* (Cambridge MA: Harvard University Press, 2007), 21. Taylor's whole book works to problematise the idea of a rigid bifurcation between secular and religious in modern society.

21 Bloch writes somewhere, 'only an atheist can be a good Christian and only a Christian can be a good atheist'. Here he stands in an ancient apophatic tradition. Pseudo-Dionysius argues that God is 'beyond every assertion and every denial', and Victorinus that 'the being of God is so different from all existence known to us that we can best point to it as non-existence'.

22 Rancière, *Shores of Politics*, 21.

the pursuit of 'self-evident' secular rights has established the society as the leading exemplar of life dedicated to a purely human prosperity and autonomy. Yet the move here is as much an exchange as a progression. The 'We' of 'the People' is elided with providential teleology ('manifest destiny'), and the shift of sovereignty from divinely ordained monarch to the *demos* is carried by a transfer of political theology, from the mediaeval doctrine of 'the King's two bodies' (one material, the other transcendent) to an implicit conception of 'the President's two bodies'. The quasi-religious aura of the Presidency, and of the Constitution's founding canonic texts, has often been noted, along with the ritualistic force of presidential inaugurations. Nowhere was this more obvious than in the recent inauguration of Barack Obama, the outsider who was now also the Chosen One, the (black) Christian 'with the funny Muslim name', who, accompanied by a 'pilgrimage' of millions, entered Washington DC – his Jerusalem, his Promised Land – to an acclamation of Hallelujahs. Actually Obama may be said to have *three* bodies, first the transcendent corpus of office, second his all-too-vulnerable human frame, but third the virtual, cyborgian body ghosting through the internet, which spiritually sustained his campaign and has much of the task of sustaining his power; thus making the quasi-Christian model complete.[23]

John Updike has one of his protagonists comment on his country's originary settler Protestantism in the following terms: 'The Holy Ghost... who the hell is that? Some pigeon, that's all... but that God-awful faith... when it burns out... it leaves a dead spot. Love it or leave it...a dead spot. That's where America is... in that dead spot.'[24] *Love it or leave it*: a key phrase surely; in the twentieth century, American popular culture projected the secular themes of the society around the world, and yet – certainly in the music – it's often shot through with residues of religious feeling. Indeed, as, in the second half of the century, US domination of secular global politics was accompanied by a paradoxical intensification of religious practice in its public culture, so the popular music saw if anything more obvious manifestations of such feeling. Rock 'n' roll called into the mainstream, via the mediation of Southern folk, country, R&B and Soul music, multiple symptoms of 'that good old way', applying them, however, to the imperatives of sex and money. Across the society, a hardening of both secular ambitions and of the ecstasies of faith located 'loving' and 'leaving' as reciprocal movements, each excluding but also implicating – implicating by excluding – the other: a paralytic *fit* worthy of the aging Nietzsche.

In a quite different philosophical register from Charles Taylor's, Jacques Derrida also engages this reciprocal movement, arguing that the contemporary 'rebirth' of religion and the hegemony of what he calls tele-technoscientific reason, far from being simply in opposition, actually co-produce each other. They 'always have made common cause, bound to one another by the band of their opposition', and for Derrida this relationship is one structured by (auto)immunity: each side protects itself against the other – 'secretes its own antidote' – but by virtue of their common foundations – in 'faith' and its rituals, in mechanical iterability – must therefore also 'protect itself against its own protection, its own police, its own power of rejection, in short against its own, which is to say, against its own immunity'.[25] Similar

23 On the transition from a patrimonial to a democratic model of sovereignty (both in their way absolutist), see Michael Hardt and Antonio Negri, *Empire* (Cambridge MA: Harvard University Press, 2000), 69–113. Hardt and Negri are much concerned with the biopolitical forces making possible 'the President's third body' – the cyborgian forces of virtual production – a factor that will become important too later in my own argument.

24 John Updike, *Bech at Bay: A Quasi-Novel* (London: Hamish Hamilton, 1999), 204.

25 Jacques Derrida, 'Faith and Knowledge: The Two Sources of "Religion" at the Limits of Reason Alone', in *Acts of Religion*, ed. Gil Anidjar (New York: Routledge, 2002), 42–101 (43, 44). The work of 'immunity' is key to Roberto Esposito's theory of community, which will feature towards the end of this essay. In the light of Derrida's analytic, it's worth drawing attention to Obama's internet campaign song, 'Yes We Can', in which Obama's words are 'tele-techoscientifically' stitched together with those of many performers and other supporters over a riff whose mechanico-ritualistic repetitions point up the intricate 'common cause' of 'faith and knowledge' in a way that is also cemented by the musical

terms characterise many of the discourses, including Derrida's own, that grappled critically with the implications of the epicentre of our own millennial moment – 'September 11'. Two fundamentalisms, two tribes (which can be personified: Bushes and Bin Ladens), each already deeply implicated in the other, both positively and negatively, struggle for control not only of souls but also of the properties of the world political body – land, oil, life itself (most obviously: control of women) – in a way that tends inexorably towards reciprocal suicides. As if the iconic faces of two brothers gradually petrify into death masks, revealing a twitching corpse for which any gain, for either faith or reason, is also a loss.

'Losing My Religion' was, it seems, probably not intended to be about religion at all in any obvious way: 'losing my religion' is a Southern phrase meaning 'losing one's patience or temper' (but then, why associate this condition with religion? Surely so as to suggest a loss of certainty, of belonging, that is, losing a place in the Symbolic order; moreover, the video is full of religious imagery). According to Stipe, the song is a response to Sting's 'Every Breath You Take', a 'stalking song'. In that sense, then, it *is* about God – about the god's eye view; and also keeping an eye on God; so altogether, one might say it's about obsessive ownership, veneration, investment – in short, fetishism: a fetishism that is of course sexual but also quasi-religious, in that, for Stipe as for Sting – and Lennon as well – the stalking scenario can't help but conjure up the economy of stardom, of *celebrity* – perhaps as close as many of us come now to a visible or audible god.

Fetishism, that nexus where religion meets human production and self-production, has been subject to a long history of displacements. But it's always centred on a transfer of human attributes on to an external object, which, however disavowed, is treated as source of power. In Michael Rogin's eloquent phrase, it's 'a story masquerading as an object'.[26] The fetish is secularised, in commodity, in erotic object (but this process had already been anticipated in Christianity, with the murder of God); and then it's vernacularised, and even inverted, in popular culture – the slave, slave-labour, mediating force of commodity-fetishism, competing, in the cultural forms of the Low, for positions of mastery.

In popular song's twentieth-century history, we find fetishism everywhere. Why do its symptoms (obsessive possession, voyeurism, perverse transfers of love-object) come to 'stalk' popular song so powerfully? This is part of a broader secularisation process; and also linked to intensifying eroticising of commodity. But it's also, maybe, because *voice*, the core of song, is (contrary to what we might at first assume) the originary attribute of a fetish: divine breath or sound typically brings the world into existence; Yahweh is invisible, disembodied, but his voice must be obeyed ('And God said…', as *Genesis* has it). The ventriloquial structure of this fetish-voice initiates the emergent economy of *possession* (possessing, being possessed, *having and being*), which reaches a specific stage in popular song (especially in the also disembodied His Masters Voice of recorded song). Here politics are organised

---

style (pop plus gospel) together with the 'providential' cast of the historical lineage summoned quite consciously in the song's lyrics ('yes we can'). See http://yeswecan.dipdive.com/

That 'faith' and 'knowledge', far from being contradictory, actually intertwine was not a new argument when Derrida put it. It's there, for example – together with reference to its underpinnings in the repetitions of ritual – in Theodor W. Adorno and Max Horkheimer, *Dialectic of Enlightenment*, tr. John Cumming (London: Verso, 1997 [1944]), 12–13; which is to say, then, that the secular forces of enlightenment itself cannot escape their debts to religion.

26 Michael Rogin, *Blackface, White Noise: Jewish Immigrants in the Hollywood Melting Pot* (Berkeley: University of California Press, 1996), 183.

most obviously around the possession-economy of *gender*, and around its mediations on the register of *race*. This regime is grounded still, however, in negotiations of *class*, in the struggles of the *Low* – or, to put this in more traditionally Marxist terms, it's rooted still in structures of *exchange*; that is, in commodity (for 'money talks' also, and commodity has a voice); and commodity here reaches a particularly complex form in the figure of the *star*. In the commodity system, as Adorno and Horkheimer put it, 'exchange itself has become a fetish';[27] and digital simulations of celebrity compound the interest to infinity. How could musical politics move beyond this?

How, that is, could it move beyond *representation*? At bottom, fetishism stands for the reduction of mimetic movement – repetition of difference – to a relationship of equivalence in a structure of possession: that is, to *representation*. Thus its history (each successive stage of which has 'vanished' as it has been naturalised) has operated as a mediator of that broader history through which the human species has pursued its self-understanding as a symbolising creature, hence as separate from 'nature'. (This is the story told by Adorno and Horkheimer's 'dialectic of enlightenment'.) But Freud ends his speculative reconstruction of early human history, *Totem and Taboo,* with the assertion: 'In the beginning was the act' – not, as later Judaeo-Christian and Platonic traditions would qualify this, the Word (word qua symbol). Not language but gesture; not text but performance; not *énoncé* but *énonciation*. God's 'Let there be...' coincides with his 'And God made...' Certainly we're confronted here with the problematic of *creation*. In a moving passage Lacan, discussing hysteria, locates the typical hysterical question (and the Judaeo-Christian god is surely the original hysteric) in the question of gender: 'Who am I? a man or a woman?' Or rather, 'what is it to be a woman?' Then he glosses this: 'Am I capable of procreating?' Which leads him to a meditation on creation. Acknowledging that the one thing the chain of signifiers cannot cover is the fact of *individuation* – the production of a singular being – leads him to the conclusion that 'In the symbolic nothing explains creation.'[28]

In the old religions, of course, it's God who explains it. The divine vocal performative – or if you prefer, the shattering noise of the big bang. But according to some recent theory, there wasn't one big bang but many – perhaps an infinite number, making the universe infinitely old, infinitely large: always already voiced. Might we draw on this de-fetishisation of physics for thinking about musical politics? If creation has no single origin (in Lacanian, there is no final signifier), might it happen, potentially, every day? And if the symbolic cannot explain it, should we perhaps look to the dimension that the symbolic displaces? – for (again in Lacanian), 'The gods belong to the field of the real.'[29]

I have no definitive theory of how we should do this. And the question opens on to a potentially enormous, multi-dimensional field of inquiry.

Excursus 2. Before narrowing this down, a few aspects may be allowed to set a scene. 'Nothing', writes Bourdieu, 'would be more futile than to search for the origins of "creative" power.'[30] But nothing, either, would be harder to resist. The psycho-political primacy of the Freudian originary act was hardly

---

27 Adorno and Horkheimer, *Dialectic of Enlightenment*, 17.

28 Jacques Lacan, *The Psychoses: The Seminar of Jacques Lacan, Book III 1955–1956*, ed. Jacques-Alain Miller, tr. Russell Grigg (London and New York: Routledge, 1993), 168–79 (171).

29 Lacan, *Fundamental Concepts*, 45.

30 Pierre Bourdieu, *The Rules of Art* (Cambridge: Polity Press, 1996), 169.

a new idea; Freud was quoting Goethe's *Faust*, and his move also brings to mind Marx's injunction to philosophers to change the world rather than interpret it, and Nietzsche's performative theory of morality ('there is no "being" behind the doing, acting, becoming; the "doer" has simply been added to the deed by the imagination – the doing is everything'[31]). Bergsonian vitalism and other fashionable essays in *Lebensphilosophie* form the background too for such contemporaneous developments as Bakhtin's philosophy of the act and Benjamin's theory of 'pure violence'.[32] Nietzsche saw the origins of music, specifically, in pure activity, mutating then into mimetic forms of gesture; only much later, he thought, did the evolution of 'symbolic means' give music the capacity to inhabit the world of 'inner life' – a perspective mirrored in varying ways in theories of language and art associated with Benjamin, Adorno and Bloch. For all these thinkers, there was no question of deed and word, act and symbol, now being separable; indeed, this is what gives this moment of thought as a whole its unmistakably nostalgic tone, all the more so since the *force* underpinning its drive-to-the-act – the Romantic lineage whereby, from Kant onwards, 'creative power' had been relocated from the divine to the human via the concept of 'genius' – was reaching a climax of intensity in the iconoclastic self-declarations of modernism at just the same time as, within the wider society, the possibility of such 'creativity' seemed irredeemably stunted by the instrumentalism of contemporary society, with its 'herd instinct', its 'bad smell, the smell of failure…ever thinner, more placid…more ordinary, more indifferent…'[33]; not to mention the apparent implications of evolutionary theory and fashionable social Darwinism.

Bourdieu's jaded tone sounds an echo of this moment. Or is it that the earlier moment installs itself as a pre-echo of what was to come? In Foucault, Nietzschian performativity tightens its sphere of operation to the subjectivating power/knowledge structures of the biopolitical *dispositifs*, a move continued by Judith Butler, with the help of Austin's speech-act theory. At which point, Deleuzian vitalism comes to the rescue, positing what in Foucault could be no more than 'folds' of agency punctuating smooth cultural space as never-ending rhizomatic eruptions of difference: 'the explosive internal force that life carries within itself'; 'evolution is actualisation', says Deleuze, and 'actualisation is creation'.[34] For Vikki Bell, the flowering of neo-Deleuzian perspectives that we have witnessed in the final decades of the twentieth century should be seen against a broader backdrop, which includes growing interest in the pre-discursive investitures of bodies; ideas of 'information' as not limited to consciousness but pervading all physical systems; and the co-production of beings and their environments via a 'self-activity' that can be identified in (for example) chemical processes, medical crisis-management and the operational protocols of cyborgian hybrids.[35] And once again, this upsurge of faith in 'life' is to be placed in the context of a second phase of the modern crisis of secular society – as if the second half of a game with who knows how many subsequent iterations of extra time – a crisis addressed also in the turn to religious themes in so much recent philosophy: Agamben, Esposito, Badiou, Nancy, Žižek, Derrida; above all, perhaps, Derrida, the Derrida whose deconstructions (including of Austin's speech-act theory[36]) had earlier, again repeating previous moves, demolished (definitively, one might think) the claims to pure presence of any act…

---

31 Friedrich Nietzsche, 'The Genealogy of Morals: An Attack', in *The Birth of Tragedy and the Genealogy of Morals*, tr. Francis Golffing (New York: Doubleday, 1956 [1887]), 178–9.

32 See Mikhail Bakhtin, *Toward a Philosophy of the Act*, ed. Vadim Liapunov and Michael Holquist, tr. Vadim Liapunov (Austin: University of Texas Press, 1993); Walter Benjamin, 'Critique of Violence' (1921), in *One-Way Street and Other Writings*, tr. Edmund Jephcott and Kingsley Slater (London: New Left Books, 1979), 132–54.

33 Nietzsche, *Genealogy*, 160, 177.

34 Deleuze, quoted in Vikki Bell, *Culture and Performance: The Challenge of Ethics, Politics and Feminist Theory* (Oxford: Berg, 2007), 97, 107.

35 Bell, *Culture and Performance*, 104–17.

36 Jacques Derrida, 'Signature Event Context', in *A Derrida Reader: Between the Blinds*, ed. Peggy Kamuf (Hemel Hempstead: Harvester Wheatsheaf, 1991), 80–111.

If it's above all the idea of *performativity* that links these two phases, it seems natural, within exploration of specifically musical contexts, to link it in turn to questions of *performance* (a branch of the broader genus whose genre-specific rules focus, illuminate and at times subvert the normative mimetic processes of its parent). Musical performance *c*. 1900 entered a crisis owing to the threat apparently posed by mechanical reproduction. The crisis persists – is even intensified – today, yet, interestingly, is complemented by a strongly emergent academic interest in performance studies. Is this rescue archaeology? Or is the complementarity more deeply motivated? What if the separable ontological status of 'performance' as such actually comes into being with the threat of its extinction? It's an 'act' whose purity is all the more valued because it has always already been lost. Some of the work in performance studies situates itself in relation to the broader arguments.[37] Carolyn Abbate, for instance, quoting the philosopher Vladimir Jankélévitch, asks: 'composing music, playing it, and singing it... are these not three modes of doing, three attitudes that are drastic, not gnostic, not of the hermeneutic order of knowledge?' 'Real music', she argues, 'the event itself, in encouraging or demanding the drastic, is what damps down the gnostic.'[38] In each performance-event, however small – is Abbate's suggestion – new life, new creation, can spring forth.

At a higher level of historical rhythm, the relationship of the two large 'events' I have sketched can hardly avoid bringing to mind Marx's notorious historiographical binary, tragedy/farce. But how would we know there aren't more phases to come: history as riff? Hal Foster, meditating on the relationship of the two artistic avant-gardes implicated in these phases, reads it through Freud's concept of *Nachträglichkeit* – deferred action, belatedness, retroactivity – a concept which, for Freud, is the key to the temporal processes of subjective self-construction, in particular, the role played by trauma. What cannot at first be accepted (cannot be represented) is repressed and must return, where it will feature as repetition of something originary. In this knotted skein of reference to encounters always already missed, Foster argues, 'even as the avant-garde recedes into the past, it also returns from the future', for 'Each epoch dreams the next, as Walter Benjamin once remarked, but in so doing revises the one before it.'[39] What is particularly interesting here, though, is that not only is 'representation' (or its failure) the motor of the trauma (that is, the failure is what motivates the repetition); 'representation' (or its crisis) is also the *object* of the trauma (it's what has gone missing: a crisis felt on all levels – politics, art, philosophy – where transcendental certainties have collapsed, where 'God' is paralysed).

---

37 Butler's, for instance, are referenced in my own *Voicing the Popular*, ch. 3, and in Suzanne Cusick, 'On Musical Performances of Gender and Sex', in *Audible Traces: Gender, Identity, and Music*, ed. Elaine Radoff Barkin and Lydia Hamessley (Zürich: Carciofoli Verlagshaus 1999), 25–48. See also Christopher Small, *Musicking: The Meanings of Performing and Listening* (Hanover NH: Wesleyan University Press, 1998); Anthony Gritten and Elaine King (eds.), *Music and Gesture* (Aldershot: Ashgate, 2006); Rachel Beckles Willson, 'A Study in Geography, 'Tradition', and Identity in Concert Practice', *Music and Letters*, 85:4 (2004), 602–13; Carolyn Abbate, 'Music – Drastic or Gnostic?', *Critical Inquiry*, 30 (Spring 2004), 50–536; Simon Frith, *Performing Rites: On the Value of Popular Music* (Oxford: Oxford University Press, 1996). Much of the performance studies literature in the field of music is pretty focused on internal issues of practice and historical recovery; see e.g. Richard Tasuskin, *Text and Act: Essays on Music and Performance* (Oxford: Oxford University Press, 1995), John Butt, *Playing with History: The Historical Approach to Musical Performance* (Cambridge: Cambridge University Press, 2002). Nicholas Cook's many writings in this area tie the specific and more general issues together well; see e.g. 'Music as Performance', in *The Cultural Study of Music: A Critical Introduction*, ed. Martin Clayton, Trevor Herbert and Richard Middleton (New York: Routledge, 2003), 204–14. On the broader context of performance studies, see Susan Melrose, *A Semiotics of the Dramatic Text* (London: Macmillan, 1994).

38 Abbate, 'Music – Drastic or Gnostic?', 505, 532.

39 Hal Foster, *The Return of the Real: The Avant-Garde at the End of the Century* (Cambridge MA: MIT Press, 1996), x, 207.

Not for the first time (as a psychoanalysist might want to say), Freudian insight and Freudian method are themselves in a relationship that is *nachträglich*; that is, 'representation' becomes both subject and object of a new conception of historical understanding.

If the nub of the crisis, then, concerns the relationship between 'event' and 'representation', a focus for the discussion might be found in those currents in recent critical philosophy addressing precisely this problematic; more specifically, the concept, or rather the possibility, of the *new* as such, a concern all the more urgent because of the way that, both on the level of official politics and that of intellectual theory in the human sciences, initiation of change seems to have been foreclosed. I'll draw mostly on Žižek's concept of *act*, elaborated in many of his writings but most usefully for my purposes here in his *On Belief*, and second, on Alain Badiou's concept of *event*, as put forward in his book *Being and Event*; but I'll also touch upon Jacques Derrida's critique of Marx and the revolutionary event, in his book *Spectres of Marx*, and Jean-Luc Nancy's theory of 'coming' (*jouissance*) in his *The Birth to Presence*.[40] Despite arriving by apparently radically different routes – (to simplify) Žižek via psychoanalysis, Badiou via set theory, Derrida by deconstruction, Nancy by phenomenology – their approaches here seem to me to contain significant congruences (no doubt derived from ancestors in common: Hegel, Marx, Heidegger, Lacan). All four, for instance, take as read that 'totality' – a One, a symbolic consistency, self-presence, authentic origin – is fraudulent, secured only at the expense of disavowing what doesn't fit: lack, the void, excess, the real, infinity, endless deferral. For both Žižek and Badiou, however, rupture is possible. Žižek carefully distinguishes act proper from the symbolic act, which simply reasserts one's existing subjective position; from the hysteric's 'acting-out', a kind of theatrical performance enabling survival of trauma; and from the psychotic *passage à l'acte*, an outburst of blind violence. The act proper comes upon us *by chance*, like a 'miracle'; it's 'an intervention in the course of which the agent's identity itself is radically changed', 'an intrusion which momentarily suspends the causal network of our everyday lives'.[41] For Badiou, event is what he calls an 'ultra-one' (by contrast with 'situations' as they normally present themselves, which, though multiple – for 'The multiple from which ontology makes up its situation is composed solely of multiplicities' – appear to us under the regime of a 'count-as-one'). Event happens, if it happens at all, at an 'evental site' – that is, a situation containing a singularity, some content not recognised in the situation's own self-understanding. It, event, belongs to itself, 'interposes itself between the void and itself'.[42] It appears when named, by an act of 'interpretative intervention', and then survives through operations of 'fidelity' which assemble a 'generic' (that is, autochthonous) network of 'truths'. (By the way, the fact that these truths, while 'indiscernible' from the standpoint of the established situation, can nevertheless be thought – but only, so far as I can see, through a transcendent act of faith, or through a god-like ontological stance situated *outside* the situation – reminds us of the Žižekian act on the one hand, the quasi- Žižekian 'god-space' of critique that I proposed earlier, on the other.)

---

40 Žižek, *Belief*; Alain Badiou, *Being and Event*, tr. Oliver Feltham (London: Continuum, 2005 [1988]); Jacques Derrida, *Specters of Marx: The State of the Debt, the Work of Mourning and the New International*, tr. Peggy Kamuf (New York: Routledge, 2006 [1993]); Nancy, *Birth to Presence*.

41 Žižek, *Belief*, 84, 85, 86.

42 Badiou, *Being and Event*, 29, 507.

Having said all that, there are, though, important differences between Žižek and Badiou – and between each of them and Derrida and Nancy – differences concerning in particular the status of the subject, and the relationships between agency, act and history; I'll come back to this.

We can work Freud into the ancestry of these ideas – notably the Freud for whom mental life is always fractured, the subject never completely 'at home', always 'beside himself'. Returning to his theory of dreams, we find that he sometimes describes the 'dream work', as he does the unconscious itself (where the dream material does its work), as a *Vorstellungsrepräsentanz* – a *performance*, an *act*, of a representation; but, as Lacan points out, the representation performed out, the surface meanings, stands in for another reality – a Real of representation, or, as Lacan would call it, a Real of illusion; for an encounter which, within this structure, can never be recalled, only repeated. 'Desire manifests itself in the dream by the loss expressed in an image at the most cruel point of the object. It is only in the dream that this truly unique encounter can occur. Only a rite, an endlessly repeated act, can commemorate this...encounter...'[43] Doesn't this describe exactly the functioning of 'Losing My Religion'? But is it truly only dream that can perform this function? In 'performance-work', as I will call it, by analogy with the Freudian dream-work, we seem to find a musical dynamic that, in twisting repetition with symbolic structure, presentation with representation, operates an analogous economy. 'Act' or 'event' is what would *cut* the structure of this economy. Cutting through the dream-economy of 'burning' (of the child, of the father's sins) would de-couple the terms of the constitutive oedipal network; what would be the equivalent move for interpretation of the dream, of the performance-work, presented, re-presented, in 'Losing My Religion'?

We should not forget here that we're talking about a *record*; which, when we play it, might itself be thought to work as some sort of *Vorstellungsrepräsentanz*. The advent of recorded voice qualifies, in my view, as an 'event' in Badiou's sense. A multifarious exercise of naming struggled to identify the significance of this technical miracle: neologisms (phonograph, gramophone) went along with re-worked topoi (notably that of *fidelity* – His Masters Voice), and with hysterical supernatural imagery (for the dead could now speak and the machine was inhabited by spirits). This provoked in turn new understandings of 'popular song' – that is, new namings of 'the people' – as images of bourgeois populism (Caruso), of the Tin Pan Alley masses, of ethic others (blacks), of established, emergent or would-be national-populars (English, Jews, Italians, Irish, etc.) swam into the perspectives of a reshaping social imaginary on the back of specific vocal registrations.

Each voice demanded its following – its 'faithful'. Fidelity – or 'authenticity', a core trope for popular song throughout the twentieth century – would, in a neat historical circularity, become the key organising thread for the operation of fidelity to this event. Evidence of miraculous 'acts', as listeners were struck dumb by uncanny disembodied voices, is all over the early history. It's worth pointing out that this event pretty well coincides with the Nietzschian deicide – as if faith transfers from one object to another – and also coincides, more or less, with Freud's invention of the part-object, object-cause of desire or *objet a* in Lacan's formulation – including object-voice, that object always already outside as well as inside, always split, but now put even more powerfully at issue by the disembodying technology of recording: a voice belonging, then, if not to a Man already dead, at least to one

---

43 Lacan, *Fundamental Concepts*, 59.

that is *dis-eased, dis-located,* transposed into an anatomy calling for constant re-imagination. As already noted, these developments bring *performance* into a new prominence. This isn't so strange as it initially might seem. Just as 'God' becomes an issue, comes into the spotlight, once he's dead, so 'performance', live performance, becomes an object of anxiety only when music has been killed, frozen, mortified, by recording; and vocal performance, in particular, becomes a site of intense indeterminacy once voice has apparently evacuated any bodily home. In all these cases, an originary event produces retroactively the threat of a loss of what 'will have been'. Right across this site, fidelity becomes the issue.

Excursus 3. I doubt that Badiou would accept this example of event. Strangely, for a philosopher with Marxist roots, he restricts the territories of possible events to four – science, art, politics and love – all of which are fields of voluntary activity, excluding the deeper ground of what in an older vocabulary was called the mode of production. (Perhaps it's not so strange, though, if we bear in mind Badiou's now-ambivalent but not disavowed debt to '1968' and the Maoist 'cultural revolution'.) There's a possibility that we find here yet another example of a mode of thought that cannot (yet) acknowledge its own foundations (it's *nachträglich*); for what if the very prominence of 'fidelity' as trope in Badiou's politics, providing the condition of his philosophy in the way that, he himself argues, philosophy always needs, owes its purchase to an event he cannot recognise? Causation (that is, the spectre of 'technological determinism') isn't the issue here; rather, a recognition that in this late-nineteenth/early twentieth-century moment something shifts that is crystallised in the phonographic voice, in the way it problematises origin, disembodies (or better, cyborgianises) performance, deconstructs presence (a century before Derrida!), imbricates representation with multiple repetitions of difference – a shift that also lubricates the emergent mechanisms of psychoanalysis and the other anti-foundationalist systems of thought characteristic of this moment, not to mention the assumptions of activist (anti-representational) politics such as Leninism. Friedrich Kittler's invocation of the new '1900 discourse network' associated with effects of the emergent media can get us some way towards grasping the traumatic (i.e. a-historicist, neo-Benjaminian) import of this moment; at least it can if we follow Ian Biddle's helpful extrapolation:

> If…the singing or spoken voice can be *recorded*, it can also be constituted as a *fixed* object of scrutiny; sounds can be transported, moved from one location to another… There is no longer a need for discourse translation… As a result, the sounds of the voice can become stable carriers of human character, and of… pathologies that hitherto resided only in the internal invisible world of the psyche. Hence, these externalised sounds become mobile…[44]

Even here, however, certain residues of a sort of medial positivism arguably obscure the role of performative *faith*. The phonographic voice presents a secularised version of the voice in the burning bush: its location, the bush (the wild – albeit a machined wild – anterior to any Heideggerian *Lichtung*); without visible body or obvious source; but (in a fashion that Freud and Lacan would elaborate) always *burning*…[45]

---

44 Ian Biddle, 'Of Mice and Dogs: Music, Gender, and Sexuality at the Long Fin de Siècle', in *The Cultural Study of Music: A Critical Introduction*, ed. Martin Clayton, Trevor Herbert and Richard Middleton (New York: Routledge, 2003), 215–26 (220). See also Friedrich Kittler, *Gramophone, Film, Typewriter*, tr. Geoffrey Winthrop-Young and Michael Wutz (Stanford: Stanford University Press, 1999).

45 This machined, technologised 'bush' calls to mind Adorno's conception of the 'hear-stripe', the background noise (the hum of Being?) characteristic of radio, phonograph and film sound, on to which 'the music' seems to be projected; see T.W Adorno, *Essays on Music*, ed. Richard Leppert (Berkeley: University of California Press, 2002), 218–19, 251. The 'hear-stripe', Adorno speculated, has its effects at the level of the unconscious; and this structure might in turn be connected to the screen/projection mechanism of the 'fantasy-scene' (as exemplified in 'Losing My Religion') and that of the Freudian 'screen-memory' which, awake or dreaming, protects us from trauma.

This transfer of the field of faith not only creates the conditions for a 'post-human' (and post-poststructuralist) politics such as Badiou advocates – a politics after God, Nation, State, Man, but also after the initial deconstructive breakthrough – it also creates ground for a critique. As I suggest in a recent article,[46] the principal gift of phonography is the revelation (a revelation of what we always already suspected) that embodiment is mutable and mobile. Fidelity to this truth would therefore have to be, as Richard Elliott has explained, a *critical* fidelity;[47] or, to use terms that Ian Biddle foregrounds in his study of musical community: in offering us the tools to operate the processes of territorialisation and deterritorialisation, phonographic fidelity produces an irreducible ethical *undecideability*.[48] Faith, we might even have to say, could require betrayal. After all, without Judas, God wouldn't have died even a first time (though of course, the thirty pieces of silver resurrected him immediately in the fetishistic form of commodity). Fidelity, then, incorporates a necessary *in*fidelity, for the *passages* of fidelity, putting at issue any fixities of the body and of time, are traced – under conditions, precisely, *after* God – in the vicissitudes of the subject, of political commitment, of identity. Fidelity – to anticipate a terminology that I will come to shortly with more focus – is a *spectre*, arising in the confluence of 'faith' and 'freedom'.

It's true that, for Badiou, fidelity to the event always struggles with processes of normalisation; history tends to turn into 'nature'. And this forces him to recognise that event has a *history*, is subject to unpredictable process: 'inasmuch as its name is a representative without representation, the event remains anonymous and uncertain'.[49] I'll come back to this. Nevertheless, for Badiou, fidelity is at the mercy of decisions made at moments of chance by subjects that are simply 'operators' – subject is just the 'local status of a procedure'.[50] But this is to risk fetishising the event itself. My own view is more Žižekian: subjects have a *substance* and a *history*, based on a certain continuity of *desire*, and they inhabit a space structured by *power*: not all fidelity-operations have an equal chance. The space set up by the event of recorded voice is crossed by vocal objects of varying degrees of fidelity to its potentials. This is precisely the space, and the content, that are at issue in both 'Imagine' and 'Losing My Religion', where the celebrity-god rears his fetishistic head. To sustain the potential of this nexus demands an occupation of the 'god-space' that is reflexive. This requires, first, that the subject recognises its own representations as 'performances', performances that hide the subject's own real foundation – that foundation which the later Lacan calls *sinthome* ('symptom' mis-spelled to signify emptiness of content; so, the meaningless substance at the heart of the subject, an object around which drive constantly circulates); and second, it requires that creative acts, of production or interpretation, are recognised as always heteronomous: if the voices of the people are the voice of God, this is of a God who consciously bars and splits himself. The God-particle, we might say (if there is one), *is sinthome* – saint-man, in Žižek's

---

46 Richard Middleton, 'Last Night a DJ Saved My Life: Avians, Cyborgs and Siren Bodies in the Era of Phonographic Technology', *Radical Musicology*, 1 (2006), http://www.radical-musicology.org.uk (12 January 2009), 31 pars.

47 Richard Elliott, 'Popular Music and/as Event: Subjectivity, Love and Fidelity in the Aftermath of Rock 'n' Roll', *Radical Musicology*, 3 (2008), http://www.radical-musicology.org.uk (12 January 2009), 60 pars.

48 Ian Biddle, '"Love thy Neighbour?": The Political Economy of Musical Neighbours', *Radical Musicology*, 2 (2007), http://www.radical-musicology.org.uk (12 January 2009), 49 pars.

49 Badiou, *Being and Event*, 206.

50 Ibid. 392.

whimsical translation (but also Saint-Thom, doubting subject of infidelity): the kernel of radical otherness that prevents 'man' as totality from ever forming, but that is also the basis for ethical choice. To put it in Badiou's language, event has always already materialised when, through an act of interpretative intervention, it is subjectively recognised; moreover, the recognition is itself an outcome of a multiplicity of previous events. At this level, as Badiou himself puts it, 'the activist constructs the means to sound, if only for an instant, the site of the unpresentable, and the means to be thenceforth faithful to the proper name that, afterwards, he or she will have been able to give to – or hear, one cannot decide – this non-place of place, the void.'[51] To act here is, literally but in more than one sense, to 'play God'.

At one level, this lineage of activism summons back into view the sounds of our two moments (or non-places) of crisis. If 'the whole program of modernism… [then and now] hinges on the tenet that *there must be an object other than the fetish*'[52] – that is, a Real of representation – then the accompanying scene set forth by recorded voice brings this programme up against a limit, its most radical gift, the potential de-subjectivation of community through the universalising of loss (of death), always in tension with the reification of record as commodity. But this kairotic meta-structure, knotting together moments decades apart, is surely animated by minor acts of (in)fidelity at a day-to-day level; as Elliott describes this, the 'rare evental' is always in dialogue with the 'everyday evental' (Event with event, as I shall now put it).[53] Derrida's deconstruction of the 'rare evental', his insistence on the boundless hinterland and spectralised deferrals of memory, which, precisely, memorialise past acts of (in)fidelity, is relevant here, and I'll return to it. But if these spectres stalk us because of the irreducible excess of representation (its Real; or what a critical Badiouian might call the void of fidelity), we might wonder whether we can find a way, somehow, to register the power of this excess; to 'exscribe' the Derridean fading that surrounds all processes of naming with the pulsing life beneath – a conjunction that I have myself elsewhere tried to locate in the ever-spiralling play of loss ('death') and reproductive rebirth ('life') conjured by the record form.[54]

This domain of 'life' is indeed, it seems to me, the level at which the post-Derridean phenomenology of Jean-Luc Nancy is aimed. At this level we find 'presence', or, 'what is born': 'this presence that comes, and only comes. As when we are born – an event [*sic*] that lasts all our lives. Coming (being in the birth, being a birth), existence misses sense as meaningful "sense." But this missing makes itself sense, and makes sense, our sense, the sense of exposed beings.' Indeed, this is the mode of presence proper to the 'exhaustion of

---

51 Ibid. 111.

52 Mladen Dolar, *A Voice and Nothing More* (Cambridge MA: MIT Press, 2006), 69.

53 Elliott, 'Popular Music', par 42. The Greek god *kairos* was god of the fleeting moment, the moment that must be grasped. In Christian theology, kairotic time relates to that knot of moments in which divine interventions are tied together. In the Eastern churches, the liturgy is initiated by the proclamation, 'It is time [*kairos*] for the Lord to act.' Walter Benjamin's concept of *Jetztzeit*, albeit indebted rather to Old Testament notions of messianic time, seems closely allied.

54 See Middleton, 'Last Night a DJ'. 'Exscription' is Nancy's term for the otherness that, he argues, governs the relation of things and their names: 'every statement would be performative but, in return, every thing would be exscription of a statement. Exscription would be the performative (*performation*) of the performative (*performatif*) itself', and its 'some thing' would be 'impossible and real, the *impossibly real* experience of some thing' (*Birth to Presence*, 176, 177). This is, surely, his take on the Lacanian Real.

transcendentals', to being that is exposed, abandoned, banned (like Jesus, by God); 'man is the being of abandoned being'. This process takes place beneath all decisionism of thought, which has always already been preceded: '"to decide" means not to cut through to this or that "meaning" of existence – but to expose oneself to the undecidability of meaning that existence *is*'; '"decision" and "decided-Being" are...that in which...existence...appropriates the unappropriable event of its advent to Being, from a groundlessness of existence', and this differentiation '"is made," or it "acts"', with the result that it 'calls us forth into the situation'. This place, however – *contra* Badiou – is *un-named*; what happens, what takes place, is place as such: 'This nothing means that nothing *takes place* in the happening, for there is no place to take; but there is the spacing of a *place* as such, the nothingness spacing time, opening up in it an otherness, the heterogeneity of existence.' Thus 'Happening means... that the origin is not and was never present'; 'History in this sense means the *heterogeneity of the origin*, of Being, and of ourselves' and event is defined as 'time full of its own heterogeneity, and therefore, spaced'.[55]

Doesn't this begin to sound like an inadvertent description of the work of records – the endless circulation of copies, performances, covers, problematising origin, opening sameness to undecidability of meaning and spaces of infinite heterogeneity? Even before the 'birth' of the self, Nancy identifies an 'awakening' at a more hypnotic, passive level, an event that is precipitated by, and persists as, an 'impartation', a sort of originary splitting for which the model is what happens in the mother's womb. His exscriptive descriptions of this – 'trembling', 'vibration', pulsation' – as sameness is 'cut through' and differentiated, can hardly help summon thoughts of the equally hypnotic reproductive activity of records, as well as of the musical pulsations they carry.[56] Similarly, the irreducible excess in this process, the 'excess of the One over and above *itself*, sameness itself as a limit', means that all continuation – 'living on', 'brimming over' – involves 'undoing the limit on the limit itself, by keeping it; by retracing it with the gesture that erases it (and what erasure does not necessarily retrace what it erases?)' – a gesture built in to record culture in all its moments. Such gestures, suspending history, spacing time, go to produce a sense of, precisely, '*our time*', 'the possibility of saying "we" and "our"', of producing community as a *togetherness of otherness*, for 'we are not a "being" but a "happening"'; a model that seems to fit the formation of communities – mutable, rhyzomatic, heterogeneous – around particular recorded music repertories as if designed for the purpose.[57]

This perspective, though exhilarating, might also seem too *comfortable* – as if politics can relax into the knowledge that the 'birth of presence' will go on whatever we do. In a sense Nancy approaches 'from below', from the point of a speculative materialist (indeed, vitalist) phenomenology, a not dissimilar position to the one that Badiou approaches, from the point of a universalising mathematical logic, 'from above', a position that in each case tends to leave begging the question of agency; what exactly might precipitate event? Nevertheless, their theories serve to open informatively on to the two-levelled structure linking (more in parallax than parallel, perhaps) the flows of Event and event, respectively. It's a structure with a general form (that is, philosophical application), but this is mirrored, again with lines of force varying with perspective, in the specific case of the phonographic E/event. Here we

---

55 Nancy, *Birth to Presence*, 2, ix, 47, 97, 103, 104, 106, 162, 163.
56 Ibid. 9–35.
57 Ibid. 67–8, 150, 155, 156.

see a meta-structure (a kairotic knot) tying together the initial instance – one founding itself on a mimetic impulse that is clearly *analogue* – with a *nachträglich* echo in the late twentieth century, where the impulse is *digital*, a relationship where the nature of 'fidelity to fidelity' is, precisely, what is put at issue;[58] and this intersects constantly with the day-to-day dialogues of (in)fidelity set up in the circulation of specific records around the communities committed to them. This structure is mirrored in turn by the related intersections played out at the broader cultural level between the Events (dis-)established within the movements of the *dispositifs* and the events precipitated by the histories of specific musical and other genres; between, that is to say, the exigencies of *performativity* and those of *performance*. The interweaving of these structures goes far to explain why what for Marx was a historical binary, following the pattern of (quasi-theatrical) representation – tragedy/farce – becomes a multiplicitous play of repetition-in-difference. The revolution will not be televised; but it will be (has been? has always already been?) recorded, and re-played. The revolution will revolve (at 78/45/33⅓ rpm) – before, then, sampling itself digitally.[59]

At whatever E/evental moment, 'Bodies call again for their creation', asserts Nancy. For '"God is dead" means: God no longer has a body.' Yet, since this body was made, mimetically, in the image of man, it's this human body that has become problematic, body as the locus of sense, the body 'trapped by the sign'. 'Not that kind of creation' is required, therefore, the kind 'that blows into them the spiritual life of the sign. But birth, the separation and sharing of bodies…'. Such bodies can be thought only by a 'voice…without vocabulary, without vocalization, and without vocalics', a voice that 'vibrates "for itself"'; 'A body is always the imminence of such a voice; it is its trace, the dull, grating noise of a weighing of a thought…', a body that is 'neither substance nor subject, but *corpus*, a catalogue without a logos, which is "logos" itself…'[60]

We hear this sound, this V*ox Dei*, in the trembling pulsations circulating round the 'nervous system' that constitutes the phonographic *corpus*. It's the sound of an 'object voice' – the 'partial object' on Freud's list that is most radically split between inside and outside, the most extimate or ex-static; which means that it's perhaps the one most susceptible to narcissistic temptations of the fetishistic mirror (via ventriloquial structures of possession); but also, maybe, the one most available to political activism: for its ambiguity is linked not just to a doubling – as Lacan has it, while its undecidable functions 'may not make for two gods, nor does it make for one alone'[61] – it is linked rather to an infinity. The political task might then be twofold. First, if fetish is a story masquerading as an object, to find ways of narrativising the vocal object, telling its story – which is to say, finding, and perhaps *acting on*, its point of enunciation. Which then, since we are talking of popular song, means to map this structure of multivalent performance-work to articulations of another multiple-that-wants-to-be-One, 'The People' – to 'extimate' its sovereign claims, connect presentations of vocalic bodies to potential acts of a vocalic body politic.

---

58 The implications of the analogue/digital divide cry out for an extended treatment; some other time.

59 Richard Elliott's discussion of John Trudell's record, 'Baby Boom Ché' ('Popular Music', par 4) deftly sketches this intersection. He quotes Trudell: 'Rock 'n' roll is based on revolutions going way past 33⅓.'

60 Nancy, *Birth to Presence*, 191, 197, 201, 206.

61 Lacan, quoted in Dolar, *Voice*, 56.

On the level of theory at least, this task has become easier in recent years. The (temporary) 'triumph' of neo-liberalism and the 'fall' of (actually existing) socialism encouraged the deconstructive impulse to target representations of 'The People' as a sovereign One – this was, after all, a god that had apparently failed – just as the predictable crisis of the neo-liberal hegemony, now upon us, mandated the urgency of a successful riposte. Agamben, for example, notes how

> One term [people]…names both the constitutive political subject and the class that is, de facto if not de jure, excluded from politics… It is as if what we call "people" were in reality not a unitary subject but a dialectical oscillation between two opposite poles: on the one hand the set of the People as a whole political body, and on the other, the subset of the people as a fragmentary multiplicity of needy and excluded bodies…[62]

Rancière puts it differently, in terms of the necessary mechanisms of a new sort of democracy, one able to resist populist hatred of the other:

> Democracy exists in a society to the degree that the *demos* exists as the power to divide the *ochlos*. This power of division is enacted through a contingent historical system of events, discourses and practices whereby any multitude affirms and manifests itself as such, simultaneously refusing both its incorporation into the One of a collectivity that assigns ranks and identities and the pure abandonment of individual focuses of possession and terror… This specific power of the *demos*, which exceeds all the dispositions of legislators, is in its simplest form the rallying-dividing power of the primal many, the power of the *Two* of division. The Two of division is the path followed by a *One* which is no longer that of collective incorporation but rather that of the equality of any One to any other One.[63]

And Nancy, taking us back to the question of enunciation, asserts that

> This question would be that of the 'voice' of a 'people,' insofar as a people would not be *a subject*, and as its voice would pass through a place, a mouth, apart – and separated from itself. There doubtless remains to be invented an affirmation of separation which is an affirmation of relation… [This] would have to be a *political* affirmation, in a sense that remains for us to discover.[64]

In searching for a route towards such a discovery, we might do well to go back to an early point in the development of the discourse and start with Badiou's discussion of Rousseau's concept of 'People', as a body politic animated by a general will. Defining this as, precisely, an originary event, as an ultra-one in his terms, Badiou slides past the notorious problem of the totalitarian (or ochlocratic) potential in Rousseau's formulation. But Badiou has already told us that the ultra-one is actually formed as an 'originary two': it looks two ways, bordering both the void and the established situation, hence inhabits a temporal interval; 'inasmuch as its name is a representative without representation, the event remains anonymous and uncertain. The excess of one is also beneath the one… This is because the essence of the ultra-one is the Two.'[65] It doesn't take much effort to force this opening further, into a wider splintering, for the void – the Real in Žižek's Lacanian language – is infinite. This, in effect,

---

62 Agamben, *Homo Sacer*, 176–7.
63 Rancière, *Shores of Politics*, 32.
64 Nancy, *Birth to Presence*, 142.
65 Badiou, *Being and Event*, 206.

is the nub of Derrida's critique of Marx's theory of revolution. Derrida starts from Victor Hugo's wonderful description of two Parisian barricades in the revolution of 1848 – a revolution that, as Hugo says, saw 'a revolt of the people against itself'. One barricade is 'furious', 'monstrous', 'terrible', governed by the 'spirit of the revolution'; from it 'growled this voice of the people which is like the voice of God; a strange majesty emanated from that hodful of refuse. It was a garbage heap and it was Sinaï.' The other barricade is 'quiet', 'ominous', 'a sepulchre... the chief of that barricade was a geometer or a spectre'. One a 'gaping mouth', the other 'a mask'.[66] This doubling is also, as we have noted, the structure of revolution in Marx: first time as tragedy, second as farce; but it fits into a longer rhythm too, a rhythm of fidelity, one might say, one that he likes to couch in terms of a relationship between *Geist* and *Gespenst*, spirit and spectre, the ghosts of history – an alterity which at the same time always interpenetrates and multiplies itself. As Derrida points out, Marx is obsessed with these figures, not least because, we might say, it's the spectralising of spirit that produces fetish, most importantly, fetishism of commodity. Marx wants to get rid of them all – and thinks we can and must; this is the meaning of revolution. Derrida demurs – as a deconstructionist must – arguing that conjurations, ghosts, are endemic to thought itself, and that fetishism, objectifying representations, are, equally, endemic to production as such. This seems partly right. There will be ghosts so long as memory produces history and history produces trauma. Whatever Marx hoped, the dead can't bury themselves. And there will be representation so long as meaning supplements practice. But neither ghosts nor representations are reducible to fetishes. To speak to the ghost – an injunction with which Derrida's book, quoting Shakespeare's *Hamlet*, concludes[67] – or better, to speak and listen, in a ventriloquistic dialogue, isn't necessarily to *bow down* before it. For Žižek, spectre covers over a contradiction in 'reality', a 'hole' that we cannot face; but 'our primary duty is not towards the spectre' and 'act' can trump it.[68]

Derrida ends up with Freud's concept of the uncanny, *das Unheimliche* – and therefore in the unconscious, where, as he points out, it's not a question of whether spectres and spirits exist, but of a narrative, an (anonymous) *act*, of haunting: in a formulation used by both Marx and Freud, '*es spukt*', it spooks.[69] The structure of the unconscious and of the dream – and therefore of the subject – no less than that of history, is that of a rhythm of repetition, a ventriloquistic dialogue; just like, also, the structure of performance-work, especially in its manifestations through the repetitions of recordings. But for Žižek, drawing on Lacan, this is a rhythm too of encounter; we are indeed called to awake (as Marx insisted) but, as Lacan suggests, 'awakening works in two directions...', looking not only to everyday 'reality' but also to what is hidden in the dream; 'The real has to be sought beyond the dream – in what the dream has developed, hidden from us, behind the lack of representation of which there is only one representative. This is the real that governs our activities more than any other...'[70] In this repeating process there is thus not just return but also a movement. Fidelity to 'the people' must become therefore, not a fetishism, but a faith in a multiplicitous Real, where the popular

66 Derrida, *Specters of Marx*, 118–19.
67 Ibid. 221.
68 Žižek, 'Spectre', 80.
69 Derrida, *Specters of Marx*, 216–20.
70 Lacan, *Fundamental Concepts*, 60.

subject is never quite at home – is everywhere and nowhere. Performance-work, dreaming through recorded voice of a meaning it cannot quite hold, enunciates it anyhow.

The greatest gift of phonographic voice – and its specific contribution to the 'biopolitics' of our time – is the revelation that embodiment is mutable, that it's articulated by the passages of voice (animated by the passages of breath, or, to use an older language, of 'soul'), but that these passages out-run, even as they cite or even fall back on, all attempts by originary authority (God, People, State; Subject as such) to appropriate them. If what this voice masks even as it pronounces is indeed a body, a body politic, this is no corpse, but a live *vocalic* body, albeit one whose 'presence' is carried by a spectral genealogy; voice, then, in corporeal dispersion, crossing perpetually between Deleuze's 'body without organs' (which opposes to the figure of *organism* the idea of a multiplicity of machinic connections) and Žižek's inversion – 'organs without a body': part-objects, here popular vocal objects, which, while never free from the possibilities of fetishistic consumption and hegemonising or ochlocratic appropriation, are called to voice the act, the materiality of production, the creativity of drive, and hence to re-configure collective subjectivity around its *sinthome*; called, certainly – as we might metaphorically hazard – to articulate the body of God, but a god whose frozen gestures can do no more than mimic the pulsations (at once sounds, movements and drive-energies: *pulsions*) of his creating creation.

That utopian moment would mark the fulfilment – in the messianic sense of a moment that initiates and extinguishes at the same time – of the originary covenant between God and People, which contained from the beginning the implicit promise, and premise, that one (and hence both) must ultimately die – or rather lapse into paralysis and unconsciousness. Hallelujah! – as Leonard Cohen, writer and performer of the great song of that title, might exclaim, right on cue. (As I write, the moment of transition between 2008 and 2009, with the globalised capitalist world falling definitively into recession, while the messianic Barack Obama rides to its rescue, is marked by a competitive race to the top of the UK singles chart by two very different covers of the song, one by talent-show winner Alexandra Burke, the other – posthumously – by sainted cult icon, Jeff Buckley. Competitive down-loading by the two followings demonstrated that commodity still talked at the same time that, through the distributed body of the internet, the differences within sameness circulated in new ways.[71]) Cohen's song, covered by innumerable other singers too, redeems (and re-invests) the

---

71 By accident, the personae of the three singers make up an intriguing trio: Cohen, Jewish (his family claimed descent from the priestly Aaron), depressive Old Testament prophet (or transitional John the Baptist?), declaiming lyrically but caustically from a bohemian wilderness; Buckley, sainted (even Christ-like) martyr, virtually abandoned by his father (Tim Buckley, who, like Cohen, came from a time when the gods walked the earth, i.e. when the rock counterculture established canonic status), his ecstatic, suffering, sexually ambivalent voice a match for all those worryingly erotic portraits of Jesus crucified; and Burke, late-come acolyte who (according to the 'true' disciples of Buckley, of Cohen, of the song) betrayed them for money, for the rewards offered by show-biz Pharisees, but whose 'kiss' (complete with over-the-top Gospel-Soul peroration) might also, like that of Judas, be regarded as grounded in the inevitable unfolding of a divine plan (here, in the theological ambivalence of the song itself as well as the performative ambivalence of her recording) (it was this 'betrayal' that set off the down-loading frenzy).

The records in question are: Leonard Cohen, 'Hallelujah', *Various Positions* (CBS 26222, 1984) [the initial studio version]; Leonard Cohen, 'Hallelujah', *Cohen Live: Leonard Cohen Live in Concert* (Columbia 471 171-2, 1994 [1988]) [live version with substantially different lyrics]; Jeff Buckley,

religious debts of the ballad genre. It was from the start, in its two Cohen versions, a song of (in)fidelity, both in its subject (in which religious faith and fracture, and sexual bond and breakdown, are inextricably interwoven) and in its own mobile history (Cohen's two 'canonic' recorded versions apparently select, in radically different ways, from around 80 verses actually written). Its lyrics negotiate between biblical and secular languages, divine and profane addressees, sexual and religious ecstasies, faith and doubt, love orgasmic and broken, separation and relation, name and its absence (an antimony that ends up in that between 'name' and 'song', when 'there is nothing on my tongue but Hallelujah'). The hymn-like tune, drawing its oscillations between major tonic and its relative minor, and the pentatonic inflections that go with this, from the very core of popular song common practice, invites responses across the stylistic range, from folk, country, rock and soul. Many covers – most notably those by John Cale, Bob Dylan, Rufus Wainwright and k.d. lang, in addition to Buckley's – traverse the gap opened up between abandonment and *jouissance* in varying ways; others – succumbing to Lennon-esque self-importrance – traverse it hardly at all. But the multiplicity of voices, points of enunciation, communities of address, articulate 'body' at a range of levels – from sensual fantasy through erotic/star/commodity fetish and social (consumer/subcultural/identitarian) affiliations of a body politic to cybo-theogonic avatar – all of which, however, open space for animations, no matter how fragmentary, tentative or compromised, of the popular.[72]

If, in this process, both voice and body refuse singularity, we may want to re-cast the slogan with which I started: *Voces Populi, Corpus Dei*, perhaps; or better: *Voces Populi, Corpora Dei*; or further (and following a lead given by Roberto Esposito): *Voces Populi, Caro Dei*. For Esposito, the flesh – the carnal – is what resists all movements of unification or sovereign subjection of life, whether in the human or the political body; it's the undifferentiated stuff of 'multitude', of *incarnation* (as against *incorporation*), and hence what always escapes or overflows the singularity of organism. In his quest for an affirmative biopolitics, 'a politics no longer over life but *of* life',[73] Esposito finds examples of such flows in biotechnology, but we can readily extend this mapping into the spheres of cyborgian 'flesh' fed by modern media, including recorded music (and here, by the way, we may discover – finally! – the location of that vocal 'grain' which Roland Barthes so influentially identified but which neither he nor his many followers have ever satisfactorily pinned down[74]).

It's an enticing prospect, and congruent with much in Nancy, Rancière and Deleuze (the common inspiration is Spinoza); but qualifications begin to enter, all the more when Esposito moves from the problematic of body/flesh to that of birth/fraternity.[75] Here he wants to shift

---

'Hallelujah', *Grace* (Columbia 475928 2, 1994); Alexandra Burke, 'Hallelujah' (Sony 88697446252, 2008).

72 *Hallelujah*: from Hebrew *hallelu* (= praise ye) and *Jah* or *Yah* (= the Lord). But Cohen's 'hallelujah' is not only ecstatic but also, he tells us, 'broken'. Placing this in critical motion against the affirmatory hallelujahs accompanying Barack Obama's inauguration, might this offer a hint – certainly no more – of how we might open the difficult question whether and how a musical politics could translate, connect to or move into a politics of a broader field?

73 Roberto Esposito, *Bíos: Biopolitics and Philosophy*, tr. Timothy Campbell (Minneapolis: University of Minnesota Press, 2008), 11. For Esposito's account of 'flesh', see ibid. 157–69.

74 Which isn't to say that it's necessarily absent from 'live' performance, only that it's a property that overflows any singular body, a function which phonographic technology enhances and reveals.

75 Roberto Esposito, *Bíos:* 169–82.

the discourse from a focus on birth as a sign of national genealogy (Latin *natio*, from *natus* = to be born; note also *natura* = nature), and fraternity therefore as denoting consanguinity in a fatherland, to a conception of birth as a perpetual process of self-reproduction whereby new forms of individuation follow each other in a fluid sequence without thresholds, each step excorporating what was inside, preserving as it surpasses what came before; with no caesura between biological levels (vegetal, animal, human), or between the physical, somatic and psychic, fraternity thus becomes radically 'transindividual', overflowing the borders of any political body. It may well be that politics does go all the way down to the furthest depths of *bíos*; but doesn't this mean the Nietzschean will-to-power goes down too, with potential sovereign claims at any level? If Nazi biopolitics had at its ideological core, as Esposito claims, the belief that 'the state is *really* [i.e. not just metaphorically] the body of its inhabitants',[76] we shall want to be wary of projects that seek to align any sovereign body with practices attached to particular assemblages of flesh (there are musical examples to warn us: Serbian 'turbofolk', for instance[77]). Or again (the psychoanalytic point), how easy is it to cancel those 'cuts' that, arguably, initiate the very structures of loss, desire, law and trauma without which psychic development couldn't take place, or to disavow the suggestion that the very concept of a 'below' (that is, a 'before') is a retroactive (*nachträglich*) construction? Sovereign insistence (something like Freud's 'His Majesty the Ego', recalling the transcendental stratum of absolutist political theology; the 'illness of man', according to Lacan) is embedded to an extent that will surely outlive the deaths of both God and Man.

Esposito attempts to forestall the psychoanalytic objection by means of a brilliant comparison between the Freud of *Totem and Taboo* – where the band of brothers murder the father, initiating the fraternal sovereignty of tribal community – and the Freud of *Moses and Monotheism*, where, he points out, the father-figure (Moses) is presented as an outsider, even an enemy (an Egyptian), and the people he founds as thus radically impure, incomplete, doubled in its origin. But an adoptive father is still a father – and Esposito builds his argument on the myth, central to Freud's account, that Moses was murdered by the rebellious Israelites; the Oedipal structure, though importantly modified, is still in place, and with it a paternal function of law and a politics of immunity (this is, of course, in action still in Palestine/Israel today). The more general point is that even if fraternity may encompass the enemy, and even if the repetitiousness of 'birth' pushes the topology of 'flesh' in a direction beyond all putative constraints, the counter-movement – the structures of exception, as Agamben has it,[78] and the constant assertions of sovereign power that follow – is also still to be reckoned with; and operating, still, within as well as without, at the level both of individual subjects and political bodies.

Word is made flesh – continually, but also vice versa; and the *act*, the making, is all-important. It's on the terrain configured by this interplay – this 'zone of indeterminacy', to borrow again a phrase from Agamben[79] – that the dialogue between the fleshly infinitudes

---

76 Ibid. 171.

77 See Bennett Hogg, 'Who's Listening?', in *Music, Power, and Politics*, ed. Annie J. Randall (New York: Routledge, 2005), 211–30.

78 Giorgio Agamben, *State of Exception*, trans. K. Attell, Chicago: University of Chicago Press, 2005.

79 Giorgio Agamben, *The Open: Man and Animal*, tr. Kevin Attell (Stanford CA: Stanford University Press, 2004), 38.

of the Body-without-Organs and the fantasies of impossible closure conjured by the lure of the Objects-without-a-Body performs out the continual production of difference and sameness (difference *as* sameness, sameness *as* difference); a production that is also one of the instabilities of power. The historical status of this knot – the 'ecceity' of its reciprocal movements constitute our reality – is why the Žižekian act-as-miracle is called upon to break, again and again, the deadlock of a site where the BwO and the OwB each constantly seeks to hold sway. Isn't it the vocal act – the *voces populi* animated by the *mobile vulgus*, always both sign and flesh but always also beyond either in a dispersion radically enhanced by the phonographic Event – that best incarnates the political potential of this moment?

Index